Investment Appraisal and Financial Decisions

Investment Appraisal and Financial Decisions

Sixth edition

Steve Lumby and
Chris Jones

THOMSON

LEARNING

Australia • Canada • Mexico • Singapore • Spain • United Kingdom • United States

Investment Appraisal and Financial Decisions

Copyright © 1981, 1984, 1991, 1994, 1999 The Lumby Family Partnership

The Thomson Learning logo is a registered trademark used herein under license.

British Library Cataloguing-in-Publication Data
A catalogue record for this book is available from the British Library

First edition published by Chapman & Hall 1981
Sixth edition published by International Thomson Business Press 1999
Reprinted 2000 by Thomson Learning

Typeset by Columns Design Ltd, Reading, Berkshire
Printed in Croatia by ZRINSKI d.d.

ISBN 1-86152-257-6

Thomson Learning
Berkshire House
168-173 High Holborn
London WC1V 7AA
UK

http://www.thomsonlearning.co.uk

Contents

To: the Chelsea People – Vanessa and the Gang
the Osset Folk – Janet, Harriet, Emily and Edward
and everyone at Anfield

Preface

A thing may look specious in theory, and yet be ruinous in practice; a thing may look evil in theory, and yet be in practice excellent.

> Edmund Burke, Impeachment of Warren Hastings,
> 19 February 1788

There is a popular feeling that 'theory' is opposed to 'practice' and the merits lie with 'practice'. This is a false conclusion, based on a false supposition. If practice has long been successful, and does not conform to theory, the theory is bad and in need of revision … The distinction should not be between theory and practice; it should be between good theory and bad theory, between good practice and bad practice. … Practice is brick; theory is mortar. Both are essential and both must be good if we are to erect a worthy structure.

> D. Paarlberg, *Great Myths of Economics*

This book is concerned with corporate financial decision making, with a particular emphasis on the evaluation and financing of long-term capital expenditure decisions. Its aim is to build an understanding of practice through the development of theory. Some of the theoretical approaches covered are relatively non-problematical such as the theoretical strength of net present value as a decision criterion; others are more controversial such as the nature of the dividend decision. However, the practical applications of techniques often cause significant difficulties and it is necessary to keep in mind that some of the assumptions underlying the theory may sometimes be questioned. In particular, the most fundamental assumption of all – that of maximization of shareholder wealth as the prime objective of management – may well be compromised by the personal objectives of managers themselves.

The book has been written to provide a comprehensive introduction to the subject of financial decision making that is appropriate for students at an introductory or intermediate level of either academic or professional study.

The authors of the book have experience of teaching financial management at a wide range of institutions (London School of Economics, Leeds Polytechnic, University of Sheffield, Sheffield Hallam University, and private sector professional centres, amongst others) and to a wide range of students both academic (HND, BA, BSc in business studies, accounting and finance, and also MBA both full-time and executive type programmes) and professional (ACCA, ICAEW, CIMA).

We have probably learned more from these experiences than our students and we have certainly found it necessary to look for new ways to present this fascinating subject so that it is made more real for them.

We have made a number of changes to the sixth edition. We have brought the issue of corporate governance up to date to include Greenbury and Hampel and the ongoing debate on the behaviour of some senior managers. We have attempted to relate some issues more closely to the UK context, particularly by recognizing the nature of the tax system. We have also extended our coverage of some of the international aspects of financial decision making. There are other topics that we feel unable to include in the text on the grounds of its length and the specialized nature of the topic. For example we have not included any material specifically related to mergers and acquisitions, although, of course there is a considerable amount of material that relates to this area in more general terms.

The introduction contains more detailed coverage of our approach along with an explanation of the book's structure.

As with previous editions, there are both 'quickie' and full-scale, exam type questions at the end of each chapter, along with a brief summary of what has been covered. The reading lists are designed to be reasonably accessible and, in general, articles based on advanced mathematical applications have been omitted. The 'quickie' questions are designed to emphasize the more significant areas of each chapter and also provide an opportunity to test understanding and give some feedback on that (answers to 'quickie' questions are in the back of the book). The exam style questions have been selected to cover the most important areas of each chapter and provide practice for both the real world and examinations. These questions have been written by the authors or taken from the examinations of professional bodies and we are very grateful for the permission of those bodies to use their questions. Tutors can obtain a solutions manual for these questions from the publisher.

This book expresses a normative theory of financial decision making. It is about developing a general understanding of the way financial decisions are made and, perhaps how these processes could be improved. Thus, whilst the book may well provide solutions to practical problems, this is not its primary objective. The authors accept no responsibility for losses incurred as the result of applying the theories discussed to real-world decisions!

So far as possible we have adopted a descriptive and graphical approach in this book. We believe that this makes the material accessible to far more readers and also that the adoption of a mathematically based approach can often obscure the reality and significance of important conclusions. We believe that the level of understanding provided by this book is a prerequisite for the use of more sophisticated mathematical approaches and that these should really be covered in a more advanced course.

Financial management is a fascinating and rewarding area for study and we hope that you enjoy the course for which you use this book.

Finally we would like to express our thanks to the people at International Thomson Business Press including Alan Nelson, Jenny Clapham and Penny Grose. Thanks also go to Professor Richard Laughlin of the University of Essex and Dominic Recauldin.

Introduction

The nature of financial decisions

An overview

This book covers a particular area of managerial economics: the theory of financial decision making by business corporations. It is concerned with how management within companies[1] *should* make[2] financial decisions,[3] and so it can be said to adopt a normative approach because it sets out to establish a standard, or norm. But such a theory cannot hope to succeed in its task if it is developed in isolation from what actually does happen in practice, and so we shall also examine how financial decisions *are* made, in order to guide and enrich the development of our normative approach.

The value base

Financial decisions are no different in their fundamental aspects from other decisions of a non-financial nature, be they in industry or commerce (such as marketing decisions) or elsewhere (such as decisions to transfer footballers, or even international diplomacy decisions). In essence, *all* decisions are based on the concept of the comparison of alternatives, and it is in this sense that the theory of financial decisions really has its roots in valuation theory, because all the alternatives in any decision-making situation have to be valued in order to be compared. Therefore, although we can say that all types of decisions involve the same fundamental process, each is given its own unique characteristics by the valuation base which it employs.

The financial decision theory developed in this book is founded on the valuation bases that come from capitalism[4] and the idea of the free market economy. It is important that this is specified from the outset, as a different valuation base would be likely to produce a different overall theory of financial decisions. However, many parts of our financial theory will be applicable to other types of economic organization, and you may wish to consider and reflect upon the implications of our theory for more social value bases, such as those which might be appropriate to the public sector and, in particular state-owned public enterprises. This is particularly interesting since the past twenty years have seen an apparent change in value bases in those particular areas and a transfer of many public sector enterprises into the private sector.

The 'model' approach and the structure of the text

We have structured this text in six sections:

1. Introduction to the context of financial decisions – Introduction and Chapters 1 and 2.
2. The capital investment decision – Chapters 3 to 8.
3. The impact of uncertainty on the capital investment decision – Chapters 9 to 12.
4. Financing decisions – Chapters 13 to 20.
5. The interaction of capital investment and financing decisions, including the dividend decision – Chapters 21 and 22.
6. Financial decisions in an international context – Chapters 23 to 25.

In the course of our development of a normative approach to financial decisions, a considerable number of abstractions from and simplifications of the 'real world' will be made, in order to distil the difficulties and focus attention on areas of major importance.

Adopting this type of 'modelling' approach is normal in the study of economics and related areas. However it brings with it a danger that it is seen as fully describing a 'real' world and providing simple solutions to real-world problems. It is important to remember that we are developing a normative theory and are therefore attempting to give advice on how financial decisions *should* be taken. In general we will work with simplified models and if the theory were to be followed in practice, without recognizing the full range of possible complicating factors the quality of financial decisions made in business might deteriorate rather than improve.

The difficulties caused by taxation, inflation and capital scarcity will all be taken into account, as will the concept of risk and the fact that the future is uncertain.[5] All these real-world complexities will be added layer by layer to the simplified model with which we start. Even though that model might be a poor reflection of the real world, it provides a logically sound framework upon which to build.

A warning

As a final point, the reader should be constantly aware that the theory of financial decisions which is presented here is neither in a state of general detailed agreement, nor does it yet provide complete solutions to many of the important problems of financial decision making. In order to reflect this state of affairs, we shall examine the causes and evidence of these controversies and point out the irrationalities, ambiguities and inconsistencies that necessarily accompany the development of any theory that aspires to real-world application.

The decision process

In order to examine the decision process and to answer the question: 'How do we make a decision?', we have first to discuss the circumstances in which a decision needs to be made. We can specify two necessary conditions for a decision situation: the existence of alternatives and the existence of an objective or goal.

The first necessary condition

The existence of alternatives is necessary because, if there are no alternatives from which to choose, then there is no need for a decision. This condition can be specified further in that not only must alternatives exist, but they must be seen to exist by the potential decision maker. There are two points of interest here.

First, notice that we talk of a decision *situation* and of a *potential* decision maker. This is because the mere existence of perceived alternatives does not necessarily mean that a decision will be made. For instance, the potential decision maker may well procrastinate, and therefore the passage of time takes him (or her) out of a decision situation and into a situation where there is only one possible course of action and no alternatives are available. (Death is the ultimate example of the passage of time removing a decision situation from an individual.)

The second point of interest is that we are *not* specifying that all possible alternatives are perceived; if they were, we could call this an optimal decision situation. We are, rather, examining how decisions are made, given that a particular decision situation exists. Whether the decision is truly optimal or non-optimal is of no concern at present.

The second necessary condition

The second necessary condition for a decision situation arises from the fact that the actual process of 'making a decision' is liable to cause the decision maker to expend both time and effort. Rationally he will be unwilling to do so unless he expects that some of the perceived alternatives will be preferred to others in relation to attaining the desired objective. Thus the existence of an objective is the second necessary condition: without it, there will be no purpose in making a decision.[6]

Valuation of alternatives

Together, these two necessary conditions provide the rationale for making decisions: if the decision maker does not perceive alternatives, or sees no reason to choose between the alternatives if they are perceived, then no decision will be made (except one of a totally arbitrary kind, as in note 6). But once these conditions do exist, a decision cannot actually be made until values are placed upon the alternatives. In fact, we can assert that the only reason why any alternative course of action is ever evaluated is in order to make a decision about it; therefore, the valuation method used must be related to the objective involved in making the decision and the way in which that objective is expressed.

For example, if our objective were to drive from A to B in the shortest possible time, then we should value the alternative routes from A to B by a common value criterion which was related to our objective of time, and choose whichever route took the shortest time. Suppose there were three alternative routes and one we valued by time, one by distance and one by scenic beauty. We obviously could not make a decision because the alternatives have different measures or yardsticks of value and so cannot be compared. Alternatively, if all three routes were measured in terms of scenic beauty, we should again be unable to make a decision, even though we could compare the routes – because the basis of the comparison is not the one which gives the rationale for the decision: the value base of the objective, which in this example is 'time'.[7]

Therefore, any decision-making process consists of these three components: a series of perceived alternatives, an expectation that these alternatives are not all equally desirable in terms of attaining an objective held by the decision maker, and a common value base related to the decision objective. So it is with all financial decisions made in business.

Financial decision making

This book focuses attention on only two of the three components that we have identified in the decision process and examines how they relate to the making of financial decisions: the expectation that the perceived alternatives are not all equally desirable in terms of attaining a specific objective, and the common value base that is related to this objective and is used to compare the alternatives.

The remaining component of the decision process is the series of perceived alternatives. We shall not be examining it in the main body of the text as it is primarily a condition for the decision *situation*, and we are concentrating on the actual decision making, assuming that the decision situation already exists. However, this omission does not mean that the 'search process' (as it is called) for alternatives is unimportant. It is in fact extremely important. If this search process is not efficient in seeking out alternatives, then there is a grave danger that the decision itself will not be optimal because the 'most preferred' alternative may go unperceived.

The decision objective

Turning to the two decision process components that we shall examine in detail, we immediately become involved in value judgements, because the objective we use for financial decision making, and the consequent value base, will determine the decision reached as to which alternative is selected. Therefore, what objective are we going to use and what valuation base are we going to set up for our theory of financial decisions?

We stated earlier that the fundamental value judgement upon which our approach is based is capitalism. The approach is thus most appropriate in largely unregulated, competitive economies. In such economies, it is reasonable to assume that companies exist for one overriding purpose: in order to benefit their owners.[8] Whilst companies provide income for their employees and the wider local community, supply the needs of a particular market, and provide other benefits such as technological advance, the fact remains that the fundamental rationale for their existence must be to bring benefit to their owners.

This rationale for existence undoubtedly holds true for the great majority of privately owned[9] companies (and also, to some extent, for state-owned industries although their rationale for existence can be more complex[10]). Therefore, management's objective in making financial decisions *should be* to further the very reason for the company's existence, of benefiting the owners, i.e. the shareholders. We shall see that there might be other managerial objectives but, in essence, we will treat those as deviating from what they should be (this is consistent with the idea of adopting a normative approach). So if the decision objective is to benefit the owners, what is the value base to be used for the comparison of alternatives?

To answer this question, we have to examine the decision objective more closely. It is obvious from what we have already said that not only should company managements make financial decisions so as to benefit the shareholders but they should also strive to maximize that benefit, otherwise shareholders will be interested in replacing them with a set of decision makers who will do this. Therefore, what is meant by the term 'maximizing owners' or shareholders' benefit'?

Maximizing shareholder wealth

We are going to assume that maximizing benefit means maximizing wealth. Although there is nothing surprising about this, we have to be careful here because we are going to assume that maximizing the increase in the owners' wealth is the *only* way in which management decisions can benefit owners.

This is a slight simplification of the real world, because it is quite possible for shareholders to gain benefit from a company other than by increases in wealth. For example, shareholders of a company such as Body Shop may gain benefit from ownership in terms of pride in the fact that the company has a proactive stance towards protecting the environment and this is reflected in various investment vehicles such as *ethical* unit trusts. However, this is a comparatively minor point and we shall proceed on the relatively sound assumption that increase in wealth is the main, if not the sole source of benefit from company ownership.

What about firms selling military arms to countries whose policies are repugnant, or firms causing pollution to land, air or water resources? Do these types of activity enter into consideration of our decision objective? On the basis of our underlying assumption about the nature of the economy, our answer must be that they should not, because if these activities were thought to be truly undesirable, governments would legislate to constrain companies' decision-choice alternatives so as to exclude them (as in many cases they do). Company decision makers should only need to perceive and analyse the decision alternatives in terms of maximizing the owners' wealth. From this viewpoint we can treat financial decisions as not being anything to do with morality. Morality, the law and other things might act as constraints on what a company does but they are entirely different issues and are generally assessed using different criteria.

In market economies, we can develop a theory of financial decisions for privately owned firms in this way because of the workings of the market system for company capital. Ordinary share capital, the substance of ownership, is normally provided through supply and demand markets (e.g. stock exchanges), which means that potential shareholders can buy shares in companies that they expect will provide them with the greatest possible increase in wealth (i.e. shareholders have to make financial decisions in much the same way as management, choosing between alternative ownership opportunities), and existing shareholders can sell their shares if they see other companies providing greater increases to their owners' wealth than they are receiving. (An important concept here, and one we have yet to deal with, is that the future is uncertain and so any decision amongst alternatives usually has a risk attached to it: the risk that the alternative chosen may not turn out as expected. Some alternatives are riskier than others and so shareholders will really want to own companies that they expect will give them the greatest possible increase in wealth, for a given level of risk. This concept will be considered much more fully later.)

Therefore, if a company were to make its decisions on bases other than that of maximizing shareholder wealth, the whole rationale for the company's existence – so far as shareholders are concerned – would be in doubt and they would be likely to take their investment funds elsewhere. In the extreme case, company law provides the opportunity for shareholders to replace a company's decision makers if enough of them believe that decisions are not being taken in their best interests.

Defining wealth

However, we still cannot determine the value base for financial decision making until we have defined 'wealth', because the purpose of the value base is to act as a common denominator with which to make the alternative courses of action directly comparable and to see which one leads furthest towards the decision objective. As the objective of financial decisions is assumed to be to 'maximize the increase in owners' wealth', let us define 'wealth' and so determine the value base.

Wealth can be defined as the capacity to consume or, to put it in more straightforward terms, money or cash.[11] Thus the objective of management becomes the maximization of shareholders' purchasing power, which can be achieved by maximizing the amount of cash paid out to shareholders in the form of dividends. But which dividends should a company's management try to maximize: this year's, next year's or what?

The point here is that it would be a relatively easy task for a company to maximize a single year's dividend, simply by selling up all the assets and paying a final liquidation dividend! (We are ignoring the niceties of company law here, but the point still remains.) Obviously this is not what is meant by our decision objective of maximizing dividends, and the trouble arises through the omission of the time dimension. When fully defined, including the time dimension, the objective of a company's financial decision makers becomes the maximizing of the *flow* of dividends to shareholders *over or through time*.

The role of accounting profit

There are two points of fundamental importance that arise from the development of this decision objective. First, the word 'profit' has not been mentioned and the emphasis has been laid on wealth defined as cash. Second, the introduction of time means that decisions must be analysed not only in terms of immediate cash gains and losses, but also in terms of *future* gains and losses.

These two points are interlinked. Profit, when used in a business sense, is a concept developed by financial accountants in order to assist them with their auditing and reporting functions, performed on behalf of shareholders.

Accounting has developed over hundreds of years from a base called *stewardship*. It was really designed to provide evidence that people holding responsibility for other people's assets could account for them (i.e. demonstrate where the resources went). In many ways this is still lies at the heart of financial accounting. Although financial reports are produced each year and contain the figure *profit* it should not be interpreted as being the same thing as the increase in the value of the company during the year. Annual reports are produced using a number of conventions and rules, the most important of which is that the figures are expressed in terms of historic cost (with one or two possible exceptions). There is also a certain amount of judgement exercised in the production of the statement and it has been said that profit is the invention rather than the discovery of the accountant. The Accounting Standards Board (the body that defines many of the rules used by accountants) has expressed the view that accounting should not be seen as being concerned with value or worth. As we will see, wealth, worth and value are all concepts related to the future (and cash flows in the future) but profit is related to the past.

Financial decisions are basically economic or resource allocation decisions. Management have to decide whether they should allocate the firm's scarce resources (land, labour, machinery, etc.) to a particular project. The economic 'unit of account' is cash, not accounting profit, because it is cash which gives power to command resources (i.e. resources are purchased with cash, not profit). Thus to use the accounting profit concept in financial decision making would be to use an entirely inappropriate concept – a concept specially developed for reporting the outcome of decisions and not developed for helping to take the actual decision itself.

However, we cannot discard the accounting profit concept completely. To do so would be rather like a sports team whose policy is that they do not mind whether they win or lose, so long as in playing they give maximum entertainment to their supporters. This is fine, and it is probably the correct attitude; but often it is on the winning or losing that the success of the team is ultimately judged and therefore that part of the game cannot be ignored. So it is with accounting profit. The company's financial decision makers should have as their major concern the maximization of the flow of cash through time to the shareholders, but they should always do so with an eye to reported profit. Profitability, as expressed in annual published accounts, forms a major criterion by which shareholders and prospective shareholders judge a company's success and, as we shall see later, it is important that people do form correct judgements about a company's performance.

A further reason why the effects of financial decisions on reported profits cannot be completely ignored is provided by the fact that the level of retained profit, in company law, can form a very substantial maximum barrier to an annual dividend payment. Thus a company that wishes to maximize its dividend flow must ensure that its dividend payout intentions are legally within the confines of company law.

Therefore, with the exception of these two provisos, we can say that the financial decision theory developed here is built on an analytical framework that is largely devoid of the accounting profit concept, although it would be correct to assume that, in the longer run, good company cash flows will result in good reported profits.

The time dimension

Turning to the second point of importance in our decision objective, the introduction of the time dimension, we have already noted that the arbitrary time segmentation of a continuous flow process has been the cause of major problems for the accounting profit concept, but to see the true significance of the introduction of this factor we have to return to our discussion on value.

An asset (such as a machine or a share in a company) is valued on the basis of the gains, or losses, that the owner receives. Furthermore, these gains and losses do not refer to just a single time period, but to the whole period of future time for which the asset will exist. (This concept is sometimes referred to as the asset's earning power.)

Let us consider an asset of company ownership: an ordinary share. Ordinary shares are traded (i.e. bought and sold) in supply and demand markets and so its market valuation represents an equilibrium value, a value at which demand for the share by people who wish to buy it equates with the supply of the share by people who wish to sell it. But what process actually gives a share its equilibrium price, what makes prospective purchasers wish to buy it at that price and what makes prospective sellers willing to sell it at that price? Let us examine the prospective purchaser's reasons.

Suppose an ordinary share of XYZ plc has a stock market price of 150p.[12] A prospective owner of that share would only be willing to buy it if he though it was worth 150p. In other words, he would expect that the gains to be received from ownership would have a value of at least 150p.

These gains of ownership consist of two elements: the stream of dividends received for as long as he owns the share, and the selling price received when the share is sold (and so ownership relinquished) at some future point in time. However, it is important to note that this future selling price of the XYZ share is itself based on the value the succeeding owner puts on the benefits that he in turn expects to receive from ownership – the dividend flow received and the selling price that he will receive upon selling the share at some future point in time. So the process goes on *ad infinitum*. Therefore, although there are two benefits of ownership, the dividends received and the future selling price, this latter benefit is itself determined by the flow of dividends expected to be generated by the share subsequent to its sale. (We can treat the cash flow received if the company were to be wound up or *liquidated* as a final dividend.)

Given this argument, our theory will assume that shares derive their (equilibrium) stock market price on the basis of the sum of the dividend flow that they will produce through time. (As the future is uncertain, it is more correct to talk of valuation based on the *expected* dividend flow, but we shall return to this later.) Thus the greater the future dividend flow, the more highly are the shares valued. Therefore if our financial decision makers are taking decisions so as to maximize dividend flow through time, then via the direct link between dividend flow and a share's market price, this action will result in the *maximization of the market value of the company's shares*. It is this that we shall take as being the operational objective of financial management decision making.[13]

The objective hierarchy

So let us summarize our assumed hierarchy of decision objectives:

1. Decisions are taken by companies so as to maximize owners' wealth.
2. Owners' wealth can be maximized through maximizing owners' purchasing power.
3. Purchasing power can be maximized through maximizing the amount of cash the company pays out to shareholders in the form of dividends.
4. With the introduction of the time dimension the objective becomes the maximizing of the value of the dividend flow through time to the shareholders.
5. The maximization of the value of the dividend flow through time maximizes the stock market's valuation of the company's ordinary share capital.

However, it is important to realize that although it is this 'fifth level' of objective we shall use in developing the theory of financial decision making, it is really only a surrogate objective for the fundamental, underlying objective of maximizing shareholders' wealth.

A fundamental assumption

As a final point, let us state the assumptions about the shareholder which have been implied in the analysis. It was earlier argued that the maximization of shareholders' wealth had to be the fundamental decision objective, because of the nature of the capital markets. However, the validity of this assertion depends entirely upon the assumption that shareholders perceive wealth in the way we have postulated and that in this perception they are rational. In essence this means that we have assumed that shareholders see wealth as the receipt of cash flows through time and that they will always prefer a greater to lesser cash flow. These appear reasonably safe assumptions, but we shall consider situations where they may not hold when we look later at dividend policies.

Technology and financial decision making

The past fifteen years have seen what amounts to a technological revolution. This has been described as an information revolution on a par with the industrial revolution of the eighteenth and nineteenth centuries. It is now most unlikely that decision makers will not have access to computer facilities and the power of the typical desktop machine is now such that sophisticated software can be used to aid their decisions. In most cases the type of software used will be based on spreadsheets such as Microsoft Excel or Lotus 123 and you are encouraged to use the software available to you when answering the problems set throughout the text. However, it is important that you understand the underlying principles so it is not advisable to rely solely on the financial functions embedded in the software. It is also worth mentioning that some of the functions can be somewhat problematical as we will see.

Summary

- The decision process consists of three elements:
  - a series of perceived alternatives;
  - an expectation that these alternatives are not all equally desirable in terms of attaining an objective held by the decision maker;
  - a common value base, related to the objective, by which the alternatives may be compared.

- As far as financial management is concerned, it is assumed that the objective of financial management decision making is the maximization of shareholder wealth. This is normally translated to mean maximizing the current worth of the company's shares.

- Given that shareholder wealth is seen in terms of an ability to consume goods and services and that it is cash which provides consumption power, so share value can be maximized by maximizing the sum of the expected stream of dividends through time generated by the share.

- Accounting profit is essentially an inappropriate concept within the context of financial management decision making because it is a *reporting* device, not a decision-making device. Finance decisions are economic or resource allocation decisions and the economic unit of account is cash; hence decisions are evaluated in terms of their cash flow impact. However, the reported profit impact of financial decisions remains an important consideration in terms of the correct communication of management's actions to shareholders and others.

Notes

1. Be these either large stock exchange quoted companies such as ICI or Unilever, or small unquoted companies such as a local printing company or car rental company.

2. The terms decision 'making' and decision 'taking' can be used synonymously. However, the term decision 'making' will be used in this book because of its more positive emphasis on deliberate creative action.

3. We will carefully define just what financial decisions are, but for now this covers such things as a decision to invest in a new machine, to borrow money from the bank or a decision to 'pass' (i.e. not pay) an annual dividend that shareholders were expecting.

4. There are many variants of capitalism (which in itself is just one type of economic system; for example, alternatives could include socialist, feudal and primitive communal economies) but its two general features are the private ownership of property and the allocation of the economy's resources (land, labour and machinery) through a supply and demand price mechanism.

5. Indeed, we shall also occasionally allude to the psychological processes behind firms' financial decisions, where conflicts of interest arise.

6. In a way, in specifying this second necessary condition, we are ignoring the situation where a decision *has* to be made, even though this second condition does not exist. For instance, if you are out for a walk with no particular destination in mind and you come to a crossroads, a decision *has* to be taken on which direction to take, even though the second necessary condition is really unfulfilled. Such situations are of little interest as far as the decision *process* is concerned; we could call them indifference decisions.

7. For the present, we shall ignore the possibility of multiple objectives, although we shall touch upon it later. However we may observe that where multiple objectives exist in real life, one objective is often regarded (either implicitly or explicitly) as being of overriding importance, with the other objectives acting as constraining factors or considerations.

8. In abstract terms we can define a company as a collection of assets. The owners of the company have therefore pooled their funds to assemble such a collection and are logically only likely to do so in order to bring benefit (either directly or indirectly) to themselves.

9. The term 'privately owned companies' can be a source of confusion. It refers to all companies which are owned by individuals, either singly or collectively, whether or not they are 'publicly quoted' (plc) on a stock exchange or otherwise. Thus both public and private companies (in financial nomenclature) are privately owned companies.

10. See, for instance, Ivy Papps, *Government and Enterprise*, Hobart Paper No. 61, Institute of Economic Affairs, 1975.

11. We shall be ignoring the effects of inflation until later.

12. This is obviously a simplification, as in practice each share has two equilibrium prices, a buying price and a selling price. The former will be the higher of the two, and the difference constitutes the market maker's 'turn'. However, for simplicity, we will ignore this complication and use a 'middle' value.

13. Of course, if the company's shares are not quoted on a stock exchange, then the objective simply reduces to the maximization of the value of the company's shares. This, however, still leaves the problem of how the shares are to be valued. In fact they should be valued on exactly the same basis as quoted shares: the future expected dividend flow. It is one of the great advantages of a stock market quotation that this value is 'automatically' and continuously provided for use both by management and by investors.

Quickie questions

1. What are the three major areas of financial decisions?
2. What is the search process?
3. What is the fundamental objective of financial management decision making?
4. Why is accounting profit an inappropriate criterion for financial decision making?
5. How are shares valued?

1 Corporate objectives, management objectives and corporate governance

Wealth maximization and the company

In the introduction we pointed out that we will assume, for the purposes of analysis and the development of our normative theory of financial decisions, that maximization of shareholder wealth is the objective of financial decisions.

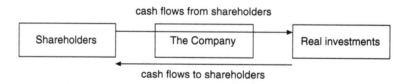

cash flows from shareholders

Shareholders → The Company → Real investments

cash flows to shareholders

If we accept this assumption, the company becomes a transparent vehicle for the transmission of resources from the shareholder into investments (investment) and back to the shareholder (return). This will generally take the form of cash. In a sense, the company only exists to allow for these cash flows and it is necessary because the individual shareholder is not otherwise in the position to make the (relatively small) investment in, say, a factory that they might wish to. However, the reality of the situation is somewhat different. The company is not a neutral vehicle because it contains decision makers (managers) who have their own interests to look after as well as those of the shareholders. In the situation where the shareholders are not the same people as the managers, this is likely to result in conflicts of interests and may well mean that decisions are not made in order to maximize shareholder wealth.

Maximizing vs. Satisficing

A company's management (or, more strictly speaking, its directors) are in what is termed a 'principal–agent' relationship with the shareholders. The shareholders are the principals – the owners of the company's assets – and the managers are employed as their agents to manage those assets on their behalf.

The major problem facing any principal (owner) is that of control: how to control the agent (manager) to ensure that the agent always acts in the best interests of the principal. The problem arises out of the fact that there may well be a conflict between the personal objectives of the agents and the objectives that their principal wishes them to pursue.

Shareholders will want their managers to take decisions so as to maximize the worth of the company's shares. However, management will have their own personal objectives. These objectives will be mainly concerned with three things: their pay, their perks (non-monetary rewards such as holiday entitlements, working conditions, company cars, etc.) and their job security.[1] The past few years have provided many examples of company bosses who appear to have paid themselves much more than would seem to be necessary especially in the area of privatized utilities. Remember that every million pounds taken out of the company by its managers is a million pounds less for its shareholders, no matter how it is presented (salary, bonus, share options, etc.)

In such circumstances, it is sometimes argued that managers will become shareholder wealth satisficers rather than maximizers. This implies that managers will do just enough to keep shareholders reasonably satisfied in terms of increasing their wealth and, at the same time, put their remaining efforts into the pursuit of their own personal objectives.

Thus a satisficing management may be thought more likely to pursue a specific target which – if achieved – would be felt to be sufficient to keep shareholders satisfied, rather than to pursue a more general target of maximization. For example, management might pursue a target of increasing the value of the company's shares by, say, 10% per year, rather than having as their objective trying to achieve the maximum possible annual growth rate in the share price.

In addition, satisficing behaviour implies that the management team will not organize the search process of alternative courses of action so as to seek out the very best, maximizing course of action. Instead, they will terminate the search process as soon as a satisfactory (but not necessarily the best) course of action is identified.

Agency theory postulates that principals respond to the problem they face in two ways. First, they develop monitoring devices to try to ensure that managers are attempting to maximize the company's share price. Second, they create incentive schemes for management so that it is in the manager's own best interest to pursue share price maximization. In practice it is very difficult to devise either monitoring or incentive schemes that can be relied upon to produce the required results for shareholders.

Ownership and control

There are many ways in which the actions of a company's managers are monitored and controlled so as to try and ensure that they act in their shareholders' best interests rather than their own.

However, before we briefly examine these, it is important to make one clarifying observation. This is that a principal–agent problem only really arises when there is a significant divorce between ownership and control.

For example, in an owner-managed business there is no such problem whatsoever, as the owners are the managers, and so the objectives of one group are also the objectives of the other. If we move on to a larger, family-owned business, where the owners are not necessarily the managers, there is still likely to be very little problem. This is because, in these circumstances, the owners will still be able to exercise close personal control over their managers. Even though the shareholders may not be the managers, the shareholders in such a company are likely to know who the senior managers are, and are likely to be able to monitor their actions directly.

It is only when a company's development reaches the point where there is a clear-cut division between owners and managers, when the company is too large and the owners are too widespread for them to be able to exercise effective personal control, that the principal–agent problem of control starts to manifest itself. For many companies, this point is reached when they decide to stop being a private company and instead become a public company, quoted on a stock exchange.

For the vast majority of private companies – especially, small private companies – the principal–agent problem does not exist in any meaningful sense. Thus, in discussing the problem, we must view it in relation to the larger company and, in particular, to the stock exchange quoted company.

Regulation of the relationship between directors and shareholders

The main vehicles for the regulation of the actions of directors are as follows:

1. The fiduciary responsibility that is imposed on directors by company law.
2. The legal requirement for an annual independent external audit of the company.
3. The 'listing rules' of the Stock Exchange.
4. The Stock Exchange's 'model code' on directors' share dealings.
5. Companies Act regulations on directors' transactions.
6. The 'City Code' on take-overs and mergers.
7. The Cadbury Committee's 'Code of Best Practice' on corporate governance.
8. The Greenbury Committee's 'Code of Best Practice'.
9. The Hampel Committee's recommendations (forthcoming).

Fiduciary responsibilities

A fiduciary responsibility arises whenever assets (either tangible or intangible) are entrusted by one party to the care of another party. Thus it can be said that fiduciary responsibilities arise directly out of principal–agent relationships.

In essence, the directors of companies have a fiduciary responsibility to their shareholders to act in their best interests. Furthermore, they must be prepared to demonstrate that they have discharged their responsibilities correctly, if challenged to do so in the law courts.

The scope of these responsibilities is not clear-cut; nor are the responsibilities unchanging. However, they are underpinned by three basic principles which have the force of law behind them:[2]

1. Directors should not place themselves in a position where their own personal interests conflict with the interests of shareholders.
2. They should not profit from their position at the expense of shareholders.
3. They cannot use information that is obtained in confidence from the company for their own benefit, or for the benefit of any other persons except the shareholders.

Annual reports and independent external audit

Another important element in the array of devices set up to monitor and control the actions of boards of directors is the annual audit requirement.

The Companies Act 1985 requires all limited companies to have an annual audit of their financial affairs, conducted by independent, external auditors. The prime purpose of this audit is to report to the shareholders on the conduct of the management's stewardship of the company's assets.

As such, this independent external audit can be seen as the bedrock control mechanism of the principal–agent relationship between shareholders and their managers. Indeed, it is interesting to note that although such an audit is now a legal requirement, independent external audits existed long before they were enforced by law. The audit not only certifies the annual report of the company but also examines the company's financial systems to ensure that proper control is being exercised.

However, as mentioned earlier, the financial statements produced by companies are based on a system known as historic cost accounting which is not really designed to disclose the economic performance of the company. A good example of this is the research carried out by companies. The standard treatment for research (and much development work) is to treat it as an expense rather than an investment. This has the effect of reducing the reported profits of the company (despite the fact that it may contribute significantly to cash flows in the future). It has been suggested that this might have the effect of reducing the amount of R&D (research and development) undertaken, particularly when the bonuses of managers are linked to company profits.

Stock Exchange rules

The London Stock Exchange is authorized by the 1986 Financial Service Act to regulate the UK Stock Exchange, in line with a series of European Community directives. These regulations are contained in what is referred to as the 'Yellow Book'.

The Yellow Book rules stipulate that the directors of a quoted company have both an individual and collective responsibility to ensure that the company complies with obligations under the regulations.

For purposes of the current discussion, the principal obligation of directors imposed by the Yellow Book rules is to release price-sensitive information to the market as a whole, so as to avoid a 'false market' in the valuation of a company's securities.

The implications of this in terms of the principal–agent problem is fairly obvious. If directors should fail to disclose information to the stock market, such that the share price is kept artificially high or low, then this could prompt action by the shareholders which would be damaging to their wealth. Shareholders might find themselves buying shares which, in reality, were over-valued; or they might sell their shares when they were under-valued.

Directors' transactions

Closely related to the foregoing is the Stock Exchange's 'model code' on directors' share dealings and the Companies Act regulations on directors' transactions.

To buy or sell shares on the basis of information which has not been publicly disclosed is known as 'insider dealing' and is illegal under the 1985 Company Securities (Insider Dealing) Act. This ruling applies to directors as well as all other potential investors. However, it causes particular problems for directors for they will, almost inevitably, be in possession of some price-sensitive information concerning the company which has not yet been disclosed to the stock market, but which would alter the market's valuation of the company's shares.

Therefore, at certain times in particular (for example, just before the company announces its annual results), the directors may have information which indicates that the shares are currently being over- or under-valued by the stock market. If directors were to deal in the shares at such times, it would clearly not be in the interests of their shareholders.

As a result, the Stock Exchange specifically requires companies to stipulate a code of practice for their directors based on the Exchange's own 'model code'. Although the provisions of the code are quite lengthy, the principal elements are:

1. Directors must not deal in their company's shares on a short-term basis.
2. Directors are not allowed to deal in the shares of their company prior to the disclosure of regularly recurring information (such as the annual results), or an announcement of an exceptional nature (such as a take-over bid).

Company law also regulates transactions between directors and their companies. The Companies Act 1985 stipulates that where a director has either a direct or indirect interest in a proposed contract with the company (for example, a director may own an asset which he intends to sell to the company), then that interest must be declared at a board meeting, and there may also be a duty to disclose the information in the company's accounts. These transactions are referred to as 'Class 4' transactions in the Yellow Book. Subject to some exceptions, the Yellow Book rules require such transactions:

1. to have the prior approval of shareholders;
2. to be fully disclosed in a circular to shareholders.

In addition, they cannot be voted on by the Class 4 party.

The City Code on take-overs and mergers

Although this is a specialized area which is not dealt with in this book, it is worth noting, within the context of the present discussion, that directors' actions are particularly constrained when the company is subject to a take-over bid.

It is easy to conceive of a situation in which a take-over bid for a company may be unwelcome to its directors, who might fear that they will lose their jobs and/or independence as a result – but which may be in the best interests of shareholders, in that the price offered values the shares at a premium to their current market value. (Or, alternatively, the directors may wish the bid to succeed although it is not in the best interests of the shareholders.) Under such circumstances, the directors may be in a position to defeat the bid through the actions that they take. In such a situation, the directors are subject to a code of best practice – known as the 'City Code' – as a Yellow Book requirement.

The City Code is based on a number of principles of best practice that are then codified into a complex set of rules. Amongst these principles are a number which are of direct interest to the current discussion:

1. All shareholders must be made the same offer.
2. Relevant information must be disclosed to all shareholders, so as to allow them to make a properly informed decision.
3. All information supplied to shareholders must be prepared with the highest standards of care and accuracy.
4. The directors must take no action, without the consent of their shareholders, which is specifically designed to 'frustrate' (i.e. defeat) the bid.

In this way, the City Code ensures that at one of the most important times in a company's life – when it is subject to a take-over bid – its directors are required to act in their shareholders' best interests.

The Cadbury, Greenbury and Hampel Reports on Corporate Governance

It is appropriate to deal with these three reports under the same heading as they are closely related. In broad terms, the Cadbury Committee was set up because of concerns about the misappropriation of what is known as *shareholder value*. More specifically, Whittington (1993) identifies four major forces driving the need for the changes in corporate governance proposed by Cadbury:

1. an increasing use of 'creative accounting';
2. a number of high profile business failures;
3. high levels of pay for directors, especially in privatized utilities;
4. short-termism (i.e. actions by managers driven by personal, short-term objectives such as bonuses rather than long-term shareholder value).

Concerns about creative accounting (i.e. manipulating financial statements so that they look the way that managers want them to look) have been with us for decades and were a major reason for the development of the system of accounting standards (rules) we have today. These concerns were further emphasised by Griffiths who published a book called *Creative Accounting* which exposed a number of ploys used by accountants to massage financial statements.

A number of well publicized and spectacular corporate bankruptcies in the late 1980s and early 1990s – two of the most notable being those of Maxwell Communication Corporation and Polly Peck – led to more general concern about the standard and quality of the stewardship function of directors of large public companies.

Numerous cases were highlighted in the financial press and in the law courts concerning ill-advised decisions on acquisitions and financing; instances of massive corporate fraud; excessive increases in directors' remuneration (particularly when corporate performance was poor) and 'one-way' incentive schemes which resulted in large financial rewards for directors when things went right, but had no adverse impact on remuneration if things went wrong.

All of these events finally led to the establishment by the Council of the Stock Exchange, together with the accountancy profession, of The Committee on the Financial Aspects of Corporate Governance under Sir Adrian Cadbury (the Cadbury Committee) which produced its report at the end of 1992.

The Committee looked directly at how directors do and should run the businesses which are under their control. In their report they set out a code of best practice which encompassed what they thought were the key principles of proper corporate governance, designed to ensure that directors meet their responsibilities and reduce their scope for exploiting the system.

The key conclusions were twofold. One was that there should be an effective balance of power between members of the board, so that no single individual can dominate or impose their views, unquestioned by their fellow directors. In this respect a separate chairman and chief executive was seen to be highly desirable, as opposed to the situation in some companies where the two roles were combined.[3]

The second key conclusion was that non-executive directors should be more numerous and play a more prominent role in the board's affairs. Cadbury envisaged them acting as a countervailing power to the executive directors, to specifically ensure that decisions taken by the board were in the interests of the company's shareholders.

There were also two other important conclusions. One was that, fairly obviously, there should be an effective system of reporting to and control by the board. The second was to highlight the role of the company secretary as the person with direct responsibility for ensuring that the board conducted its affairs in a fit and proper way.

The Cadbury Code is not legally binding on boards of directors. However, a 'statement of compliance' with the code has been made a Yellow Book rule. This means that all publicly quoted companies must state in their annual report and accounts whether or not they have implemented the code. If they have not implemented it in all aspects, then they must state which aspects have not been complied with, and for what reason. In this way, it is hoped, the decision is then put into the hands of the company's shareholders to decide whether or not they wish to demand greater compliance.

The code is reproduced in full in Table 1.1.

Table 1.1 Cadbury Report: Code of Best Practice on Corporate Governance

The board of directors
- The board should meet regularly, retain full and effective control over the company and monitor the executive management.
- There should be a clearly accepted division of responsibilities at the head of a company which will ensure a balance of power and authority such that no one individual has unfettered powers of decision. Where the chairman is also the chief executive, it is essential that there should be a strong and independent element on the board, with a recognized senior member.
- The board should include non-executive directors of sufficient calibre and number for their views to carry significant weight in the board's decisions.
- The board should have a formal schedule of matters specifically reserved to it for decision to ensure that the direction and control of the company is firmly in its hands.
- There should be an agreed procedure for directors in the furtherance of their duties to take independent professional advice if necessary, at the company's expense.
- All directors should have access to the advice and services of the company secretary, who is responsible to the board for ensuring that board procedures are followed and that applicable rules and regulations are complied with. Any question of the removal of the company secretary should be a matter for the board as a whole.

Non-executive directors
- Non-executive directors should bring an independent judgement to bear on issues of strategy, performance, resources, including key appointments, and standards of conduct.
- The majority should be independent of management and free from any business or other relationship which could materially interfere with the exercise of their independent judgement, apart from their fees and shareholding. Their fees should reflect the time which they commit to the company.
- Non-executive directors should be appointed for specified terms, and reappointment should not be automatic.
- Non-executive directors should be selected through a formal process and both this process and their appointment should be a matter for the board as a whole.

Executive directors
- Directors' service contracts should not exceed three years without shareholders' approval.
- There should be full and clear disclosure of directors' total emoluments and those of the chairman and highest-paid UK director, including pension contributions and stock options. Separate figures should be given for salary and performance-related elements and the basis on which performance is measured should be explained.

- Executive directors' pay should be subject to the recommendations of a remuneration committee made up wholly or mainly of non-executive directors.

Reporting and controls
- It is the board's duty to present a balanced and understandable assessment of the company's position.
- The board should ensure that an objective and professional relationship is maintained with the auditors.
- The board should establish an audit committee of at least three non-executive directors with written terms of reference which deal clearly with its authority and duties.
- The directors should explain their responsibility for preparing the accounts next to a statement by the auditors about their reporting responsibilities.
- The directors should report on the effectiveness of the company's system of internal control.
- The directors should report that the business is a going concern, with supporting assumptions or qualifications as necessary.

The Greenbury code of practice provides a framework setting out board responsibilities for pay issues and has meant that more information about this has been made available. Indeed, the quality of information to be provided to shareholders is a major part of the code. The Cadbury and Greenbury codes of practice have had some significant effects on the relationship between directors and shareholders and Hampel has observed that Cadbury has indeed led to higher standards of governence. The Hampel Committee was set up to review the recommendations of Cadbury and also took in Greenbury. Its basic findings are that the previous two committees were on the right track but that the implementation of their proposals has tended to be more about the letter than the spirit of the reports. It also emphasizes the importance of disclosure of information and reasserts the responsibility shareholders have to themselves for controlling their executives. At the time of writing (early 1998) the Stock Exchange had not yet produced the code of practice that it is expected to produce based on the three reports.

However it seems unlikely that rules and codes will ever be able to fully protect shareholders. The business failures have continued (e.g. BCCI and Barings) as have the high profile salary increases of certain directors. For example the *Financial Times* reported on 19 August 1997 that the chief executive of British Biotech took a 59% pay increase for the year to April 1997, despite a fall in the share price of the company during the year from 288p to 242p and a reported loss of £28.5 million. It also reported that four directors who resigned during the year made £9 million by exercising share options.

Incentive scheme criteria

Early in our general discussion about principal–agent relationships we stated that principals have two responses to the problem that they face. One response is the development of regulatory devices, as we have just seen. The second response is the creation of management incentive schemes, to try to ensure that there is much greater congruence between management's own personal objectives and the shareholders' objective of wealth (or share price) maximization.

To be successful, an incentive scheme must fulfil a number of criteria:

1. It should reward management effort and ability, not luck.
2. Its rewards should be potentially large enough to have a significant impact on management total remuneration.
3. The incentive reward system must work each way – rewarding good performance and penalizing poor performance.
4. The incentive scheme must take the concept of risk into account.
5. Reward should be related to performance over a time horizon which matches that of the shareholders.
6. It should be simple and inexpensive to operate and be difficult to manipulate or exploit.

Let us expand a little on each of these points in turn. Shareholders are interested in wealth maximization which, as we know, translates through into the maximization of the value of the company's shares. The first criterion in the list given above relates to the fact that the performance of all companies is, to a greater or lesser extent, dependent on general economic conditions within both the domestic and international economy. Therefore management should not be rewarded for a rise in the company's share price which has simply occurred through an improvement in general economic conditions. Nor should they be penalized for a share price fall resulting from depressed economic conditions.

What the foregoing implies is the need for an incentive scheme based on relative share price performance. In other words, management should be rewarded when the movement in the company's shares (either up or down) is more favourable than their competitors' share price movements – they should be rewarded for a greater rise in the share price, or a smaller fall.

The second criterion is required because, rationally, a manager will always have in mind the trade-off that exists between his incentive scheme gain from trying to maximize the worth of the shares and the likely gain from directly pursuing personal objectives through satisficing activities. Therefore if the incentive reward is relatively small, it is unlikely that the scheme will result in the desired modification of managerial behaviour.

The third criterion is necessary if the incentive scheme is to be proactive in affecting managerial behaviour. In other words, satisficing activity must be seen to have a negative rather than just a neutral impact on managerial rewards. A one-way incentive scheme rewards good performance, but does not penalize poor performance.

The danger with a one-way scheme is that it encourages management to take risks, without them suffering as a result from a potential adverse outcome: management might be tempted to undertake a risky venture on the basis that if it turns out to be successful there will be a favourable impact on their remuneration. However, if the outcome is unsuccessful only the shareholders – and not management – bear the resulting costs.

This is therefore the reasoning that lies behind the fourth criterion. Any incentive scheme must force management to look at both possible outcomes (i.e. good and bad) of a risky investment.

The fifth criterion relates to the problem that shareholders wish management to maximize the value of their shares over the time period that they intend to hold them. Therefore it becomes necessary to avoid any incentive scheme that might encourage management to make decisions which have a favourable short-term impact on the share price, but an adverse longer-term impact.

Finally, the need for the last criterion is fairly self-evident. If the incentive scheme is complex and expensive to operate, it may well be that the benefits that it brings are outweighed by the monitoring costs. Furthermore, if the incentive scheme is capable of being manipulated, then shareholders may find themselves rewarding management for illusionary gains to themselves.

Types of scheme

Fundamentally, there are two types of managerial incentive schemes, with many potential variations. One is based on accounting numbers – typically profitability (although it may be on sales growth). The other is based directly on share price performance.

A typical incentive scheme based on accounting numbers would reward management with a bonus based on either the growth rate of profitability or the absolute level of profitability (usually in excess of some minimum level), where 'profitability' may be defined either pre- or post-tax and interest charges.

Out of our six specified criteria, such a scheme is likely to be satisfactory on only one count: it is likely to be simple and cheap to operate. In all other respects (with the possible exception of criterion two) such a scheme is unlikely to bring about the desired effects from the shareholders' point of view.

Incentive schemes based on share price performance are usually *option-based*. In such a system key decision makers in the senior management team are allocated share options. These give the individual the right, (but not the obligation), to buy a specific number of the company's shares at a fixed price per share at any time over a specific future time period (typically, between three and ten years).

Having stated earlier that there are basically two types of managerial incentive schemes, they do of course both have the same objective of trying to ensure that managers take decisions which are in their shareholders' best interests. The great advantage of this second type of scheme is that it is directly related to shareholder wealth through the market value of the company's shares. Incentive schemes based on accounting profit only have, at best, an indirect relationship to shareholder wealth.

The key point about share option schemes is that management have the right to buy shares in the company at a *fixed* price. Therefore, the higher the actual share price, the greater is the worth or value of the option. Consequently, management have a very direct interest in maximizing the value of the company's shares.

Share option incentive schemes are likely to be more effective than profit-related bonus schemes, in that they will satisfy more of the criteria that we specified. However, they are likely to be far from ideal. The main problems with share option schemes are:

1. they represent a type of 'one-way' incentive;
2. they can reward management for share price movements which arise out of general economic conditions, rather than superior managerial performance;

3. they fail to deal adequately with the question of risk in decision making.

Can a 'perfect' incentive scheme be devised that satisfies our six criteria and results in a congruence of managers' and shareholders' objectives? The answer is probably not.

There are two main reasons for this assertion. The first is that a really effective scheme is likely to be complex and expensive to administer. Therefore, the sixth criterion is unlikely to be satisfied. The second reason relates to the fact that – particularly with respect to the first criterion specified – what is really required is a scheme that rewards *relative* share price performance. The problem here is one of being able to identify a genuinely similar company for comparison purposes.

We mentioned earlier that although the performance of all companies is affected, to some extent, by general economic conditions, all companies are not affected to the same extent. For share price performance comparability purposes, we need to identify companies whose performance is affected by general economic conditions in a very similar way to that in which our company is affected. Such a genuinely comparable company may be extremely difficult to identify in many cases.

It is generally recognized that executive incentive schemes have not been particularly successful (except, of course for the executives concerned). A review of 103 companies by the corporate governance consultancy Pirc found that 72% of the new share option schemes in 1997 paid out awards for annual earnings growth of 2% above inflation and that this had been achieved in seven of the last ten years.

Conclusion

What conclusion can be drawn from this discussion? We began by assuming that the objective behind financial management decision making was the maximization of the shareholder wealth, which is 'operationalized' in terms of maiximizing the value of the company's shares.

We then asked the question: are managers really maximizers, or are they more likely to be shareholder wealth satisficers? This point is important because, as was mentioned earlier, if management really have as their objective the satisficing rather than the maximizing of shareholders' wealth, then our normative theory of financial decision making would change. It is clear from the discussion above that some managers have been criticized for taking more out of companies than would seem appropriate. However, it is very difficult to judge the value of top managers to companies, in the same way as it is difficult to place a financial value on the contribution a top footballer makes to his team. We are of the view that although satisficing behaviour may well exist in the short term, it is unlikely to do so in the medium to long term – particularly in stock exchange quoted companies.

There are two principal reasons for this argument:

1. the competitive market for the shareholders' funds;
2. the competitive market for management jobs.

In a stock exchange quoted company, shareholders can monitor their management's performance through their company's share price performance, relative to that of similar companies. If one set of management is only satis-ficing, whilst the management of a similar company is striving to maximize shareholder wealth, then this fact can be expected to be reflected in the respective share price performance of the two companies (because of the resulting lower flow of dividends). Under such circumstances the satisficing company's management are likely to suffer adverse criticism in the financial press and their shareholders are likely to 'vote with their feet' – selling their shares and buying into the maximizing company. The resulting selling pres-sure on the company's shares is likely to depress their market price and, unless the situation is corrected fairly rapidly, market forces – perhaps in the form of an 'unwelcome' take-over bid – will lead to a change in manage-ment.[4] Thus the competitive market for shareholders' funds can help to ensure adherence to the maximizing objective. So, a manager might be paid a very large amount of money but the shareholders of the company can make up their own minds as to whether or not she is worth it.

In addition, one way for a manager to pursue his own objectives in terms of pay and perks is through job promotion. Given that most managers per-ceive that promotion can be gained through doing a job well, then it follows that in a competitive market for managerial jobs – as exists within a company – individual maximizing managers will look to advance their own personal objectives by replacing satisficing managers. Thus a satisficing manager runs the risk of being displaced by an ambitious maximizing manager.

It is never going to be possible to ensure that all actions by the executives of companies are in the best interests of their shareholders. It is thus not possible to argue that all decisions made in companies will necessarily fol-low the theories and 'good practices' we will be describing throughout this book. However, this does not mean that we should simply throw up our hands and surrender to management self-interest. Indeed, one measure of management performance that might be used by shareholders is how far decisions do follow the good practices we describe.

Summary

This chapter has covered the following major points:

- Shareholders and managers are in a principal–agent relationship where the principal is faced with the problem of controlling the agent's actions to ensure that the agent works in the best inter-ests of the principal.

- The principal's response to the problem is to develop monitoring devices and create incentive schemes.

- Managerial, (and especially directors') performance is monitored and controlled by a range of different legal and quasi-legal devices, which include fiduciary responsibilities, external audits, Yellow Book rules, the 'model code' on directors' share dealings, Companies Act regulations on directors' transactions and the Cadbury/Greenbury Committees' codes of best corporate gover-nance practice.

- Incentive schemes are desirable to bring about goal congruence between directors and shareholders. However the design of such schemes is fraught with problems and they are, in reality, unlikely to provide really effective control.

- Financial managers are unlikely to be able to sustain satisficing rather than maximizing behaviour for more than the short run. This is because of the competitive market for shareholders' funds causing the shareholders of satisficing companies to switch to maximizing companies; and because of the competitive market for management jobs both within the firm and between firms.

Notes

1. Job security refers here to the risky nature of a company's business. The more risky the company, the more likely it is to go bankrupt, so causing the management to lose their jobs. Hence management may be concerned to reduce the company's exposure to risk and such action may not be in the shareholders' best interests. This point will be explored further at a later stage.

2. The seriousness of these fiduciary responsibilities should not be underestimated. A director was subject to a claim of £406 million by the liquidators of a company called Bishopsgate Investment Management for alleged breaches in fiduciary duties.

3. The great stress placed upon this point by Cadbury resulted in a significant early victory when Barclays Bank gave way to public criticism over its proposal to combine these two roles. However it appears that Hampel is moving away from this position.

4. Changes in management, and hence changes in objectives, may come about in several ways. Shareholders, either behind the scenes or in the open at the company's annual general meeting, might force a change or, alternatively, a company's non-executive directors may be the catalyst responsible for action to be taken.

Further reading

1. Three articles which given an interesting overview of finance are: J.F. Weston, 'Developments in Finance Theory', *Financial Management*, Spring 1981; S.C. Myers, 'Finance Theory and Financial Strategy', *Midland Corporate Finance Journal*, Spring 1987; and W. Beranek, 'Research Directions in Finance', *Quarterly Review of Economics and Business*, Spring 1981.
2. Pike reports survey data on managers' perceived objectives (amongst other things) in R.H. Pike, 'An Empirical Study of the Adoption of Sophisticated Capital Budgeting Practices and Decision-Making Effectiveness', *Accounting and Business Research*, Autumn 1988; and R.H. Pike, *Capital Budgeting Survey: An Update*, Bradford University Discussion Paper, 1992. In addition, two interesting earlier articles on objectives are R.N. Anthony, 'The Trouble with Profit Maximization', *Harvard Business Review*, November–December 1960; and B. Branch, 'Corporate Objectives and Market Performance', *Financial Management*, Summer 1973.

3. For a discussion on conflicts between managers' and shareholders' objectives, see: G. Donaldson, 'Financial Goals: Management vs. Stockholders', *Harvard Business Review*, May–June 1963; C.M. Findley and G.A. Whitmore, 'Beyond Shareholder Wealth Maximization', *Financial Management*, Winter 1974; N. Seitz, 'Shareholders' Goals, Firm Goals and Firm Financing Decisions', *Financial Management*, Autumn 1982; and J.R. Grinyer, 'Alternatives to Maximization of Shareholder Wealth', *Accounting and Business Research*, Autumn 1986.

4. The ideas of satisficing and of the principal–agent problem can be found in: H.A. Simon, 'Theories of Decision Making in Economics and Behavioural Science', *American Economic Review*, June 1959; M.C. Jensen and W.H. Meckling, 'Theory of the Firm: Managerial Behaviour, Agency Costs and Ownership Structure', *Journal of Financial Economics*, October 1976; and E.F. Fama, 'Agency Problems and the Theory of the Firm', *Journal of Political Economy*, Spring 1980.

5. For a lengthy discussion of the search process (among other things) see: J. Grieve Smith, *Business Strategy*, Blackwell 1985.

6. For a more extended discussion on the control and monitoring of directors' activities see: R.R. Montgomerie, 'Responsibilities of Directors and Advisors' in *Handbook of UK Corporate Finance* second edn, eds J. Rutterford and R.R. Montgomerie, Butterworths 1992. See also *Corporate Governance: Responsibilities, Risks and Remuneration* eds K. Keasey and M. Wright, John Wiley and Sons and ICAEW, 1997.

7. The Cadbury Report is essential reading, ranging as it does over the whole of the corporate governance debate: 'Report of the Committee on the Financial Aspects of Corporate Governance', Gee, 1992.

8. In addition, two good books on corporate ethical responsibilities are W. Shaw and V. Barry, *Moral Issues in Business*, Wadsworth 1992; and N.E. Bowle and R.F. Duska, *Business Ethics*, Prentice-Hall 1990.

9. For a really different view of the relationship of managers to their company and shareholders which is fun to read see *Barbarians at the Gate*, B. Burrough and J. Helyar, Arrow Books 1990 (there is also a film based on this book but the portayal of the central character, Ross Johnson, as some sort of innocent is somewhat misleading).

10. Finally, for two thought-provoking articles, see: F.A. Hayek, 'The Corporation in a Democratic Society: in whose interests ought it and will it be run?' reprinted in H.I. Ansoff, *Business Strategy*, Penguin 1978; and J.J. Chrisman and A.B. Carroll, 'Corporate Responsibility – Reconciling Economic and Social Goals', *Sloan Management Review*, Winter 1984.

Quickie questions

1. What is the principal–agent problem?
2. List the main ways in which directors' actions are monitored and controlled.
3. What are the main criteria for an effective managerial incentive scheme?

Problems

1. How might you go about devising an incentive scheme for top management?
2. What is meant by the term 'a risky investment'? What makes some investments more or less risky than others?
3. What might be the financial management objectives of state-owned industries?
4. Discuss the means by which management's actions are monitored and controlled by shareholders.

2 Strategic planning and the finance function

Introduction

In the introduction, we discussed the concept of financial decision making and the need for an objective in order to make a choice amongst alternative courses of action. Then in Chapter 1 we put forward the generally accepted assumed objective that managers take decisions so as to 'maximize shareholder wealth', (or 'value', as it is sometimes termed). We saw that this implied that they were effectively trying to maximize the value of a company's shares.

We then posed the question about whether such an objective was realistic – given human nature – and that led us to consider the nature of the principal–agent relationship that exists between shareholders and their managers. In doing so, we examined the various control mechanisms that are imposed on managements and the way in which management incentive schemes might be designed to provide agreement between the shareholders' objective (that of wealth maximization) and management's own personal objectives.

Finally, we concluded that because of the potential threat of an unwelcome take-over bid and the competitive market for management jobs, the objective approximating to shareholder wealth/share price maximization was probably a reasonably reliable representation of reality. It was also pointed out that even if managers do have agendas other than the creation of shareholder value, we can still put forward a framework for 'good' decision making.

However, before we turn to look at the area of financial management decision making in more detail, we need to set out the context within which these decisions are taken.

First we need to consider the strategic business planning process out of which are developed the company's financial plans. Secondly we need to look at the broad role of financial management generally in order to highlight the specific aspects which are focused upon in this book. We then need to review how the finance function is organized within the firm and finally we need to look at the place of the firm within the general economy and, in particular, the role of the financial markets which supply the finance that enables companies to undertake their activities.

Strategic business planning

Although the idea of maximizing shareholder wealth is the fundamental objective underlying business activity, it is insufficient as an objective on its own in order to guide decision making. What is required is the addition of some substance to the objective, to explain how it is to be achieved. This is the area of strategic business planning.

The key planning questions

The strategic planning process for a business begins with trying to obtain answers to three simple questions (in the order stated):

1. Where are we now?
2. Where do we want to be?
3. How are we going to get there?

Just how the company should obtain answers to these three question is not something that is universally agreed upon. Strategic planning has more theories – and more fashionable 'flavours of the month' – than does financial management (which has its fair share!).

Strategic planning is not the focus of this book's attention and so we will not dwell too long on the area. But what we will do here is try to provide fairly straightforward answers to these questions and so avoid much of the controversy.

SWOT analysis

The first question – 'Where are we now?' – is normally answered through the use of SWOT analysis. SWOT is an acronym standing for Strengths, Weaknesses, Opportunities and Threats. It provides a useful framework for analysing a company's existing situation, both in terms of its own strengths and weaknesses and in terms of the opportunities and threats posed by the external environment within which it operates.

To undertake SWOT analysis, the company first undergoes a self-critical review of its existing strengths and weaknesses. In doing so it looks at its existing product range; its fixed asset base; its human resources and its managerial capability. This 'inward look' is then followed by an 'outward look' at its operating environment.

In looking at both the opportunities and the threats that it may face, the company would examine such issues as changes in consumer demand for the company's products and services; the range of competitors that the company faces in the market-place and the way in which technological change is affecting the company, its products and its organization.

Matrix analysis

Once the company feels it has a clear response to the first question, it can then turn to the second, related question: 'Where do we want to be in three to five years' time?'[1] Attempts to answer this question cause the greatest controversy in terms of management (as opposed to financial management) theorists.

In the 1970s and early 1980s the 'portfolio grid matrix' approach was fashionable. This is, essentially, a very simplistic approach to try and attempt to identify those business areas which hold greatest promise. The most famous, and original, of these was the Boston Consulting Group's so-called 'Boston Box'. This consisted of a two-dimensional grid, with 'market growth rate' on one axis and 'market share' on the other. Out of this came four different types of business definition: Stars, Dogs, Cash Cows and Question Marks. Fig. 2.1 illustrates the concept.

The idea is that the company should invest in the 'star areas' of its business operations, where there is strong growth potential and the company has a high market share. Conversely, the company should divest itself of operations in 'dog' areas, where growth prospects are low and the company has low market share. In business areas where the company has a high market share but low prospects for future growth, further investment should not be pursued. Instead the company should simply concentrate on trying to maximize the cash flow that can be generated from the existing investment. Finally, in 'question mark' areas of the company's operations, a strategic decision has to be taken: whether to increase investment in the hope of gaining market share or to maintain the company's existing limited presence in the market and await further developments and opportunities.

Although the ideas behind the Boston Box approach generated many more sophisticated variations, they all suffered from the need for a great deal of qualitative data which could not easily be transformed into a quantitative – that is, financial – analysis.

Furthermore, it is not at all clear whether the basic advice of the Boston Box would turn out to be correct. Cash Cows may well be worth further investment, as might Dogs, as long as they were profitable.

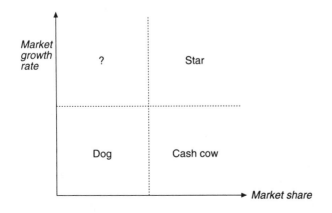

Fig. 2.1 *The 'Boston Box' matrix grid*

Competitive analysis

These rather simplistic approaches to the company's attempt to answer the question 'Where do we want to be?' gave way in the 1980s to the 'Competitive Analysis', developed by Michael Porter at the Harvard Business School.

Porter believed that the objective of businesses is to create 'competitive advantage', which he defined as the difference between the worth of the company's output to its customer and the cost to the company of producing the output. From a financial standpoint therefore, competitive advantage is really gross profit: the difference between revenues and cost of sales.

Companies go about maximizing their competitive advantage by utilizing competitive strategy – that is, they move into those areas of business that hold out the potential of creating the greatest competitive advantage for the company. These areas will be where the company can create 'superior value' for its customers, either by charging a lower price than its competitors (because its cost of sales is lower), or by offering customers unique benefits that are not available from its competitors.

The value drivers

According to Porter, there are five key factors which determine how attractive an area of business will be to a company:

1. buyer power;
2. supplier power;
3. entry opportunities;
4. substitute possibilities;
5. competitor rivalry.

These 'competitive forces' are termed 'profit' or 'value' drivers, and it is these that the company must take into account in answering the question 'Where do we want to be?' in terms of:

1. What business areas should we expand into?
2. What business areas should we withdraw from?
3. How can we improve a business area's level of profitability?

'Buyer power' relates to the industry's fundamental level of competitiveness. The greater the scope of the customer to play one supplier off against another, the less profitable the industry is likely to be.

'Supplier power' relates to the company's ability within an industry to keep down its cost of sales. The scarcer the alternative sources of supply of the company's inputs, the less profitable will be the industry.

'Entry opportunities' refer to the ease with which competitors can gain access to the market-place. The lower the barriers to entry, the lower will be the industry's profitability.

'Substitute possibilities' concern the degree of competition from other industries in related areas. For example, if you were to manufacture sausages, not only would you be concerned about other sausage manufacturers, but you might also be concerned about hamburger manufacturers, as your customers could switch from eating sausages to eating hamburgers. The greater the threat of substitutability, the less profitable the industry.

Finally, there is the degree of rivalry between existing competitors. Rivalry will tend to be more intense the more equally matched are the competitors, the lower is the growth rate of the industry and the greater is the proportion of fixed operating costs within the industry. In such circumstances, intense rivalry brings lower profitability.

The strategic approaches

Going through this detailed analysis helps the company to understand the competitive setting within which it exists and, on this basis, reach decisions as to the direction in which it wants to go in the future. Porter believes that the choice about which business areas the firm should position itself in and how it should compete in those areas to successfully generate competitive advantage relates to the ideas of creating 'superior value' for the customer.

Porter suggests that there are four strategic approaches available to the company, of which just one should be focused upon. If not, there is a danger that by focusing on multiple strategies, the company loses clarity of purpose. These strategic approaches are:

1. Broad product differentiation where the company tries to specifically differentiate all its products across the complete range from those of its competitors, looking to add unique benefits (such as better quality or greater convenience).
2. Narrow product differentiation where the company aims for product differentiation in a very narrow, specialized product range.
3. Broad-based cost leadership where the company drives towards creating superior value by concentrating on minimizing operating costs over its complete product range.
4. Focused cost leadership where the company looks to specialize in a very narrow product range and go for maximum scale economies and production cost efficiency.

Investment and financing strategy

Having made these crucial, strategic decisions, the company is then faced with the third question: 'How do we get to where we want to go?'

In many cases there is a blurring between the process of answering the second and the third questions. In answering the second question the company is setting up its strategic objectives; whilst in answering the third question it is required to appraise the financial and operational viability of the different strategic approaches suggested above. This is the subject matter of much of the remainder of this book.

The planning objective of financial management is to maximize shareholder wealth through the maximization of the value of the company's shares. In order to do this, the management must first of all identify a suitable business strategy. The choice of this strategy is through understanding the competitive environment, specifically in relation to those five key value drivers. It is characteristics of these five factors which are going to determine the firm's net cash flow generated over time in terms of the rate of sales growth and the level of profit margins.

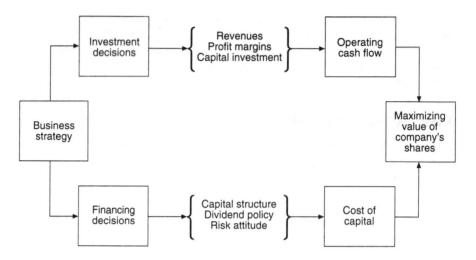

Fig. 2.2 *The strategic planning process*

Therefore it is at this stage that the company formulates its investment strategy in terms of the capital (fixed asset) expenditure decision.

The other factor involved with shareholder wealth maximization is the cost of capital to the company. Maximizing shareholder wealth is achieved not only through maximizing revenues and revenue growth and minimizing cost of sales through the investment strategy; it is also achieved through minimizing the cost of the finance put into these investments. Thus the firm will need to develop a financial strategy covering such elements as the company's capital structure (i.e. its debt–equity capital mix), its dividend policy and its attitude towards risk (and hence its credit rating).

It should be stressed that the company's overall financial strategy is crucial. It is very easy to concentrate too much on investment decisions and by doing this neglect other areas of the total picture. If the company's cost of capital is higher than that of its competitors it will be at a serious competitve disadvantage. Not only will the competitor company be more profitable overall but the company might find that certain projects are not worth pursuing whilst this is not the case for its competitors.

Suppose the cost of capital for company A is 20% but that company B's cost of capital is only 15% (because of a different capital structure for instance). If both companies take on projects yielding 25%, company A will enjoy a margin of 25% − 20% = 5% whilst company B enjoys a margin of 10%. Also, an investment yielding 18% will be worthwhile for company B but not for company A. Company A is at a considerable disadvantage compared to company B when it comes to creating wealth for its shareholders.

The overall planning process is shown in Fig 2.2.

The role of financial management

Before moving on to look more closely at the theory and practice of financial decision making, it is important to see the place of financial decision making within the overall financial management function. This book is not concerned about the whole spectrum of financial management, but it is concerned with what are probably the most fundamental elements within that spectrum and, as such, they have important implications for the other elements.

Essentially, the financial management function can be divided up into five principal areas:

1. Translating the company's business plan into a financial plan.
2. Evaluating the financial plan to ensure its validity, given the company's objective as far as shareholder wealth maximization is concerned.
3. Ensuring that sufficient finance is made available in order to undertake the planned activities.
4. Controlling the plan's implementation.
5. Reporting the outcome of the business plan's implementation to all interested parties.

Therefore, the starting point is where the company – either formally or informally – draws up a business plan. This would normally be done in non-financial terms: sales targets, percentage market shares, capacity levels and manpower levels, etc. These plans would then have to be examined and analysed (and modified, if need be), to ensure that their financial implications are satisfactory and that they will help to increase shareholder wealth.

In addition to evaluating the financial feasibility of the business plan, financial management has also to ensure that the company has adequate financial resources at its command to enable it to undertake the plan. If those resources do not already exist within the company, then arrangements have to be made to raise additional finance from the financial markets.

The business plan is then implemented and controlled, typically through standard costing, budget-setting and variance analysis. Finally, the outcome of all this activity has to be reported to the company's own management in the form of management accounts, and to its shareholders in the form of financial accounts (i.e. the profit and loss account, balance sheet and cash flow statement). In addition, financial reports to other interested parties such as the employees, the company's bankers and the tax authorities may also be required.

Organization of the finance function

Fig. 2.3 is a typical organizational chart for the finance function of a large company. From it can be seen how these different elements of financial management are normally split up between the three major participants: the Finance Director, the Chief Accountant and the Treasurer. The main responsibilities of the Finance Director are as follows:

1. the setting of the company's broad financial strategy;
2. decisions on major capital expenditure on new assets and the acquisition of other companies;
3. interpretation and implications of macro- and micro-economic financial developments for the company;
4. implications for the company of government economic and fiscal (tax) legislation and proposals;
5. the dividend decision.

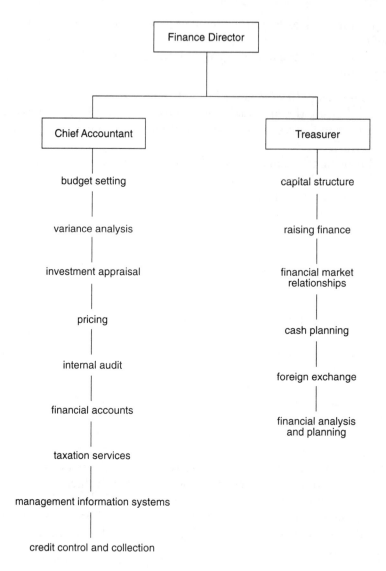

Fig. 2.3 *The finance functions*

Finance Director

Chief Accountant

budget setting

variance analysis

investment appraisal

pricing

internal audit

financial accounts

taxation services

management information systems

credit control and collection

Treasurer

capital structure

raising finance

financial market relationships

cash planning

foreign exchange

financial analysis and planning

The Chief Accountant is responsible for the following tasks:

1. preparation of financial reports to all internal and external user groups including: management, employees, shareholders, bankers, other creditors and tax authorities;
2. installation, maintenance, updating and review of the company's management information systems;
3. preparation and control of budgets;
4. pricing policies (in conjunction with marketing);
5. capital investment appraisals;
6. management of working capital.

The Treasurer's main responsibilities concern the following seven areas:

1. the establishment and maintenance of good relationships with shareholders and financial institutions;
2. ensuring that sufficient finance, and credit facilities, are available to meet all foreseeable contingencies;
3. the issue of securities and investment of surplus cash;

4. cashier and payroll activities;
5. management of the company's exposure to foreign exchange risk;
6. corporate financial planning;
7. interest rate planning.

The firm in the economy

The are basically two major groupings within a simple economic system: households and firms. 'Households' is the term used by economists to refer to individuals within the economy (like you, the reader) who own the physical resources such as land, property, machinery, raw materials or labour. Households then transfer these resources to firms who use them to produce outputs (which can be anything from cornflakes to theatre tickets) that people want. This process is shown by the innermost pair of arrows in Fig. 2.4. It is known as the 'real' sub-system in the economy's flow of funds, as it deals with the flow of real or physical inputs (resources) and outputs (goods and services) in the economy.

Firms pay households for their resources with money in the form of wages, rents and prices. In turn, households pay for the outputs of firms also by using money. Thus there is a secondary pair of arrows in Fig. 2.4 which is referred to as the monetary sub-system, as it relates to the flow of cash between households and firms.

The money that households receive from firms in payment for their resources is known as their income. The money households pay to firms in order to buy the outputs of firms is their expenditure. Households generally have an excess of income over expenditure, known as savings. Similarly, the households' income represents the firms' costs and the households' expenditure represents the firms' revenues.

In aggregate, within an economy, the household sector usually has a surplus (of income over expenditure), while the firm sector is in deficit (i.e. it

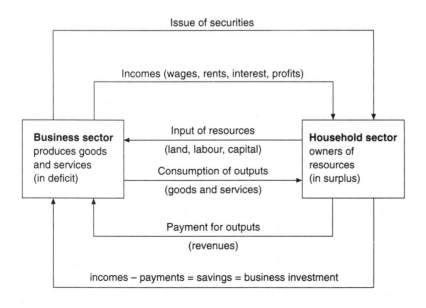

Fig. 2.4 *Simple two-sector economy*

requires additional cash). Therefore households lend their savings to firms and, in return, firms pay out interest and dividends to households. This flow is represented by the outermost pair of arrows on Fig. 2.4 – the financial sub-system.

Obviously, what has been described here is a very simplistic analysis; a more complete picture of the flow of funds within the economy would involve at least three other sectors: the government, the financial intermediaries (of which more later) and overseas economies. However, our purpose for the moment is sufficiently served by this very simple illustration.

The problem of liquidity

Within this simple illustration of the flow of funds in an economy, there lies a problem. Generally speaking, households dislike lending their savings to firms unless they have the ability to get their money back again quickly and easily, if they so wish (because some unforeseen need to spend their savings on goods and services has arisen). In other words, households only like to invest their savings if they have a considerable degree of liquidity.

On the other hand, firms want to be able to keep the money that they borrow from households for lengthy periods of time, because they will often want to invest it in long-term or permanent assets such as machinery or buildings. It would be no good a firm borrowing £1 million from households one week, and then the households asking for their money back the next week (because some unforeseen circumstances have arisen) if, in the meantime, the firm has bought a new factory with the money. Thus the problem is that there is a mis-match between firms and households in their liquidity requirements. Because of their liquidity preference, households generally only want to lend short term, but firms want to borrow medium to long term.

Within the economy, this problem is overcome in two ways: by the existence of financial intermediaries (such as banks), and financial markets (such as the stock market). Both financial intermediaries and financial markets stand between the firms and the households in order to solve the mis-match in liquidity requirements.

Taking a bank as the best-known example of a financial intermediary, the role they play can be simply illustrated as follows. Suppose a household has £1000 of savings. They want to invest those savings, but they also require to be able to recall their money (liquidate their investment) if an unforeseen need for it arises. Instead of lending the money directly to a firm, which is likely to want to keep the money medium to long term, and will not want (or be able) to offer the household the facility of returning the money at short notice, the household lends the £1000 to a bank. In other words, the money is placed on bank deposit. The bank undertakes to repay the contents of the deposit account to the household at any time, but then promptly lends £900 of the £1000 to a firm. The loan to the firm may be for, say, a five-year term. The result of this is that the household has the required liquidity for its savings and the firm has got its required illiquidity.

But what happens if, shortly after the loan is made to the firm, the household demands their money back? The bank has only got £100 of the original £1000. It is here that the bank takes advantage of being able to pool the savings of many households. Knowing that it is unlikely that *all* the households who have placed money on deposit will simultaneously want their money back, the bank tries to keep sufficient liquid resources (the £100 kept back would be part of these) available to be able to satisfy those households who do actually want to liquidate the investment of their savings.

This mis-match of liquidity requirements between households and firms is also reconciled through the existence of capital markets like the stock exchange. Basically the stock exchange provides a market-place where medium- to long-term securities (loans and shares) issued by firms to households can be sold (or liquidated).

For example, the household which wanted to invest £1000 of its savings could, instead of going through a financial intermediary, invest the money in the firm directly. In return the firm might issue £1000 worth of share certificates. If a stock market did not exist, a household would be extremely reluctant to take this course of action because ordinary shares form part of the firm's permanent capital and are unlikely ever to be repaid unless the firm is itself wound-up. Thus the household's investment would be completely illiquid.

However, the problem is overcome through the existence of stock markets. If the firm's shares are quoted on the stock market, it means that there are institutions known as market makers whose function is always to be prepared to buy (and sell) shares in the firms from households. Thus if our household which has invested £1000 in the shares of the firm wishes to liquidate the investment because unforeseen circumstances have arisen and the money is needed, they can simply sell their shares – not back to the company, but on the stock market (to the market maker) – and so liquidate their investment.

Risk and return

There is, of course, an important difference between the two examples used of the household with £1000 of savings. When the bank deposit account is liquidated, the household will recover the precise amount placed on deposit – £1000 (plus any interest that has accrued). However, when the £1000 investment in the company's shares is liquidated, just how much money will be recovered – it could be more or less than £1000 – is uncertain, because the market maker sets a price according to the levels of supply and demand for the shares. This is in turn a function of expectations at the time of the future performance of the company. Thus the household suffers a degree of uncertainty in the latter case which is avoided in the former.

This problem of risk – that is, uncertainty of outcome – will play a major role in the development of the theory of financial decision making. In many ways it is what financial decision making is all about. Householders (i.e. investors) dislike risk – they are risk averse – and will only be willing to take on risk if they can be expected to be rewarded for so doing. This reward comes in the form of the expected level of return. Thus much of financial decision making is concerned with the risk and return trade-off – is the expected return worth the risk involved?

In fact we can identify two factors that determine the rate of return we expect to receive. The first is that we receive a reward for forgoing consumption now in exchange for consumption later. It is a reward for forgoing the convenience of access to resources now and it is called the *liquidity premium*. At the time of writing this stands at around 6% (although there is a significant range of returns available from the market). The second is that we receive a reward for taking risks (or at least on average we do, because the whole thing about risk is that sometimes we come out ahead whilst at other times we do not). This is called the *risk premium* and it will vary according to the perceived risk of the investment.

For this reason, the householder in our example would expect to get a higher return on savings invested in shares (coming in the form of dividends plus a possible capital gain on subsequent sale) than when they were placed on bank deposit (coming in the form of interest). In fact, the capital markets provide a whole spectrum of different risk (and expected return) investments in which households can place their savings. The nature of this risk and the determinants of the reward structure will be returned to at a later point.

Summary

This chapter has covered the following major points:

- There are three key planning questions: where are we now?; where do we want to be?; and how are we going to get there?

- The 'where are we now' question is usually answered using SWOT analysis, which looks at the business's strengths, weaknesses, opportunities and threats.

- There are many approaches to tackling the second question. In the 1970s and early 1980s, matrix analysis such as the Boston Box, was fashionable.

- This simplistic approach has given way to Porter's 'competitive analysis' and the need to identify the company's 'value drivers'.

- The five value drivers are: buyer power, supplier power, entry opportunities, substitute possibilities and competitor rivalry. Their analysis determines the business areas the company might expand into and withdraw from.

- Out of this analysis, Porter suggests that the company selects one strategic approach out of the four possibilities: broad or narrow product differentiation or, broad or narrow cost leadership.

- Once the overall business strategy is formulated, management then needs to formulate the company's investment strategy and its financing strategy.

- The role of financial management can be split into five broad elements:
  - the translation of the business plan into financial terms;
  - the financial evaluation of the plan;
  - the raising of finance for the plan;
  - the implementation and control of the plan;
  - the reporting to interested parties as to the financial outcome of the plan's implementation.

- The mis-match in liquidity requirements between households and firms can be resolved through the use of financial intermediaries and capital markets. However, there is a significant difference in the risk a household/investor is exposed to through each means and this is reflected in the expected returns on investment each provides the household.

Notes

1. The duration of a company's planning horizon is, in itself, a problematical area. How far ahead in time companies will try and plan depends partially upon the type of business that the company is engaged in and partially on the stability of its operating environment. Some types of business require the acquisition of very long-lived assets, and in such companies the planning process, out of necessity, also has to be very long-term – attempting to look 15–25 years into the future. On the other hand, if the company's assets are essentially short-term and it operates in a very unstable and ever-changing environment, the planning horizon will be likely to be far shorter.

Further reading

1. For a discussion of the development of the matrix approach to corporate strategy, see K. Davidson, 'Strategic Investment Theories', *Journal of Business Strategy*, Summer 1985.
2. The two classic books by Porter that introduced the ideas of competitive analysis are M.E. Porter, *Competitive Strategy*, Free Press 1980 and *Competitive Advantage*, Free Press 1985.
3. For more specific articles on financial planning see J.F. Weston, 'Forecasting Financial Requirements', *Accounting Review*, July 1958 and W.T. Carleton, C.L. Dick and D.H. Downes, 'Financial Policy Models: Theory and Practice', *Journal of Financial and Quantitative Analysis*, December 1973.
4. Finally, on the role of the financial management function, a useful booklet to read is J.A. Donaldson, *The Corporate Treasury Function*, Institute of Chartered Accountants of Scotland 1988.

Quickie questions

1. What are the three key strategy questions?
2. What is SWOT analysis?
3. Describe the Boston Box.
4. List the five 'value drivers' of a business.
5. What does the firm's investment strategy cover?
6. Why is financing strategy important?
7. What are the typical responsibilities of the chief accountant?
8. Sketch out a basic flow of funds diagram for an economy.
9. What role does the stock market play?
10. What do we assume about investors' risk attitude?

Problems

1. Outline the strategic business planning process.
2. Investors want to be able to get their money back at short notice; companies want to borrow money for long-term investments. How is this mis-match in liquidity requirements overcome in practice?

3 Traditional methods of investment appraisal

Introduction

In its simplest form, an investment decision can be defined as one which involves the firm making a cash outlay with the aim of receiving, in return, future cash inflows. Numerous variations on this definition are possible, such as a cash outlay with the aim of reducing or saving further cash outlays, but these can all generally adapt to the initial definition with little trouble.[1]

Decisions about buying a new machine, building a factory, extending a warehouse, improving a delivery service, instituting a staff training scheme or launching a new product line are all examples of the investment decisions that may be made in industry. In order to help in making such decisions, and to ensure that they are consistent with each other, a common method of appraisal is required which can be applied equally to the whole spectrum of investment decisions and which should, in terms of the decision structure so far outlined, help to decide whether any particular investment will assist the company in maximizing shareholder wealth (via share price maximization).

A warning

In looking for such an investment appraisal method we shall begin by examining two of the most widely used[2] methods: payback, and return on capital employed, to see how well they fit in with our financial decision objective and value base. However, before doing so we should be clear that neither of these two methods, nor any other method of investment appraisal can give a definitive decision. They cannot tell a company's financial decision maker to 'invest' or 'not invest', but can only act as a decision *guide*. This extremely important point will become obvious as we develop our theory, but it is all too easy to slip back into the erroneous (and sometimes comforting) belief that the techniques that we shall develop here will make decisions for us. They will not do this. All they will do is help to communicate information to the decision maker; but when the actual decision is finally made, it is based on a whole range of very diverse considerations which are beyond our present capabilities to encompass in 'overall' decision-making formulae.[3]

There has sometimes been a considerable amount of resistance and resentment on the part of financial managers to the introduction of any new investment appraisal technique, based partially on the belief that with such methods their decision-making function would be replaced by a formula, 'handle-turning' function. Such a belief is ill-founded, not only for the reason already given, but also because investment is about the future. Almost all investment decisions will involve making forecasts/ estimates/guesses about the investment's future performance, and appraisal techniques are applied to the numbers that emerge from that process. The future is, almost without exception, uncertain and so any investment appraisal technique can only produce *advice* based on these forecasts and not a decision that is guaranteed to turn out to be optimal given hindsight. So, investment appraisal techniques can never replace managerial judgement, but they can help to make that judgement more sound.

The payback method

Let us start by looking at the first of these two traditional methods of investment appraisal: the payback method.[4] This is one of the most tried and trusted of all methods and its name neatly describes its operation, referring to how quickly the incremental benefits that accrue to a company from an investment project 'pay back' the initial capital invested – the benefits being normally defined in terms of after-tax cash flows.

The payback method can be used as a guide to investment decision making in two ways. When faced with a straight accept-or-reject decision, it can provide a rule where projects are only accepted if they pay back the initial investment outlay within a certain predetermined time. In addition, the payback method can provide a rule when a comparison is required of the relative desirability of several mutually exclusive investments.[5] In such cases projects can be ranked in terms of 'speed of payback', with the fastest paying-back project being the most favoured and the slowest paying-back project the least favoured. Thus the project which paid back quickest would be chosen for investment.

Given below are examples of the payback method operating in both decision-making situations. With Project A, assuming that the criterion for project acceptance is a four-year (maximum) payback, then we can see that it should be accepted because it pays back the initial outlay of £4000 within this time period:

Project A Year[6]	Cash flow (£)
0	−4000
1	+1000
2	+1000
3	+2000 payback period
4	3000
5	1000

If Projects B and C are mutually exclusive, Project C has the faster 'speed of payback' and so is the preferred investment. B pays back within three years (i.e. $2\frac{3}{5}$ years: years 1 and 2 cash flow plus three-fifths of year 3 cash flow), whereas C pays back in two years exactly:

Project B		Project C	
Year	Cash flow (£)	Year	Cash flow (£)
0	− 10 000	0	− 12 500
1	+ 3 000	1	+ 5000
2	+ 4 000	2	+ 7500
3	+ 5 000	3	+ 1000
4	+ 6 000	4	+ 1000
		5	+ 1000

Working capital

Most projects involve an expenditure not only on capital equipment, but also on working capital. For example, suppose a company was considering investing in a sausage-making machine. Not only would the company have to incur the capital expenditure on the machine itself, but they would also have to invest in working capital: raw material stocks, finished goods stocks and debtors. However, the point to be recognized is that, at the end of the project's life, although the capital equipment will only have (at best) a scrap value, the working capital should be recovered in full. This is because, at the end of the project's life, the firm can run down its stocks of raw materials and finished goods and, hopefully, all outstanding debtors will pay up.

The following question then arises: should working capital be included as part of the project's outlay and so be included in the payback calculation? Example 1 illustrates such a situation. It is probably the case that for payback calculations (only), working capital should be excluded from the analysis, and so the advice given by payback is to accept the sausage machine project.[7] However it should be noted that there are no real rules in making decisions such as this. We will use the cash flows that we judge to be most appropriate.

Example 1

Ajax plc is considering the purchase of a sausage machine. The machine would cost £12 000, have an expected life of five years and a zero scrap value (net of disposal costs) at the end of that time. In addition, an expenditure of £8000 on working capital will be required throughout its life. The firm's management accountants have estimated the net, after-tax, operating cash flows of the project as follows:

Year	Operating cash flow (£)
1	+6000
2	+6000
3	+6000
4	+4000
5	+3000

Ajax evaluates investment opportunities using a three-year maximum payback criterion. The problem here is what set of cash flows should be evaluated using payback: Alternative 1 or 2?

Year	Alternative 1 Capital expenditure (£)	Working capital (£)	Operating cash flow (£)	Year	Alternative 2 Capital expenditure (£)	Operating cash flow (£)
0	−12 000	−8000		0	−12 000	
1			+6000	1		+6000
2			+6000	2		+6000
3			+6000	3		+6000
4			+4000	4		+4000
5		+8000	+3000	5		+3000

If working capital is taken into account, the project should be rejected, as it takes more than three years to recover the total initial outlay of £20 000. But if working capital is excluded from the analysis, the project is acceptable as it has a two-year payback.

The logic behind the approach of excluding working capital is as follows. Payback is concerned about how long it will take the project to reach its break-even point where at least the outlay has been recovered. Management are interested in this point, because they recognize the uncertainties that surround any estimate of a project's future cash flow. Thus the more quickly a project achieves payback, the less risky is that project in the eyes of many managements. As a project's working capital is likely to be recovered whenever the project comes to the end of its life (i.e. working capital is automatically paid back), it is excluded from the analysis of the break-even point.

Advantages of payback

As can be seen from the two initial illustrations, payback is quick and simple to calculate (once the project's cash flow forecasts have been made) and is likely to be readily understood by management. This is one of its greatest advantages as an appraisal technique, but it has other advantages in addition.

A second advantage is that it is thought by many managements to lead to automatic selection of the less risky project in mutually exclusive decision situations. The point has already been mentioned that one of the most difficult tasks in investment appraisal is the forecasting of future project cash flows. In this respect, generally speaking, the further ahead in time is the cash flow estimate, the less reliable is that estimate. Therefore by emphasizing 'speed of return' and selecting the project, from a series of alternatives, that pays back quickest, the appraisal method is – almost by definition – choosing the least risky project, in that it chooses the one which reaches break-even most quickly. However, this is a complex point and we shall return to it later when the problem of risk is more fully discussed.

A further advantage of payback, and one that is connected to what has been said previously, is that it saves management the trouble of having to forecast cash flows over the whole of a project's life. Given that the forecasting process is difficult, and the further ahead in time the forecast has to be made the greater the difficulty, the fact that project cash flows need not be forecasted beyond the maximum payback criterion (by which time the project either is or is not acceptable) is an obvious advantage. For instance, in Example 1, although the sausage machine was thought to have had a five-year life, there really was no need to forecast its cash flows beyond three years (the decision criterion) in order to evaluate it.

A final advantage of payback, that is seen by many managers, is that it is a convenient method to use in capital rationing situations. Capital rationing is a subject which we shall return to later to look at in more detail. However, it basically refers to a situation where a company does not have unlimited capital expenditure funds. (Perhaps the limit has been imposed by the company itself in the form of an annual capital expenditure budget.) Example 2 illustrates the situation.

Example 2

Alpha plc has identified five independent[8] investment opportunities and wishes to evaluate their desirability. The company normally uses payback with a three-year criterion and has specified a maximum capital expenditure budget for the year of £200 000. The project's net after-tax cash flows are estimated as follows:

Project:	1	2	3	4	5
			(all cash flows in £000s)		
Year					
0	−100	−300	−100	−200	−250
1	+ 50	+100	+ 20	+ 50	+ 50
2	+ 50	+100	+ 80	+ 50	+100
3	+ 50	+100	+ 50	+100	+ 80
4		+ 80	+ 30	+ 50	+ 80
5		+ 50			

Using payback, Projects 1 to 4 are all acceptable as they each pay back within the three-year criterion. Project 5 is unacceptable. However, Alpha has a problem. To undertake all four acceptable projects will require total expenditure of £700 000 and only £200 000 has been budgeted. How is the firm to 'ration out' the available cash among the competing projects?

The solution is to reduce the payback criterion from three down to two years. Projects 2 and 4 are now undesirable, leaving just 1 and 3 which, between them, will utilize the available capital.

Example 2 shows how the capital rationing problem can be met by reducing the payback criterion and so reducing the number of acceptable projects. In addition, the approach can also claim to have yet another advantage in that, in such a situation, it appears to accept the most 'sensible' projects. If capital is in short supply, it could be argued that the best projects to accept would be those which returned the expenditure rapidly – which is exactly what the payback method does.

The decision criterion

Nothing has so far been said about how the decision criterion is set. There are a number of possible methods that management might utilize. One would simply be to base the criterion on past experience; for example if the firm's experience is that most successful projects have paid back within four years, then that time period might be set as a criterion. Alternatively, general 'industry practice' might be taken as the guideline.

One obvious, and very sensible, basis for setting the decision criterion would be forecasting ability. For example, if a firm believed that, realistically, it could not forecast project cash flows with sufficient accuracy beyond five years ahead, then five years might be set as the criterion. Here management would be recognizing their forecasting limitations and would be sensibly deciding not to evaluate a project on cash flow forecasts which might be seen more as guesses than estimates.

Disadvantages of payback

Having looked at the advantages – true or otherwise – claimed for the method, let us now turn to the disadvantages. The first is the problem of what is meant by the term 'investment outlay'. If we look at Projects D and E, just how should the investment outlay be defined in each case?

Project D		Project E	
Year	Cash flow (£)	Year	Cash flow (£)
0	−10 000	0	−5000
1	+ 5000	1	+1000
2	+ 5000	2	−5000
3	+ 5000	3	+3000
4	− 2000	4	+3000
		5	+4000

Is Project D's outlay £10 000 or £12 000? Is Project E's outlay £10 000 or £9000? The point is that in each case we *can* come to a decision, say, Project D's outlay is £10 000 and E's is £9000, but the decision rule as it stands is too ambiguous in its definition of terminology to give a definitive ruling.

The problem of ambiguity can also be seen in the definition of the *start* of the payback time period. In other words, from what point do we begin counting? Suppose that Project E will be accepted only if it pays back within three years. If this means that E must pay back its outlay by Year 3 – that is, three years after its commencement – clearly, it should not be accepted. On the other hand, if the payback criterion means that it should pay back within three years of the completion of its outlays – that is, by Year 5 – then it is acceptable. Once again, as it stands, the decision rule is too ambiguous to give a definitive ruling.

This ambiguity is an important problem. When any technique, designed as a decision-making aid, is open to ambiguity in interpretation, then it is likely to be manipulated so as to lend backing to the *desired* decision, rather than the *right* decision. Any decision rule open to such misuse is dangerous and must be viewed with suspicion.

A further problem, and probably the most important one, arises from the fact that the decision is concentrated purely on the cash flows that arise *within* the payback period, and flows that arise outside this period are ignored. Projects F and G illustrate the problem that this can cause:

Project F		Project G		Project H (do nothing)	
Year	Cash flow (£)	Year	Cash flow (£)	Year	Cash flow (£)
0	−100 000	0	−100 000	0	0
1	+ 10 000	1	+ 50 000		
2	+ 20 000	2	+ 50 000		
3	+ 40 000	3	+ 10 000		
4	+ 80 000				
5	+160 000				
6	+320 000				

According to the payback rule, if the two projects are mutually exclusive, Project G is preferred because it pays back the outlay more quickly. If the two projects are independent (i.e. either one or both could be accepted or rejected) and the company has a three-year payback period criterion, again Project G would be accepted and F rejected. In both situations, looking at the cash flows over the whole life of each project, we can see that the wisdom of the decision advice given by the payback method is open to some doubt.

There is a further problem with the logic of payback. The option not to invest is generally one of the options open to the decision maker. If we call this project H and compare it with F and G above we find that it pays back immediately (because no cash was paid out!). An investment of zero will always produce an immediate payback.

The time value of money

A final problem with the payback method is that, in the format used above, it suffers from the fundamental drawback of failing to allow for the 'time value of money'.[9] However, this difficulty can easily be overcome by applying the method – not to ordinary cash flows – but to 'present value' cash flows. In such circumstances, the technique is usually referred to as 'discounted' payback. The concept of the time value of money has a central place within financial decision theory and will be developed formally in the next two chapters. Nevertheless, it will be useful to introduce the idea briefly, at this point.

Essentially what is meant by the term 'the time value of money' is that a given sum of money has a different value depending upon when it occurs in time. The idea is not directly concerned with inflation or deflation (let us assume that neither exists, so that price levels are stable through time) but really concerns the fact that money can be invested so as to earn interest.

Suppose you were owed £100 and were given the choice of having your £100 returned to you either now or in one year's time (assume that if you choose £100 in a year's time the event is 'certain' – i.e. you are certain to be alive then and you are certain to be paid the money). Most people would instinctively take the £100 now – even if they did not need the money – and this would be the correct decision in terms of the time value of money.

The reason why £100 in a year's time has a smaller value than £100 now is because if you took the £100 *now*, the money could be placed on deposit at (say) a 6% interest rate and so turn into £106 in one year's time. Therefore if the person who was in debt to you offered the choice of £100 now or £106 in one year's time (again both events are certain to occur), you would have no preference for either alternative. Thus we could say that the present value of £106 received in a year's time is £100, or that the future value of £100 now is £106 in a year's time, assuming a 6% interest rate.

This concept of the time value of money will be much more fully discussed when we talk about the discounted cash flow methods of investment appraisal in Chapter 5, but the point to be made here is that the payback method does not make any allowance for the time value of money, its emphasis on the speed of return being purely a consideration of project risk. For example, the payback method would be indifferent between Projects I and J whereas, as the reader may well discern, if allowance is made for the time value of money, Project J is preferable to Project I, as money received nearer in time is more valuable than money received later in time.

	Project I		Project J
Year	Cash flow (£)	Year	Cash flow (£)
0	−4000	0	−4000
1	+ 500	1	+3000
2	+ 500	2	+ 500
3	+3000	3	+ 500
4	+ 500	4	+ 500

A worked example of discounted payback will be shown when the time value of money concept is more fully explored in Chapter 5.

In conclusion

Despite these criticisms, it is still possible to say that, to a great extent, payback has been unfairly maligned in the literature on financial decisions. However, it obviously has a robust ability to survive, because surveys reveal it to be the most widely used of all appraisal methods. This popularity stems mainly from two of the reasons that we have already given, that of ease of comprehension and its apparent bias towards less risky projects. Indeed it can be strongly argued that the payback method does provide a very useful 'rule of thumb' check mechanism for the very many minor investment decisions that companies have to make, which are financially too small (either in relative or absolute terms) to justify the time and expense that would necessarily be incurred in using a complex, but more theoretically correct appraisal method.[10] Furthermore, as shall be seen at the end of Chapter 5, a particularly supportive case can be made for the discounted payback technique.

The real problem does not stem from the payback concept itself, but more from the way the method is *used* in the decision-making process. Except in the case of very minor investment decisions, it should not really be used to give decision *advice* at all, but only to give *information* on the speed of return of the initial outlay, which may or may not be of relevance (depending upon the firm's liquidity) in the decision process. It cannot really be considered as an investment appraisal technique because of its major defect: its inability to report the expected return over the *whole* life of an investment, through its disregard of the investment's post-payback period flows. Using the payback method to choose between alternative investments or to set a minimum criterion for investment acceptance is really applying it to a task which is well beyond its ability to handle. At best, for large investments, it can act successfully only as an initial screening device before more powerful methods of appraisal are applied.[11]

The return on capital employed

The second traditional approach to investment appraisal is the return on capital employed (ROCE) which, like payback, has many different names (perhaps the most common is the accounting rate of return) and a wide variety of different methods of computation. In its basic form, it is calculated as the ratio of the accounting profit generated by an investment project to the required capital outlay, expressed as a percentage. There are many variations in the way these two figures are actually calculated, but normal practice in its use for investment appraisal is to calculate profit after depreciation but before any allowance for taxation, and to include in capital employed any increases in working capital that would be required if the project were accepted.

There are two common ways of expressing the ROCE in practice. One is the ratio of the average annual profit generated over the life of the project, to its average capital value (i.e. the average capital employed). The other approach is to take the average annual profit as a ratio of the initial outlay. Example 3 illustrates these calculations.

The ROCE can be employed in the investment appraisal of both independent projects and mutually exclusive projects. First, a decision criterion is set in terms of a minimum acceptable level of ROCE. (The figure used here often reflects the firm's overall return on capital.) Then, for an independent project to be acceptable, its ROCE must at least equal the 'hurdle' or criterion return specified. In a situation of mutually exclusive projects, the best of the alternatives is the project with the highest ROCE. However, this 'best' project will only be accepted by the firm if it, too, meets the set criterion.

Advantages of ROCE

The ROCE investment appraisal technique is widely used in practice, although it is probably declining in popularity. It has three main advantages. The first is that by evaluating the project on the basis of a percentage rate of return it is using a concept with which all management are familiar. For example, being told that a project had a four-year payback would not immediately convey whether that was good or bad; but being told that a project is expected to produce a 35% return on capital would appear obviously desirable (given that we know the going rate of return on, say, the overall company).

The second advantage is connected to the first. It is the fact that the method evaluates the project on the basis of its profitability, which many managers believe (despite comments in Chapter 1) should be the focus of the appraisal. Finally, a third advantage that exists is that of logic. Managers' own performance is often evaluated by shareholders in terms of the company's *overall* return on capital employed. Therefore there does seem to be a certain logic in evaluating individual capital investment opportunities on a similar basis. (This line of thinking then often leads to the specification of the ROCE criterion being set equal to the company's actual or desired overall return on capital.)

Example 3

The Beta Company wished to evaluate an investment proposal using the ROCE technique. The project requires an initial capital expenditure of £10 000, together with £3000 of working capital. The project will have a four-year life, at the end of which time the working capital will be fully recovered and the project will have a scrap value of £2000.

The project's net pre-tax cash flows are as follows, and the company uses straight-line depreciation:

Year	Net cash flow (£)
1	+4000
2	+6000
3	+3500
4	+1500

In these circumstances (and lacking further information) 'profit' can be calculated as equal to cash flow minus depreciation. The annual depreciation charge would be:

$$\frac{£10\,000 - £2000}{4} = £2000/\text{year depreciation.}$$

Annual profit or (loss):

Year			(£)
1	4000 − 2000	=	2000
2	6000 − 2000	=	4000
3	3500 − 2000	=	1500
4	1500 − 2000	=	(500)
	Total profit	=	£7000

$$\text{Average annual profit} = \frac{£7000}{4} = £1750$$

The initial capital employed would equal £13 000 (capital expenditure plus working capital). The average capital employed would be calculated as:

$$\frac{\text{Capital expenditure} - \text{scrap value}}{2} + \text{scrap value} + \text{working capital}$$

that is:
$$\frac{£10\,000 - £2000}{2} + £2000 + £3000 = £9000.\,[12]$$

Hence return on initial capital employed equals

$$\frac{£1750}{£13\,000} = 0.135 \text{ (approx.) or } 13.5\%$$

and return on average capital employed equals

$$\frac{£1750}{£9000} = 0.194 \text{ (approx.) or } 19.4\%.$$

Disadvantages of ROCE

To set against these advantages, there are a number of major disadvantages, the first of which is the ambiguous nature of the ROCE concept. There are so many variants that no general agreement exists on how capital employed should be calculated, on whether initial or average capital employed should be used or on how profit should be defined. As a result, the method lays itself open to abuse as a technique of investment appraisal by allowing the decision maker to select a definition of ROCE which best suits his preconception of a project's desirability.

Second, because the method measures a potential investment's worth in percentage terms it is unable – in an unadjusted form – to take into account the financial size of a project when alternatives are compared.

For example, suppose a company was considering whether to build a large factory, at a cost of £10 million, or a small factory at a cost of £3 million. If the large factory turned out to have an ROCE of 20% while the small factory's

ROCE was 24%, then the latter investment would be the one chosen (assuming 24% exceeded the ROCE criterion). However, it is not at all certain that the small factory would be a wise choice. While the small factory would result in an aggregate profit of £720 000 (24% of £3 million), the large factory would produce a profit of £2 million for the firm.

However, these two criticisms are relatively insignificant when compared to two further difficulties. The first concerns the fact that accounting profit rather than cash flow is used as the basis of evaluation. As our earlier discussion in Chapter 1 showed, this is an entirely incorrect concept to use in a decision-making context. Accounting profit is a *reporting* concept; it is a creation of accountants. A capital investment decision is an economic or resource allocation decision and the economic unit of account is cash, because it is cash which gives power over resources.

The other major criticism of the ROCE is that it also ignores the time value of money. Furthermore, unlike payback, where discounted payback can be used, there is no way that the ROCE can be modified to take the time value of money into account.

However, despite these criticisms, the method is still widely applied to investment decisions in industry and it may be fair to say that, like payback, although there are many problems associated with its application, it may give acceptable decision advice when applied to relatively minor, short-run investment projects.

Nevertheless, there is survey evidence which does indicate a decline in the technique's popularity. There are perhaps two reasons for this, both of which arise from the high rates of inflation suffered by the economy in the late 1970s and the 1980s. The first is that high rates of inflation led to high interest rates and this high time value of money sharply brought home to management the importance of taking it into account in decision making. With interest rates of around 20% it becomes obvious that the timing of cash flows is important. A second reason for the ROCE's decline in popularity could be that the high rates of inflation – and the failure of the inflation accounting debate – taught management about the doubtful validity of the accounting profit number. Thus a method that uses accounting profit and ignores the time value of money has little to recommend it as a decision-making tool.

The use of ROCE tends to result in the adoption of short-term approaches to decision making; so-called *short-termism*. This is related to its use for measuring the performance of managers and the fact that it emphasizes the effects of the investment on reported earnings rather than long-term cash flows.

In conclusion

Comparing these two 'traditional' investment appraisal techniques, each has its own advantages and disadvantages and it is not clear whether either is superior. Each has its own group of advocates and it is common to find both used in conjunction so as to produce a 'two-tier' decision rule, e.g. projects may be accepted only if (say) they pay back within five years *and* have a minimum ROCE of 12%.

In the final analysis, our conclusion must be that, apart from the possible exception of the evaluation of relatively small, short-lived investments, neither method has sufficient advantages to offset its disadvantages, and particularly the failure of both normally to allow for the time value of money.[13] In the next chapter we shall start to examine investment appraisal methods that do attempt to make such an allowance.

Summary

This chapter has covered the following major points:

- The two 'traditional' methods of capital investment appraisal – payback and the return on capital employed – were examined to see how they are calculated and how they are applied, both to individual project evaluation and to situations involving mutually exclusive projects.

- As far as payback was concerned, the technique was usually applied to a project's after-tax cash flows, but working capital was excluded entirely from the evaluation.

- Basically there were four advantages to payback:
  — quick and simple;
  — seen as automatically selecting the less 'risky' project from amongst alternatives;
  — seen as helpful in capital rationing situations;
  — saves management from having to forecast project cash flows beyond the criterion time period.

- Payback's main disadvantage was its failure to consider project cash flows outside the payback period. However, it was argued that, to some extent, this omission might be understandable where management felt that their forecasting ability was suspect beyond the criterion time period.

- The other disadvantage is payback's failure to account for the time value of money, but this can be taken into account through the use of discounted payback.

- The ROCE also had advantages:
  — it is evaluated using the familiar percentage concept;
  — it evaluated projects on the basis of profitability;
  — management's success or failure in taking financial decisions in aggregate is judged on the basis of the company's return on capital employed (amongst other things). Therefore it appears sensible that individual investment decisions should be taken on the same basis.

- However, to be set against these advantages were two major disadvantages: a failure to consider cash flow and a failure to take the time value of money into account.

- In sum, these two techniques may be suitable as initial screening devices, or to evaluate small, short-lived projects. However, they should not be used otherwise, with the possible exception of discounted payback.

Notes

1. Although this point will be expanded upon later, it is worth specifying now that an investment's 'cost' can be defined as all cash outflows and/or reduced cash inflows through time that result (either directly or indirectly) from the investment decision. Similarly, an investment's 'benefit' can be described as all cash inflows and/or reduced outflows through time that result (directly or indirectly) from the investment decision. Thus all costs and benefits of an investment are defined in terms of being incremental to the firm through time and are expressed in cash terms.

2. Various empirical surveys both in the UK and the USA and elsewhere have shown that these two investment appraisal methods have widespread popular appeal. Their familiarity and directness will make the task of replacing them by superior appraisal techniques a difficult one.

3. Not least amongst these diverse considerations is the decision maker's own psychology; one survey (Scapens, Sale and Tikkas, CIMA 1982) concludes that concern with an investment's financial viability is of almost secondary importance to whether or not it 'fits in' with the company's strategic plans.

4. There are a variety of names given to this method. Others include pay-back period, pay-off period, capital recovery period, cash recovery factor.

5. The term 'mutually exclusive' when applied to investment projects is best explained by means of an example. Suppose a company requires a new warehouse and there are two possible sites under consideration, then the decision could be analysed in terms of two mutually exclusive investments: building the warehouse at Site A and building the warehouse at Site B. The projects are said to be mutually exclusive because only *one* new warehouse is required, so if it is built at Site A, the acceptance of this project excludes the other project from being chosen, and vice versa. More generally a pair of projects are mutually exclusive if the acceptance of one means that the other would not or could not be accepted. This definition can be extended to any number of alternative investment projects of which only one can be chosen.

6. It is important to note that throughout this book we shall use the following convention when dealing with all types of financial flows (e.g. profit, dividend, cash or tax flows): all flows will normally be assumed to occur instantaneously on *the last day of the year in which they arise*. Thus a cash flow in the second year of a project's life will be assumed to occur on the last day of the second year. The main exception to this rule is that a project's outlay (or cost) which arises in the first year of its life is assumed to occur on the first day of the year.

These rather unrealistic assumptions are made for arithmetical convenience, but, in most circumstances, they do not affect the realism of our results in any substantial way. (See the Appendix to Chapter 5 on Compounding and Discounting.) Diagrammatically:

Thus 'Year 0' (or t_0) refers to the start of the first year (i.e. 'now'). 'Year 1' refers to the *end* of the first year and – simultaneously – the start of the second year. 'Year 3' refers to the end of the third year, and so on. References in the text to, for example, 'the second year' will refer to events that happen during the second year, whilst references to 'year 2' (or t_2) will refer to a financial flow that is assumed to arise at the end of the second year (or, the start of the third year).

7. However, it is important to notice that payback is the *only* appraisal technique which excludes working capital from the analysis.

8. Project independence can be defined as a situation where the expected financial flows that arise from a project will occur irrespective of any other project being or not being undertaken.

9. There do exist special cases where the ordinary payback decision rule effectively allows for the time value of money, but such situations are simply fortuitous and of little more than arithmetical interest.

10. This may be especially true of very small companies which may be lacking the resources and knowledge to undertake a more complex appraisal.

11. Even this is really open to doubt. Original writers on the topic such as Joel Dean and Ezra Solomon believed that payback could be used as a coarse screening device to pick out projects whose desirability (in terms of profitability) is so obvious as to remove the need for more refined appraisal. For similar reasons it is held that the method could also be used to reject 'obviously' highly unprofitable projects. There is little evidence to support this belief, neither has there been an operational definition of 'obvious' in this context.

12. The rationale for this calculation can be most easily seen with the help of a diagram:

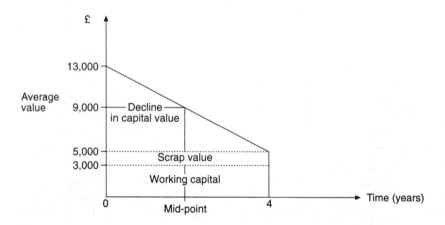

13. Even allowing for the discounted payback variant referred to earlier, payback still suffers the major criticism of not considering a project's financial flows outside the payback period.

Further reading

1. Most of the literature concerning payback and ROCE is fairly old, and the more up-to-date contributions have tended to contrast them with the DCF techniques which are to be discussed in Chapter 5. Nevertheless, an interesting starting point is the discussion in: D. Bodenhorn, 'On the problem of capital budgeting', *Journal of Finance*, December 1959.
2. Even older, but also of interest is: J. Dean, 'Measuring the Productivity of Capital', *Harvard Business Review*, Jan–Feb 1954; as is: E.A. Ravenscroft, 'Return on Investment: Fit the Method to your Needs', *Harvard Business Review*, Mar–Apr 1960.
3. Specifically on payback, see: M.J. Gordon, 'The Payoff Period and the Rate of Profit', *Journal of Business*, October 1955; A. Rappaport, 'The Discounted Payback Period', *Management Science*, Jul–Aug 1965; H. Levy, 'A Note on the Payback Method', *Journal of Financial and Quantitative Analysis*, December 1968; and M.H. Weingartner, 'Some New Views on the Payback Period and Capital Budgeting Decision', *Management Science*, August 1969.
4. Two interesting articles which discuss reasons for the continuing popularity of payback are: M. Statman, 'The Persistence of the Payback Method: A Principal–Agent Perspective', *Engineering Economist*, Winter 1982; and R.H. Pike, 'Owner Manager Conflict and the Role of the Payback Method', *Accounting and Business Research*, Winter 1985.
5. The ROCE method is generally recognized as being inadequate, but see: M.J. Mepham, 'A Reinstatement of the Accounting Rate of Return', *Accounting and Business Research*, Summer 1968, and C.G. Hoskins and G.A. Mumey, 'Payback: A maligned method of Asset Ranking?', *Engineering Economist*, Autumn 1979.

Quickie questions

1. What is the payback decision rule for mutually exclusive projects?
2. What is the payback of Project W:

   Capital expenditure: £11 000   Net cash flow: Yr 1   +4000
   Working capital: £4000   Yr 2   +4000
   Scrap value: £1000   Yr 3   +4000
   Life: 5 years   Yr 4   +3000
                                           Yr 5   +2000

3. What are the advantages of payback?
4. How is payback used in capital rationing situations?
5. How might the payback criterion be set?
6. What is 'discounted payback'?
7. What is the single most important criticism of payback?
8. Why does money have a 'time value'?
9. What is Project W's (see question 2) ARR/ROCE, assuming straight-line depreciation?
10. What are the main advantages of ARR/ROCE?
11. What are the two most serious disadvantages of ARR/ROCE?

Problems

1. Gamma plc is a diversified industrial conglomerate. Its head-office accounting staff are currently evaluating investment proposals put up by different divisions for approval.

   The Electronics division have put forward a proposal to produce a new type of calculator which, because of rapid technological change, can only be expected to have a four-year life, once the production facilities have been set up during the first twelve months.

   The Property division propose taking a four-year lease on a building which already has a tenant paying an annual rent.

   The Mining division propose to spend £1.5 million developing a small copper mine. The mine would only have a three-year life. At the end of that time, the environmental damage the company had caused would need to be rectified at a cost of £0.75 million.

   The net cash flows of the projects (excluding working capital) are as follows (£000s):

Year	Electronics	Property	Mining
0	−1000	−1000	−1500
1	−1000	+ 200	+ 500
2	+ 800	+ 400	+1000
3	+ 800	+ 400	+ 800
4	+ 800	+ 400	− 750
5	+ 800		

   Gamma normally uses payback to evaluate projects with a decision criterion of three years.

   Required:
   (a) Calculate the payback of all three projects and determine the decision advice.
   (b) If the Electronics and Property division projects were mutually exclusive, which project would you advise the company to accept? Think carefully before reaching a decision and then justify your decision.
   (c) If the Property and Mining division projects were mutually exclusive, which project would you advise the company to accept? Again, think carefully and justify your decision.
   (d) Comment on the company's use of the same decision criterion for projects from all three divisions. Would you think this wise?

2. Zeta plc is a manufacturer and distributor of ice-cream. The management are presently considering a project which will require capital expenditure of £200 000, together with £50 000 of working capital. The capital equipment is expected to have a scrap value of £80 000 at the end of its four-year life and 80% of the working capital will also be recovered. (The remaining 20% of unrecovered working capital will consist of bad debts and spoilt stocks.)

   The project's annual revenues and operating cash costs are estimated as follows (£000s):

Year	Revenues	Operating costs
1	200	150
2	260	200
3	400	290
4	100	80

   The company calculates depreciation on a straight-line basis. Normally projects are evaluated using both payback and the return on initial capital employed. The criterion used is three years for payback and 13% for the ROCE.

Required:
(a) Evaluate the project using the company's normal decision criteria. What advice would you give?
(b) The chairman, after receiving your advice, is puzzled over your treatment of working capital in the payback calculation. Explain to her your reasonings.
(c) The chairman also wondered whether the returns on *average* capital employed should be used instead of initial capital. What would your advice be and would the decision advice change? Think carefully before giving your answer; your promotion depends upon it!
(d) If Zeta decides to use only one appraisal technique, which would you advise – payback or ROCE/ARR – and why?

4 The single-period investment consumption decision model

Introduction to the model

In the previous chapter, two widely-used investment appraisal decision rules, payback and ROCE/ARR, were examined. One criticism of payback was that it ignored the time value of money – unless discounted payback was used. A similar criticism was made of the ROCE/ARR approach but, in addition, that was also criticized for evaluating projects on the basis of profit, not cash flow.

The other two main methods of capital investment appraisal are net present value (NPV) and the internal rate of return (IRR). These will be examined in detail in Chapter 5. However, in this chapter we take the opportunity to expand upon our initial discussion about the time value of money, and then look at how, in theory, capital investment decisions should be taken. This will then enable a judgement to be made as to how closely the four alternative investment appraisal techniques accord with the theoretically correct approach.

In order to look at the theory of investment decision making, we are going to develop a simple graphical analysis.[1] *In no way does this analysis purport to represent the real world*, but it will be useful in that it allows conclusions to be reached that do have real-world validity.

The basic assumptions

So as to simplify the analysis and to lay bare the problem of investment decision making, we shall specify six assumptions about the real-world environment within which investment decisions are made.

Assumption 1

The decision maker is only concerned with making investment decisions over a single period time horizon, which we will treat as one year for the sake of simplicity. Given this horizon, there are only two points of time that concern us – the start of the year or now (i.e. t_0 or Year 0) and the end of the year (i.e. t_1 or Year 1). Therefore all the available investment opportunities possess the general characteristic of requiring a cash outlay now, in return for a cash inflow at the end of the year. No investment cash flows extend beyond t_1.[2] (We will show later that this analysis can be easily expanded to cash flows that extend over many years and, indeed, different times during those years.)

Assumption 2

The size and timing of any investment's cash outflow and subsequent cash inflow is known with certainty by the decision maker and so no risk is involved in the investment decision.[3]

Assumption 3

Only 'physical' investment opportunities are available, i.e. investments involving the use of factors of production (land, labour and machinery) to produce a future return. This means that there is no 'capital market' where money can be lent or borrowed at a rate of interest.[4]

Assumption 4

All investment projects are infinitely divisible; therefore fractions of projects may be undertaken, and they exhibit decreasing returns to scale.

Assumption 5

All investment project cash flows are entirely independent of each other. Therefore the return produced at the end of the year from any investment now is fixed and known for certain and is unaffected by any other investment decision.

Assumption 6

The person in receipt of the benefits from investment decisions is rational, in that 'more cash' is always preferred to 'less cash' in any period.

These are the six major assumptions that we are going to make initially (although there are several other assumptions which we shall specify later as we develop the analysis), and obviously most of them are very unrealistic and in no way reflect the real world: investors are almost invariably faced with making decisions where the effects stretch over many periods; the future is largely unknown and so future cash flows cannot be certain; non-physical investments, such as placing money on deposit at a bank, are usually available to investors; investment projects are often indivisible and so must either be undertaken completely or not at all; many investment project cash flows depend upon what other investment decisions have or have not been made. However, such simplifying assumptions do provide a starting point for our analysis; we shall examine later the effect of replacing them with more realistic descriptions of the real world, but for the moment let us accept them.

The time value of money

We have already defined an investment decision by a company as one which involves the company in cash outlay (now) with the aim of receiving a (future) cash inflow in return. If we also make the simplistic but basically correct assumption that a company can do either of two things with any 'spare' cash[5] it has – pay it out to shareholders as a dividend[6] or retain it within the company and invest it – then if a company makes a decision to invest, it is in fact deciding not to pay that cash to shareholders now but instead to put it into a project with the aim of obtaining an increased amount of cash in the future, which can then be paid out as a dividend.

Therefore, a decision to invest by a company means that shareholders forgo the opportunity of consumption now (i.e. a dividend now) with the aim of increasing future consumption (i.e. an enlarged dividend later). At this stage we will ignore the complications caused by the possibility of selling shares and the linkage of their value to investment decisions. So investment decisions are about the delaying of current consumption in order to increase future consumption. (Or in non-economic terms, not spending money on consuming goods and services now, but investing the money instead so as to produce more money later which can then be spent on an increased quantity of goods and services.)

To look more closely at the investment decision, let us first consider the case of the single-owner firm (i.e. one in which the company has only one shareholder, who owns all the shares, and whose entire wealth is represented by the company) in which the owner is also the decision maker. In deciding to invest, the owner is forgoing some present consumption in order to increase future consumption and, in taking such action, he must also have decided that the future consumption so gained is somehow of greater value than the present consumption sacrificed in making the investment.

To make such investment decisions in a consistent manner,[7] the owner requires a specific criterion that will enable him to judge whether or not any particular investment opportunity will produce sufficient compensation, in terms of increased future consumption, for having to reduce current consumption in order to make the investment.

Suppose our owner-manager requires a minimum of £1.20 back at the end of the year in order to persuade him to invest £1 now. Thus he requires compensation of 20p for every £1 of current consumption he forgoes. This requirement – which is a type of exchange rate of money between points in time and is, in fact, the owner's time value of money (TVM)[8] – can be expressed as a percentage:

$$\frac{£1.20}{£1.00} - 1 = 0.20 \text{ or } 20\%.$$

So an investment appraisal decision rule could be formulated in which a project is only undertaken if it produces at least a 20% return on capital.

The owner-manager would not be willing to invest in a project which produced less than a 20% return, because 20% represents his time value of money.

It is important to realize that this time value of money is unlikely to remain a constant but will probably increase as more and more present consumption is sacrificed for investment so as to produce a greater amount of future consumption. That is to say, with each successive reduction in current consumption the owner is likely to demand a higher and higher minimum future return in order to persuade him to invest, because each additional £1 of current consumption forgone is likely to be of increasing value (in terms of the benefits received from consumption), and each additional £1 of future consumption gained is likely to be of decreasing value. This is an example of the economic concept of diminishing marginal utility.

The basic graphical analysis

The single-owner firm case

The one-period graphical analysis, made under our six assumptions, is shown in Fig. 4.1. The curve AB is called the physical investment line[9] (PIL) and is composed of all the physical investment opportunities available to the company at t_0, arranged in order of decreasing return.[10] Thus the most 'profitable' investments – in terms of greatest return – would be undertaken first by the firm.

The physical investment line represents the complete range of maximum consumption combinations that the owner can obtain between the two points in time[11] by applying varying amounts of the company's existing resources to physical investment opportunities. Therefore as the owner gives up increasing amounts of current consumption in order to make physical investments, the company locates further and further up and around the physical investment line. (For instance if it locates at point A, no investment

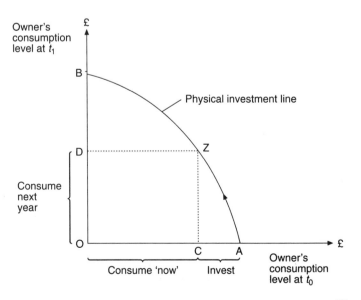

Fig. 4.1 *The physical investment line*

is undertaken and if it locates at point B, all possible physical investments are undertaken.)

Using Fig. 4.1, OA represents the owner's total wealth now (i.e. at t_0) and can be regarded as the (unforced) liquidation value of the company. If all this wealth is consumed now and none is invested, then there will be zero wealth available for consumption next year (i.e. t_1). If only part of this year's wealth is consumed, say OC, and the rest, CA, is invested, then the company locates itself at point Z on the physical investment line and this level of investment will produce OD available for consumption next year.

The return received by the company from the last (i.e. marginal) £1 of investment made at t_0 – the final piece of investment that brings the company to locate at point Z – can be found from the slope of the physical investment line at that point.[12] But besides being the return on the marginal investment, this slope represents something else. The company has located at point Z because the owner must feel that further investment is not worthwhile. In other words, the gain in next year's consumption generated by a marginal increase in investment now, does not provide sufficient compensation for the further reduction in present consumption that would be necessary to finance the increased investment. Therefore the marginal return on investment being obtained at Z must be equal to the owner's time value of money (TVM).

If the marginal return at Z was greater than the owner's TVM, the company would continue to invest, and if it were less than the TVM, the company would have stopped investing *before* reaching point Z, because the return gained from a move along the PIL from below Z to point Z would have been insufficient compensation for the present consumption that would have to be forgone to make the investment.

Introduction of indifference curves

We can derive this result better by asking the question: given that the physical investment line represents a whole series of infinitely divisible and independent opportunities for investment projects, arranged in decreasing order of rate of return, so that the investment with the greatest return is ranked (and undertaken) first and the one with the smallest return last, how does the company know when to stop investing? In order to answer this fully, we have to use another economic concept: the indifference curve.

It is assumed that the reader is familiar with the derivation and meaning of this term – it is explained in most basic economic textbooks. In rough terms, indifference curves are curves of constant utility or welfare, and when mapped on to our graph of consumption 'now' and consumption 'next year', an individual indifference curve indicates all possible combinations of consumption at the two points in time which give the same level of utility. The curves are convex to the origin, indicating that there is diminishing marginal utility attached to consumption at any single point of time, and each indifference curve, moving from left to right, gives the individual a higher overall level of utility.

Their place here concerns the fact that the set of indifference curves belonging to the company's owner can be mapped on the Fig. 4.1 graph, as shown in Fig. 4.2, and can be used to indicate at what point the company should stop investing; it is that point on the physical investment line which enables the owner to achieve his highest indifference curve, that is, his highest level of utility. This is found at the point of tangency between an indifference curve and the physical investment line. In terms of Fig. 4.2, the company invests CA 'now' because the two time-point pattern of consumption that results for the owner – OC 'now' and OD 'next year' – places him on his highest possible indifference curve and so maximizes his welfare.

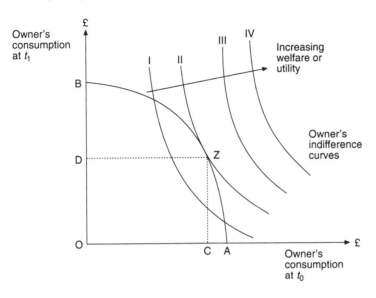

Fig. 4.2 *Indifference curves*

The point of tangency between the two curves represents a point where the slopes of each equate. As the slope of the indifference curve reflects an individual's marginal time value of money and the slope of the physical investment line represents the rate of return on the marginal project, then the point where the slopes of these two curves equate must be the point at which the owner's TVM equals the return on the marginal investment made by the company. Thus the investment decision rule is that the company continues to make physical investments until the return from the marginal investment (i.e. the last one made) equals the owner's marginal time value of money. Any further investment will not produce the necessary return required and so will have the effect, in terms of our indifference curve analysis, of placing the owner on a lower indifference curve.[13]

Introduction of capital markets

From this simple analysis, under a series of restrictive assumptions about the real world, we have seen how investment decisions would be made and why money is said to possess a 'time value'. If we now make our analysis slightly more realistic by relaxing our third assumption so as to make available to the single-owner firm the opportunity of being able to lend and borrow money on a capital market at a rate of interest, we can then develop a second reason for money having a time value.

With the introduction of capital markets, the firm is faced with three possible courses of action at t_0: consumption, physical investment or capital market investment. Making the very important assumption that there is a perfect capital market[14] and therefore only one market rate of interest[15] (which is both the borrowing and lending rate), we can use the one-period graphical analysis to illustrate how the company makes investment decisions so as to allow the owner to distribute his consumption between the two points in time in such a way that he maximizes his welfare.

The financial market line

In terms of Fig. 4.3, suppose the single-owner firm has amount OG available for consumption at t_0 and OH available at t_1. The capital market can be represented by a straight line, AE, which passes through point F, the coordinate of the existing consumption distribution. The slope of this line[16] is given by $-(1 + r)$, where r is the perfect capital market rate of interest, and the line is termed the financial investment line (FIL).

This line shows the range of capital market transactions available to the single-owner firm, given the existing distribution of cash resources of OG now (i.e. t_0) and OH next year (i.e. t_1). A move *down* the financial investment line from F to (say) point L means that the firm borrows GM on the capital market now – so increasing consumption at t_0 from OG to OM – and repays (capital plus interest) HN next year – so reducing consumption at t_1 from OH to ON. Notice that the maximum that can be borrowed now is amount GA; if the firm attempts to borrow more than this, there will not be sufficient resources available next year to repay the capital and accrued interest.

A move *up* the financial investment line to (say) point I means that the firm is lending JG on the capital market so as to reduce consumption now (to OJ) and to increase consumption next year (to OK). Again notice that a maximum of OG can be lent now – reducing current consumption to zero – and this results in having OE available for consumption next year.

Fig. 4.3 *The financial investment line*

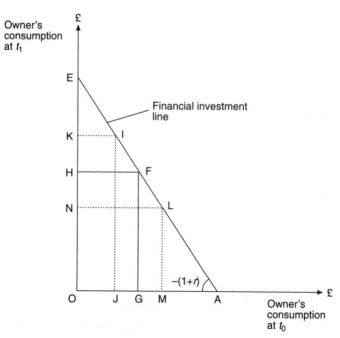

The separation theorem

Having seen how the financial investment line works, we can now combine the physical and financial investment lines on a single graph. This allows us to examine how both physical investment decisions and capital market borrowing or lending decisions are made in conjunction with each other, in order to allow the owner to achieve his highest possible indifference curve and so optimize his consumption spread over the period and maximize his utility.

However, up to this point we have taken as our decision-making entity the single-owner firm, where the investment decision maker and the owner are one and the same person. Introducing the possibility of using the capital market allows us to analyse the investment decision process not only in the single-owner case, but also in the much more important situation where there are many owners (i.e. shareholders) and they are separate from the investment decision makers (i.e. management). This is the Separation Theorem.[17]

The capital investment decision rule now becomes: the company (i.e. managers) undertakes physical investments until the return from the marginal physical investment equates with the perfect capital market interest rate/rate of return. This level of physical investment results in some particular dividend flow, at t_0 and t_1, to the shareholders. The shareholders then make financial investment decisions (by either borrowing or lending on the capital market) until their individual marginal time values of money equate with the capital market rate of interest. Such action will result in them achieving their highest possible indifference curves by producing a distribution of consumption over the period, which maximizes their individual levels of utility.

Graphical derivation of the decision rule

We can see how these separation theorem decision rules are derived and why they help to maximize the shareholder's utility by examining Fig. 4.4. Here the financial investment line is superimposed on the Fig. 4.1 situation. Let us assume for the moment that although ownership is separate from management, the company has only one shareholder.

The current liquidation value of the company is OA. In the absence of a capital market we know that the company management will invest amount AC, and so make physical investments up to point Z on the physical investment line. This represents the point of tangency between the physical investment line and the owner's indifference curve (UT_1), and therefore at this point the return from the marginal investment (derived from the slope of the physical investment line) equates with the shareholder's time value of money (given by the slope of the indifference curve tangential to point Z). Thus in our one-period world, the shareholder would receive a 'dividend' of OC now and OD next year. This distribution of consumption over the period places him on his highest attainable indifference curve: UT_1, and so maximizes his utility.

With the introduction of a capital market, the company's management now invest amount QA, so as to undertake physical investments up to the point where the return on the marginal physical investment equates with the capital market interest rate/rate of return (derived from the slope of the

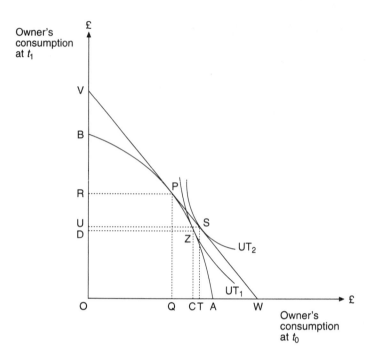

Fig. 4.4 *The separation theorem*

financial investment line). This occurs at point P where the financial investment line is tangent to the physical investment line. Thus the shareholder now receives a different dividend distribution: OQ now and OR next year. The company has undertaken physical investments up to point P because this has the effect of placing the shareholder on the highest possible financial investment line (VW).

Unlike the situation where capital market opportunities did not exist, the shareholder now does not have to accept the pattern of dividend distribution given by the company for consumption. Instead, he can borrow or lend on the capital market (i.e. move down or up VW from point P) so as to adjust his received dividend flow to suit whatever consumption pattern is preferred.

This preferred pattern is given by the point on the financial investment line which is tangent to one of his indifference curves, because this indifference curve will be the highest attainable. Thus the shareholder either lends or borrows on the capital market until his marginal time value of money (derived from the slope of the indifference curve) equates with the perfect capital market rate of interest. In Fig. 4.4 the shareholder achieves this point, S, by moving down the financial investment line and borrowing an amount QT to make a total of OT available for consumption 'now' and OU available for consumption 'next year'. (A dividend of OR is received from the company next year, but part of this, RU, is used to repay the borrowed capital and accrued interest.)

Whether the shareholder lends or borrows or even omits to use the capital market at all depends solely upon the location of the point of tangency between the financial investment line and the shareholder's indifference curve, as Fig. 4.5 shows. What Fig. 4.4 illustrates is how, by taking advantage of both physical *and* financial investment opportunities, the shareholder can attain a higher indifference curve, UT_2 (and so increase his utility),

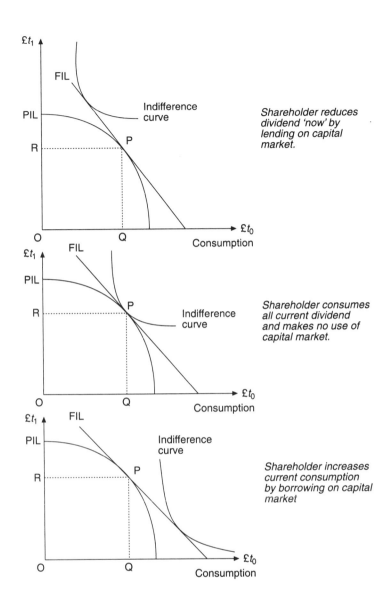

Fig. 4.5 *Lending and borrowing decisions*

Shareholder reduces dividend 'now' by lending on capital market.

Shareholder consumes all current dividend and makes no use of capital market.

Shareholder increases current consumption by borrowing on capital market

than would have been possible from making physical investments alone. In fact this can unambiguously be seen occurring in Fig. 4.4, because the shareholder has managed to increase his consumption in both periods through using the capital market: by amount CT 'now' and UD 'next year'.[18]

The multi-owner firm

The development of this separation theorem is extremely important. It results in a company's management making only *physical* investment decisions and leaving individual shareholders to adjust their received dividend pattern to fit their particular consumption requirements by using the capital market. In the owner-manager firm and in the situation where ownership and management are separate but there is only one owner, it makes no difference to the analysis whether the individual owner/shareholder uses the capital market or the company uses the capital market on the owner's/shareholder's behalf (as long as, in the case where owner and management are separate, the managers are aware of the owner's marginal time value of money).

However, the crucial importance of the separation theorem comes when ownership is separated from management *and* there is more than one owner. Quite simply, different individuals have different time values of money, and so a company would be able to undertake the physical investment decisions but not the financial investment decisions, because there would be more than one marginal time value of money.[19] The use of the separation theorem avoids this problem by leaving the financial investment decisions to the individual shareholders.

Fig. 4.6 shows a situation where a company is owned by two shareholders: one with 75% of the equity (Shareholder 1) and the other with 25% of the equity (Shareholder 2). The firm continues to make physical investments until the marginal return on investment equates with the market rate of interest, and then pays out the resulting dividends to each shareholder in proportion to his equity holding. In so doing, the company would still be ensuring that each individual shareholder is placed on the highest possible financial investment line. It is then up to the individual shareholder to make whatever decision is best, in the knowledge of his own set of indifference curves and time value of money, with regard to using the capital market in order to adjust his received dividend flow.

In the example shown in Fig. 4.6, Shareholder 1 (75% holding) will use the capital market to borrow and so increases consumption 'now' at the expense of a reduced future consumption level. Shareholder 2 will use the capital market to lend, thereby reducing consumption 'now' but, in return, having an increased level of consumption 'next year'.

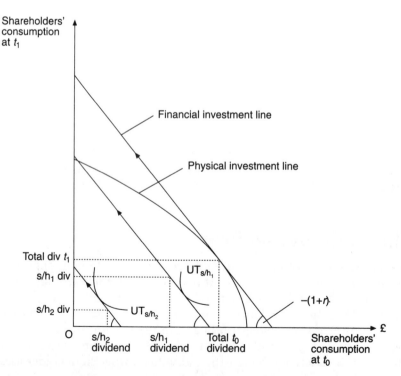

Fig. 4.6 *The multi-owner case*

The conclusions of the basic model

This development of the single-period investment–consumption model, as it is called, is important not only for illustrating how and why money has a time value, but also as acting as an introduction to financial decision making in general. In this respect, we stated that management's objective must be to try to maximize shareholders' wealth and this would be achieved through the maximization of the dividend flow through time. The separation theorem places this latter statement in a clearer light.

Management must make investment decisions so as to maximize the dividend flow to shareholders. But this is only the first stage of a two-stage process, because the individual shareholder then uses the capital market to adjust the timing of this dividend flow so that it accords with his desired pattern of consumption.

The conclusions of our one-period investment–consumption model, *and the assumptions upon which it is based*, are important and wide-ranging (as we shall see later). The model implies that we require a technique of investment appraisal which will ensure that companies undertake physical investment until the return from the marginal investment equates with the perfect capital market rate of return. In other words, companies should undertake capital investment projects as long as the return generated (from each one) is *not less* than the market rate of interest.

Introducing uncertainty

At this point, it should also be noted that, just as individuals have their own personal time value of money, so the capital market interest rate represents the economy's average time value of money. Therefore the capital investment decision rule for companies could be restated as: undertake capital investment projects as long as the rate of return generated from each one is not less than the market's time value of money. However, it should also be noted that this decision rule, as it stands, is set in a world of certainty. In an uncertain world, as we shall see, there is a whole range of different market interest rates. Therefore this decision rule will require some slight modification.

The problem of uncertainty will be developed fully in later chapters, but it will be helpful to introduce the basic idea at this stage. In a certain world, an investment's outcome is known with certainty by the decision maker. In an uncertain world, an investment's outcome is uncertain and hence is referred to as a 'risky' investment. With such investments, decision makers are not entirely uninformed about the possible outcome, in that they *expect* a particular outcome (or cash inflow) from an investment, but realize that the *actual* outcome may differ from what was expected. (Notice too, therefore, that risk is a two-way street. An investment's actual outcome may be either better or worse than was expected.)

Generally speaking, investors dislike uncertainty of outcome. This does not mean that they are unwilling to take on a risky project. Instead it means that they require a reward for doing so and this reward is a higher level of expected return. Therefore, in an uncertain world, there is not just a single capital market interest rate/rate of return, but a whole series of different rates of return – one for each level of risk: the higher the risk, the higher the capital market rate of return.

As a result, in an uncertain world, our capital investment decision rule for companies now has to be modified. Projects should only be undertaken as long as they generate a rate of return which is not less than the capital market's rate of return *for a risk level equivalent to that of the project*.

Payback and ROCE

Clearly, the payback investment appraisal method does not meet the requirements of our decision rule that has been derived through this graphical analysis. The reason being that – even allowing for the fact that it can be adapted to allow for the time value of money – it uses speed of return, rather than rate of return, as its criterion of project desirability.

Equally unsuitable is the return on capital employed because, although it is a rate-of-return concept, it ignores the time value of money.[20] In the next chapter we shall turn to the discounted cash flow methods of investment appraisal and examine the extent to which they meet the requirements of our model.[21]

Summary

This chapter dealt with the Hirshliefer single-period investment-consumption model to examine what was required of a capital investment appraisal decision rule. The following were the main points covered:

- The model was developed initially under six basic assumptions:
  — single time period horizon;
  — certainty of investment outcome;
  — only physical investment opportunities;
  — investments exhibit infinite divisibility and diminishing returns to scale;
  — investments are all independent;
  — investors are rational.

- The concept of the investor's marginal time value of money was introduced, which would be likely to be an increasing function of the amount invested.

- The firm's physical investment line was introduced and it was seen that the slope of the function represented the marginal rate of return on investment projects at any point.

- As a result, firms would locate on the physical investment line at the point where the slope of the line (the marginal project rate of return) equated with the investor's own marginal time value of money.

- In terms of indifference curves, this optimal investment point occurs at the point of tangency between the PIL and the investor's indifference curve set: the slope of the indifference curve reflecting the investor's marginal time value of money.

- With the introduction of capital markets and the financial market line, the graphical analysis can now handle cases other than the single-owner firm. The decision rule is that the firm should invest in projects as long as their return is not less than the market rate of return – given by the slope of the FIL, which reflects society's average time value of money.

- This capital investment decision rule then allows each individual shareholder to adjust the received pattern of dividends/cash flow by using the capital market to locate on the highest possible indifference curve.

- This analysis is known as the Hirshliefer Separation Theorem in that the capital investment decision (made by managers) can be separated from the capital market decision (made by owners/investors/shareholders).

- Finally, the concept of risk was briefly examined. It was argued that, in an uncertain world, the investment decision rule that arose out of the Hirshliefer analysis had to be modified: the firm should accept projects as long as they were expected to produce a return that was not less than the capital market rate of return for that level of risk.

Notes

1. This approach was first used by the American economist Irving Fisher (and hence has become known as Fisherian Analysis) in *The Theory of Interest* (New York, Macmillan 1930). Its use was revived specifically in terms of financial decision theory by Jack Hirshliefer, 'On the Theory of Optimal Investment Decisions', *Journal of Political Economy*, August 1958.

2. Alternatively we could say that all investment opportunities have a life-span of just one period of time, t_0 to t_1.

3. In this assumption of no risk, we are also implicitly assuming that our investor will be alive to enjoy the fruits of his or her decisions.

4. We are also assuming here that the relative price levels of these factors of production are unchanging and so no 'holding gains' (in inflation accounting parlance) are possible.

5. Here we are using the term 'spare cash' in the sense of the residual cash resources of a company after allowing for the claims of all creditors.

6. In this simple case we are obviously ignoring the possible constraining influence of legislation in respect of company dividends.

7. We can define a consistent criterion for investment decisions as one which would produce the following decision: if Project A is preferred to Project B and Project B is preferred to Project C, then the decision criterion should result in Project A being preferred to Project C. If not, the criterion is not producing consistent decisions. Technically, the decision making must exhibit 'transitivity'.

8. This time value of money could be either positive or negative. For instance, an individual could be willing to take 5p less 'next year' for every

£1 invested 'now', so his exchange rate would be $95/100 - 1 = -0.05$ or -5%. However, there is considerable evidence to suggest that TVMs are usually positive, with the ultimate, although somewhat morbid, argument being the inevitability of death. So in a one-period case, in order to be persuaded to forgo £1 of consumption 'now', the owner will have to be offered £1 + 'next year', just to cover the risk that he may not be around next year to collect the return from the investment – he may be dead!

As an individual's time value of money is likely not to remain constant but to change with events, it is more correct to call any TVM a *marginal* time value of money.

9. The literature gives this curve a variety of names, e.g. investment opportunity line, productive opportunity line or time-exchange function.

10. As a result of this arrangement and of our assumption that all physical investment opportunities are infinitely divisible and display decreasing returns to scale, the physical investment line is likely to be generally smooth and concave to the origin. In the real world of investments that are not infinitely divisible it is anything but smooth.

11. The term 'maximum consumption combinations' is meant in the sense that with any given amount of current consumption, no higher consumption next year is possible with the company's existing resources and similarly, with any given amount of consumption next year, no higher level of current consumption is possible.

12. The return on the marginal investment – the marginal return – can properly be found from the first derivative of the function of the physical investment line. For illustration purposes it can be very roughly approximated by:

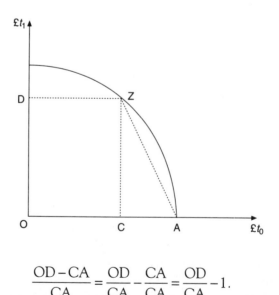

$$\frac{OD - CA}{CA} = \frac{OD}{CA} - \frac{CA}{CA} = \frac{OD}{CA} - 1.$$

Therefore if the company has a total value now of £1000 (OA) of which the owner consumes £600 (OC) and invests the remainder (CA) in order to produce £450 (OD) next year, we can obtain a rough approximation of the return on the marginal project (point Z) as:

$$\frac{450}{400} - 1 = 0.125 = 12\tfrac{1}{2}\%.$$

Graphically, we are finding the slope of the dotted line ZA. In fact this calculation of $12\tfrac{1}{2}\%$ does not provide the return on the marginal investment, but the *average* return on the *total* investment.

13. It is worth noting that under our present assumptions it makes no difference to our analysis whether or not the company represents the owner's sole source of consumption. However, we shall see later that when some of the assumptions are varied, this factor becomes important.

14. The concept of a perfect capital market will prove extremely important to us, in later developments of the theory. For the time being we shall define it – under the assumption of a world of certainty – as a market where everyone can borrow or lend as much money as they wish (within their ability to repay) at a single rate of interest which is applicable to all, whether borrowing or lending. Additionally there are no transaction costs involved in using the market, no single investor or group of investors dominate the market and all information is freely available.

15. Up to this point, no mention has been made of taxation. It is easiest to assume that taxation does not exist, but it makes little difference to the analysis if tax is levied on gain as long as all investors face the same level of taxation and there is no differentiation between gain from physical and capital market investment. In such circumstances the return on investment referred to in the analysis is, of course, the after-tax return.

16. This term is negative because the line AE has a negative slope – it slopes downwards from left to right.

17. This is often referred to as the Hirshliefer Separation Theorem.

18. The reader must be careful not to be misled here. The test of being 'better off' or increasing utility is whether or not a higher indifference curve is reached. So we could just as easily get a situation where the shareholder achieves a higher indifference curve through using the capital markets but this results (say) in a decrease in consumption 'now' and an increase 'next year'. As a higher indifference curve has been reached the reduction in consumption 'now' must be more than offset (in the shareholder's mind) by the gain in consumption 'next year'.

19. It would be possible, although somewhat unlikely, for all of a company's shareholders to have an identical set of indifference curves/time value of money. In such cases the separation theorem would lose its importance.

20. In fact there do exist chance circumstances when ROCE will provide correct investment appraisal advice, but such situations are likely to be highly artificial and of little practical significance.

21. It may be wise to correct here a mistaken impression that the reader could possibly gain from this presentation and development of the theory. Historically, payback and ROCE were derived (largely) in ignorance of the single-period investment–consumption model. It is therefore not surprising that neither method meets the model's requirement for an investment appraisal technique. However, the two major discounted cash flow methods, which are to be discussed in the next chapter, were *not* developed

in isolation from the model but arise out of the logic which lies behind the model's construction.

The reader should not hold the belief that it is just fortuitous that these later two methods of investment appraisal accord (as we shall see) with the model.

Further reading

1. The basic reading for the ideas discussed in this chapter is: J. Hirshliefer, 'On the Theory of Optimal Investment Decisions', *Journal of Political Economy*, August 1958. The article is not easy reading, especially the second half, but is very much worthwhile.
2. Although the idea of risk has only been introduced very briefly at this stage, an accessible article to read would be: J. Hirshliefer, 'Risk, the Discount Rate and Investment Decision', *American Economic Review*, May 1961.

Quickie questions

1. Why is an individual's personal time value of money likely to increase as more investment is undertaken?
2. What does the physical investment line represent?
3. What determines the slope of the physical investment line?
4. What is an indifference curve?
5. Given a single owner-manager firm, how does the firm decide on its level of capital investment?
6. If an owner wants to lend money at t_0, does he move up or down the financial investment line?
7. What is the two-part decision rule that arises out of the Hirshliefer separation theorem?
8. Define a risky capital investment.
9. Taking risk into consideration, what is the capital investment decision rule that managers should follow if they wish to maximize shareholder wealth?
10. What are the four main assumptions (remember, two were dropped at later stages in the analysis) of the single period investment–consumption model?
11. What is the generally assumed attitude of investors to risk?
12. If your personal marginal time value of money was less than the market interest rate, would you want to lend or borrow?

Problem

1. Phonetic plc has £500 of cash resources available at t_0. It has identified three investment projects, as follows:

Project	I	II	III
Outlay at t_0	100	200	200
Inflow at t_1	120	300	210

Assume that all projects exhibit *constant* returns to scale.

Required:
(a) Draw, to scale, the physical investment line facing the firm.

(b) Given that the market interest rate is 8% show, graphically, the firm's investment decisions and the resulting t_0 and t_1 cash flow to the owner.

(c) How might the investment decisions of the firm change if the market interest rate moved:

   (i)   to 25%?

   (ii) to 10%?

   (iii) to 20%?

(d) Given the market interest rate of 8%, before the firm can implement the investment plan given in your answer to part (b) an extra project is identified:

Project	IV
Outlay at t_0	250
Inflow at t_1	330

Show the new situation graphically. What is your revised investment decision advice to management?

5 The discounted cash flow approach

Net present value

Having examined the two 'traditional' methods of capital investment appraisal, it is now time to turn to the other two main appraisal techniques. These are net present value (NPV) and internal rate of return (IRR) both of which are described as discounted cash flow (DCF) methods. We shall start by first examining the net present value technique.

The NPV investment appraisal method works on the simple, but funda-mental, principle that an investment is worthwhile undertaking if the money got out of the investment is greater than the money put in (assum-ing of course that our objectives can be described in financial terms). On this very commonsense principle, project A is worth investing in. For an outlay of £500, it produces a total cash inflow of £600. Thus it has a net value of plus £100.

Project A

Year	Cash flow (£)
0	−500
1	+200
2	+200
3	+200
	+100 net value

It is clear that, with such a straightforward approach, the decision rule would be: accept all investments with a positive or zero net value (as they produce a return either equal to or greater than their cost), and reject all those with a negative net value.

However, let us take a totally different situation. Suppose you were made an offer: if you pay £500 now, you will immediately receive 200 French francs, 200 Japanese yen and 200 German marks. How would you go about deciding whether the offer was worthwhile? What you certainly would *not* do is to say: I have to give up 500 pieces of paper and, in return, I'll get 200 + 200 + 200 = 600 pieces of paper. As I end up with 100 more pieces of paper, the deal is worthwhile! Instead, you would recognize that in order to evaluate the offer, you have to convert all the different currencies to a *common* currency, and *then* undertake the comparison.

Although it does not *look* as silly as that which was initially suggested with the currency offer, our suggested approach to evaluating Project A *is* just as silly. In the same way that money in different currencies cannot be compared directly, but first have to be converted to a common currency, cash flows in the same currency (as in Project A), but occurring *at different points in time* cannot be compared directly, but must first be converted to a common point of time. This is because of the *time value of money*.

Therefore the net present value investment appraisal decision rule basically takes the same approach as that used with Project A, but with one vital difference. That difference is that the time value of money is taken into account in assessing whether the investment has a positive or negative net value.

The discounting process

The time value of money is taken into account through the discounting process. The arithmetic of discounting is dealt with in an appendix to this chapter and the reader is advised to become familiar with its contents. However, it will help to explain the NPV technique if the basic concepts of discounting are developed here.

We have already seen from our initial discussion on the time value of money in Chapter 3 that, given the choice between £100 now, or £100 in twelve months' time, most people would intuitively take the £100 now. This is because the £100 could be placed on deposit at (say) 6% interest and so turn itself into £106 in twelve months' time. (And, being rational investors, £106 in twelve months' time will be preferred to only £100 in twelve months' time.) Therefore, in this case, 6% – the interest rate – represents the time value of money.

The mathematics of this process works through the compound interest formula:

$$A(1 + r)^n$$

where A is the initial amount invested or deposited, r is the (annual) rate of return (which could be interest) and n is the number of years for which A is left deposited. In the example used above, these three variables have the respective values of: £100, 0.06 and 1. So, £100 left on deposit for twelve months is turned into:

$$£100(1 + 0.06)^1 = £100 + £6 = £106.$$

Using this compound interest formula, but switching it around, we can also calculate that to receive £106 in twelve months' time, the amount to be invested now is:

$$\frac{£106}{(1+0.06)} = £106\,\frac{1}{(1+0.06)} = £100.$$

Therefore £100 is the 'present value' (PV) of £106 received in twelve months' time and £106, the 'future' or 'terminal' value (FV) of £100 deposited twelve months' previously, assuming a 6% interest rate in each case.

Similarly, £100 invested for two years at a 6% compound interest rate would turn into:

$$£100(1 + 0.06)(1 + 0.06) = £100(1 + 0.06)^2 = £112.36$$

and £112.36 received in two years' time is equal to:

$$\frac{£112.36}{(1+0.06)^2} = £112.36 \, \frac{1}{(1+0.06)^2} = £100 \text{ now.}$$

Thus the terminal value in two years' time of £100 invested now is £112.36, whilst the present value of £112.36 received in two years' time is £100. In each case we are assuming an annual compound interest rate of 6%.

In general terms, $A(1 + r)^n$ is the terminal value of an amount A that has been placed on deposit for n years at an annual compound interest rate of r. Similarly: $A[1/(1 + r)^n]$ is the *present value* of an amount A received in n years' time, where r is the annual compound interest rate.

In the calculation of the terminal value, an amount of money is being 'compounded' *forward* through time, whereas in the calculation of the present value, an amount of money is being 'discounted' *backwards* through time. To distinguish between these two processes, it is usual to refer to the compound interest rate, when used in the discounting process, as the *discount rate*. Also, usually a slightly easier notation is used for the present value expression: $A(1 + r)^{-n}$. Thus in the previous example, the present value of £112.36 received in two years' time, when the annual rate of discount was 6%, is given by:

$$\frac{£112.36}{(1+0.06)^2} = £112.36 \, (1+0.06)^{-2} = £112.36 \times 0.8900 = £100.$$

A discounting example

The NPV method makes use of the idea of present values by expressing the project's cash flows in terms of its net *present* value, although the cash flows could just as easily be expressed in terms of net *terminal* values. It is really for no reason other than convention that present values are used.

To see how the NPV method works, let us return to Project A, but this time, instead of just netting out the cash inflows and outflows to produce a net value of plus £100, we first of all convert (or 'discount') the cash flows to *present value* cash flows, in order to allow for the time value of money, and then net out the inflows and outflows. Thus with a discount rate of (say) 8%, the net present value of Project A is £15.40:

Project A

Year	Cash flow (£)	×	Discounting factor				=	Present value cash flow (£)
0	−500	×	$(1 + 0.08)^0$	=	−500 × 1		=	−500.00
1	+200	×	$(1 + 0.08)^{-1}$	=	+200 × 0.9259		=	+185.18
2	+200	×	$(1 + 0.08)^{-2}$	=	+200 × 0.8573		=	+171.46
3	+200	×	$(1 + 0.08)^{-3}$	=	+200 × 0.7938		=	+158.76
						NPV		+ 15.40

From this analysis we can see that Project A is worth undertaking, because the cash outflows associated with it are exceeded by the cash inflows produced by it. The time value of money has been taken into account by the fact that all the cash flows of the project, for the purposes of comparison, are converted to values at one point in time: the present.

To emphasize this important point further, it is vital to understand that once the fact is accepted that money has a time value, then it follows that money at different points in time is not directly comparable: £1 now cannot be directly compared with £1 next year, and so the cash flows of a project that arise at different points through time all have to be converted to a value at one particular point in time. By convention, and because it has many practical advantages, the point in time normally chosen is the present.

Thus our original netting procedure with Project A which produced a net value of +£100 was nonsensical, because we were not comparing like with like, but were trying to compare directly the net money flows arising at different points in time without first converting them to a common point in time. The NPV approach tells us that in terms of present values (i.e. converting all the cash flows to money values *now*) Project A produces a return which is £15.40 in excess of the investment outlay (i.e. in present value terms the cash outflow is £500 and the total cash inflow is £515.40) and is therefore a worthwhile investment.

Project B

Year	Cash flow (£)	×	Discounting factor	=	Present value cash flow (£)
0	−1000	×	$(1 + 0.08)^0$	=	−1000.00
1	+ 100	×	$(1 + 0.08)^{-1}$	=	+ 92.59
2	+ 200	×	$(1 + 0.08)^{-2}$	=	+ 171.46
3	+ 200	×	$(1 + 0.08)^{-3}$	=	+ 158.76
4	+ 550	×	$(1 + 0.08)^{-4}$	=	+ 404.25
Net value + 50				NPV	− 172.94

As another example, evaluating Project B without taking into account the time value of money, the cash inflows exceed the cash outflows by £50 and so the project appears to be a worthwhile investment. However if we do take into account the time value of money by discounting the cash flows into present values at an 8% discount rate, then we can see that Project B is *not* a worthwhile investment, because the cash outflow required exceeds the cash inflows produced, resulting in a *negative* net present value.

Calculating present values

The discounting factors, such as $(1 + 0.08)^{-3}$, can be calculated quite easily on any basic calculator that has a 'powers' function, i.e. x^y. In addition, a table of discounting factors for a variety of values of n and i is given on page 606. These tables can be used to find that $(1 + 0.08)^{-3}$ equals 0.7938. In other words, the present value of £1 in three years' time at an 8% rate of discount is 79.38 pence. Therefore, £200 in three years' time has a present value of: £200 × 0.7938 = £158.76.

It is also very easy to use computer spreadsheets to find the present value of a series of cash flows. If you have access to a PC with a spreadsheet, use it to caculate the NPV of example B above. If you use the NPV function built into the spreadsheet you will probably have come up with the answer −£160.1. This is because the function was incorrectly defined in the first spreadsheets to have an NPV function and, presumably for the sake of consistency, it has been incorrectly defined ever since. It is actually present value and not net present value. Using the notation below, the function in the spreadsheet is

$$\sum_{t=1}^{n} \frac{A_t}{(1+r)^t}$$

but for NPV t should equal 0 to n and not 1 to n. Thus the spreadsheet function is incorrect by one power of $1 + r$ for each period calculated.

The timing of cash flows

For the sake of simplicity we will continue to assume, in the examples that follow, that cash flows are discrete and occur at the end of the time period in question. Obviously, in the real world this will often not be the case. Many cash flows in business happen throught the year (e.g. sales, purchases and expenses). To be strictly accurate we should work on the basis that both cash flows and compounding are continuous. The formula for calculating the present value of cash flows like this is an exponential function:

$$1/r \, (1 - e^{-r}).$$

Applying this to a discount rate of 11% gives a discount factor of 0.947 for cash flows taking place during the first year. Thus if we received £100 every day this would total £36 500 (spread over the year) and its present value would be £36 500 × .947 = £34 566.

However, it is not always convenient to work figures out using exponential functions and there is an extremely good approximation that is much easier to use. All we need to do is to assume that the cash flows take place discretely but half way through the year, so in year one (still using 11%) this would produce the discount factor

$$1/(1.11)^{0.5} = 0.95.$$

Applying this to our cash flow of £36 500 produces a present value of £34 675 which is less than 0.5% out. Had we assumed a year end cash flow, 1/1.11 gives us a discount factor of 0.90 and if we apply this to £36 500 we find a present value of £32 850 which is nearly 5% out.

Discount tables using mid-point cash flows are included in the tables that start at page 606.

The NPV decision rule

In general terms, we can express the net present value of an investment project as the sum of its net discounted future cash flows:

$$\sum_{t=0}^{n} \frac{A_t}{(1+r)^t}$$

where A_t is the project's cash flow (either positive or negative) in time t (t takes on values from year 0 to year n, where n represents the point in time when the project comes to the end of its life) and r is the annual rate of discount or the time value of money (which is here assumed to remain a constant over the life of the project). If the expression has a zero or positive value, the company should invest in the project; if it has negative value, it should not invest.[1] (This general mathematical expression for the net present value of an investment project is more fully explained in the appendix on compounding and discounting at the end of this chapter.)

Let us take a closer look at Project B to see why the NPV method tells us not to invest. Project B requires an outlay of £1000 and would produce cash inflows for the four following years. However, if we did not invest £1000 in B we could, presumably, put the money on deposit (i.e. lend the money on the capital market) at the going rate of interest of 8%. At the end of four years' time this would produce $£1000 \times (1 + 0.08)^4 = £1360.50$.

Suppose we *did* invest in Project B and as the generated cash inflows arose we placed them on deposit (at 8% compound interest). How much cash would we be able to accumulate by the end of four years (i.e. by the time the life of the project was completed)? This is shown below, where the £100 Project B produces in twelve months' time can be invested for three years, the £200 it produces in 24 months' time can be invested for two years, and so on:

Year	Project's cash inflow (£)	×	Compounding factor	=	Terminal value (end of year 4) (£)
1	+ 100	×	$(1 + 0.08)^3$	=	+ 125.97
2	+ 200	×	$(1 + 0.08)^2$	=	+ 233.28
3	+ 200	×	$(1 + 0.08)^1$	=	+ 216.00
4	+ 550	×	$(1 + 0.08)^0$	=	+ 550.00
			Total terminal value	=	+ 1125.25

So putting the £1000 on deposit for four years produces £1360.50, whereas if we invest our £1000 in Project B and place on deposit any cash flows that arise, at the end of four years this will produce only £1125.25.

Therefore, looking at the two alternatives, the project is not the most desirable investment: we should be better off placing the £1000 on deposit in the capital market. This is the basis of the advice given by the NPV appraisal method because the present value of £1360.50 received in four years' time with an 8% discount rate is:

$$£1360.50(1 + 0.08)^{-4} = £1000$$

whilst the present value of £1125.25 received in four years' time with an 8% discount rate is:

$$£1125.25(1 + 0.08)^{-4} = £827.06.$$

The difference between these two sums (£1000 – £827.06) is £172.94, which is the amount of Project B's negative net present value.

So we can see that the NPV method of investment appraisal evaluates projects by looking at the *alternative* to an investment in that project, such as lending the money out on the capital market at the market rate of interest. It automatically carries out this comparison of alternatives through the decision rule: only invest in projects which produce zero or positive NPVs. As we have seen, the value of a project's NPV represents the increase or decrease (depending upon whether the NPV is positive or negative) in return that would arise from investing in the project rather than lending the money on the capital market at the market rate of interest, and it is this rate that is used as the discount rate.

Alternative interpretations of NPV

There are some equally valid, alternative interpretations of the meaning behind a project's net present value which might be helpful to examine in order to gain a deeper understanding. We will take another project as an example. Project C is expected to produce the following net cash flows:

Year	Cash flow (£)
0	−100
1	+ 30
2	+ 40
3	+ 50
4	+ 20

Referring back to our brief discussion at the end of the previous chapter about risk, suppose that the capital market rate of return available from an investment of similar risk to Project C is 10%. Thus 10% is the relevant time value of money and so is the appropriate discount rate to use in an NPV analysis.

Project C's NPV is calculated as:

Year	Cash flow (£)		Discount factor		PV cash flow (£)
0	− 100	×	$(1 + 0.10)^0$	=	− 100.00
1	+ 30	×	$(1 + 0.10)^{-1}$	=	+ 27.27
2	+ 40	×	$(1 + 0.10)^{-2}$	=	+ 33.06
3	+ 50	×	$(1 + 0.10)^{-3}$	=	+ 37.57
4	+ 20	×	$(1 + 0.10)^{-4}$	=	+ 13.66
					+ £11.56 NPV

Project C has a positive NPV and therefore, according to the decision rule, is worthwhile undertaking. There are three obvious interpretations that can be made of this result:

1. An investment of £100 in Project C produces £11.56 more, in t_0 terms, than investing on the capital market. In this sense, the £11.56

is an *excess* return or a measure of *economic profit*. (This is our original interpretation.)

2. As Project C produces a positive NPV, it is generating a return which is greater than 10%, the discount rate used.
3. If £100 were borrowed at 10% interest, in order to undertake Project C, then the project would generate a sufficient cash flow to pay the interest, repay the loan *and* leave a surplus of £11.56 in present value terms.

Given these three interpretations, the logic of the NPV decision rule becomes even more obvious:

1. A negative NPV project is unacceptable because it indicates that the project makes a loss *relative* to a capital market investment (i.e. an opportunity loss).
2. A negative NPV project is unacceptable because it is producing a return less than that available for a similar level of risk on the capital market.
3. A negative NPV project is unacceptable as it would not generate sufficient cash flow to repay the financial cost of undertaking it.

Also notice, given these interpretations, that a zero NPV project *would* be acceptable – but we would not be overjoyed if we identified one.

Finally, there is a fourth interpretation of a project's NPV that can be made. In many ways, this is the most important interpretation and how it arises will be seen in the next section when we return to the Hirshliefer analysis. Quite simply, a project's net present value indicates the increase in shareholders' wealth that it will generate if it is undertaken. Hence, the technique links directly into our fundamental objective of financial management decision making.

NPV and the investment–consumption model

When looking at our single-period investment–consumption model, we saw that in order to act in the best interests of its owners, a company should move along the physical investment line until the return from the marginal investment becomes equal to the return given by the capital market (i.e. the market rate of interest). How does the NPV method of investment appraisal help us achieve this point?

Returning to Project A, we saw that, using an 8% discount rate, the project had an NPV of plus £15.40 whilst Project B had an NPV of minus £172.94. On the basis of what we already understand about the net present value, we can also say – using the two examples above – that as Project A has a positive NPV when discounted at 8%, it must be producing a rate of return *greater* than 8%, and similarly, as Project B has a negative NPV when discounted at 8%, then it must be producing a rate of return of *less than* 8%.

Just what the exact rate of return is in each case we shall consider later, but looking at Project D, since it gives a zero NPV when discounted at 8%, we can conclude that it has a rate of return exactly *equal* to 8%:

Project D

Year	Cash flow (£)	×	Present value factor		Present value cash flow (£)
0	− 400	×	$(1 + 0.08)^0$	=	− 400.00
1	+ 200	×	$(1 + 0.08)^{-1}$	=	+ 185.18
2	+ 100	×	$(1 + 0.08)^{-2}$	=	+ 85.73
3	+ 162.62	×	$(1 + 0.08)^{-3}$	=	+ 129.09
				NPV	£0

Therefore, if a company follows the NPV rule and invests in all physical investment opportunities available to it that possess either zero or positive net present values, using the market rate of interest as the discount rate, it will automatically move along the physical investment line until a point of tangency is reached with the financial investment line.

If a company makes physical investments beyond this optimal point, these projects will have a rate of return which is less than the market rate of interest and therefore *negative* net present values. As long as investment decision makers within companies follow the NPV decision rule and *only* invest in projects with zero or positive NPVs, then the company is ensured of optimally locating on the physical investment line.

The graphical interpretation

In Fig. 5.1, if management assess the company's total resources (i.e. the full, liquidated value of the company at time t_0) as OA and they have sought out all the investment alternatives available to them, expressed by the physical investment line AB, then using the NPV method of investment appraisal, they will invest in all projects with positive or zero NPVs when discounted at the market rate of interest.

Fig. 5.1 *Using the NPV rule*

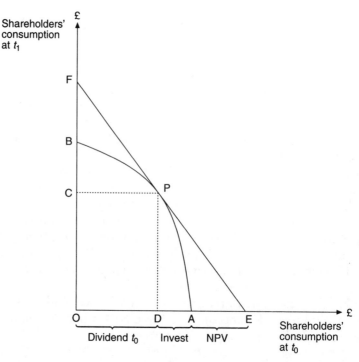

This simple decision rule will lead to DA of the company's resources being put into productive investments at t_0 and the remainder, OD, being paid out to shareholders as dividends. This investment will result in a total dividend of OC being paid out at t_1. Shareholders can then adjust their individual dividends to fit their desired consumption pattern by lending or borrowing on the capital market. This two-stage process, with the company first making physical investment decisions and then the individual shareholder making financial investment decisions, will ensure that individual shareholders will achieve their highest possible indifference curves and hence maximize their level of utility.

We should also note that if the company does invest up to the optimal point P in Fig. 5.1 (i.e. the point of tangency between the physical and financial investment lines), then the present value of the cash *inflows* generated by all the company's investment project undertakings is given by DE, the cash expenditure made on these investments is given by DA and so, by difference, AE represents the total *net* present value of the investment projects undertaken by the firm. (Alternatively, OE can be said to represent the present value of the sum of dividend OD at t_0 and dividend OC at t_1.)

From this we can see the derivation of that important fourth interpretation of the idea of net present value. Notice that with no investment undertaken, the total worth of the company's resources (in t_0 terms) is given by AO. If amount AD is invested to yield OC at t_1, then the worth of the company (again, in t_0 terms) increases to amount OE. Thus undertaking the investments required to locate at point P on the physical investment line has resulted in an increase in the current worth of the company – in other words, in shareholders' wealth – of AE, which of course represents the total NPV of the investments undertaken. Therefore the net present value of a project represents the amount by which shareholders' wealth (measured in t_0 terms) will change as a result of accepting the project. (It thus becomes obvious why management should not accept *negative* NPV projects – they will cause shareholders' wealth to be reduced.)

In general, the single-period investment–consumption diagram can measure the NPV of a company's total physical investments as the distance between the point at which the physical investment line cuts the horizontal axis and where the financial investment line, passing through the point at which the firm has located on the physical investment line, also cuts the horizontal axis.[2] As can be seen from Fig. 5.2, if a company either under-invests and locates at (say) point X, or over-invests and locates at (say) point Y, or optimally invests and locates at point Z on the physical investment line, in each case the total NPV earned by the company's investment decisions is given by the distance on the horizontal axis between the physical investment line and the financial investment line passing through the location point: respectively AB, AC and AD.[3] Locating at the optimal point on the physical investment line (at the point of tangency with the market line) also maximizes NPV and so here is yet another surrogate for the financial decision-making objective of maximizing shareholder wealth, that of maximizing total net present value.

One final point of interest from this graphical analysis is to use it to look at the effect of a change in the market rate of interest. A *fall* in the market rate of interest will cause the financial investment line to pivot anticlockwise and become flatter. This would then have the effect of moving the point of tangency (and hence the optimal physical investment point) higher

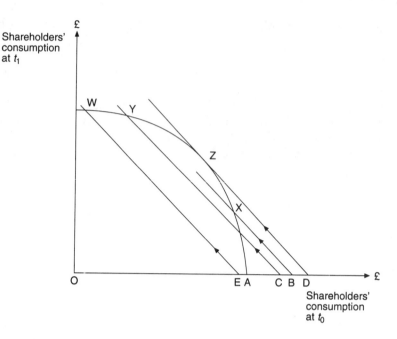

Fig. 5.2 *Under and over investments*

up the physical investment line, thus increasing the amount of investment that a company must undertake to reach its point of optimality. This is just as we would expect, as is the case where the market rate of interest rises and the reverse effect is observed.

(The reader no doubt has noticed how the analysis has slipped in and out of the assumption of a single-period time horizon. The assumption was made in the Hirshliefer analysis in order to allow a graphical/two-dimensional presentation. However, the conclusions drawn can be quite simply applied to a multi-time period example, such as that of Project D.)

Internal rate of return

Before looking more carefully at this analysis and specifically at the implicit and explicit assumptions that lie behind the NPV method, let us turn to the second major discounted cash flow investment appraisal technique, the internal rate of return (IRR) or yield.[4] As we shall see later on in the discussion, the IRR has some very great theoretical and practical difficulties as a method of investment appraisal, and indeed it may be questioned whether it is truly a method of appraisal at all, or just an arithmetic result.

The IRR model

To discover what the IRR is, let us return briefly to our discussion of NPV. We stated that if a project had a positive NPV at a certain discount rate (say) 10%, this meant, amongst other things, that the project's return was actually greater than 10%, whilst if the project had a negative NPV then its return was less than the discount rate, and if it had a zero NPV, then its return was equal to the discount rate.

The IRR of a project can be defined as the rate of discount which, when applied to the project's cash flows, produces a zero NPV (hence the method could be seen as just an arithmetic result of the NPV method). In general terms, the IRR is the value for r which satisfies the expression:

$$\sum_{t=0}^{n} \frac{A}{(1+r)^t} = 0.$$

For a very simple project, such as E, where cash flows only extend over two periods, the internal rate of return is easy to calculate using simple algebra:

Project E

Year	Cash flow (£)
0	+ 200
1	+ 218

The IRR of Project E is equal to r, where:

$$-200 + \frac{218}{1+r} = 0.$$

Multiplying both sides by $(1 + r)$ gives:

$$-200(1 + r) + 218 = 0$$

and rearranging: $218 - 200 = 200r$
$$18 = 200r$$

$$\frac{18}{200} = r = 0.09 \text{ or } 9\%.$$

Thus if Project E's cash flows were discounted by 9% they would have a zero NPV:

Project E

Year	Cash flow (£)	×	Present value factor		Present value cash flow (£)
0	− 200	×	$(1 + 0.09)^0$	=	− 200
1	+ 218	×	$(1 + 0.09)^{-1}$	=	+ 200
				NPV	£0

And with a slightly more complex project, with cash flows occurring at three points of time, t_0, t_1, and t_2, the IRR can still easily be found through the solution to a quadratic equation, as with Project F:

Project F

Year	Cash flow (£)
0	− 100
1	+ 60
2	+ 55

IRR $= r$, where:

$$-100 + \frac{60}{1+r} + \frac{55}{(1+r)^2} = 0.$$

Multiplying both sides by $(1 + r)^2$, we produce a quadratic equation in $1 + r$ that can be solved via the quadratic formula:

$$-100(1+r)^2 + 60(1+r) + 55 = 0$$

$$(1+r) = \frac{-60 \pm \sqrt{60^2 - (4 \times -100 \times 55)}}{(2 \times 100)}$$

$$(1+r) = +1.10 \text{ or } (1+r) = -0.50.$$

This second (negative) result can be discarded as meaningless for our purposes, so that $1 + r = 1.10$ and $r = 0.10$ or 10%. This is the internal rate of return of Project F, and therefore if the project's cash flows were discounted at this rate they would have a zero NPV.

Estimating the IRR via linear interpolation

To find the IRR of projects whose cash flows extend over more than three points in time, we become involved with finding solutions to complex polynomial equations. There are many computer programs that will carry out this task, including spreadsheets. Try the example in the last section using the spreadsheet package on your PC to calculate IRR if you have access to one. If you don't have access to a computer (and this must be very rare for corporate decision makers) a fairly good *approximation* of an investment project's IRR can be found through the mathematical technique called linear interpolation.

Returning to Project F, although we have found its IRR to be 10%, let us now estimate it by using the *linear interpolation* method.

If a whole series of different discount rates were applied to Project F's cash flow, the resulting NPVs could be plotted out on a graph against the discount rate. Fig. 5.3 illustrates the sort of result that might occur, termed the *NPV profile*. Notice that the project's IRR is given by the point where the NPV profile cuts the horizontal axis.

We will first deal with the *mechanics* of linear interpolation, and then examine its rationale. The approach used is to select a pair of discount rates so that one of them, when applied to the project's cash flow, produces a positive NPV and the other produces a negative NPV. From observing Fig. 5.3, it can be seen that as the discount rate (the time value of money) gets larger, the positive NPV gets progressively smaller, passes through zero, and then becomes an increasingly large negative value. (This result is, of course, not surprising, knowing as much as we do about the time value of money concept.) Therefore a low and a high discount rate should be chosen to provide the required positive and negative NPVs.

Using 4% and 20% discount rates (the extreme discount rate values given in the table on page 606), the NPV of Project F can be calculated as:

0	−	100 $(1.04)^0$	=	− 100.00	0	−	100 $(1.20)^0$	=	− 100.00

$$
\begin{array}{lllll}
0 - 100\,(1.04)^0 & = & -100.00 & \quad 0 - 100\,(1.20)^0 & = & -100.00 \\
1 + 60\,(1.04)^{-1} & = & +57.69 & \quad 1 + 60\,(1.20)^{-1} & = & +50.00 \\
2 + 55\,(1.04)^{-2} & = & +50.85 & \quad 2 + 55\,(1.20)^{-2} & = & +38.19 \\
\text{NPV} & = & +8.54 & \quad \text{NPV} & = & -11.81
\end{array}
$$

Given the IRR is that discount rate that produces a *zero* NPV, Project F's

IRR must lie somewhere between 4% and 20%. As the IRR is more than 4%, *how much* more than 4% is estimated by taking the NPV at 4% as a proportion (0.42) of the difference between the two NPVs calculated. That proportion is then taken of the difference between the two discount rates used (16%):

$$IRR = 4\%\left[\frac{+8.54}{+8.54-(-11.81)}\times(20\%-4\%)\right]$$

$$IRR = 4\%+[0.42\times16\%]=10.72\%.$$

Figure 5.3 shows the linear interpolation method diagrammatically. The IRR is only estimated, because the NPV profile is being approximated by a straight line.

This 'bracketing' of discount rates around the true IRR so as to produce a positive and negative NPV is not strictly necessary, but it does make the

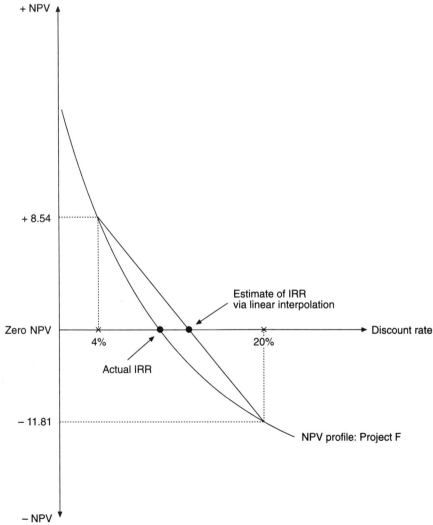

Fig. 5.3 *Estimating the IRR (not to scale)*

approximation calculation easier. Furthermore, the narrower the bracketing around the actual IRR, the more accurate the estimate of the IRR. For example, using 8% and 12% discount rates, linear interpolation estimates Project F's IRR as:

At 8% discount rate: +2.70 NPV

At 12% discount rate: −2.58 NPV

$$IRR = 8\% \left[\frac{+2.70}{+2.70 - (-2.58)} \times (12\% - 8\%) \right] = 10.04\%.$$

This gives a much closer result to the actual IRR. However, for most investment appraisal purposes, a highly accurate estimate of the IRR is not justified and an estimate with the accuracy of our initial calculation is usually more than sufficient.

Finally, notice that the arithmetic of linear interpolation can still be used, even if the two discount rates used do *not* produce one positive and one negative NPV, as they have done in the examples used so far.

The general rule for using linear interpolation is as follows. Select any two discount rates, a lower rate and a higher rate. Calculate the project's NPV at each discount rate. Given that:

LRNPV = NPV of the project when calculated at the lower discount rate
HRNPV = NPV of the project when calculated at the higher discount rate
LDR   = Lower discount rate, and
HDR   = Higher discount rate, then:

$$IRR = LDR + \left[\frac{LRNPV}{LRNPV - HRNPV} \times (HDR - LDR) \right].$$

This is illustrated in Example 1.

Example 1

Arnold Ltd wish to estimate the IRR of a project that is under evaluation. Its cash flows are as follows:

Year	Cash flow (£)
0	−10 000
1	+ 5 000
2	+ 8 000
3	+ 3 000

Again using 4% and 20% as the two discount rates, the NPV of the project is as follows (but remember, any two discounts could be used although, of course, they will give a different answer because the linear interpolation method is only estimating the IRR. Thus, using a different pair of discount rates will produce a different estimate):

At a 4% discount rate, the NPV is + £4871
At a 20% discount rate, the NPV is + £1458

Therefore the project's IRR can be estimated as:

$$IRR = 4\% + \left[\frac{£4871}{£4871 - £1458} \times (20\% - 4\%) \right] = 26.8\%.$$

The IRR decision rule

Having seen how to calculate a project's internal rate of return, how are we to use it for investment appraisal purposes? The decision rule is that only projects with an IRR greater than or equal to some predetermined 'cut-off' rate should be accepted. This cut-off rate is usually the market rate of interest (i.e. the discount rate that would have been used if an NPV analysis were undertaken instead). All other investment project opportunities should be rejected. Therefore Project F would be acceptable if the decision criterion has been set at 10%, or less.

The reasoning behind the IRR decision rule is similar to that behind NPV. The market interest rate reflects the *opportunity* cost of the capital involved. Thus to be acceptable, a project must generate a return at least equal to the return available elsewhere on the capital market.

IRR and the investment–consumption model

Again, just as the NPV method fitted into our single-period investment–consumption model, so too does the IRR method. We originally described the physical investment line as representing the whole series of infinitely divisible physical investment projects which were available to the company, arranged in order of decreasing rate of return. This rate of return can be viewed as the individual project's internal rate of return and can be derived (as we have already seen) from the slope of the physical investment lines.[5]

In Fig. 5.4 therefore, moving progressively along the line from point A to B, the slope gets less and less steep, indicating that the company initially

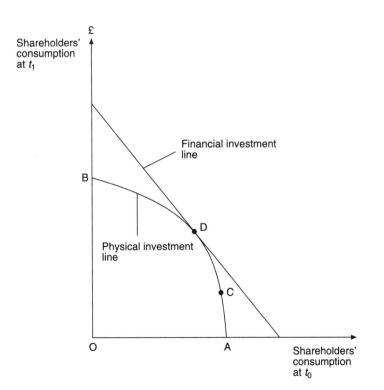

Fig. 5.4 *Using the IRR rule*

invests in projects with high internal rates of return and then works its way through to projects with much smaller IRRs. Thus from the slope of the physical investment line at point C can be derived the IRR of the marginal physical investment represented by that point.

The IRR decision rule tells a company to invest in all projects with IRRs greater than or equal to the market rate of interest. Thus a company will move up and around its physical investment line until it reaches the point of tangency with the financial investment line. Up to this point, all investment projects that the company has undertaken will have IRRs *greater than* the market rate of interest. At point D on Fig. 5.4, the marginal project will have an IRR *equal* to the market interest rate, and it is at this point that the company will cease further investment, because the remaining investment opportunities will all have IRRs which are *less than* the market interest rate. Therefore, the internal rate of return investment appraisal rule, like the NPV rule, will ensure that a company locates at the optimal point on its physical investment line.

Discounted payback

Having examined the basic application of the two discounted cash flow techniques of capital investment appraisal, it is appropriate to return briefly to look at the discounted payback technique, which was referred to in Chapter 3. There it was stated that a major limitation of payback was that it did not take the time value of money into account. However, this criticism could be overcome through the use of discounted payback.

All that discounted payback does is to see how quickly a project takes to pay back its outlay in *present value* (rather than undiscounted), cash flow terms. Example 2 illustrates the approach.

Example 2

Phonate plc wishes to evaluate an investment opportunity using discounted payback, for which it uses a four-year decision criterion. For discounting purposes, the company uses a 10% discount rate which, it is judged, reflects the return available elsewhere in the capital market for a similar risk investment. The project, code-named G, has a five-year life and the following estimated cash flows are as follows:

Year	Cash flow (£)
0	−250 000
1	+100 000
2	+100 000
3	+102 000
4	+ 50 000
5	+ 35 000

The discounted payback of Project G is calculated as follows:

Year	Cash flow (£)	×	Discount factor	=	PV cash flow (£)	
0	− 250 000	×	1	=	− 250 000	
1	+ 100 000	×	0.9091	=	+ 90 910	
2	+ 100 000	×	0.8264	=	+ 82 640	
3	+ 102 000	×	0.7513	=	+ 76 633	3-year payback
4	+ 50 000	×	0.6830	=	+ 34 150	
5	+ 35 000	×	0.6209	=	+ 21 731	

Project G has a discounted payback of approximately three years and so is acceptable, according to the company's decision criterion.

Truncated NPV

Discounted payback can be looked upon as a variation of the basic payback technique. However it is perhaps instructive to see it more as a variation on the NPV method.

In Example 2 the decision rule used by the company implied: accept the project as long as its NPV is at least zero (if not positive) at the end of four years. If a project complies with this requirement then it does pay back within the criterion period. Thus discounted payback is no more than a truncated version of NPV. Instead of calculating the project's NPV over the whole of its life, the NPV is effectively calculated up to some specified cut-off point which, in this example, happened to be four years.

Discounted payback still suffers from the criticism made of standard payback – that of ignoring project cash flows that lie outside the payback time period. However, as before, the point should be made that setting this artificial time horizon on a project's life may be no more than making a realistic allowance for management's limited forecasting abilities.

Finally, despite the foregoing, it should be pointed out that the use of discounted payback will not necessarily lead to the firm's optimal physical investment line location. This is because some positive NPV projects may well be rejected because they do not generate that positive NPV sufficiently quickly. A further criticism will be made of discounted payback in the following chapter.

Summary

This chapter has looked at the basic application of the two discounted cash flow (DCF) methods of investment appraisal. The main points covered were as follows:

- The fact that money has a time value (i.e. an opportunity cost in terms of a rate of interest) means that cash flows that arise at different points in time cannot be compared directly but must first be converted to common point of time (usually t_0, the present time).

- The NPV decision rule states:
  — accept a project if its NPV ≥ 0 (i.e. positive or zero);
  — reject a project if its NPV < 0 (i.e. negative).

- Although a number of different (but correct) interpretations can be made about the meaning of NPV, the most important is that the magnitude of a project's NPV represents the increase in shareholder wealth that can be expected to come about through its acceptance.

- It was seen that the NPV decision rule (see above) would lead the company to locate at the optimal point on the physical investment line of the Hirshliefer analysis. It was from this analysis that the connection between NPV and shareholder wealth can be seen.

- The internal rate of return (IRR) of a project is that discount rate which, when applied to a project's cash flow, produces a zero NPV. It is therefore a simple arithmetic result.

- The IRR decision rule is:
  - accept a project if its IRR ≥ decision criterion or 'hurdle rate';
  - reject if its IRR < decision criterion.

- Like NPV, use of the IRR decision rule will also lead to the company optimally locating on its physical investment line.

- Discounted payback, in which the speed of payback is computed in present value cash flow terms, was seen to be simply a version of NPV with an artificially truncated project life.

Appendix: compounding and discounting

Tables A to H can be found on pp. 606–9.

1 Compound interest factors

The amount to which a sum of £1 accumulates when placed on deposit for N years at a constant annual rate of interest of i is given by:

$$(1+i)^N.$$

Thus, £500 placed on deposit for six years at an annual rate of interest of 12%, accumulates to:

$$£500\,(1.12)^6 = £500 \times 1.9738 = £986.90.$$

Similarly, if £200 is placed on deposit for three years at 10% and two years at 8%, then the accumulated sum at the end of five years is:

$$£200\,(1.10)^3\,(1.08)^2 = £200 \times 1.3310 \times 1.1664 = £310.50.$$

Table A provides compound interest factors for various values of N and i.

2 Present value factors

The value now (i.e. the present value) of £1 arising in N years' time when the rate of discount (interest) is i, is given by:

$$1/(1+i)^N \text{ or } (1+i)^{-N}.$$

Thus, £500 arising in six years' time, when the annual rate of discount is 12%, has a present value of:

$$£500 \, (1.12)^{-6} = £500 \times 0.5066 = £253.30.$$

Similarly, £200 arising in five years, where the annual rate of discount is 10% for three years and 8% for two years, has a present value of:

$$£200 \, (1.10)^{-3} \, (1.08)^{-2} = £200 \times 0.7513 \times 0.8573 = £128.82.$$

Table B provides present value factors for various values of N and i.

3 Perpetuities

A perpetuity is a special pattern of cash flows. It is a fixed cash flow that continues for ever. The best known examples of this are undated government securities. The first of these were created during the Napoleonic wars at a time when the British Government did not have the money to repay some debt that was falling due. Thus they 'consolidated' the loan stock and promised to pay 2.5% (which was then above the market rate) for ever rather than repaying the principal. This was called Consolidated Loan Stock (Consols for short). If you had held £100 of this loan stock in 1805 you would have received £2.50 per annum in interest.

So PV (£100) $\times r$ (the interest rate of 2.5%) = C (the 'coupon' or cash flow of £2.50).

Rearranged this becomes PV = C/r.

The Consols still pay 2.5% but the market rate of interest varies and so does their present value. So if the rate of interest is now 6%, the PV of the block of Consols will be £2.50/6% = £41.67.

Have a look at today's price for 2.5% consolidated loan stock in a good newspaper (*Guardian*, *The Times*, *Telegraph*, *Financial Times*). It comes under undated government securities and the price quoted is for a block of Consols with a nominal (face) value of £100.

A perpetuity cannot have a terminal value simply because it does not have a foreseeable end.

4 Annuities

An annuity can be defined as a constant amount of cash which arises for a given number of consecutive years. Three main types of annuity can be specified:

1. an annuity due, where the first sum arises immediately;
2. an immediate annuity, where the first sum arises in one year's time;
3. a deferred annuity, where the first sum arises in two or more years' time.

Examples of the cash flows of four-year £100 annuities of each type are given below:

Year	0	1	2	3	4	5
1. Annuity due	£100	£100	£100	£100		
2. Immediate annuity		£100	£100	£100	£100	
3. One-year deferred annuity			£100	£100	£100	£100

5 Present value of an annuity

The present value of an *immediate* annuity of £1 per year for N years, where the rate of discount is i, is given by:

$$\frac{1-(1+i)^{-N}}{i}, \text{ denoted as } A_{N \neg i}.$$

Thus the present value of a four-year £100 immediate annuity, where the rate of discount is 16%, is:

$$£100 \frac{1-(1.16)^{-4}}{0.16} = £100 \, A_{4 \neg 0.16} = £100 \times 2.7982 = £279.82.$$

The present value of a four-year £100 annuity *due*, where the rate of discount is 16%, is:

$$£100 + £100 \, A_{3 \neg 0.16} = £100 + (£100 \times 2.2459) = £324.59.$$

Whereas the present value of a four-year £100 annuity, deferred for (say) one year (so that the first sum arises at year 2), at a rate of discount of 18%, is:

$$£100 \, A_{4 \neg 0.18}(1.18)^{-1} = £100 \times 2.6901 \times 0.8474 = £227.96.$$

Notice the precise function of the $A_{N \neg i}$ factor. It gathers the annuity together and brings it to a point in time that is *one year earlier than the point of time when the first annuity amount arises*. For an *immediate* annuity, one year earlier than when the annuity commences is t_0. Thus $A_{N \neg i}$ will provide the present value of an immediate annuity; but for a deferred annuity the $A_{N \neg i}$ factor will have to be applied with an additional discount factor – as in the example above – to get it back to present value. Table C provides factors for the present values of £1 immediate annuities for various values of N and i.

Another way of defining an immediate annuity is that it is effectively the difference between a perpetuity that starts immediately (i.e. first cash flow in one year's time) and a perpetuity that starts in n periods' time. A perpetuity starting in n periods' time would be worth $C/r \times 1/(1+r)^n$ and, as we know, a perpetuity starting immediately is worth C/r. So the value of an annuuity is $C[(1/r) - (1/(r(1+r)^n))]$.

6 Terminal value of an annuity

The amount to which an annuity of £1 per year for N years accumulates when the annual rate of interest is i takes the form of a geometric progression, which simplifies to:

$$\frac{(1+i)^N - 1}{i}, \text{ denoted as } S_{N \neg i}.$$

Thus the 'terminal value' of a four-year £100 immediate annuity (the amount to which it accumulates at the end of its life), where the rate of interest is 14%, is:

$$£100\frac{(1.14)^4 - 1}{0.14} = £100\,S_{4\neg0.14} = £100 \times 4.9211 = £492.11.$$

Table D provides the terminal values of annuity factors for various values of N and i.

7 Annual equivalent factors

The annual value of an immediate annuity which lasts for N years, where the prevailing rate of discount is i, and which has a present value of £1, is given by:

$$\frac{i}{1-(1+i)^{-N}}, \text{ denoted as } A_{N\neg i}^{-1}$$

In other words, the reciprocal of the $A_{N\neg i}$ factor.

Thus the annual value of an immediate annuity which lasts for five years, where the rate of discount is 8%, and which has a present value of £2000, is:

$$£2000\frac{0.08}{1-(1.08)^{-5}} = £2000 \times 0.2505 = £501 \text{ per year.}$$

If this was a five-year annuity, deferred for (say) three years, then its annual value would be:

$$£2000\,A_{5\neg0.08}^{-1}(1.08)^3 = £2000 \times 0.2505 \times 1.2597 = £631.11.$$

In other words, a £631.11 five-year annuity, deferred for three years, would have a present value of £2000 if the annual rate of discount was 8%. Table E provides these factors for immediate annuities with a present value of £1, for various values of i and N.

8 Sinking fund factors

Sinking funds were once fairly commonly used as a way of saving to replace assets or paying for some other obligation in the future. The idea is that the terminal value (i.e. the amount that is going to be paid out) is converted into a series of annual cash payments.

The annual value of an annuity which lasts for N years, where the prevailing rate of interest is i, and which has a terminal value of £1, is given by:

$$\frac{i}{(1+i)^N - 1}, \text{ denoted as } S_{N\neg i}^{-1}.$$

Thus the annual value of a four-year annuity which has a terminal value of £100, where the interest rate is 16%, is:

$$£100\frac{0.16}{(1.16)^4-1}=£100\times0.1974=£19.74 \text{ per year.}$$

In other words, a four-year £19.74 annuity would have a terminal value of £100 when the annual interest rate is 16%. Hence, the annual amount of £19.74 would be known as the sinking fund. Table F provides sinking fund factors for annuities with terminal values of £1, for various values of i and N.

Notes

1. There is a widely advocated DCF method of investment appraisal (but not widely used), variously called the 'excess present value index', the 'profitability index', the 'discounted profitability index', or even the 'benefit–cost ratio'. This method arises directly out of the NPV method (and so gives equivalent decision advice) and can be defined as:

$$\frac{\text{Present value of project cash inflows}}{\text{Present value of project cash outflows}}.$$

If the index is less than 1, the project should be rejected (equivalent to a negative NPV). If the index is greater than or equal to one, the project should be accepted. Thus in terms of Project B:

$$\text{Index} = \frac{827.06}{100000} = 0.8271.$$

and as the index is less than 1, Project B should be rejected.

2. To a limited extent a similar analysis can be performed on the vertical axis in terms of net *terminal* values (i.e. at t_1) rather than net present values. For instance, in the situation illustrated in Fig. 5.1, OF represents the terminal value of the sum of dividend OD in t_0 and OC in t_1; OC represents the terminal value of the cash inflows generated from the company's investments; and CF represents the net terminal value of the investments undertaken.

3. Notice that if the company were to over-invest up to point W, the *total* net present value of its investment decision would be negative. In other words, the shareholders would have been better off if management had undertaken no investment at all, rather than over-investing to such an extent. This analysis does serve to support management's general inclination to invest conservatively (i.e. a tendency to under-invest, or to invest less than the optimal amount). Under-optimal investment must always lead to an increase in shareholders' wealth, relative to their wealth if management undertook zero investment, as long as negative NPV projects are not undertaken. However, with over-investment, a situation like point W is possible where shareholders are actually worse off as a result of the company's investment decisions. In the real world, a management with poor appraisal ability may well do right to err on the side of conservatism, rather than taking a very sanguine or cavalier attitude to investment decisions.

4. This method of investment appraisal has unfortunately suffered a confusing array of alternative names in the past, such as the 'marginal efficiency of capital', 'true yield' and even (to really add to the confusion) 'discounted cash flow'. Some of these alternatives still persist in the literature, but it is now most widely known as the 'internal rate of return'.

5. Strictly speaking, this is not correct. The IRR of a project is its *average* rate of return, whilst under our assumptions of infinite project divisibility and diminishing returns, the IRR of each incremental piece of a project will be slightly lower than that of the previous increment. Hence the physical investment line is composed of the IRRs of each incremental investment in the projects that are available, rather than of the IRRs of each complete project that is available.

Further reading

1. At this stage we are only midway through our evaluation of the two discounted cash flow investment appraisal techniques. Therefore many relevant articles will not yet be appropriate. However, a very interesting starting point is two articles which question the whole basis of the investment decision making developed here: P.F. King, 'Is the Emphasis of Capital Budgeting Theory Misplaced?', *Journal of Business Finance and Accounting*, Spring 1975; and D. Cooper, 'Rationality and Investment Appraisal', *Accounting and Business Research*, Summer 1975.
2. In addition, a further article which is of interest at this stage is: E.M. Lerner and A. Rappaport, 'Limit DCF in Capital Budgeting', *Harvard Business Review*, September–October 1968.
3. Finally, it is perhaps a good idea to introduce a dose of realism at this early stage and an interesting article to pursue is T. Crick and S.H. Kim, 'Do Executives Practice what Academics Teach?', *Management Accounting*, November 1986.

Quickie questions (including questions on the appendix)

1. Using a 14% discount rate, what is the NPV of the following project?

Year	Cash flow
0	−1000
1	+ 500
2	+ 600
3	+ 400

2. If a project costing £1000 has an NPV of +£120 at a 10% discount rate, how would you interpret the NPV figure and what should be the investment advice?
3. Estimate the IRR of the following project:

Year	Cash flow
0	−500
1	+200
2	+300
3	+200

4. Using the project in question 3, what is its discounted payback, given a 10% discount rate?
5. In the real world where the outcomes of investment projects are uncertain, what should the NPV discount rate represent?
6. What is the connection between the NPV discount rate and the IRR hurdle rate?
7. Given a 10% discount rate, what is the present value of the following annuity?

Year	Cash flow
0	−1000
1	+ 350
2	+ 350
3	+ 350
4	+ 350

8. What are the three main types of annuity?
9. A project costs £1000 and produces a cash inflow of £100 per year for ever. What is its IRR?
10. Using annuity factors, what is the NPV of this project at a 16% discount rate?

Year	Cash flow
0	−1000
1	+ 200
2	+ 200
3	+ 500
4	+ 500
5	+ 500

Problems

1. Trionym plc is a manufacturer of confectionery, based in the West Midlands. It has recently merged with a sugar refiner, West Indian Sugar Supplies plc (WISS). For some weeks, the accountants in the two companies have been discussing investment appraisal techniques. Trionym traditionally uses payback and the return on average capital employed, while WISS has used NPV for a number of years.

   The discussion on appraisal techniques has now reached a crisis as a decision is required on a proposal to invest £1.8 million on a new chocolate-coating machine in order to move into the chocolate biscuit market. The financial details are as follows:

Outlay:	£1.8 million at t_0
Life:	10 years
Net cash flow:	Years 1–6 +£500 000/year
	Years 7–10 +£300 000/year
Scrap value:	£0.5 million

   The company uses straight-line depreciation and has a target rate of return, for both ROCE and NPV of 18%, and a payback criterion of five years.

   Required:
   (a) Calculate the project's NPV.
   (b) Calculate the ROCE in line with company practice.
   (c) Calculate the project's payback.

(d) On the basis of your calculations, formulate your investment decision advice. Write a report to the chairman which justifies your decision and mention any reservations which you might have.

(e) In order to try and resolve the conflict between the two managements you suggest that the company uses discounted payback as a compromise. Estimate the project's discounted payback and write a memo to the chairman outlining its advantages and disadvantages.

(f) Comment critically on the company's existing decision criteria.

2. Congo Ltd is considering the selection of one of a pair of mutually exclusive investment projects. Both would involve purchasing machinery with a life of five years.

Project 1 would generate annual cash flows (receipts less payments) of £200 000; the machinery would cost £556 000 and have a scrap value of £56 000.

Project 2 would generate annual cash flows of £500 000; the machinery would cost £1 616 000 and have a scrap value of £301 000.

Congo uses the straight-line method for providing depreciation. Its cost of capital is 14% per annum. Assume that annual cash flows arise on the anniversaries of the initial outlay, that there will be no price changes over the project lives and that acceptance of one of the projects will not alter the required amount of working capital.

Required:

(a) Calculate for each project:
  (i) the accounting rate of return (ratio, over project life, of average accounting profit to average book value of investment) to nearest 1%;
  (ii) the net present value;
  (iii) the internal rate of return (DCF yield) to nearest 1%;
  (iv) the payback period to one decimal place.

(b) State which project you would select for acceptance, if either, giving reasons for your choice of criterion to guide the decision.

Ignore taxation.

3. Stadler is an ambitious young executive who has recently been appointed to the position of financial director of Paradis plc, a small listed company. Stadler regards this appointment as a temporary one, enabling him to gain experience before moving to a larger organization. His intention is to leave Paradis plc in three years, with its share price standing high. As a consequence, he is particularly concerned that the reported profits of Paradis plc should be as high as possible in his third and final year with the company.

Paradis plc has recently raised £350 000 from shareholders, and the directors are considering three ways of using these funds. Three projects (A, B and C) are being considered, each involving the immediate purchase of equipment costing £350 000. One project only can be undertaken and the equipment for each project will have a useful life equal to that of the project, with no scrap value. Stadler favours Project C because it is expected to show the highest accounting profit in the third year. However, he does not wish to reveal his real reasons for favouring Project C and so, in his report to the chairman, he recommends Project C because it shows the highest internal rate of return. The following summary is taken from his report:

Project	Net cash flows (£000) Years									Internal rate of return %
	0	1	2	3	4	5	6	7	8	
A	−350	100	110	104	112	138	160	180	–	27.5
B	−350	40	100	210	260	160	–	–	–	26.4
C	−350	200	150	240	40	–	–	–	–	33.0

The chairman of the company is accustomed to projects being appraised in terms of payback and accounting rate of return, and he is consequently suspicious of the use of internal rate of return as a method of project selection. Accordingly, the chairman has asked for an independent report on the choice of project. The company's cost of capital is 20% and a policy of straight-line depreciation is used to write off the cost of equipment in the financial statements.

Required:
(a) Calculate the payback period for each project.
(b) Calculate the accounting rate of return for each project.
(c) Prepare a report for the chairman with supporting calculations indicating which project should be preferred by the ordinary shareholders of Paradis plc.
(d) Discuss the assumptions about the reactions of the stock market that are implicit in Stadler's choice of project C.

Ignore taxation.

6 Net present value and internal rate of return developed

NPV and project interdependence

In Chapter 3, when examining the payback and ROCE/ARR techniques, two investment decisions were dealt with:

1. decisions involving single, independent projects where a straightforward 'accept' or 'reject' decision was required;
2. decisions involving mutually exclusive projects, where a decision on the single best project from a series of alternative projects was required.

In Chapter 5 when examining the two discounted cash flow techniques of NPV and IRR, our discussion only covered the decision rule for single independent project decisions. In this chapter, we start by looking at the NPV and IRR decision rules when faced with mutually exclusive projects and other forms of project decision interdependence.

NPV and mutually exclusive projects

We have already seen from the single-period investment–consumption model that, in terms of net present value, the higher the aggregate NPV of a firm's investments, the higher will be the level of wealth achieved by its shareholders. Therefore, as far as deciding between mutually exclusive investment alternatives is concerned, the decision rule would appear to be quite straightforward in terms of using the NPV: accept whichever alternative projects that result in the greatest positive NPV, because this will produce the greatest addition to the shareholders' wealth.[1]

As an example, suppose a company has to make an investment decision concerning two mutually exclusive projects, A and B, whose cash flows and NPV calculations are set out below:

Project A

Year	Cash flow (£)	×	10% discount factor	=	Present value cash flow (£)
0	− 1500	×	1	=	− 1500
1	+ 500	×	0.9091	=	+ 454.55
2	+ 800	×	0.8264	=	+ 661.12
3	+ 1000	×	0.7513	=	+ 751.30
				NPV	+ 366.97

Project B

Year	Cash flow (£)	×	10% discount factor	=	Present value cash flow (£)
0	− 1900	×	1	=	− 1900
1	+ 500	×	0.9091	=	+ 454.55
2	+ 800	×	0.8264	=	+ 661.12
3	+ 1000	×	0.7513	=	+ 751.30
4	+ 700	×	0.6830	=	+ 478.10
				NPV	+ 445.07

Assuming that the appropriate discount rate is 10%, when the project cash flows are converted to present values, Project B is preferred to A because it has the larger positive NPV. It is important to realize that the appraisal method in such circumstances is entirely unaffected by the fact that these two projects have differing capital outlays and life-spans. The whole decision is based purely on the absolute size of the positive NPV.

The mutually exclusive investment decision can be made in this way because of two important assumptions underlying the analysis. When developing the single-period investment–consumption model, a number of simplifying assumptions about the real world were specified. However, when we then moved on to examine the DCF investment appraisal techniques, many of these assumptions (such as a single time period and a world of certainty) were either implicitly or explicitly dropped. Nevertheless, there are two important assumptions that underlie the use of DCF techniques. They are:

1. The existence of a perfect capital market. Reference has already been made to this concept, when the existence of a capital market was introduced in the Hirshleifer analysis in Chapter 4. A perfect capital market describes a market where investors can lend and borrow money and which has a number of particular characteristics. We will examine the concept in greater detail at a later stage but, for the present, all that is required is to specify that characteristic which is of particular importance as far as the DCF techniques are concerned. It is that investors/companies will always be able to raise finance to undertake any project that they identify as having a non-negative NPV (or whose IRR meets the decision criterion hurdle rate). Therefore, decision makers will never find themselves in a position where they are unable to take on a positive NPV project because of

lack of finance. In addition, we should add to this condition the assumption that the cost of the finance raised will always be at the going rate of return for investments of that particular risk level.

2. The discount rate used in an NPV analysis, or the hurdle rate used in an IRR analysis, correctly reflects the degree of risk involved in the project. This refers to the fact that the discount rate should represent the return available elsewhere in the (perfect) capital market on a similar risk investment. Therefore notice how this assumption is, itself, dependent upon the first assumption.

As a result of these two assumptions the choice between Projects A and B can be made on the basis used. The fact that B is a more costly project than A is irrelevant, given the first assumption. Project B is preferred to A simply because it is capable of generating a cash flow that will pay back its outlay and its financing costs and leave an economic profit, in present value terms (a rise in shareholder wealth), of £445.07. Project A will also repay its outlay and its financing costs, but will only cause shareholder wealth to rise by £366.97.

Also, the fact that B is more expensive than A, and has a longer life than A, might suggest that it is more risky. (Neither fact will *necessarily* make B more risky than A.) However, these differences can also be ignored in the decision analysis because of our second assumption. In other words, the whole problem of riskiness is taken account of in the discount rate. The fact that both projects are being discounted at 10% implies that a judgement has been made that they are equally risky.

In this respect, if it were felt that two mutually exclusive projects were of different risk levels, then different discount rates should be used to evaluate each one. However, the decision – with its focus on maximizing the increase in shareholder wealth – would remain unchanged. Example 1 illustrates such a situation.

The point to notice about Example 1 is that the decision has been taken on the basis of what would be the resulting increase in shareholder wealth. The fact that the amusement park development produces a return in excess of 18% (in fact its IRR is approximately 18.6%), whilst the private housing development only produces a return in excess of 10% (its IRR is approximately 12.5%), is irrelevant. Rates of return cannot be compared in isolation, but must be looked at relative to the risk involved. In this example, given the risk involved, the private housing development is the better project from the viewpoint of shareholder wealth.

Finally, the operation of this modified NPV rule for mutually exclusive projects requires an additional assumption in the face of unequal project lives (but not unequal investment outlays). This is that the mutually exclusive projects are 'isolated' investments in the sense that they do not form part of a replacement chain. In other words, it is assumed that the nature of the mutually exclusive projects is such that, whichever project is chosen, it will not be replaced when it reaches the end of its life. If this assumption does not hold, then we are involved with a different type of project interdependence which requires a more complex decision rule. This issue is treated separately when the Replacement Decision is examined.

Epitasis plc is a small company engaged in house-building. The company is presently considering whether to purchase a piece of land that has come up for sale at a cost of £10 million. Two suggestions have been made for the use of the land. One is to construct a number of private houses for sale and the other is to construct and operate an amusement park.

The company's management accountants have made the following estimates of both projects' net cash flows (including the cost of the land):

Year	Private house development (£m)	Amusement park (£m)
0	−10	−10
1	− 5	− 8
2	+ 7	+ 4
3	+ 9	+ 6
4	+ 4	+ 8
5		+ 7
6		+ 9

The company uses NPV to evaluate projects and normally takes 10% as a discount rate, as this reflects the return available elsewhere on house-building investments. In the present situation this appears to be a suitable rate for the private housing development, but not for the amusement park. After much research, the company has decided that the minimum required rate of return that they should expect on this more risky project is 18%.

On this basis, the project's NPVs were calculated:

Private housing development: + £0.733 million.
Amusement park development: + £0.264 million.

Therefore the company's decision was to purchase the land and undertake a private housing development.

Interlinked projects

Another type of project interdependence can arise when a project's cash flows are affected by investment decisions taken elsewhere. It would be highly unusual to find *any* project which had truly independent cash flows, as almost certainly the magnitude and timing of a project's cash flows will be affected to some extent by other investment decisions. This problem really arises out of uncertainty about the future, and will be examined later in that context.

The case of interdependence to be examined here is the simpler case in which the cash flows of an investment opportunity are directly affected by the company's decision regarding another investment project. For example, when two non-mutually exclusive projects, C and D, are appraised it is found that Project C has the following cash flows, which are independent of any other investment decisions made by the company:

Project C

Year	Cash flow (£)	×	10% discount factor	=	Present value cash flow (£)
0	− 1000	×	1	=	− 1000
1	+ 400	×	0.9091	=	+ 363.64
2	+ 500	×	0.8264	=	+ 413.20
3	+ 200	×	0.7513	=	+ 150.26
			NPV		− £72.90

When discounted by 10% (assumed to be the appropriate rate), Project C has a negative NPV of £72.90. Viewed in isolation, and following the NPV rule for independent projects, it would be rejected as an unsuitable investment.

However, suppose Project D, which is also under consideration, has two alternative sets of cash flows and NPVs, depending upon whether Project C is accepted by the company (cash flow 1) or rejected (cash flow 2):

Project D

Year	Cash flow 1 (£)	×	10% discount factor	=	Present value cash flow (£)
0	− 2000	×	1	=	− 2000
1	+ 500	×	0.9091	=	+ 454.55
2	+ 800	×	0.8264	=	+ 661.12
3	+ 1000	×	0.7513	=	+ 751.30
4	+ 1000	×	0.6830	=	+ 683.00
			NPV		+ 549.97

Year	Cash flow 1 (£)	×	10% discount factor	=	Present value cash flow (£)
0	− 2000	×	1	=	− 2000
1	+ 500	×	0.9091	=	+ 454.55
2	+ 800	×	0.8264	=	+ 661.12
3	+ 1200	×	0.7513	=	+ 901.56
4	+ 600	×	0.6830	=	+ 409.80
			NPV		+ 427.03

The correct way to analyse this situation, within the assumptions made, is to treat the problem as three mutually exclusive investments: Project C, Project D, and Project C + D. Whichever alternative produces the largest positive NPV should be accepted. In this example:

Project C   = − £72.90
Project D   = + £427.03
Project C + D = − £72.90 + £549.97 = + £477.07

Thus the correct investment decision, in terms of maximizing shareholder wealth, is to accept Projects C and D jointly, because it is this alternative which produces the largest net present value.

IRR rule and interdependent projects

Introduction

We have seen that in the face of these two types of non-independent cash flow, the NPV investment decision rule can be fairly easily modified so as to produce the correct decision advice. In terms of the single-period investment–consumption model, these modified decision rules would ensure a company's attainment of the optimal point on the physical investment line and the consequent maximization of shareholder wealth. But what modifications would have to be made to the IRR decision rule?

In a situation of mutually exclusive investment projects, a modification, apparently similar to that made to the NPV rule, is traditionally advocated: accept whichever project has the greatest IRR, as long as it exceeds the decision criterion/hurdle rate. Such an approach is incorrect, but it has been widely advocated because of a misunderstanding concerning the process involved in using both NPV and IRR as criteria for investment decisions.

We have already seen that when an individual project is evaluated by NPV, an 'automatic' comparison is made between the cash flows produced by the project and the cash flows that would have been produced (but were forgone, and so represent an opportunity cost under the assumption of a perfect capital market) if the project's outlay had been invested on the capital market for the period of the project's life-span. Therefore, the decision whether to accept or reject the project is not an absolute decision, but a *relative* one – relative to what the forgone alternative would have yielded. As a result, when faced with mutually exclusive investments, the choice between projects is carried out on the basis of this automatic comparison with the capital market. Whichever project performs best, *relative to the capital market*, is chosen – given that the chosen alternative out-performs the capital market alternative, i.e. has a positive NPV.

Incremental cash flows

We can approach this idea another way. Suppose we have a pair of mutually exclusive projects, E and F, which have the following cash flows, lives and present values when discounted at the appropriate market rate of return of 10%:

Project E

Year	Cash flow (£)	×	10% discount factor	=	Present value cash flow (£)
0	−1500	×	1	=	− 1500
1	+ 550	×	0.9091	=	+ 500.00
2	+1400	×	0.8264	=	+ 1156.96
				NPV	+ 156.96

Project F

Year	Cash flow (£)	×	10% discount factor	=	Present value cash flow (£)
0	−1900	×	1	=	−1900
1	+ 400	×	0.9091	=	+ 363.64
2	+ 800	×	0.8264	=	+ 661.12
3	+ 800	×	0.7513	=	+ 601.04
4	+ 700	×	0.6830	=	+ 478.10
				NPV	+ 203.90

Project F would be preferred to E, as it has the larger, positive NPV.

Now, let us look at the present value of the extra, or incremental, cash flows that the firm would obtain from investing in Project E, rather than F and vice versa:

Year	Project E c/f	−	Project F c/f	= Incremental E–F c/f	×	10% PV factor	=	Present value cash flow
0	(−1500)	−	(−1900)	= + 400	×	1	=	+ 400
1	(+ 550)	−	(+ 400)	= + 150	×	0.9091	=	+ 136.36
2	(+1400)	−	(+ 800)	= + 600	×	0.8264	=	+ 495.84
3		−	(+ 800)	= − 800	×	0.7513	=	− 601.04
4		−	(+ 700)	= − 700	×	0.6830	=	− 478.10

$$\text{NPV} - \ 46.94$$

Year	Incremental F–E c/f	×	10% PV factor	=	Present value cash flow
0	− 400	×	1	=	− 400
1	− 150	×	0.9091	=	− 136.36
2	− 600	×	0.8264	=	− 495.84
3	+ 800	×	0.7513	=	+ 601.04
4	+ 700	×	0.6830	=	+ 478.10

$$\text{NPV} \ + \ 46.94$$

In our initial analysis of this decision problem, Project F was preferred to E. The incremental analysis shown above helps to explain further the reason for the decision: if F is chosen in preference to E, this will produce an NPV which will be £46.94 greater than if E was preferred to F.

(Notice the NPV of Project F, less that of Project E, is: £203.90 − £156.96 = £46.94.)

Therefore, F is chosen.

Use of the IRR

In the case of mutually exclusive investments, use of the IRR decision rule causes problems. Unlike the NPV calculation which automatically compares the project with the alternative capital market investment forgone, the IRR method makes the comparison on a somewhat different basis by using the decision rule: does the project yield a greater or lesser return than the capital market? In doing so, however, it does not give a consistently reliable indication of *how much* better or worse the project is, relative to the capital market investment alternative.

Thus the IRR decision rule is safe to apply to single, independent decision situations (when all that is required is an answer to the question: does the project produce a return better or worse than that of the capital market?), but it cannot reliably be used to judge between *alternative* projects. This is a rather subtle, but important point, and it requires some further explanation.

Using linear interpolation, the IRRs of the two projects, E and F can be estimated. For E the IRR is estimated at 17%, and for F at 15%. As E has the larger of the two IRRs and this is greater than the decision criterion hurdle rate (10%), the IRR decision rule would suggest that Project E is accepted and F rejected. However, to formulate decision advice on this basis is to forget that the IRR method only compares a project with the capital market alternative in the operation of the accept/reject decision rule. (Indeed the fact that this standard IRR decision rule gives unreliable decision advice is made obvious in this example, because the decision reached is the *opposite* of that reached by NPV.)

The IRR method can correctly advise in this case that both projects are worthwhile: Project E is worthwhile as it produces a return that is greater than that of the capital market, likewise with Project F. But it does not necessarily follow that E is *better* than F because it has an IRR of 17% as opposed to 15%. Indeed we know from operating the NPV decision rule that the advice is incorrect: F is a better investment than E; and selecting E will result in a £46.94 loss of NPV.

IRR and incremental cash flows

The correct approach to evaluating mutually exclusive investments using the IRR is to examine the incremental cash flows that arise between the alternatives. In order to clarify the problem and derive the correct IRR decision rule in such circumstances, we shall make use of a device which was used earlier to examine the IRR concept: the net present value profile.

Fig. 6.1 graphs the NPV profiles of Projects E and F and both the differential cash flows (E–F, F–E). This demonstrates one of the real problems of using the IRR as a decision criterion when choice between alternatives is involved.

Project E always has a higher IRR than F, whatever the rate of discount, and therefore, basing the choice between mutually exclusive investments on size of IRR, the decision is independent of the capital market rate of

Fig. 6.1 *NPV versus IRR*

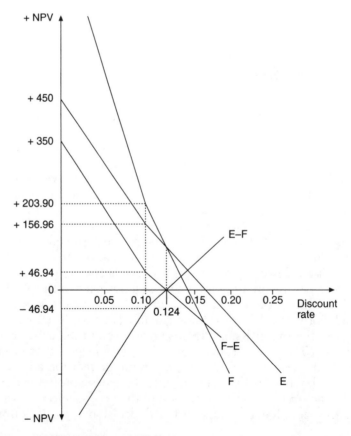

interest. In contrast, when the decision is based on the NPV rule, the choice of project changes as the discount rate/market rate of interest changes. It can be seen from Fig. 6.1 that at rates of discount below 12.4%, Project F is preferred because it has the higher NPV; but at discount rates above 12.4%, Project E is preferred.

The intersection point of the two cash flow profiles is at a discount rate of 12.4% and so, at this rate, the decision would be indifferent between the two projects because they both produce the same NPV. Also notice that, as we would expect at that discount rate, the NPV of both differential cash flows is zero: both projects are equally acceptable, and the differential cash flows reflect this indifference.

On the basis of Fig. 6.1, a number of firm conclusions can be made about the use of both methods in appraising mutually exclusive projects. The NPV can be used to give the correct decision advice with just a small (and commonsense) modification to the basic rule: accept whichever alternative has the highest positive NPV when discounted at the perfect capital market rate of interest. The use of the IRR involves a more complex decision rule. This complexity arises both from the fact that the IRRs of the differential cash flows have to be computed and (as can be seen from Fig. 6.1) from the fact that the IRRs of both incremental cash flows are identical. The complete modified decision rule is as follows.

Calculate the IRRs of the two projects and the IRR of *either* of the differential cash flows, then:

1. If the differential cash flow IRR is *greater* than the cut-off rate, and
    (a) less than both project IRRs, then accept the project with the *smallest* IRR;
    (b) greater than both project IRRs, then accept the project with *highest* IRR.
2. If the differential cash flow IRR is *less* than the cut-off rate, and
    (a) the IRRs of one or both projects are higher than the cut-off rate, then accept the project with the *highest* IRR;
    (b) if neither project's IRR is greater than the cut-off rate, *reject* both.

In the example used, therefore, using the NPV decision rule, Project F should be accepted because it has the highest positive NPV when discounted at 10% – the perfect capital market interest rate. The modified IRR decision rule also leads to the acceptance of F because the IRR of the differential cash flow (12.4%) is greater than the cut-off rate (10%) and less than the IRR of both projects (15% and 17%). Therefore, the project with the smallest IRR, Project F, is chosen.

A less complex, but somewhat incomplete decision rule can also be used in most cases:

1. If the IRR of the differential cash flow is less than the cut-off rate, accept the project with the largest IRR.
2. If the IRR of the differential cash flow is greater than the cut-off rate, accept the project with the smallest IRR.

In the example used above, as the IRR of the differential cash flow, at 12.4%, is greater than the 10% cut-off rate, then project F should be accepted as it has the smallest IRR – 15% as against 17% for Project E.

The conclusion that can be drawn from this example is that the IRR decision rule is excessively complex and unwieldy when compared against the

NPV decision rule. What is more, the example used only two mutually exclusive projects. If faced with a choice between (say) a dozen alternatives, the NPV rule simply requires the calculation of each project's NPV and the project with the largest positive NPV is selected. With the IRR rule, the IRRs of *pairs* of projects and their differential cash flow have to be calculated, making a choice between each pair of projects in turn, until an outright 'winner' is found – an extremely tedious operation.

A further example

Example 2 may help to clarify this approach to resolving the conflict that can occur between the advice given by the NPV decision rule and the advice given by the standard IRR decision rule for mutually exclusive decision situations.

Given Example 2, it should be made clear that it is very unlikely that any company actually uses this modified IRR decision rule in practice. To use it in this way implies a belief in the correctness of the NPV decision rule – because the modified IRR rule is designed always to give the same advice as NPV. But in that case it is both simpler and easier to use the NPV rule itself. Example 2 illustrates how it would be possible to use the IRR decision rule in mutually exclusive project situations so as to provide correct (i.e. shareholder wealth-maximizing) decision advice.

Example 2

Parabiotic plc is involved in making a decision between a pair of mutually exclusive projects: X and Y. The cash flows of the two projects are as follows:

Year	Project X (£000s)	Project Y (£000s)
0	−1000	− 450
1	+ 400	+ 300
2	+ 600	+ 150
3	+ 187	+ 106

Given the risk involved, it is judged that 6% would be an appropriate NPV discount rate and IRR hurdle rate.

NPV calculation

Year	Cash flow (£) X		Discount factor		
0	− 1000	×	1	=	− 1000
1	+ 400	×	0.9434	=	+ 377.36
2	+ 600	×	0.8900	=	+ 534.00
3	+ 187	×	0.8396	=	+ 157.00
					+ 68.36 NPV

Year	Cash flow (£) Y		Discount factor		
0	− 450	×	1	=	− 450
1	+ 300	×	0.9434	=	+ 283.02
2	+ 150	×	0.8900	=	+ 133.50
3	+ 106	×	0.8396	=	+ 89.00
					+ 55.52 NPV

Using the NPV decision rule for mutually exclusive projects, Project X is preferred to Project Y as it has the largest positive NPV and so will give the greatest increase in shareholder wealth.

IRR calculation

Project X: At 6% it has an NPV of +68.36 NPV

At 20%:	-1000	$\times$	1	=	-1000
	$+\ 400$	$\times$	0.8333	=	$+\ 333.32$
	$+\ 600$	$\times$	0.6944	=	$+\ 416.64$
	$+\ 187$	$\times$	0.5787	=	$+\ 108.22$
				=	$-\ 141.82$ NPV

Project Y: At 6% it has an NPV of +55.52 NPV

At 20%:	$-\ 450$	$\times$	1	=	$-\ 450$
	$+\ 300$	$\times$	0.8333	=	$+\ 249.99$
	$+\ 150$	$\times$	0.6944	=	$+\ 104.16$
	$+\ 106$	$\times$	0.5787	=	$+\ 61.34$
				=	$-\ 34.51$ NPV

Linear interpolation can now be used to estimate the IRR of both projects:

$$\text{Project X}: 6\% + \left[\frac{68.36}{68.36 - (-141.82)} \times (20\% - 6\%) \right] = 10.5\% \text{ IRR}$$

$$\text{Project Y}: 6\% + \left[\frac{55.52}{55.52 - (-34.51)} \times (20\% - 6\%) \right] = 14.6\% \text{ IRR}$$

Using the *standard* IRR decision rule for mutually exclusive projects, Project Y is the better project as it has the higher IRR and should be accepted because its IRR exceeds the hurdle rate of return of 6%.

Therefore, in this case, we are getting a *conflict* between the advice given by NPV and the advice given by the IRR decision rule. However, if the *modified* IRR decision rule is used, we require to calculate the IRR of the differential cash flow: X minus Y.

Year	Cash flow X (£)	–	Cash flow Y (£)	=	Differential cash flow
0	-1000	–	(-450)	=	$-\ 550$
1	$+\ 400$	–	$(+300)$	=	$+\ 100$
2	$+\ 600$	–	$(+150)$	=	$+\ 450$
3	$+\ 187$	–	$(+106)$	=	$+\ 81$

At a 4% discount rate:

	$-\ 550$	$\times$	1	=	$-\ 550$
	$+\ 100$	$\times$	0.9615	=	$+\ 96.15$
	$+\ 450$	$\times$	0.9246	=	$+\ 416.07$
	$+\ 81$	$\times$	0.8890	=	$+\ 72.01$
				=	$+\ 34.23$ NPV

At a 20% discount rate:

	$-\ 550$	$\times$	1	=	$-\ 550$
	$+\ 100$	$\times$	0.8333	=	$+\ 83.33$
	$+\ 450$	$\times$	0.6944	=	$+\ 312.48$
	$+\ 81$	$\times$	0.5787	=	$+\ 46.87$
				=	$-\ 107.32$ NPV

Again, using linear interpolation:
Differential cash flow IRR:

$$4\% + \left[\frac{34.23}{34.23 - (-107.32)} \times (20\% - 4\%) \right] = 7.9\%.$$

Note that linear interpolation has been used here for illustrative purposes. It is to be expected that the calcualtions would normally be carried out using a computer spreadsheet

Now, using the simplified, modified IRR decision rule for mutually exclusive projects: as the IRR of the differential cash flow is *greater than* the hurdle rate of 6%, Project X – the project with the *smaller* IRR – should be accepted. Notice that there is now no conflict with the advice given by NPV.

The 'opportunity cost of cash' assumption

The fact that, in a decision choice involving mutually exclusive projects, selecting the project with the highest positive NPV will give a correct decision but selecting the project with the highest IRR will, *only by chance*, also give the correct decision, has been explained on the basis that the IRR ranks projects in an order of preference which is independent of the capital market rate of return. But we have not really answered the question of why, in the example used, the NPV rule accepts Project F and rejects E. After all, Project E produces a higher return (17%) than F (15%). The reason lies in what is (somewhat misleadingly) called the *reinvestment assumption* of each decision rule. Perhaps a more apt description would be the *opportunity cost of capital* assumption.

The NPV decision rule assumes that project-generated cash flows are reinvested to earn a rate of return equal to the discount rate used in the NPV analysis. (More strictly, remember, it is not so much a reinvestment rate of return, but an opportunity cost or benefit.) In contrast, the IRR method assumes project-generated cash flows are reinvested to earn a rate of return equal to the IRR of the project which generated those cash flows. Therefore using Project E as an example:

Project E:	Year	Cash flow (£)	
	0	– 1500	NPV at a 10% discount
	1	+ 550	rate = +£156.96
	2	+ 1400	

IRR is approximately 17%

The NPV decision rule assumes that the £550 and £1400 cash flows generated at Years 1 and 2 respectively can be reinvested to earn a 10% rate of return. The IRR method assumes they can be reinvested to earn a 17% rate of return.

This difference can be seen in the general forms of the two models. With the NPV model, the discount rate used is the market rate of interest:

$$\sum_{t=0}^{N}\frac{A_t}{(1+i)^t} = NPV$$

where A_t = project cash flow at time t;
  i = market discount rate;
  N = number of years of the project's life.

However, with the IRR model, the discount rate used is the project's own internal rate of return:

$$\sum_{t=0}^{N} \frac{A_t}{(1+i)^t} = 0 \quad \text{where } r = \text{project's IRR.}$$

A simple example will help to illustrate the point. Suppose that the following project, G, is available, where the market rate of discount is 5%. The project has an NPV of +£12.39 and an IRR of 10%. What these results mean is shown in Example 3, where the reinvestment assumptions can actually be seen to be in operation.

Example 3

Project G:	Year	Cash flow (£)	At a 5% discount rate
	0	− 173.55	NPV = + 12.39
	1	+ 100	
	2	+ 100	At a 5% hurdle rate
			IRR = 10%

The project's NPV is arrived at by calculating the sum of money that can be accumulated from the project by the end of its life (where intermediate cash flows are reinvested at 5%), and comparing this with the amount of money that could be accumulated by placing the project's outlay in a similar-risk capital market investment. £205 can be accumulated from the project and only £191.34 from the capital market investment. This difference of £13.66 in Year 2 terms has a present value of £12.39: the project's NPV.

The project has an IRR of 10%. If it truly does produce a 10% return it must be capable of generating the same amount of cash by the end of its life that would be generated from investing the project's outlay to yield a 10% return. Investing £173.55 for two years at 10% generates £210. The only way that Project G can accumulate £210 by the end of its life is to assume that the intermediate cash flow (£100 at Year 1) can be reinvested to earn 10%.

The IRR approach assumes that the project cash flows can yield a return equal to the IRR of the project that generated those cash flows. Now the important point is that investments yielding such returns may well be available to the company but, the flaw in the IRR's assumption is that these investments will be available *independently* of whether or not the company accepts the particular project under consideration. The NPV model accepts this argument, taking the market rate of interest, as the opportunity cost of the project cash flows.

The market rate of interest is viewed as the opportunity cost because, even if a project's cash flow *is* used by a company to undertake an investment with a very high yield, if that cash flow were *not* available, the high-yielding investment could still be undertaken by using money borrowed from the capital market, *at the market rate of interest*. What the IRR model does is to credit some of the assumed profitability of those other investments to the project being appraised, by assuming that the opportunity cost of the project-generated cash flows is equal to the project's own IRR or yield.

Therefore, we can conclude that, given the presence of a perfect capital market, it is the NPV model and not the IRR model which makes the correct assumption about the opportunity cost of a project's cash flow. Hence it is the NPV decision rule that gives the correct decision advice. As a result, if we are to use the IRR, then we have to make use of the type of complex decision rule that was derived earlier. However there is no real logic to that type of rule – it simply ensures that the same decision is produced as that given by the (much simpler) NPV decision rule.

Finally, there is also a logical inconsistency in the IRR's reinvestment assumption. As an example of this, take Projects H and I.

Project H:	Year	Cash flow (£)		Project I:	Year	Cash flow (£)
	0	− 100			0	− 150
	1	+ 30			1	+ 70
	2	+ 70			2	+ 70
	3	+ 19.80			3	+ 74.41

Project H has an IRR of 10%, while Project I has an IRR of 20%. Therefore the implicit assumption is that Project I's cash flows can be reinvested to earn 20%, but Project H's cash flows can only be reinvested to earn 10%. Therefore why, for example, can the £70 generated at Year 2 by Project I be reinvested at twice the rate as the same amount of cash, generated at precisely the same point in time, by Project H? There is a fault in the logic of the assumption. There is no logical reason why cash flows which arise at the same time from two different sources should be reinvested at different rates (i.e. have different opportunity benefits).

Extending the time horizon

Introduction

Having examined the case of mutually exclusive projects, let us now turn to another issue. This concerns the fact that the Hirshleifer's single-period graphical analysis was undertaken under the assumption of a single-period investment time horizon. Certainly since starting to examine the DCF methods of investment appraisal, examples have been used of projects which involve cash flows extending over more than one period. But what we must now ask is whether the assumption of a single-period time horizon is simply an assumption of convenience which allows the model to be developed graphically.

In short, the answer to the question is that it is not. In a single-period world we have seen that both the NPV and IRR decision rules will give the same, correct decision advice (even if some fairly complex adjustments sometimes have to be made to the IRR rule). Both methods should enable a company to locate optimally on its physical investment line. However, problems can occur for the IRR decision rule once this two-dimensional world is left behind.

Average and marginal rates of return

As soon as the assumption of a single time period (t_0-t_1) is explicitly relaxed, we get new support for the rationale of the NPV approach (to the detriment of IRR) and a new perspective from which to view the 'reinvestment' assumption. So far, in all the examples used, we have implicitly assumed that the capital market interest rate remains fixed over time. However, suppose a company is evaluating Project J, whose cash flows are given below. In this case, the annual market interest/discount rate is expected to be 10% over the coming year and 15% over the following year.

Project J:

Year	Cash flow (£)		Discount factor		
0	− 100	×	1	=	− 100
1	+ 60	×	$(1.10)^{-1}$	=	+ 54.55
2	+ 60	×	$(1.10)^{-1} \times (1.15)^{-1}$ =		+ 47.43
			NPV	=	+ 1.98

The IRR of Project J is approximately 13%.

As far as the NPV decision rule is concerned, known fluctuations in the discount rate do not cause any problems. Project J has a positive NPV after its cash flows have been discounted by the appropriate market discount rate for each time period.

But what of the IRR decision rule? Project J should be accepted if its IRR is greater than the decision criterion/hurdle rate, but in this example, the IRR of J is *greater* than the market interest rate in one period, and *less* than the rate in the other period. In such circumstances, a single-figure IRR is just not valid for decision-making purposes.

This is a very real problem with the IRR decision rule. Unless future market interest rates can be assumed to be, at least, approximately constant, the rule breaks down. What we are seeing in this example is that, although both DCF methods recognize that money has a time value and so cash flows that occur at different points of time cannot be directly compared, but first have to be converted to values at just one point of time via a weighting mechanism,[2] the IRR uses the *average*, or long-run, rate of return for weighting, whilst the NPV uses the *marginal*, or period-by-period, rate of return.

Multiple IRRs

Another problem for the IRR decision rule, which arises out of the mathematics of its computation, comes to light when the investment time horizon is extended. The IRR of a project's cash flow is the root of a polynomial equation,[3] the problem is that, as the fifteenth-century French mathematician Descartes proved with his 'rule of signs', there are possible solutions to polynomial equations for each change of sign. Thus any particular investment project may have more than one internal rate of return (i.e. there may be more than one rate of discount which will reduce the project's cash flow to a zero NPV), or it may not have any IRR at all. This important (and not uncommon) phenomenon can be examined in terms of the NPV profiles of projects on the basis that the IRR is given by the point at which the profile line cuts the graph's horizontal axis (along which the discount rate is measured).

To start with, we must define what have become known as 'conventional' and 'non-conventional' cash flows.[4] A conventional project cash flow is one where a cash outflow, or a series of cash outflows, is followed by a cash inflow or series of cash inflows. The essence of the definition is that in a conventional cash flow, there is only one change in sign $(+, -)$ between the time periods. All three cash flows given below are therefore conventional:

			Year		
Project	0	1	2	3	4
K	− 1000	+ 400	+ 500	+ 800	+ 50
L	− 1000	− 500	− 600	+ 1500	+ 2000
M	− 500	− 600	+ 2000		

The one change of sign for Project K comes between year 0 and year 1, for Project L it comes between year 2 and year 3, and for Project M it comes between year 1 and year 2. In each project cash flow there is only one sign change. Such projects will only have one IRR each (there is an exception to this, to which we shall return), and so no problems arise for the IRR decision rule.

Non-conventional cash flows can therefore be defined as those which involve more than one change in sign, such as shown below:

			Year			
Project	0	1	2	3	4	
N	− 100	+ 20	− 50	+ 80	+ 170	3 changes of sign
P	− 100	+ 60	+ 80	− 20		2 changes of sign

Such projects are likely to have more than one IRR and, as a general rule of thumb, a project will have as many IRRs as its cash flow has changes in sign.

Example 4

Ossett Roadstone Ltd has been given permission to extract gravel. It will cost £1 050 000 to set up the project. It will then produce cash flows of £800 000 for five years. At the end of the five years, it will cost £3 000 000 to landscape the area which is a requirement for planning permission. Assess the project using IRR.
   The cash flows produce two solutions 2% and 43% and the pattern of its NPV is graphed in Fig. 6.2.

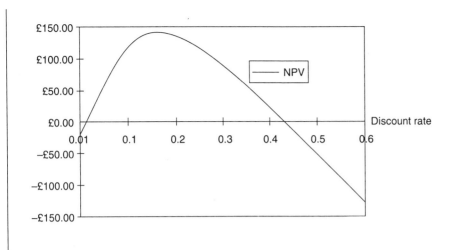

Fig. 6.2 *Multiple IRRs*

As we have already suggested, most people would use a computer spreadsheet to calculate the IRR of a pattern of cash flows. Try Ossett Roadstone using a spreadsheet. You will find that the solution presented by the computer depends upon the level of the guess that you entered into the formula. The lesson here must be that the use of such software without a knowledge of the problems being discussed here could lead to inappropriate decisions.

Non-conventional cash flows can make life very difficult for the IRR decision rule. For example, suppose that Project Q's NPV profile is illustrated in Fig. 6.3. This project has three IRRs: 10%, 15% and 18%. In itself, this is not too disturbing if the cut-off rate is either less than 10% or greater than 18%, because the IRR rule still manages to give unambiguous (and operationally correct) decision advice. But if the cut-off rate is (say) 12%, the IRR decision can only give – at best – highly ambiguous advice (which may be incorrect). In such circumstances, the NPV rule would have no difficulty in giving the correct advice: to reject the project because it has a negative NPV.

However, it can be shown that with most project cash flows that are likely to occur in practice, and where multiple IRRs occur, the variations in the project's NPV between the IRRs are usually very small, and the value of the

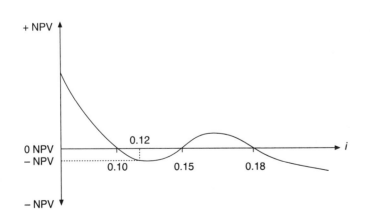

Fig. 6.3 *A misleading IRR*

NPV itself is likely to be close to zero. Therefore it follows that with a simple accept-or-reject decision, the problem of multiple IRRs is not too serious. If a project is accepted on the basis of (say) the majority of its IRRs being greater than the cut-off/discount rate, whereas when evaluated using NPV it turns out to have a negative NPV, then the IRR-based decision would not be disastrous as the magnitude of the negative NPV would be likely to be relatively small. Nevertheless, the problem of multiple IRRs does remain to cause difficulties in the case of mutually exclusive investment decisions. In such circumstances, the differential cash flow may well have multiple IRRs, which causes the decision rule to become non-operational.

Despite the foregoing argument concerning the practical unimportance of multiple IRRs, the conclusion reached must still be that the possible presence of multiple IRRs is yet one more factor to count against the use of that particular DCF technique. The argument that, while the IRR rule may give the wrong decision, it will not be *very* wrong, is not a persuasive one.

Extended yield method

One approach that is often suggested, and sometimes used in practice, to handle the problem of multiple IRRs, is the *extended yield* method. Project R is an example of a project which would cause difficulties for the IRR decision rule. The extended yield method solves the problem by eliminating the offending second change in sign. This is achieved by discounting the unwanted cash flow back to present value at the hurdle rate, and then netting the figure off against the Year 0 outlay. Example 5 illustrates the approach.

However, it should be noted that the extended yield method only *gets around* the problem of multiple IRRs – it does not *solve* the problem.

Although a single IRR has been calculated for Project R, the point remains that in reality Project R has *two* IRRs (and neither is likely to be the 13.4% estimated).

Example 5

A company wishes to evaluate Project R using the IRR decision rule with a 10% hurdle rate:

Year	Cash flow
0	− 100
1	+ 50
2	+ 80
3	− 10

The Year 3 cash flow is discounted back to present value at 10%: $-10(1.10)^{-3} = -7.51$ and this figure is then netted off with the Year 0 cash flow to provide a *revised* cash flow for Project R:

Year	Cash flow
0	− 107.51
1	+ 50
2	+ 80

At 4%, the project has an NPV of: +14.53
At 20%, the project has an NPV of: −10.29

Using linear interpolation, the IRR of Project R can be estimated as:

$$4\% + \left[\frac{14.53}{14.53 - (-10.92)} \times (20\% - 4\%) \right] = 13.4\% \text{ IRR.}$$

Other problems with the IRR rule

If we return to the example of Ossett Roadstone we find another problem with IRR. As before it will cost £1 050 000 to set up the project. It will then produce cash flows of £800 000 for five years. However, at the end of the five years, it will cost £3 090 000 to landscape the area which is a requirement of planning permission. Assess the project using IRR.

The answer to Example 6 is shown in Fig. 6.4 and illustrates another problematical situation for the IRR rule where there is only a single IRR for the project, but at no rate of discount does the project yield a positive NPV. If, in this example, the discount rate were 10%, the NPV rule would correctly reject the project. However, the IRR rule would accept it because its IRR (20%) is greater than the hurdle rate.

Fig. 6.5 illustrates an NPV profile which causes the IRR decision rule to break down completely. Here we assume that all the conditions for Ossett Roadstone remain the same except for the fact that the landscaping will cost £3 200 000 and it can be seen that no internal rate of return exists![5]

A further difficulty that arises out of the IRR approach is caused by the fact that it evaluates projects on the basis of a percentage rate of return. In other words, it examines a project's return relative to its outlay, rather than in absolute terms as with NPV.

For example, suppose a company is evaluating a pair of mutually exclusive projects: a large factory or a small factory. The large factory has an outlay of £10 million, the small factory has an outlay of £2 million. Suppose the large factory has an IRR of 18% and the small factory 24%, and the hurdle rate is 15%. Therefore both alternatives are acceptable in their own right, but the standard IRR decision rule would accept the small factory, as it produces the higher IRR. The problem is that the company would end up with a significantly better incremental cash flow from an 18% return on £10 million, than from a 24% return on only £2 million. This is, of course, yet another reason for the possible existence of conflicting advice between NPV and the standard IRR decision rule.

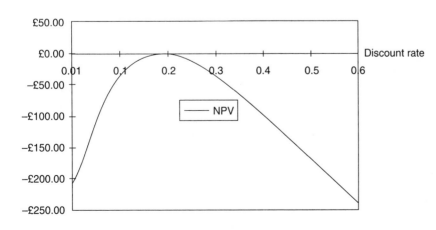

Fig. 6.4 *A non-existent IRR*

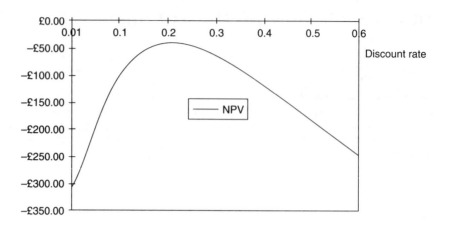

Fig. 6.5 A non-existent IRR

The modified IRR

Whilst there can be little argument about the theoretical superiority of NPV as a decision rule, surveys of managers suggest that many of them feel that they understand the idea of IRR better than NPV simply because it is expressed in percentage terms rather than an absolute figure. Managers are used to dealing with percentages, e.g. return on capital, dividend yields, gross profit margins, etc. It may also be that they (mistakenly) believe that it is not necessary to be able to work out the company's cost of capital in order to use IRR. This has led to the development of modified IRR. It is thus an attempt to overcome the theoretical difficulties of the normal IRR technique, whilst retaining an evaluation of the project based on a percentage rate of return and so avoiding the perceived 'user-unfriendliness' of NPV.

The approach is really founded on an NPV analysis which is then converted into a rate of return. However, instead of *discounting* the project cash flows – at the appropriate opportunity cost of capital – to *present value*, the cash flows (with the exception of the project's outlay) are *compounded* forward to a total *terminal* value. On the basis of these two cash flows – the project's outlay and the terminal value of its net cash inflows – the IRR is then calculated. This is illustrated in Example 7.

This particular modification to the IRR technique has two great technical advantages. First, it eliminates any potential problem of multiple IRRs. Second, it will not provide decision advice involving mutually exclusive projects which conflicts with that given by the NPV technique. If you recall, that particular problem arose out of the fact that the IRR technique made an incorrect assumption about the reinvestment rate of project-generated cash flows. With this modification, the problem is avoided by compounding the project's net cash inflows forward at the correct reinvestment rate – the project's opportunity cost of capital or hurdle rate.

Example 7

Year	(£)	
0	(100)	Hurdle rate is 10%
1	50	
2	40	
3	50	

The terminal value of the project's net cash inflows can be calculated as:

Year	(£)		
1	$50 (1.10)^2$	=	60.5
2	$40 (1.10)^1$	=	44.0
3	$50 (1.10)^0$	=	50.0
Total terminal value		=	£154.50

The project has a modified cash flow of:

Year	(£)
0	(100)
3	154.5

The IRR can now be estimated, as usual, using linear interpolation:

NPV at 4%	:	37.50
NPV at 20%	:	(10.59)

$$\text{IRR} = 4\% + \left[\frac{37.50}{37.50 - (-10.59)} \times (20\% - 4\%) \right] = 16.5\% \text{ IRR.}$$

In Example 7, the project is shown to have an IRR of approximately 16.5%. In fact the modified *actual* IRR is 15.6%. What we have to ask is: does the project genuinely produce a rate of return of 15.6%? The answer is that it does, if the project-generated cash flows can accumulate at the end of the project's life to the same amount that could be accumulated by investing the project's outlay to earn an annual rate of return of 15.6%.

Investing £100 for three years at an annual rate of return of 15.6% yields a terminal value of:

$$£100. (1 + 0.156)^3 = £154.50$$

This is *precisely* the terminal value of the project's net cash inflows calculated in Example 7. In other words, the project does genuinely earn a rate of return of 15.6%.

In many ways this modified IRR calculation achieves the best of all worlds. Its theoretical underpinning is that of NPV, but its method of evaluation is through the use of a user-friendly rate of return. Therefore it can be seen as a cosmetic restatement of an NPV analysis.

In conclusion

Our analysis puts forward a very strong case for the use of the NPV decision rule for investment appraisal. At best, the IRR method (or the modified IRR) might be used as a support and as a communication device on the basis of management's familiarity with rates of return, rather than net present values, for the decision advice given by the NPV rule.[6]

As a result of this conclusion, from now on, we shall be implicitly assuming that the NPV technique will be the approach that should be used by companies in making investment appraisals. It is the only technique from the four investigated that can be relied upon to give advice that will lead towards the maximizing of shareholder wealth.

The replacement cycle problem

Optimal replacement cycle

It was noted earlier that, when faced with a mutually exclusive investment decision, the NPV decision rule was to accept whichever project had the largest positive NPV. This decision rule was based on the assumption of a perfect capital market *and* on the assumption that the projects involved were 'one-offs'. In other words, they did not form part of a continuous replacement cycle.

However, where a project *does* form part of a continuous replacement cycle, the NPV decision rule needs to be modified. This situation is referred to as the *replacement cycle problem*, and Example 8 illustrates the approach.

Example 8

Photolysis plc uses a 10% discount rate for project appraisal. It is considering purchasing a machine which, when it comes to the end of its economic life, is expected to be replaced by an identical machine and so on, continuously. The machine has a maximum life of three years but, as its productivity declines with age, it could be replaced after either just one or two years. The financial details are as follows (all figures in £000s):

Year	0	1	2	3
Outlay	– 1000			
Revenues		+ 900	+ 800	+ 700
Costs		– 400	– 350	– 350
Scrap value		+ 650	+ 400	+ 150

The choice of when to replace this machine can be seen as a choice between three mutually exclusive alternatives, the cash flows and NPVs of which are as follows:

Cash flows

Dispose of machine at end of:		0	1	2	3
First year	Outlay	– 1000			
	Revenue		+ 900		
	Costs		– 400		
	Scrap		+ 650		
	Net cash flow	– 1000	+ 1150		
Second year	Outlay	– 1000			
	Revenue		+ 900	+ 800	
	Costs		– 400	– 350	
	Scrap			+ 400	
	Net cash flow	– 1000	+ 500	+ 850	

Third year	Outlay	− 1000			
	Revenue		+ 900	+ 800	+ 700
	Costs		− 400	− 350	− 350
	Scrap				+ 150
	Net cash flow	− 1000	+ 500	+ 450	+ 500

Disposal point

					NPV
Yr 1	− 1000	$+ 1150\,(1.10)^{-1}$			= + 45.46
Yr 2	− 1000	$+ 500\,(1.10)^{-1}$	$+ 850(1.10)^{-2}$		= + 156.99
Yr 3	− 1000	$+ 500\,(1.10)^{-1}$	$+ 450(1.10)^{-2}$	$+ 500(1.10)^{-3}$	= + 202.08

If these were straightforward mutually exclusive projects, then the decision could be based on whichever alternative has the largest positive NPV. However, the machine – whenever the decision is taken to replace it – will be replaced by an identical machine which will itself be replaced by another identical machine and so on. Therefore, purely on the basis of the NPVs alone, like is not being compared with like as each NPV is generated over a different span of time: one, two or three years.

In order to place the three alternatives on a comparable basis, the equivalent *annual* cash flow of each has to be computed:

Disposal point	NPV	÷	$A_{n \dashrightarrow 0.10}$	=	Equivalent annual cash flow
Yr 1	+ 45.46	÷	$A_{1 \dashrightarrow 0.10}$	=	+ 50.00
Yr 2	+ 156.99	÷	$A_{2 \dashrightarrow 0.10}$	=	+ 90.46
Yr 3	+ 202.08	÷	$A_{3 \dashrightarrow 0.10}$	=	+ 81.26

In order to understand the meaning of the *equivalent annual cash flow* figures, let us take the two-year replacement option as an example. Quite simply, the cash flow of the machine over its two-year life has an NPV which is equivalent to that of a two-year immediate annuity of £90.46 per year:

Year 0	Year 1	Year 2		
− 1000	+ 500	+ 850	=	+ 156.99 NPV
	+ 90.46	+ 90.46	=	+ 156.99 NPV

As a result, replacing the machine every two years is equivalent to a cash flow of £90.46 at the end of every year:

Year	0	1	2	3	4	5	6 → ∞
1st machine	− 1000	+ 500	+ 850				
2nd machine			− 1000	+ 500	+ 850		
3rd machine					− 1000	+ 500	+ 850
etc., etc.							− 1000
Equivalent c/f		+ 90.46	+ 90.46	+ 90.46	+ 90.46	+ 90.46	+ 90.46

Therefore, the optimal replacement cycle of the machine can be decided on the basis of which replacement cycle gives the most favourable equivalent annual cash flow. In this example, it is two-year replacement. Both one- and three-year replacement will result in a lower equivalent annual cash flow.

Repair versus replace

The repair versus replace decision is very common. How long should the company continue to spend money on keeping an existing machine working, and when should it be replaced with a new machine?

With this situation, it is important to realize two decisions are involved:

1. When should the *existing* machine be replaced?
2. What is the optimal replacement cycle of the *new* machine?

Furthermore, decision 2 *must* be made before decision 1 can be made. Example 9 continues on from Example 8 to illustrate the procedure.

Finally, a major drawback of the repair or replace decision procedure should be pointed out. The drawback is the implicit assumption of unchanging technology. In other words, the assumption in the optimal replacement cycle that the new machine will be replaced by an *identical* machine, *ad infinitum*, is clearly unrealistic. Thus the technique's real-world usefulness should be seen with this limitation in mind.

Example 9

Photolysis plc, referred to in Example 8, already have an existing machine doing the job of the new machine whose optimal replacement cycle has been identified as every two years. Therefore, the only remaining decision is: when should the company's existing machine be scrapped? The financial details are as follows (all figures in £000s):

Existing machine

Year	0	1	2
Scrap value	+ 250	+ 200	+ 50
Repair cost	– 100	– 250	
Revenue		+ 600	+ 600
Costs		– 300	– 340

On the basis of this information, the existing machine could be kept operational for a maximum of two more years. To be kept operational for the next twelve months would require £100 000 of repairs to be carried out now. To extend the machine's life up to the end of Year 2 would require a further £250 000 to be spent on repairs in twelve months' time. However, the repair costs in any particular year could be avoided by scrapping the machine in that year. The cash flows of the different options are as follows, based on the assumption that when scrapped, the existing machine will be replaced by the new machine (referred to in Example 8) which is itself replaced every two years and so locks the company into an equivalent annual cash flow of + £90.46: in perpetuity.

Scrap the existing machine at:	Year	0	1	2	3 → ∞
Year 0	Scrap value	+ 250			
	New machine		+ 90.46	+ 90.46	+ 90.46
	Net cash flow	+ 250	+ 90.46	+ 90.46	+ 90.46
Year 1	Scrap value		+ 200.00		
	Repair cost	– 100			
	Revenue		+ 600.00		
	Cost		– 300.00		
	New machine			+ 90.46	+ 90.46
	Net cash flow	– 100	+ 500.00	+ 90.46	+ 90.46
Year 2	Scrap value			+ 50.00	
	Repair cost	– 100	– 250.00		
	Revenue		+ 600.00	+ 600.00	
	Cost		– 300.00	– 340.00	
	New machine				+ 90.46
	Net cash flow	– 100	+ 50.00	+ 310.00	+ 90.46

The NPV of each of these perpetuity cash flows is:
Scrap at Year 0: + 250 + (90.46 ÷ 0.10) = + 1154.60 NPV
Scrap at Year 1: – 100 + 500 $(1.10)^{-1}$ + (90.46 ÷ 0.10) $(1.10)^{-1}$ = +1176.92 NPV

Scrap at Year 2: $-100 + 50 (1.10)^{-1} + 310 (1.10)^{-2} + (90.46 \div 0.10)(1.10)^{-2} = +949.20$ NPV

Therefore the best option for the company is to scrap the existing machine in twelve months' time (the largest NPV option) and replace it by the new machine, which itself is replaced every two years thereafter (see Example 8).

Summary

This chapter has looked at the application of the two DCF investment appraisal methods in the context of decisions between mutually exclusive projects. Arising out of this have come a number of difficulties with the IRR decision rule. The main points made are:

- The NPV decision rule for mutually exclusive decisions is: accept whichever project has the largest positive NPV. The logic behind this was obvious, given the objective of shareholder wealth maximization and the meaning of NPV.

- The decision rule holds even when the alternative investments are of unequal magnitude, duration or risk, assuming a perfect capital market and that the discount rate used properly reflects the return available elsewhere on the capital market from a similar-risk investment.

- The standard IRR decision rule for mutually exclusive investments is:
  — the 'best' project has the highest IRR;
  — accept the best project if its IRR > hurdle rate.

- This *standard* IRR decision rule gives unreliable investment decision advice in situations of mutually exclusive projects: the problem arises from the arithmetic of the IRR and the fact that it assumes project-generated cash flows will be reinvested to earn a rate of return equal to the IRR of the project generating those cash flows.

- The reinvestment assumption is, strictly speaking, an assumption about the opportunity cost of project-generated cash flows. Given a perfect capital market, the assumption made by the IRR is incorrect – their opportunity cost equates with the capital market rate of return for the risk level involved. The NPV method makes this, correct, assumption.

- The problem of the IRR can be resolved, in an artificial way, by a modified decision rule which, in its simplest form, states:
  — if IRR of the differential cash flow is > hurdle rate, accept the project with the smallest IRR;
  — if IRR of the differential cash flow is < hurdle rate, accept the project with the largest IRR.

- A further problem for the IRR arises out of the possible existence of multiple IRRs, when the decision rule then breaks down completely.

- The problem of multiple IRRs can be resolved, again in a purely artificial way, through the use of the extended yield technique. However, this was shown not to deal with the problem, merely to avoid it.

- The theoretical objections to the IRR can be overcome by the use of the *modified* IRR technique, but in reality it is more akin to a cosmetic restatement of NPV.

- The strong conclusion to the chapter is that, for several reasons, the IRR investment appraisal technique is – just like payback and ROCE/ARR – unsatisfactory. Therefore only NPV remains as an investment appraisal technique which will give consistently reliable advice leading to shareholder wealth maximization.

- Finally, a related area was examined: the repair-or-replace decision. This was seen to be a special case of mutually exclusive projects involving the use of the annuity discounting factors.

Notes

1.   This, of course, would be the decision rule for revenue-generating projects. For purely cost-generating projects (such as the installation of air conditioning equipment in a factory), the best project would be that which produces the smallest negative NPV.

2.   The processes of discounting and compounding can be viewed simply as a method of assigning weights to cash flows.

3.   The IRR calculation simply involves finding the roots of a polynomial equation of n terms (where n = the number of periods of the project's life). In general, the IRR equation of a project which lasts for n years will have n roots or solutions or IRRs. However, with a conventional type of cash flow, only one of these solutions is a real number and the rest will be imaginary (e.g. $\sqrt{-2}$), with mathematical, but no economic importance. However, a non-conventional project cash flow can produce a polynomial equation of a type which may have several real number roots, each one of which is an equally valid IRR. (Conventional and non-conventional cash flows are defined in the following paragraph in the main text.)

4.   The use of these terms should not lead the reader into the all-too-easy substitution of 'usual' and 'unusual'. Non-conventional cash flows can be extremely common in practice, as we shall discover when we examine the impact of taxation on investment appraisal.

5.   The IRR is said not to exist only as a 'real' number, in such cases. It will exist, and so there will be roots to the polynomial, in terms of imaginary numbers. This mathematical result, however, has little relevance for our purposes.

6.   Even this may be a disadvantage in that management may falsely believe that the IRR is essentially the same as the Accounting Rate of Return (ROCE), when in fact the two measures are totally distinct.

Further reading

1. On the problems with the IRR technique, see R. Dorfman, 'The Meaning of Internal Rates of Return', *Journal of Finance*, December 1981; A Herbst, 'The Unique, Real Internal Rate of Return: Caveat Emptor!', *Journal of Financial and Quantitative Analysis*, June 1978; S.M. Keane, 'The Internal Rate of Return and the Reinvestment Fallacy', *Journal of Accounting and Business Research*, June 1979 and C.R. Beidleman, 'DCF Reinvestment Rates Assumptions', *Engineering Economist*, Winter 1984.
2. For a description of the modified IRR technique, see W.R. McDaniel, D.E. McCarty and K.A. Jessell, 'DCF with Explicit Reinvestment Rates: Tutorial and Extension', *The Financial Review*, August 1988.
3. There are many articles reporting the results of surveys on capital budgeting practice. Amongst these, the following are of particular interest: M. Ross, 'Capital Budgeting Practice in Twelve Large Manufacturers', *Financial Management*, Winter 1986, R.H. Pike and T.S. Ooi, 'The Impact of Corporate Investment Objectives and Constraints on Capital Budgeting Practices', *British Accounting Review*, August 1989, S.H. Kim and L. Guin, 'A Summary of Empirical Studies on Capital Budgeting Practices', *Business and Public Affairs*, Autumn 1986, and S.C. Weaver *et al.*, 'Capital Budgeting: Panel Discussions on Corporate Investments', *Financial Management*, Spring 1989.
4. Finally, two rather thoughtful articles are S.C. Myers, 'Notes on an Expert System for Capital Budgeting', *Financial Management*, Autumn 1988, and M. Bromwich and A. Bhimani, 'Strategic Investment Appraisal', *Management Accounting*, March 1991.

Quickie questions

1. Project A has an outlay of £1 million and when using a discount rate of 10%, to reflect its risk, it has an NPV of + £20 000. Project B has an outlay of £10 million and when discounted at 20%, to reflect its risk, has an NPV of + £15 000. If A and B are mutually exclusive, which project should the firm accept?
2. In question 1, what assumptions are you making in giving your answer?
3. What are the reinvestment assumptions of NPV and IRR, which is correct, and under what circumstances?
4. Under what circumstances can multiple IRRs occur, and what can be done to avoid the problem?
5. Project C has the following cash flows:

0	− 100
1	+ 60
2	+ 80
3	− 20

Using the 'extended yield technique', what is its IRR, given a 10% hurdle rate?
6. Sketch out a diagram showing how the conflict between NPV and IRR can occur.
7. What is the simple modification to the IRR decision rule?
8. Project D has the following cash flows:

0	− 80
1	+ 40
2	+ 80
3	− 30

Given the minimum required rate of return is 10%, what is its modified IRR?

Problems

1. Saucy Steamboats Ltd is currently evaluating a proposal to invest in a new inshore rowing boat. Two possible types, A and B, have now been identified, each of which would have a five-year life and zero scrap value. Their costs and associated net revenues are:

Year	Type A (£)	Type B (£)
0	− 1000	− 2000
1	+ 350	+ 640
2	+ 350	+ 640
3	+ 350	+ 640
4	+ 350	+ 640
5	+ 350	+ 640

The appropriate discount rate is 10% per annum. Both alternatives can be considered marginal investments and acceptance of either one would leave the company's risk unchanged. The company operates in a perfect capital market. Ignore taxation and inflation.

Required:
(a) The managing director of Saucy Steamboats Ltd insists that the investment alternatives should be appraised using the internal rate of return. You are therefore required to appraise these projects on that basis alone. State the decision rule you use, making sure that it will produce the correct investment decision advice in terms of maximizing shareholders' wealth.
(b) Present a careful and detailed outline of the argument you might put forward to the managing director for using the net present value appraisal technique, rather than the internal rate of return, given the present conditions surrounding Saucy Steamboats Ltd.

Note that your answer to part (b) should *not* be confined to a discussion of the two investment opportunities under consideration in part (a). Assume that all cash flows arise on the last day of the year to which they relate, with the exception of the project outlays, which occur at the start of the first year.

2. Mr Cowdrey runs a manufacturing business. He is considering whether to accept one of two mutually exclusive investment projects and, if so, which one to accept. Each project involves an immediate cash outlay of £100 000. Mr Cowdrey estimates that the net cash inflows from each project will be as follows:

Net cash inflow at end of:	Project A (£)	Project B (£)
Year 1	60 000	10 000
Year 2	40 000	20 000
Year 3	30 000	110 000

Mr Cowdrey does not expect capital or any other resource to be in short supply during the next three years.

Required:
(a) Prepare a graph to show the functional relationship between net present value and the discount rate for the two projects (label the vertical axis 'net present value' and the horizontal axis 'discount rate').
(b) Use the graph to estimate the internal rate of return of each project.

(c) On the basis of the information given, advise Mr Cowdrey which project to accept if his discount rate is (i) 6%, (ii) 12%.

(d) Describe briefly any additional information you think would be useful to Mr Cowdrey in choosing between the two projects.

(e) Discuss the relative merits of net present value and internal rate of return as methods of investment appraisal.

Ignore taxation.

3. Charles Pooter (Investment) plc are considering which, if any, of four independent projects to undertake. The forecast cash flows for each project are listed below; receipts arise at the end of each year.

Project	Immediate outlay	Net cash inflows Year 1	Year 2	Year 3
1	− 2500	+ 1000	+ 1000	+ 1000
2	− 1000	+ 100	+ 1400	0
3	− 1000	+ 800	+ 600	0
4	− 4000	0	0	+ 5000

The company faces a perfect capital market, in which the interest rate for the projects' risk level is 10%.

Required:

(a) Using the NPV decision rule, indicate which projects the company should accept. State clearly the reasons for your decisions.

(b) How would your conclusions in (a) differ if the projects were mutually exclusive?

(c) Estimate the IRRs of Projects 2 and 3. Would it be valid to choose between Projects 2 and 3 on the basis of their expected IRRs? If not, present revised calculations so that the internal rate of return method, and the method you have used in (a), lead to the same, unambiguous conclusions.

(d) In practice, the IRR method has been observed to be far more widely used than NPV. Suggest reasons for this relative popularity. Why might the supposed superiority of NPV be an illusion or an irrelevance, in reality?

4. Demeter Ltd owns a machine of type DK which could be used in production for two more years at most. The machine originally cost £45 000 five years ago. Its realizable value is currently £8000 (because a special opportunity for sale has arisen), but it would be zero at all subsequent times. If the machine were to be used for two more years, it would require a major overhaul at a cost of £9000 at the end of one year.

A new model of the machine is now being marketed. It costs £40 000 and has a maximum life of ten years, provided that special maintenance is undertaken at a cost of £10 000 after five years, and at a cost of £20 000 after eight years. The new model would have no realizable value at any time. Assume that no other new models are expected to become available in the foreseeable future, and that no changes are expected in costs or demand for output of the machine. Demeter's cost of capital is 15% per annum.

Required:
Prepare calculations to show whether Demeter's existing machine should be replaced now, or after one or two years.

7 Project appraisal cash flows

Investment appraisal and inflation

Up to this stage in the analysis, we have implicitly assumed, within our world of managerial investment decision making, that prices have been stable. That is not to say that we have excluded the possibility of any price changes, but that we have assumed that there are no general price movements within the economy, either upwards (inflation) or downwards (deflation). Indeed it was made clear when dealing with the concept of the time value of money that the concept, fundamentally, has nothing to do with inflation, and so inflation was assumed not to exist.

In this section we will now drop this assumption and examine how the existence of general price movements within an economy affect investment appraisal and decision making, and how appraisal techniques can be adapted, if need be, to cope with such circumstances. These effects will be examined mainly by analysing the inflation case, but the approach used and conclusions drawn will also apply, by analogy, to the case of deflation.

The problem of inflation

Inflation can be simply defined as a situation where prices in an economy are, in general, rising over time. Its expected (or unexpected) presence is likely to cause problems for the appraisal of investment opportunities in two main ways.

The first problem is that it will make the estimation of a project's expected cash flow more difficult. When a project is being appraised, management will have to provide estimates of its inputs and outputs. With inflation, the prices of these inputs and outputs are likely to change, and management will hence have to estimate the magnitude of these changes. In other words, management will have to estimate the expected future rates of inflation. Thus there is a *forecasting* problem caused by the presence of inflation.

The second problem is, in one sense, an extension of the first. Market interest rates, or rates of return, can be viewed as representing the price of money, and so interest rates – like other prices – can be expected to rise when there is general inflation within the economy. Thus management have the additional task of estimating the effects of inflation on the project appraisal discount rate.

'Real' and 'market' rates of interest

The effects of inflation on market interest rates can most easily be seen by way of an example. We know from the discussion about the concept of the time value of money that suppliers of investment capital make a trade-off between consumption now and consumption at some future point in time. Generally speaking, current consumption is preferred to future consumption and so, in order to be persuaded to forgo consumption now (and invest instead), investors have to be rewarded with the promise of increased consumption at a later point in time. Market interest rates reflect this time 'exchange rate' of consumption.

Example 1

For the moment, suppose that within the economy there is no inflation. An investor, we are told, is willing to lend you £100 for a year in return for £110 in twelve months' time. In other words, he is willing to give up £100 worth of consumption now, as long as he is rewarded with an extra 10% consumption in twelve months' time. Thus the 10% interest rate that he is demanding can be seen both in money terms – he wants an extra ten £1 coins – and in terms of consumption or purchasing power. However, it is this latter interpretation that is of fundamental concern to the investor – how much additional consumption he is to receive in the future for giving up current consumption. (Pound coins by themselves are of little use. What makes them desirable is that they give the power to consume; consumption and consumption power – or purchasing power – is the point of importance.)

Now let us take a slightly different situation, with inflation expected to raise the general level of prices in the economy by 5% over the next twelve months. Our investor would still be willing to give up £100 worth of current consumption as long as he is rewarded with an extra 10% of *consumption* in twelve months' time. However, an extra £10 will not be sufficient cash to buy this additional consumption, because of the presence of inflation.

In order to consume, in twelve months' time, the *same* amount of consumption as that given up now, the investor will need £100 (1 + 0.05) = £105, because of the rise in prices. But our investor has to be able to consume 10% *extra* in order to be persuaded to give up current consumption and so, in money terms, he will require £105 (1 + 0.10) = £115.50. This therefore represents a *money* interest rate of 15.5%: because of 5% inflation, 15.5% extra cash is required to purchase 10% extra consumption.

It follows from the analysis in Example 1 that, in inflationary conditions, two interest rates can be identified – a money (or nominal) interest rate and a consumption (or purchasing power) interest rate. In Example 1 these were 15.5% and 10% respectively. We shall refer to the former rate as the 'market' interest rate (as it would be the rate quoted on the capital market) and to the latter as the 'real' interest rate. (It is real in the sense that it represents the market interest rate, *deflated*, to take out the effects of inflation.) The general relationship, which is often referred to as the Fisher Effect, after the American economist who first developed it, is shown below:

$$\begin{pmatrix} \text{Real} \\ 1+\text{interest} \\ \text{rate} \end{pmatrix} \begin{pmatrix} \text{General} \\ 1+\text{rate of} \\ \text{inflation} \end{pmatrix} = \begin{pmatrix} \text{Market} \\ 1+\text{interest} \\ \text{rate} \end{pmatrix}$$

Substituting in here the data from the example:

$$(1 + 0.10)(1 + 0.05) = (1 + 0.155)$$

Therefore, the real interest rate: $\dfrac{(1 + 0.155) - 1}{(1 + 0.05)} = 0.1$ or 10%

the market interest rate: $(1.10)(1.05) - 1 = 0.155$ or 15.5%

and the general inflation rate: $\dfrac{(1 + 0.155) - 1}{(1 + 0.1)} = 0.05$ or 5%.

Two possible approaches

The example used above shows that under inflationary conditions we can identify two possible interest or discount rates: the market interest rate and the real interest rate. The question that immediately arises is: which one should be used in an NPV investment appraisal analysis? The answer to this question is that either rate can be used, but they must each *only* be applied to an appropriate definition of the project cash flow. Specifically, we can state either:

1. *money* cash flows of the project can be discounted by the *market* interest rate to present value cash flows; or
2. *money* cash flows of the project can be discounted by the rate of general inflation to *current general purchasing power* cash flows, and then these current general purchasing power cash flows can be discounted by the *real* interest rate to present value cash flows.

Either approach will generate exactly the same NPV for the project.

In these statements the term 'money' cash flow can be defined as the physical quantity of money (i.e pound coins) that the project will generate at any particular point in time, and the term 'current general purchasing power' (CGPP) cash flow refers to the money cash flow, deflated by the *general* rate of inflation, so as to reflect the current general purchasing power of that future cash flow. Example 2 can clarify the definition and can also be used to show that these two alternative discounting approaches are entirely consistent with each other.

In Example 2 we should have expected the present values to be exactly the same for obvious reasons: in the first approach, the cash flow is being discounted by 15.5%, whereas in the second approach the cash flow is being discounted by 10% and 5%. Thus in each alternative the cash flow is being discounted by the same amount because:

$$(1 + 0.155) = (1 + 0.10)(1 + 0.05)$$

Example 2

Rhotacine plc wishes to evaluate a project. The company has taken great care to estimate how future rates of inflation will affect the prices charged for the project's output (and hence its revenue), and how inflation will affect the costs incurred in generating those revenues. The project's actual (money) cash flows have been estimated as:

Year	Cash flow (£)
0	−1000
1	+ 800
2	+ 600

The company believes that a 15.5% return is available elsewhere on the capital market for a similar risk project (i.e. the market rate of return) and that prices in general, as measured by the retail price index (RPI), will increase by 5% per year over the next two years.

Approach 1: Take the project's money cash flows and discount by the market rate of discount to NPV.

Year	Cash flow (£)	×	15.5% discount	=	PV c/f
0	−1000	×	1	=	−1000
1	+ 800	×	0.8658	=	+ 692.64
2	+ 600	×	0.7496	=	+ 449.76
					+ 142.40 NPV

Approach 2: Take the project's money cash flows and discount by the RPI to CGPP cash flow. Then discount the CGPP cash flow by the real discount rate to NPV.

Year	Cash flow (£)	×	5% discount	=	CGPP c/f
0	−1000	×	1	=	−1000
1	+ 800	×	0.9524	=	+ 761.92
2	+ 600	×	0.9070	=	+ 544.20

The real discount rate can be found from the Fisher Effect relationship:

$$\frac{(1+0.155)}{(1+0.05)} - 1 = 0.10 \text{ or } 10\%.$$

Year	CGPP c/f	×	10% discount	=	PV c/f
0	−1000	×	1	=	−1000
1	+ 761.92	×	0.9091	=	+ 692.66
2	+ 544.20	×	0.8264	=	+ 449.73
					+ 142.39 NPV

Notice that the two NPVs are (virtually) identical. (The fact that they are not identical simply arises from rounding errors because only four-figure discount factors were used.)

Therefore, it is for this reason that it was stated earlier that either the market discount rate or the real discount rate could be used in an investment appraisal analysis, *as long as each was applied to an appropriate definition of cash flow.*

The market discount rate is an interest rate expressed in money terms and so it is applied to the actual money cash flows that the project is expected to produce. The real discount rate is an interest rate expressed in consumption or purchasing power terms, and so it should be applied to the project cash flows that are similarly expressed; in other words it is applied to the money cash flows after they have had the inflationary element taken out. To illustrate this we can make use of the Year 2 cash flow from Example 2.

In Year 2 the project is expected to produce a physical cash flow of £600. Given an annual rate of general inflation of 5%, this money would buy the same 'basket of goods' that £544.20 would buy *today* (i.e. Year 0).

However, because of the time value of money of investors, £600 at Year 2 is not equivalent to £544.20 at Year 0. The present value of £600 at Year 2 (taking into account the time value of money, expressed in real terms, of 10%) is £449.73.

There are two further points to be noticed about this example. The first is that discounting the money cash flow by the general rate of inflation has nothing to do with the idea of the time value of money, it is simply a calculation to express the project cash flow – not in money terms, but in consumption/purchasing power terms. The idea of the time value of money is not taken into account until the discounting of these deflated cash flows by the *real* discount rate.

The second point to notice is that the project money cash flows are deflated (or discounted) by the general rate of inflation, *not* by the specific rate of inflation that applies to a particular cash flow. For example, suppose that although the general rate of inflation (as given by changes in the RPI) is 14%, the rate of *wage* inflation is 20%. The actual money cash flow paid out in wages would be discounted by 14% and not by 20%. This is because we wish to express the money cash flows of a project in terms of their ability to purchase a *general* range or collection of goods, not their ability to purchase any one *particular* good.

A final example

The above analysis shows that the two possible approaches to project appraisal are exactly equivalent. Both start with the actual 'money' cash flows that the project is expected to produce, and both result in an identical set of present value cash flows from which the net present value can be found.

Given this equivalence, it does not much matter which approach is used, although discounting the money cash flows by the market interest rate would appear more straightforward because it only involves a single set of discounting calculations and is the recommended approach to use. However, sometimes the easiest approach is to use a mixture of both, if there are some simplification benefits to be had through cancellations. Example 3 demonstrates the principle.

Example 3

Project A:	Outlay:	£1000
	Life:	30 years
	Scrap value:	£100
	Net revenues:	£20 per year in current (t_0) terms.

The net cash flow is expected to increase each year by 8%.

| | RPI: | 6% per year. |
| | Market discount rate: | 14.48% |

It would be possible to set out the project's money cash flows and discount by 14.48% to present value. However, 14.48% is a rather awkward discounting number to use, and thirty years of

---

cash flows would be hard work! Therefore we could instead discount the money cash flows by a combination of RPI (6%) and the real discount rate.

Using the Fisher Effect:

$$\frac{1.1448}{1.06} - 1 = 0.08 \text{ or } 8\% = \text{real discount rate.}$$

Therefore, the project's money cash flows can be expressed as:

Year	Outlay (£)	Scrap (£)	Net revs. (£)
0	−1000		
1			$+120 (1.08)^1$
2			$+120 (1.08)^2$
.			.
.			.
.			.
30		+100	$+120 (1.08)^{30}$

The outlay is already in present value terms and so does not require discounting. The scrap value can be discounted back either at 14.48% or at a combination of 6% and 8%:

$$\text{Year 30: } +100 (1.448)^{-30} = +100 \times 0.0173 = +1.73$$

or

$$\text{Year 30: } +100 (1.08)^{-30} (1.06)^{-30} = +100 \times 0.0994 \times 0.1741 = +1.73.$$

As far as the net revenue cash flows are concerned, it is convenient to discount them to present value using a combination of 8% and 6% in order to be able to simplify the calculation through cancellation:

Year	Net revs. (£)			Discount factors
0				
1	$+120 (1.08)^1$	$\times$	$(1.08)^{-1}$	$(1.06)^{-1} = +120 (1.06)^{-1}$
2	$+120 (1.08)^2$	$\times$	$(1.08)^{-2}$	$(1.06)^{-2} = +120 (1.06)^{-2}$
.				.
.				.
.				.
30	$+120 (1.08)^{30}$	$\times$	$(1.08)^{-30}$	$(1.06)^{-30} = +120 (1.06)^{-30}$

Therefore, we are left with a thirty-year annuity cash flow:

$$+120 \, A_{30-0.06} = 120 \times 13.7648 = +1651.78.$$

Hence, the project's NPV is:

$$-1000 + 1.73 + 1651.78 = +653.51 \text{ NPV.}$$

Inflation and the IRR rule

This discussion about allowing for inflation in investment appraisal has been conducted within the context of an NPV analysis. Nevertheless it is simple to transfer the conclusions into the context of an IRR calculation. Either the IRR of the money cash flows of the project can be compared against the hurdle rate of the market interest rate or, alternatively, the IRR of the project's current general purchasing power cash flows can be matched against the real interest rate. However, in order to be able to use the IRR successfully, it is important to remember that it is necessary to assume that either the market interest rate or the real interest rate will remain constant over the project's life.

Investment appraisal and taxation

Introduction

Taxation has an important role to play in investment appraisal, as it can have a substantial impact on the desirability, or otherwise, of an investment opportunity. Furthermore, taxation considerations affect virtually every area of financial decision making both in a practical and in a theoretical context. Indeed, the complexity of the tax system and the fact that its application to individual financial decision-making situations can sometimes be difficult to generalize mean that it causes problems for the development of a realistic theory of financial decision making.

In this section we shall deal briefly with only a relatively simple aspect of taxation – its impact on investment project cash flows and their subsequent evaluation. However, in many of the later chapters we will be returning to examine some of the more complex problems that the presence of taxation poses for financial decision making.

The impact of tax

The theory of financial decision making is developed on the basis of an important underlying assumption: management are taking decisions so as to maximize the wealth of the shareholders. It therefore follows that in the appraisal of an investment project, what is of importance is the cash flows that will be generated by the project, and *that are available for shareholders*. In other words, as far as investment appraisal is concerned, we would wish to evaluate the *after-tax cash flows* of a project.

In this analysis of the impact of tax on project appraisal, only a simplified version of the UK corporate tax system will be used. Furthermore it is assumed that the reader is aware – in outline – of this tax system but, for those who lack knowledge in this area, a brief appendix at the end of the chapter outlines the very basic elements. It should also be remembered that tax rates are set in the budget each year. Thus it is important to note that any tax rates used in this book may or may not be correct.

There are three ways in which the UK corporation tax regime impacts upon project appraisal:

1. Tax relief is available on capital expenditure through the system of *writing-down allowances*.
2. A tax liability will arise on any *taxable profit* generated by the project.
3. There will also be a tax impact caused by how the project is financed. If it is financed with the help of debt capital, then there will be *tax relief* available on the interest payments. Alternatively, if the project is financed with shareholders' funds (i.e. equity capital), then dividends will be paid on the equity, which in turn will give rise to a liability for advance corporation tax.

With these three factors in mind, the approach taken to project appraisal is to evaluate the *after-tax project cash flows* using the *after-tax discount rate*. The after-tax project cash flows take into account effects 1 and 2 above, and the after-tax discount rate takes into account effect 3.

Financing cash flows

Up to this stage of our analysis of investment appraisal, very little has been said about how a project should be financed and the effect of the financing method on the project appraisal. This is how the position will remain until the capital structure/financing decision is discussed in detail in later chapters.

However, the basic philosophy of the approach of investment appraisal – and the NPV technique in particular – will be outlined now. This approach is that the financing method, and hence *all* the cash flows associated with the financing method, including interest payments, divided payments and loan repayments, can be ignored. This is because, in effect, they are implicitly taken into account in the discount rate used in the NPV analysis. Example 4 attempts to show the underlying rationale to this advice using a very simple situation.

Example 4 shows why an NPV analysis can (apparently) ignore how a project is financed. The costs of finance are taken into account within the discount rate used. In a similar way – although this will not be explained in detail until a later chapter where the *cost of capital* is examined more fully – using an *after-tax* discount rate also takes into account the taxation impact on the financing cash flows.

Example 4

Suppose a company wishes to acquire a machine which costs £1000 and has a three-year life. The machine is expected to generate a net revenue (i.e. revenues less cash *operating* – not financing – costs) of £450 per year.

The company approaches its bank for a £1000 three-year term loan in order to buy the machine. The bank agrees to the loan, after examining the riskiness of the proposed investment, and sets an interest rate of 10%. (Notice that this interest rate, like any rate of return, reflects the risk of the investment involved.)

Normally the company would then evaluate the NPV of the project, *ignoring* how it was to be financed and the cash flows (interest payments and loan repayments) associated with the financing method. Using a 10% discount rate (as this reflects the project's risk – it is the return available elsewhere from a similar risk investment) the NPV is:

$$-1000 + 450A_{3-0.10} = +119.06 \text{ NPV.}$$

However, it *could* be argued that this does not represent the true company cash flow, as effectively the bank, not the company, buys the machine. Thus, from the company's standpoint the true cash flows associated with the project are:

Year	0	1	2	3
Interest		−100	−100	− 100
Loan repayment				−1000
Net revenue		+450	+450	+ 450
Net cash flow[1]	0	+350	+350	− 650

However, when this cash flow is discounted to NPV at 10%, the result is exactly as before:

$$+350A_{2-0.10} - 650 (1.10)^{-3} = +119.06 \text{ NPV.}[2]$$

The reason for this is important: it is that the present value of the financing cash flow always equals the amount of the finance. Hence the present value of the bank loan cash flow equals the amount of the bank loan:

$$-100A_{3\to0.10} - 1000(1.10)^{-3} = -1000 \text{ PV.}[3]$$

Therefore, in the original NPV analysis of the project, the financing method is not *really* being ignored, because the project's outlay represents the present value of the financing cash flows.

Finally, care should be taken in not being misled by this simple example. The NPV analysis would have been undertaken in exactly the same way (with exactly the same +119.06 NPV) if the project had been financed with (say) a £600 bank loan and £400 of retained earnings. The £1000 NPV analysis outlay would implicitly represent the present value of *all* the financing cash flows, *however* the project was financed.

Writing-down allowances

If a company spends money on capital equipment (such as a machine) the tax authorities do not usually allow that *whole* expense to be used to affect the tax liability in the year in which it is incurred. Instead, the expense – and so the tax relief – has to be spread over the project's life, in accordance with a specific schedule. That schedule is the system of 25% writing-down allowances on the reducing balance of the project's worth.

Just how many tranches of writing-down allowance (WDA) the company will receive depends upon when the project is bought. In our simplified tax world, we can set up two alternative scenarios:

1. The project is bought on the first day of the company's accounting year.
2. The project is bought on the last day of the *previous* accounting year.

In both cases the expenditure is effectively made at t_0, but it is made one day earlier in case 2. One day makes no significant difference as far as an NPV discounting analysis is concerned, but it can make a significant difference as far as writing-down allowances are concerned.

Therefore, in general, we can state that a project will have as many WDAs as there are years in its life in case 1, whilst there will be one *extra* WDA in case 2. Furthermore, assuming that corporation tax is paid twelve months after year end, in case 1 the first WDA tax relief is received by the firm in t_2, whilst in case 2 the first WDA is received by the firm in t_1. (This therefore is the advantage of case 2. By buying the machine one *day* earlier, the tax relief comes through one *year* earlier.) Example 5 shows the calculations.

Example 5

A machine costs £1000 and has a four-year life, at the end of which time it will be sold for £400 scrap. The corporation tax rate is 35%, payable twelve months in arrears and a system of 25% WDA, on the reducing balance, is in operation. The WDA tax relief is as follows.

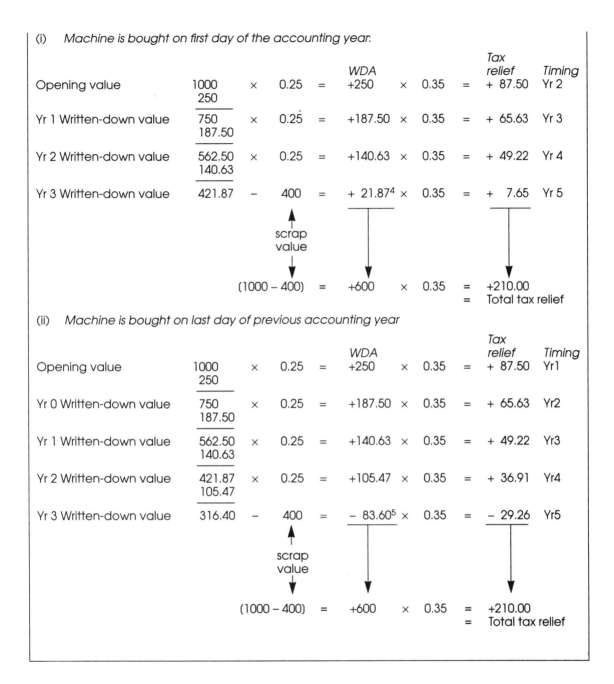

(i) *Machine is bought on first day of the accounting year.*

					WDA				Tax relief	Timing
Opening value	1000	×	0.25	=	+250	×	0.35	=	+ 87.50	Yr 2
	250									
Yr 1 Written-down value	750	×	0.25	=	+187.50	×	0.35	=	+ 65.63	Yr 3
	187.50									
Yr 2 Written-down value	562.50	×	0.25	=	+140.63	×	0.35	=	+ 49.22	Yr 4
	140.63									
Yr 3 Written-down value	421.87	−	400	=	+ 21.87[4]	×	0.35	=	+ 7.65	Yr 5

scrap value

(1000 − 400)	=	+600	×	0.35	=	+210.00
					=	Total tax relief

(ii) *Machine is bought on last day of previous accounting year*

					WDA				Tax relief	Timing
Opening value	1000	×	0.25	=	+250	×	0.35	=	+ 87.50	Yr1
	250									
Yr 0 Written-down value	750	×	0.25	=	+187.50	×	0.35	=	+ 65.63	Yr2
	187.50									
Yr 1 Written-down value	562.50	×	0.25	=	+140.63	×	0.35	=	+ 49.22	Yr3
	140.63									
Yr 2 Written-down value	421.87	×	0.25	=	+105.47	×	0.35	=	+ 36.91	Yr4
	105.47									
Yr 3 Written-down value	316.40	−	400	=	− 83.60[5]	×	0.35	=	− 29.26	Yr5

scrap value

(1000 − 400)	=	+600	×	0.35	=	+210.00
					=	Total tax relief

'Profit' tax charge

In our world of a simplified UK tax system, a straightforward tax charge, at whatever is the going rate, can be made on the project's net operating cash flow. (Depreciation is, of course, not an allowable expense against tax as it is substituted by the WDA system and, in any case, it is not a cash flow.) This tax liability then will be offset, to some extent, by the WDA tax relief. Example 6 shows a fully worked situation.

Example 6

Stanchion plc is considering investing in a project which will require a capital expenditure outlay of £250 000. It will have a four-year life and, at the end of that time, the equipment used will be sold off for £100 000.

In addition, £38 000 of working capital will be required from the start of the project, and this figure will have to be increased to £50 000 at the end of the second year. All the working capital will be recovered at the end of the project's life.

The project is expected to generate annual revenues of £200 000 and to incur annual cash operating costs of £80 000. The company believes that an after-tax discount rate of 10% would be appropriate.

The project would be bought on the last day of the company's previous financial year and would be financed with a three-year term loan of £250 000 at 3% over bank 'base rate'. Bank 'base rate' is currently 12%. The working capital would be financed out of Stanchion's own retained earnings.

Corporation tax is charged at 35%, payable twelve months after year end. 25% writing-down allowances on the reducing balance are available on capital expenditure. The company expects to have a substantial annual tax liability arising from other operations that it undertakes:

WDA calculations (£000s)

				WDA				Tax relief	Timing
250	×	0.25	=	+ 62.5	×	0.35	=	+ 21.9	Yr 1
62.5									
187.5	×	0.25	=	+ 46.9	×	0.35	=	+ 16.4	Yr 2
46.9									
140.6	×	0.25	=	+ 35.1	×	0.35	=	+ 12.3	Yr 3
35.1									
105.5	×	0.25	=	+ 26.4	×	0.35	=	+ 9.2	Yr 4
26.4									
79.1	−	100	=	− 20.9	×	0.35	=	− 7.3	Yr 5

Tax charge on project's profits (£000s)

Annual revenues	200
Less annual costs	80
Taxable 'profit'	120
Tax at 35%	£42

NPV calculation (£000s)

Year	0		1		2		3		4		5
Capital expenditure	− 250										
Scrap value									+ 100		
WDA tax relief		+	21.9	+	16.4	+	12.3	+	9.2	−	7.3
Working capital	− 38			−	12	+		+	50		
Revenues		+	200	+	200	+	200	+	200		
Costs		−	80	−	80	−	80	−	80		
Corporation tax				−	42	−	42	−	42	−	42
Net cash flow	− 288	+	141.9	+	82.4	+	90.3	+	237.2	−	49.3
10% discount factor	× 1	×	.9091	×	.8264	×	.7513	×	.6830	×	.6209
PV cash flow[6]	− 288	+	129.0	+	68.1	+	67.8	+	162.0	−	30.6

NPV: +£108 300

Notes
(i) Because of the company's substantial tax liability from other operations it is assumed that the company will be able to take the WDA tax relief that is available at Year 1. If not, this tax relief

would have to be carried over to Year 2 when there would be a sufficient tax liability from the project to offset against the WDA relief.

(ii) At the end of Year 2 an *additional* £12 000 has to be spent on working capital to raise the total expenditure up to the required £50 000.

(iii) All financing cash flows have been ignored for the reasons outlined earlier in this section.

Investment appraisal and the relevant cash flow

In an earlier chapter it was stated that in order properly to appraise an investment opportunity, we have to appraise all the cash flows that arise either directly or indirectly as a result of the project. Some of the cost or benefit cash flows that arise as a result of undertaking a project are both obvious and easy to identify. For example, if a project consists of buying a machine, operating it and selling its output, there are some 'obvious' cash flows involved, such as the cost of the machine and the revenue generated from the sale of the output. However, the identification of cash flow costs and benefits that are relevant to a project's appraisal are not always obvious.

Guiding rules

A set of 'guiding rules' will be used to outline the most important points and then a comprehensive example will be used to illustrate their application.

Rule 1: All costs incurred (and revenues generated) *prior* to the investment appraisal decision should be excluded. They are *sunk costs*, in that they are unaffected by the investment decision under appraisal. Example 7 illustrates this logic.

Rule 2: Ignore depreciation charges. Depreciation is a *non-cash flow* and so does not enter into the NPV *cash flow* analysis.

Rule 3: Ignore all financing cash flows (e.g. interest charges, loan repayments, dividends, etc.) and all their tax effects (e.g. interest tax relief and advance corporation tax (ACT)). This is because, as was seen in the previous section, these are all implicitly taken into account through the discounting process.[7] The UK government has decided to phase out ACT.

Example 7

Suppose a company has spent £100 000 undertaking research (R&D) in order to develop a new product. They have now reached the stage where they need to take a decision on whether to invest in manufacturing facilities for the new product. In this investment appraisal, the £100 000 spent on R&D is a sunk cost and so is irrelevant to the decision to be made.

To see how misleading it could be to include the R&D expenditure, suppose the manufacturing equipment costs £500 000 and the product is expected to produce net revenues of £580 000. (For this simple example, we will ignore any discounting.) If the sunk costs were ignored, the

---

decision would be to accept, but if the sunk costs were included in the analysis, the decision would be to reject:

Sunk cost excluded (£)		Sunk cost included (£)	
Cost	: – £500 000	Cost	: – £500 000
Net revenues	: + £580 000	R&D expenses	: – £100 000
		Net revenues	: + £580 000
'Profit'	: + £80 000	'Loss'	: – £20 000
Decision	: Accept	Decision	: Reject

The point here is that if the company accepts the project, at least they have the £80 000 'profit' to offset the £100 000 spent on R&D. If they reject the project, they are simply left with a £100 000 R&D expense.

Rule 4: Ignore all *non-incremental* cash flows. This is the more general case of Rule 1. Only those cash flows that arise because of the project should be included in an NPV analysis. Any cash flow that would arise *whether or not* the project was undertaken should be excluded.

An example of Rule 4's application would be *allocated* fixed costs. If a company normally allocated a particular proportion of its fixed Head Office costs to any new project, as part of its budgeting/costing process, these should be *excluded* from the investment appraisal. They would be cash flows that are non-incremental to the investment decision, in that the Head Office costs would still be incurred whether or not the project was accepted.

Rule 5: This concerns the cost, to the project, of using resources (usually raw materials) that the firm already holds in stock. Here there are three possible 'costs':

1. original purchase price/historic cost;
2. current replacement cost;
3. resale value or disposal cost.

The first of these is *never* relevant – the historic cost of the raw material stock is a sunk cost. However, which of the other two costs is relevant depends upon the particular circumstances.

Where the resources held in stock are used elsewhere in the company, then the cost to the project of using them is their replacement cost. This is because if the resources are used on the project, then those stocks will have to be replaced. Hence the current replacement cost is the *opportunity* cost[8] of their use.

If the resources already held in stock have no other use in the company than their use on the project, they will not be replaced. (Such a situation might arise through, say, the company using those particular resources in the past but no longer doing so, although some surplus stocks still remain.) Under these circumstances, if the stocks have a resale value then their resale value would be the (opportunity) cost to the project of their use. (The company, in using them on the project, forgoes the opportunity to sell them off.) If they only have a disposal cost, then their use on the project would *save* these costs. Hence the project would be credited with a benefit – or cash inflow – the saved disposal cost.

Rule 6: This concerns the use, by the project, of resources already in use with the company and where the company cannot obtain further supplies of those resources. In other words, this is the situation where the project utilizes 'scarce' or limited resources. The rule is that the cost of their use on the project is their *total* opportunity cost. Example 8 illustrates this situation.

Example 8

Suppose that there is a shortage of well-qualified mining engineers. A mining company at present employs 100 mining engineers and they are all fully utilized undertaking various projects. The company is now considering the development of an additional mine which would require five mining engineers. Because of the shortage of such staff, they cannot recruit any more, and so, if they undertook the new mining project, the engineers would have to be taken away from their existing tasks elsewhere in the company.

Suppose that each engineer is currently contributing £80 000 per year to the company's profits (i.e. revenue generated, less the engineer's salary, less the material and incremental costs incurred, equals £80 000). This will be lost if the company redeploys the engineer onto the new project: it would be the *internal* opportunity cost of using each engineer on the new project.

Thus the *total* cost of each engineer used on the new project would be the forgone contribution (the internal opportunity cost), *plus* the engineer's salary (the external opportunity cost, or *the market price* of the scarce resource).

These rules are now used together in Example 9.

Example 9

Radiometric plc has been offered a contract to manufacture six special communication systems for the government. Manufacture would take a total of three years at a rate of two machines per year. Payment would be in two instalments: £350 000 at the start of manufacture and another £350 000 upon completion.

The company is now evaluating the contract to see if it is worthwhile undertaking, and its management accounting department has produced the following estimates about the resources required to produce the special communication systems:

1   *Materials*

Type of material	Quantity per system (tonnes)	Amount in stock now (tonnes)	Original cost of stock per tonne (£)	Current purchase price per tonne (£)	Current realizable value per tonne (£)
Copper	20	60	700	1000	800
Radium	10	20	500	750	See below

Copper is used regularly by the company on many contracts. Radium is used rarely, and if the existing stock is not applied to this contract it will have to be disposed of immediately at a net cost of £100 per tonne. Materials required for the contract must be purchased and paid for annually in advance. Replacement costs of copper and radium and the realizable value of copper are expected to increase at an annual compound rate of 20%.

2   *Labour*
Each of the six systems will require 3000 hours of skilled electronic engineering and 5000 hours of unskilled labour. Current wage rates are £4 per hour for skilled electronic engineers and £3 per hour for unskilled labour.

Radiometric expects to suffer a shortage of skilled electronic engineers during the first year so that acceptance of the contract would make it necessary for the firm to give up other work on which a contribution of £7 per hour would be earned. (The 'other work' would require no unskilled labour.)

Again, in the contract's first year only, the company expects to have 20 000 surplus unskilled labour hours. Radiometric has an agreement with the in-house trade union whereby it lays off employees for whom there is no work and pays them two-thirds of their normal wages during the lay-off period.

All wage rates are expected to increase at an annual compound rate of 15%.

3 Overheads

Overhead costs are currently allocated to contracts at a rate of £14 per skilled electronic engineer, calculated as follows:

	£
Fixed overheads (including equipment depreciation of £5)	11.00
Variable overheads	3.00
	£14.00

Special equipment will be required to undertake this contract, and will be purchased at a cost of £200 000 payable immediately. It will be sold once the contract is completed for £50 000. Both fixed and variable overheads are expected to increase in line with the retail price index.

The special equipment will be financed with the first contract instalment paid by the government.

Radiometric have considerable experience in manufacturing this type of equipment and believe that a return of 20% would be available elsewhere on the capital market for a similar risk investment. The retail price index is expected to increase by 15% per year over the life of the contract.

It can be assumed that all current prices will hold for the next twelve months, before increasing in line with inflation. Therefore the material costs incurred for the second year's production will be 20% higher than the current market prices. Also it can be assumed that all cash flows arise on the last day of the year to which they relate, unless otherwise stated. Taxation should be ignored for the purposes of this evaluation (to simplify the analysis).

		Project cash flows (£000s)		
Year	0	1	2	3
Revenues	+ 350			+ 350
Equipment cost	− 200			
Scrap value				+ 50
Copper cost	− 40	− 48	− 57.6	
Radium cost	+ 2	− 18	− 21.6	
Elec. engin. cost		− 66	− 27.6	− 31.7
Unskilled labour		− 10	− 34.5	− 39.7
Variable o/hs.		− 18	− 20.7	− 23.0
Net cash flow	+ 112	− 160	− 162	+ 305.6
20% discount factor	× 1	× .8333	× .6944	× .5787
PV cash flow	+ 112	− 133.3	− 112.5	+ 176.8

Contract's NPV: +£43 000   Therefore it is worth undertaking.

Data calculations

1   Materials:

Copper	Year 1:	Use 40 tonnes from stock. As this will have to be replaced, its cost is the current purchase price of £1000 per tonne.
	Year 2:	Buy in 40 tonnes at £1000 (1.20) = £1200 per tonne.
	Year 3:	Buy in 40 tonnes at £1000 (1.20)^2 = £1440 per tonne.
Radium	Year 1:	Use 20 tonnes from stock. This will save a disposal cost of £100 per tonne. (Opportunity benefit.)
	Year 2:	Buy in 20 tonnes at £750 (1.20) = £900 per tonne.
	Year 3:	Buy in 20 tonnes at £750 (1.20)^2 = £1080 per tonne.

<table>
<tr><td>2</td><td>Labour:</td><td></td><td>6000 hours of skilled engineers required per year.
10 000 hours of unskilled labour required per year.</td></tr>
<tr><td></td><td>Skilled</td><td>Year 1:</td><td>6000 hours taken from elsewhere in the company. Cost is wage rate
plus lost contribution: £4 + £7 = £11 per hour.</td></tr>
<tr><td></td><td></td><td>Year 2:</td><td>Hire 6000 hours at £4 (1.15) = £4.60 per hour.</td></tr>
<tr><td></td><td></td><td>Year 3:</td><td>Hire 6000 hours at £4 (1.15)^2 = £5.29 per hour.</td></tr>
<tr><td></td><td>Unskilled</td><td>Year 1:</td><td>Utilize 10 000 hours of surplus labour. Cost is the incremental wages
paid: £1 per hour.</td></tr>
<tr><td></td><td></td><td>Year 2:</td><td>Hire 10 000 hours at £3 (1.15) = £3.45 per hour.</td></tr>
<tr><td></td><td></td><td>Year 3:</td><td>Hire 10 000 hours at £3 (1.15)^2 = £3.97 per hour.</td></tr>
<tr><td>3</td><td>Overheads</td><td></td><td></td></tr>
<tr><td></td><td>Fixed:</td><td></td><td>Exclude as non-incremental.</td></tr>
<tr><td></td><td>Depreciation:</td><td></td><td>Exclude as non-cash flow.</td></tr>
<tr><td></td><td>Variable:</td><td>Year 1:</td><td>£3 per skilled labour hour.</td></tr>
<tr><td></td><td></td><td>Year 2:</td><td>£3 (1.15) = £3.45 per skilled labour hour.</td></tr>
<tr><td></td><td></td><td>Year 3:</td><td>£3 (1.15)^2 = £3.97 per skilled labour hour.</td></tr>
</table>

Summary

Having concluded in the previous chapter that of the four basic investment appraisal techniques, only one – the NPV – was satisfactory, this chapter then turned to examine some of the possible problems that may be encountered with the application of NPV: inflation, taxation and relevant project cash flows. The main points made are as follows:

- Inflation is not the cause of the time value of money, but it does affect its value through the Fisher Effect relationship.

- The simplest approach to take in an investment appraisal in an inflationary environment is to discount a project's actual *money* cash flows by the market (or money) discount rate to NPV.

- *Real* cash flows should not be confused with cash flows in *current* terms. 'Real' refers to expressing an actual money cash flow in current *general* purchasing power terms. This will only be the same as a cash flow in current terms if the latter is expected to inflate at the *general* rate of inflation.[9]

- With taxation, there are three impacts on project appraisal:
  — tax relief on capital expenditure;
  — tax charge on the project's profit;
  — tax effects on the project's financing method: tax relief on debt interest and/or ACT liability caused by dividends (ACT is however being phased out).

- The approach to use is to evaluate the after-tax project cash flows with the after-tax discount rate. The after-tax project cash flows take account of the capital expenditure tax relief and the tax charge on the project's profit. The third tax impact is taken into account through the after-tax discount rate.

- As far as the relevant project cash flows are concerned, an investment appraisal should only include the *incremental* cash flows. This is the key concept. Any cash flows that have already occurred prior to the investment decision, or any subsequent cash flows that will occur whether or not the project is undertaken, are irrelevant.

- In addition, use has to be made of the opportunity cost concept to ensure that the *full* costs and benefits of undertaking the project are captured in the investment appraisal.

Appendix: the UK corporate tax system

This appendix briefly outlines the basics of the UK corporate tax system as it affects investment appraisal. In no way does it purport to represent a complete analysis. However, some familiarity with the tax regime is necessary in order to be able to appreciate how it is likely to impact on project appraisal.

1. Company 'profits' are subject to a rate of tax – which can vary depending upon the situation – and the tax is paid approximately one year in arrears.
2. Profit can be defined as revenues less allowable costs. Within these costs, depreciation is not an allowable cost, nor are dividend payments or working capital expenses. However, interest payments are an allowable cost. Most normal business expenses such as labour, materials and overhead costs are allowable against tax.
3. As a substitute for depreciation, writing-down allowances are allowable costs. These are calculated annually at a rate of 25% of the reducing value of the capital expenditure. (Notice in the WDA calculations in Example 6, the tax relief was taken into account separately. It could have been incorporated into the 'taxable profit' calculations.)
4. If a company pays out a dividend, this has the effect of bringing forward part of the corporation tax payment. That part of the corporation tax liability that is brought forward for immediate payment is known as advance corporation tax (ACT) and that which remains payable twelve months after year end is known as mainstream corporation tax. However this is being phased out from 1998.

Notes

1. Alternatively, the cash flows could be shown as:

Year	0	1	2	3
Loan from bank	+ 1000			
Interest		– 100	– 100	– 100
Loan repayment				– 1000
Capital expenditure	– 1000			
Net revenue		+ 450	+ 450	+ 450
Net cash flow	0	+ 350	+ 350	– 650

but the net effect is the same.

2. Actually, using four-figure discount tables the NPV is + 119.08, but the difference between the two NPVs is solely brought about through rounding error.

3. Again, the two-pence difference is caused by rounding error in the discount factors used.

4. This value is referred to as the 'balancing allowance'.

5. This value is referred to as the 'balancing charge'.

6. Notice how tax produces a non-conventional cash flow and hence multiple IRRs.

7. There are two important possible exceptions to this rule. One is in a special investment appraisal situation: the lease versus purchase decision. The other is in the case of overseas project appraisal. Both topics will be covered at a later stage.

8. The concept of 'opportunity cost' is important in all forms of economic analysis. See the suggested reading.

9. An example might help to make this statement clear. Suppose the current wage rate is £5 per hour and we require 100 hours of labour at Year 2. Therefore the Year 2 labour cost in *current* terms is £500. This may or may not equal the Year 2 labour cost in *real* terms, depending upon the inflation rate of labour costs. If labour costs inflate at 10% per year and the RPI is also inflating at 10% per year, the current labour cost will equal the real cost. But if labour costs inflate up at a different rate from the RPI, then the two things are not equal:

(a) Labour inflates up at 10% per year.
   RPI inflates up at 10% per year.
   Actual Year 2 cash flow: $£500 (1.10)^2 = £605$.
   Real Year 2 cash flow: $£605 (1.10)^{-2} = £500$.
   Current Year 2 labour cost = £500.

(b) Labour inflates up at 15% per year.
   RPI inflates up at 10% per year.
   Actual Year 2 cash flow: $£500 (1.15)^2 = £661.25$.
   Real Year 2 cash flow: $£661.25 (1.10)^{-2} = £546.46$.
   Current Year 2 labour cost = £500.

Further reading

1. A good overview article on the problem of inflation and capital investment appraisal is: N.J. Coulthurst, 'Accounting for Inflation in Capital Investment: State of the Art and Science', *Accounting and Business Research*, Winter 1986.
2. Other interesting articles include: B. Carsberg and A. Hope, *Business Investment Decisions Under Inflation: Theory and Practice*, ICAEW 1976; A. Rappaport and R.A. Taggart, 'Evaluation of Capital Expenditure Proposals Under Inflation', *Financial Management*, Spring 1982; M.K. Kim, 'Inflationary Effects in the Capital Investment Process', *Journal of Finance*, September 1979; and S.N. Chan, 'Capital Budgeting and Uncertain Inflation', *Journal of Economics and Business*, August 1984.
3. Finally, on the whole area of relevant cash flows and opportunity costs see: L. Amey, 'On Opportunity Costs and Decision Making', *Accountancy*, July 1961; J.R. Gould, 'Opportunity Costs: the London Tradition', in *Debits, Credits,*

Finance and Profits, H.C. Edey and B.S. Yamey (eds), Sweet and Maxwell 1974; and N.J. Coulthurst. 'The Application of the Incremental Principle in Capital Investment Project Evaluation', *Accounting and Business Research*, Autumn 1986.

Quickie questions

1. If the market interest rate is 13% and the general rate of inflation is 4%, what is the real interest rate?
2. What approaches can be taken to an NPV investment appraisal in inflationary conditions?
3. What is a *real* cash flow?
4. Rent is paid each year. This year's rent – £10 000 – has just been paid. How much rent will need to be paid in two years' time if:
   (a) the rent remains constant in real terms;
   (b) the rent remains constant in money terms?
   In both of the above cases, what is the PV of the Year 2 rent? Assume that the market discount rate is 15.5% and the RPI is 5% per year.
5. A machine costs £500 and has a three-year life and a zero scrap value. It is bought on the first day of the accounting year. What are the amounts of WDA tax relief received if the corporation tax rate is 35%, paid twelve months in arrears, and the WDAs are calculated as 25% of the reducing balance?
6. A company owns a machine which is presently lying unused in the factory. The machine was bought five years ago at a cost of £60 000 and has now been depreciated down to a book value of £10 000. It could be sold now for £3000. Alternatively it could be rented out for a year at £2500. The company's chief engineer believes the machine will be totally obsolete in twelve months' time and would then have a scrap value of £800. The company is considering using the machine to undertake a one-year project. If it did, the machine's scrap value at the end of the year, net of dismantling costs, would be zero. Ignoring the time value of money, what is the cost of using the machine on the project?
7. What is the approach used to handling tax in investment appraisal?
8. Why should *allocated* fixed costs be excluded from project cash flows in an NPV analysis?
9. A company pays an annual rent of £20 000 for its factory of 10 000 m². All space is fully utilized and no more space is available for rent. Each square metre of space generates a contribution of £15. A project is being considered that would require 150 m² of factory space. What would be the cost, to the project, of that space?

Problems

1. Sanglo Radios plc is considering buying a machine to make printed circuit boards. The machine costs £1.2 million and will last for five years. Scrap value of these machines is £200 000. An investment of £150 000 in working capital will be needed initially. The accountant has prepared the following estimated annual trading account for the project:

	(£)
Sales	1 400 000
Materials	(300 000)
Labour	(500 000)
Depreciation	(200 000)
Allocated fixed overheads	(250 000)
Annual profit	£150 000

The machine would be financed with a four-year term loan from Barclays Bank at an interest rate of 3.5% over base. Currently, the bank base rate is 8%. The interest payments attract tax relief.

The machine would be bought on the last day of the company's previous fiscal year and would attract a 25% writing-down allowance. Corporation tax is payable at 40%, one year after year end.

The company believes that 10% would be the minimum after-tax return acceptable from a project with this level of risk and, if that return is achieved, then they will be able to increase dividends to shareholders by £50 000 a year over each of the next five years.

Required:
Calculate the project's net present value.

2. Sparrow Ltd is a construction company based in the southwest of England. Mr and Mrs Hawk each own 50% of the company's issued share capital. The company's latest accounts show a balance sheet value for share capital and reserves of £250 000 and an annual turnover of £1.25 million.

The company has recently been offered two contracts, both of which would commence almost immediately and last for two years. Neither contract can be delayed. The prices offered are £700 000 for contract 1 and £680 000 for contract 2, payable in each case at the contract's completion. The skilled labour force of Sparrow is committed during the coming year to the extent that sufficient skilled labour will be available to support only one of the two contracts. Due to a shortage in the area, the company will not be able to expand its skilled labour force in the foreseeable future. If necessary, Sparrow could subtract one entire contract, but not both, to a nearby company, Kestrel Ltd, which is of a similar size to Sparrow. If one contract were subcontracted, all work would be undertaken by Kestrel, subject to regular checks of progress and quality by Mr Hawk. Kestrel has quoted prices of £490 000 for contract 1 and £530 000 for contract 2, payable in either case by two equal instalments, half at the start of the contract and the remainder at the end of the first year.

Sparrow maintains a standard costing system and normally prices contracts on a cost-plus basis. Total cost is calculated by adding to direct costs 60% for overheads, this percentage being based on previous experience. A target price is then calculated by adding a 25% profit mark-up to total cost. Mrs Hawk has calculated the following target prices for the two contracts under consideration:

	Contract 1 (£)	Contract 2 (£)
Materials: Special materials (at original cost)	50 000	—
Other materials (at standard cost)	200 000	24 000
Labour: skilled (at standard cost)	80 000	80 000
Unskilled (at standard cost)	112 000	126 000
Direct costs	442 000	446 000
Overheads: 60% of direct costs	265 200	267 600
Total cost	707 200	713 600
Profit mark-up: 25% of total cost	176 800	178 400
Target price	884 000	892 000

The following additional information is available:

Materials: Contract 1 would require the immediate use of special materials which were purchased one year ago at a cost of £50 000 for a contract which was not completed because the customer went into liquidation. These special materials have a current purchase price of £60 000 and a current realizable value of £30 000. The company foresees no alternative use for these special materials. Usage of the other materials would be spread evenly between the two years of each contract's duration. These other materials are all used regularly by the company. Their standard costs reflect current purchase prices which are expected to continue at their present level for the next twelve months. In the following year, prices are expected to rise by 10%.

Labour: Skilled labour costs for each contract represent 8000 hours each year for two years at a standard cost of £5 per hour. Unskilled labour hours required are 16 000 hours per annum for contract 1 and 18 000 hours per annum for contract 2, in each case at a standard cost of £3.50 per hour. Standard costs are based on current wage rates. Hourly wage costs for both skilled and unskilled labour are expected to increase by 5% in the current year and then by a further 10% in the following year.

Overheads: An analysis of Sparrow's most recent accounts shows that total overheads may be categorized as follows:

Fixed administrative and office costs	60%
Depreciation of plant and equipment	30%
Costs which vary directly with direct costs	10%
	100%

Fixed administrative and office costs are expected to increase as a result of inflation by 5% in the current year, and by a further 10% in the following year.

Sparrow expects to have sufficient surplus plant and equipment capacity during the next two years for either contract 1 or contract 2.

Sparrow has a money cost of capital of 10% per annum in the current year. Mr Hawk expects this to increase to 15% per annum in the second year of the contract.

Assume that all payments will arise on the last day of the year to which they relate, except where otherwise stated.

Required:
Provide calculations, on the basis of the estimates given, showing whether Sparrow should accept either or both contracts, and which one, if any, should be subcontracted to Kestrel.

3. Bailey plc is developing a new product, the Oakman, to replace an established product, the Shepard, which the company has marketed successfully for a number of years. Production of the Shepard will cease in one year, whether or not the Oakman is manufactured. Bailey plc has recently spent £75 000 on research and development relating to the Oakman. Production of the Oakman can start in one year's time.

Demand for the Oakman is expected to be 5000 units per annum for the first three years of production and 2500 units per annum for the subsequent two years. The product's total life is expected to be five years.

Estimated unit revenues and costs for the Oakman, at current prices, are as follows:

	(£)	*(£)*
Selling price per unit		35.00
less costs per unit:		
Materials and other consumables	8.00	
Labour (see (a) below)	6.00	
Machine depreciation and overhaul (see (b) below)	12.50	
Other overheads (see (c) below)	9.00	
		35.50
Loss per unit		0.50

(a) Each Oakman requires two hours of labour, paid at £3 per hour at current prices. The labour force required to produce Oakmans comprises six employees, who are at present employed to produce Shepards. If the Oakman is not produced, these employees will be made redundant when production of the Shepard ceases. If the Oakman is produced, three of the employees will be made redundant at the end of the third year of its life, when demand halves, but the company expects to be able to find work for the remaining three employees at the end of the Oakman's five-year life. Any employee who is made redundant will receive a redundancy payment equivalent to 1000 hours' wages, based on the most recent wage at the time of the redundancy.

(b) A special machine will be required to produce the Oakman. It will be purchased in one year's time (just before production begins). The current price of the machine is £190 000. It is expected to last for five years and to have no scrap or resale value at the end of that time. A major overhaul of the machine will be necessary at the end of the second year of its life. At current prices, the overhaul will cost £60 000. As the machine will not produce the same quality of Oakmans each year, the directors of Bailey plc have decided to spread its original cost and the cost of the overhaul equally between all Oakmans expected to be produced (i.e. 20 000 units). Hence the combined charge per unit for depreciation and overhaul is £12.50 ([£190 000 + £60 000] / 20 000 units).

(c) Other overheads at current prices comprise variable overheads of £4.00 per unit and head office fixed costs of £5.00 per unit, allotted on the basis of labour time.

All wage rates are expected to increase at an annual compound rate of 15%. Selling price per unit and all costs other than labour are expected to increase in line with the retail price index, which is expected to increase in the future at an annual compound rate of 10%.

Corporation tax at 35% on net cash income is payable in full one year after the income arises. A 25% writing-down allowance is available on the machine which will be bought on the first day of the company's accounting year. Bailey plc has a money cost of capital, net of corporation tax, of 20% per annum.

Assume that all receipts and payments will arise on the last day of the year to which they relate. Assume also that all 'current prices' given above have been operative for one year and are due to change shortly. Subsequently all prices will change annually.

Required:
(a) Prepare calculations, with explanations, showing whether Bailey should undertake production of the Oakman.
(b) Discuss the particular investment appraisal problems created by the existence of high rates of inflation.

8 Capital market imperfections

Capital rationing

In Chapter 4 we set up a single-period investment–consumption model to use as a guide to effective financial investment appraisal. The model was a crude and unrealistic simplification of the real world, but it was used so that the underlying principles of investment decisions could be examined, without becoming embroiled in elaborate complications (such as the existence of taxation, inflation and an uncertain future). In addition, a time horizon of only one time period was used so that the conclusions could be presented graphically rather than algebraically.

We saw that neither payback nor ROCE/ARR were satisfactory investment appraisal rules in terms of the Hirshleifer analysis, as they did not lead to the firm optimally locating onto the physical investment line. In contrast, both the DCF techniques – NPV and IRR – did lead the firm to locate optimally.

However, a closer examination of the IRR method uncovered a number of problems with its use and so, at the end of Chapter 6, we were able to conclude that the NPV decision rule was the only one of the four investment appraisal techniques which would consistently lead to investment decisions being taken that would help to maximize shareholder wealth. Even so, the NPV decision rule required the assumption of a perfect capital market.

In this chapter we are going to examine what happens to the NPV decision rule in the absence of a perfect capital market. In particular, we are going to examine the case where the company may not be able to undertake all the positive NPV projects it has discovered, because of a shortage of capital investment funds. This particular capital market imperfection is known as *capital rationing*.

Capital market borrowing

A great deal of attention, in both the applied and theoretical literature, has been paid to the problem of capital rationing but, even so, there is no general agreement on what precisely is meant by the term, and this has resulted in a certain amount of confusion. In an effort to avoid adding to this, it is important that we state from the outset what we shall take to be the meaning of capital rationing.

From the viewpoint of the making of investment decisions by financial management within companies, capital rationing is a *managerial* problem. It is, most certainly, a theoretical problem for our decision-making model but, more importantly, it is also a practical problem.

Up to this point, we have followed the NPV investment appraisal rule because it is most likely to indicate (in a practical sense) consistently good investment decisions. In its basic form the NPV decision rule is: accept all projects whose cash flows, when discounted by the market interest rate and then summated, have a positive or zero net present value. Such projects are acceptable because they yield a return that is either greater than (+ NPV), or at least equal to (zero NPV) the return that is available on the capital market for a similar-risk investment (which is defined by the rate of discount used).

Therefore, in terms of opportunity cost, the discount rule can be viewed as the minimum return that management must earn from investing shareholders' money in physical investment opportunities. It represents the minimum acceptable rate of return because it is the return that shareholders themselves can earn by placing their money in *financial* investment opportunities (i.e. investing on the capital market). Hence management should not invest shareholders' money to earn a lower rate of return than can be obtained on the capital market.

Implicit in the NPV decision rule is the idea that as long as a company's management can find investment opportunities that yield at least the capital market return (i.e. they satisfy the NPV decision rule), then capital will be available to finance them. This is because investing borrowed funds in projects with non-negative NPVs ensures that the project will yield a return that will at least be sufficient to repay the borrowed capital plus interest. In terms of the single-period investment–consumption diagram, this implies that if a company identifies so many acceptable projects (i.e. + or 0 NPV) that the company's existing resources at t_0 provide insufficient investment capital to undertake them all, then additional finance can be borrowed from the capital market.

In Fig. 8.1, OA represents the company's existing resources at t_0 and AB represents the physical investment line. The point of tangency between the physical and financial investment lines is at point C.

Therefore the company has identified acceptable projects that require a total investment outlay at t_0 of AD. As the company's existing resources only amount to OA, OD will have to be borrowed from the capital market.

The investment AD undertaken at t_0 will produce a cash inflow at t_1 of OE. The amount required to repay the loan, plus interest, is given by EF, leaving an amount OF for shareholders. Notice what the net result has been of borrowing on the capital market by the company. Without borrowing, the maximum amount of cash that could have been generated at t_1 would have been OG; but with borrowing (and hence undertaking additional

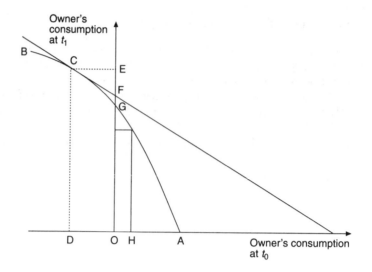

Fig. 8.1 *Capital market borrowing*

Owner's consumption at t_1

Owner's consumption at t_0

physical investment), the company has been able to increase the t_1 cash flow available to the owner by the amount FG.

The term 'capital rationing' refers to the situation where the implicit assumȚ tion within the NPV decision rule, that capital will always be available to finance acceptable projects, *does not hold.* For example, using the situation as found in Fig. 8.1, suppose that the company was unable to raise OD on the capital market, then a situation of capital rationing would exist: acceptable projects requiring a total outlay of AD had been identified, but they cannot all be accepted because only OA of finance is available. Management have therefore to 'ration out' this limited amount of investment capital between the available projects.

It should be clear from the above that the existence of capital rationing need not only apply to externally raised funds. For example, not only may the company not be able to raise any capital market finance, but the shareholders (in the example used in Fig. 8.1) may be unwilling to allow the company to invest the *whole* of OA. Suppose that for some reason the maximum that shareholders will allow to be applied to physical investments is AH. Then the company has an even tighter capital constraint than before: only AH of capital available, although they have identified acceptable projects which require a total of AD of capital.

It should be clear from the above that the existence of capital rationing represents a capital market imperfection: investment funds are no longer freely available at the market rate of return. The reasons why such capital rationing may occur in practice are many and varied, but in the context of our analysis they are only of passing interest. The point that we wish to examine is, given a situation of capital rationing, how does it affect the efficiency of the investment decision advice given by the NPV appraisal technique, and can NPV be adapted to operate successfully in such situations?

Hard and soft capital rationing

Two types or classes of capital rationing are usually specified: 'hard' capital rationing (which has received the lion's share of attention in the literature but which is probably of little importance in practice, as far as investment decisions in companies are concerned), and 'soft' capital rationing.

Hard capital rationing describes the situation where forces external to the company, usually either the capital market itself or the government (which may or may not act through the capital market), will not supply unlimited amounts of investment capital to a company, even though the company has identified investment opportunities which would be able to produce the required return. Soft capital rationing arises from forces internal to a company, such as a capital budget, which limits the amount of capital available for investment. In certain situations and in certain cases, the distinction between hard and soft capital rationing and between the various different causes of hard rationing may be important for the analysis. Where they are, such a distinction shall be made, but for the moment we shall concentrate on the problems which capital rationing *per se* causes for investment appraisal.

An example

In a situation where capital rationing is non-existent (and hence we are assuming a perfect capital market), investment decision making involves a comparison between the investment funds being applied to the particular investment under consideration and their being applied to a similar-risk capital market investment, because this latter alternative reflects the opportunity cost of undertaking the investment. With the introduction of capital rationing, choice is still involved, but the alternative to the application of capital to a proposed investment project is not *necessarily* the capital market investment, but may instead be another of the firm's investment projects.

In other words, the opportunity cost of undertaking a particular investment is now not necessarily reflected in the capital market rate of return, but may be a higher value, represented by the return yielded by another project which could not be undertaken by the company because the supply of capital is limited. An example can help to illustrate the point.

Suppose a company has discovered two independent projects, A and B. Each requires £500 of investment capital, and Project A yields a return[1] of 12%, whereas B yields a return of 15%. If the company's cost of capital were 10% and funds were unlimited, both projects would be accepted because both would have positive NPVs. The acceptance procedure, using the NPV method, would involve the comparison of the return given by each project *in turn*, with the return available on the capital market.

However, if capital rationing exists, and the company's investment funds are limited to a *total* of £500, then a different decision process is required. The company must now choose, *not* between each project and the capital market return, but first between the two projects themselves and then, once it has decided which is the best project, must compare its return with the alternative given by the capital market. Thus in a non-rationing situation the company would be making two decisions: accept/reject Project A, accept/reject Project B; whilst in a rationing situation they would be making one, two-stage decision: select Project A or B, then accept/reject the selected project.

Single-period capital rationing

It appears at first sight that capital rationing involves little more than another type of the 'mutually exclusive projects' decision, which we dealt with earlier. In fact, as we shall see, the existence of capital rationing produces a much more difficult decision problem.

Most readers will be familiar with the idea of a budget as a means of planning and control[2] and so, for the sake of presenting a clear argument, we shall assume that for each decision period (say, a year), management have a capital budget within which to keep, i.e. total capital expenditure must not exceed some stated upper limit: the capital budget or (to avoid terminology confusion) the capital constraint. Therefore we shall assume a *soft* rationing situation, but the conclusions we derive will be equally applicable to hard rationing.

Let us begin with the most simple and straightforward capital rationing problem: a situation where capital is rationed at present (i.e. t_0) but will be freely available in the future – a rather unlikely situation in practice – or one where the collection of investment projects the company wishes to appraise involve capital outlays *only* in the current period (i.e. the capital outlay required for the project does not extend over more than one point in time). In addition, it is assumed that projects are infinitely divisible, so that fractions of projects may be undertaken, and that they exhibit constant returns to scale.

In such a situation, only a slight modification to the standard NPV decision rule is required. Each investment opportunity should have its expected future cash flows discounted to net present value by the appropriate market discount rate. This NPV is then expressed as a ratio of the capital outlay which the project requires in the rationed time period, and is often termed the *benefit–cost ratio*.

All projects which have a positive or zero benefit–cost ratio would normally be accepted in a non-rationed situation. However, because capital rationing exists and a choice has to be made between the alternative projects, they should be ranked in order of decreasing benefit–cost ratio. Starting with the project with the largest (positive) ratio, and working down the rankings, as many projects as possible (with positive or zero ratios) should be accepted, until all the available capital is allocated.

Examples of benefit–cost ratios

Example 1 shows this decision method in operation. It assumes that capital rationing will only exist in the current time period (Year 0), all the projects are independent and divisible, and exhibit constant returns to scale and none can be delayed.

Example 1

In a non-rationing situation all the projects in the table below would be accepted, except for Project F which has a negative NPV when discounted at the market interest rate. In order to undertake them all, the company would require a total of £460 of capital now (Year 0) and this would produce a total NPV of £283.09. Therefore acceptance of Projects A to E would cause shareholders' wealth to rise by £283.09.

Project			Year				NPV when discounted at 10%
	0	1	2	3	4		
A	− 100	+ 20	+ 40	+ 60	+ 80	⇒	+ 50.96
B	− 150	− 50	+ 100	+ 100	+ 140	⇒	+ 57.94
C	− 60	+ 20	+ 40	+ 40	–	⇒	+ 21.29
D	− 100	+ 60	+ 60	+ 100	–	⇒	+ 79.26
E	− 50	+ 20	+ 40	+ 60	+ 40	⇒	+ 73.64
F	− 100	+ 30	+ 30	+ 30	+ 30	⇒	− 4.91

Suppose that capital rationing exists at Year 0 (but not in Years 1 to 4) and as a result the company has only £300 of investment capital available. It therefore cannot undertake all of the five positive NPV projects. Which projects should be selected to be undertaken? The second table ranks the projects in decreasing order of benefit–cost ratio. (Note in particular, how project B's benefit–cost ratio is calculated. Although B requires two capital outlays, at Year 0 and Year 1, the ratio concerns the NPV and the outlay in the rationed time period only. Hence the denominator of the ratio is simply B's Year 0 outlay.)

Project	$\dfrac{NPV}{\text{Yr 0 Outlay}}$	=	Benefit–cost Ratio	Ranking
A	50.96/100	=	+ 0.51	3
B	57.94/150	=	+ 0.39	4
C	21.29/60	=	+ 0.35	5
D	79.26/100	=	+ 0.79	2
E	73.64/50	=	+ 1.47	1
F	− 4.91/100	=	− 0.05	6

Benefit–cost Project	Outlay ranking	Yr 0	
E	1	50	
D	2	100	Accept: E, D, A, ⅓B
A	3	100	
B	4	150	
C	5	60	
F*	–	100	

* Note that in this simple type of rationing situation, Project F would never be accepted because it has a negative benefit–cost ratio.

$$\text{Total NPV} \quad = \quad £73.64 + £79.26 + £50.96 + 1/3 \,(£57.94)$$
$$= \quad £223.17$$

The table shows that the £300 of available capital should be applied to Projects E, D, A and one-third of Project B. This gives the company, for its £300 capital outlay, a total positive NPV of £223.17, which is the maximum possible total NPV, given the capital expenditure constraint. Therefore, because investment capital is scarce, shareholder wealth will only rise by £223.17 as a result of the investment decisions made, rather than by the possible total of £283.09. Thus, we can see that, as far as shareholders are concerned, there is a definite cost to capital rationing. In this case, because of the presence of capital rationing, shareholders' wealth will be approximately £60 below the value it would have otherwise attained.

However, given the situation specified, the process of selecting projects on the basis of their benefit–cost ratios ensures that the company will maximize the total amount of positive NPV gained from the available projects, assuming limited investment capital. This is because the terms in which the benefit–cost ratio focuses attention on the size of a project's NPV are not absolute, but *relative* to the scarce resources required to undertake it. In other words, projects are ranked in order of preference, in terms of the NPV they produce, for every unit (i.e. £1) of the limited investment capital which they require. In the example used above, Project A is preferred to Project B (even though B has the larger total NPV) because it produces 51p of (positive) NPV for every £1 of the scarce investment capital applied to its undertaking in Year 0, whereas Project B only produces 39p of NPV per £1 of investment outlay.

Example 2 is divided up into two separate single-period capital rationing situations. In the first situation there is straightforward Year 0 rationing. However in the second situation a further element is added to the analysis. This shows that the standard NPV decision rule for independent projects – accept all non-negative NPV projects – breaks down in capital rationing situations. This means that not only will some positive NPV projects (like Project C in Example 1) not be accepted, but there may also be circumstances where it is advantageous to accept a *negative* NPV project.

Example 2

The management accounting department of Septillion plc have identified six independent investment opportunities, codenamed G to L. The Year 0 and Year 1 cash flows of these projects, together with their NPVs, are as follows:

		(£000s)		
Year	0	1	....	NPV
Project				
G	− 100	− 500	....	+ 25
H	− 200	− 90	....	+ 36
I	− 150	− 220	....	+ 44
J	− 300	− 100	....	+ 30
K	− 50	+ 100	....	+ 10
L	− 100	+ 80	....	− 12

Under normal circumstances, Septillion plc would accept Projects G to K, as they all have positive NPVs, and Project L would be rejected. However, to undertake Projects G to K, a total of £800 000 would be required at Year 0, and an additional £910 000 at Year 1. (Notice that Project K does not require a further cash outlay at Year 1.)

In the first situation, Septillion's board of directors have stipulated that, although there will be no capital expenditure constraint at Year 1, the company is only willing to undertake £275 000 of capital expenditure at Year 0. Thus the company faces a single time-period capital rationing situation. In order to solve the problem, benefit–cost ratio rankings are used:

Project	NPV	÷	Year 0 outlay	=	Benefit–cost ratio	Rank
G	+ 25	÷	100	=	+ 0.25	2
H	+ 36	÷	200	=	+ 0.18	4
I	+ 44	÷	150	=	+ 0.293	1
J	+ 30	÷	300	=	+ 0.10	5
K	+ 10	÷	50	=	+ 0.20	3
L	− 12	÷	100	=	− 0.12	−

			NPV
Investment decision:	275	available	
	150	invested in I, producing	: +44
	125	balance	
	100	invested in G, producing	: +25
	25	balance	
	25	invested in 50% of K, producing	: +5
	–	all funds invested	
		Total NPV	+74

Thus the company should undertake Projects I and G, and 50% of K. This will generate a total positive NPV of £74 000, which will be the maximum possible, given the expenditure constraint.

The second situation is somewhat contrived, but serves to show an important point. Suppose that, instead of constraining capital expenditure at Year 0, the board of directors decided that there is *no* constraint on expenditure at Year 0, but at *Year 1* there is only £290 000 of *external* finance available. However, this figure can be added to by any internally generated funds that arise from projects at Year 1.

Once again, the management face capital rationing and, although there is no constraint at Year 0, they must be careful at that time only to undertake projects for which there will be sufficient finance available at Year 1 for them to be continued. (It would be no good accepting every non-negative NPV project available at Year 0, only to find that many would subsequently have to be abandoned at Year 1 through insufficient finance.)

The revised set of benefit–cost ratios are now:

Project	NPV	÷	Year 1 outlay	=	Benefit–cost ratio	Rank
G	+25	÷	500	=	0.05	4
H	+36	÷	90	=	0.40	1
I	+44	÷	220	=	0.20	3
J	+30	÷	100	=	0.30	2
K	+10	÷	–			
L	–12	÷	–			

Obviously Septillion will undertake Project K: it has a positive NPV and does not require any outlay in the rationed time-period. Furthermore, because it actually generates a cash *inflow* of £100 000 at Year 1, this amount can be added to the external funds available for capital expenditure. Thus the investment decision is:

			NPV
	290	available	
plus	100	from investment in K, producing	: +10
	390	balance	
	90	invested in H, producing	: +36
	300	balance	
	100	invested in J, producing	: +30
	200	balance	
	200	invested in 91% of I, producing	: +40
	–	all funds invested	
		Total NPV	+116

However, this is not the end of the decision. Although the £390 000 of funds has been fully utilized, it is possible to obtain additional funds at Year 1 by investing in Project L. The question is: does the additional *positive* NPV generated from investing Project L's Year 1 cash inflow compensate for the *negative* NPV arising from Project L directly? The answer lies in examining Project L's *cost–benefit* (rather than benefit–cost) ratio and comparing it with the benefit–cost ratio of the 'marginal' project.

Project L has a cost–benefit ratio of –12/+80 = –0.15. In other words, every £1 generated at Year 1 from investing in Project L has a cost of 15 pence of negative NPV.

The 'marginal' project in Septillion's investment decision is I, because it was into Project I that the last £1 of the available expenditure was spent. Project I can have a total of £220 000 invested in it at Year 1. So far, only £200 000 has been invested and so, if any further investment funds are available – up to a maximum of £20 000 – they too would be invested in I. The benefit gain from a further investment in I is given by its benefit–cost ratio of 0.20. In other words, every £1 extra invested in I generates an additional 20 pence of positive NPV.

From this comparison of Projects I and L, it can be seen that the benefit generated from a further investment in I *does* exceed the cost arising from the investment in L (i.e. 0.2 > 0.15). Investing in the whole of L will produce £80 000 at Year 1, but as only a further £20 000 can be invested in I, for the moment, the decision will be to undertake just 25% of project L to produce the required cash flow:

		NPV
Invest in 25% L to yield 20, costing	:	–3
invest 20 in 9% of I, yielding	:	+4
Net gain		+1

Septillion has now undertaken the whole of Projects K, H, J *and* I, as well as 25% of L. On the benefit–cost ratio rankings, if any *more* investment funds were available, the next best project is G. Therefore is it worthwhile undertaking the remaining 75% of L – which would produce an extra £60 000 of funds at Year 1 – in order to invest in 12% of Project G (60 ÷ 500)?

Again comparison of the ratios provides the answer: every £1 generated from L costs 15 pence of negative NPV; every £1 invested in Project G produces 5 pence of positive NPV. Therefore further investment in L in order to invest in Project G is *not* worthwhile.

Thus the optimal investment decision is: undertake Projects K, H, J, I and 25% of L. This will yield a maximum total of positive NPV of: 10 + 36 + 30 + 44 – 3 = +£117 000 NPV.

Divisibility assumption

The benefit–cost ranking approach to the situation of single-period capital rationing depends heavily on the assumption that investment projects are divisible (i.e. that fractions of projects can be undertaken, such as 25% of Project L in the example). Where this assumption does not hold, benefit–cost ratios do not work and instead, the investment selection decision has to be undertaken by examining the total NPV values of all the feasible alternative combinations of whole projects (where the term 'feasible' refers to the fact that the total outlay required to undertake the combination does not exceed the amount available). Therefore using as an example the situation as in Example 1, if none of the investment projects were divisible, the combination of accepting Projects B, D and E would produce the greatest amount of NPV, keeping within the £300 capital expenditure limit.

Mutually exclusive investments

A variation on the infringement of the divisibility assumption occurs when projects are mutually exclusive. Suppose the same example is again taken, but now it is assumed that Projects A and E are mutually exclusive. Therefore either one or the other, or neither, can be accepted, but both *cannot* be accepted. In order to obtain the optimum selection of projects we would proceed as we did originally, going down the list of projects ranked by their benefit–cost ratios until all the capital is utilized, but now this process has to be undertaken *twice* – once excluding Project A from the list and then again, but now excluding Project E from the list:

Project	Benefit–cost rank	Outlay	
E	1	50	⎫
D	2	100	⎬ Accept E, D, B:
B	3	150	⎭ Total NPV = £210.84
C	4	60	

Project	Benefit–cost rank	Outlay	
D	1	100	⎫
A	2	100	⎬ Accept D, A, ⅔B:
B	3	150	⎭ Total NPV = £168.84
C	4	60	

Preferred combination: Projects E, D and B.

Single-period rationing and the IRR

Before leaving the single-period rationing case, it is worth noting that the IRR investment appraisal technique cannot cope adequately with this situation. Ranking projects in terms of their IRRs is *not* the same as ranking via benefit–cost ratios. The reason why the IRR technique fails to adapt to capital rationing is because of the fact that the IRR is simply an absolute percentage rate of return, whereas what is required is a measure of project performance *relative* to the rationed investment outlay. Hence this is just one more example of the limitations of the IRR technique.

Multi-period capital rationing

Introduction

The problem of investment decision making in the face of capital rationing which extends over more than one period is both complex and, at present, not completely resolved. The complexity of the problem has not been helped by general confusion and differences in the literature over what precisely is meant by capital rationing and by the range of differing assumptions that have been made, both explicitly and implicitly. The main source of confusion over capital rationing, as far as the theory of corporate investment decision making is concerned, has occurred through a failure to isolate the problem from general capital market theory. As a result, a number of paradoxical problems have arisen.

In attempting to outline a normative theory of investment decision making, we shall try to be both as practical and realistic as possible. In doing so, we will assume that hard (or external) capital rationing, both for individuals and companies, is likely to be only a relatively short-run phenomenon which may well arise, in practice, out of poor forward planning.[3] It is certainly true to say that unlimited amounts of investment capital are not immediately available to companies, because capital-raising operations can take some time to arrange. Thus there can be a definite limit to capital supplies in the very short run. However, as long as a company plans its future operations carefully and well ahead of time, and its management appears competent, it is unlikely that it will be unable to raise the capital it requires for any planned project which is expected to be 'profitable', i.e. it is unlikely that it will run into any serious, externally imposed capital rationing. We are not assuming that hard capital rationing never occurs but that, in the majority of cases, for most of the time, it is an unlikely phenomenon.

Soft capital rationing

If we make the assumption that externally imposed constraints on the supply of capital to a company are unlikely to be anything but relatively short-term phenomena, we are left with the task of examining the effects of internally imposed or soft capital rationing on the investment decision-making process. We can define soft capital rationing as a capital expenditure constraint which is imposed on a company by its own internal management, rather than by external capital markets, and which limits the amount of capital investment funds available in any particular time period.

This capital limit will normally be imposed by a capital expenditure budget, of which, in a well-managed company, there are likely to be two: a short-term capital budget for the immediate twelve months ahead and a medium-term capital budget which covers the next three to five years ahead.[4] Both budgets are likely to impose relatively inflexible capital constraints upon management.

When looking at how the NPV appraisal method could be adapted to deal with the single-period rationing problem, we saw that when the capital constraint was binding (i.e. there was insufficient capital available to invest in all projects with positive NPVs), companies would have to forgo undertaking some projects which they would have otherwise undertaken. Such a situation is understandable when imposed from outside the company, but it seems ludicrous when imposed from within the company. Why should a company wish to constrain itself in this way?

The reason is that companies require to plan for the future and to monitor, control and evaluate the implementation of these plans, so that future planning and control can be further improved upon. A capital budget is just one part of these plans and of the controlling process. It requires the imposition of a ceiling on capital expenditure, because capital investment is not a simple operation but one which takes time and a range of resources.

For example, the decision to invest in a particular project does not consist simply of the evaluation and appraisal process. Capital may have to be raised for the project (an operation which cannot be carried out instantaneously), the company must have the trained manpower available to implement the project and monitor its performance (again, not an instantaneous process), and even the evaluation and decision procedure itself is likely to have its own manpower and resource constraints, as is the whole of the company's organizational structure. Thus, in order to plan carefully and to control efficiently, limits may quite properly have to be imposed – in the short and medium terms – on the level of capital investment expenditure that a company allows itself to undertake.[5]

The existence of capital budgets within companies is likely to mean that management is faced with the problem of decision making in a situation of multi-period capital rationing (i.e. where capital rationing extends over a number of future periods). In such circumstances, the simple benefit–cost ratio technique cannot be used to place investment opportunities in an order of preference. This is because, in the single-period rationing case, the problem was to allocate investment capital amongst competing projects in the face of a *single* constraint, in order to maximize the total amount of positive NPV gained. In the multi-period case, this allocation procedure has to be carried out simultaneously under more than one constraint, as each period's rationing forms a separate constraint. To assist in this simultaneous allocation problem, we employ the mathematical programming optimizing technique of linear programming (LP). It is assumed that the reader is familiar with the basic mechanics of this technique, which can be found in most introductory books on operational research methods. However, a brief outline of the technique is provided in an appendix to this chapter.

The opportunity cost of capital dilemma

The presence of multi-period capital rationing does not alter the objective of financial management decision making: the maximization of shareholder wealth. This, we know, can be achieved through making investment decisions so as to maximize the total amount of positive NPV generated. The NPV figure gains its significance from the fact that it represents the result of netting out project cash flows and comparing this net cash flow with the opportunity cost, which is embodied in the perfect capital market discount rate.

In examining how investment resources can be allocated to projects in a situation of multi-period capital rationing, we will assume that the *suppliers* of capital to a company do not themselves impose any form of capital rationing. It is self-imposed, rather than market-imposed capital rationing. This assumption releases the analysis from one of the major difficulties of the multi-period rationing problem: the choice of discount rate.

We know that the discount rate used in the NPV calculation represents the opportunity cost of cash which, in a perfect capital market, is reflected in the market rate of interest. Once a perfect capital market no longer exists, then the market interest rate no longer necessarily reflects the opportunity cost of capital. In such circumstances, as we saw when looking at the single-period rationing problem, the opportunity cost of investment capital is represented by the return gained from the marginal project in the rationed period. Therefore, in a multi-period rationing situation, the appropriate discount rate for any period is given by the return on the marginal project in that particular period. This is the dilemma.

The company needs to know the opportunity cost of cash in each period to use as the discount rate, in order to make the correct selection. Each period's opportunity cost of cash is represented by the return on the marginal project in that particular period, but this marginal project can only be identified *after* the correct project selection has been made. In other words, in order to make the correct investment project selection, the opportunity cost of capital in each rationed period needs to be known, but this can only be known once the correct selection of projects has been made. Thus, we are firmly on the horns of a dilemma, unless we assume that the company faces a perfect capital market and it is the company alone which imposes capital rationing. In such circumstances, the market interest rate still represents the opportunity cost of capital to shareholders and so can be used as the discount rate to aid project selection. Hence the need to assume soft capital rationing.

The LP solution to capital rationing

Example 3 illustrates how, in multi-period capital rationing, linear programming can help to allocate scarce investment capital to projects so as to maximize the total amount of positive NPV.

Example 3

A company has found the following independent investment opportunities (all figures in £000s):

Project	Year 0	1	2	3	4	5
A	− 100	− 50	− 25	+ 100	+ 100	+ 100
B	− 50	− 70	+ 100	+ 100		
C		− 100	− 30	+ 150	+ 200	
D	− 10	− 20	+ 50	− 100	+ 100	+ 100
E	− 100	− 100	+ 200	+ 100	+ 50	
F			− 200	+ 300	+ 100	+ 100

We shall assume that none of these projects can have the timing of its cash flow brought forward or delayed, and none can be undertaken more than once. Furthermore, we shall again assume that all projects exhibit constant returns to scale. Finally, the perfect capital market rate of interest is 10% and this rate is expected to remain constant over the next five years, and can be assumed to reflect the capital suppliers' opportunity cost.

Calculating the NPVs of the projects, using a 10% discount rate, we can see that the company would normally undertake them all, because each has a positive NPV:

Project	NPV (£)
A	+ 39.4
B	+ 44.1
C	+ 133.6
D	+ 68.4
E	+ 83.6
F	+ 190.5

In order to do so, however, the company would require the expenditure of £260 000, £340 000, £255 000 and £100 000 of investment capital in the next four time periods (Years 0–3) respectively.

Suppose that the company has an internally imposed capital constraint, such that external finance raised in any one period must not exceed £150 000. In addition, internally generated finance (from projects) cannot be used to increase the amount of capital expenditure. Clearly, in these circumstances the company cannot undertake all six projects, and so which should be selected to be undertaken and which should be rejected?

There are several ways in which this problem could be formulated into a linear programme, but each alternative formulation would produce a solution giving exactly the same selection of investment projects to undertake. One approach, which fits directly into our NPV approach, is to take as the LP's objective function the maximization of the total amount of NPV which the company can generate over the next five years, given the imposed constraints. Thus, taking a, b, c ... f to represent the proportion of Projects A, B, C ... F undertaken:

Objective function:

$$39.4a + 44.1b + 133.6c + 68.4d + 83.6e + 190.5f \text{ Max.}$$

Constraints:

$$100a + 50b + 10d + 100e \leq 150 \text{ (Year 0)}$$
$$50a + 70b + 100c + 20d + 100e \leq 150 \text{ (Year 1)}$$
$$25a + 30c + 200f \leq 150 \text{ (Year 2)}$$
$$100d \leq 150 \text{ (Year 3)}$$
$$a, b, c, d, e, f \leq 1$$
$$a, b, c, d, e, f \leq 0$$

Solving this linear programme on a computer gave the following selection of projects: the whole of both Projects C and D should be undertaken, together with 0.3 of Project E and 0.6 of Project F; Projects A and B should not undertaken.[6] This selection results in a total NPV of +£341 400 being generated, which is the maximum possible total sum, given the circumstances specified.[7]

The assumptions behind LP

In using linear programming to solve this type of capital rationing problem, a number of assumptions and limitations are involved, one of which we have already touched upon: the specification of the rate of discount to be used. In addition, the technique assumes that all the relationships expressed in the model are linear (for example, all the projects are assumed to exhibit constant returns to scale) and that the variables are infinitely divisible. There is also an assumption that the project cash flows are known with certainty because, as yet, no way has been found of satisfactorily adjusting the technique to take account of risk.

The first of these three assumptions does not necessarily cause too much trouble because, where non-linear relationships are involved, they can often be adequately described in the LP formulation as a number of linear approximations. Similarly, the second assumption also may not be too troublesome, especially if the LP is being applied to the solution of the capital rationing problem within a company operating in a process industry (e.g. oil or chemicals), because the output is (approximately) infinitely divisible. (Integer programming – another type of allocation technique – avoids this assumption, but in doing so involves a number of new, and often more difficult, problems.) However, what really is a serious practical drawback to the use of LP in capital rationing situations, is the inability of the technique to handle uncertainty. There have been some attempts to allow for uncertainty,[8] but by and large they represent mathematical solutions to mathematical, rather than practical, problems.

The dual values

In Example 3, where the objective was to maximize the total amount of positive NPV generated, the solution involved the company undertaking the whole of Projects C and D, together with 30% of Project E and 60% of Project F. The reader will be able to confirm from the project cash flow information that this solution results in the utilization of only £40 000 of the £150 000 available for investment in Year 0, and of only £100 000 of the £150 000 available in Year 3. Therefore, although the company's capital expenditure is constrained in these two periods, the constraints are 'nonbinding', i.e. they do not bind or constrain the company in its efforts to achieve its objective. For this reason, there is no *additional* opportunity cost of the cash used for capital expenditure in these two periods (i.e. there is no opportunity cost incurred in addition to that opportunity cost already allowed for in the discounting process used to convert the project cash flows to NPVs), because the company does not forgo any of its investment project opportunities as a result of these two constraints.

The situation is different in respect of the Year 1 and Year 2 capital expenditure constraints. In these periods, the linear programme's project selection results in the £150 000 available (in both Years 1 and 2) being *fully* utilized and therefore the constraints are said to be *binding*: their existence limits the company's freedom of action in pursuit of its objective of NPV maximization because it limits the amount of investment the company can undertake. As a result, there is an additional opportunity cost attached to the use of investment cash in each of these two periods.

These additional opportunity costs are represented by the 'dual' values produced by the linear programme. In the example used above, the LP solution produced the following dual values for the four capital expenditure constraints:

Year	Dual value (£)
0	0
1	0.837
2	0.952
3	0

The dual values which are produced from LP with a maximizing objective function represent the increase (decrease) in the total value of the objective function that would arise if a binding constraint were marginally – i.e. by one unit – slackened (tightened). Thus, in the example, the investment capital constraints result in the company achieving a total NPV value (i.e. the objective function's value) of £341 400. If £150 001 were available for investment in Year 1 (keeping the £150 000 limit in force in each of the three other periods), then the value of the objective function would rise by £0.837 to £341 400.837.

In this very simple example this increase in the objective function would be achieved by increasing the level of investment in Project E (the marginal project in Year 1) from 30% of E to 30.001%.[9] Also, because the use of LP assumes linear relationships, a *reduction* in the amount of capital available in Year 1 to £149 999 would result in the value of the objective function *falling* by £0.837.

A similar analysis can be made in terms of the Year 2 capital constraint dual value of £0.952 which is caused by a 0.0005% change in the level of investment in Project F. Because the capital constraints in Years 0 and 3 are non-binding their dual values are both zero: a marginal change in either constraint will leave both the original project selection and the value of the objective function unaltered.

There are a number of points to be made here. The first is that the example used is a highly simplified one and the practical application of the use of LP to solve capital rationing problems is far more complex and problematical. We have only outlined the approach and specified the main theoretical difficulties. Second, if we accept that Projects E and F are the marginal projects in Years 1 and 2 respectively (i.e. investment levels in these two projects change in response to marginal changes in available investment capital in these two years), it is important to realize that the relative IRRs of these two projects do *not* produce their dual values, because the IRR represents a project's *average* return over the *whole* of its life, whilst the dual value refers to a project's *marginal* return in *just* the period specified.

A third point of importance is that dual values apply only to incremental/marginal changes in binding constraint values. To identify the effect of any non-marginal change – i.e. a substantial change – the LP has to be reformulated accordingly and re-solved. Finally, dual values apply only to individual marginal changes in binding constraints, i.e. they operate under a *ceteris paribus* assumption that all other variables in the formulation remain unchanged. Thus, in the example used, if an extra £1 of investment capital is available in both Years 1 *and* 2, the resulting change in the value of the objective function is not necessarily the sum of the two individual dual values. Therefore we can see that dual values can be informative in that they represent part of the opportunity cost of investment capital, but their usefulness is relatively limited because of their marginal nature.

A more complex example

Example 4 deals with a more complex multi-period capital rationing problem.

Example 4

Butyrin Ltd is the subsidiary of a large holding company. It is formulating capital investment plans. The company has identified the following independent projects (all figures in £000s):

		Year		
Project	0	1	2	3
A	– 100	– 50	– 60	+ 300
B	– 80	+ 40	+ 50	
C	– 200	– 100	+ 400	

The company judges that 10% is the correct discount rate to use, which produces the following NPVs:

Project	NPV
A	+ 30.35
B	– 2.36
C	+ 39.65

However, the company finds itself in a capital rationing situation imposed by its parent and there is only £170 000 available at Year 0 and £65 000 available at Year 1.

In addition, the following facts are relevant:
1. Projects A and C each use a particular type of raw material which is in short supply. Project A requires 32 tonnes and Project C requires 17 tonnes. Butyrin can only purchase 25 tonnes in total.
2. Any surplus funds the company has can be placed on deposit from Year 0 to Year 1 at 8% interest. However, all surplus funds available at the end of any subsequent year must be returned to the parent company.
3. Butyrin's bank has indicated that it is willing to give a two-year term loan of any amount up to £120 000. Interest would be payable at each year end at 15%, and the loan would have to be repaid at Year 2.
4. The parent company will allow Butyrin to reinvest any project-generated cash flows.

Before this problem can be formulated into an LP, points 2 and 3 above have first to be dealt with. Placing money on deposit can be viewed as a mini-project and so, like Projects A, B and C, we need to calculate its NPV:

NPV of £1 placed on deposit

	Year	
	0	1
Cash flow	− 1	+ 1.08
10% discount factor	× 1	× 0.9091
	− 1	+ 0.98 = − 0.02 NPV

Similarly with the bank loan:

NPV of £1 bank loan

	Year		
	0	1	2
Cash flow	+ 1	+ 0.15	− 1.15
10% discount factor	× 1	× 0.9091	× 0.8264
	+ 1	+ 0.14	− 0.95 = − 0.09 NPV

We are now ready to formulate the LP:

Let *a* equal the *proportion* of Project A undertaken.
Let *b* equal the *proportion* of Project B undertaken.
Let *c* equal the *proportion* of Project C undertaken.
Let *d* equal the *amount* of cash placed on deposit: Yr 0 to Yr 1.
Let *L* equal the *amount* of cash borrowed: Yr 0 to Yr 2.

The *objective function* is:

$$30.35a - 2.36b + 39.65c - 0.02d - 0.09L \quad \text{Max.}$$

Notice that the negative, as well as the positive NPV variables are included. It should be left to the LP to decide the investment plan and, as we saw with single-period capital rationing, negative NPV projects can sometimes be acceptable.

The set of *capital expenditure constraints* are:

$$
\begin{aligned}
100a + 80b + 200c + d &\le 170 + L \\
50a + 100c + 0.15L &\le 65 + 40b + 1.08d \\
L &\le 120 \\
a, b, c &\le 1
\end{aligned}
$$

Notice that *only* the cash flows in the rationed time periods need be specified in the LP. Hence the LP doesn't need to know explicitly about the loan repayment because it occurs in Year 2 when there is not expected to be any capital expenditure constraint. The LP implicitly is aware of the *overall* effect of the loan because it knows what its NPV is.

Finally, there is the raw material constraint and the non-negativity conditions:

$$
\begin{aligned}
32a + 17c &\le 25 \\
a, b, c, d, L &\ge 0
\end{aligned}
$$

With the raw material constraint, there is no need to enquire when the constraint will occur. Time is only important in the LP as far as money flows are concerned because of the differing capital expenditure constraints. Also, notice that the non-negativity conditions not only prevent negative projects, but they also prevent a negative deposit account and bank loan.

Therefore, the complete LP formulation, ready for solution via a computer package, is:

$$
\begin{aligned}
30.35a - 2.36b + 39.65c - 0.02d - 0.09L & \quad \text{Max.} \\
100a + 80b + 200c + d &\le 170 + L \\
50a + 100c + 0.15L &\le 65 + 40b + 1.08d \\
L &\le 120 \\
a, b, c &\le 1 \\
32a + 17c &\le 25 \\
a, b, c, d, L &\ge 0
\end{aligned}
$$

Two applications of dual values

Two Examples, 5 and 6, of possible applications of dual values will serve to indicate their usefulness and will also help to demonstrate the different procedures required. The first example concerns the evaluation of an additional investment, and the second shows how to determine the value of additional sources of cash.

In order to do so, use will be made of our original multi-period example in this section, involving six independent projects (A to F), where the LP's solution to the multi-period capital rationing problem was:

Investment plan:	Project A: reject
	Project B: reject
	Project C: undertake 100%
	Project D: undertake 100%
	Project E: undertake 30%
	Project F: undertake 60%
Dual values:	Cash at Year 0: 0
	Cash at Year 1: £0.837
	Cash at Year 2: £0.952
	Cash at Year 3: 0

Example 5

Suppose that, before the investment plan can be undertaken, a new project is identified: Project W. This project involves the following cash flows (all figures in £000s):

Year	Cash flow
0	−100
1	+ 20
2	+ 90

The dual values can be used to indicate either that the project is *not* worth considering or that it *is* worth considering and so the LP should be reformulated to include Project W's cash flows, and then re-solved.

If the original LP formulation dual values are to be used, the project's NPV has first to be determined and then the opportunity cost of its cash flows. If the *net* effect is positive, the project is worth considering and the LP should be reformulated and re-solved. If the net effect is negative, the project can be discarded without further analysis. The calculations are as follows:

Year	Cash flow		10% discount rate		PV cash flows
0	− 100	×	1	=	− 100
1	+ 20	×	0.9091	=	+ 18.18
2	+ 90	×	0.8264	=	+ 74.38
			NPV	=	£ − 7.44

Year	Cash flow		Dual value		Opp. cost cash flows
0	− 100	×	0	=	0
1	+ 20	×	0.837	=	+ 16.74
2	+ 90	×	0.952	=	+ 85.68
			Opportunity cost		+102.42

Net effect of project: NPV + opportunity cost = − £7.44 + £102.42 = + £94.98.

As the overall net effect of the project is positive, this indicates that the project is worthwhile considering further and the LP should be reformulated (now including Project W's cash flows) and re-solved. This analysis is in fact very similar to the analysis made in Chapter 7 when looking at relevant cash flows. There we saw that the cost of utilizing a scarce resource was equal to its *total* opportunity cost: the internal opportunity cost, plus the external opportunity cost (the market price of the resource).

That is exactly the approach used to evaluate Project W. The NPV analysis evaluates the project's use of cash in terms of the market 'price' of cash (the discount rate); and then the subsequent analysis evaluates the project in terms of its impact on the firm's capital rationing problem – the internal opportunity cost.

On this basis, therefore, Project W could have been evaluated directly on the total opportunity costs involved:

	10% discount rate	+	Dual value of cash	=	Total opportunity cost of cash
Year 0	1	+	0	=	1
Year 1	0.9091	+	0.837	=	1.7461
Year 2	0.8264	+	0.952	=	1.7784
Year 3	0.7513	+	0	=	0.7513

Project W

Year	Cash flow		Opportunity cost		
0	– 100	×	1	=	– 100
1	+ 20	×	1.7461	=	+ 34.92
2	+ 90	×	1.7784	=	+ 160.06
					+ 94.98

Thus, if Project W is accepted, it should enable the total NPV generated by the projects under consideration to be increased.

Example 6

Now suppose that the company, having formulated its production plan from the original six available projects, is then offered an opportunity to borrow additional cash at Year 2 as long as it is repaid (with interest) at Year 3. What is the maximum interest rate that the company would be willing to pay to take out such a loan?

The maximum interest rate represents the point of indifference or *equality* between what would be *gained* (in terms of the objective function) by borrowing (say) £1 at Year 2 and what would be *lost* from the resulting repayment of capital plus interest at Year 3. Using the *total* opportunity cost figures calculated in Example 5 makes for a simple solution to the problem:

$$£1 \times \text{opportunity cost of cash at Year 2} = £1(1 + i) \times \text{opportunity cost of cash at Year 3}$$

$$£1 \times 1.7784 = £1(1 + i) \times 0.7513$$
$$1.7784 = 0.7513 + 0.7513i$$

$$\frac{1.7784 - 0.7513}{0.7513} = i = 1.367 \text{ or } 136.7\%$$

This very high rate of interest should not come as a surprise. The firm should be willing to pay such a rate of interest (at a maximum) for the sake of gaining extra cash in a time period when cash is constrained, and repaying in a time period when it is unconstrained.

Lend–borrow interest differentials

Introduction

Up to this point in the chapter, we have been examining the investment decision in the face of one particular capital market imperfection, that of soft capital rationing. Let us now turn to examine another common imperfection: the existence of a gap between the borrowing and the lending interest rate, caused by the presence of market transaction costs, where the borrowing rate is somewhat higher than the lending rate. Perhaps the best way to lay bare the problem here is to make use of the single-period investment–consumption diagram.

Identification of the opportunity cost

In the basic model we saw that, because of the so-called 'separation theorem', it made little difference to the appraisal of physical investment opportunities whether a company had one or several owners and, if it had several owners, whether their indifference curve sets were similar or dissimilar; in fact the company did not even require knowledge of its owners' indifference curve sets.

In the face of a perfect capital market, a company would invest in physical investment opportunities until the return from the marginal project equated with the market rate of interest (i.e. it would invest in all projects which had positive or zero NPVs). This investment decision rule determined the dividend flow pattern which the individual shareholder could adjust, if he wished, by using the capital market. The company used the market interest rate as the investment appraisal discount rate because it reflected the opportunity cost of cash to the shareholders.

Let us now start with the simple case of a single-owner company and a perfect capital market, except that transaction costs result in the borrowing interest rate being higher than the lending interest rate. In such a case the separation theorem (i.e. separation between management investment decisions and shareholder consumption decisions) breaks down, as there is no longer a single opportunity cost of cash because there are now two market interest rates.

Fig. 8.2 illustrates this situation with the steeper of the two financial investment lines (BC) representing the borrowing rate and the other (DF) representing the lending rate. In these circumstances the shareholder's indifference curve may be tangential at any point along the non-linear boundary BCDF. We can specify three separate cases:

1. If a point of tangency occurs on the BC segment then, at time t_0, the company should undertake physical investments up to point C, and then the shareholder should add to his received dividend by borrowing on the capital market. For the company to locate itself correctly at point C on the physical investment line, the market *borrowing* rate should be used as the NPV discount rate because it would represent the opportunity cost of cash. The borrowing rate reflects the opportunity cost in these circumstances because the shape and location of the shareholder's indifference curve set is such that preference

emphasis is placed on consumption at time t_0. Thus, if cash is to be invested rather than consumed at time t_0, the investment should earn a return at least equal to the borrowing rate, because the shareholder will be borrowing to replace (at least in part) the investment outlay undertaken.

2. If a point of tangency occurs along segment DF, then the company should locate itself at point D on the physical investment line and the shareholder should then lend out some part of his received dividend on the capital market. In this case, the company can ensure optimally locating at point D by undertaking all physical investments which produce positive or zero NPVs when discounted at the market *lending* rate. This rate represents the shareholder's opportunity cost of cash for reasons analogous to those cited in the previous case, except that his indifference curve set is now shaped so as to bias preference towards consumption at time t_1. Thus the company should undertake physical investments as long as they earn a return which is at least equal to that which the shareholder could earn by lending on the capital market.

3. If the point of tangency between the shareholder's indifference curve set and the boundary curve BCDF occurs along the segment CD, then this also represents the optimal point of location for the company on its physical investment line. In such circumstances, the opportunity cost of cash is represented by the slope of the shareholder's indifference curve at the point of tangency (his *personal* time value of money) and it is also represented by the return on the marginal investment at the point of tangency on the physical investment line. Therefore, this is the rate of discount which the company should use in its investment appraisal, to ensure that it locates itself at the optimal point on the physical investment line.

In practical terms, the company's management is unlikely to be aware of the location of its shareholder's indifference curve set in relation to the boundary BCDF and so will not know whether to use the borrowing rate (case 1),

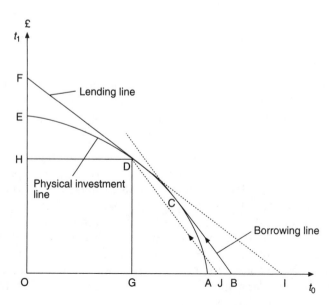

Fig. 8.2 *Lending and borrowing*

the lending rate (case 2) or some intermediate rate between the borrowing and lending rates (case 3) as the investment appraisal discount rate. However, even if the company were aware of its single shareholder's indifference map and so could optimally locate on the physical investment line, in the more realistic case where there are several shareholders, their indifference curve sets are unlikely to be the same, which may well lead to a direct conflict over the value at which the discount rate should be set in order to reflect the opportunity cost of cash.

Quite simply, then, the real-world solution to the problem is indeterminate, and all that a company can hope to do is to use a single discount rate both consistently and publicly, so that it attracts shareholders whose opportunity cost of cash approximates to this rate.

Three further points

There are three further points worth noticing in this analysis. First, suppose that the company is aware of the indifference curve set of shareholders and, as a result, uses the lending rate for discounting and so locates at point D in Fig. 8.2. The total net *present* value of the company's investments (given by AI) does not have any real meaning in the sense that the dividend flow produced of OG at t_0 and OH at t_1 cannot be converted by the shareholder into a cash flow of zero at t_1 and OI at t_0. Such a dividend flow can only have a present value of OJ.

This presents an interesting problem in terms of management's objective function, which we have stated as the maximization of the stock market's current valuation of the company. To do this – and assuming the stock market valuation is based on the present value summation of the future dividend flow – it could be argued that the company should use the borrowing rate as the discount rate, because this is the only meaningful way a 'present value' could be stated, but then in this example, maximization of the market value of the company's equity capital would not bring maximum benefit to the shareholders, in terms of assisting them to obtain the highest possible indifference curve.

A second point is that, if the company selects a discount rate between the market borrowing and lending rates (inclusively) and it makes an *incorrect* selection, the smaller the gap between the borrowing and lending rate, the less serious (in terms of lost utility) will be the mistake.

Finally, it is interesting to speculate upon the situation of a company which was either totally ignorant of its shareholders' indifference curve sets or which had shareholders with widely different indifference maps. In these circumstances, and still using a one-period analysis, the most conservative action for the company to take would be to use the borrowing rate for discounting when evaluating projects.

If that is the correct rate (i.e. case 1) then there is no problem. If either the lending rate or some intermediate rate is correct, then, although shareholders will not maximize their utility, the utility level achieved will *always* be higher than if the company did not undertake any investment at all. If either the lending rate or an intermediate rate is chosen to evaluate investment possibilities and this chosen rate proves to be incorrect, then shareholders *may* find themselves at a *lower* utility level than if the company had undertaken no investment at all, but instead had liquidated itself at time t_0.[10] Taking immediate corporate liquidation as the ultimate alternative, investing in projects with positive NPVs when discounted at the borrowing rate will always raise the shareholders' utility level. The use of a discount rate above the borrowing rate *may* reduce the utility level to below that achieved through immediate liquidation.

In conclusion

We have seen that the presence of different lending and borrowing interest rates can cause an insurmountable difficulty to investment appraisal (or at least to the theory). However, if we can conclude that in the real world the difference between lending and borrowing rates is likely to be relatively small, then the problem does not disappear, but it does take on considerably less significance. In such circumstances the detrimental effect on the owners' wealth and utility is likely to be fairly small. We shall touch upon this problem once again at a later stage.

Summary

Principally, this chapter has covered the capital rationing problem; but, in addition, another capital market imperfection, that of differential interest rates for lending and borrowing, has also been examined. The main points made are as follows:

- Capital rationing refers to a situation where a company cannot undertake all positive NPV projects it has identified, because of a shortage of capital.

- Two different types of capital rationing situation can be identified, distinguished by the source of the capital expenditure constraint. Hard capital rationing occurs when the constraint is externally imposed on the firm by the capital market. Soft capital rationing occurs when the constraint is internally imposed on the firm, by its own management.

- In a situation of capital rationing the standard NPV decision rule for independent projects no longer holds and so has to be modified.

- In the single-period capital rationing situation, the NPV decision rule is replaced with a benefit–cost ratio analysis which evaluates the project's NPV relative to the required outlay in the rationed time period.

- In multi-period capital rationing, the optimal investment solution can only be obtained through solving the individual capital rationing constraints simultaneously via linear programming.

- The solution to a multi-period capital rationing LP not only provides advice on the capital investment decision (the LP's primal solution), but it also provides a dual solution. The dual solution indicates the (internal) opportunity cost of the scarce resources which, in this type of situation, is principally cash.

- The usefulness of the dual values is limited because of their marginal nature. However, they can be used to help evaluate some decisions that arise after the capital rationing LP has been solved.

- Finally the problem of differential lending and borrowing rates of interest was examined. It was concluded that, in such circumstances, the optimal investment decision is indeterminate because of lack of knowledge as to which market interest rate (lend or borrow) should be used to evaluate projects. However, it was judged that, in the real world, the sub-optimal decisions that might arise as a result would be likely to have only a small impact on shareholder wealth.

Appendix: linear programming

A company has identified two independent projects with the following cash flows:

Project	Year 0	Year 1	Year 2
A	−100	−50	+200
B	− 80	−60	+170

Assuming a discount rate of 10% correctly reflects the return available elsewhere on the capital market, their NPVs are approximately:

Project	NPV
A	+20
B	+ 6

However, to undertake both projects requires an outlay of £180 at Year 0 and 110 at Year 1. The company has imposed a capital expenditure constraint of £65 at Year 0 and £90 at Year 1. This problem can be formed into a linear programme (LP) in order to solve the investment decision, where a equals the proportion of Project A undertaken and b equals the proportion of Project B undertaken.

a and b can take on values between 0 (where *none* of the project would be undertaken), and 1 (where the whole of the project would be undertaken). Thus if the solution turns out to be $a = 0.25$ and $b = 0.80$, it means 25% of Project A should be undertaken and 80% of Project B.

Every LP consists of just *three* elements: an objective function, a set of constraints and a set of non-negativity conditions. Here, the objective is to make an investment decision (that is select values for a and b) in order to maximize the total NPV generated. Therefore, the objective function will be:

$$20a + 6b \quad \text{Max.}$$

where $20a$ is the amount of positive NPV generated from the investment in A (i.e. if $a = 0.40$, then $20a$ equals: $20 \times 0.40 = 8$; undertaking 40% of Project A produces a positive NPV of 8), and similarly with $6b$.

There are two constraints on the investment decision: the fact that capital is limited in Year 0 and in Year 1. The formulation of the Year 0 capital expenditure constraint would be:

$$100a + 80b \leq 65$$

where 100*a* is the capital invested in Project A at Year 0 (i.e. if *a* = 0.40, then 100*a* equals: 100 × 0.40 = 40; undertaking 40% of Project A will require a Year 0 outlay of 40), and similarly for Project B. Thus this constraint simply indicates that the amount of cash spent on undertaking Project A at Year 0 (100*a*), plus the cash spent on undertaking B at Year 0 (80*b*) must not exceed (≤) the £65 of investment finance available at Year 0.

The Year 1 capital expenditure constraint is similarly:

$$50a + 60b \leq 90.$$

In addition, to prevent the LP from suggesting that any project should be undertaken more than once, the values that can be placed on *a* and *b* are limited to a maximum of 1 (i.e. 100%). Therefore:

$$a, b \leq 1.$$

The non-negativity condition is simply there to prevent nonsensical negative values being assigned to *a* and *b*:

$$a, b \geq 0.$$

Thus the complete LP formulation is:

$20a + 6b$		Max.
$100a + 80b$	≤	65
$50a + 60b$	≤	90
a, b	≤	1
a, b	≥	0

There are many computer packages available which will solve this LP. What is being solved is the values of *a* and *b* in a pair of simultaneous equations (the two constraints), so as to maximize the total NPV generated. The solution to this particular, very simple, problem is

$$a = 0.65$$
$$b = 0$$

In other words, 65% of Project A should be undertaken and Project B should be rejected. This produces a total NPV of 13, the maximum possible amount, given the constraints.

Notes

1. This return would be the project's IRR. For simplicity, we are abstracting from the problems which may arise in calculating or using an IRR.

2. If not, any book on management accounting will outline the basic principles. For example, see J.C. Drury, *Management and Cost Accounting*, Chapman & Hall, 1992.

3. We will shortly discuss the reason for making this assumption.

4. In addition, there may be a very much longer-term capital budget which might stretch as far as 20–25 years ahead, depending upon the company and the industry in which it operates and upon the gestation period of its major capital investment projects.

5. It could be argued that even this internally imposed capital rationing is, in reality, produced by external – but not exclusively financial – market inefficiencies, in that there is a time-lag between demand signals and the subsequent supply.

6. The primal solution reads: $a = 0, b = 0, c = 1, d = 1, e = 0.3, f = 0.6$.

7. If it *were* possible to relieve the capital expenditure constraint through the use of internally generated funds (from projects), then the LP formulation would have to be revised and a different solution would result:

$$39.4a + 44.1b + 133.6c + 68.4d + 83.6e + 190.5f \text{ Max.}$$
$$100a + 50b + 10d + 100e \leq 150$$
$$50a + 70b + 100c + 20d + 100e \leq 150$$
$$25a + 30c + 200f \leq 150 + 100b + 50d + 200e$$
$$100d \leq 150 + 100a + 100b + 150c + 100e + 300f$$
$$a, b, c, d, e, f \leq 1$$
$$a, b, c, d, e, f \geq 0$$

8. By including 'chance' constraints into the LP formulation, whereby some level of cash flow must be provided by the solution, with a given level of probability.

9. Project E produces a total NPV of + £83 700, and 0.001% of this amount is £0.837, the dual value for Year 1. This information on how the dual value arises is supplied by the computer solution to the problem. In a more complex example the source of the dual value is likely to involve more than merely an adjustment to the level of investment in a single project.

10. We are assuming here that liquidation can be achieved without incurring costs.

Further reading

1. For a good starting point on the literature of capital rationing, see J.H. Lorie, L.J. Savage, 'Three Problems in Rationing Capital', *Journal of Business*, October 1955, and H.R. Fogler, 'Ranking Techniques and Capital Budgeting', *Accounting Review*, January 1972.
2. For an approach equating with the Hirshleifer analysis, see F.D. Arditti, R.C. Grinold, H. Levy, 'The Investment–Consumption Decision under Capital Rationing', *Review of Economic Studies*, July 1973.
3. For application of LP to multi-period capital rationing, see two articles by K.N. Bhaskar, 'Linear Programming and Capital Budgeting: a Reappraisal', *Journal of Business Finance and Accounting*, Autumn 1976, and 'Linear Programming in Capital Budgeting: the Financing Problem', *Journal of Business Finance and Accounting*, Spring 1983.
4. Perhaps the most thoughtful article of all on the subject is H.M. Weingartner, 'Capital Rationing: n Authors in Search of a Plot', *Journal of Finance*, December 1977; whilst also of interest is G.W. Trivol and W.R. McDaniel, 'Uncertainty, Capital Immobility and Capital Rationing in Investment Decision', *Journal of Business Finance and Accounting*, Summer 1987.

Quickie questions

1. What are the two types or classes of capital rationing?
2. Why does capital rationing cause problems for the NPV decision rule?
3. Given these projects:

	t_0	t_1	....	NPV
A	-100	-50	....	$+60$
B	-200	-200	....	$+90$
C	-40	-150	....	$+20$
D	-100	$+20$	....	-10

If only 200 is available at t_0, which projects should be selected?

4. Given the projects in question 3, if only 240 external capital was available at t_1 (no capital rationing at t_0), which projects should be selected?

5. Given these projects:

	t_0	....	NPV
A	-100	....	$+40$
B	-100	....	$+30$
C	-200	....	$+50$
D	-100	....	$+10$
E	-50	....	$+4$

Only 300 is available at t_0 and Projects B and C are mutually exclusive. Which projects should the firm accept?

6. Given the projects:

	t_0	t_1	t_2	....	NPV
A	-100	-200	$+50$	....	$+40$
B	-150	$+70$	$+70$	....	$+20$
C	-200	-120	-30	....	$+50$

External capital is limited to 190 at t_0, 110 at t_1 and zero at t_2. Formulate the problem into an LP.

7. A capital rationing LP produces the following dual values for cash:

t_0	1.86
t_1	0.73
t_2	0.64
t_3	1.21

A bank loan is available at t_1, repayable at t_2. What is the maximum rate of interest you would be willing to pay, given the firm uses a 10% discount rate for project appraisal?

8. Given the dual values in question 7, the firm now discovers an additional project:

Year	Cash flow
0	-100
1	$+40$
2	$+90$

What action should be taken?

Problems

1. Sporangium plc is a large bakery company with other interests including ice-cream manufacture and specialized catering. For investment appraisal purposes, it uses a 15% rate of discount.

The management are considering the company's capital investment plans for the coming year. One project under consideration is the purchase of a fleet of delivery vans. Two alternative proposals have been put forward. One is to purchase a fleet of petrol-powered vans; the other is to purchase electrically-powered vans.

Investment in the petrol-powered fleet would yield an internal rate of return (IRR) of 25% whilst the electrically-powered fleet would only yield a return of 20%. However, when the two alternatives are evaluated using net present value (NPV), the electrically-powered fleet has the larger positive NPV.

In addition to the above, the company has identified four other projects (all independent). Their outlays and NPVs are shown below:

Project	Outlay (t_0) (£000)	NPV (£000)
A	50	+ 60
B	80	+ 40
C	140	+ 84
D	80	+ 32
Petrol fleet	100	+ 80
Electric fleet	170	+ 110.5

All projects require only a single outlay at t_0, except Project A which requires a further £70 000 one year later at t_1.

The company has only £290 000 available for capital investment projects at t_0. Capital is expected to be freely available from t_1 onwards. None of the above projects can have their starts delayed. All projects are divisible, exhibit constant returns to scale and have the same level of risk, which is the same as that of the projects already being undertaken by the company.

Required:
(a) Carefully explain the reasons for the conflict in the investment advice about the fleet of delivery vans. In the absence of capital rationing which vehicle fleet should be purchased and why?
(b) When faced with capital rationing which projects should the company undertake at t_0? Explain the reasons for your decision.
(c) How would your advice in (b) above be modified if the start of the delivery fleet project could be delayed until t_1? What would be the resulting gain in shareholder wealth?

2. Hyalophane plc has identified the following investment projects:

Project	t_0 Immediate outlay (£000)	t_1 Year 1 (£000)	t_2 Year 2 (£000)
A	− 100	− 100	+ 302
B	− 50	− 100	+ 218
C	− 200	+ 100	+ 107
D	− 100	− 50	+ 308
E	− 200	− 50	+ 344

Required:
(a) The company faces a perfect capital market, where the appropriate discount rate is 10%. All projects are independent and divisible. Which projects should the firm accept?
(b) The company faces capital rationing at t_0. There is only £225 000 of finance available. None of the projects can be delayed. Which projects should the firm accept?
(c) The situation is as in (b) above, except that you are now informed that Projects A and B are mutually exclusive. Which projects should now be accepted?

(d) All projects are now independent but indivisible. Which projects should be accepted? What will be the maximum NPV available to the company?

(e) All projects are independent and divisible. There is capital rationing at t_1 only. No project can be delayed or brought forward. There is only £150 000 of external finance available at t_1. Which projects should be accepted?

(f) Given the information as in (e) above, except that there is capital rationing at both t_0 (£225 000 available) and t_1 (£150 000 available), formulate the linear programme to solve the problem, so as to maximize the total NPV generated.

(g) Suppose that the solution to the above linear programme produces the following dual values for cash:

$$
\begin{array}{ll}
t_0 & 0.92 \\
t_1 & 0.84 \\
t_2 & 0
\end{array}
$$

If money can be transferred from t_0 to t_1, via a deposit account, under what circumstances would it be worthwhile?

(h) Given the circumstances in (g) above, what minimum rate of interest would be required to make the linear programme transfer cash from t_1 to t_2?

In all the above questions, none of the projects can be accepted more than once.

3. Raiders Ltd is a private limited company which is financed entirely by ordinary shares. Its effective cost of capital, net of tax, is 10% per annum. The directors of Raiders are considering the company's capital investment programme for the next two years, and have reduced their initial list of projects to four. Details of the projects are as follows:

Cash flows (net of tax)

Project	Immediately (£000)	After one year (£000)	After two years (£000)	After three years (£000)	Net present value (at 10%) (£000)	Internal rate of return (to nearest 1%)
A	− 400	+ 50	+ 300	+ 350	+ 157.00	26%
B	− 300	− 200	+ 400	+ 400	+ 150.0	25%
C	− 300	+ 150	+ 150	+ 150	+ 73.5	23%
D	0	− 300	+ 250	+ 300	+ 159.5	50%

None of the projects can be delayed. All projects are divisible; outlays may be reduced by any proportion and net inflows will then be reduced in the same proportion. No project can be undertaken more than once. Raiders Ltd is able to invest surplus funds in a bank deposit account yielding a return of 7% per annum, net of tax.

Required:
(a) Prepare calculations showing which projects Raiders should undertake if capital for immediate investment is limited to £500 000, but is expected to be available without limit at a cost of 10% per annum thereafter.

(b) Provide a linear programming formulation to assist the directors of Raiders Ltd in choosing investment projects if capital available immediately is limited to £500 000, capital available after one year is limited to £300 000 and capital is available thereafter without limit at a cost of 10% per annum.

(c) Outline the limitations of the formulation you have provided in (b).

(d) Comment briefly on the view that in practice capital is rarely limited absolutely, provided that the borrower is willing to pay a sufficiently high price, and in consequence a technique for selecting investment projects which assumes that capital is limited absolutely, is of no use.

9 Traditional and technological approaches to risk

Introduction

In this chapter we examine some of the more traditional approaches that management use to cope with the problem of risk in capital investment decision making. We will also, briefly, consider an alternative approach to risk, utilizing the power of desktop computers.

We have already introduced the concept of risk in Chapter 2, when we put forward the idea that investors are risk-averse and so require a reward for taking on risk. This reward is represented by the rate of interest or rate of return they expect to get (but which, of course, they may not receive, given the nature of risk).

In the next chapter we will start to take a very much more careful and systematic look at the concept of risk and its implications. However, for the purposes of the current chapter, we will define risk quite simply: it describes the situation where the future is uncertain. Therefore a risky capital investment would be an investment whose outcome is uncertain.

Expected net present value

In an uncertain world, even assuming the presence of perfect capital markets, use of the NPV method of investment appraisal cannot be said necessarily to lead to optimal investment decisions or to the maximization of shareholder wealth. All it can lead to is the *expected* maximization of wealth. Hindsight, that is knowledge about the actual outcome of past events, may suggest different advice from that given by the NPV appraisal rule, because the latter is based only upon estimates of the future.

When we examined the rationale and operation of the NPV appraisal method, we paid very little attention to how the estimates of a project's future net cash flows were derived. In practice, management is *unlikely* to produce a series of 'point' (i.e. single figure) estimates of each year's net cash flow but instead is likely to construct a *range* of estimates.

For example, a project may have an initial cost of £1000 and a life of three years, but the level of the net cash flows may be uncertain, depending, say, on the general state of the industry in which the company operates. Example 1 shows a simple illustration of the estimated annual net cash flows based on three economic states: boom, normal and depressed conditions. From these data the project's NPV is calculated in each state and a figure is attached expressing the probability or likelihood of each state actually occurring. These NPVs are combined to produce the arithmetic mean (i.e. average) NPV of the project: the *expected* NPV of the project, given the different estimates and their probabilities of occurrence. It is upon the value (and more importantly, the sign) of this expected net present value (ENPV) that the normal investment appraisal decision rule is applied.

Example 1

Paraiso plc is considering whether to purchase a machine to produce glue for ceramic tiles. The machine costs £1000 and is expected to have a productive life of three years. However, the estimate of the annual net revenue from the machine is uncertain and depends on the state of the house-building industry. The company's management have produced the following estimates:

	State of industry	0	1	2	3
(I)	Boom	− 1000	+ 500	+ 700	+ 980
(II)	Normal	− 1000	+ 500	+ 600	+ 700
(III)	Depressed	− 1000	+ 300	+ 300	+ 250

Paraiso normally use a 10% discount rate in project appraisal, believing that this correctly reflects the risk of the project. On this basis, the project NPVs have been calculated as follows:

State	NPV
I	+ 769
II	+ 477
III	− 291

Latest figures from the Building Trades Research Institute suggest the following probabilities for the industry's future prospects:

State	Probability
Boom	0.20
Normal	0.60
Depressed	0.20

On this basis, Paraiso plc estimate the project's expected (i.e. arithmetic mean) NPV:

State	Prob.		NPV		
I	0.20	×	+ 769	=	+ 153.8
II	0.60	×	+ 477	=	+ 286.2
III	0.20	×	− 291	=	− 52.2
					+ 387.8 ENPV

As the project has a positive expected net present value (ENPV), it is accepted.

It is important to notice that, as this example shows, management not only has the task of estimating the project's annual net cash flow in each of the different states of the industry, but must also estimate the probability of the occurrence of each state. (Strictly, these are *subjective* probabilities, because they are based upon management's subjective judgement, rather than on past observations of similar events.)

In addition, it is also assumed in Example 1 that, whichever state of the industry occurs, the industry will remain fixed in that state over the duration of the project. If this assumption is unrealistic, further adjustments will need to be made to the ENPV calculation. Example 2 illustrates this more complex type of situation.

Example 2

Maravista plc design and manufacture clothes for the 13–15 years segment of the fashion industry. The success or otherwise of their products depends upon whether they are in fashion in any particular year.

The company's management are considering investing £40 000 to produce a range of leather belts which, they believe, will have a two-year fashion life. However, the outcome of the project is dependent upon whether the belt design turns out to be in fashion and hence, successful (State I) or out of fashion and so a relative failure (State II), or a marketing disaster (State III).

Maravista's marketing analysts have studied the situation carefully and have estimated the following net revenue figures for the project (£000):

Year 1 State	Prob	Net rev.	Year 2 State	Prob.	Net rev.
I	0.5	+ 80	I	0.6	+ 100
			II	0.3	+ 80
			III	0.1	+ 20
II	0.3	+ 30	I	0.4	+ 80
			II	0.3	+ 40
			III	0.3	+ 10
III	0.2	+ 10	I	0.1	+ 70
			II	0.4	+ 40
			III	0.5	+ 5

For example, as Maravista's marketing analyst explained to the chief executive, we believe that in the first year of the product's life it has a 50% chance of being in fashion and, hence, a success. Given it is successful in the first year, then there is a 60% chance of being similarly successful in its second year, a 30% chance of it then being a relative failure and, finally, a 10% chance of it turning into a marketing disaster.

On this basis, the analysis can be simplified by estimating the expected (i.e. arithmetic mean) revenue in the second year, for each possible first year state:

Year 1 state	Year 2 rev.		Prob.		
I	+ 100	×	0.6	=	+ 60
	+ 80	×	0.3	=	+ 24
	+ 20	×	0.1	=	+ 2
					+ 86 Expected Yr 2 net revenue
II	+ 80	×	0.4	=	+ 32
	+ 40	×	0.3	=	+ 12
	+ 10	×	0.3	=	+ 3
					+ 47 Expected Yr 2 net revenue

III	+ 70	×	0.1	=	+ 7
	+ 40	×	0.4	=	+ 16
	+ 5	×	0.5	=	+ 2.5

+ 25.5 Expected Yr 2 net revenue

Now, the project's expected cash flows have been simplified to:

Year 1 state	Prob.	Year 0 outlay	Year 1 net rev.	Year 2 expected rev.
I	0.5	– 40	+ 80	+ 86
II	0.3	– 40	+ 30	+ 47
III	0.2	– 40	+ 10	+ 25.5

Maravista usually uses a 20% discount rate to reflect the high-risk nature of the fashion industry and, on this basis, the project's expected NPV can be calculated:

Year 1 state	Prob.		NPV		
I	0.5	×	+ 86.4	=	+ 43.2
II	0.3	×	+ 17.6	=	+ 5.3
III	0.2	×	– 14.0	=	– 2.8

+ 45.7 ENPV

As the project has a positive expected net present value of approximately £45 700, Maravista PLC decides to proceed with production.

Limitations of ENPV

The concept of *expected* NPV (indeed an expected IRR could be similarly calculated) has been found by management to be useful for project appraisal in an uncertain world because it provides an average value of the proposed project's performance. However, it is important to realize that it *cannot* be said to take account of risk, because all that the ENPV calculation provides is a measure of the investment's *expected* performance, whereas risk is concerned with the likelihood that the *actual* performance may diverge from what is expected.

Example 3 illustrates this point very simply. Two mutually exclusive projects have identical expected NPVs. Therefore on the basis of the ENPV decision rule, the management should be indifferent between them – they are both expected to make a positive NPV of £8.5 million.

However, almost certainly, the management of Armacao plc will *not* be indifferent, but instead will strongly prefer the silicon chip project. The reason for this is that this project is likely to be viewed as being less risky than the semi-conductor project.

Armacao plc wants to enter the electronics industry and is considering two possible projects. Both projects require the same outlay of £10 million and both have the same expected net present value. However, because this is a venture into a new area of business, Armacao only want to undertake *one* of the projects. The figures are as follows (£m.):

State of world	Prob.	Semi-conductor project NPV	Silicon chip project NPV
Strong growth	0.20	+ 30.6	+ 13.0
Slow growth	0.60	+ 8.5	+ 8.5
Recession	0.20	− 13.6	+ 4.0

Semi-conductor project:	0.2	×	+ 30.6	=	+ 6.12
	0.6	×	+ 8.5	=	+ 5.10
	0.2	×	− 13.6	=	− 2.72
					+ 8.5 ENPV

Silicon chip project:	0.2	×	+ 13.0	=	+ 2.6
	0.6	×	+ 8.5	=	+ 5.1
	0.2	×	+ 4.0	=	+ 0.8
					+ 8.5 ENPV

Risk is to do with the fact that the project's actual outcome can vary from what is expected. In this respect the actual outcome can either be better (the *upside potential*) or worse (the *downside risk*) than the expected outcome. A 'gambling' investor will focus most of his attention on the upside potential, but a 'risk-averse' investor will be more concerned with looking at the expected outcome and the downside risk.

Given the assumption (which is generally correct) that investors *dislike* risk – they are *risk-averse* – the managers of Armacao plc are likely to view the silicon chip project as less risky because, even in the *worst* state of the world, it is still expected to produce a small positive NPV. In contrast, the semi-conductor project will produce a large negative NPV of £13.6 million if the economy moves into recession.

There is however one set of circumstances in which the ENPV approach does 'allow' for risk. That is to say, there is one set of circumstances when, if faced by the two alternative projects in Example 3, it would be correct to conclude that the company would be indifferent between them because they produce the same ENPV.

Those circumstances would be where the company intended to undertake a *large number* of similar or identical projects. In that case the ENPV indicates (quite correctly) the average outcome of each individual investment. Thus if the company were to undertake (say) 100 semi-conductor projects, then twenty of them would produce an NPV of + £30.6 million, sixty would produce an NPV of + £8.5 million and the remaining twenty would produce negative NPVs of £13.6 million. Thus the *average* outcome *per project* would be a positive NPV of £8.5 million.

Similarly, the average outcome of 100 silicon chip projects would be a + £8.5 million NPV per project. Twenty of the projects would produce an

NPV of + £13 million, and so on. Therefore, in these circumstances, the company would be indifferent between the two projects, given they have the same ENPV.

Unfortunately, most capital investment projects are *not* undertaken a great number of times, but are unique, one-off investments. It therefore follows that the idea of ENPV remains as an inadequate way of 'allowing for' or 'indicating' a project's risk.

Value of additional information

One interesting use of the ENPV technique is that it can help to indicate the value of additional information. Example 4 illustrates such a situation.

Example 4

Alvor plc has developed a new product and has now reached the stage of making a decision whether or not to undertake manufacture. The manufacturing machinery would cost £90 000 and the project is expected to have a life of six years. However, the performance of the product in the market-place is uncertain.

Alvor's marketing director has indicated that there are four possible outcomes (states I, II, III or IV): very successful, moderately successful, disappointing and complete failure. On this basis, the company's management accountants have estimated the possible NPVs and the project's overall expected NPV (£000):

State of world	Prob.		NPV		
I	0.2	×	+ 110	=	+ 22
II	0.5	×	+ 70	=	+ 35
III	0.2	×	+ 5	=	+ 1
IV	0.1	×	− 25	=	− 2.5
				ENPV	+ 55.5

As the ENPV is positive, the company decides to go ahead with production but, just before this decision is implemented, Carvalho Intelligence plc, a market research company, offers to undertake a survey of the new product which will indicate, *in advance of production*, what outcome is likely to occur. The cost of the survey would be £2000 and the management of Alvor plc are now trying to decide what should be done.

The approach to take is to examine what action the company would take in response to the various possible outcomes of the market research. Clearly, if the market research indicated that either states I, II or III would occur, the company would undertake manufacture, as to do so would generate a positive NPV. However, if the market research indicated that state IV would occur, the company would *not* proceed with manufacture, as manufacture would lead to a negative NPV of £25 000.

Survey indicates: State	Company's investment decision	Prob. of survey result		NPV outcome of decision		
I	Accept	0.2	×	+ 110	=	+ 22
II	Accept	0.5	×	+ 70	=	+ 35
III	Accept	0.2	×	+ 5	=	+ 1
IV	Reject	0.1	×	0	=	0
					ENPV	+ 58

Therefore:

	(£)
ENPV of project *with* market research survey	58 000
ENPV of project *without* market research survey	55 500
Maximum worth of survey	2 500
Cost of survey	2 000
Net benefit of survey to Alvor plc	£+ 500

On the basis of this analysis, the survey is worthwhile. The company should undertake the survey prior to manufacture and only proceed to manufacture if the survey indicates that either states I, II or III will occur.

In Example 4 the additional information was always correct. A more complex analysis involving the opportunity cost concept is required if the additional information may be incorrect. This situation is illustrated in Example 5.

Example 5

Centianes plc is considering undertaking a project as follows:

Outcome	Prob.		NPV			
Success	0.6	×	+ 100	=	+ 60	
Failure	0.4	×	− 40	=	− 16	
				ENPV	+ 44	

A market research survey will indicate *with 90% accuracy* which outcome will actually occur. The maximum worth of the survey can be estimated as follows:
There are four possible states of the world:

State	
A:	Survey indicates 'success' and is correct.
B:	Survey indicates 'success' and is wrong.
C:	Survey indicates 'failure' and is correct.
D:	Survey indicates 'failure' and is wrong.

There is a 60% chance the survey will indicate 'success' and a 40% chance that it will indicate 'failure'. There is a 90% chance that the survey result will be correct and a 10% chance that it will be wrong. The probabilities of each of the four 'states of the world' will be given by the product of the individual probabilities:

State					Prob.
A	0.6	×	0.9	=	0.54
B	0.6	×	0.1	=	0.06
C	0.4	×	0.9	=	0.36
D	0.4	×	0.1	=	0.04

Therefore:

State	Decision	Prob.		Outcome		
A	Accept	0.54	×	+ 100 NPV	=	+ 54.0
B	Accept	0.06	×	− 40 NPV	=	− 2.4
C	Reject	0.36	×	0 NPV	=	0
D	Reject	0.04	×	− 100 NPV*	=	− 4.0
				ENPV	=	+ 47.6

ENPV with survey	:	+ 47.6
ENPV without survey	:	+ 44.0
Max worth of survey	:	+ 3.6

*Notice that this is an opportunity cost. If the survey incorrectly forecasts 'failure' and we act on the survey's advice, we forgo the opportunity of gaining an NPV of +100.

The abandonment decision

Another 'special case' of the ENPV decision is the evaluation of an option to abandon a project before it reaches the end of its life. Such an analysis is illustrated in Example 6.

However, the limitations of the abandonment analysis should be noted. The first is that when *multiple* abandonment points are available – such as at the end of Years 1, 2 and 3 of a project with a life of four years – there is a real-world information problem as to how reliable future abandonment values are to be estimated. The second problem is that the analysis of a multiple abandonment point decision is much more complex than that of Example 6. A *dynamic programming* analysis is required. The problem here is that the more complex the analysis required, the more reluctant management often are to accept its advice, as they lack an understanding as to how the advice was generated.

Example 6

Irmaos plc operates a series of photocopier shops in which customers can walk off the street and have their photocopying done immediately. The company normally only keeps its machines for two years before disposing of them on the second-hand market.

They have recently been approached by a photocopier manufacturer who is trying to break into the UK market. Each machine will cost £10 000.

Irmaos believe that the crucial factor is the reliability of the new photocopiers. On past experience they believe that there is only a 60% chance that they will prove to be reliable.

On this basis they have estimated the following net cash flows produced by an individual photocopier:

Photocopier	Yr 1	Yr 2	Scrap
Reliable	+ 8000	+ 6000	+ 400
Unreliable	+ 4000	+ 3000	+ 200

A 15% discount rate is used to reflect the risk of the photocopying business and, on this basis, the project's NPV and ENPV are calculated:

		NPV		Prob.		
Reliable	$-10\ 000 + 8000(1.15)^{-1} + 6400(1.15)^{-2} =$	$+1796$	$\times$	0.6	$=$	$+1078$
Unreliable	$-10\ 000 + 4000(1.15)^{-1} + 3200(1.15)^{-2} =$	-4102	$\times$	0.4	$=$	-1641
				ENPV		-563

On this basis, Irmaos declines to purchase the machines. However, in order to try to get the company to change their mind, the photocopier manufacturer offers to buy back the machines at the end of the first year for 50% of their purchase cost. In other words, Irmaos are being offered an abandonment option. This decision can be analysed as follows:

Assuming that the company purchases a photocopy machine and then, at the end of the first year, decides *not* to abandon, the resulting NPVs of the decision are as follows:

Photocopier	Yr 1	Yr 2		NPV	Decision taken
Reliable	$-5000(1.15)^{-1}$	$+6400(1.15)^{-2}$	$=$	$+491$	Don't abandon
Unreliable	$-5000(1.15)^{-1}$	$+3200(1.15)^{-2}$	$=$	-1928	Abandon

In each case, the negative cash outflow at Year 1 is an opportunity cost. If the photocopier is *not* abandoned, the company forgo the opportunity to sell it back to the manufacturer for £5000.

This analysis allows the abandonment decision (at Year 1) to be made. If the photocopier turns out to be reliable, the machine should not be abandoned, as this generates a positive NPV outcome. However, if the photocopier turns out to be unreliable then the company *should* abandon the project at the end of Year 1, because not to do so would incur a negative NPV of £1928.
Having made the abandonment decision, the overall investment decision can then be made:

Photocopier reliable:

Outlay	:	− 10 000			
Net revs	:		+ 8000	+ 6000	
Scrap	:			+ 400	
Net cash flow	:	− 10 000	+ 8000(1.15)$^{-1}$	+ 6400(1.15)$^{-2}$	= + 1796 NPV

Photocopier unreliable:

Outlay	:	− 10 000		
Net revs	:		+ 4000	
Abandon value	:		+ 5000	
Net cash flow	:	− 10 000	+ 9000(1.15)$^{-1}$	= − 2174 NPV

Photocopier	Prob.		NPV		
Reliable	0.6	×	+ 1796	=	+ 1078
Unreliable	0.4	×	− 2174	=	− 870
			ENPV		+ 208

As the project has a positive ENPV, Irmaos should go ahead and purchase the photocopiers, but should abandon the project by selling them back to the manufacturer at the end of the first year if they prove to be unreliable.

Example 7 works through a more complex expected net present value question (which includes a little inflation for added interest!). It is designed to illustrate how the basic principles outlined in some of the earlier, simple examples may be applied in a more complex situation.

Example 7

The directors of Starlite plc are considering the purchase and exploitation of a disused tin mine which is being offered for sale for £50 000. A review of the mine's history shows that the total amount of pure tin that can be extracted depends upon the type of rock formations in the area and that only the following three possibilities exist:

Rock type	Total tin output	Probability
A	240 tonnes	0.4
B	120 tonnes	0.4
C	72 tonnes	0.2

If Starlite purchases the mine, the first year of ownership will be spent in making the mine and associated smelting plants operational, at a cost of £95 000 payable at the end of the year. Production will start at the beginning of the second year of ownership, when the output of pure tin will be 2 tonnes per month, whatever the type of rock formation. This production rate will remain unchanged until the mine is exhausted. During the first year of production, the directors expect that the resale value of the tin will be £9900 per tonne and that labour and other production costs will be £187 000. These revenues and costs are expected to rise by 10% per annum in subsequent years. These cash flows can be assumed to occur at the end of the year in which they arise.

Special mining equipment will also be purchased at the beginning of the first year of production at a cost of £48 000. This equipment will be sold immediately on the cessation of production, at an amount expected to equal its purchase price, less £200 for every tonne of tin produced during its life. Other revenues from the sale of the mine at the end of production are expected to equal the closure costs exactly.

The company has received permission from the present owners of the mine to carry out a geological survey of the area. The survey would cost £10 000 and would reveal for certain the type of rock formations in the area and hence how much tin could be produced from the mine.

Starlite plc has a money discount take of 21% per annum for this type of project.

The ENPV of the project – without the geological survey – can be calculated as follows.

If the output of tin per month is constant, whatever the rock type, then the different rock types simply affect the *life* of the mining operation:

$$\text{Annual rate of production: 2 tonnes} \times 12 = 24 \text{ tonnes}$$

Life of mine:

$$\text{Rock type A:} \quad \frac{240}{24} = 10 \text{ years}$$

$$\text{Rock type B:} \quad \frac{120}{24} = 5 \text{ years}$$

$$\text{Rock type C:} \quad \frac{72}{24} = 3 \text{ years}$$

Whatever the rock type, the following cash flows will be incurred:

t_0	− £50 000		purchase cost	
t_1	− £95 000		plant purchase	
t_1	− £48 000		equipment purchase	
t_2	$24 \times £9900$	=	+ 237 600	1st year's revenue
			− 187 000	1st year's costs
			+ £50 600	1st year's net revenue

The net revenue increases at 10% per year

Disposal value of mining equipment:

Rock type A:	£48 000	−	(240×200)	=	£	0
Rock type B:	£48 000	−	(120×200)	=	£	24 000
Rock type C:	£48 000	−	(72×200)	=	£	33 600

The discount factor is $(1.21)^{-n} \equiv (1.1)^{-n}(1.1)^{-n}$.

Rock type A
PV of mine, plant and equipment purchase costs:

						£
t_0	− £50 000	×	1	=	−	50 000
t_1	− £143 000	×	$(1.21)^{-1}$	=	−	118 182
					£ −	168 182

PV of net revenue flows: (£000)

t_2	t_3	t_4		t_{11}
$\dfrac{50.6}{(1.1)^2(1.1)^2}$	$\dfrac{50.6\,(1.1)}{(1.1)^3(1.1)^2}$	$\dfrac{50.6\,(1.1)^2}{(1.1)^4(1.1)^2}$	....	$\dfrac{50.6\,(1.1)^9}{(1.1)^{11}(1.1)^2}$

$$50.6\,(1.1)^{-2}\,A_{10-10} \times (1.1)^{-1}$$
$$50.6 \times 0.83 \times 6.14 \times 0.91 \quad = \quad £ + 234\,660$$
$$\text{Net present value: } £ + 66\,478.$$

Rock type B
PV of mine, plant and equipment purchase costs: £–168 182
PV of net revenue flows: (£000)

$$50.6(1.1)^{-2} A_{5\frown 0.10} \times (1.1)^{-1}$$
$$50.6 \times 0.83 \times 3.79 \times 0.91 \quad = \quad £+144\ 847$$

PV of disposal of mining equipment:

$$24\ 000\ (1.21)^{-6} \quad = \quad 24\ 000\ (1.1)^{-6}(1.1)^{-6}$$
$$= \quad 24\ 000 \times 0.56 \times 0.56 \quad = \quad £+7526$$

Net present value: £– 15 809.

Rock type C
PV of mine, plant and equipment purchase costs: £–168 182
PV of net revenue flows: (£000)

$$50.6\ (1.1)^{-2} A_{3\frown 0.10} \times (1.1)^{-1}$$
$$50.6 \times 0.83 \times 2.49 \times 0.91 \quad = \quad £+95\ 163$$

PV of disposal of mining equipment:

$$33\ 600\ (1.21)^{-4} \quad = \quad 33\ 600\ (1.1)^{-4}(1.1)^{-4}$$
$$= \quad 33\ 600 \times 0.68 \times 0.68 \quad = \quad £+15\ 537$$

Net present value: £– 57 482.

Expected net present value:

			(£)
+ 66 478	×	0.4 =	+ 26 591
– 15 809	×	0.4 =	– 6 324
– 57 482	×	0.2 =	– 11 496
		ENPV =	£ + 8771

Hence, on the basis of the expected NPV, the project is worthwhile undertaking without the survey.

We can now move on to examine whether or not the survey is worthwhile. From the previous set of calculations, it can be seen that the project would not go ahead if the company knew, *ex ante*, that either rock type B or rock type C existed. This is because both would involve negative NPVs. Thus the company would only go ahead with the mine if rock type A was indicated. Hence, assuming a survey is undertaken, the expected value of the outcome would be:

Rock type	NPV		Probability		(£)
A	+ 66 478	×	0.4	=	+ 26 591
B	0	×	0.4	=	0
C	0	×	0.2	=	0
					£+ 26 591

The expected net present value of the mine project, without the survey is approximately + £8800; whilst if the survey is undertaken, this rises to + £16 500[1] approximately. Therefore, on this basis, it would suggest that the survey is worthwhile undertaking. Although the expected net present value approach is a rather unsatisfactory method of selecting between alternative financial opportunities as it takes no account of the risk involved, inspection of the alternative NPVs that might occur under the two options does support the initial advice that the survey should be undertaken:

	Survey NPV	No survey NPV
Rock type A	+ £56 478	+ £ 66 478
Rock type B	– £10 000	– £ 15 809
Rock type C	– £10 000	– £ 57 482

The appraisal of almost any investment project in the real world will involve the making of a great number of estimates. For example, the outlay required to undertake the project, its life, the annual cash inflows and out-flows it will generate, the scrap value it will have, and even the correct rate of discount to reduce the cash flows to present values. Estimates will be made for all these factors and the project will then be appraised by calculating an expected net present value.

If this NPV is positive then the appraisal is in favour of acceptance. But, in terms of downside risk, the decision maker is also interested in how sensitive the advice is to changes in the estimates made about the project. In other words, he is likely to be interested in the *margin of error* that there can be in the estimates made about the individual components of the project (i.e. outlay, life, etc.) *before* the advice that the appraisal gives (in this case to accept) becomes incorrect.

The decision pivot point

The decision whether to accept or reject a particular project *pivots* around the zero NPV. If the NPV is greater than zero, then the advice is to accept. On the other hand, if the NPV is negative, then the advice is to reject. Thus a zero NPV becomes the decision *pivot point*.

Sensitivity analysis is the term used to describe the process where each estimated element of a project's cash flow is taken in turn (with a *ceteris paribus* assumption holding all other estimates constant) to see the extent to which it can vary before the project's positive NPV is reduced to a zero value. Therefore if the estimated element varies by *more* than this amount, then the decision advice given by the original estimate of the project's NPV will be incorrect. These sensitivity calculations are illustrated in Example 8.

Example 8

Suppose the following estimates have been made about an investment proposal:

Outlay:	£1000
Life:	3 years
Annual revenues:	£2000
Annual costs:	£1500
Appropriate discount rate:	10%

On the basis of these estimates, the NPV can be calculated as follows:

	Year			
	0	1	2	3
Capital outlay	– £1000			
Revenues		+ £2000	+ £2000	+ £2000
Costs		– £1500	– £1500	– £1500
Net expected cash flows	– £1000	+ £500	+ £500	+ £500

$$\text{ENPV} = -1000 + 500\,A_{3\neg 0.10} = +£243$$

Taking each of the five estimated factors in turn (and holding all the others constant at their initial estimated values), we shall examine the degree of variation necessary to reduce the +£243 NPV to zero.

Outlay: Let the outlay value be x.

$$-x + 500\, A_{3\neg 0.10} = 0$$
$$\therefore x = 500\, A_{3\neg 0.10} = 1243$$

The outlay can be as high as £1243 before the appraisal advice to invest (i.e. + NPV) becomes incorrect; in other words the original estimate can increase by £243 or by $(243/1000) = 0.243$ or 24.3%.

Life: Let the life be x years.

$$-1000 + 500\, A_{x\neg 0.10} = 0$$

Thus the value for x that produces a zero NPV lies between 2 and 3:

$$x = 2 + \left[\frac{132}{243 + 132} \times (3 - 2)\right] = 2.35 \text{ years.}$$

The project life can be as short as 2.35 years before the advice of the original investment appraisal is incorrect; i.e. the original estimate can decrease by 0.65 year or by $0.65/3 = 0.217$ or 21.7%.

Revenues: Let the annual revenue be x.

$$-1000 + x\, A_{3\neg 0.10} - 1500\, A_{3\neg 0.10} = 0$$

$$x = \frac{1000 + 1500\, A_{3\neg 0.10}}{A_{3\neg 0.10}} = \pounds 1902.$$

Thus the annual revenues can be as low as £1902, over the three years, before the original advice is incorrect; i.e. the original estimate can decrease by £98 per year or $98/2000 = 0.049$ or 4.9%.

Costs: Let the annual costs be x.

$$-1000 + 2000\, A_{3\neg 0.10} - x\, A_{3\neg 0.10} = 0$$

$$x = \frac{1000 + 2000\, A_{3\neg 0.10}}{A_{3\neg 0.10}} = -\pounds 1598.$$

The annual costs can be as high as £1598 in each of the three years before the original investment advice is incorrect, i.e. the original estimate can increase by £98 per year or $98/1500 = 0.065$ or 6.5%.

Discount rate: Let the discount rate be x (i.e. the project's IRR).

$$-1000 + 500\, A_{3\neg x} = 0$$

$$A_{3\neg x} = \frac{1000}{500} = 2.0.$$

Using linear interpolation, $A_{3\neg 0.20} = 2.11$ and $A_{3\neg 0.25} = 1.95$.

$$x = 0.20 + \left[\frac{2.11 - 2.0}{2.11 - 1.95} \times (0.25 - 0.20)\right] = 0.234.$$

Thus the estimate for the discount rate can be as high as 23.4% before the original investment advice is incorrect; i.e. the original estimate can be increased by 13.4% or $0.134/0.10 = 134\%$.

Variable	Original estimate	Maximum value	Maximum change	% Change
Outlay	1000	1243	+ 243	+ 24.3%
Life	3	2.35	− 0.65	− 21.7%
Revenues	2000	1902	− 98	− 4.9%
Costs	1500	1598	+ 98	+ 6.5%
Discount rate	10%	23.4%	+ 13.4%	+ 134%

Using linear interpolation, we know that when $x = 3$ the NPV equals + £243. Trying $x = 2$:

$$- 1000 + 500\, A_{2 \neg 0.10} = -132 \text{ NPV.}$$

The sensitivity table in Example 8 shows that the decision to invest is most sensitive to the estimates of annual cash flows (where an actual outcome of only 4.9% below estimate would cause the NPV decision advice to be incorrect) and the annual cash outflows (a decision sensitivity of 6.5%). The decision advice is fairly insensitive to all the other estimates. We would conclude from this that management should review both of these decision-sensitive estimates to ensure that they are as accurate as possible.

Example 8 outlines the general approach of the sensitivity analysis technique, which is a good working tool in that it makes the decision maker more aware of the possible effects of uncertainty on his investment decisions. In addition, it can also help to direct attention to those particular estimates which require a special forecasting effort on account of their effect on the decision's sensitivity.

Non-annuity cash flows

However, Example 8 is rather unrealistic, because most of its cash flows are annuities. It was this characteristic that allowed us to take the approach that we did. Example 9 illustrates the approach to be taken when there are only non-annuity cash flows.

Example 9

Benagil plc is considering undertaking a project and has made the following estimates:

Outlay: £2300
Life: 3 years
Discount rate: 10%

Revenues:	Yr 1	:	+ £2000	Costs:	Yr 1	:	− £ 900
	2	:	+ £2400		2	:	− £1100
	3	:	+ £1600		3	:	− £ 800

On this basis, the project's NPV has been estimated at + £375.
The management of Benagil now wish to analyse how sensitive is the NPV's decision advice to accept, to changes in the estimates:

Outlay: Let the outlay be *x*.

$$-x + 1100\,(1.10)^{-1} + 1300\,(1.10)^{-2} + 800\,(1.10)^{-3} = 0 \text{ NPV}$$
$$-x + 2675 = 0$$
$$x = 2675$$

Therefore the outlay can increase by as much as £375 (or 375 ÷ 2300 = 16.3%) before the original decision advice is changed.

Life: Let the life be *x*.

When *x* = 3, the project's NPV is + 375
When *x* = 2, the project's NPV is:

$$-2300 + 1100\,(1.10)^{-1} + 1300\,(1.10)^{-2} = -226.$$

Using linear interpolation to estimate a value for *x* that gives a zero NPV:

$$x = 2 + \left[\frac{-226}{226 - (+375)}(3 - 2) \right] = 2.38 \text{ years.}$$

Therefore the project's life can be shortened by up to 0.62 year (approximately 7.5 months) or 0.62 ÷ 3 = 20.7% before the original decision advice is incorrect.

Discount rate: Let the discount rate be *x*.
When *x* = 10%, the project's NPV is + 375
When *x* = 20%, the project's NPV is:

$$-2300 + 1100\,(1.20)^{-1} + 1300\,(1.20)^{-2} + 800\,(1.20)^{-3} = -18.$$

Using linear interpolation to estimate a value for *x* that gives a zero NPV:

$$x = 10\% + \left[\frac{375}{375 + 18}(20\% - 10\%) \right] = 19.5\%.$$

Thus the correct discount rate for the project can be as high as 19.5%, an increase of 9.5% (or 9.5% ÷ 10% = 95% on the original estimate), before the NPV's decision advice to accept is incorrect.

Revenues
If the revenues were to decrease by 5% per year, they would become:

Yr 1	+ 1900
2	+ 2280
3	+ 1520

and the NPV would become:

$$-2300 + 1000\,(1.10)^{-1} + 1180\,(1.10)^{-2} + 720\,(1.10)^{-3} = +125.$$

If the revenues were to decrease by 10% per year, then the project's NPV would become:

$$-2300 + 900\,(1.10)^{-1} + 1060\,(1.10)^{-2} + 640\,(1.10)^{-3} = -125.$$

Costs
If the costs were to increase by 5% per year, they would become:

Yr 1	− 945
2	− 1155
3	− 840

and the NPV would become:

$$-2300 + 1055\,(1.10)^{-1} + 1245\,(1.10)^{-2} + 760\,(1.10)^{-3} = +259.$$

If the costs were to increase by 10% per year, then the project's NPV would become:

$$-2300 + 1010\,(1.10)^{-1} + 1190\,(1.10)^{-2} + 720\,(1.10)^{-3} = +142.$$

		Sensitivity table		
Variable	Original estimate	Maximum value	Maximum change	% change
Outlay	2300	2675	+ 375	+ 16.3%
Life	3	2.38	− 0.62	− 20.7%
Discount rate	10%	19.5%	+ 9.5%	+ 95%

Revenues : Decision advice *not* sensitive at the 5% level, but *is* sensitive at the 10% level.

Costs : Decision advice *not* sensitive at either the 5% or the 10% level.

Therefore, the advice to management is that the decision given by the NPV calculation is insensitive to changes in most of the estimated variables. However, if the revenues were to fall by 10% of their estimated value the original decision advice would turn out to be incorrect. Hence it may be worthwhile to re-examine the estimates of annual revenues to see if the company's confidence in their accuracy can be improved.

Limitations of sensitivity analysis

The technique suffers, in particular, from an obvious and important drawback: the fact that each estimated component is varied *in turn* whilst all the others are held constant. Thus, in Example 9, the discount rate can be as high as 19.5% (approximately) before the NPV calculation advises rejection of the project, but this degree of sensitivity only holds (except through a chance ordering of factors) if all the other estimates turn out to be accurate. In other words, the technique ignores the possible effects on the decision of two or more of the estimated components varying simultaneously.[2]

Even if this problem with sensitivity analysis is set to one side, it can also be criticized on the basis that it makes no attempt to analyse risk in any formal way. Nor does it give any indication as to what the decision maker's reaction should be to the data presented in a sensitivity table.

In the examples set out above, the original NPV calculations indicated a decision to accept. Sensitivity analysis provides no rules to guide the decision maker as to whether the initial appraisal advice should or should not be amended in the light of the sensitivity data. With these limitations in mind, let us now look at other approaches which may be used to deal with the problem of uncertainty in investment appraisal.

The risk-adjusted discount rate

Risk and return

The risk-adjusted discount rate approach attempts to handle the problem of risk in a more direct and thoughtful way. As we know, investors are risk-averse and so require a reward for undertaking a risky investment in the form of the rate of return that it is expected to produce. The more risky the investment, the greater must be its expected return if investors are going to be persuaded to undertake it.

It is this idea – the relationship between risk and return – that the risk-adjusted discount rate approach picks up on. We have seen from our analysis of the NPV decision rule that a positive NPV means that the project produces a return greater than the discount rate – which itself represents the minimum acceptable rate of return. Thus the risk-adjusted discount rate idea takes the commonsense approach to handling risk in investment appraisal of adjusting the *level* of the minimum acceptable return to reflect the project's level of risk.

The approach taken is usually to add a risk *premium* to the 'risk-free' rate of return. The greater the project's perceived level of risk, the greater is the risk premium. The risk-free rate of return is usually taken to be the going rate of return on long-term government bonds (on the basis that such bonds have no *default risk*: a situation is never realistically going to occur where the government defaults on its loan obligations – after all, governments are allowed to print money!).

For example, suppose that the current rate of return on government long-term bonds is 8%. Management may decide to classify investment proposals into three broad categories, low-, medium- and high-risk, and assign risk premiums of 3%, 5% and 9% respectively. Therefore the cash flows of low-risk projects would be discounted to present value using a discount rate of 8% + 3% = 11%, whilst projects of medium- or high-risk would be evaluated by discounting their cash flows to present value using 13% and 17% discount rates respectively.

In one very important way, the risk-adjusted discount rate approach to the problem of uncertainty is much more useful to the decision maker than sensitivity analysis, in that it does actually produce decision *advice*, in the form of a risk-adjusted net present value. In addition, the method is easily understandable and appears to be intuitively correct: investors *do* require a higher expected return on riskier investments. However, we can identify several drawbacks in this essentially correct (but too casual) analysis.

The problems

The two main problems are the allocation of projects into risk classes and the identification of the risk premiums. In addition there is a technical problem with this approach to allowing for risk, in that it implicitly implies that risk increases over time (which may or may not be the case).

The problems of the risk class and the risk premiums simply arise from the casual nature of the analysis. Thus the allocation of a project to a particular risk class and the premia assigned to each class will be based on the *manager's* own personal attitude towards risk, and on the manager's personal perception as to the nature of risk and the reward required for accepting risk. Our earlier discussion on objectives is sufficient for us to realize that the manager's view of risk – and the required rewards – may not be the same as those of the shareholders. (This whole area will be examined much more closely in the three chapters which follow.)

Certainty-equivalents[3]

The 'technical' problem is easy to illustrate, as is shown in Example 10. The problem is that a *constant* risk premium implies *increasing* risk over time. In Example 10 a risk-adjusted discount rate of 8% implies that a project's cash flows become more risky over time. It is debatable whether the riskiness of a project's cash flows do correspond with this assumption.

Example 10

An investment produces an uncertain cash flow at Year 1 which is expected to be £100. If you would be willing to accept £90 for certain at Year 1, instead of the uncertain £100, then £90 is said to be the 'certainty-equivalent'.

Given that you are indifferent between the two amounts, the certainty-equivalent *factor* at Year 1 – a_1 – can be identified by:

$$£90 = a_1 \times £100$$
$$a_1 = \frac{£90}{£100} = 0.90$$

What this certainty-equivalent factor of 0.90 means is that at Year 1, every £100 of uncertain cash flow is valued as being equivalent to £90 of certain cash flow. Therefore the smaller the certainty-equivalent factor, the *more risky* is the uncertain cash flow and the less valuable it is. For example, if the certainty-equivalent factor was 0.70 this implies that investors would be willing to accept £70 for certain for every uncertain £100: the less you are willing to accept for certain, the more risky is your perception of the equivalent uncertain cash flow.

Furthermore, given that these two amounts are seen as equivalents, their *present values* should also be the same. Therefore the present value of the *certain* £90, discounted at the risk-free interest rate, should be the same as the present value of the *uncertain* £100, discounted at a rate which has been adjusted to reflect the risk involved.

If we let the risk-free interest rate be R_f and the risk-adjusted discount rate be R, then, in our example:

$$\frac{£90}{(1+r_F)^1} = \frac{£100}{(1+r)}$$

and given that £90 = $a_1 \times £100$

then

$$a_1 \times \frac{£100}{(1+r_F)^1} = \frac{£100}{(1+r)^1}.$$

This can be rearranged to give:

$$a_1 = \frac{(1+r_F)^1}{(1+r)^1}.$$

More generally, the certainty-equivalent factor at any time period *t* is:

$$a_t = \frac{(1+r_F)^t}{(1+r)^t}.$$

To see what this implies, let's put in some numbers. Suppose the risk-free interest rate is 5% and you judge that a satisfactory *risk-adjusted* discount rate is 8% (i.e. there is a 3% risk premium being added to the risk-free rate of return).

The certainty-equivalent factors will be as follows:

Year 1	:	$(1.05/1.08)^1$	=	0.9722
Year 2	:	$(1.05/1.08)^2$	=	0.9452
Year 3	:	$(1.05/1.08)^3$	=	0.9190
		etc.		etc.

As can be seen, over time the certainty-equivalent factor is getting *smaller*. In other words, the implicit assumption is that, over time, the project's cash flows are getting more risky and so less valuable.

Use of the normal distribution[4]

Another attempt to take a more analytical approach to the problem of risk makes use of the properties of normal probability distributions. The approach starts from the premise that if a project's risk can be defined as the degree of possible variability between its expected outcome and its actual outcome, then what is of prime importance to the risk-averse decision maker (or more correctly, the risk-averse owner on whose behalf the decision is being made) is just *one* side of this variability: the risk of project underperformance. Therefore, what would be of interest to the decision maker is the probability of the project actually producing a negative NPV, even though the *expected* result was a positive NPV. On the assumption that the range of possible outcomes for the project are normally distributed, then the properties of the normal curve can be used to provide the required probability.

The discount rate

A problem arises, however, in the choice of the discount rate to be used to calculate the possible NPVs of the project being appraised. One possibility is to use the risk-free discount rate. The investment decision advice is then based on whether or not the probability of a negative NPV exceeds some maximum acceptable probability, in much the same way as a risk-premium is utilized when using the risk-adjusted discount rate. If the probability of a negative NPV were sufficiently small, the project would be acceptable.

An alternative approach is to discount the project cash flows using an appropriate *risk-adjusted* discount rate in order to calculate the expected NPV and then use the properties of the normal curve to estimate the probability of a negative NPV. This latter approach uses the probability of a negative NPV as an *additional* piece of decision information, almost as an extension of the sensitivity analysis concept. By contrast, the former approach attempts to use the properties of the normal curve to allow directly for risk in investment decision making. In doing so it avoids the element of 'double-counting' risk which occurs when using a risk-adjusted discount rate to calculate the range of possible NPVs.

A simple illustration, such as that set out in Example 11, can be used to explain the mechanics of both approaches. From the results of this example it can be seen that when using a risk-free discount rate, the decision advice is based on whether a 13.8% probability of the project actually producing a return below the riskless return is acceptable for the perceived level of risk of the project concerned. Alternatively, the second approach informs the decision maker that the project can be expected to produce a positive NPV of £492 when discounted at a rate thought appropriate for its degree of risk, but that if a decision is made to accept the project there is an 18.4% probability that this decision will turn out to be incorrect (i.e. that the project actually produces a negative NPV).

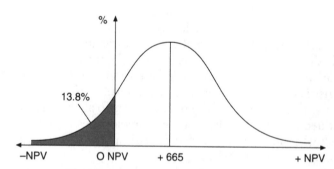

Example 11

A project under evaluation is thought to involve a medium degree of risk. The risk-free discount rate is 4% and the appropriate risk premium is believed to be 6%. The project has the following estimated cash flows:

Cash outlay (year 0): £1000

Cash inflows:

		Year			
		1	2	3	Prob.
	Good	+ 1000	+ 1000	+ 1000	0.10
	Med./good	+ 800	+ 800	+ 800	0.20
Market conditions:	Medium	+ 600	+ 600	+ 600	0.40
	Med./poor	+ 400	+ 400	+ 400	0.20
	Poor	+ 200	+ 200	+ 200	0.10

(a) Using the risk-free discount rate of 4%:

Market conditions	NPV		Prob.			$(NPV - ENPV)^2$	×	Prob.		
Good	+ 1775	×	0.10	=	+ 177.5	$(1775 - 665)^2$	×	0.10	=	123 210
Medium good	+ 1220	×	0.20	=	+ 244.0	$(1220 - 665)^2$	×	0.20	=	61 605
Medium	+ 665	×	0.40	=	+ 266.0	$(665 - 665)^2$	×	0.40	=	0
Medium Poor	+ 110	×	0.20	=	+ 22.0	$(110 - 665)^2$	×	0.20	=	61 605
Poor	− 445	×	0.10	=	− 45.5	$(-445 - 665)^2$	×	0.10	=	123 210
			ENPV		+ 665.0			Var	=	369 630

Whilst the ENPV = + 665, the standard deviation = $\sqrt{369\,630}$ = 608 NPV

Probability of a negative NPV: $\dfrac{0 - 665}{608}$ = 1.094 Std. units

Using area under the normal curve tables (page 610) this gives a value for the shaded area (− NPV) of 0.1379.

Therefore there is a 13.8% probability that the project will produce less than the risk-free return of 4%.

(b) Using the risk-adjusted discount rate of 4% + 6% = 10%:

Market conditions	NPV		Prob.			$(NPV - ENPV)^2$	×	Prob.		
Good	+ 1487	×	0.10	=	+ 148.7	$(1487 - 492)^2$	×	0.10	=	99 002.4
Medium good	+ 989	×	0.20	=	+ 197.8	$(989 - 492)^2$	×	0.20	=	49 401.8
Medium	+ 492	×	0.40	=	+ 196.8	$(492 - 492)^2$	×	0.40	=	0
Medium poor	− 5	×	0.20	=	− 1.0	$(-5 - 492)^2$	×	0.20	=	49 401.8
Poor	− 503	×	0.10	=	− 50.3	$(-503 - 492)^2$	×	0.10	=	99 002.4
			ENPV		+ 492.0			Var.	=	296 808.4

ENPV = + 492
Standard deviation = √296 808.4 = 545 NPV.

Probability of a negative NPV: $\dfrac{0 - 492}{545}$ = 0.903 Std. units.

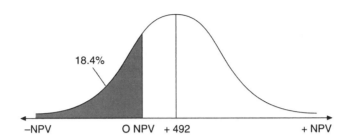

Using area under the normal curve tables this gives a value for the shaded area (–NPV) of: 0.1841.

Therefore there is an 18.4% probability that the project will produce less than the required return of 10%.

Simulation

Over the past ten years or so there has been a massive expansion in the accessibility of computer software designed for simulation. The idea of simulation is to create a computer model that will allow for the variables in a model to be related to each other in any way that might be required and also to allow them to be varied singly or together in almost infinite combinations. By doing this it is possible to form a view as to what the possible outcomes of a decision might be. Of course, it will still be necessary to make predictions but the predictions should be more reliable in nature. For example, a mining company might be making a decision about the exploitation of a new mine and wishes to calculate its NPV. Traditionally a best estimate of the variables would have been used in the model and, eventually a single value would have been arrived at for the NPV of the project. However, by using a simulation package it is possible to enter ranges of values in the cells of the spreadsheet and the packages allow for the inputting of most statistical distributions into individual spreadsheet cells. In the case of the mining company, they might well have access to scientific data that will tell them (for instance) that the expected yield of ore from rock is normally distributed with a mean of 150 grammes per kilogramme and a standard deviation of 40 grammes.

Once the spreadsheet has been written the simulation goes ahead. This involves the generation of the distributions in the spreadsheet in random or structured combinations with the NPV of the project being calculated each time. The more iterations of the model that are run, the more reliable will be the distributions generated. The only limit to the number of iterations in practical terms is the power and capacity of the computer being used. Let us assume that it has been decided that it is appropriate to run 2500 iterations.

The spreadsheet model would be recalculated 2500 times and the distributions for the various cells would be generated in a random manner. Each run will generate a value for the NPV of the project which is stored. By the end of the process there will be 2500 possible values for NPV and these will be reported. This might be in the form of a graph or it might be in the form of statistical information that discloses the possibility of differing levels of return (including, perhaps, the possibility of negative returns).

The results of such a process are likely to be far more reliable than those resulting from guesswork as to a single most likely outcome. However, they are still dependent upon the availability of information about possible future outcomes. There is also the problem of the 'black box' syndrome. The whole approach has the very strong feel of science about it and, generally speaking, the results are presented in a way that is extremely plausible. This might have the effect of removing some of the healthy scepticism that all decision makers should have. In other words, this is still an approach based on predictions and whilst its results might be rather more reliable than those produced by other approaches, this should never be forgotten.

A particular strength of the approach is that it encourages decision makers to pay attention to the underlying factors that are likely to have a significant impact on the outcome of the project.

Summary

This chapter has looked at some of the approaches used to cope with the problem of risk in capital investment appraisal. None of these can be said really to tackle the issue except in a rather intuitive, rule-of-thumb way. However, it could be argued that their use in practice is better than ignoring the presence of risk completely. The major points made were as follows:

- The expected net present value (ENPV) approach examines the *average* outcome of a project. However, because of this it fails to capture what is the essence of risk, by ignoring *variability* of outcome.

- However, the analysis can be useful for examining the value of additional information to a company.

- The abandonment decision analysis can help to evaluate investment appraisal situations where an option is available to abandon the project before it reaches the end of its life.

- The abandonment decision analysis suffers from the difficulty of obtaining reliable abandonment value data and requires a complex mathematical analysis in all but the simplest problems.

- Sensitivity analysis examines the degree to which the various estimates made about a project can change, before the decision advice given by NPV is overturned.

- There are two main advantages. The first is that it highlights those estimates to which the decision advice is most sensitive. Management can then go back and take more time and trouble to ensure those particular estimates are as accurate as possible.

The second advantage is that it gives the decision maker more information to use in deciding whether or not to accept the advice of the original NPV analysis.

- There are two disadvantages of sensitivity analysis. The first is the more serious: it only looks at the effect of changing one estimate at a time. It doesn't examine the effects of simultaneous changes in two or more estimates. The second disadvantage is that it gives no indication as to *how* the decision maker should evaluate and make use of the sensitivity data.

- The risk-adjusted discount rate approach described in this chapter represents an intuitive attempt to recognize the relationship between risk and return.

- It can be faulted on a number of grounds. First, on the basis of how the risk premiums are derived and the project's risk category is determined. Secondly, we saw that using a risk-adjusted discount rate makes an assumption about implicit project risk which may not be justified.

- The use of the normal probability distribution was examined. This is an interesting approach to the handling of risk in decision making, although little used in practice. The most sensible approach is to obtain a probability that the investment project will produce a return that is less than the *risk-free* return. The alternative approach, looking at the probability of a negative NPV calculated on the basis of a discounted rate assumed to reflect the project's risk, is simply a variation on sensitivity analysis.

- Finally we described the use of computer simulation. This is rather more sophisticated than most of the other options and whilst it is still not used very extensively, its use is becoming more common. It is likely that it will become much easier to use this approach as software improves and it is probable that it will improve the quality of decision making.

Notes

1. £26 591 minus the cost of the survey.

2. In theory this problem can be overcome by use of the operational research technique of simulation; in practice, however, this does little to enhance or clarify the decision maker's view of the effects of uncertainty on a project's desirability.

3. These are discussed further in Chapter 10.

4. This statistical area is examined in the Appendix to Chapter 13.

Further reading

1. The articles in this general area of the more traditional approaches to handling risk are not particularly rewarding. However, two interesting pieces are: G.J. Grayson, 'The Use of Statistical Techniques in Capital Budgeting', in *Financial Research and Management Decisions*, ed. A.A. Robicheck, John Wiley 1967, which looks at the use of sensitivity analysis; and A.A. Robicheck and S.C. Myers, 'Conceptual Problems in the Use of the Risk Adjusted Discount Rate', *Journal of Finance*, December 1966.
2. Other articles of interest are: D.B. Hertz, 'Risk Analysis in Capital Investment', *Harvard Business Review*, January–February 1964; J.F. Magee, 'How to Use Decision Trees in Capital Investment', *Harvard Business Review*, September–October 1964; A. Rappaport, 'Sensitivity Analysis in Decision Making', *Accounting Review*, July 1967; and E.F. Brigham, D.F. Shone and S.R. Vinson, 'The Risk Premium Approach to Measuring a Utility's Cost of Equity', *Financial Management*, Spring 1985.
3. On the abandonment decision, see J.E. Jarrett, 'An Abandonment Decision Model', *Engineering Economist*, Autumn 1973.
4. Finally, on certainty-equivalents, see A.A. Robicheck and S.C. Myers, 'Conceptual Problems with the Use of Risk-adjusted Discount Rates', *Journal of Finance*, December 1966, and G.A. Sick, 'A Certainty-Equivalent Approach to Capital Budgeting', *Financial Management*, Winter 1986.

Quickie questions

1. A machine costs £1000 and has a life of three years. It can either be a success or a failure. If it is successful – and it has a probability of 45% – then it will produce an annual net cash flow of £500. If it is a failure, the annual net cash flow will be only £350. The discount rate is 10%. What is its ENPV?
2. What is the maximum worth of a survey that would tell you, in advance of the decision, whether the machine in question 1 would be a success or failure?
3. What would be the maximum worth of the survey in question 2 if it was only 75% accurate?
4. Given the following information:

State	Prob.	£NPV
I	0.3	+ 100
II	0.5	+ 50
III	0.2	– 300

What would be the maximum worth of a survey which could tell you, in advance, which state of the world would occur?

5. A machine costs £140. It has a two-year life and a 15% discount rate correctly reflects its risk. Its performance depends upon the state of the world:

State	Yr 1	Yr 2	Prob.
I	+ 100	+ 100	0.70
II	+ 60	+ 60	0.10
III	+ 40	+ 40	0.20

The company can sell the machine at the end of Year 1 for £60. At the end of Year 2 the machine will be worthless. Advise the company.

6. Given the following information about a project:

Outlay:	£1000
Life:	5 years
Net cash flow:	+ £280 per year
Discount rate:	10%

How sensitive is the decision advice to changes in the estimate of the life and the annual net cash flow?

Problems

1. The directors of Linnet Oil plc are considering whether to make an immediate payment of £20 million for a licence to drill oil in a particular geographical area. Having acquired the licence, the company would commission a seismic survey to determine whether the area is a suitable prospect, i.e. whether there are any geological structures present which could contain oil. If the area is a suitable prospect, exploration wells would be drilled to discover if oil is in fact present. If oil is present, appraisal wells would be drilled to ascertain the size and characteristics of the potential field.

   The company's development expert has produced the following data about the licence area, based upon the results from adjoining areas. If oil is discovered by the exploration wells, the appraisal wells will indicate one of the three following types of oilfield:

Type	Probability of occurrence	Millions of barrels	Expected life (years)
I	60%	negligible	zero
II	32%	42	4
III	8%	2250	10

The annual oil production will decline over the life of the field. To approximate the decline, the expert argues that a sensible approach would be to assume that the annual production of the field during the first half of its life is twice the annual production during the second half. For example, for a type II field the first two years' annual production rate would be 14 million barrels per annum and the second two years' annual production rate would be 7 million barrels per annum.

During the entire life of the field, a barrel of oil is expected to sell for $26.4 and the $/£ rate is expected to be 1.2$/£. The annual operating cash surplus is expected to be 45% of sales revenue. The combined tax costs for the company are usually 77% of the operating cash surplus and these tax cash flows can be assumed to arise one year after the cash flows relating to sales and other costs. Production of oil would start in one year's time and the first annual net revenues would arise at the end of the first year of production.

   The cost of drilling the appraisal well will be £100 million and drilling the exploration well will cost £10 million. Both costs will be paid in one year's time. The seismic survey costs of £2 million will be paid immediately. All three of the costs, together with the cost of the licence to drill oil, will give rise to tax relief equal to 50% of the cost, receivable one year after the cost is paid.

   It is expected that there will be a 50% chance that the seismic survey will indicate the prospect of oil and a 30% chance that the exploration drilling will find oil. The company's after-tax cost of capital for this type of project is 15% per annum.

Required:
(a) Calculate the expected net present value of the venture.

(b) Calculate the maximum price the company should pay for an alternative type of seismic survey which will reduce the probability of indicating a positive prospect from 50% to 30% and so increase from 30% to 50% the chance that the exploration drilling will find oil.

2. Southgate Ltd is investigating the introduction of a new alcoholic drink, to be called Mildmay. Extensive market research by an outside agency, at a cost of £10 000, has suggested that a price of £5 per bottle to the retail trade would be acceptable.

Production of Mildmay will require specialized distilling and flavouring equipment which, it is estimated, would cost £200 000. As with most distilling equipment, this installation is likely to have a long production life but, due to its rather specialized nature, when production of Mildmay ceases it will only be able to be sold for scrap for about £2000 (net of dismantling costs). Variable costs of production are estimated at £3 per bottle and overheads are estimated at £25 000 per year, avoidable only if production ceases.

At the proposed selling price, the drink trade is expected to demand 50 000 bottles per year, well within the capacity of the production equipment, but after four years interest is expected to decline and so production will cease. However, the company believes that it may well be able to extend product life for a further two years by either running a small trade advertising campaign at the start of years 5 and 6 at a cost of £10 000 per year, or alternatively by reducing the price per bottle by 40p in these two years. The market research company believes that the two alternatives would achieve similar sales results, but just what these sales would be is uncertain. If the campaign is successful in year 5 then sales of 35 000 bottles could be expected in that year, with sales of 28 000 or only 9000 bottles being equally likely in year 6, or alternatively the year 5 promotion may be relatively unsuccessful with sales of only 7000 bottles in that year and an equal likelihood of either 12 000 or 5000 bottles in the following year. The market research agency believes that the campaign has only a 60% chance of being successful in year 5.

All expenses and revenues will be paid or received in cash at the end of the year in which they arise, with the exception of the production equipment, for which payment is due at the start of the first year of manufacture and the advertising expenditure which must be paid for at the start of each year in which a campaign is mounted. The company normally uses a 10% discount rate for project evaluation purposes.

Required:
(a) Evaluate the financial feasibility of the proposed new drink, in respect of its normal expected life of four years, including in your presentation details about the sensitivity of the decision advice to changes in all the estimates made, except the scrap value and discount rate.
(b) Briefly, advise management on the results of the sensitivity analysis.
(c) Evaluate which of the two alternative methods (if any) should be used to extend the product life.

3. A small company in the house-building industry has £201 000 cash which is surplus to current requirements. The cash will eventually be used to help finance the construction of a small housing development. The housing development depends upon obtaining permission to build the houses from the local government planning department. It is believed that this permission will be given in two years' time.

The £201 000 can be invested in the money market to yield a return of 10% per year.

Alternatively an opportunity exists for the funds to be invested on a temporary basis in Goer, a family-owned car hire business which wishes to expand its car hire fleet by thirty cars costing £6700 each. Goer is temporarily short of funds because of recent inheritance tax payments. If the funds are invested with Goer they will produce an annual net cash inflow to the building company, but the size of this cash flow is now known with certainty, and the cash flow at the end of the second year is dependent upon the cash flow at the end of the first year. Estimates of the net cash inflows to the building company are detailed below.

End of Year 1		End of Year 2	
Probability	Cash inflow (£)	Probability	Cash inflow (£)
0.6	80 000	0.6	80 000
		0.4	90 000
0.4	100 000	0.6	100 000
		0.4	110 000

In addition Goer will make a payment to the building company at the end of the first year of £141 000, or at the end of the second year of £81 000. The building company has to choose at the end of the first year whether to receive payment of £141 000 then or £81 000 a year later. If the payment of £141 000 is received by the building company at the end of the first year the investment will be terminated and there will be no further cash flows to the building company from Goer.

18% per year is considered to be an appropriate discount rate for investments in the car hire business.

Required:
(a) Prepare a report recommending whether the building company should invest in the car hire business or in the money market. All relevant calculations must be included in your report.

Ignore taxation. State clearly any assumptions that you make.
(b) Discuss the practical problems of incorporating abandonment opportunities into the capital investment decision-making process.

Suggest possible reasons why a company might decide to abandon an investment project part way through its expected economic life.

4. The management of Haydn Ltd is planning the launch of a new micro-computer, the SQ. The market for micro-computers is very competitive and the anticipated product life of the SQ is only three years. The marketing director of Haydn Ltd has produced the following table showing three different estimates of likely demand for the SQ during each year of its life.

Demand predictions	Probability	Year 1 Units	Year 2 Units	Year 3 Units
Most optimistic	0.2	32 000	16 000	12 000
Best guess	0.5	16 000	8 000	6 000
Most pessimistic	0.3	4 000	2 000	1 500

The above estimates assume a constant selling price of £500 over the three years. The variable production cost per unit of an SQ is £400.

The production director has indicated that the factory is in a position to produce 32 000, 16 000 or 4000 units per annum, but, once decided, the chosen production level could not be increased until the start of the following year. The total cost of setting up the production line would consist of fixed costs of £1 million, and variable costs of £50 for each unit of production capacity. These costs would be paid at the start of the year's production.

A market research firm has offered, for a fee of £300 000, to carry out a detailed survey which would determine precisely the level of demand for the SQ. The management of Haydn Ltd wishes to know whether the market survey is likely to be worthwhile.

In order to assess whether the survey is worth undertaking, the directors of Haydn Ltd have asked that the following simplifying assumptions be made:

(i) cash flows relating both to sales and variable production costs are to be deemed to arise at the end of the year in which they are incurred;

(ii) demand can be represented by only one of the three sets of probabilities envisaged by the marketing director;

(iii) the level of the demand in the first year will determine the levels demanded in the second and third years;

(iv) the appropriate discount rate for the venture is 10% per annum; and

(v) stock levels will remain unchanged.

Required:

(a) Determine the initial production capacity that Haydn Ltd should choose, and compute the resulting expected net present value of producing and selling at that level.

(b) Calculate whether the market survey should be commissioned, and comment on any reservations you might have relating to the use of expected values as an aid in decision making.

(c) Discuss the advantages to the company of conducting a market survey of this kind.

10 Risk and expected return

Risk and return

Having looked at some of the less theoretically sound approaches that are used in the handling of risk in investment appraisal, we now begin to take a much more analytical and structured approach to the problem.

Introduction to uncertainty

We will begin by examining how investment appraisal can cope with the fact that the future is largely unknown and that decision making has to be carried out on the basis of *expectations*. That is, in an uncertain world, capital investment decisions have to be taken on the basis of *expected* project cash flows, which may or may not turn out to be the same as the cash flows that *actually* arise.

In a world where the future in uncertain, decision making involves taking a risk: the risk that the actual outcomes may differ from what was expected. In our analysis of the handling of uncertainty in financial decision making we shall use the two terms 'risk' and 'uncertainty' interchangeably. Although it is possible to distinguish between the two terms, there is little purpose in doing so for our present needs. Thus when reference is made to a risky investment decision, we are concerned with a situation where we are uncertain about that investment's *actual* future outcome.

A simple approach

Our original approach to the problem of investment decision making in an uncertain world was to assert that investors are averse to uncertainty – in other words they dislike risk. Therefore, in order to be persuaded to take on an investment for which the outcome is uncertain, they have to be offered the expectation of a higher return[1] from the investment as a *reward*, or as *compensation* for taking on the risk involved. Further, it followed that the greater the degree of uncertainty surrounding an investment's outcome, the greater would have to be the level of expected return in order to make the investment attractive to investors.

In such a world as outlined above, the perfect capital market would not display just a single rate of interest, but a whole continuum of interest rates – one for each level of risk: the higher the risk, the higher the interest rate. We could therefore adapt the NPV appraisal technique by using as the discount rate for any particular project's appraisal, the perfect capital market discount rate which related to that particular project's level of risk.

In such a way the discount rate would still correctly reflect the opportunity cost of undertaking the investment: the investment should only be undertaken if it produces a return that is at least equal to the return that could be obtained on the capital market, *for a similar level of risk*. (The IRR appraisal technique could be similarly adapted. The perfect capital market interest rate appropriate for the project's level of risk would be used at the hurdle/cut-off rate.)

However, this simple analysis – although fundamentally and conceptually correct – does beg two rather problematic questions: how are we to identify the degree of risk associated with a particular investment project and, given that we can measure a project's risk level, how are we then to identify the corresponding perfect capital market interest rate? These two questions will form the basis for much of the following discussion.

A caution

The impact of uncertainty has a fundamental and pervasive impact on the whole of financial decision making. It is often useful to assume away its existence in order to clarify the basic analysis of investment decision making; however, if our theory is to have any real-world validity then we must come to grips with the problems it poses.

In the introduction to this book it was pointed out that the theory of financial decision making is still under development, and many areas of the theory contain considerable controversy. In fact, there is still much to find out about how financial decisions should be made, or indeed, how they are made and there are probably more unanswered questions than answered questions.

However, when we look at the research work that is currently being undertaken, we find that a very substantial proportion of it is concerned with the presence of risk in decision making, because it is our lack of understanding about risk – its nature, measurement and investor's attitude towards it – that causes the greatest number of problems and unanswered questions. The more traditional approaches to risk are not seen as providing satisfactory solutions and so recent years have seen the development of different approaches such as chaos theory.

Given the situation as outlined above, we must treat our analysis of uncertainty with considerable caution. Generally speaking, it is believed that the analysis that we shall develop does move in the right direction – it is relatively sound – but the conclusions reached can only be tentative, and can be expected to alter over time as our understanding improves.

The expected utility model

We are concerned with the construction of a theory of financial decision making by a company's management on behalf of its shareholders. Given the fact that management will have to take decisions about investment proposals whose outcomes are uncertain, it is important that we should be aware of how the individual shareholders would themselves come to a decision in such circumstances. Therefore we require a model that adequately reflects the risk attitudes of shareholders: how they perceive risk and how they react to its presence. Unlike our theory of financial decisions, which is a normative theory outlining how management *should* make financial decisions, the model of shareholders' risk attitudes needs to be a *positive* model – it should try to reflect their *actual* attitudes, rather than what should be their attitudes. Only in this way will we be able to construct successfully a normative theory of managerial financial decision making based on shareholders' actual desires. To this end we have to make some carefully specified assumptions about shareholders and investors generally.

Investors' behaviour axioms

Stated succinctly, we shall assume that when faced with making risky financial decisions, individual shareholders or investors act *rationally* and *consistently*. More specifically, we can formulate four basic axioms[2] regarding the behaviour of investors when making decisions:

1. Investors are able to choose between alternatives by ranking them in some order of merit, i.e. they are capable of actually coming to a decision.
2. Any such ranking of alternatives is 'transitive', i.e. if alternative A is preferred to B and alternative B is preferred to C, then alternative A *must* be preferred to C.
3. Investors do not differentiate between alternatives which have the same degree of risk, i.e. their choice is dispassionate in that it is based solely upon consideration of the risk involved, rather than on the nature of alternatives available.
4. Investors are able to specify for any investment whose returns are uncertain, an exactly equivalent alternative which would be equally preferred but which would involve a *certain* return, i.e. for any gamble, investors are able to specify a *certainty-equivalent*.[3]

These four axioms of investors' decision-making behaviour can be used to construct an expression or function of utility. This utility function[4] can then be used as the basis of a model of investors' risk attitudes which will enable us to explore the way in which individuals make decisions about risky alternatives, on the assumption that they do so in order to maximize their own expected utility index.

Given below is an example which goes through the process by which an individual's utility function may be derived. Although this process may appear rather unrealistic, it is perfectly practical as long as the individual's decisions are both consistent and rational, in line with the four axioms stated above.

Utility function construction

The process shown in Example 1 could be carried on indefinitely, because there are an unlimited number of different pairs of probabilities (each adding up to 100%) which can be attached to the project's two outcomes. Eventually we shall have gathered sufficient utility indices of certainty-equivalents to enable us to plot the individual's personal utility index. Fig. 10.1 illustrates such a function.

Example 1

Suppose that we inform an individual that a project will be made available to him and that we wish to know the maximum amount he would be willing to pay to be allowed to undertake it. There are just two possible outcomes from this project: one is a gain of £5000 (+£5000) and the other is a loss of £2000 (–£2000).[5]

In order to construct the utility function we need a measure or index of utility. This measure is completely arbitrary, but for convenience we shall assign the utility index number of 1 to the +£5000 outcome and 0 to the –£2000 outcome:[6]

	Utility function
Outcome	index
+£5000	1
–£2000	0

Alternatively this could be written as:

$$U(+£5000) = 1 \qquad U(-£2000) = 0$$

If the probability of an outcome of +£5000 is ρ and of –£2000 is $(1 - \rho)$, then the *expected* utility of the project will be:

$$\rho \times U(+£5000) + (1 - \rho) \times U(-£2000).$$

As $U(+£5000) = 1$ and $U(-£2000) = 0$, then the expected utility of the project reduces to:

$$\rho \times 1 + (1 - \rho) \times 0 = \rho$$

From axiom 4 we assume that for any project with a risky outcome, an investor can specify an equivalent certain alternative: the certainty-equivalent or (C-E). This represents the maximum sum an investor would be willing to pay to undertake the risky project. In this case, the utility of the certainty-equivalent can be specified:

$$U(C\text{-}E) = \rho U(+£5000) + (1 - \rho) U(-£2000),$$
$$U(C\text{-}E) = \rho \times 1 + (1 - \rho) \times 0 = \rho.$$

We are now in a position to construct a utility function for a specific individual investor. However, before doing so, it is important to emphasize that the utility function we shall construct will be unique to this particular (hypothetical) investor. Different investors are likely to have different utility functions because they are based on each individual's personal attitude to risk.

The approach that we shall use is to ask the individual to state the maximum (certain) price he would be willing to pay to be allowed to undertake the project, for a whole range of different probabilities attached to the two outcomes. For example, if we said that the probability of the project producing +£5000 is 0.80 and the probability of producing –£2000 is $(1 - 0.80) = 0.20$, then he may state that he would be willing to pay a maximum of (say) £2000. This is the project's certainty-equivalent, and its utility index can be calculated as:

$$U(C\text{-}E) = \rho U(+£5000) + (1 - \rho) U(-£2000),$$
$$U(+£2000) = 0.80 \times 1 + 0.20 \times 0 = 0.80.$$

Again we might specify that the probability of the project producing +£5000 was 0.40, and the investor may allocate this project a certainty-equivalent of (say) –£500. In other words, with probabilities of 0.40 and 0.60 attached to the project's two possible outcomes of +£5000 and –£2000 respectively, the investor would have to be *paid* £500 to induce him to undertake the project.

The utility index of this certainty-equivalent would be:

$$U(-£500) = 0.40 \times 1 + 0.60 \times 0 = 0.40.$$

This procedure could be continued indefinitely, with a variety of different probabilities.

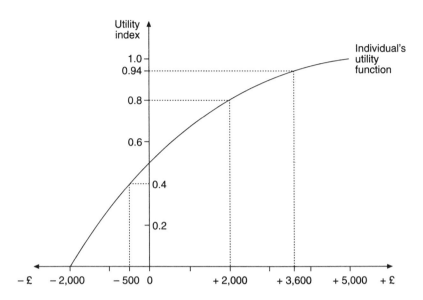

Fig. 10.1 *A utility function*

The shape of the utility function

The general shape of this utility function is of interest. Let us return to the first pair of probabilities attached to the project's outcome in Example 1, where there was an 80% chance of an outcome of +£5000 and a 20% chance of an outcome of –£2000.

	Project outcome	×	Probability		
	+£5000	×	0.80	=	+£4000
	–£2000	×	0.20	=	–£ 400
	Expected outcome			=	+£3600

The project's expected outcome has a value of +£3600, whereas our individual assigned it a certainty-equivalent of only +£2000. That is, the expected utility of the project to the individual is *less than* the utility of the project's expected outcome or value. This can be written using the following notation:

$$E[U(\text{PROJ.})] < U[E(\text{PROJ.})]$$

In this particular case, the expected utility of the project is the utility of the certainty-equivalent value assigned by the individual of +£2000, and the utility of the project's expected value is the utility of +£3600. Using the (hypothetical) utility function in Fig. 10.1 we can read off the following utility index values for these amounts:

$$E[U(+\pounds2000)] = 0.80$$
$$U[E(+\pounds3600)] = 0.94$$

$$0.80 < 0.94$$

The second pair of probabilities, where our investor assigned a certainty-equivalent of –£500, also has this characteristic:

Project outcome	×	Probability		
+£5000	×	0.40	=	+£2000
–£2000	×	0.60	=	–£1200
Expected outcome			=	+£ 800

We see that once again, the project's expected outcome of +£800 is higher than the certainty-equivalent assigned of –£500.

We will find that this holds for *all* the probability combinations offered to our investor: he would assign a certainty-equivalent value which was below the project's expected value. This result is caused by the fact that the derived utility function is *concave* to the origin. If our individual always assigned a certainty-equivalent value which was *equal* to the project's expected value, the utility function would be a *straight line*, whilst if the individual assigned certainty-equivalent values consistently *greater* than the project's expected value, the utility function would be *convex* to the origin. Fig. 10.2 illustrates these alternatives.

Our individual consistently assigns certainty-equivalent values that are less than the project's corresponding expected value; he is *risk-averse* – in other words, he dislikes risk and shows this by being only willing to pay a sum of money to undertake the project (the C-E) which is less than the project's expected worth. The difference between the two figures is seen by the individual as the compensation he requires to bear the risk involved with the project. Thus when our individual indicated that £2000 was the maximum he would pay to undertake a project with an expected value of +£3600, the difference of £1600 is the expected compensation required because of the risk involved.

Fig. 10.2 *Utility function shapes*

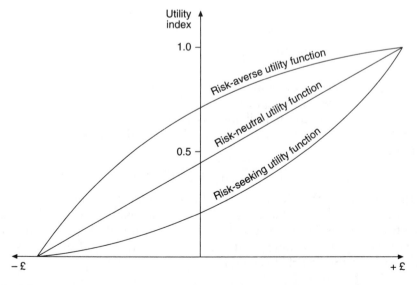

Similarly, if an individual assigns certainty-equivalents *equal* to the project's expected value, he is termed 'risk-neutral' in that he requires no compensation for undertaking a risky project. If the assigned certainty-equivalents are *greater than* the project's expected value, the investor is termed a 'risk-seeker', because he is willing to pay a premium in order to be allowed to bear a risk. It is difficult to imagine why any investor should be indifferent towards risk let alone why they should actively seek it. If we ignore the 'buzz' that some individuals might get from gambling, there are good reasons why investors should be risk-averse. Indeed, even gamblers will generally be prepared to pay insurance premiums, which might seem a little inconsistent.

So why should investors be risk-averse? The answer is that other things being equal, each £1 we stand to lose in a gamble is worth more to us in relative terms than each £1 we stand to gain. Let us take a simple example. If I were to give a destitute person £10 it would probably represent quite a significant amount of money to them. If I were to give £10 to somebody who already had £100, it would still be fairly significant to them. However, if I were to give £10 to a millionaire it would make no practical difference to his or her financial position. In other words, although each individual experiences the same absolute increase in wealth, their perceptions of the increase are very different. We can see that this is to do with the increase in wealth relative to existing wealth. We can take this a stage further and consider the situation where I am offered an even chance bet that I will win or lose £5. Should I take it? The answer is no. Let us say I start from the position where I have £100. The relative difference between £95 and £100 is greater than the relative difference between £100 and £105 (it is 5.26% compared to 5%) so, relatively speaking, the £5 I stand to lose is worth more than the £5 I stand to gain. Buying a lottery ticket isn't really the same thing as the risks involved in investment since the purchaser compares the possible millions to be won with the £1 spent on the ticket and whilst the odds against winning are huge, they see that the amount to be won can change their life whilst the £1 risked will not.

Fig. 10.2 illustrates the possible utility functions for the three categories of attitudes to risk. It follows that the greater the aversion or attraction to risk, the more pronounced will be the concavity and convexity respectively of the utility functions, and vice versa. However as we have already pointed out, it is probable that only risk-averse functions exist in the real world.

Individual choice amongst risky investments

Once an individual's utility function has been constructed in this way, it can be used to indicate how she or he would choose between alternative risky projects, on the assumption that she or he will attempt to achieve the greatest possible amount of utility, i.e. the individual selects whichever alternative is expected to produce the highest utility index value. This process is illustrated in Example 2.

Suppose our individual, whose utility function is displayed in Fig. 10.1, wishes to decide between two alternative investments: A and B. Once again, we shall assume that the returns produced by both investments occur almost immediately after their required outlays, so as to avoid the need for discounting.

The possible net returns from these two investments and their relevant probabilities are set out below, together with the calculation of the utility that the individual would expect to derive from each:

Investment A Possible net return	×	Prob.			Investment B Possible net return	×	Prob.		
– £1000	×	0.3	=	– £ 300	+ £ 500	×	0.2	=	+ £ 100
+ £2000	×	0.4	=	+ £ 800	+ £1500	×	0.6	=	+ £ 900
+ £5000	×	0.3	=	+ £1500	+ £2500	×	0.2	=	+ £ 500
Expected return:				+ £2000	Expected return:				+ £1500

$$E(U(\text{Inv.A})) = 0.3U(-£1000) + 0.4U(+£2000) + 0.3U(+£5000),$$
$$E(U(\text{Inv.B})) = 0.2U(+£500) + 0.6U(+£1500) + 0.2U(+£2500).$$

Using the utility function in Fig. 10.1 to determine the utility index value:[7]

$$E(U(\text{Inv.A})) = (0.3 \times 0.28) + (0.4 \times 0.8) + (0.3 \times 1) = 0.704,$$
$$E(U(\text{Inv.B})) = (0.2 \times 0.59) + (0.6 \times 0.74) + (0.2 \times 0.85) = 0.732.$$

As $E(U(\text{Inv.B})) > E(U(\text{Inv.A}))$, the individual will select investment B in order to maximize his or her utility.

From the above, it can be seen that although investment A has the largest expected return, the individual would actually select investment B because it produces a higher level of expected utility: a utility index of 0.732 as opposed to 0.704. In other words, investment B is preferred because our risk-averse individual judges that it possesses a superior risk–expected return combination than does investment A.

The problem with this expected-utility model of investment decision making is that its practical usefulness is virtually zero because of its elaborate procedure. To derive an accurate representation of an individual's utility function is both difficult and time-consuming. In fact, it could be argued that it is virtually impossible to measure it in a real-world way. Deriving the function from answers to questions when real money is not at stake might be very different from the real risk attitude of the individual. In addition, an individual's attitude to risk can be expected to change over time as his or her personal attitudes and circumstances change, thus necessitating a periodic re-estimation of the function.

In addition, in terms of our normative theory of managerial financial decision making, the model presents another problem. Assuming that a company has several shareholders, the company's management would need to be aware of each individual's utility function. Even assuming that such a feat were possible, the utility functions of these individuals are likely to be different, and there is no way in which they can sensibly be aggregated to assist managerial decision making. However, the expected utility model does provide a starting point for a more analytical approach to the problem of handling risk. In particular, of greatest interest is the fact that risk-averse investors generally are likely to have *concave to the origin* utility functions in the forms of a quadratic equation: $U(x) = a + bx - cx^2$, as shown in Fig. 10.1.

Risk, return and the investment decision

Introduction

Accepting the fact that the operational usefulness of the expected utility model is severely limited, we must look elsewhere for a means of measuring an investment's risk. One particularly fruitful approach that can be seen as having its foundations in the expected utility model is that of portfolio theory. This theory was originally developed within the context of a risk-averse individual investor who was concerned with how to combine shareholdings in several different (stock exchange) quoted companies in order to build an investment portfolio that would maximize the amount of expected return, given a specified level of risk. (Such a portfolio is termed 'efficient', and could also be defined as one that minimizes risk for a given level of expected return.)

Following on from Chapter 7 we outline the main characteristics of portfolio theory within the context of an investor constructing a share portfolio. We also examine the implications and validity of the theory for managerial financial decision making.

However, before we can do that we need to define two terms: the *risk* and the *return* on an investment in the shares of a company.

Return on investment

We shall continue to avoid the problems that can arise through the discounting process by considering the return on a share over just a *single* time period. Therefore the return on an investment in the shares of a company takes on a very simple definition:

$$\text{Return} = \frac{(\text{Selling price}^8 - \text{Purchase price}) + \text{Dividends received}}{\text{Purchase price}}.$$

Thus the return is simply the amount of the capital gain (or capital loss) plus the dividends received while the share was held, expressed as a ratio of the original purchase price. For example, if a share was bought for 100p and was sold for 114p and during the time it was held a 3p dividend was received, then the return on the share was:

$$\frac{(114p - 100p) + 3p}{100p} = \frac{14p + 3p}{100p} = 0.17 \text{ or } 17\%.$$

There are two things to note about this example. The first is that although the return is defined as a single-period return, it can be applied to *any* single time period: a week, a month, a year or whatever – because it is determined solely by the lapse of time between when the share was bought and when it was sold. However, because we are so used to dealing with *annual* rates of return, we will assume from now on that the period of time under consideration is that of a year.

The second point to note is that the example tells us a piece of history: what *has been* the return that was received on this investment. However, we are interested in decision making and so, although the actual achieved return on an investment is of interest in assessing decision-making performance, we are really concerned with what *will be* the future return on an investment that can be expected.

Expected returns

If we are trying to calculate the return that we would be likely to receive from an investment, we need to estimate the future selling price and the dividends expected to be received while holding the share. In such an exercise it is unlikely that just a single estimate would be made, but instead a *range* of estimates, which might be determined by (say) general economic conditions. Example 3 illustrates such a situation.

Example 3

If the current price of a share is 100p and the following estimates are made:

Prevailing economic conditions	Estimated selling price	Estimated dividends received
Boom	128p	7p
Steady growth	117p	3p
Slump	105p	0p

then we estimate that the return will be 35% if the economy booms, 20% if it exhibits steady growth and only 5% if there is an economic slump. Although this information is of interest, it is of limited use for decision-making purposes unless we have some idea about *how likely* each possible set of economic conditions is, and hence each possible investment outcome is. In other words, we need to apply some (subjective) probabilities to each outcome in order to produce a probability distribution of possible returns.

Suppose the following probability estimates are made:

Economic conditions	Probability	Return on investment
Boom	0.30	35%
Steady growth	0.40	20%
Slump	0.30	5%

This is obviously a very crude representation of a probability distribution as it only allows for three possible returns on the investment: 35%, 20% and 5%, and ignores the possibility of some intermediate return such as 18%. However such a degree of unsophistication is acceptable for our present purposes.

The probability distribution illustrated in Example 3 is symmetrical in its range of possible returns and if constructed with greater complexity could be represented graphically as in Fig. 10.3.

The returns are symmetric, in that they are evenly or regularly distributed around the most likely outcome. Such a distribution is termed a Normal probability distribution and it can be fully described in terms of just two attributes: a measure of central tendency of the returns and a measure of the dispersion of the returns around the central tendency.

If the returns are not distributed symmetrically around the central tendency, as for example in Fig. 10.4, then the distribution is said to be asymmetrical

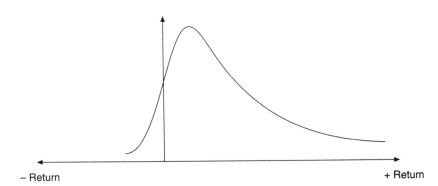

Fig. 10.3 A *symmetrical distribution*

Fig. 10.4 A *skewed distribution*

or skewed and so a third attribute is required: a measure of *skew*. For the moment, we shall assume that the returns on the investment are symmetrically distributed, but we shall return to the point at a later stage.

The measure of central tendency of returns we shall use is the *arithmetic mean* return (usually referred to as the expected return[9]) and the measure of dispersion, the *variance* (or the square root of the variance, the *standard deviation*).

The expected return, variance and standard deviation of returns are calculated in Example 4, using the data from Example 3.

Example 4

The expected return is given by:

$$E(r) = \Sigma r_i \rho_i$$

The variance is given by:

$$\sigma^2 = E(r^2) - E(r)^2$$
$$= \Sigma r^2_i \rho_i - (\Sigma r_i \rho_i)^2$$

The standard deviation is given by:

$$\sigma = \sqrt{\sigma^2}$$

Expected return:

	Return r_i		Probability ρ_i		
	35%	×	0.30	=	10.5%
	20%	×	0.40	=	8.0%
	5%	×	0.30	=	1.5%
	$E(r) = \Sigma r_i \rho_i$			=	20.0%

Risk, return and the investment decision   221

Variance of returns:	$(Return)^2$		Probability		
	r_i^2		p_i		$r_i^2 p_i$
	1225	×	0.30	=	367.5
	400	×	0.40	=	160.0
	25	×	0.30	=	7.5
		$E(r^2) = \Sigma r_i^2 p_i$		=	535

$$\sigma^2 = E(r^2) - E(r)^2 = 535 - 20^2 = 135$$

Standard deviation of returns: $\sigma = \sqrt{\sigma^2} = \sqrt{135} \approx 11.62\%$

Summary:[10] $E(r) = 20\%$; $\sigma^2 = 135$; $\sigma = 11.62\%$

Risk

In Example 4, the investment under consideration is 'expected' to produce a return of 20%. That is, 20% represents the average or arithmetic mean return, but the actual return may turn out to be considerably better (up to 35%) or considerably worse (down to 5%) than the 20% expected. Thus the investment is risky: it involves some uncertainty, meaning that it is possible for the actual return to be somewhat different from what is expected. We really require a means by which the risk of the investment can be measured or quantified: *how risky* is the investment?

If risk is defined as being concerned with the probability that the actual outcome may be something other than expected, then one way of obtaining a measure of risk would be to use the *range* of possible outcomes. Thus in the example used above, the possible return ranged from 5% to 35%, and this 30% difference could be used as a measure of the risk involved. However, such a measure is rather crude and simplistic, as Example 5 shows.

Example 5

Suppose a choice has to be made between two alternative investments, A and B, whose probability distribution of return is given below:

r_a	Probability	r_b	Probability
20%	0.30	20%	0.20
8%	0.40	8%	0.60
−4%	0.30	−4%	0.20

Both investments have an expected return of 8% and both have the same range of outcomes (24%), but are they equally risky? Having defined risk as being concerned with the probability of actual outcomes differing from the expected outcomes, it would (correctly) appear to intuitive judgement that investment A was the more risky of the two alternatives as the extreme outcomes of A (20% and −4%) have a greater probability of occurrence than the extreme outcomes of B. Conversely, the expected outcome of B has a greater probability of occurrence (0.60) than with A (0.40).

What we are looking for in a measure of risk is not the simple *range* of outcome, but how this range is *dispersed* around the expected outcome. Both the variance and the standard deviation provide acceptable measures of this dispersion, with the standard deviation being *especially* useful as it provides a measure in the same units as the expected return.[11]

Thus we can conclude that the risk of an investment can be measured by the variance or standard deviation of possible returns around the expected return: the greater the dispersion, the greater the risk, the greater the variance or standard deviation and vice versa; and where there is no dispersion of possible returns, then the expected return is a *certain* return, there is *no* risk and both variance and standard deviation give a measure of zero.

Therefore returning to the data used in Example 4, the return expected from the investment is 20% and its risk can be indicated by the standard deviation of 11.62% or by the variance of 135. In Example 5, which considered two investments, A and B, we concluded that A intuitively appeared to be more risky than B. The standard deviation of returns for A is 9.3% and for B is 7.6%, which confirms A as the riskier investment as it has the larger standard deviation.

Further, if we continue to assume that the possible returns on an investment are symmetrically distributed around the expected return, then quoting the risk of an investment by means of its standard deviation can be converted into an intuitively more meaningful measure by using the properties of the area under the normal curve.[12]

Thus if an investment has an expected return of 10% and a standard deviation of returns of 7%, then it can be said that:

1. there is a 65% chance (approximately) that the actual return will lie somewhere between 17% and 3% (i.e. 10% ± 7%); and
2. there is a 95% chance (approximately) that the actual return will be somewhere between 24% and −4% (i.e. 10% ± (2 × 7%)).

Therefore, the greater the standard deviation, the greater the dispersion of possible return around what is the expected return.

Downside risk

One factor in the above discussion that may strike the reader as rather strange is that investment risk is defined as both the probability of the investment doing worse than expected *and* the probability of it doing better than expected. This does not seem to fit in precisely with our initial assertion that investors are risk-averse – that they dislike risk and require a reward or compensation for taking it on. This would tend to suggest that risk is really concerned with the chance that the investment's outcome will be *worse* than expected.

In one sense, this is quite correct. A risk-averse investor is concerned with the chance of the investment performing below expectation, often referred to as the *downside risk* of the investment. However, part of the reward for holding this risk is the chance that the investment's performance might exceed expectation: the *upside potential* of the investment; therefore both elements are of interest to the investor and are illustrated in Fig. 10.5.

The distinction between the two elements of investment performance variability is important if the distribution of returns is *asymmetrical*.

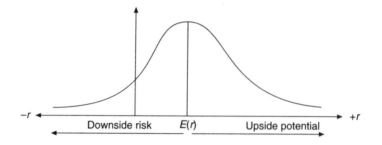

Fig. 10.5 *The 'two sides' of risk*

With a symmetrical distribution, the expected return divides the probability distribution into two identical halves. Thus standard deviation (or variance) measures both upside potential and downside risk equally well.

Where the distribution is skewed, the standard deviation measure describes neither type of investment risk adequately, but produces a measure of dispersion which is an unhelpful average of the two risk types.

As an illustration of the problem caused by asymmetric distributions try calculating the mean and variance of the returns on the two mutually exclusive investment opportunities shown below with possible returns shown in the columns headed r_a and r_b along with the probability of these returns being achieved.

	Investment A		Investment B	
r_a	Probability		r_b	Probability
−10%	0.10		10%	0.60
10%	0.10		20%	0.10
20%	0.40		30%	0.20
30%	0.30		60%	0.10
40%	0.10			

We find that returns for investment A have a mean value of 21% and a standard deviation of 13% whilst investment B has a mean value of 17% and a standard deviation of 15.8%. It looks at first sight as though A would be preferred as it has both a higher mean and a lower standard deviation. However, A can produce a loss whilst not only is B guaranteed to produce a positive result but also has a chance of producing a higher return than the best result A can produce. In fact, it is not really possible to say what decision an investor should make in these circumstances unless we can assess their attitudes towards risk in terms of the value they place on each possible outcome. The possibility of loss might carry a very high (negative) value, especially if it was an important decision that could lead to a manager losing her job.

One possible solution would be to use a specific measure of the dispersion of each risk type. This can be provided by a statistic called the *semi-variance*, which measures the dispersion of each half of the distribution individually. However, use of the semi-variance tends to complicate several of the calculations involved, and therefore for the sake of convenience – if nothing else – we will assume symmetrically distributed returns and so continue to make use of the standard deviation and variance.

Risk and expected utility

The above analysis contained what could be called a casual justification for measuring investment risk by the standard deviation or variance of returns.

However, it is possible to give a more analytical justification for these risk measures.

Our analysis of the expected utility model allowed us to conclude that risk-averse investors would be expected to have a utility function of the general form:

$$U(x) = a + bx - cx^2$$

and, therefore, in terms of the utility an investor could expect to obtain from the return on an investment in the shares of a company, we can express the utility function as:

$$E[U(r)] = a + bE(r) - cE(r^2).$$

In other words, the expected utility of the investment is determined by the distribution of the possible returns (which produce values for $E(r)$ and $E(r^2)$) and by the investor's personal attitude towards risk (which determines the values for the constants a, b, c).[13]

Given the definition for variance that we have used:

$$\sigma^2 = E(r^2) - E(r)^2,$$

then the third term of our general utility function can be re-expressed as:

$$- cE(r^2) = - c[\sigma^2 + E(r)^2]$$

and multiplying this out, the general utility function can be re-expressed as:

$$E[U(r)] = a + bE(r) - c\sigma^2 + cE(r)^2.$$

The advantage of undertaking this bit of algebraic manipulation is that we can now see that the expected utility produced by an investment is determined by the three risk-attitude constants (a, b, c), and two of the characteristics of the probability distribution of the investment's return: the expected return $[E(r)$ and $E(r)^2]$ and the variance of returns (σ^2).

We know that if an investment's return is certain, then the variance has a value of zero, whereas if the investment's actual return is uncertain, the variance will have a positive value. However, because the constant attached to the measure of variance (c) in the utility function is negative for the risk-averse investor (it is this that causes the utility function to be concave to the origin), a *positive* variance results in a *reduction* in the value of the utility expected from the investment.

Thus the more uncertain the actual return on the investment, the greater will be the value of the variance and the less will be the utility expected from the investment by the investor. This is exactly what we would expect for a risk-averse investor: the more risky the investment, the less attractive is the investment, and hence the lower is the utility it is expected to provide.

Required assumptions

This analysis provides us with a much more carefully reasoned justification for using variance or standard deviation as a measure of investment risk. However, at least one of two alternative conditions must hold true for this analysis to be seen to have real-world validity.

The first is that the variance is acceptable as a measure of risk so long as the probability distribution of possible returns is symmetrical. If it is strongly *asymmetrical* then we know that the arithmetic mean and variance no longer provide a complete description, as a measure of skew would also be required. Furthermore, neither the standard deviation nor variance would then provide an adequate measure of downside risk.

Alternatively, the conclusion only holds if investors' utility functions do follow the quadratic form developed earlier and are therefore solely determined by the expected return and variance of return variables. If utility functions of investors have a more complex form than that of a simple quadratic (and assuming returns are asymmetrically distributed) it follows that any measure of risk is also likely to be more complex.

The practical validity of these two alternative assumptions is troublesome. For example, there is evidence to suggest that investors' utility curves may exhibit both convexity and concavity – i.e. they may be risk-seekers or risk-averse, depending upon the size of the investment under consideration. They might also be prepared to take greater risks if they feel that it is the only way to achieve targets. However, perhaps the question of skew in investment returns poses the greater problems.

Intuition tells us that investment returns *must* be skewed: the maximum downside risk on an investment in a limited liability company is −100%, but the upside potential return can quite easily exceed that percentage. Further, there is some evidence to suggest that investors *are* interested in skew and do recognize that skewed returns can exist.

However, we shall continue our analysis on the assumption that variance (or standard deviation) of return is an adequate measure of risk, based on the reasoning that even if returns are skewed, the amount of skew is likely to be relatively small, and so will not be too much at odds with the assumption of symmetry.

Limitation of the analysis

Our analysis up to this point remains extremely limited as far as investment decision making is concerned. Assuming an investor is interested in maximizing expected utility and is risk-averse, then if a choice has to be made between two investments with identical expected returns, we can state that the alternative with the smaller amount of risk (either standard deviation or variance) will be preferred. Alternatively, given a choice between two investments with an identical amount of risk, the investor will prefer whichever has the highest expected return. Thus A is preferred to B and C is preferred to D:

Choice 1:
$$\begin{cases} E(r_A) = E(r_B) \\ \\ \sigma_A < \sigma_B \end{cases}$$

Choice 2:
$$\begin{cases} E(r_C) > E(r_D) \\ \\ \sigma_C = \sigma_D \end{cases}$$

However, the decision here is extremely limited. Certainly, we can conclude that A should be *preferred* to B, but we cannot say whether or not the investor will actually *choose* to undertake A, i.e. we cannot tell whether A gives a sufficiently large expected return to provide adequate compensation for the risk involved.

Furthermore, once we move away from this rather special choice situation, we cannot even make a preference statement: we cannot reach any conclusion as to which of the following pair of alternatives would be preferred:

$$\text{Choice 3:} \quad \begin{cases} E(r_E) > E(r_F) \\ \\ \sigma_E > \sigma_F \end{cases}$$

For a possible solution to these decision problems, we now have to look at portfolio theory. In addition, thinking back to the two questions that were posed at the start of this chapter: 'how are we to identify the degree of risk associated with a particular capital investment project?', and 'how can we identify the corresponding capital market interest rate that is appropriate for that level of risk?', it would appear that the analysis outlined above goes some way to providing an answer to the former, but not to the latter. We shall not comment further on these two questions at this stage, but wait until our understanding of the risk and expected return relationship has been further developed.

Summary

This chapter has taken a closer look at the relationship between risk and return in investment decision making. In particular, it considers how the risk and expected return of an investment might be measured. The main points covered are as follows:

- Four axioms of investor behaviour are specified:
  — choice is possible;
  — choice is transitive;
  — choice is dispassionate;
  — certainty-equivalents can be specified for any gamble situation.

- Given these axioms, it is possible to construct a utility function for a risk-averse investor, of the general form: $U(x) = a + bx - cx^2$, where the constants a, b and c reflect the investor's own personal risk attitude.

- With such a utility function, when faced with an investment the following relationship holds: the expected utility of the investment will be less than the utility of the investment's expected outcome. The difference is the required reward for risk-taking.

- As far as stock exchange investment is concerned, the expected return on a share can be measured as its arithmetic mean return and the risk of the share can be measured either as its variance or – more conveniently – its standard deviation of returns.

- However, standard deviation (or variance), whilst fitting in with the utility function concept of risk, is only a satisfactory measure of risk if either investment returns are symmetrically distributed around the expected return, or if investor's utility functions actually follow the quadratic form specified:

$$E[U(r)] = a + bE(r) - cr^2 + cE(r)^2.$$

- Finally, the analysis developed so far is highly limited. It can allow choice to be made either between projects of equal risk, or between projects of equal expected return. It does not allow choice between projects where there is neither equal risk nor expected return (unless of course one alternative enjoys both a higher return and lower risk). Nor does it allow decision making on any investment's *absolute* desirability (i.e. accept or reject), but just on *relative* desirability (when compared with another project).

Notes

1. 'Higher', that is, than what they would have received if the investment's outcome was known for certain. They would get a higher return as a reward for taking on the risk involved.

2. An axiom can be defined as a statement which is generally accepted without any need for proof or verification.

3. For example, suppose an investor is offered an investment which has a 60% chance of producing £5000 and a 40% chance of producing only £1000. We are assuming that the investor will be able to specify a *certain* sum of money which would be equally acceptable to this uncertain investment. This sum might be £3000. Thus £3000 is said to be the certainty-equivalent of the uncertain investment: the investor would be indifferent between receiving £3000 for certain, or receiving £5000 with a 60% probability and £1000 with a 40% probability.

4. We have already come across the idea of utility or indifference curves in the development and use of the single-period investment–consumption model.

5. We will assume that the project's outcome will occur almost immediately and so avoid – at this stage – the need to consider discounting.

6. Quite literally *any* utility index numbers could be used; for instance we could give +£5000 an index of 75 and –£2000 an index of 36 if we wished. The advantage of assigning index numbers of 1 and 0 to these two outcome extremes is simply that it eases the arithmetic.

7. Fig. 10.1 is not sufficiently detailed for the reader to obtain these values. However, they were obtained from the utility index as shown.

8. To calculate the return on a share, you do not need to have actually sold the share. You may continue to hold the share and simply wish to know what return you have made to date. In such circumstances the 'selling price' would be replaced by the 'current market price'.

9. Note that the word 'expected' is now being used in a technical sense, meaning the arithmetic mean.

10. Notice that the standard deviation can be expressed as a percentage, just as can the expected return. However the variance involves a 'squaring-up' of the data and so cannot be viewed as a percentage, but simply as an uncategorized measure of dispersion.

11. The standard deviation is stated in rates of return whilst the variance represents 'rates of return squared'. Because it is easier to discuss risk as a percentage rate of return, rather than a rate of return squared, the standard

deviation is now commonly used to measure risk. However, it is sometimes mathematically more convenient to measure risk by variance. Either definition of risk is conceptually valid, since they are mathematically equivalent. The two measures cannot be used interchangeably, but they do give consistent rankings of risk.

12. Any introductory textbook on inferential statistics will discuss these properties in detail, but see the Appendix to Chapter 13.

13. The c constant is negative to ensure that the utility function is that of a risk-averse individual and hence concave to the origin.

Further reading

1. Utility theory is not a simple area, but for an easy introduction see: R.O. Swalm, 'Utility Theory – Insights into Risk Taking', *Harvard Business Review*, November–December 1966.
2. For an example of an actual attempt to construct utility functions, see: C.J. Grayson, 'The Use of Statistical Techniques in Capital Budgeting', in *Financial Research and Management Decisions*, ed. A. Robicheck, John Wiley 1967.
3. Finally, for a more complete discussion on utility functions, see Chapter 11 of J.C. Francis and S.H. Archer, *Portfolio Analysis* second edn, Prentice-Hall 1979.

Quickie questions

1. If the NPV discount rate should reflect the return available elsewhere in the capital market for an investment of similar risk to the project being appraised, what two *practical* problems arise?
2. What is meant by the term 'transitive' with regards to ranking alternatives?
3. What is a certainty-equivalent?
4. If an investment has two outcomes: +£10 000 and –£5000 and an investor indicates that £3500 is the certainty-equivalent of a 60% chance of a +£10 000 outcome, what is the utility measure of £3500 on a 0 to 1 scale?
5. If a utility function is concave to the origin, what risk attitude does this indicate?
6. What would the utility function of a risk-neutral investor look like?
7. For a risk-averse investor what is the relationship between an investment's expected outcome and its certainty-equivalent?
8. Define the return on a share.
9. Given the following information, what is the expected return and risk of an investment in the following shares?

Economic conditions	Probability	Investment return
Strong growth	0.20	+40%
Weak growth	0.60	+15%
Economic decline	0.20	–10%

10. What is downside risk?
11. Why is it a potential problem in terms of choice if returns are not distributed symmetrically about the mean?

Problem

1. An investor carefully considers a number of gambles and decides that he is indifferent between a certain income of £2500 p.a. and each of the following probabilities:
    - (i) A 60% chance of receiving £4500 p.a. and a 40% chance of receiving £500 p.a.
    - (ii) A 75% chance of receiving £1600 p.a. and a 25% chance of receiving £4500 p.a.
    - (iii) A 55% chance of receiving £1600 p.a. and a 45% chance of receiving £3500 p.a.
    - (iv) A 75% chance of receiving £2000 p.a. and a 25% chance of receiving £3500 p.a.
    - (v) A 50% chance of receiving £2000 p.a. and a 50% chance of receiving £3000 p.a.
    - (vi) An 85% chance of receiving £2000 p.a. and a 15% chance of receiving £4000 p.a.

    The investor has an occupation which gives him an income of £1000 p.a. which he regards as certain. He is now considering which of the two alternative additional activities he should undertake:
    - (1) Offers a 50% chance each of an income of £1500 p.a. and £2000 p.a.
    - (2) Offers a 50% chance each of an income of £1000 p.a. and £2500 p.a.

    Assume that he will accept one of these opportunities and that he has no borrowing and investment opportunities available: the utility function measures the utility derived from the present contemplation of an income of the specified amount in any year.

    Required:
    - (a) Sketch a utility function for the investor. What does this function indicate about his attitude towards risk?
    - (b) Use utility analysis to indicate which new opportunity he should accept.
    - (c) Calculate the variance of each possible income stream available to the investor.
    - (d) Comment briefly on the implications for the usefulness of variance calculations in analysing decisions subject to uncertainty.

11 Portfolio theory

The nineteenth-century Scottish/American millionaire philanthropist, Andrew Carnegie, is reported to have said 'The way to make a fortune is to put all your eggs into one basket and then watch the basket very carefully'. In fact, as we shall see, this is a high-risk strategy. Choosing the right basket might indeed lead to the making of a fortune but choosing the wrong basket could turn out to be the way to lose one! As we will demonstrate, a more logical approach to investment is to diversify and thus spread our risks.

Two-asset portfolios

Portfolio theory – as its name implies – is concerned with the construction of investment portfolios; which is to say collections of investments. Essentially it is based on the application of fairly simple mathematics recognizing that if we know the arithmetic means and variances of multiple, individual distributions together with the degree to which their returns co-vary, then the arithmetic mean and variance of a probability distribution resulting from the combining of the individual distributions can be specified.

Thus if the shares of several different companies are combined into an investment portfolio and the expected returns, variances of returns and covariances of returns are known for each company's shares, then the expected return and variance of the investment portfolio can be determined.

However the importance of portfolio theory does not lie so much in this statistical result, but in what arises out of it. Although the expected return of the investment portfolio is simply a weighted average of the expected returns on the individual investments that go to make up the portfolio, the risk of the portfolio (measured by its standard deviation of returns) is *less than* the weighted average risk of the individual constituent investment.[1] In other words, the statistical result upon which portfolio theory is founded supports the wisdom of not keeping all your (investment) eggs in one basket. Risk can be reduced through diversification without an associated reduction in returns.

Risk and expected return

Suppose that an individual investor has a sum of money with which she wishes to construct an investment portfolio by buying the ordinary shares of different companies. In order to keep the arithmetic simple, we shall initially assume that she is going to purchase the shares of just *two* companies – therefore she is constructing what can be termed a *two-asset risky portfolio*. Later on we will see how the approach used can be directly expanded to involve portfolios that consist of shareholdings in many companies.

Let the two companies whose shares comprise the individual's investment portfolio be called A and B, respectively. The individual uses a proportion, x, of her investment funds to buy shares in company A, and the remainder of her funds $(1 - x)$ is used to buy shares in company B. The statistical result that is the foundation of portfolio theory allows us to determine the expected return, $E(r_p)$, and variance of return, σ_p^2, of the resulting investment portfolio:

$$E(r_p) = xE(r_A) + (1 - x)E(r_B),$$
$$\sigma_p^2 = x^2\sigma_A^2 + (1 - x)^2\sigma_B^2 + 2x(1 - x)\,\text{Cov}(r_A,r_B).$$

For the moment it will be more convenient for us to deal with portfolio risk in terms of the standard deviation of returns, σ, and so the second expression becomes:

$$\sigma_p = \sqrt{[x^2\,\sigma_A^2 + (1 - x)^2\,\sigma_B^2 + 2x(1 - x)\,\text{Cov}(r_A,r_B)]}.$$

The covariance

We are familiar with all the notation used in these expressions, except for $\text{Cov}(r_A,r_B)$. This notation represents the measure of the covariance between the returns on the shares in A and in B. In other words, the covariance examines the degree to which the returns on the shares of both companies vary in relation to each other.

This covariance can either be positive or negative and can also be weaker or stronger. Positive covariability indicates that the returns on the two shares will tend to move in the same direction as each other (i.e. if, in a particular period, the return produced by the shares in company A is above what was expected, then there will be a tendency to find that the return on the shares in B is similarly above expectations), whereas negative covariability indicates that the returns will tend to move in opposite directions.

In addition, the greater the strength of covariability (say, positive covariability) then the stronger will be the tendency for the variability in returns between the two companies to move in unison. It helps to explain the meaning of the covariance if its components are examined. We can express the covariability of returns as follows:

$$\text{Cov}(r_A,r_B) = \sigma_A \times \sigma_B \times \rho_{AB}$$

In other words, the covariance of returns in A and B represents the product of the risks of A and B (measured by the standard deviation of returns) and the *correlation coefficient* (ρ_{AB}), between the returns in A and in B.[2]

The correlation coefficient expresses the strength of the linear relationship between the two variables – in this case the returns of the shares of A and B

– and can take on any value between +1 and −1. A correlation coefficient of +1 indicates perfect positive correlation, such that the returns of the two shares will vary in perfect lock-step, whereas a correlation coefficient of −1 indicates perfect negative correlation. In this case the returns on the two shares will move in perfect negative lock-step. A positive correlation coefficient, but one which is less than +1, indicates that there is a tendency for the returns on the two shares to move together in the same direction; and a negative correlation coefficient, one which is less than 0 but greater than −1, indicates that there is a tendency for the returns to move in opposite directions. Given the relationship above, the sign attached to the correlation coefficient determines the sign of the covariance.

The further away the correlation coefficient is from +1 or −1 (and hence the closer it is to zero) the weaker is the general tendency indicated by the sign of the correlation – or the greater is the tendency for the share return movements to be unrelated, or *uncorrelated*. A correlation coefficient of 0 indicates that there is no relationship between the two shares in terms of the variability of their returns.

In fact, almost all shares are positively correlated with each other.

The covariance calculation

This may be a good stage at which to provide a simple example of the calculations required to determine the covariance: Example 1.

Example 1

Suppose the shares of two companies, C and D, have the following probability distributions:

State of economy	Probability	Returns on C	Returns on D
Boom	0.2	24%	5%
Steady growth	0.6	12%	30%
Slump	0.2	0%	−5%

Then their expected returns and standard deviation of returns can be calculated as:

$$E(r_C) = 12\% \qquad\qquad E(r_D) = 18\%$$
$$\sigma_C = 7.59\% \qquad\qquad \sigma_D = 15.03\%$$

and the covariance of returns is given by:

$$\Sigma(r_C - E(r_C)) \, (r_D - E(r_D)) \, \text{Pr}.$$

That is:

$$(24\% - 12\%) \times \quad (5\% - 18\%) \times 0.2 = -31.2$$
$$(12\% - 12\%) \times \quad (30\% - 18\%) \times 0.6 = \quad 0$$
$$(\,0\% - 12\%) \times (-5\% - 18\%) \times 0.2 = +55.2$$
$$\text{Cov}(r_C, r_D) = \overline{+24.0}$$

Given that $\text{Cov}(r_C, r_D) = \sigma_C \, \sigma_D \, \rho_{C,D}$, then

$$\rho_{C,D} = \frac{\text{Cov}(r_C, r_D)}{\sigma_C \sigma_D} = \frac{+24}{7.59 \times 15.03} = +0.21.$$

This is a relatively low, positive correlation. It indicates that although the returns on the shares in the two companies *tend* to vary in the same direction, the tendency is rather weak.

Given the above information, if an investor were to construct a two-asset portfolio consisting of shares in companies C and D, such that 75% of her funds were placed in the shares of C (i.e. $x =$

0.75) and the remainder of her funds placed in D (i.e. $1 - x = 0.25$), then the resulting portfolio would have an expected return ($E(r_p)$) and risk (σ_p) as follows:

$$E(r_p) = (0.75 \times 12\%) + (0.25 \times 18\%) = 13.5\%,$$
$$\sigma_p = \sqrt{((0.75^2 \times 7.59\%^2) + (0.25^2 \times 15.03\%^2) + (2 \times 0.75 \times 0.25 \times 24.0))},$$
$$\sigma_p = \sqrt{(32.40 + 14.12 + 9.0)} = \sqrt{55.52} = 7.45\%.$$

The risk-reduction effect

Returning to the expression for the risk and expected return of a two-asset portfolio, but now expanding the covariance term in the risk expression, we can examine the cause of the risk-reduction effect of investment diversification:

$$E(r_p) = xE(r_A) + (1 - x)E(r_B),$$
$$\sigma_p = \sqrt{[x^2 \sigma_A^2 + (1 - x)^2 \sigma_B^2 + 2x(1 - x)\, \sigma_A \sigma_B \rho_{AB}]}.$$

The first of these two expressions does not give cause for much excitement. It simply shows that the portfolio's expected return is an average of the expected returns on the two component investments ($E(r_A)$ and $E(r_B)$), weighted by their respective importance (by value) in the overall portfolio. This is just as we would have thought; however, the second expression is of considerably greater interest. This interest is caused by the last element in the expression – the correlation coefficient of returns – which can take on any value between $+1$ and -1 (including zero).

The third term in the expression for portfolio risk: $2x(1 - x)\sigma_A\sigma_B\rho_{AB}$ is at its largest value[3] when the correlation coefficient is $+1$. The further away the correlation coefficient is from $+1$, the smaller is the value of this third term and hence the smaller is its contribution to the portfolio's risk. (In fact when the correlation coefficient becomes negative, the term actually makes a *negative* contribution to risk, which reaches a maximum when the returns are perfectly negatively correlated, i.e. -1.)

It is this third term (and in particular the correlation coefficient it contains) that is the cause of the risk-reduction effect of investment diversification. Measuring portfolio risk as the standard deviation of returns, we can say that the portfolio risk is a weighted average of the risk of the component investments (just as with the expected return), but *only* if the returns on the shares in the two companies are perfectly positively correlated (i.e. $\rho_{AB} = +1$). If the correlation coefficient is *less than* $+1$ (as will normally be the case) then the risk of the portfolio is *less than* a weighted average of the risk of the individual investment components. The further away the correlation coefficient is from $+1$, the greater will be the risk reduction effect.

Example 2 will help to clarify matters at this point.

Example 2

An investor wishes to construct a portfolio which consists of placing 60% of his available funds into the shares of company E and the other 40% into the shares of company F.
Companies E and F have the following expected returns and risk:

$$E(r_E) = 30\% \qquad\qquad E(r_F) = 10\%$$
$$\sigma_E = 12\% \qquad\qquad \sigma_F = 3\%$$

The expected return on the investor's portfolio will be a weighted average of the expected returns on the portfolio's component investments:

$$E(r_p) = (0.60 \times 30\%) + (0.40 \times 10\%) = 22\%.$$

But what of the portfolio's *risk*? That will depend upon the correlation coefficient between the returns on the shares of the two companies. If the correlation coefficient is: +1 then there will be *no* risk-reduction effect and the portfolio's risk:

$$\sigma_p = \sqrt{((0.6^2 \times 12\%^2) + (0.4^2 \times 3\%^2) + (2 \times 0.6 \times 0.4 \times 12\% \times 3\% \times +1))} = 8.4\%.$$

This is simply a weighted average of the risk of the portfolio's components:

$$\sigma_p = (0.6 \times 12\%) + (0.4 \times 3\%) = 8.4\%.$$

However, the further away the correlation coefficient is from +1, the greater will be the amount of risk eliminated through the *diversification* effect. To illustrate this effect, three examples will be used:

(i)   If $\rho_{E,F} = + 0.5$, then $\sigma_p = 7.9\%$
(ii) If $\rho_{E,F} = \quad 0$, then $\sigma_p = 7.3\%$
(iii) If $\rho_{E,F} = \quad -1$, then $\sigma_p = 6.0\%$

From Example 2 it can be seen how portfolio risk, but *not* portfolio expected return, is progressively reduced as the correlation coefficient moves further and further away from perfect positive correlation (i.e. $\rho = +1$).

A diagrammatic example

Example 3 is designed to illustrate graphically the points made above and to show how the portfolio risk and return can also be varied by varying the proportions of the investment funds placed in each risky asset.

Example 3

Suppose that the ordinary shares of the companies (G and H), with which the investor has chosen to construct her portfolio, exhibit the following characteristics:

Company G	Company H
$E(r_G) = 25\%$	$E(r_H) = 18\%$
$\sigma_G = 8\%$	$\sigma_H = 4\%$

From the foregoing analysis, we know that the expected return and risk of any portfolio made up of the shares in these two companies depends not only on the above information, but also on the proportions of the available funds invested in each company's shares (i.e. x and $(1 - x)$) and the correlation coefficient of the probability distributions of the returns from each company's shares (i.e. ρ_{GH}).

Fig. 11.1 illustrates the range of possible portfolio risk and expected returns that the investor could obtain by varying the proportions of her funds between the two companies, in three particular cases: when the correlation coefficient of returns has a value of +1, 0 and −1. For example, if the investor chose to construct a portfolio that consisted of splitting her investment funds equally between the shares of the two companies (i.e. $x = 0.50$ and $(1 - x) = 0.50$), then the expected return of the portfolio would be:

$$E(r_p) = (0.50 \times 25\%) + (0.50 \times 18\%) = 21.5\%.$$

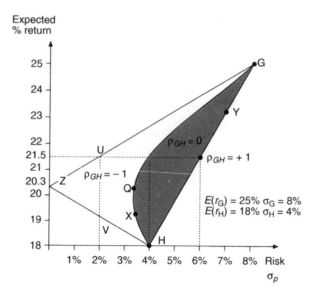

Fig. 11.1 *The impact of the correlation coefficient*

Expected
% return

$P_{GH} = 0$

$P_{GH} = +1$

$P_{GH} = -1$

$E(r_G) = 25\%$ $\sigma_G = 8\%$
$E(r_H) = 18\%$ $\sigma_H = 4\%$

1% 2% 3% 4% 5% 6% 7% 8% Risk
σ_p

However, the risk of this portfolio varies, depending upon the value of the correlation coefficient:[4]

ρ_{GH}	σ_p
+1	6%
0	4%
−1	2%

Once again we see that portfolio risk is maximized where the two components are perfectly positively correlated and minimized where they are perfectly negatively correlated. For correlation coefficients between these two extremes, then portfolio risk will be less than 6%, but more than 2% (e.g. when $\rho_{GH} = 0$, $\sigma_p = 4\%$).

Portfolio risk (and simultaneously, expected return) can also be varied by varying the proportions of investment funds placed in the two shares. Assuming that $\rho_{GH} = +1$, then we know that splitting the investment funds evenly between G and H produces a risk of 6% and an expected return of 21.5%; but any of the risk–expected return combinations that lie along the straight line GYH in Fig. 11.1 could be obtained, simply by varying the proportions of G and H held.

At one extreme the portfolio would consist only of shares in G, then $E(r_p) = E(r_G) = 25\%$ and $\sigma_p = \sigma_G = 8\%$. At the other extreme the portfolio could consist solely of H, when the risk and expected return would be 4% and 18% respectively. Alternatively any intermediate portfolio could be constructed such as Y which consists of 75% of funds being placed in G and the remainder in H. This portfolio has a risk and expected return of 7% and 23.25%, respectively.

Notice that where G and H are perfectly positively correlated, all the possible portfolio risk–expected return combinations that are available (through varying x and (1 − x)) lie along a *straight line*. In other words both the expected return *and* the risk of the portfolios constructed are simple weighted averages.

In contrast, the risk–expected return portfolio combinations for all other correlation coefficient values (i.e. except for $\rho = +1$) lie along *non-linear* lines, with the non-linearity becoming more pronounced as the correlation coefficient moves further away from +1. Indeed the non-linearity is a graphical representation of the risk-elimination effect.

Thus the curved line GQXH represents all the possible portfolio combinations available by varying the proportion of G and H when the correlation coefficient is zero. For example, portfolio X consists of 80% of portfolio funds in H and the balance in G. The expected return is 19.4% (the same as it would have been if $\rho_{GH} = +1$) but the risk is only 3.58% (whereas it would have been 4.8% if $\rho_{GH} = +1$). The degree of curvature of GQXH signifies the degree of risk reduction possible in the circumstances given.

The third example represented diagrammatically in Fig. 11.1 is where the two risky assets display perfect *negative* correlation. Here the dog-legged line GUZVH reflects all the possible portfolio combinations that would be available by varying the investment portfolios. One unique feature about this set of circumstances is that, as can be seen from the diagram, it is now possible to construct a portfolio with *zero* risk. This is portfolio Z. The exact make-up of this portfolio can be found by solving for x in the expression:[5]

$$\sigma_p = x \times 8\% - (1-x) \times 4\% = 0.$$

In this case the solution is $x = 0.33$. In other words, if one-third of the portfolio funds were placed in the shares of G and the rest in H, then the risk of the portfolio would be zero and the expected return (which would in fact be a *certain* return, as no risk is involved), would be:

$$E(r_p) = (0.33 \times 25\%) + (0.66 \times 18\%) = 20.13\%.$$

However, it should be noted that the ability to reduce risk to *zero* in this way is a characteristic *only* of risky portfolios which consist of perfectly negatively correlated components. Where the correlation coefficient between portfolio components is greater than -1 (but less than $+1$), risk reduction is possible, but *total* risk elimination is impossible.

In practice the ordinary shares of most companies exhibit correlation coefficients (with shares in other companies) with values greater than zero but less than $+1$, thereby limiting the degree of risk reduction possible through portfolio manipulation. The shaded area on Fig. 11.1 therefore gives the likely risk–return combinations that might be possible in practice with a two-component portfolio consisting of ordinary shares in companies G and H.

Dominance

Continuing with the example where the two portfolio components are perfectly negatively correlated, we can use it to illustrate the fact that, under some circumstances, there would be portfolios available to investors that will be seen as being unambiguously undesirable. This is demonstrated in Example 4.

Example 4

Suppose an investor wishes to construct an investment portfolio consisting of shares in I and J, when I and J are perfectly negatively correlated. In Fig. 11.2 the line IKLMJ can be termed the *portfolio boundary*, because it represents all possible portfolios constructed with the shares of the two companies, given the correlation coefficient.

Fig. 11.2 *Perfect negative correlation*

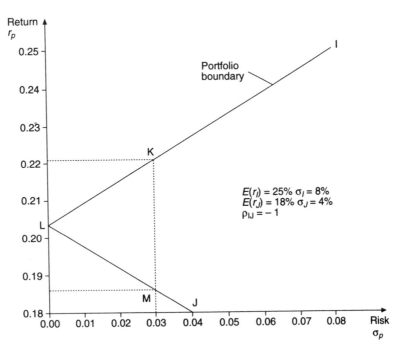

$E(r_I) = 25\%$ $\sigma_I = 8\%$
$E(r_J) = 18\%$ $\sigma_J = 4\%$
$\rho_{IJ} = -1$

From Fig. 11.2 we can see that a rational risk-averse investor would not choose *any* portfolio lying along the lower part of the IKLMJ dog-leg, i.e. between L and J. The reason for this is that there will always be a *better* portfolio lying along the upper part of IKLMJ (where 'better' is defined in terms of a portfolio giving a higher expected return for the same amount of risk).

For example, our investor is always going to prefer portfolio K to portfolio M. Both involve the same amount of risk, but K is expected to produce a substantially higher return: K is said to *dominate* M. In fact all the portfolios lying along the lower part of the dog-leg are dominated by portfolios lying along the upper part. The portfolios that lie along the boundary between points I and L are therefore termed *efficient*, in that each represents the maximum expected return for a given level of risk.

Returning to Fig. 11.1, along the portfolio boundary for which the correlation coefficient is zero, portfolios lying between points G and Q are similarly efficient and those lying between points Q and H, inefficient.

Multi-asset portfolios

A three-asset portfolio

So far, we have considered two-asset portfolios only. However, the analysis can be quite easily extended to portfolios containing many assets (e.g. the ordinary shares of many different companies), although the calculations become much more lengthy. The risk (measured by variance) and the expected return of a portfolio consisting of N different assets can be calculated from the expressions given below, where x_i represents the proportion of funds invested in component i:

$$E(r_p) = \sum_{i=1}^{N} x_i E(r_i),$$

$$\sigma_p^2 = \sum_{i=1}^{N} \sum_{j=1}^{N} x_i x_j \sigma_i \sigma_j \rho_{ij}.$$

It is the calculation of the portfolio variance that is particularly time-consuming, because it is calculated as the sum of the weighted variance of all possible combinations of pairs of assets. However, expanding the number of assets has a particularly significant effect. As we have seen from the formulae for the variance of portfolios, the total variability of the portfolio is made up of two groups of components. One comes from the variability of the individual assets whilst the other comes from their variability relative to each other. As the number of assets increases, the variability of individual assets becomes less significant in determining the variability of the portfolio and in the end what really matters is how the assets are correlated.

Example 5 illustrates the computations necessary for a simple three-component portfolio.

Example 5

An investment portfolio consists of shares in companies N, P and Q, in the respective proportions: 20%, 70%, 10%. The resulting portfolio, termed Z, has an expected return of 26.2% and a standard deviation of return of 8.04%.

Company	Portfolio proportion	$E(r_i)$	σ_i	ρ_{ij}
N	0.20	20%	6%	N, N = +1
				N, P = +0.7
				N, Q = +0.4
P	0.70	30%	10%	P, N = +0.7
				P, P = +1
				P, Q = +0.8
Q	0.10	12%	2%	Q, N = +0.4
				Q, P = +0.8
				Q, Q = +1

$$E(r_p) = \sum_{i=n}^{q} x_i E(r_i)$$

$$= (0.20 \times 20\%) + (0.70 \times 30\%) + (0.10 \times 12\%) = 26.2\%$$

$$\sigma_p^2 = \sum_{i=n}^{q} \sum_{j=n}^{q} x_i x_j \sigma_i \sigma_j \rho_{ij}$$

$$
\left.
\begin{aligned}
&= 0.20 \times 0.20 \times\ 6\% \times\ 6\% \times 1\ = 1.44 \\
&\ \ \ 0.20 \times 0.70 \times\ 6\% \times 10\% \times 0.7 = 5.88 \\
&\ \ \ 0.20 \times 0.10 \times\ 6\% \times\ 2\% \times 0.4 = 0.096 \\
&\ \ \ 0.70 \times 0.20 \times 10\% \times\ 6\% \times 0.7 = 5.88 \\
&\ \ \ 0.70 \times 0.70 \times 10\% \times 10\% \times 1\ = 49.0 \\
&\ \ \ 0.70 \times 0.10 \times 10\% \times\ 2\% \times 0.8 = 1.12 \\
&\ \ \ 0.10 \times 0.20 \times\ 2\% \times\ 6\% \times 0.4 = 0.096 \\
&\ \ \ 0.10 \times 0.70 \times\ 2\% \times 10\% \times 0.8 = 1.12 \\
&\ \ \ 0.10 \times 0.10 \times\ 2\% \times\ 2\% \times 1\ = 0.04
\end{aligned}
\right\} +
$$

$$\sigma_p^2 = \underline{64.672}$$

$$\sigma_p = \sqrt{\sigma_p^2} = \sqrt{64.672} = 8.04\%$$

Therefore the portfolio (we shall term it portfolio Z), consisting of 20% of investment N, 70% of investment P and 10% of investment Q has the following characteristics:

Expected return = 26.2%
Risk = 8.04%

A graphical representation

Whereas all possible portfolios that can be constructed from just two assets (with a specified correlation coefficient) can be illustrated graphically as lying along a line (as in Figs 11.1 and 11.2), when dealing with multi-asset portfolios, all possible combinations are represented by an *area*.

Fig. 11.3 illustrates the area of possible portfolios that may be obtained from combining the shares of companies N, P and Q. Point Z represents the location of the portfolio actually constructed in Example 5.

From our previous discussion of dominance we know that, for risk-averse investors, the only portfolios of interest will be those lying along the north-west boundary of the portfolio area, PXYQ, the 'efficiency boundary' or 'efficient frontier'. These portfolios represent the greatest possible expected return for a given level of risk. Therefore a risk-averse investor would not be interested in holding portfolio Z: portfolio X would give a superior expected return for the same level of risk, whilst portfolio Y would give the same return for a much-reduced level of risk. Indeed, all the portfolios lying along that part of the efficiency boundary between X and Y would be preferred to portfolio Z.[6]

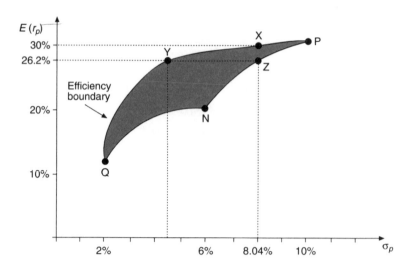

Fig. 11.3 *Dominance*

An investor faced with holding a portfolio consisting of shares in the three companies N, P and Q would consider only the portfolios lying along the efficiency boundary and select the one which maximized her utility, given her own particular attitude to risk and return. In terms of indifference curves, the investor would select that portfolio which allowed her to obtain her highest possible indifference curve. Fig. 11.4 illustrates this situation.

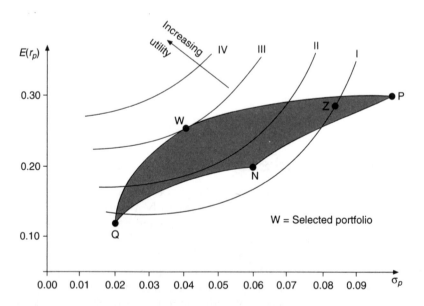

Fig. 11.4 *The optimal portfolio*

Considerations of practicality

Up to this point, although the analysis has been useful in identifying that it is the risk and expected-return characteristics of combinations of investments that is of importance, rather than the risk and expected-return characteristics of single investments, the *practical* usefulness of the analysis is limited.

Individual investors themselves, never mind others who may be taking decisions on their behalf, are unlikely to be aware of the nature of their set of indifference curves. Thus in Fig. 11.4, although in the circumstances given portfolio W would be optimal for the investor with that set of indifference curves (some of which are shown), in practice the investor can do little more than follow her own rather poorly formed 'judgement' as to the combination of the three investments which will produce the 'best' risk–return combination.

The main stumbling block to the practical application of the ideas we have developed so far is the vast numbers of calculations that would be needed to identify the efficiency boundary in practice. The example used above involved the consideration of just three risky assets – and only looked at one possible portfolio – but we still saw that a substantial number of calculations were required as each possible combination of pairs of investments had to be considered. In the real world the investor faces a vast number of risky assets and so the data and computations necessary to identify the efficiency boundary become astronomical in number and, to all intents and purposes, totally impractical.

For example, the total amount of data required – in terms of expected returns, variances and covariances – is given by $N(N + 3)/2$, where N is the number of different shares. An investor dealing with the London Stock Exchange has over 7200 securities from which to choose. In terms of portfolio theory, this would require almost 26 million calculations! (For 7200 securities it would actually be $(7200^2/2) + 7200$ which is 25 927 200.) Thus even if an investor were knowledgeable about his own set of indifference curves, it is unlikely that he would be able to identify the efficiency boundary, let alone the optimal portfolio lying along that boundary.

Introduction of a risk-free investment

A two-asset portfolio

A move towards greater practical usefulness can be made if a *risk-free* investment is introduced into the analysis. With such an investment, the return is known for certain and exhibits no variability. Short-term government bonds (stocks), held to maturity are usually considered such an investment.[7]

To see the effect of introducing a risk-free investment we will start by examining the characteristics of a two-asset portfolio where one asset is a risk-free investment (e.g. government stock) and the other is a risky investment (e.g. the shares of company A). The risk-free return will be designated as r_F (it is no longer an *expected* return, but is now certain), and because its return is certain, its risk – measured by either the standard deviation (σ_F) or the variance (σ_F^2) – is zero.

The resulting portfolio has the following characteristics:

$$E(r_p) = xE(r_A) + (1 - x) r_F,$$
$$\sigma_p^2 = x^2 \sigma_A^2 + (1 - x)^2 \sigma_F^2 + 2x (1 - x) \sigma_A \sigma_F \rho_{AF}.$$

As the risk-free investment has a zero variance and standard deviation, the expression for portfolio risk reduces to:

$$\sigma_p^2 = x^2 \sigma_A^2 \text{ or } \sigma_p = \sqrt{(x^2 \sigma_A^2)} = x\sigma_A.$$

The risky–riskless boundary

Fig. 11.5 illustrates the range of portfolio risks and expected returns that are possible from combining risky investment A, with an expected return of 18% and a standard deviation of 5%, with a risk-free investment producing a certain 8% return. The different portfolios that are available from combining the two investments lie along a straight line because, as the above expression for portfolio risk shows, when combining a risk-free and a risky investment, portfolio risk becomes a simple weighted average of the risk of the components.

To identify this particular type of portfolio boundary, we will term it the 'risky–riskless' boundary. Portfolio P on this boundary consists of 75% of risky investment A and 25% of the risk-free investment. In other words, portfolio P is three-quarters of the way up the boundary line between the risk-free asset (government stock) and the risky asset (shares in company A). It produces the following characteristics:

$$E(r_p) = 0.75 \times 18\% + 0.25 \times 8\% = 15.5\%,$$

$$\sigma_p = 0.75 \times 5\% = 3.75\%.$$

The slope of this boundary is particularly interesting. It is calculated as $[E(r_A) - r_F]/\sigma_A$ and gives the *additional* amount of expected return produced by the portfolio for each unit increase in its risk. Therefore in this example, every 1% increase in portfolio risk (σ_p) produces an extra $(18\% - 8\%)/5 = 2\%$ of expected return.

Fig. 11.5 *The risky–riskless boundary*

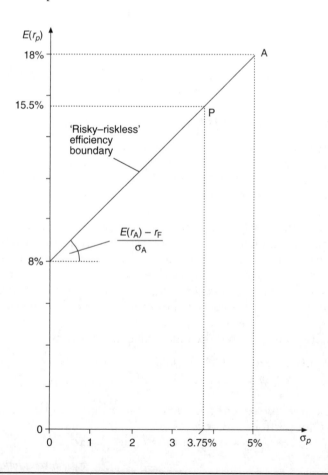

For example, if we wished to undertake a portfolio investment which involved taking on a risk of 4.75% (measured by standard deviation), then this should provide an expected return of $4.75 \times 2\% = 9.5\%$ *in excess of the* risk-free return of 8%. Thus the total expected return from the portfolio would be $9.5\% + 8\% = 17.5\%$.

This can be seen to fit in with the portfolio risk and expected return expressions. If the portfolio is to display risk of 4.75%, then:

$$\sigma_p = x \times 5\% = 4.75\%$$

This gives $x = 4.75\% \div 5\% = 0.95$
and so $(1 - x) = 0.05$
Therefore, $E(r_p) = 0.95 \times 18\% + 0.05 \times 8\% = 17.5\%$.

A riskless asset plus a risky portfolio

Extending this approach further, suppose that an investor is faced with a choice amongst many alternative risky investments (such as the London Stock Exchange). The shaded area in Fig. 11.6 represents all possible risky investment portfolios open to her, and AB represents the boundary of efficient portfolios[8] available.

If the possibility of undertaking a risk-free investment is introduced, we can now consider constructing another two-asset portfolio where one asset is risk-free and the other is risky. The difference between the situation here and that in the previous example is that now the risky asset is not a single investment (e.g. shares in a single company) but an investment in an *efficient portfolio of risky assets*.

Suppose such an investment was efficient risky portfolio C in Fig. 11.6, then the two-asset portfolios available would lie along the line r_F, C. The point of interest to us here is that the introduction of this two-asset portfolio dominates part of the original efficiency boundary AB. Those portfolios lying along BC of the efficiency boundary are dominated by those lying along r_F, C. Fig. 11.7 shows this situation in more detail.

Returning to Fig. 11.6, it can be seen that combining government stock (r_F) with efficient risky portfolio C is not the *best* two-asset combination. For example government stock and portfolio D dominate all the r_F, C

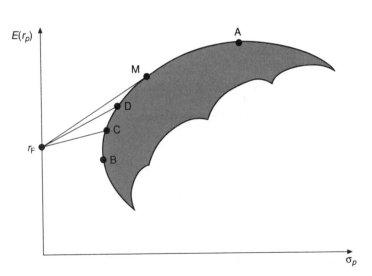

Fig. 11.6 *Combining risk-free and risky investments*

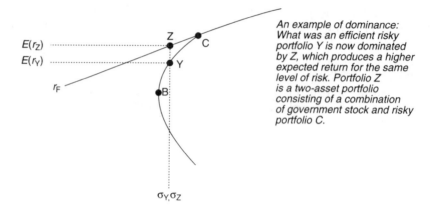

Fig. 11.7 *An example of dominance*

E(r_Z) ⋯⋯⋯⋯⋯⋯⋯⋯⋯⋯ Z C
E(r_Y) ⋯⋯⋯⋯⋯⋯⋯⋯⋯ Y
r_F
B

σ_Y, σ_Z

An example of dominance: What was an efficient risky portfolio Y is now dominated by Z, which produces a higher expected return for the same level of risk. Portfolio Z is a two-asset portfolio consisting of a combination of government stock and risky portfolio C.

portfolios, as well as all those portfolios from B to D on the original risky portfolio efficiency boundary.

Another way of looking at this analysis is in terms of the slope of the risky–riskless efficiency boundary. We saw in the previous section that the slope of this boundary gave the additional amount of expected return (in excess of the risk-free return), for each unit increase in risk taken on. It therefore follows that it is in the investor's best interests to combine government stock with that efficient risky portfolio that creates the *steepest possible* risky–riskless boundary slope. This portfolio is found at the point of tangency of a line drawn from the risk-free return to the risky portfolio efficiency boundary: portfolio M in Fig 11.6.

Under these circumstances the original efficiency boundary AB has now been radically modified to AMr_F. An investor who wishes to locate somewhere along A to M has to specifically identify the particular portfolio of risky investments. However, an investor who wishes to locate along M to r_F will simply place a proportion of her investment funds in government stock and the remainder in risky portfolio M. Investors will no longer be interested in any portfolio lying along M to B as these are all dominated by portfolios lying along the risky–riskless boundary of M, r_F.

The possibility of borrowing

Buying government stock can be viewed as simply lending money to the government, and therefore the return on government stock, r_F, is the risk-free *lending* interest rate. In the previous section we saw how the original efficiency boundary was modified and extended by the introduction of a risk-free investment: lending at the risk-free interest rate. A complementary extension and modification can also be achieved by the introduction of the possibility that the investor can add to her investment funds by *borrowing*.

Assuming that investors can borrow unlimited amounts (given their ability to repay) at an interest rate of r_B, and assuming that both the interest payments and loan repayments are certain, then Fig. 11.8 illustrates the modification and extension possible to the *original* boundary of efficient risky portfolios: the line AB. The revised efficiency boundary now becomes BNX, where X extends without limit (i.e. unlimited borrowing capacity).

For reasons similar to those of the previous analysis, portfolios lying along that part of the original efficiency boundary of A to N are no longer desirable, as they are dominated by portfolios lying along NX. However the composition of the portfolios lying along NX are somewhat different to those lying along r_F M in Fig. 11.6.

In Fig. 11.6 the portfolios on the risky–riskless boundary were composed of investments split between risky portfolio M and risk-free government stock. In Fig. 11.8, the investments lying along NX are constructed by the investor placing *all* her own investment funds into risky portfolio N, borrowing additional funds and placing these additional funds also in risky portfolio N. The greater the amount of money borrowed, relative to the investor's own funds, the further up the line NX, towards (and beyond) X will her resulting investment portfolio be located.

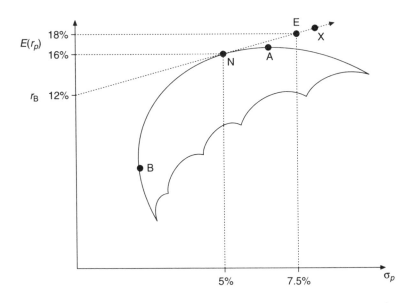

Fig. 11.8 *Borrowing extra funds*

An illustration of a portfolio lying along NX is shown in Example 6 in conjunction with Fig. 11.8.

Example 6

Suppose the following facts apply:

$$E(r_N) = 16\% \quad r_B = 12\%$$
$$\sigma_N = 5\% \quad \sigma_B = 0\%$$

If the investor has investment funds of £1000 available, and she wishes to increase her investment funds by 50% (0.50), by borrowings of £500, then the risk and expected return of the resulting portfolio E will be given by:

$$x = 1.5 \, (1 - x) = -0.5$$
$$E(r_E) = 1.5 \times E(r_N) + (-0.5) \times r_B$$
$$\sigma_E = 1.5 \times \sigma_N$$
$$E(r_E) = (1.5 \times 16\%) - (0.5 \times 12\%) = 18\%$$
$$\sigma_E = 1.5 \times 5\% = 7.5\%$$

An alternative way of calculating the expected return would be as follows:

£1500 invested in N at 16%	=	£240	expected annual return
less £500 borrowed at 12%	=	£ 60	annual interest
	=	£180	net expected annual return

An annual return of £180 on an outlay of £1000 of the investor's own cash represents a percentage return of 18% = $E(r_p)$.

Combined borrowing and lending possibilities

Fig. 11.9 combines the possibilities of borrowing money at an interest rate of r_B and the possibilities of lending money at an interest rate of r_F, by buying government bonds, where $r_B \neq r_F$. The resulting efficiency boundary is now r_F, M, N, X. As this stands we have not advanced the practicality of portfolio theory to any great extent, because we still have to rely on knowledge of the investor's set of indifference curves to identify which portfolio of risky assets is to be held and we still have the problem of identifying the composition of that risky portfolio. For example, Fig. 11.9 shows the points of tangency between the indifference curves and efficiency boundary for three different investors: I, II and III.

Investor I will hold portfolio W, which involves her placing a proportion of her investment funds in government bonds and the balance in risky portfolio M. Investor II holds portfolio Y, which simply consists of placing all her investment funds in the collection of risky assets of which portfolio Y is composed. Finally investor III holds portfolio Z, which consists of placing all her own investment funds in risky portfolio N, plus borrowing additional funds at a rate of interest of r_B and placing these funds also in portfolio N.

The situation displayed in this example is a slight improvement (in practical terms) when compared to the original situation, where neither borrowing nor lending took place. We no longer have to identify the composition of the *complete* risky portfolio efficiency boundary of AB, but we still have to be able to identify a considerable proportion of this boundary. In terms of Fig. 11.9, we still have to identify the set of risky portfolios lying between M and N.

Fig. 11.9 *Borrowing and lending possibilities*

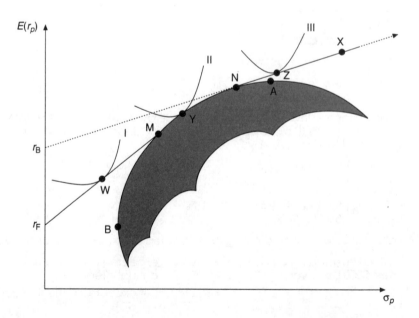

The capital market line

From the above analysis, and from Fig. 11.9, we can see that the only efficient portfolios which are composed *solely* of risky investments lie along that part of the efficiency boundary represented by MN. It follows that the smaller is the gap between the borrowing (r_B) and lending (r_F) interest rates, then the smaller will be the segment of the *original* efficiency boundary of interest to investors.

Therefore, let us now assume that the individual can lend and borrow funds at the *same* risk-free interest rate (i.e. $r_B = r_F$). In such circumstances the efficiency boundary simply becomes the straight line drawn from r_F which is a tangent to the original risky portfolio efficiency boundary. The efficiency boundary that arises out of this assumption of identical risk-free lending and borrowing rates leads to some very important conclusions and is termed the *Capital Market Line* (CML). It is illustrated in Fig. 11.10.

The separation theorem

Fig. 11.10 shows that there is now *only one* collection or portfolio of purely *risky* assets that investors would be interested in holding. This is labelled portfolio M. Thus investors who wished to locate on the CML somewhere between r_B and M would invest a proportion[9] of their funds in that portfolio of risky assets represented by M, and the remainder of their funds would be placed in the risk-free security. Those investors who wished to locate on the CML above M would place all their own investment funds in the portfolio of risky assets M, borrow additional funds[10] at an interest rate of r_F and invest those additional funds also in M.

This case, where it is assumed that investors can lend and borrow unlimited amounts at the risk-free interest rate of r_F, is important because of the fact that in such circumstances *all* risk-averse investors will be interested in only *one* portfolio of risky investments: portfolio M in Fig. 11.10. They will either

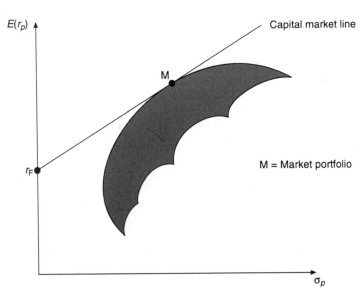

Fig. 11.10 *The capital market line*

put all their investment funds into this portfolio; or only part of their funds and lend the rest at the risk-free interest rate; or borrow additional funds and place all their own funds plus the borrowed funds into portfolio M. Therefore, whatever investment portfolio is constructed by an investor – in other words, wherever he or she chooses to locate on the CML – he or she will only be interested in one collection or portfolio of purely risky assets. This will be portfolio M. As a result we are now in a position of being able to identify the portfolio of risky assets that an investor would wish to hold (i.e. M), without any knowledge of his or her set of indifference curves (except to assume that he or she is generally risk-averse). This is the so-called Separation Theorem.[11] It has a significance similar to the separation theorem of the single-period investment–consumption model, in that decisions about investment in risky assets can be made on behalf of investors without the need for any knowledge about the *specific* characteristics of their indifference curves.

In other words, we can distinguish between the individual investor's risk and expected return choice (i.e. *where* he or she decides to locate on the CML) and the choice of the optimal (share) portfolio. The optimal share portfolio is simply portfolio M and the investors can adjust the riskiness of their own portfolio, *not* by changing portfolio M, but by changing the level of lending or borrowing at the risk-free rate. Therefore investors with different risk preferences will *all* hold the same *risky* portfolio of shares (i.e. portfolio M) but will have different proportions of borrowing or lending.

The introduction of the idea of the risky portfolio M helps to improve the practicality of portfolio theory for reasons other than just the separation theorem. We saw earlier that one of the main drawbacks of identifying the original risky-asset efficiency boundary was the astronomical number of calculations that would be required. The presence of the CML neatly gets around this difficulty, as long as the location of the CML can be determined. Given that the CML represents a linear function, its location can be determined with knowledge of just two points: the risk-free return and the expected return and risk of the risky portfolio, M. Identification of the former is relatively straightforward whilst an acceptable proxy for the latter point – as we shall see in the following section – can be given by the expected return and risk of a general stock market index; for example, the Financial Times Stock Exchange (FTSE) index.

The market portfolio

If all investors display the characteristics we ascribed earlier to a single investor (general risk aversion, rationality and consistency), then under the assumptions listed below, *all* investors[12] will wish to invest some or all of their funds in portfolio M of Fig. 11.11. Further, as this will be the *only* combination or portfolio of risky investments that will be of interest to investors, and given that *someone* must hold each risky investment that is available, then it follows that risky portfolio M must contain *all the risky investments that are available*. That is to say, portfolio M must consist of shares in all the companies quoted on the stock exchange. Hence it is termed the *market portfolio*.

An investor who wishes to hold the market portfolio as part of her overall investment portfolio would (at least in theory) hold shares in *all* the companies quoted on the stock market, in amounts proportionate to their

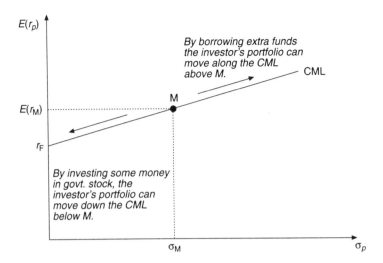

Fig. 11.11 *Moving along the CML*

total market values. As an example, suppose that there were only three quoted companies: A, B and C and their total market values were £20 million, £10 million and £30 million, respectively. An investor who wished to invest £1800 in the market portfolio would buy £600 of shares in A, £300 of shares in B and £900 of shares in C.

The concept of the market portfolio produces a definition of equilibrium market prices. If the market portfolio contains the shares of all the quoted companies, then the market prices of those shares (and hence the return they are expected to produce) must be such that they are acceptable investments for inclusion in the market portfolio. In other words, share prices are at equilibrium when they produce an expected return that is just sufficient compensation for the risk that they involve.

It should also be noted that, given the risk reduction effect of diversification, then the market portfolio represents the *ultimate* diversified portfolio: it represents that portfolio of risky assets in which all the risk that is possible to eliminate, has been eliminated. However, the reader may understandably wish to question the practicality of the market portfolio concept. How can any investor seriously attempt to hold a risky portfolio that consists of shares in *all* quoted companies? Furthermore, what exactly do we mean by 'the market'? Do we mean all the shares quoted on the London stock exchange or all the world's stock exchanges? Do we limit our definition to shares or do we extend it to cover all assets? If we do extend it to include all assets, what about the ones that are not tradable or divisible?

Fortunately, several studies have shown that constructing a randomly selected portfolio of shares consisting of only between fifteen and twenty different securities (instead of the approximately 7200 different securities that are quoted on the UK stock exchange) results in the elimination of around 90% of the maximum amount of risk which it would be possible to eliminate through diversification. As a result, it is relatively easy to hold a portfolio of risky assets which closely resembles the market portfolio (defined as shares quoted on the UK stock exchange) in terms of both risk and expected return. Fig. 11.12 illustrates this relationship.

Fig. 11.12 illustrates not only the risk elimination effect of diversification but also the fact that not *all* risk can be diversified away. There is an underlying rump of non-diversifiable risk. Various studies have shown that about

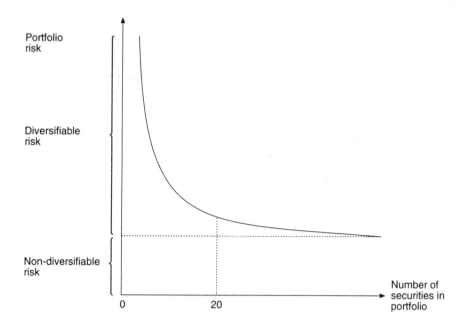

Fig. 11.12 *The risk-reduction effect*

65% of total risk can, on average, be diversified away. The remaining 35% of total risk is *non-diversifiable*. So while we can say that there are some theoretical problems in defining markets, etc. it is clear that it is possible to at least move towards the theoretical position we have been describing.

The assumptions

Many of the assumptions necessary for the conclusions reached in the foregoing analysis will be familiar, because they were used earlier in our development of the theory of financial decision making. There are six main assumptions in total:

1. The investor's objective is to maximize the utility of wealth.
2. Investors make choices on the basis of risk and return. Return is measured by the arithmetic mean return from a portfolio of assets, and risk is measured by the standard deviation or variance of those returns.
3. All investors can lend and borrow unlimited amounts of cash at the risk-free interest rate.
4. No taxation, transaction costs or other market imperfections.
5. All investors have the same knowledge and expectations about the future and have access to the complete range of investment opportunities. Investors are all price-takers and have free access to all relevant information.
6. All investors have the same decision-making time horizon, i.e. the expected return on investments arises from expectations over the same time period.

These assumptions are important, and some of them are clearly unrealistic. However the lack of realism of the model's assumptions is an issue of secondary importance. The main issue surrounds the predictive ability of the model: does the model correctly predict the expected return on portfolios of a particular level of risk? If it has substantial predictive power, then the lack of realism of its assumptions is of little concern. We shall touch upon the model's predictive ability in the next chapter, but (generally speaking) it does seem to possess fairly good (but not prefect) predictive power. Furthermore, when many of the above assumptions are relaxed we do find that the model appears to be remarkably robust and that its general conclusions continue to hold.

The market price of risk

The slope of the CML is of some interest. It can be calculated as:

$$[E(r_M) - r_F]/\sigma_M$$

where $E(r_M)$ and σ_M are the expected return and risk of the market portfolio and r_F is the risk-free return.

The slope of the CML indicates the risk–expected return relationship of the whole capital market: in other words, it indicates the reward that investors will get (in terms of an expected return in excess of the risk-free return) for taking on risk. For this reason it is often referred to as the market price of risk.

As an example, suppose that the following values held:

$$E(r_M) = 16\%$$
$$\sigma_M = 3\%$$
$$r_F = 10\%$$

then the market price of risk would equal:

$$\frac{E(r_M) - r_F}{\sigma_M} = \frac{16\% - 19\%}{3\%} = 2.$$

Thus the CML would have a slope of +2. This can be interpreted as indicating that for every 1% point of risk (standard deviation) taken on, the investor can expect to receive a return of 2% above the risk-free return. So, an investor willing to take on 4% of risk in her portfolio (i.e. $\sigma_p = 4\%$) could expect to receive (on the basis of the figures above) a return of:

$$10\% + (2 \times 4\%) = 18\%.$$

That is to say, an investor who was willing to accept an investment risk of 4% could construct a portfolio yielding an expected return of 18%.

In general terms, the expected return from efficient portfolio j (where the term 'efficient' refers to a portfolio lying along the CML), is given by the expression for the CML function:

$$E(r_j) = r_F + \frac{[E(r_M) - r_F]}{\sigma_M}\sigma_j$$

or, more simply:

$$E(r_j) = r_F + \lambda\sigma_j$$

where $\lambda = [E(r_M) - r_F]/\sigma_M$ = the market price of risk.

Thus, the expected return on an efficient investment portfolio is equal to the risk-free return (r_F), plus the risk premium ($\lambda\sigma_j$). The premium reflects the portfolio's own risk (σ_j), together with the market's *risk attitude* or *risk–expected return trade-off* (λ).

Market portfolio risk

Finally, there are two interconnected points about this analysis that are very important and which should be understood clearly. The first is to notice that the market price of risk indicates the amount of additional return that can be expected for each 1% of 'market portfolio risk' taken on (σ_M).

We know that the market portfolio represents the ultimate diversified portfolio and hence, by definition, the risk it contains is the risk that cannot be eliminated through diversification. Therefore the market price of risk indicates the additional expected return (in excess of the risk-free return) provided by the market to investors for each 1% of *non-diversifiable* risk taken on. The implied assumption here is that the market would not be willing to give investors any reward (in terms of expected return) for taking on risk that it is possible to eliminate through the diversification process. This is a conclusion of great importance and it will be expanded upon in the next chapter.

The second point is connected to the first. It is that the CML expression:

$$E(r_j) = r_F + \lambda \sigma_j$$

gives the return that should be expected from an *efficient* investment portfolio. Thus it only applies to investment portfolios lying along the CML (a rational risk-averse investor would not be interested in any other portfolios). The point of importance here is that this analysis, and in particular the expression for the CML does *not* apply to *individual* investments (for example, it does not apply to the return we should expect from the shares of an individual company) – which could be termed inefficient investments – but only to efficient investments, i.e. efficient portfolios. Once again, this point will be picked up in the following chapter.

Diversification within companies

We have seen that diversification is a logical strategy for investors in that it can be shown to allow for the reduction of risk without a corresponding reduction in returns. So, if diversification is good for investors, does this mean that managers should be seeking to diversify within companies? To an extent, the answer to this is that it all depends from whose viewpoint we are looking at the company.

In the same way that diversification can lead to less variability in the returns enjoyed by a shareholder, so it can lead to reduced variability in the returns of a company. On a basic level, it might be expected that a business that sells both hot soup and ice-cream can expect that some of the effects of variation in the weather would be reduced because of the relationship between the two products. However, it is not necessary for companies to diversify for the benefit of their shareholders. They can diversify for themselves. Managers, on the other hand cannot diversify in the same way. They cannot decide that they will have 10% of their employment in ICI and the rest spread around a further 19 companies. Thus it might be expected that at least some managers will see it as being a good idea to diversify within the company. This might be achieved on a number of levels ranging from developing a wider range of products produced right up to adopting a policy of taking over unrelated businesses to form a conglomerate.

So long as there are no costs associated with the diversification within the company, the shareholders should, in theory, be indifferent to the level of internal diversification as they will merely take this into account when they make their own portfolio decisions. However, there is evidence that internal diversification is not always costless. There is a limit to how thinly the management of most businesses can be spread and it appears that it is often the case that the take-over of an unrelated business fails to produce the required returns because of a lack of management expertise. The other side of this can be seen in the many examples of companies disposing of subsidiaries so that they can concentrate on what are described as 'core activities', in other words, what they do best.

So, to sum up this section, internal diversification is neither good nor bad in itself, so far as the investor in a company is concerned. Thus, if it emerges as the result of an otherwise sound investment decision it will be welcomed. However, if it is an end in itself that reduces the present value of the company, it will be contrary to the interests of the investor and as such, should not be undertaken.

Summary

This very brief analysis of portfolio theory can be summarized as follows:

- The expected return on a share can be measured by its arithmetic mean return and its risk can be measured by the standard deviation of returns.

- When investments are combined in a two-asset portfolio, the expected return on the portfolio is equal to a weighted average of the returns expected on the two-component investments.

- However, the risk of the portfolio is less than a weighted average of the risk of the two-component investments. This is the risk reduction or elimination effect of diversification.

- Portfolio risk can easily be reduced by investing in less risky investments; but, as a result, the portfolio's expected return will also be reduced. However, portfolio diversification can reduce portfolio risk *without* a consequent reduction in expected return: this is the true meaning of the risk-reduction effect of diversification.

- From the two-asset portfolio analysis it follows that the greatest possible risk-reduction effect must be achievable with the greatest possible amount of diversification. This occurs when the portfolio includes investments in the shares of *all* quoted companies, and is termed the market portfolio.

- Not all risk is capable of being diversified away and so the market portfolio does contain a significant element of risk. However, risk which is capable of being diversified away will be eliminated from the market portfolio, leaving only non-diversifiable risk.

- The market portfolio, in terms of its risk-reduction characteristics, can be fairly easily approximated by a portfolio of fifteen to twenty investments in different segments of the stock market. This is because the risk-reduction benefits of diversification arise fairly rapidly and most of the risk-reduction effect is achieved with only a relatively limited amount of diversification.

- Given that investors are rational and risk-averse, this means that they *like* expected return, but *dislike* risk. Thus investors will only be interested in holding one portfolio of shares (risky assets): the market portfolio (or its more practical twenty-investments equivalent). This is because it provides the minimum possible amount of risk for its given level of expected return.

- Investors can then adjust the risk of their own personal portfolios (σ_p) so that they hold more or less risk than the market portfolio (σ_M) by either borrowing or lending at the risk-free rate of return, and so sliding their own personal investment portfolio up or down the CML from point M (see Fig. 11.11).

- Therefore the equation of the CML indicates the return that can be expected by an investor from an efficient portfolio, which can be defined as one which is located on the CML.

- This return:

$$E(r_p) = r_F + \lambda\sigma_p$$

consists of two elements. The first is the return available on an investment with no risk at all (r_F). The second is the risk premium, ($\lambda\sigma_p$), the additional return available as a reward to investors for taking on risk.

- The risk premium itself consists of two elements: λ and σ_p. The first element, λ, is the market price of risk and represents the going rate of reward on the stock market (in terms of expected return) for taking on risk. The second element, σ_p, is the number of percentage points of risk taken on by the particular efficient portfolio chosen (j).

- Finally, it is important to realize that the *only* source of an efficient portfolio's risk (σ_p) is the market portfolio risk. The risk of the market portfolio is, by definition, all non-diversifiable and so the risk premium only relates to non-diversifiable risk.

- Although diversification is in the interests of investors, they can achieve this for themselves through their portfolio choices. It is thus not necessary for companies to include diversification as an objective and internal diversification will only be acceptable, so far as investors are concerned, when it is costless.

Notes

1. This is the case in all but the most exceptional circumstances, as will be seen later.

2. It is assumed that the reader is familiar with the statistical term, correlation coefficient. This is the term, often used in conjunction with two-variable linear regression analysis, that expresses the strength of the linear relationship between two variables. A fuller explanation than that given in the text will be found in any introductory book on general statistics.

3. That is, for any given set of values for x, σ_A and σ_B.

4. These values have been calculated from the portfolio risk and expected return expressions, but they could have been estimated from Fig. 11.1.

5. This expression is a simplified version of the original expression for portfolio risk, which can be applied when the correlation coefficient is perfectly negative, i.e. $= r_p - 1$.

6. Indeed, any portfolio lying to the northwest of Z would be preferred, but the only portfolios that would not – in turn – be dominated themselves, are those lying along the boundary line.

7. These investments are held to be risk-free as there is thought to be no chance of default either on the interest payments or on the redemption. (The reason for such a view is based on the fact that the government can never 'run out' of money – if they do, then they can always print some more.) However, it is important to notice that this assumption only holds in the absence of inflation. If inflation is anticipated, then only the monetary return is certain; the *real* return remains uncertain.

8. The efficient portfolios lying along AB could be called efficient risky portfolios in that they are all portfolios that consist of risky investments – the shares of companies.

9. Just *what* proportion would depend upon where the investor wished to locate between r_F and M.

10. Just how much would be borrowed would depend upon how far up the CML, above M, the investor wished to locate.

11. In fact it is often referred to as the 'Tobin' Separation Theorem – after the author who developed the idea – in order to distinguish it from the Hirshleifer separation theorem that we dealt with in an earlier chapter.

12. With the exception of the investor who wishes to hold a totally risk-free portfolio. That investor would place all his or her investment funds in government stock, in order to earn a certain return of r_F.

Further reading

1. Many articles on portfolio theory are very mathematical and make difficult reading. A good overview is provided in J. Dickinson, 'Portfolio Theory', in *Issues in Finance* by M. Firth and S.M. Keane (eds) Philip Allen, 1986.
2. Also of great interest, from the father of portfolio theory is H.M. Markowitz, 'Foundations of Portfolio Theory', *Journal of Finance*, June 1991.
3. Finally, three other useful articles are W.H. Wagner and S. Lau, 'The Effects of Diversification on Risk', *Financial Analysts Journal*, November–December 1971; W.F. Sharpe, 'Risk Aversion in the Stock Market: Some Empirical

Evidence', *Journal of Finance*, September 1965 and B.H. Solnik, 'Why not Diversify Internationally rather than Domestically?', *Financial Analysts Journal*, July–August 1974.

Quickie questions

1. In a two-asset portfolio, what determines the degree of risk-reduction effect?
2. What is the expression for the risk of a two-asset portfolio?
3. Given the following:

State of world	Probability	Possible return: A	Possible return: B
I	0.30	28%	35%
II	0.40	18%	15%
III	0.30	6%	20%

   What is the correlation coefficient of returns between investments A and B?
4. Given the information in question 3, how would you construct a portfolio to produce an expected return of 20%?
5. What is the expression for the risk and expected returns of an *N*-asset portfolio?
6. What is an *efficient* portfolio?
7. What is the expression for the capital market line?
8. If the risk-free return (i.e. government stock) was 10% and the expected return on the FTSE index was 16% (and risk measured by standard deviation was 3%), how would you construct an efficient portfolio to produce a 15% expected return, and what would be its risk?
9. Given the information in question 8, and the fact that you have personal funds of £1000 to invest, how would you construct a portfolio giving an expected return of 20%, and what would be its risk?
10. Define the market portfolio.

Problems

1. In Utopia, a very restrictive investment market exists. Investors are able to invest in four types of security (in any combination): A, B, C and X. Securities A, B and C are all risky investments; their current market-derived expected (period) returns $E(r)$ and the standard deviation of these returns (σ) are given below:

Security	$E(r)$	σ
A	0.10	0.02
B	0.15	0.04
C	0.20	0.07

   All are perfectly positively correlated with each other. Security X is a risk-free investment which yields a period return of 8%. Investors can also borrow unlimited amounts of cash at an interest rate of 8% per period. There is no taxation in Utopia.

   Required:
   (a) Draw to scale the area of possible risky portfolios. Draw the capital market line and identify the market portfolio.
   (b) Calculate the market price of risk and explain what it represents.
   (c) State briefly what conclusions you draw from your answer to (a) about the current state of the market for risky assets in Utopia.

(d) An investor in Utopia wishes to hold an efficient portfolio yielding a 10% expected period return. How would this portfolio be composed and what would its risk be?

(e) Show how an investor in Utopia might construct an efficient portfolio yielding a 20% expected period return.

(f) State the main assumptions underlying portfolio theory and indicate briefly why its conclusions may be of importance for investment decision making within individual companies.

2. Alpha plc, a UK manufacturing company, wishes to diversify its operations internationally by establishing equal-sized subsidiaries in two other countries. Because of the company's trading relationships that exist, one should be in Europe and the other in the Far East.

Five countries have been considered and the forecasts of possible present values of net cash flows (excluding outlay) have been calculated using a 20% discount rate. In addition, the calculation of the expected net present value and the risk (measured by standard deviation of NPV) has also been completed. These data are given below:

Hong Kong (HK$m)		Switzerland (SFrm)		Greece (DRm)	
Prob.	PV	Prob.	PV	Prob.	PV
0.30	+63.8	0.35	+15.39	0.30	+16.20
0.40	+64.4	0.40	+15.80	0.50	+17.00
0.30	+64.9	0.25	+16.34	0.20	+17.30

Singapore (S$m)		Austria (ASch.m)	
Prob.	PV	Prob.	PV
0.30	+18.1	0.35	+100
0.40	+19.3	0.40	+125
0.30	+25.9	0.25	+ 84

The expected initial outlay in all cases is approximately £5.2 million and all of the projects have an expected life of five years.

An investment analyst employed by Alpha has already started work on the decision and has calculated the expected NPV [E(NPV)] and the risk of the Austrian project:

ASch.m		£m	Outlay	£NPV	Prob.	
100 ÷ 20.8250	=	4.80	− 5.2	= −0.4	× 0.35	= −0.14
125 ÷ 20.8250	=	6.00	− 5.2	= +0.8	× 0.40	= +0.32
84 ÷ 20.8250	=	4.03	− 5.2	= −1.17	× 0.25	= −0.29

$$E(NPV) = £-0.11m$$

(£NPV)^2		Prob.		
0.16	×	0.35	=	0.06
0.64	×	0.40	=	0.26
1.37	×	0.25	=	0.34
$E(NPV)^2$		=		0.66

$$Risk = \sqrt{0.66 - (-0.11)^2} = £0.80m$$

The corporate finance department of Alpha plc have estimated the following average exchange rates (number of units of overseas currency per £1) for the next five years:

HK$/£	:	12.7625
SFr/£	:	2.4400
DRm/£	:	225.7250
S$/£	:	3.4422
ASch/£	:	20.8250

They have also estimated the correlation coefficients of ENPV between the countries.

Hong Kong/Switzerland	:	−0.15
Hong Kong/Austria	:	+0.40
Hong Kong/Greece	:	+0.60
Switzerland/Singapore	:	+0.30
Greece/Singapore	:	+0.60
Austria/Singapore	:	+0.85

Required:
(a) The analyst looking at this investment decision has now left the firm. You are asked to complete the task by using the above information to advise the management of Alpha plc in which two countries to locate its proposed subsidiaries. Alpha is concerned with both the profitability and the riskiness of its investments.
(b) Critically discuss the shortcomings of your analysis.

3. Europium plc has been specially formed to undertake two investment opportunities. The risk and return characteristics of the two projects are shown below:

	A	B
Expected return	12%	20%
Risk	3%	7%

Europium plans to invest 80% of its available funds in Project A and 20% in B. The directors believe that the correlation coefficient between the returns of the projects is +0.1.

Required:
(a) Calculate the returns from the proposed portfolio of Projects A and B.
(b) Calculate the risk of the portfolio.
(c) Comment on your calculations in part (b) in the context of the risk-reducing effects of diversification.
(d) Suppose the correlation coefficient between A and B was −1.0. How should Europium plc invest its funds in order to obtain a zero-risk portfolio?

12 The capital asset pricing model

The security market line

In the previous two chapters we have introduced approaches to the financial decision-making process in the face of uncertainty. We saw that on the basis of several assumptions concerning investors and their environment, investment decisions can be made on the criteria of expected return and the variability of return.

We then developed the idea of the CML which (if it can be held to apply in the real world) leads us to conclude that the capital markets display a linear risk–expected return relationship of the type:

$$E(r_j) = r_F + \lambda \sigma_j.$$

Further, our analysis indicates that this relationship is not based simply on the *total* risk of individual investments – in other words, the variability of their possible returns – but on just one part of that risk: the non-diversifiable risk. The market would not provide a reward (in terms of an increased expected return) for that part of an investment's risk that could be eliminated by holding it as part of a well-diversified portfolio.

At this point it is worth recalling the purpose of our enquiry into the handling of uncertainty. We are concerned with building up a normative theory of managerial financial decision making: a theory about how company managements should make physical capital investment decisions on behalf of their shareholders. Therefore, although the analysis in the previous chapter was concerned with investors (rather than managers) making financial decisions, its relevance to our purpose is obvious. We are interested in how shareholders, as *investors*, take decisions in the light of uncertainty because of the guidelines it can give us about how managers should take similar decisions on their behalf.

Our brief consideration of capital investment appraisal under conditions of uncertainty that was made at the beginning of Chapter 10 led us to try to seek out two things: how to measure the risk of a capital investment project and how to identify the return that should be expected from it, given its level of risk. Although our development of portfolio theory will have given us some clues as to how both these questions should be answered, it has done no more than that, because it focused on the risk and expected return relationship of *collections* (or portfolios) of assets. Our concern is with the relationship as it applies to *individual* assets. It is this point that is tackled in the current chapter.

In particular, we are going to develop a share price valuation model. In other words, for the time being at least, we are going to continue to look at stock exchange investment decision making, but now in relation to investment in shares of *individual companies*, rather than *portfolios*. This share price valuation model is usually referred to as the *capital asset pricing model* (CAPM) and it arises directly out of the ideas and conclusions of portfolio theory.

However, it also involves the many unrealistic assumptions of our previous analysis. Nevertheless, the model is useful, in that it provides several significant insights into the major factors of share price determination, and so is of direct interest to decision makers within companies. Indeed, it is worthwhile remembering that the realism or otherwise of a model's assumptions is an irrelevant issue in considering its validity. What is important is the predictive power of the model. In other words, despite its (unrealistic) assumptions and simplifications of the real world, does it appear to capture the main elements of the relationship it seeks to portray? We shall conclude that although the CAPM is not a perfect and complete representation of the real world, it appears to be a fairly good representation of the real world and is, in many ways, the best tool available to us.

Derivation of the security market line

The CML function provides an expression for the return that can be expected from an efficient portfolio investment, i.e. an investment in the market portfolio, plus either lending or borrowing at the risk-free rate of return. However, we can also use it to derive an expression for the expected return on an *inefficient* investment, such as a risky portfolio other than the market portfolio or, more importantly, an investment in the shares of a single company.

The expression for the expected return on an inefficient investment (e.g. on the shares of an individual company) is derived mathematically in the Appendix to this chapter. What we shall do in this section is put forward a more reasoned argument.

We already know from our analysis of the risk and expected return of a two-asset portfolio that the risk is given by the expression:

$$\sigma_p = \sqrt{[x^2\sigma_A^2 + (1-x)^2\sigma_B^2 + 2x(1-x)\sigma_A\sigma_B\rho_{A,B}]},$$

and that the risk-reduction effect of diversification is 'caused' by the correlation coefficient. The further away the correlation coefficient is from +1, the greater is the risk-reduction effect.

From this expression, we can see that portfolio risk is made up of three elements. The first element – given by the term $x^2\sigma_A^2$ – is the contribution that investment A makes *independently* to the portfolio. Similarly, the second element – $(1-x)^2\sigma_B^2$ – is investment B's independent contribution to portfolio risk.

However, the third element, $2x(1-x)\sigma_A\sigma_B\rho_{A,B}$, is really composed of *two* identical parts:

$$x(1-x)\sigma_A\sigma_B\rho_{A,B}.$$

This represents the contribution made to the risk of the portfolio by the two investments *jointly*, and which is determined by their tendency to co-vary (i.e. $\rho_{A,B}$).

Because investment A co-varies with investment B in an identical fashion to how investment B co-varies with investment A, there are two identical parts to the third element. Within each part, the term $\sigma_A\sigma_B\rho_{A,B}$ – known as the *covariance* of returns between investments A and B – effectively represents the *non-diversifiable* risk that each investment contributes to the portfolio.

We saw that when the correlation coefficient was +1, there was *no* risk reduction effect. This is because the total risk of each investment would be all non-diversifiable. Hence, when $\rho_{A,B} = +1$, the portfolio risk expression becomes:

$$\sigma_p = \sqrt{[x^2\sigma_A^2 + (1-x)^2\sigma_B^2 + 2x(1-x)\sigma_A\sigma_B]},$$

which simplifies to:[1]

$$\sigma_p = x\sigma_A + (1-x)\sigma_B.$$

That is, the portfolio risk is just a weighted average of the risk of the portfolio components.

However, when $\rho_{A,B} < +1$, then not *all* the total risk of each investment is non-diversifiable. Some of it can be diversified away and so:

$$\sigma_p < x\,\sigma_A + (1-x)\sigma_B,$$

which is the risk-reduction effect of diversification.

Furthermore, from our discussion of the capital market line, we derived the expression for the expected return from an efficient portfolio as:

$$E(r_p) = r_F + \lambda\sigma_p,$$

where *all* the portfolio's risk – σ_p – consisted of non-diversifiable risk derived from the portfolio's holding of the market portfolio.

From this expression can be derived an expression for the return on an *inefficient* investment, such as the shares in company S:

$$E(r_S) = r_F + \lambda\sigma_S\rho_{S,M}.$$

Indeed, this is the general expression for the expected return from *any* non-'efficient portfolio' investment and is termed the *security market line* – the SML.

The CML and the SML

An examination of the equation for the SML shows how closely related it is to the CML equation:

$$CML : E(r_p) = r_F + \lambda\sigma_p$$
$$SML : E(r_S) = r_F + \lambda\sigma_S\rho_{S,M}.$$

In fact, in interpretation, they have *exactly* the same meaning.

The CML indicates that the return on an efficient portfolio consists of two elements. The first is the return available for holding an investment with no risk at all – r_F – and the second is the *additional* return that can be expected as a reward for holding the investment's risk – the *risk premium* – $\lambda\sigma_p$.

The risk premium is the product of the market price risk (λ) and the risk taken on by the particular efficient portfolio chosen (σ_p).[2] The important point to remember here is that the risk taken on arises *purely* from the portfolio's holding in the market portfolio. As the riskiness of the market portfolio is all non-diversifiable (by definition – it is the ultimate diversified portfolio), thus the risk premium given by the market is *only for non-diversifiable risk*.

Turning to the SML expression we can see that, similar to the CML, the expected return on the shares in an individual company consists of two elements: the risk-free return and a risk premium. However, the risk premium is now not simply the product of the market price of risk (λ) and the investment's risk (σ_S), but is:

$$\lambda\sigma_S\rho_{S,M},$$

where $\sigma_S\rho_{S,M}$ is that part of investment S's total risk that contributes to the non-diversifiable risk of the market portfolio. In other words, $\sigma_S\rho_{S,M}$ represents the non-diversifiable risk of the shares in company S. Thus the risk premium is based, not on the total risk of investment S, but only on that part of total risk that cannot be diversified away – because the market provides a risk premium *only for non-diversifiable risk*. Example 1 puts some figures on this discussion to help clarify the point.

Example 1

Suppose we are given the following information about the (total) risk of company S shares (σ_S) and the degree to which they are correlated with the expected return on the market portfolio ($\rho_{S,M}$):

$$\sigma_S = 8\%$$
$$\rho_{S,M} = +\,0.70$$

Also, if $r_F = 10\%$
and $\lambda = 2$
then:

$$E(r_S) = 10\% + 2(8\% \times + 0.70)$$
$$E(r_S) = 10\% + 2 \times 5.6\%$$
$$E(r_S) = 10\% + 11.2\% = 21.2\%$$

Therefore, the risk premium of 11.2% is not based on S's *total* risk of 8%, but only on part of that risk, 5.6%. This is because:

$$8\% \times 0.70 = 5.6\% = \text{non-diversifiable risk of S.}$$

The market will only give a premium for non-diversifiable risk because S's *diversifiable* risk can be eliminated by holding the shares of S as part of a well-diversified (i.e. efficient) portfolio. Whether or not the investor in company S shares *does* actually hold them as part of a well-diversified portfolio is irrelevant as far as the stock market is concerned. The stock market will not provide a risk premium for holding a risk which can be easily eliminated through diversifying.

Thus if an investor *just* held company S shares, he would be holding a risk of 8%, but the return he could expect would only be based on a risk of 5.6%. So it can be seen how important it is to hold a well-diversified portfolio for an investor to get the expected return deserved, given the risk taken on.

The CAPM expression

In the foregoing discussion we have seen that the expected return on any inefficient investment is determined only by its non-diversifiable risk. More technically, this risk is referred to as *systematic* or *market* risk. Similarly, the diversifiable risk is known as *unsystematic* or *unique* risk.

The SML expression gives the return that an investor *should* expect from any inefficient investment, given its level of systematic risk. The relationship thus described is usually known as the *capital asset pricing model* or the CAPM. Thus, it would state that the return that should be expected on ICI shares (for example) is:

$$E(r_{ICI}) = r_F + \lambda \sigma_{ICI} \rho_{ICI,M}.$$

That is to say, the return that should be expected from an investment in ICI shares is equal to the risk-free return, plus a risk premium. The risk premium is determined by the market price of (systematic) risk and the systematic risk level of ICI shares.

Interpreting systematic and unsystematic risk

The CAPM provides the relationship between an investment's systematic risk and its expected return. Therefore, given the general risk-aversion of the market, investments with high levels of systematic risk can be expected to provide a high return, and vice versa.

On the other hand, it would be possible to have an investment with a relatively high amount of *total* risk, but only a low expected return: conversely, an investment with a low level of total risk might have a relatively high expected return. In each case, the actual level of expected return depends upon the degree of correlation concerned. The former case would hold where the correlation coefficient was low, whereas the latter case might hold where the correlation coefficient was strongly positive. Example 2 illustrates such a situation.

Because we will be interested in applying the CAPM to project investment appraisal, it is useful to consider the *source* or *cause* of systematic and unsystematic risk. Remembering that risk has to do with the variability of a share's return, and the return is, in turn, dependent upon movements in the market price (i.e. the capital gain or loss) and the level of dividends, then the determinants of risk are really the same as the determinants of share price movements and dividend levels.

Example 2

Given the following data concerning the stock market:

$$r_F = 10\% \qquad \lambda = 2$$

Company C: $\sigma_C = 20\%$
$\rho_{C,M} = +0.20$

Company D: $\sigma_D = 8\%$
$\rho_{D,M} = +0.90$

Therefore, in terms of *total* risk, company C shares are significantly more risky than company D shares.

However:	Systematic risk of company C:	$20\% \times 0.2 = 4\%$
	Systematic risk of company D:	$8\% \times 0.9 = 7.2\%$
	Expected return on company C:	$10\% + (2 \times 4\%) = 18\%$
	Expected return on company D:	$10\% + (2 \times 7.2\%) = 24.4\%$

Most of company C's risk is capable of being diversified away and so its expected return is relatively low, although its total risk is high. Conversely, most of company D's risk is systematic and so cannot be diversified away. As a result, although its total risk is relatively low, its expected return is relatively high.

This is an important area of the theory of financial decision making and we will return to analyse it in depth in a later chapter. However, for the moment we will simply (and very tentatively) conclude that both share price movements and dividends are determined by the level of a firm's cash flow.[3] (Indeed, we should not consider such a conclusion as being contentious, given our discussion in Chapter 1.) Therefore it follows that the *total* risk of a company is determined by the variability of its cash flow: the greater the variability, the greater the risk, and vice versa.

Many factors affect the level, or variability, of a firm's cash flow over time. For example, the quality of its management, the state of its labour relations, the level of its advertising and the effectiveness of its research and development efforts will all affect the level of cash flow. However, in addition, there are other more general factors that will also affect a firm's cash flow. Examples would include such things as the rate of growth of investment in the economy, the level of consumer demand, movements in exchange rates, rates of corporation tax and the level of interest rates.

All these factors can be roughly divided up into two groups. There are those factors that are *specific* or special to the company (such as the quality of its management and the effectiveness of its research and development); and there are the more general factors that affect *all* firms in the economy (to a greater or lesser extent) and not just the individual firm (e.g. the level of consumer demand). Roughly speaking, it is these former factors that are the determinants of *specific* or *unsystematic* risk, whereas the latter set of factors are the determinants of *market* or *systematic* risk.

The logic of this division of 'risk causes' is fairly easy to follow. Factors that are special or specific to an individual company will be 'washed out' or diversified away, when the shares are held as part of a well-diversified portfolio. However, there is no such escape from the market-wide macro-economic type factors that affect all firms and hence cannot be eliminated by diversification.

Unique risk relates to the individual company. So something in the nature of a food safety scare like an e-coli outbreak or the death of an especially important member of the management team like Laura Ashley will have an adverse effect on that company alone. We can expect that in a portfolio, the bad luck associated with one company will be balanced by better luck for others. However, an increase in the level of corporate taxation or a rapid rise in interest rates will adversely affect *all* firms (although not to the same extent in each), and there is no offsetting effect.[4]

We shall return to the problem of identifying the sources of systematic risk at a later stage. However, it is worthwhile pointing out that, in practice, the identification of systematic and unsystematic risk factors is not as clear-cut as the foregoing discussion might seem to imply. There is a considerable 'grey area' of boundary between the two sets of factors.

The determinants of the systematic risk level

Finally, this is an appropriate place to discuss what determines the degree to which a particular firm's shares are exposed to systematic risk. In other words, why do some companies have high systematic risk and other companies have low systematic risk?

If systematic risk can be defined as the extent to which a company's cash flow is affected by economy-wide or non-company-specific factors, then there are likely to be three main determinants of that systematic risk exposure:

1. The sensitivity of the company's revenues to the general level of economic activity in the economy and other macro-economic factors.
2. The proportion of fixed to variable costs (i.e. the degree of cost sensitivity).
3. The level of financial gearing or leverage (i.e. the amount of interest bearing debt compared to shareholder equity).

In other words, what makes a company risky in systematic risk terms is the degree to which the company's revenues are determined by macro-economic factors largely outside the control of its management. This risk can then be either increased or reduced by the proportions of fixed and variable costs involved and further increased by exposure to debt.

A company manufacturing machine tools might be seen as an example of high revenue sensitivity. If the economy is booming and wage levels are rising demand for all kinds of products will increase. Manufacturers will take this opportunity to buy new machines either to replace old ones or to increase capacity. However, if the economy is depressed then demand for many products will decline and it may not be necessary for manufacturers to buy any machinery at all, preferring to make do with existing machines until the economy begins to pick up. Thus the cash flows for a machine tool manufacturer can be expected to be particularly volatile, being especially sensitive to general economic conditions, and these general economic conditions cannot be diversified away in a portfolio.

On the other hand, a food retailer, such as Tesco or Sainsburys, might be taken as an example of a business with a low degree of revenue sensitivity. Generally speaking, in both good times and bad, the supermarket's revenue is likely to be little changed. In bad times people have still got to eat to live, while in good times spare cash will probably be spent on other things (such as holidays and cars), rather than increasing the consumption of food.

Where a company has a high level of fixed costs relative to total costs its net cash flows will be more volatile than would otherwise be the case. This is because it will still have to pay the fixed costs, no matter how high or low its income might be. The relationship of debt to equity is similar in that the company will still have to pay interest on the debt whether or not it is generating positive cash flows before interest.

These factors are particularly important for companies that have relatively volatile income flows. However for a firm with low revenue sensitivity, the proportion of fixed to variable costs will make little difference to its riskiness. As its revenues are relatively stable, it should at all times be able to cover its operating and financing costs, whether they are fixed or variable.

Given the foregoing, and assuming that managers – like investors – are risk-averse, it should not surprise us to find that firms with high revenue sensitivity try to minimize the proportion of both fixed financing and fixed operating costs. On the other hand, the management of firms with low revenue sensitivity can afford to be more relaxed about such issues.

The beta value

We now move on to the practical application of the CAPM. The model will provide the return that should be expected from an individual risky investment. But how are we to identify the several variables that are required?

If the 'market price of risk' (λ) term is expanded, the CAPM expression becomes:

$$E(r_j) = r_F + \frac{[E(r_M) - r_F]}{\sigma_M} \sigma_j \rho_{jM}.$$

Assuming that the values of r_F and $E(r_M)$ are relatively easy to identify (using the return on government stock and the expected return on the FTSE stock market index, respectively), there still remains the problem of identifying σ_M, σ_j and ρ_{jM}. These *could* be estimated individually by examining the historical variability of the returns on the market portfolio, the returns on the shares in company j and their correlation. However, fortunately, a much more straightforward estimation procedure exists (which we will examine shortly).

These three 'troublesome' elements (σ_M, σ_j and ρ_{jM}) are usually combined together and termed the *beta value of company j shares*, so that the CAPM is then re-expressed in the much neater form:

$$E(r_j) = r_F + [E(r_M) - r_F] \beta_j,$$

where

$$\beta_j = \frac{\sigma_j \rho_{jM}}{\sigma_M}.$$

Interpreting beta

The numerator of the beta value ($\sigma_j \rho_{jM}$) represents the systematic risk of company j, and the denominator (σ_M) represents the total risk of the market portfolio which (as we know) is *all* systematic risk. Hence the beta value of company j shares is an *index* of the amount of company j's systematic risk, *relative* to that of the market portfolio. Example 3 illustrates this point.

Example 3

Suppose we have the following data about company j and the market portfolio:

$$\left. \begin{array}{l} \sigma_j = 10\% \\ \rho_{j,M} = +0.70 \\ \sigma_M = 5\% \end{array} \right\} \text{Therefore, } \beta_j = \frac{10\% \times (+0.70)}{5\%} = 1.40.$$

In other words, company j has a systematic risk of: $10\% \times (+ 0.70) = 7\%$ and, as the market portfolio has only 5% of systematic risk, company j has 40% *more* systematic risk than the market portfolio:

$$\left(\frac{7\% - 5\%}{5\%}\right) = 0.40 \text{ or } 40\%.$$

Hence, company j's beta value of 1.40 indicates company j's systematic risk level *relative* to the average systematic risk level on the stock market (i.e. the risk of the market portfolio).

As further examples, a share with a beta of 2 would have *twice* as much systematic risk as the average, while a share with a beta of 0.67 would only have *two-thirds* the average level of systematic risk on the stock market.

The beta value of a company's shares also indicates the degree of responsiveness of the expected return on the shares, relative to movements in the expected return on the market. Beta does *not* indicate the degree of total volatility that can be expected in an investment's return, but only indicates the extent to which expected return is likely to react to overall *market* movements. For example, if the expected return on the market portfolio rises or falls by (say) 10%, then the expected return on the share will react as follows:

$E(r)$ will tend to rise or fall by > 10% if $\beta > 1$
$E(r)$ will tend to rise or fall by < 10% if $\beta < 1$
$E(r)$ will tend to rise or fall by ≈ 10% if $\beta \approx 1$[5]

Beta can also be interpreted in terms of a share's risk premium. The beta value of a share indicates the relative magnitude of the change in the share's risk premium that will result from a change in the risk premium of the market portfolio. Example 4 provides some figures to illustrate this.

As a result, we can conclude that high beta shares (i.e. where $\beta > 1$) will tend to *outperform* the return on the market portfolio (the return on the FTSE index) and low beta shares (i.e. where $\beta > 1$) will tend to *underperform* the average return on the stock market. But, of course, this under- or over-performance comparison with the return on the market portfolio applies to both rises *and* falls in the return on the market portfolio. Therefore high beta shares can either be a good or a bad thing, depending on what is happening to the return on the FTSE index.

Finally, it is worthwhile making one point completely clear. The beta value can indicate the expected *change* in a share's return, relative to a change in the return on the market portfolio. What it cannot do is indicate the expected return on a share, relative to the expected return on the market portfolio. For this latter information, we also need to know the risk-free return. For example, if a share has a beta of 1.4, then a *rise* of 10% in the expected return on the market portfolio would be expected to lead to a *rise* of $10\% \times 1.4 = 14\%$ in the expected return on the share. However, if the expected return on the market portfolio is 18%, then we *cannot* say that the expected return from the share is $18\% \times 1.4 = 25.2\%$. This can only be found from using the CAPM itself:

$$E(r_j) = r_F + (18\% - r_F) \times 1.4.$$

Example 4

Given the following information:

$$r_F = 10\%$$
$$E(r_M) = 16\%$$
$$\beta_T = 1.50$$

Therefore the expected return on company T shares is:

$$E(r_T) = 10\% + (16\% - 10\%) \times 1.50 = 19\%.$$

Thus an investment in company T provides an expected risk premium of 9%. That is: 19% − 10%.
  Suppose that the expected return on the market portfolio now increases by 2% to 18%. (Assume that r_F remains unchanged.) The risk premium on the market portfolio will then have risen by 2%, from 6% to 8%. However, company T's risk premium will tend to rise by 3%, because of its beta value: 2% × 1.50 = 3%. And so its overall expected return will become:

$$E(r_T) = 10\% + (18\% - 10\%) \times 1.50 = 22\%.$$

Conversely, a share whose beta value was only 0.50 would find its return only increasing by: 2% × 0.50 = 1% in such circumstances.

Portfolio betas

Thinking back to the discussion in the previous chapter about the risk and expected returns of a two-asset portfolio, we saw that although the expected return was a weighted average of the expected returns of the two portfolio components, the risk of the portfolio was *less* than the weighted average of the risk of the components. This risk reduction was caused by the effects of diversification.

However, systematic risk, by definition, cannot be diversified away, and hence the *systematic* risk of a two-asset portfolio[6] *is* a weighted average of the systematic risk of the component investments. As beta gives an index of relative systematic risk, we can conclude that the beta value of a portfolio (as well as the expected return) *is* a weighted average of the betas of its component investments.

Thus if we were to construct a three-asset portfolio as follows:

Asset	E(r)	β	Proportion of invested funds
A	14.4%	1.6	0.60
B	12.8%	1.2	0.10
C	10.8%	0.7	0.30

Then:

$$E(r_p) = (14.4\% \times 0.6) + (12.8\% \times 0.1) + (10.8\% \times 0.3) = 13.16\%,$$
$$\text{and } \beta_p = (1.6 \times 0.6) + (1.2 \times 0.1) + (0.7 \times 0.3) = 1.29.$$

This is an important characteristic of beta and we shall return to it later.

Measurement of beta

Example 3 illustrated how a share's beta value could be estimated from its constituent components:

$$\beta_j = \frac{\sigma_j \rho_{jM}}{\sigma_M}$$

However, for real-world applications, there are obvious difficulties in being able to obtain the required data easily. Fortunately, a much more convenient method of estimating beta exists.

The beta value measures the degree to which a share's risk premium varies as the average risk premium on the stock market varies. It is not surprising, therefore, that this relationship can be observed directly from the stock market, by looking at how the return on a share varies as the return on the general stock market index (used as a surrogate for the market portfolio) varies.

If the *historical* average market risk premium is plotted on a graph against the *historical* risk premium on the shares of a particular company, then the resulting scatter diagram will reflect the general nature of the relationship that exists between the return on the company's shares and the return on the market portfolio.

The points plotted on the graph can be expected to scatter upwards to the right, indicating a positive relationship between the two variables:[7] in other words, movements in the return on the shares (whether up or down) will tend to follow movements in the return on the market portfolio. Fig. 12.1 illustrates the situation. In practice, the return on the stock market index (the FTSE index, for instance) is used to approximate the market portfolio.

Linear regression analysis can then be used to plot a straight 'line of best fit' through the scatter data.[8] This reflects the average relationship between the share's risk premium and the risk premium of the market portfolio/ FTSE index. This observed relationship is usually referred to as the *market model*, and the linear regression line is termed the share's *characteristic line*. Example 5, together with Fig. 12.2, illustrates this general procedure.

In the example of the regression equation in Example 5, the 'a' coefficient had a value of 2% and the 'b' coefficient a value of 1.30. Both of these have important meanings and we shall begin by looking at the meaning of the 'a' coefficient's value.

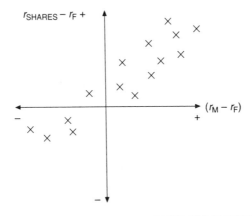

Fig. 12.1 *Scatter diagram of the share's risk premium plotted against the market portfolio's risk premium*

Example 5

To find a share's characteristic line, we look backwards to the recent past – say over the last three years – and compare the share's risk premium with the market portfolio's risk premium or the stock market index risk premium.

Therefore suppose it is now June 1994. Going back three years takes us back to June 1991. What we would do is to calculate what has been the annual risk premium on the shares, ($r_{SHARES} - r_F$), and the risk premium on the market portfolio, ($r_M - r_F$) over the last three years, moving up one month at a time.

For example:

	$r_{SHARES} - r_F$	$r_M - r_F$
June 1991 – June 1992	4%	3%
July 1991 – July 1992	6%	4.5%
August 1991 – August 1992	5%	4%
June 1993 – June 1994	7%	6%

Each of these pairs of data are then plotted onto a scatter diagram, such as in Fig. 12.2, and a regression analysis undertaken to identify the a (alpha) and b (beta) coefficients of the regression equation, the characteristic line:

$$(r_{SHARES} - r_F) = a + b(r_M - r_F).$$

Suppose the regression equation is found to be:

$$(r_{SHARES} - r_F) = 2\% + 1.30 (r_M - r_F).$$

The alpha coefficient (a) gives the vertical intercept point of the regression line and the beta coefficient (b) gives the slope of the regression line.

Fig. 12.2 *The characteristic line*

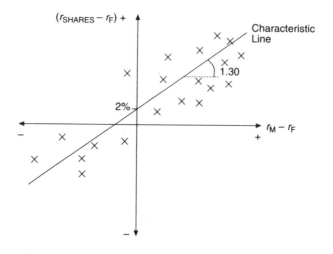

The alpha coefficient

In a perfect world the alpha coefficient of the regression equation should be zero. In other words the regression line should go through the graph's origin (where the horizontal and vertical axes cross).

The regression/characteristic line shows the relationship between the average market risk premium (on the horizontal axis) and the share's risk premium (on the vertical axis). Logically, therefore, it follows that in a situation where the market portfolio risk premium is zero, the share should not have any risk premium either.

We can look at this another way. We have seen that a share's total risk is composed of both systematic and unsystematic elements. Systematic risk describes the exposure of the company's cash flow (and hence its financial performance, value and rate of return) to changes in the macro-economic environment within which it operates. On the other hand, unsystematic risk is caused by factors specific to the individual company, such as the quality of its top management team and the state of its labour relations.

Portfolio theory shows us that investors can only expect to receive a return for holding systematic risk. The market will not provide a return for unsystematic risk because there is no need for any investor to hold it – it can easily be eliminated through holding a well-diversified investment portfolio.

However, it is very important to understand that this does *not* mean that unsystematic risk factors will not affect a company's financial performance and rate of return on its shares: *of course* they will. It is just that – as was explained earlier in this chapter – in a well-diversified investment portfolio, the good and bad effects of unsystematic risk will tend to be cancelled out. Similarly, these good and bad effects of unsystematic risk that affect a single company will tend to be cancelled out over time. Example 6 illustrates this situation and its implication as far as the alpha coefficient is concerned.

Example 6

Suppose that the risk-free return is 5%, the return on the market portfolio is 12% and the beta value of a share in the ABC company is 1.30. Therefore, according to the CAPM, the return that we should expect on ABC shares is:

$$E(r_{ABC}) = 5\% + (12\% - 5\%) \times 1.30 = 14.1\%.$$

This, of course, does not mean that each year the shares will produce a return of 14.1% but that, *on average*, that should be the annual return.

If we now look at the *actual* return on ABC shares over the last few years, suppose that we observe the following:

Year	1	2	3	4
Actual return:	15.9%	13.2%	9.7%	17.6%
Abnormal return:	+1.8%	−0.9%	−4.4%	+3.5%

The 'abnormal return' indicates by how much the *actual* return has been above or below the *expected* return. Now notice in this example that the *average* actual return is 14.1%, (the expected return predicted by the CAPM), and the average abnormal return is zero:

$$15.9\% + 13.2\% + 9.7\% + 17.6\% = 56.4\% \div 4 = 14.1\%$$
$$1.8\% - 0.9\% - 4.4\% + 3.5\% = 0\% \div 4 = 0\%$$

This is what *should* happen in a perfect world. The abnormal return each year is caused by the unsystematic risk factors (which are sometimes 'good', as in Year 1 and sometimes 'bad', as in Year 3) that affect the company's financial performance. However, over time, these effects should cancel out, leaving a zero abnormal return and, therefore, leaving an average return equal to that expected by the CAPM.

It is in this sense that we say that a share's characteristic line *should* pass through the graph's origin because the *a* or alpha coefficient of the regression equation measures the share's average abnormal return. However, life does not always work out quite so precisely as this example does. Suppose the actual returns on the ABC shares were:

Year	1	2	3	4
Actual return:	17.2%	12.8%	20.4%	14.0%
Abnormal return:	+3.1%	−1.3%	+6.3%	−0.1%

In these circumstances the average return on the shares is 16.1% and the average *abnormal* return is +2%. In other words, although CAPM says that given the share's relative systematic risk, they *should* give an average return of 14.1%, they have in fact actually given an average return which is 2% greater, at 16.1%.

This is the type of situation illustrated in Fig. 12.2, where the share's characteristic line has an alpha value of +2%.

Some investors believe that alpha values can be used to provide investment decision advice. On the basis that on average, over time, the alpha value (or average abnormal return) should be zero, some investors believe that shares with *negative* alpha values should be sold and those with *positive* alpha values should be bought.

To see the logic at work here, we will use the ABC company shares from the latter part of Example 6. In that example, according to the CAPM the shares should be expected to produce an annual return of 14.1% but, over the last few years they have actually produced an average return of 16.1%: a positive abnormal return of 2%. Given that the average abnormal return *should* be zero, it follows that over the next few years the actual average return on the shares should be only 12.1% – therefore having a *negative* alpha value of 2% – so as to bring the longer run average return back to its expected level of 14.1% and a zero alpha value.[9]

However, there is a well-known statistical fallacy in this logic. Suppose you toss a coin. We know that there is a 50% chance of heads and a 50% chance of tails, and on average we should get as many heads as tails. Suppose we toss a coin five times and each time it comes up heads; what's the chance of tails when we toss the coin a sixth time? We may be tempted to think (as do the followers of alpha values) that, given there should be as many heads as tails, with five heads in a row there must be a great chance that next time it will be tails. However, statistics has no 'memory': the chance of a tail on the sixth throw remains 50% as usual.

The beta value

Let us now return to Example 5. We have been looking at the meaning of the 'a' coefficient in the regression equation of the characteristic line. We can now look at the meaning of the regression equation's 'b'coefficient.

The 'b' coefficient describes the *slope* of the characteristic line and so indicates the degree to which the share's risk premium reacts to changes in the market portfolio's risk premium.

A slope (or 'b' coefficient) of *greater* than 1 indicates that movements in the share's risk premium will be *greater* than movements in the market portfolio's risk premium. In our example, therefore, where the 'b' coefficient had a value of 1.30, this means that a 1% increase or decrease in the market portfolio's risk premium will lead to a 1.3% increase or decrease in the share's risk premium.

Similarly, a 'b' coefficient of *less* than 1 indicates that the share's risk premium *under*-responds to movements in the market portfolio risk premium. A 'b' coefficient of 0.75 would imply that a 1% change in the market portfolio risk premium would lead to only a 0.75% change in the share's risk premium.

Finally, if the characteristic line has a slope of 1, then movements in the share's risk premium will tend to be the *same* as movements in the market portfolio's risk premium.

This description of the behaviour of the share's risk premium relative to the market portfolio's risk premium is, of course, directly comparable to our earlier discussion of the meaning of beta. And it is from the 'b' coefficient of the regression equation that the beta values of shares are, in practice, estimated. Thus, in Example 5, the shares would have had a beta value of 1.30.

Beta stability

The main problem with this approach to estimating a share's beta value is that, for decision making, we really require an estimate of what *will be* the company's beta value in the future, so that we can estimate what will be the expected return. However, the approach used for estimating beta looks at the *past*, or historical, relationship between the share and the stock market, not the future relationship.

Therefore, whether this method is a satisfactory approach to estimating beta depends upon a single issue: how stable are betas over time? If a company's beta value is found to change very little over time, then estimating the *future* beta on the basis of the *past* relationship may well be acceptable.

The beta value expresses the degree to which the company is exposed to systematic risk (relative to the market portfolio). Therefore it measures the degree to which the company's performance is affected by macro-economic forces in the economy (e.g. the rate of national economic growth, inflation levels, exchange rate movements, interest rates, etc.). Commonsense would lead us to suppose that companies are unlikely to change their sensitivity to these factors *rapidly*, unless some major event (such as a large-scale move into a new area of business) takes place within the company.

This is indeed what the evidence tends to show. Although there is some tendency over time for shares with high and low betas to move towards a beta of 1 (i.e. a general tendency for betas to regress towards the mean), generally speaking, beta values are fairly stable and do not change substantially over relatively short (say, five years) periods of time.

A further estimation approach

Finally, as well as estimating beta from first principles using the equation for beta:

$$\beta_A = \frac{\sigma_A \rho_{A,M}}{\sigma_M} \text{ or } \beta_A = \frac{\text{Cov}(r_A, r_M)}{\sigma_M^2}$$

and in addition to estimating beta through regression analysis, Example 7 shows how a 'rough and ready' approximation of beta might be generated quite simply. (Notice that these two expressions in the above equations are identical; if the covariance term is expanded, the expression reduces, through cancellation, to equal the first expression.)

Example 7

Given the following data, the beta value of company A shares could be estimated.

Year	Company A Average share price (p)	Dividend per share (p)	Average FTSE index	FTSE dividend yield	FTSE Return on govt stock
3 years ago	139	7	1300	3%	7%
2 years ago	147	8.5	1495	5%	9%
1 year ago	163	9	1520	5.5%	8%
Current year	185	10	1640	5.5%	8%

Expected return on company A shares:

(i) Average percentage annual capital gain

   Let g = average annual capital gain:

$$139p\ (1 + g)^3 = 185p$$
$$\therefore\ g = (185 \div 139)^{\frac{1}{3}} - 1 = 0.10\ \text{or}\ 10\%.$$

(ii) Average annual dividend yield

Year	Div. ÷ sh. price	=	Div. yield
3 years ago	$7 \div 139$	=	0.050
2 years ago	$8\frac{1}{2} \div 147$	=	0.058
1 year ago	$9 \div 163$	=	0.055
Current year	$10 \div 185$	=	0.054

$$0.217 \div 4 = 0.054\ \text{or}\ 5.4\%$$

Therefore the expected return on company A shares can be given as:

$$E(r_A) = \text{Av. ann. capital gain} + \text{av. dividend yield}$$
$$E(r_A) = 10\% + 5.4\% = 15.4\%.$$

Expected return on the market portfolio (FTSE):

(i) Average annual percentage capital gain

   Let g = average annual capital gain:

$$1300\ (1 + g)^3 = 1640$$
$$\therefore\ g = (1640 \div 1300)^{\frac{1}{3}} - 1 = 0.08\ \text{or}\ 8\%.$$

(ii) Average annual dividend yield

$$3\% + 5\% + 5.5\% + 5.5\% = 19\% \div 4 = 4.75\%.$$

Therefore the expected return on the stock exchange index (FTSE) acting as a surrogate for the market portfolio is:

$$E(r_M) = 8\% + 4.75\% = 12.75\%$$

Average annual risk-free return:

$$7\% + 9\% + 8\% + 8\% = 32\% \div 4 = 8\%$$

Given the information gathered above:

$$E(r_A) = 15.4\%$$
$$E(r_M) = 12.75\%$$
$$r_F = 8\%$$

the CAPM can be used to estimate the beta value of company A shares:

$$E(r_A) = r_F + E(r_M) - r_F \beta_A$$
$$15.4\% = 8\% + (12.75\% - 8\%)\beta_A$$
$$\frac{15.4\% - 8\%}{(12.75\% - 8\%)} = \beta_A = 1.56.$$

The validity of the CAPM

The assumptions behind the CAPM

Does the CAPM accurately predict the return that, on average, is produced on the shares of a particular company? This is the key question. Does it work?

The CAPM is built upon a number of assumptions, some of which are realistic, others of which are not. Effectively we can divide the CAPM assumptions up into two groups. The model makes assumptions about investors and it makes assumptions about the financial market environment within which investments are bought and sold.

As far as investors are concerned, the model assumes:

1. They are rational, risk-averse, utility maximizers.
2. They perceive utility in terms of return.
3. They measure risk by the standard deviation of returns.
4. They have a single-period investment time horizon.
5. They all have the same expectations about what the uncertain future holds.

Furthermore, the model assumes that financial markets are perfect and, specifically, that:

1. There are no taxes.
2. There are no transaction costs.
3. Investors can both lend and borrow at the risk-free rate of return.

To see whether these assumptions about the real world are reasonable, we first have to be clear as to what they mean. Saying that investors are 'rational' means that they always like more than less – in other words, they always prefer a higher return to a lower return.

Risk-aversion means, as we know, that investors dislike investments whose outcome is uncertain. This does not mean that they are unwilling to take on risky investments, but that they require a reward for doing so: the greater the risk, the greater the required reward.

Utility maximization, again as we know, means that we assume investors want to make themselves as well-off as possible. In economic terms, they wish to achieve their highest possible utility/indifference curve.

All these assumed characteristics of investors appear fairly reasonable and do not pose any real problems. We can probably also agree that investors do measure being better-off in terms of the return that the investment produces. However, whether they measure risk as the standard deviation of returns must be somewhat doubtful. A cynic might say that most investors don't even know what a standard deviation is, never mind what it measures! However, technically, the problem with standard deviation (and we touched upon this problem in our earlier discussion on utility) is that it is really only a satisfactory measure of risk if we can assume that the distribution of returns is symmetrical (i.e. normal). This is because when we say that investors are risk-averse, what we really mean is that investors dislike *downside* risk – nobody minds the upside potential of an investment. If the probability distribution of an investment's returns is normally distributed then standard deviation adequately measures *both* sides of risk. However, a problem arises if the distribution is not symmetrical, but is skewed either towards the upside or towards the downside. In such a situation, standard deviation is not going to provide an adequate measure of downside risk. Logically, the distribution of returns on a share *must* be skewed, because the upside potential is unlimited, whereas the maximum downside risk is limited to a loss of 100%.

The assumption that all investors have an investment time horizon of a single time period is highly suspect. People invest for different reasons.

Some are investing on a speculative basis, looking for short-term profits. Others are investing with a much longer time horizon in view, saving for when they retire.

Finally, the assumption that all investors have the same expectations of the future – in other words, that they make a similar assessment of the probability distribution of returns on investments – must also be suspect. The future is unknown, and so we can only guess at what might happen. Human nature being what it is, some investors may well take a more optimistic view of the future than others.

We cannot accept that all the assumptions made about the financial environment are realistic. There are taxes and, more importantly, there are differences between the tax treatment of dividends and of capital gains. It is not simply a case of saying that the return on an investment is a combination of a dividend yield and a capital gain (or loss) on the share price. Because the two are taxed differently, how that total return is to be split will be important. Not only that, investors in the same securities but with different tax situations will therefore receive different effective (i.e. after-tax) returns for the same risk.

Transaction costs also exist. Investors have to pay commission to stock-brokers on share transactions, and there is a further cost to consider in the fact that there is a difference between the buying price and the selling price of a share.

Lastly, although investors can lend at the risk-free rate of interest, (by investing in government securities), they certainly cannot borrow at that rate.

Thus we must conclude that many of the assumptions which underlie the CAPM are clearly unrealistic. However, whether or not the assumptions which underlie the model are realistic is not a matter of importance. The real question is the one we started with: Does it work? Does the model have 'predictive power'?

The empirical evidence

A model may have highly realistic assumptions, but if it has no predictive power it is largely worthless. On the other hand, a model may be constructed on very unrealistic assumptions and yet, if it works, who cares?

So does the CAPM work? Do we, in an efficient equilibrium stock market, observe the linear risk–return relationship shown in Fig. 12.3? Unfortunately, the answer is not quite as simple as 'Let's take a look'. The reason, as was pointed out by Richard Roll in a now famous article (known as Roll's critique), published in 1977, is that in order to test the CAPM, we need to be able to identify the return on the market portfolio. In practice, it is virtually impossible to do so.

Most researchers who have tried to test the CAPM to see if it works have used a stock market index as a surrogate of the market portfolio. But no stock market index includes *all* the companies quoted on the stock market but only (what they hope is) a representative selection. For example, in the UK there are almost 2500 quoted companies, but the Financial Times All-Share Index contains only 850 of those investments.

Not only that but, as Roll pointed out, even if you did include all the companies quoted on the stock exchange, you are still excluding a wide range of *other* types of investments. These might include shares in unquoted

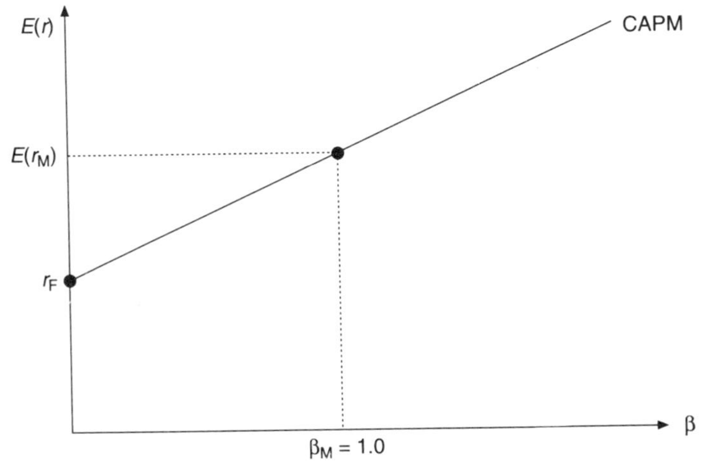

Fig. 12.3 *The capital asset pricing model relationship*

companies, antiques, precious metals and stamp collections. Therefore it is virtually impossible to be able to identify the return on the *true* market portfolio of capital assets.

Nevertheless, despite the problems put forward by Roll, hundreds of researchers have attempted to test the CAPM to see if it works, looking at the relationship between observed beta values and average returns.

The model is normally tested on the basis of 'risk premiums'. In other words, if we take the basic CAPM:

$$E(r_Z) = r_F + [E(r_M) - r_F] \times \beta_Z,$$

and subtract the risk-free return from both sides of the equation:

$$E(r_Z) - r_F = [E(r_M) - r_F] \times \beta_Z.$$

This then gives the risk premium on investment Z, $[E(r_Z) - r_F]$, equals the average risk premium on the stock market $[E(r_M) - r_F]$ times the beta value. We also add into the equation an 'intercept term' – a – which should be zero. Thus:

$$E(r_Z) - r_F = a + [E(r_M) - r_F] \times \beta_Z.$$

This intercept term plays an important role in the testing of the CAPM. As we know, the CAPM is a very simple model which states that the risk premium on an investment is *purely* a function of the average risk premium on the stock market *times* beta – a factor which is designed to measure the systematic risk of the investment relative to the average systematic risk of the stock market. If the 'a' term does *not* turn out to be zero, it indicates that some other factor(s) besides relative systematic risk are determining the investment's return.

The results of these tests show up three important things. The first is that there *does* appear to be a positive linear relationship between beta and the investment's return. So, fundamentally, we could conclude the CAPM does appear to be correct: high beta shares give high returns, and low beta shares give low returns.

However, the conclusion that the tests show the CAPM to be fundamentally correct is controversial. Others would argue the reverse, because of the other two points the results show up. The first of these is that the 'a' intercept is *not* zero, but is positive. This indicates that there *are* other factors beside relative systematic risk that determine return.

A number of researchers have followed up this point and have tried to identify what these other factors may be. Two promising factors appear to be the company size and dividend policy. Smaller companies tend to give slightly higher returns than larger companies with the same beta value. Similarly, companies with high dividend yields give slightly greater returns than companies with similar beta values, but with lower dividend yields. However, it may well be that once the tax differences between dividend income and capital gains are taken into account this effect ceases to be significant.

Other researchers have found an apparent relationship between a company's price–earnings ratio (PER), (the ratio of share price/earnings per share), and its return. Companies with low PERs give higher returns than similar beta companies with high PERs. However, it needs to be recognized that the earnings figure is based on historic accounting data whilst the price is based on market expectations. This does however, imply that earnings figures might be a better predictor of future returns than we might often give them credit for.

Finally, other research has found evidence that returns on shares may have some element of seasonality or even variability related to the day of the week. However, once year end tax effects in the USA are removed these effects are very small.

There is other evidence also, which shows up problems with the CAPM. This is specifically in terms of Roll's criticisms that our usual measures of the market portfolio are inadequate. Evidence has been found that for some industries – such as companies in the oil industry and in natural resources – the CAPM is a particularly poor predictor because, it is argued, the market portfolio is under-representative of those areas.

We said earlier that the empirical research has unearthed three real points of interest. The third of these is that the *actual* slope of the CAPM appears to be slightly less than the *predicted* slope. This is illustrated in Fig. 12.4. In other words, low beta shares (those with $\beta < 1$) tend to give slightly *higher* returns than CAPM would predict while high beta shares ($\beta > 1$) tend to give slightly *lower* returns than CAPM would predict. No really convincing explanation for this phenomenon has been forthcoming.

Fig. 12.4 *High and low betas*

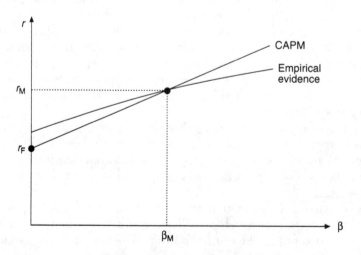

Despite all the foregoing, the arguments should be kept in perspective. Although the CAPM is not perfect, it probably is a fairly good predictor of returns and it is certainly better than anything else that is available. The other point which should not be lost sight of is that although there may be a number of other factors (e.g. company size and dividend policy) which go towards determining returns, it still appears that relative systematic risk (beta) is by *far* the most important of these factors.

Sources of information about Beta

It is relatively easy to find out the betas for quoted companies. The London Business School Risk Management Service has produced its 'Beta Book' for many years and the information is also available through on-line data services such as Datastream.

Arbitrage pricing theory (APT)

Detractors of the CAPM believe that a superior asset pricing model exists: the Arbitrage Pricing Model or APM. In many ways, the CAPM can be viewed as being a special case of this more general model and, in that sense, the APM is probably superior to the CAPM. The 'only' problem is that, so far, researchers have been unable to identify precisely the information needed to make it work in practice.

The APM looks very similar to the CAPM, but its origins are significantly different. Whereas the CAPM is a *single*-factor model, the APM is a *multi*-factor model. Instead of just a *single* beta value there is a whole set of beta values – one for each factor.

Arbitrage Pricing Theory (APT), out of which the APM arises, states that the expected return on an investment is dependent upon how that investment reacts to a set of individual macro-economic factors (the degree of reaction being measured by the betas) and the risk premium associated with each of those macro-economic factors.

This is, of course, exactly what the CAPM does – except that it only looks at *one* factor, the return on the market portfolio. CAPM looks at how the return on an investment reacts to changes in the return on the market portfolio, (the investment's beta value) and the risk premium on the market portfolio, $(E(r_M) - r_F)$.

In contrast, APM states that the expected return on investment, A, is given by:

$$E(r_A) = r_F + (r_{F_1} - r_F) \beta_{F_1} + (r_{F2} - r_F) \beta_{F_2} + \ldots$$

where F_1 and F_2 etc. refer to these individual macro-economic factors.

The first problem with using the APM is that we are unclear about the identity of these macro-economic factors (i.e. F_1, F_2, F_3, etc.). Secondly, we are unsure of how to measure the investment's sensitivity to changes in each of these factors (i.e. β_{F_1}, β_{F_2}, etc.). Finally, it is difficult to identify the risk premium of each of these macro-economic factors, (i.e. $(r_{F_1} - r_F)$, $(r_{F_2} - r_F)$, etc.).

In many ways the APM is a good idea but certainly, at present, it is still a long way from being, (and may never be), of practical use. Nevertheless, some advances have been made, especially in terms of trying to identify the macro-economic factors which determine an investment's return.

Several factors appear to have been identified as being important (some of which, such as inflation and money supply, industrial production and personal consumption, do have aspects of being interrelated). In particular, researchers have identified:

1. Changes in the level of industrial production in the economy.
2. Changes in the shape of the yield curve.
3. Changes in the default–risk premium (i.e. changes in the return required on bonds with different perceived risks of default).
4. Changes in the inflation rate.
5. Changes in the real interest rate.
6. The level of personal consumption.
7. The level of money supply in the economy.

All of these accord with commonsense. Given that the value of the firm can be seen as the discounted present value of the future cash flow it is expected to generate, then it is changes to this value which will bring about changes to the return on the firm's securities. The index of industrial production (which is obviously similar in reality to the CAPM's market portfolio) is an obvious indicator of the firm's ability to generate future cash flows. Similarly, the other factors are all – to some extent – going to impact either on the level of the cash flows that the company is able to generate or on the discount rate used by the market to convert those expected cash flows to present value.

The idea is that all firms in the economy will react – to some extent – to change in these seven factors. Furthermore, all firms will react in a similar way. For example, an increase in the level of industrial production will be good news for them all, and so these factors will not be capable of being diversified away. However, not all firms will react to the *same* extent – some will be more greatly affected than others. This degree of sensitivity would be measured by a *set* of beta values for each firm – one beta value for each factor. Finally, as none of these factors can be diversified away, they will each have a risk premium. In other words, there will be a reward for accepting the risk, of say, the impact of an unanticipated change in the level of inflation on a company's cash flow.

If we describe these seven factors as F_1–F_7, then we could try to measure the beta value of each factor on the same basis as we measure beta values for the CAPM. Thus for company A:

$$\beta_{A_{F_1}} = \frac{\sigma_A \times \rho_{A,F_1}}{\sigma_{F_1}}, \beta_{A_{F_2}} = \frac{\sigma_A \times \rho_{A,F_2}}{\sigma_{F_2}}, \text{etc.}$$

where σ_A = standard deviation of returns on A shares, σ_{F_1} = standard deviation of the level of industrial production, ρ_{A,F_j} = correlation coefficient between the returns on A shares and the level of industrial production, etc.

Some research has been undertaken applying the APM and, in particular, comparing its results with those of the CAPM. The outcome has been mixed. Some research has shown that the APM does give superior predictions to the CAPM in certain situations (usually when the industry group is effectively under-represented in the market portfolio). Other research, however, has indicated that the APM tells us very little that we don't already know from the far simpler CAPM.

Therefore the conclusion that we reach is the same conclusion that we reach in many other areas of corporate finance theory: we are a long way from the end of the road of truly knowing what the answers are to all the questions.

Betas and project investment appraisal

The project discount rate

The link between the CAPM and our quest for an NPV discount rate for project investment appraisal seems obvious. The CAPM can be used to generate the appropriate discount rate $(E(r_{project}))$ having taken into account the systematic risk of the project:

$$E(r_{project}) = r_F + [E(r_M) - r_F] \beta_{project}.$$

However, there are two major difficulties: one conceptual and one practical.

The conceptual difficulty concerns the fact that the CAPM is a *single-period return* model, whereas the discount rate required for an NPV calculation is obviously a multi-time period rate of return. As a result, strictly speaking, the CAPM-generated rate of return cannot be applied to an NPV calculation. One solution would be to derive a multi-time period capital asset pricing model – such models do exist. However, there are considerable difficulties involved with them which restricts their practical usefulness.

If it can be assumed that the risk-free return and the excess market return, i.e. $E(r_M - r_F)$, will remain approximately constant over the life of the project, then the single-period CAPM model *can* be used safely in a multi-time period analysis such as an NPV analysis. If such assumptions cannot be made with reasonable confidence – and one problem here is that the excess market return does show some degree of volatility over time – then at least we can try to allow for some of the multi-time period effects. For example, the annual yield to redemption on government stock which has the same number of years to maturity as the life of the project can be taken as the estimate of the risk-free return. However, the basic problem of CAPM being a single-period model does remain.

Nevertheless, using the CAPM to provide an NPV discount rate is certainly a considerable improvement on estimating a discount rate on the basis of management's own subjective value judgement (as we saw in Chapter 9), or not taking risk into account at all. The pragmatic solution is to conclude that, in the light of these circumstances, if a CAPM-generated expected rate of return is to be used as an NPV discount rate, it should only be used with caution. But, having stated that, the CAPM does at least provide a *framework* for analysing what should be a project's discount rate, and it is likely to provide an estimate which is of the correct order of magnitude, given the project's systematic risk. In short, the CAPM may not be the perfect way to estimate a project's discount rate, but it is the best way that we have available.

The project beta

The second difficulty concerns the identification of the project's beta value. Obviously this cannot be estimated in the way that a share's beta is estimated;

nor would it be fruitful to consider trying to estimate a project's beta through estimating the individual components of the beta value expression. One possible approach to solving the problem is to use the beta value of the industry within which the project could be classified, as a surrogate for the beta value of the project. The industry beta value would simply be an average of the beta values of the firms within that industry.[10] Thus, if the project under appraisal was a cement production facility, then the average beta value of the quoted companies in the cement industry could be taken as an estimate of the project's beta. However, some adjustments might have to be made to the beta value obtained in this way, if it were thought that the project's systematic risk characteristics differed from those of the cement industry generally.

Adjusting beta

How should such adjustments be made? What happens if a project does not fall neatly within an industrial classification (or the classification is thought to be too wide to be appropriate)? The answer to both these questions is that we require a clearer idea of the identification of systematic risk.

We know that systematic risk refers to the degree of sensitivity to macro-economic changes. Thus to form a view about the systematic risk of a particular project, we need to examine the degree to which its cash flows – its revenue and cost flows – react to changes in the economy, such as changes in the business cycle or in rates of taxation. In other words, how closely tied are the project's cash inflows and outflows to macro-economic forces?

The greater the degree to which the cash inflows are tied (that is, the greater is their sensitivity to macro-economic changes), then the greater is their systematic risk and the greater should be the project's beta value. The reverse will apply to the project cash outflows; thus, if the cash outflows are also sensitive to macro-economic changes – i.e. the costs are variable rather than fixed – then this will tend to reduce the degree of the project's systematic risk. Conversely, if most of a project's costs are fixed and do not vary with macro-economic changes, then this adds to the systematic risk.

A project whose cash inflows are highly sensitive to changes in macro-economic factors, but whose cash outflows are mostly fixed and therefore are not sensitive to macro-economic changes, would be classified as a highly (systematic) risky project. The opposite would be a project with mainly variable costs and a revenue flow that was relatively insensitive to macro-economic changes.

Thus, if it is possible to identify a fairly narrow industrial classification within which a particular investment falls, then the beta value of that industry could be taken as an initial estimate of the project's beta. This can then be adjusted (on a necessarily subjective basis) to allow for the project's particular revenue and cost cash flow sensitivities, when they are thought to differ from the industry norm. In situations where a suitable industry classification does not exist, the relevant characteristics of the project's revenue and cost cash flows would have to be examined and an attempt made to match them to an industry (and its beta value) whose cash flows exhibit similar characteristics.

Finally, there is the situation where a stock exchange quoted company is involved in the appraisal of a project that falls within the normal area of its business. Here the company's own beta value can provide the starting point, with adjustments being made to allow for the *atypical* aspects of the project's sensitivity to macro-economic factors. However, even in these circumstances, the *industry* beta (if possible) is likely to be a more satisfactory starting point than the individual company beta. This is because the individual company beta – estimated from the slope of the regression line through the historical market relationship – will contain some estimation error.[11] Using an industry beta, which is an average of individual company betas, helps to reduce substantially the amount of this error (in much the same way that unsystematic risk is reduced through diversification).

This whole problem of identifying a suitable beta value to generate a discount rate for a project's investment appraisal is complex and we will return to this discussion at a later stage.

One final point

The CAPM is a model for pricing capital assets, e.g. shares. We know from the previous chapter that in the single-period world of the CAPM, the return on a share is given by:

$$r_j = \frac{(P_j 1 - P_j 0) + \text{Divs}}{P_j 0},$$

where $P_j 0$ is the current price per share in company j and $P_j 1$ is the end of period price per share. Suppose we take the simplest possible case and assume that no dividend is paid during the time that the share is held. In such circumstances:

$$r_j = \frac{(P_j 1 - P_j 0)}{P_j 0}.$$

From this, we can use the CAPM to determine what should be the current market price of the share:

$$\frac{E(P_j 1) - P_j 0}{P_j 0} = r_F + [E(r_M) - r_F]\beta_j$$

$$\frac{E(P_j 1)}{P_j 0} - \frac{P_j 0}{P_j 0} = r_F + [E(r_M) - r_F]\beta_j.$$

Rearranging:

$$\frac{E(P_j 1) - P_j 0}{P_j 0} = r_F + [E(r_M) - r_F]\beta_j$$

In this expression, the denominator can be thought of as a *risk-adjusted discount rate*, where $[E(r_M) - r_F]\,\beta_j$ represents the share's rise premium. Therefore, the equilibrium current share price is equal to the expected future share price, discounted to present value using a risk-adjusted discount rate: in other words the discount rate reflects the (systematic) risk of the shares.

This way of looking at CAPM is useful in the context of the foregoing discussion because it shows CAPM as providing a risk-adjusted discount rate – albeit for just one time period. It was precisely this that we are seeking to use as a capital investment appraisal discount rate in the face of uncertainty.

This is not the end of our consideration either of the investment appraisal discount rate or the CAPM. We shall find that in the chapters that follow we will make repeated references to both topics. However, for the time being we will turn to look at some other aspects of risk and ways in which a company's management can respond.

Summary

This chapter discussed how the CAPM is developed out of portfolio theory, and examined its meaning and use. The main points made were as follows:

- The CML expression deals with the expected return on an efficient portfolio investment. From this can be derived the expected return on an *inefficient* investment: the expected return on the shares of an individual company. Such an expression is termed the capital asset pricing model.

- In the CAPM, the risk premium is determined by the product of the market price of risk and the share's systematic risk level. This latter value is given by the product of the share's total risk (σ) and the degree to which the returns on the share are correlated to the returns on the market portfolio.

- Normally, in practice, a share's systematic risk is not measured in absolute terms, but in terms relative to the (systematic) risk of the market portfolio. This is indicated by the beta value.

- Shares with betas greater than one will have more systematic risk than the average level of systematic risk on the stock market (indicated by the risk of the market portfolio), and their share price behaviour will tend to be more volatile than the general stock market index.

- Shares with betas of less than one will have less systematic risk than the average, and their share price behaviour will tend to underperform movements in the general market index.

- As high beta shares are more risky than average, they will be expected to produce a return higher than average. Low beta shares will similarly be expected to produce a return lower than average.

- Unsystematic, or diversifiable, risk is principally caused by company-specific factors (such as labour relations and management quality) which affect the performance of a company's cash flow. Such effects will be washed out in a well-diversified portfolio.

- Systematic, or non-diversifiable, risk is principally caused by macro-economic factors which affect *all* firms in the stock market, to a greater or lesser extent. Such factors would include the rate of national economic growth and the level and volatility of exchange rates. The impact of these effects cannot be eradicated through diversification.

- A company's exposure to systematic risk is determined by the degree of its revenue sensitivity to these macro-economic-type effects and also by its cost sensitivity, that is, its ratio of fixed to variable costs. Most importantly, the greater the revenue sensitivity, the greater the degree of systematic risk.

- Beta can, in theory, be measured from first principles using the beta expression of covariance over market variance: $Cov(r_A, r_M)/\sigma^2_M$. However, it is usually estimated by the slope of the regression line of the relationship between the returns on the share and the returns on the market portfolio.

- Although the CAPM is developed under a set of rather unrealistic assumptions, the empirical evidence does tend to suggest that a positive, linear risk–return relationship, of the type described by the CAPM, does really exist. Despite the theoretical problems that exist in the testing of the model, and despite the evidence which suggests that systematic risk is not the sole determinant of return, we can conclude that the CAPM does appear to capture the essence of the relationship between risk and return on the stock market.

- The CAPM can be viewed as being a special, single-factor model, of a more general model: the Arbitrage Pricing Theory Model. However, although research has indicated that there may be a whole range of factors which determine an investment's return, the capture of the determinants within a multi-factor APT model is not yet developed as a practical tool.

- Finally, the use of CAPM to generate NPV discount rates for project appraisal was examined. A number of problems arise in this use of the CAPM, not least of which are the facts that the CAPM is a single-period model and NPV is a multi-period analysis and that project betas have to be estimated on the basis of industry betas. However, this application of the CAPM will be further developed at a later stage.

Appendix: the security market line

Perhaps the simplest way of deriving an expression for the expected return on an inefficient investment is to examine the characteristics of a two-asset portfolio where one of the assets is an investment in the market portfolio and the other asset is an investment in the shares of a single company: company A. The risk and expected return characteristics of the resulting (inefficient) investment portfolio would be:

$$E(r_p) = xE(r_A) + (1 - x) E(r_M)$$

$$\sigma_p = \sqrt{\{x^2\sigma_A^2 + (1-x)^2\sigma_M^2 + 2x(1-x)Cov[r_A, r_M]\}}$$

Suppose that Fig. 12.5 illustrates the range of possible risk–expected return combinations AM, available from the two-asset portfolio. By the use of calculus, the slope of the line AM at point M can be identified and from this can be derived a general expression for the expected return on an inefficient investment (assuming market prices are in equilibrium).

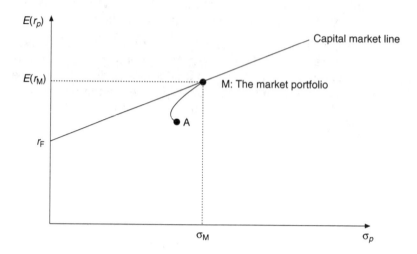

Fig. 12.5
Development of the SML

If the expected return of the portfolio is given by:

$$E(r_p) = xE(r_A) + (1 - x) E(r_M),$$

then the expected return from a marginal investment in the inefficient portfolio p can be found by differentiating $E(r_p)$ with respect to x:

$$\frac{dE(r_p)}{dx} = E(r_A) - E(r_M).$$

Similarly, the risk produced by a marginal investment in the inefficient portfolio p can be found by differentiating the expression for the portfolio's risk:

$$\frac{d\sigma_p}{dx} = \frac{1}{2}[x^2\sigma_A^2 + (1-x)^2\sigma_M^2 + 2x(1-x)\text{Cov}(r_A, r_M)]^{-\frac{1}{2}}$$

$$\times [2x\sigma_A^2 - 2\sigma_M^2 + 2\sigma_M^2 + 2\text{Cov}(r_A, r_M) - 4x\text{Cov}(r_A, r_M)].$$

At point M on the line AM, all the portfolio funds are invested in M and therefore the value of $x = 0$. This simplifies the expression for marginal risk:

$$\frac{d\sigma_p}{dx} = \frac{1}{2}[\sigma_M^2]^{-\frac{1}{2}} \times [(2\text{Cov}(r_A, r_M) - 2\sigma_M^2]$$

which reduces further, to

$$\frac{d\sigma_p}{dx} = \frac{\text{Cov}(r_A, r_M) - \sigma_M^2}{\sigma_M}$$

Given that the slope of the CML was $E(r_M) - r_F/\sigma_M$, then similarly, the slope of the line AM at point M is given by:

$$\frac{dE(r_p)}{dx} / \frac{d\sigma_p}{dx} \equiv \frac{dE(r_p)}{d\bar{x}} \times \frac{dx}{d\sigma_p} = \frac{dE(r_p)}{d\sigma_p},$$

that is:

$$\frac{\sigma_M[E(r_A) - E(r_M)]}{Cov(r_A, r_M) - \sigma_M^2}$$

However, at point M the slope of the line AM must also equal the slope of the CML. Therefore at point M, the following relationship holds:

$$\frac{\sigma_M[E(r_A) - E(r_M)]}{Cov(r_A, r_M) - \sigma_M^2} = \frac{E(r_M) - r_F}{\sigma_M}$$

This equality can then be rearranged to provide an expression for the expected return on the shares of company A:

$$E(r_A) = r_F + \frac{E(r_M) - r_F}{\sigma_M^2} \times Cov(r_A, r_M).$$

In fact this is the general expression for the return on *any* inefficient asset, and is termed the equation of the security market line (SML):

$$E(r_j) = r_F + \frac{E(r_M) - r_F}{\sigma_M^2} \times Cov(r_j, r_M).$$

This is graphed in Fig. 12.6. Examination of the SML function shows that it is a linear function (as was the CML function) of three variables: the risk-free return (r_F), the market's risk–expected return trade-off ($E(r_M) - r_F/\sigma_M^2$) and the covariance of returns between the market portfolio and the inefficient investment j [$Cov(r_j, r_M)$]. In other words, the expected return from an investment in the inefficient asset j is equal to the risk-free return, plus a risk premium:

$$F + \frac{E(r_M) - r_F}{\sigma_M^2} \times Cov(r_j, r_M)$$

↑

Risk-

free   Risk premium

return

Fig. 12.6 *The security market line*

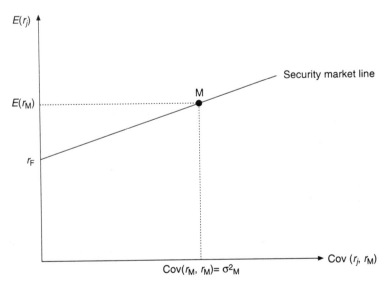

Expanding the covariance term and given the definition of λ, the market price of risk:

$$E(r_A) = r_F + \frac{E(r_M) - r_F}{\sigma_M^2} \sigma_M \sigma_A \rho_{A,M},$$

this expression simplifies to:

$$E(r_A) = r_F + \lambda \sigma_A \rho_{A,M}.$$

Notes

1. The portfolio risk expression – when $r_{A,B} = +1$ – can be given as:

$$\sigma_p = \sqrt{[x^2 \sigma_A^2 + (1-x)^2 \sigma_B^2 + 2x(1-x)\sigma_A \sigma_B]}.$$

Remembering that : $\quad (a+b)^2 = a^2 + b^2 + 2ab$

then: $\qquad\qquad \sigma_p = \sqrt{[x\sigma_A + (1-x)\sigma_B]^2}$

and : $\qquad\qquad \sigma_p = x\sigma_A + (1-x)\sigma_B.$

2. That is, the risk taken on by the particular point the investor has chosen to locate his portfolio on the CML.

3. Perhaps a safer description at this stage would be to say that share price movements and dividends are determined by the fortunes of the company.

4. Although it is not considered here, there may well be a possibility of eliminating some country-specific macro-economic factors by holding an internationally diversified portfolio.

5. The sign '$\approx$' means 'approximately equal to'.

6. Or of an n-asset portfolio.

7. The relationship would be positive in a 'correlation coefficient' sense. In other words, the return on the shares in the individual company will tend to move in the same direction as the return on the FTSE market index.

8. Most introductory textbooks on statistics will show how such a line of best fit might be calculated from scatter diagram data.

9. The rationale of this advice is dealt with more fully in Chapter 16. Basically, there is an *inverse* relationship between a share's price and its return. Therefore, where the alpha value has been negative, the return has been too *low* in the past and so can be expected to *rise* in the future – by the share price *falling*. Hence the advice to sell negative alpha shares, before the share price does actually fall.

10. In making such a calculation, the differing capital structures of the companies (i.e. the ratio of equity to fixed interest capital) must be taken into account. This topic will be returned to in a later chapter, after the issue of capital structure has been discussed.

11. Indicated by the scatter of the plots on the graph around the regression line. The greater the degree of scatter, the greater the degree of possible error.

Further reading

1. Much of the CAPM literature is mathematically demanding. However, an excellent article which is very readable is the two parts of: F. Modigliani and G.A. Pogue, 'An Introduction to Risk and Return: Concepts and Evidence', *Financial Analysts Journal*, March–April and May–June 1974.
2. Another excellent review article is K. Peansell, 'The Capital Asset Pricing Model', in *Issues in Finance*, M. Firth and S.M. Keane (eds), Philip Allen 1986.
3. Two further excellent articles can be found in the book of readings edited by J.M. Stern and D.H. Chew, *The Revolution in Corporate Finance*, Blackwell 1992. They are: J. MacQueen, 'Beta is Dead! Long Live Beta!' and B. Rosenberg and A. Rudd, 'The Corporate Uses of Beta'.
4. On the empirical evidence and testing of the CAPM, see F. Black, M.C. Jensen and M. Scholes. 'The CAPM: Some Empirical Tests', in *Studies in the Theory of Capital Markets*, M. Jensen (ed.), Prager 1972; S.A. Ross, 'The Current Status of the Capital Asset Pricing Model', *Journal of Finance*, June 1978; R.W. Banz, 'The Relationship Between Return and Market Value of Common Stock', *Journal of Financial Economics*, March 1981; and H. Levy, 'The CAPM: Theory and Empiricism', *The Economic Journal*, March 1983.
5. Roll's criticism of the CAPM tests makes difficult, but worthwhile, reading: R. Roll, 'A Critique of the Asset Pricing Theory's Tests', *Journal of Financial Economics*, March 1977. The article by Ross is also fairly demanding, but it is particularly interesting to see how the APT model is developed in an entirely different way to the CAPM: S.A. Ross, 'The Arbitrage Theory of Capital Asset Pricing', *Journal of Economic Theory*, December 1976.
6. Of direct relevance to the application of the CAPM to investment appraisal, there are a number of good articles, including: S.C. Myers and S. Turnbull, 'Capital Budgeting and the Capital Asset Pricing Model: Good News and Bad News', *Journal of Finance*, May 1977; H. Levy, 'Another Look at the CAPM', *Quarterly Review of Business and Economics*, Summer 1984; D.W. Mullins, 'Does the CAPM Work?', *Harvard Business Review*, January/February 1982; J.C. Van Horne, 'An Application of the CAPM to Divisional Required Returns', *Financial Management*, Spring 1980; and T.E. Conine and M. Tamarkin, 'Divisional Cost of Capital Estimation: Adjusting for Leverage', *Financial Management*, Spring 1985.
7. Finally, on APT a clear overview is given by R. Bower and D. Logue, 'A Primer on Arbitrage Pricing Theory', in J. M. Stern, D.H. Chew (eds), *The Revolution in Corporate Finance*, Blackwell, 1992. Some empirical testing can be seen in N.F. Chen, R.W. Roll and S.A. Ross, 'Economic Forces and the Stock Market: Testing the APT and Alternative Asset Pricing Theories', *Journal of Business*, Autumn 1986. For a discussion on the possible APT model inputs, see C.B. McGowan and J.C. Francis, 'APT Factors and their Relationship to Macroeconomic Variables', in C.F. Lee *et al.*, *Advances in Quantitative Analysis of Finance and Accounting*, JAI Press, 1991.

Quickie questions

1. Write down the standard CAPM expression for the expected return on company A shares.
2. What does beta measure?
3. What is unsystematic risk and what are its sources?
4. What determines a share's exposure to systematic risk?
5. Given the following information, what is company B's systematic risk, unsystematic risk and beta value?:

$$\sigma_B = 20\%$$
$$\sigma_M = 10\%$$
$$\rho_{B,M} = + 0.6$$

6. What is company C's beta value, given the following information?:

$$Cov(r_C, r_M) = + 73.5$$
$$\sigma_M = 7\%$$

7. Company D has a beta value of 1.2. It is thinking of undertaking a project with a beta value of 1.7. If, when accepted, the project will comprise 10% of the firm's total worth, what will be the subsequent beta value of the company?
8. Does an over-valued share lie above or below the CAPM line?
9. What is the principal difference between the CAPM and the arbitrage pricing model?
10. Given the following information, what would be your advice concerning project X:

	Cash flow		
0	-100	r_F	= 8%
1	+60	$E(r_M)$	= 12%
2	+50	$\beta_{industry}$	= 1.75

Problems

1. Vanhal plc is a widely-diversified company listed on the Stock Exchange. As it is not yet involved in the construction industry, the directors would like to broaden further the company's activities by acquiring all of the issued share capital of a construction company dealt in on the Unlisted Securities Market. Vanhal plc would issue shares with a current market value of £4 million to the shareholders of the company to be acquired. Three construction companies (A, B and C) have been identified as possible target acquisitions, each with a market value of approximately £4 million. Details of the market performance of these three companies are:

Company	Beta factor	Total risk*	Risk specific to the company*	Current gross dividend yield	Price–earnings ratio
A	0.67	30%	28%	11.1%	4.2
B	1.14	36%	31%	9.5%	5.4
C	0.88	50%	48%	12.2%	4.7

*Risk is defined in terms of standard deviation and the unit of measurement is percentage returns.

The directors are unsure which of the three companies to acquire. At present, Vanhal plc has a beta factor of 0.67, total risk of 30%, company-specific risk of 28% and a market capitalization of £62 million. The return on the Financial Times All Share Index currently has a standard deviation of 16%.

Required:
(a) Calculate the new market value and the new systematic (or market) risk of Vanhal plc that would occur in each of three independent circumstances:
   (i) if Vanhal plc acquires company A;
   (ii) if Vanhal plc acquires company B; and
   (iii) if Vanhal plc acquires company C.

You may assume that the stock markets are perfect, that the diversification opportunities of investors are unrestricted and that no synergy is involved.

(b) Explain how diversification can reduce the total risk associated with Vanhal plc's share returns.

(c) Discuss why the directors of Vanhal plc might wish to diversify, and suggest which of the three companies best meets the directors' requirements.

(d) Discuss whether the shareholders of Vanhal plc should welcome the proposed diversification.

2. Mr Swift maintains a well-diversified portfolio containing a large number of different quoted shares. He is considering investing in the quoted ordinary shares of one of two companies, Dove plc and Jay plc, an amount which is small in relation to the total value of his portfolio. He wishes to include those shares which will lead to a reduction in portfolio risk as measured by the variance of portfolio returns. The correlation coefficient of the returns on Dove's shares with the return on the market portfolio and with the returns on Mr Swift's existing portfolio are expected to be 0.30 and 0.16 respectively over the coming years. The corresponding correlation coefficients for the returns on shares in Jay are 0.25 and 0.21, respectively. The standard deviations of returns for Dove and Jay are expected to be 35% and 30% respectively for the coming year and their expected returns for that period are 9% and 7% respectively.

Required:
(a) Advise Mr Swift on which of the two shares he should select for his portfolio in order to meet his objectives.

(b) Demonstrate why the expected return on an ordinary share in Dove is greater than that for Jay.

(c) Discuss how your advice might change if Mr Swift's portfolio contained shares in only a very small number of listed companies.

(d) Discuss why the relevant measure of risk may vary between a company's shareholders, debt holders and managers.

3. The government of Trinka is considering how to protect its domestic cement industry. There is only one cement manufacturer in the country – Cemenco Ltd – which is coming in for severe competition from imported cement. Presently the government are considering banning imports of cement and – because that would leave Cemenco Ltd with a monopoly – imposing government controls on the price of cement.

In this respect the government wish to be able to compare the systematic riskiness of Cemenco with that of its overseas competitors. With this knowledge, they hope to be able to determine a fair return for the company's shareholders and hence, the price which should be set for cement.

As a result, you have been called in by the government to try to estimate the company's beta value. Trinka has an active stock exchange and Cemenco are one of the quoted companies. The government has provided you with the following information:

	Cemenco Ltd		Trinka Stock Exchange		Return
	Av. share price T$	Dividend yield	Average TSE index	Average div. yield	govt. stocks
Current year	16.42	10%	1983	16%	15%
12 months ago	15.50	12%	1665	16%	16%
24 months ago	12.10	8%	1789	10%	14%
36 months ago	9.50	10%	1490	18%	15%

Required:
(a) Estimate the beta value of Cemenco Ltd.
(b) Comment on what effects you think that the government's action might have on the riskiness of Cemenco Ltd.

4. John Smith has savings of £12 000. Of this amount he has invested £6000 in Treasury Bills which currently yield a return of 6%. The remainder has been invested in a portfolio of four different companies' shares. Details of this portfolio are as follows:

Company	Expected return	β shares	Worth of shareholding
W	7.6%	0.20	£1200
X	12.4%	0.80	£1200
Y	15.6%	1.20	£1200
Z	18.8%	1.60	£2400

Required:
(a) Calculate the expected return and β value of Mr Smith's savings portfolio.
(b) Mr Smith has decided that he wants an expected return of 12% on his savings portfolio. Show how he would achieve this by selling some of his Treasury Stock and investing the proceeds in the market portfolio.
(c) If Mr Smith were *only* to invest in Treasury Bills and the market portfolio, what savings portfolio would be required to give him an expected return of 10.32%?
(d) If Mr Smith wants to choose between his existing savings portfolio (as in (a)) and the one constructed in (c), which would you advise, and why?
(e) Explain the significance, if any, of both *a* (alpha) and *b* (beta) values to investors in quoted securities.

13 The valuation of options

Introduction

The three previous chapters have looked at the nature of risk. In particular, we have seen that the total risk of an investment can be split into that part that can be eliminated through diversification, and that part of total risk which cannot be diversified away. Furthermore, we have seen that all investors should dislike risk – they dislike the fact that an investment's outcome is uncertain – and therefore they demand a reward for undertaking a risky investment. The reward for risk-taking is in the form of the return that the investment is expected to yield; the more risky the investment, the greater must be the anticipated return. An alternative approach to understanding the implication of risk aversion is to say that *more* risky investments will be *less* valuable (and therefore be priced lower) than less risky investments. Suppose an investment is expected to produce a cash inflow of £110 with great certainty (i.e. very little risk). As such, you judge that you would require the reward of a 10% return to persuade you to undertake the investment. This implies that you would be willing to pay £100 to undertake the investment because, for an outlay of £100, the investment gives the required rate of return of 10%: (£110 − £100) ÷ £100 = 0.10 or 10%.

Now suppose another investment is also expected to produce a cash inflow of £110 but there is much greater uncertainty about whether this expected cash flow will actually occur, (i.e. this investment is more risky). As a result, let us say that you decide that you require a 37.5% return to persuade you to undertake the investment. This means that you are only willing to pay £80 to undertake that investment: (£110 − £80) ÷ £80 = 0.375 or 37.5%

Thus it can be seen that the more risky investment is less valuable – £80 – than the less risky investment, which was worth £100. However, remember that our analysis also taught us that it is only the amount of an investment's *systematic* risk which determines its required level of return.

Options and futures contracts

In this and the following chapter, we are going to look at another aspect of risk. Instead of looking at the nature of risk and the relationship between an investment's risk and its expected return, we are going to look at some other types of risk that companies are exposed to and at the techniques that are available for controlling, reducing and eliminating that exposure.

Given that we have defined risk as uncertainty of outcome, there are two important areas of financial management – other than the capital investment decision – where companies are exposed to such uncertainty. These are the areas of interest rates and foreign exchange rates.

Uncertainty exists because both of these rates move in essentially unpredictable ways. Therefore a company that borrows money is exposed to the risk of a subsequent adverse movement in interest rates. Similarly an importer who receives an invoice denominated in a foreign currency, or an exporter who invoices a customer in a foreign currency, is exposed to the risk of an adverse movement in foreign exchange rates.

The two main types of hedging[1] instruments for dealing with these sorts of risk are *futures contracts* and *option contracts*. To begin with we will examine option contracts and, in particular, we will examine a type of option contract which, while not of *direct* interest (in most circumstances) to financial managers, is of interest to investors: share options. But, as we shall see, other types of option contracts are of very great and direct interest to managers.

Option terminology

There are two types of share option contract: 'call' options and 'put' options. The holder of a *call* option has the right to *buy* a share in a particular company at a fixed price on or before a specific future date. The fixed price is known as the option's *exercise price*, and the future date is known as the *expiry date* of the option.

One very important point to notice is that the call option gives the holder the *right* to buy the share – but there is no *obligation* on them to do so unless they want to. This choice is the key feature of all options, as we shall see. If the holder of an option decides to take up their right and actually buy the share, the option is said to be 'exercised'. If they decide *not* to take up their right to buy, then the option is said to have been allowed 'to lapse'.

A *put* option is similar in all respects to a call option, except that it gives the holder the right to *sell* a share in a particular company at a specific price on or before a specific future date.

There are in fact two types of call and put options: *European* calls and puts, and *American* calls and puts. Our definition of a share option was really a definition of an American option. With European options the shares can only be bought (a call option) or sold (a put option) *at* the future expiry date, and *not* before. In contrast, American options can be exercised *at any time* up to, and including, the expiry date.

In practice, European share options are less common and less important in the real world. For the moment however, the distinction between European and American options is unimportant. At a later stage, when the distinction *does* become important, we will take care to specify precisely what type of option we are dealing with. However, don't be misled by the names given to these option types. The terms 'American' and 'European' have nothing to do with the geographical locations of the option. The vast majority of share options dealt with in the UK (and in Europe generally) are American options.

Intrinsic value

Share options are valuable securities in their own right. The price or value of an option is known as its *premium*. In order to look at what makes options valuable, we first need to distinguish between an option's *intrinsic* price or value and its actual *market* price. The intrinsic value of a *call* option is found as follows:

Intrinsic value = Current share price − Exercise price.

Example 1 demonstrates this relationship.

Example 1

Suppose you have an option to buy a share in the ABC company at any time over the next twelve months (the expiry date) at a fixed price (the exercise price) of 100p. If today, ABC company shares have a market price of 140p each, then your option's intrinsic worth is 140p − 100p = 40p.

In other words, the intrinsic value of the option is the gain that you would make if you exercised the option immediately. In this case, if you exercised your right immediately to buy an ABC share for 100p, you could then sell it at its market price of 140p, making a 40p gain.

For a *put* option, its intrinsic value is the reverse relationship:

Intrinsic value = Exercise price − Current share price.

This is demonstrated in Example 2.

Example 2

If you had a put option on XYZ company shares with an exercise price of 80p and the current share price was 50p, it would have an intrinsic value of 80p − 50p = 30p. In other words, you could buy a share in the company today for 50p and then exercise your option to sell it for 80p, thereby making a gain of 30p.

The relationship between the share price, the option exercise price and the gain made from the exercise is illustrated in Figs 13.1 (for the ABC call option) and 13.2 (for the XYZ put option). Notice that the vertical axis on both of these diagrams is the *net profit*. For a call option this would be the difference between the gain on exercise (current share price − exercise price) *less* the option's premium/price. (In other words, less what it cost you to buy originally.)[2]

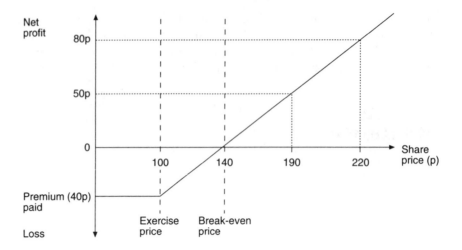

Fig. 13.1 *ABC call option*

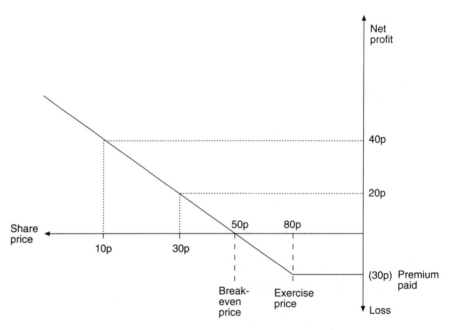

Fig. 13.2 *XYZ put option*

Intrinsic and market values

There are two very important things to notice about the intrinsic value of share options. The first is that the market value of the option will always be greater than the intrinsic value – the fundamental reason being that the option includes a 'gamble' element which is valuable, and so this increases the option's market worth. This is seen in Example 3.

Example 3

Let us return to our initial example of a call option on an ABC share at an exercise price of 100p and with twelve months until the option's expiry. We saw that if the current share price was 140p then you could make a 40p gain by exercising the option *immediately*. However, the option is not going to expire today – it doesn't expire for twelve months. The option can be exercised at any time over the next twelve months and so, if you wait, ABC's share price may rise further and then you would make an even greater gain when you come to exercise the option. For example, suppose that in two months' time ABC's share price had risen to 190p. Then you could make a 90p gain from exercising the option ((190p – 100p) – 40p – see Fig. 13.1).

This gamble element that is inherent in share options – the chance that you may make an even greater gain if you don't exercise the option immediately – is valuable, and means that the actual worth of the option – its market value – will always be greater than its intrinsic value. The one exception to this rule is that on the actual day of the option's expiry the intrinsic value and the market value *will* be the same. On the expiry date, the option runs out of gamble time and so the profit that you can make from exercising the option on that day represents its market value.

Exercise before expiry

This leads us to an important observation. Although with American share options you can exercise them at any time up to the expiry date, in normal circumstances you would *never* exercise them *before* the expiry date. The reason for this is that they are more valuable unexercised (their market value) than exercised (their intrinsic value). Returning to our original example, an investor would be willing to pay you *more than* 40p for your ABC call option; therefore if you no longer wanted to hold the option, it would be better to sell it on to another investor than to exercise it.

Option values cannot be negative

Let us now turn to the second important point about a share option's value. This is that the *minimum* value that an option can have is *zero*. In other words, the worst thing that can happen to an option is that it becomes worthless – its value can never become *negative*. Therefore with our ABC call option at an exercise price of 100p, if the current share price is 80p, then the intrinsic value is zero, *not* minus 20p:

$$\text{Intrinsic value} = 80p - 100p = 0$$

The reason for this is because with a call option although you have the *right* to buy a share – no one can *force* you to buy it, if you don't want to. You can always choose to allow the option to lapse. Thus its worst possible value can only be zero. (Also notice in the example, although the intrinsic value is zero, the actual value may well be positive. If there is a long time before the option expires then there may be a good chance that the share's market price will rise above the option's exercise price of 100p before the expiry date.)

In and out of the money

We can take this opportunity to introduce a little more share option market terminology. When a call option has a positive intrinsic value, i.e. the current share price exceeds the exercise price, the options are said to be 'in the money'. In other words, you would make a gain if you exercised today. When the opposite situation occurs – the current share price is below the exercise price – the options are said to be 'out of the money'. Furthermore, when the current share price equals the exercise price, the options are said to be 'at the money'.

Intrinsic values and the share price

Finally notice that a 1p change in the share price will lead to a similar change in the intrinsic value of the option. With the current share price of 140p our ABC call option with an exercise price of 100p has an intrinsic value of 40p. If the share price were to rise (or fall) by 5p, then the intrinsic value of the option would also rise (or fall) by 5p: 145p − 100p = 45p (135p − 100p = 35p).

The reverse relationship occurs with put options. An ABC put option with an exercise price of 200p will have an intrinsic value of 60p if the current share price is 140p (200p − 140p). If the share price were to rise (or fall) by 10p then the value of the put option would fall (or rise) by 10p. Figs 13.3 and 13.4 illustrate both these situations.

Fig. 13.3 *ABC call option premium*

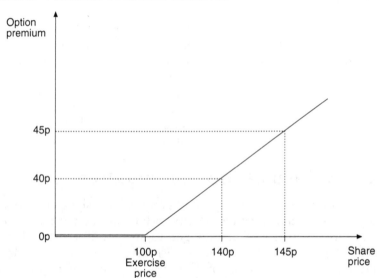

Fig. 13.4 *XYZ put option premium*

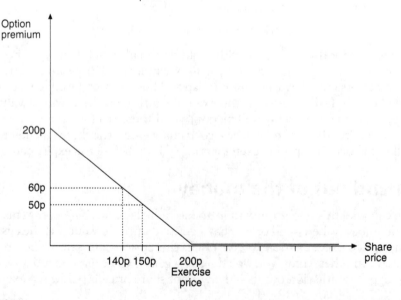

The gearing effect

So far, we have dealt only with calculation of the intrinsic value of share options. Before we turn to examine how we calculate the market value of an option, let us first look at why investors find share options such desirable investments. In order to illustrate this we will simply consider the intrinsic values of the options, but keep in mind that exactly the same effect will occur if we were to use the actual market value of the options.

There are two reasons why share options are such desirable investments. The first is termed their 'gearing effect'. We can make use of Example 4 to illustrate this phenomenon.

Example 4

You have been analysing the XYZ company's shares and decide that you want to invest £10 000 in the shares, in the belief that the share price is likely to rise soon from the current level of 100p. As an alternative to buying shares in XYZ you could buy share call options (i.e. you could buy options to buy shares) in the company with an exercise price, say 90p for a cost or premium of 10p each. (This price has been based on the intrinsic worth of the options.)

Therefore you could invest your £10 000 buying 10 000 XYZ shares, or you could invest your £10 000 buying *options* to buy 100 000 XYZ shares (i.e. 100 000 XYZ call options at 10p each). Suppose that, one way or another, you invest your £10 000 and that shortly afterwards the XYZ share price does go up – as you thought it would – to 125p. Thus the share price has gone up by 25p and so too has the (intrinsic) value of the options: 125p − 90p = 35p. (Remember a 1p increase in the share price will also give a 1p increase in the value of the call options.)

If you had bought 10 000 XYZ shares, you would therefore have made a profit of £2500 (10 000 × 25p), which represents a rate of return of 25% on the money invested (£2500 ÷ £10 000). Not bad!

However, if you had bought 100 000 XYZ call options, you would have made a profit of 100 000 × 25p = £25 000, representing a 250% (£25 000 ÷ £10 000) return on your investment! Even better!

This is what is meant by the *gearing effect* of share options, and it is one of the reasons why they are such desirable investments. If you invest and the share price rises, the gain you make on options is far greater than the gain you make from investing the same amount of money in the shares themselves. Options magnify or *gear-up* the potential gain.

Limiting exposure to downside risk

The second reason why options are such desirable investments is that they can limit the investor's exposure to downside risk. We came across this term in Chapter 10 – it refers to the unpleasant aspect of risk – the risk of doing worse than you expect. Let us take another example to highlight this particular characteristic of share options.

Suppose that you again wish to invest in XYZ company shares, because you think that the share price will rise from its current level of 100p. As an alternative, you could invest in options to buy XYZ shares – call options – with an exercise price of 90p, at a current (intrinsic) price of 10p each. Suppose you decide to buy 50 000 shares; alternatively, you could buy options to buy 50 000 shares (in other words, you could buy 50 000 XYZ call options).

After you have invested, and contrary to your expectations, XYZ's share price starts to *fall*. What loss will you make on your investment? The answer depends upon how far the share price falls. (Remember a 1p *fall* in the share price leads to a 1p *fall* in the call option price, *except* that the price of the options cannot be negative):

XYZ share price falls to:	Loss on 50 000 shares	Loss on 50 000 call options
99p	£500	£500
95p	£2 500	£2 500
90p	£5 000	£5 000
80p	£10 000	£5 000
50p	£25 000	£5 000
10p	£45 000	£5 000
worthless	£50 000	£5 000

Example 5 illustrates the ability of options to limit the investor's exposure to downside risk. If you invest in 50 000 XYZ shares you will lose £500 for every 1p fall in the share price, with a maximum potential loss (if the company goes into receivership) of £50 000. On the other hand, if you invest in 50 000 XYZ call options, you will also lose £500 for every 1p fall in the share price, but *only* up to a maximum loss of £5000, because once XYZ's share price falls below the options exercise price, the options become worthless and you suffer no further loss in value. Putting this advantage of options another way, you require less money to invest in options than you need to invest in shares. Thus your downside (in terms of your potential loss) is limited.

Using put options

The above examples illustrate how investors might use call options to speculate on an expected rise in the share price. In the first case, when the share price does in fact rise, we saw how much more rewarding it is to invest through options rather than through the shares themselves. In the second case we saw that if the share price actually falls, then options limit the potential maximum loss that the investor might suffer.

Put options can be used to speculate on a fall in the share price in much the same way that call options are used to speculate on a rise in the share price. However, let's look at a different use of put options. Suppose you already hold 10 000 ABC company shares which are currently priced at 100p each. The company is due to make an announcement about whether or not a newly tested product has proved to be successful. If the news is good, the share price can be expected to rise; if the news is bad, the share price will fall. One way of avoiding the risk of a fall in the share price would be to sell your current shareholding. The problem with this action is that although you will avoid the possibility of a loss, you also forgo the opportunity to profit from a rise in the share price if the tests prove successful.

A better solution is to use put options in order to take advantage of their characteristic that their value increases if the share price falls. Thus by using put options, you can insure yourself against any possible loss on your shares from a fall in the share price whilst, at the same time, remaining in a position to benefit from any increase in the share price. Example 6 illustrates this situation.

Example 6

Suppose ABC put options, with an exercise price of 105p, are available at a premium based on their intrinsic worth of 5p each (105p − 100p). If you bought options to *sell* 10 000 ABC shares they would cost 10 000 × 5p = £500. This cost is just like the premium that you would pay on an insurance policy.

The effect of these put options is as follows. Suppose the announcement made by the ABC company is bad news and the share price falls by 25p to 75p. You have made a total loss on your *shareholding* of 10 000 × (100p − 75p) = £2500. However, the value of each of your put options will have risen to 30p (105p − 75p).

Given that the options originally cost you 5p each to buy, they can now be sold for a 25p profit each, making a total profit of £2500 (10 000 × 25p). Therefore the loss on the shares has been matched with a profit on the options. Fig. 13.5 shows the position.

Alternatively, suppose the announcement had been good news and, consequently, the share price had risen to say, 120p. Under such circumstances the put options would be worthless but a profit would have been made on the shareholding. Therefore the put options are used here as an insurance against an adverse movement in the share price.[3]

A straddle

Suppose we take the same scenario as we have just discussed. The ABC share price is currently 100p, but there is uncertainty as to whether the share price will move up (on the disclosure of good news) or down (on the disclosure of bad news). However in this case, unlike the previous example, you do not at present hold any shares in the company. How might you seek to profit from the situation?

You could buy shares and buy puts (and so recreate the previous situation). This would mean that you would gain if the share price rose, without losing if the share price fell. But you could do better than that, by simultaneously buying *both* call options and put options at the same exercise price (and expiry date) on the ABC shares. Such an arrangement is known as a straddle.

Under such circumstances, if the share price goes *up*, you gain on the call options (and you simply lose the premiums paid on what are now worthless puts). On the other hand, if the share price goes *down*, you gain on the puts (and you lose the premium paid on what are now worthless calls). Therefore whichever way the ABC share price moves, you win!

Such an investment possibility may seem too good to be true, but it is not. The only problem is that to profit from a straddle, there does need to be a significant movement – in *either* direction – in the share price. If the share price only moves a little, the gain on one side of your options may be insufficient to cover the cost of the premiums paid on the other, now worthless, options. The straddle pay-off is illustrated in Fig. 13.6.

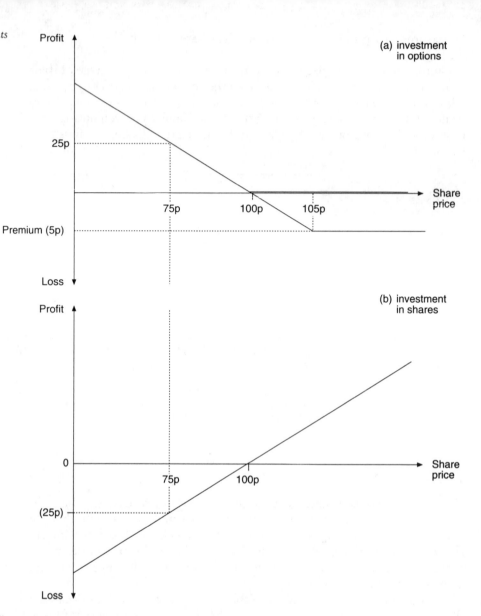

Fig. 13.5 *Investments in options (a) and in shares (b)*

(a) investment in options

Profit

25p

Premium (5p)

Loss

75p 100p 105p

Share price

(b) investment in shares

Profit

0

75p 100p

(25p)

Loss

Share price

Fig. 13.6 *The straddle*

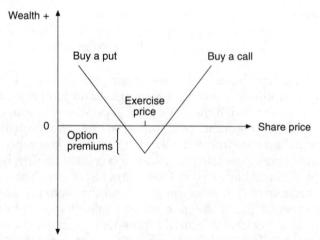

Wealth +

Buy a put

Buy a call

Exercise price

0

Option premiums {

Share price

Writing options

So far, in these examples, we have looked at situations where options have been *bought*. However share options can be *sold* (usually referred to as 'writing' an option) as well as bought.

We saw that if you buy a call option, then as the share price rises, so too does the value of the call option. Conversely, if you buy a put option then, as the share price rises, the price of the put option falls. Figs 13.1 and 13.2 illustrated these situations.

One important point to note about both option transactions is that the potential *loss* that you may make on options is always limited to their *cost*: the option premium paid. On the other hand, and this is especially true of call options, the potential for profit is virtually unlimited: the higher the share's market price rises, the higher goes the worth of the option and the greater is your gain.

Writing, or selling, options has the opposite characteristic. Your maximum gain equals the option's premium, (i.e. the price you receive from selling the option), but your potential for loss can be unlimited. If you sell a call option at an exercise price of 100p for a premium, say, of 15p, you are selling to someone the right to buy a share for 100p. Provided the share's market price doesn't exceed the exercise price of 100p, the option will not be exercised and you profit from the premium you have received from the sale of the option. However, suppose the share price rises to 150p. If the option is then exercised by the person to whom you sold it, you will have to supply them with a share worth 150p, while only receiving 100p in return. Thus your loss will be 50p, less the premium that you received of 15p, giving a net loss of 35p. The point here is that, quite obviously, the higher the share price goes, the greater will be your loss. Fig. 13.7 illustrates this situation from the viewpoint of both the buyer and the seller of call options.

A similar, but opposite effect, arises with put options. This is illustrated in Fig. 13.8. The further the share price falls below the exercise price of the put, the greater the loss to the option seller.

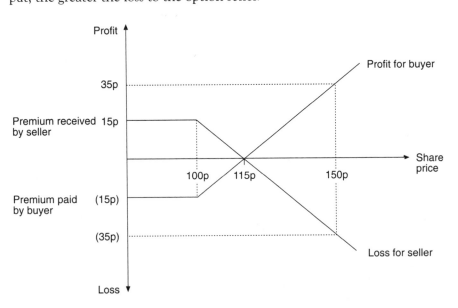

Fig. 13.7 *Writing call options*

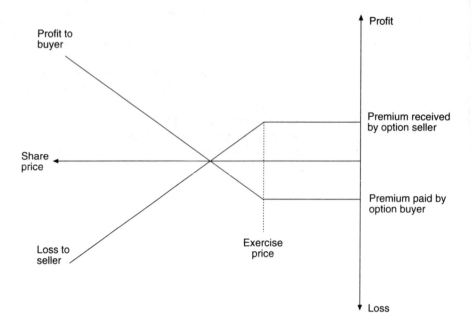

Fig. 13.8 *Writing put options*

Buying a call and selling a put

One interesting implication of this is the outcome that can arise if you simultaneously buy a call option and sell a put option, each with the same exercise price (and expiry date). The possible outcomes are illustrated in Fig. 13.9. You have to pay a premium to buy the call, and you receive a premium from selling the put. If the share price rises above the exercise price, the put option that you have sold is never exercised and so you profit from the premium that you received from its sale; you also make a profit on the call option you have bought. Conversely, if the share price falls below the exercise price, it is never worth exercising the call option you have bought and so you have the loss of the premium that you paid; you also make a loss on the put option that you have sold.

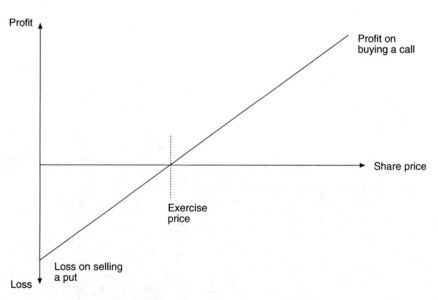

Fig. 13.9 *Buying a call and selling a put*

In short, if you simultaneously buy a call and sell a put at the same exercise price, you make a profit if the share price goes up and you make a loss if the share price goes down. This, of course, is *exactly* what would happen if, instead of buying calls and selling put options, you simply bought the shares instead. But there is one important exception to this. Buying a share is *not* the same as simultaneously buying a call and selling a put because, as we know, it is cheaper to invest in options than it is to invest in shares. Therefore buying a call and selling a put has the same profit and loss effect as simply buying the shares themselves, but at *much lower cost* in terms of the investment required.

The market value of an option

Having seen some of the reasons why share options might make desirable investments, it is now time to turn to the question of option pricing. How do we determine what should be the *market* value (as opposed to the intrinsic value) of a share option?

Let us begin by looking at the value of a call option. We observed earlier that we can distinguish between the intrinsic value of the option and the market value of the option, with the market value being greater than the intrinsic value at all times except on the expiry date, when they are the same. The justification that we gave for this relationship was as follows. The intrinsic value was the gain that you would make if you exercised the option immediately. However, you can exercise the option *at any time* up to the expiry date, and so if you don't exercise the option now, there is a chance that you may make an even greater gain in the future. We said that this gamble element attached to an option is valuable and it is this which causes the market value of the option to be greater than its intrinsic value. This gamble element is sometimes referred to as the 'time value' of the option, because one of the fundamental determinants of its value is the length of time remaining until the option's expiry date.

On this reasoning we can therefore say that:

$$\text{Market value of an option} = \text{Intrinsic value} + \text{Time value}.$$

Determinants of intrinsic value

Let us now look more closely at what factors determine each of these two components of an option's market value. We will begin with the intrinsic value. For a call option, the intrinsic value is the difference between the current share price and the exercise price (with the very important proviso that the intrinsic value can never be *negative*; its minimum possible value is zero). In other words, the intrinsic value of an option is the gain you would make if you exercised it immediately because it was about to expire. Therefore its intrinsic value is obviously a function of two variables: the current share price and the exercise price.

The intrinsic value of the option is a *positive* function of the current share price: a rise in the share price causes a rise in the intrinsic value of the option, and vice versa. In contrast, it is a negative function of the option's exercise price: the *lower* the exercise price, the *higher* the value of the option, and vice versa.

However, less obviously, the intrinsic value of an option is a function of two more variables: the risk-free rate of interest (r_F) and the time to expiry. This is because we have defined the intrinsic value as the gain that you would make if you were to exercise the option immediately because it was about to expire. But, if the option is *not* about to expire, you do not have to pay over the exercise price *until* that future expiry date. Therefore the intrinsic value is really the difference between the current share price and the present value of the *future* exercise price. The exercise price is discounted back to present value from the time of the future expiry date at the risk-free rate of interest, because the exercise price is a certain, known amount. With this more careful definition of the intrinsic value of an option:

$$\text{Intrinsic value} = \text{Current share price} - \text{Exercise price} (1 + r_F)^{-t},$$

(where t = number of years to expiry) we can see that there are two more variables to which its value is a function: the risk-free rate of interest and the time to expiry. The *higher* the risk-free rate of interest (r_F) and the *longer* the time to expiry (t), the lower will be the present value of the exercise price and the *higher* will be the intrinsic value of the option. Thus the intrinsic value is a positive function of both the risk-free interest rate and the time to expiry.

Determinants of the time value

Let us now turn to the second element in an option's actual value: its time value – what we earlier called the 'gamble element'. In terms of a call option, it is the value of the chance that the share price will rise further between now and the expiry date, so pushing up the intrinsic value of the option.

The value of this gamble element is a function of two variables. One, obviously, is time: the longer the time to expiry, the more chance there is of the share's price rising further. So, yet again, we can see that the value of an option is a positive function of the length of time to expiry.

The other variable which determines the value of the gamble element is the volatility (or variability) of the market price of the shares to which the option relates. If you have a call option in respect of a company's shares where, in the past, the share price has been very stable and unchanging, then you may reason that there is little chance of the share price going up significantly in the future. Hence the option will be less valuable.

On the other hand if, in the past, the price of the company's shares had been very volatile, then you might conclude that there is a much greater chance of the share price going up in the future. As a result, the option is seen as being much more valuable, as it allows you to profit from a rise in the share's price.

We saw from our earlier discussion on portfolio theory that the volatility or variability in the price of a share can be measured by the standard deviation, and this is how we will measure it for option valuation. However, we should also recall from our discussion of portfolio theory that investors are risk-averse – they dislike risk. What this means in simple terms is that the more risky an investment, the less valuable it is. In other words, the more risky an investment, the less people are willing to pay for it, because they will demand a higher return. However, we now seem to be saying the *opposite* of this. We are now saying that the *more* risky the share, the *more* valuable is the option to buy the share. Why do options appear to turn our normal attitude to risk on its head?

The reason is as follows. As we saw in our discussion of portfolio theory, risk is a 'two-way street'. In other words there are *two* aspects to the uncertain outcome of an investment. One aspect is the unpleasant side of risk – the downside risk, the risk of doing *worse* than you expect. The other aspect is the nice side of risk – the upside potential, the risk of doing *better* than you expect. Investors are risk-averse not because of the nice side of risk, but because of its unpleasant side – the downside risk. However, as we have seen earlier in this chapter – and it is illustrated in Example 5 – options limit our exposure to downside risk: with options, the most that you can lose is the option premium that you have paid. Therefore suddenly, with options, we start to *like* risk, because options allow us to get the benefit of an investment's upside potential, while protecting us from the downside risk.

Black–Scholes option valuation model

The market value of a share option is therefore a function of five variables:

1. the current share price;
2. the future exercise price;
3. the risk-free rate of interest;
4. the time to expiry;
5. the price volatility of the related shares.

These five variables were combined by two American researchers, Black and Scholes, into a mathematically complex option valuation formula. It would be unhelpful to go through the very formidable mathematical derivation of the model (which involves stochastic calculus) within the context of this discussion, but what is important is that we see the model and know how to operate it, as well as knowing the reasoning which underlies it.

Before we start to look at the Black–Scholes model, we should make two points clear. One is that a number of different option valuation models have been developed over time. The Black–Scholes model was the first really useful model to be developed, and is still the most generally applicable. Furthermore, although there are some difficulties in applying the model, the empirical research that has been undertaken does tend to show that although the model is not perfect, it remains an extremely good predictor of options values. The second point is that we shall initially use the model to value European options, although it is possible for it to be adapted to value American options, but not without some extra complexity.

The notation

The Black–Scholes Option Valuation Model (OPM) is as follows:

$$C = S.N(d_1) - Xe^{-r_F T}.N(d_2).$$

At first, the model looks rather difficult but, as we shall see, it is very easy to use. (However, in order to use the model, you will need to remember one piece of statistics concerning the area under the normal curve. This is reviewed in an appendix to this chapter.)

Let us begin this process by explaining the symbols used in the OPM equation:

C = Value of a call option
S = Current market price of the related shares
X = Future exercise price
r_F = Risk-free interest rate (per annum)
T = Time (in years) to expiry
σ = Volatility (the standard deviation) of the share price
e = mathematical fixed constant: 2.718 ... (you will find this value on most 'scientific' calculators)

The purpose of the constant e is that the formula uses continuous discounting. In our look at discounting in the appendix to Chapter 5, we only looked at periodic – usually annual – discounting. Although not strictly correct, it would make very little practical difference in many circumstances if you were to replace $e^{-r_F.T}$ in the Black–Scholes model with $(1 + r_F)^{-T}$. For example, if r_F = 10% and T = 2 years, then:

$$e^{-0.10 \times 2} = 0.819 \text{ and}$$
$$(1 + 0.10)^{-2} = 0.826.$$

$N(d_1)$ and $N(d_2)$ represent the cumulative area under the normal curve for a 'Z value' of d_1 and d_2, where:

$$d_1 = \frac{\log(S \div X) + r_F T}{\sigma \sqrt{T}} + \frac{1}{2}\sigma\sqrt{T}$$

$$d_2 = d_1 - \sigma\sqrt{T}$$

and $\log(S \div X)$ is the 'natural log' (or 'log to the base e') of $(S \div X)$ (again, you will find natural logs on most scientific calculators, but there is a table of natural logs given at the end of this book).

The next step is to see how the model works by using an example.

Example 7

Suppose we have the following information about the ABC company's shares and call options:

Current share price	= 165p
Option exercise price	= 150p
Risk-free interest rate	= 6%
Time to the option's expiry	= 2 years
Volatility (standard deviation) of share price	= 15%

In other words:

S = 165
X = 150
r_F = 0.06
T = 2
σ = 0.15

Our first calculation is d_1:

$$d_1 = \frac{\log(S \div X) + r_F T}{\sigma \sqrt{T}} + \frac{1}{2}\sigma\sqrt{T}$$

$$d_1 = \frac{\log(165 \div 150) + (0.06 \times 2)}{0.15 \times \sqrt{2}} + \frac{1}{2} \times 0.15 \times \sqrt{2}$$

$$d_1 = \frac{(\log 1.10) + 0.12}{0.2121} + 0.1061$$

$$d_1 = \frac{0.0953 + 0.12}{0.2121} + 0.1061 = +1.12 \text{ (approx)}.$$

Then calculating d_2:

$$d_2 = d_1 - \sigma\sqrt{T}$$

$$d_2 = 1.12 - 0.15 \times \sqrt{2} = +0.91 \text{ (approx)}.$$

Remembering that d_1 and d_2 represent Z values relating to the area under the normal curve, looking these values up in the tables at the back of the book:

$$d_1 = +1.12 \text{ gives}: +0.3686$$
$$d_2 = +0.91 \text{ gives}: +0.3186$$

$N(d_1)$ and $N(d_2)$ are the *cumulative* probabilities and therefore:

$$N(d_1) = 0.50 + 0.3686 = 0.8686$$
$$N(d_2) = 0.50 + 0.3186 = 0.8186$$

Finally, we can use the Black–Scholes model to calculate the value of the call options on ABC company shares:

$$C = S \times N(d_1) - Xe^{-r_F T} N(d_2)$$
$$C = (165 \times 0.8686) - (150 \times e^{-(0.06 \times 2)} \times 0.8186)$$
$$C = 143.32 - (150 \times e^{-0.12} \times 0.8186)$$
$$C = 143.32 - (150 \times 0.8869 \times 0.8186)$$
$$C = 143.32 - 108.90 = 34.42.$$

Therefore the call options will have a current market value of 34.42p. (Notice that if you had replaced $e^{-r_F T}$ by $(1 + r_F)^{-T}$, the calculated value of the call option would change to 34.04p. Notice also how much more this is than their intrinsic value of 15p (165p − 150p), largely because of the length of time – two years – to expiry.)

The Black–Scholes model deals with the valuation of European *call* options. That leaves a number of problems, the first of which concerns how are we to value *put* options? The answer is that we don't have to develop another, separate model to value puts; instead, we can make use of what is termed the 'put–call parity' relationship.

The building blocks of investment

There are four basic financial securities out of which all other investments can be constructed. They are:

1. investing in a company's shares;
2. investing in risk-free bonds;
3. investing in call options in the shares;
4. investing in put options in the shares.

With each one of these investments they can be either bought or sold. Thus you might buy shares in the hope that the price will go up, or you can sell shares in the expectation that the price will go down. Similarly you can buy risk-free bonds, (that is, lend money), or you can sell risk-free bonds, (that is, borrow money). Finally, with options, as we have seen, you can also either buy or sell them.

For each of these four fundamental financial securities, in the diagrams that follow, we illustrate graphically their impact on an investor's wealth arising out of a change in the price of the underlying shares. This change in wealth (in pence) is given on each of the vertical axes and the change in the share price (again, in pence) is given on the horizontal axes.

We use the notation S to represent investments in shares: $+S$ for buying shares and $-S$ for selling shares. Similarly, we use the notation B, C and P for investments in bonds, call options and put options respectively.

Finally, the 'starting point' of each analysis is the graph's origin, where the axes intersect. The *solid* line shows the change in investment or wealth, caused by a changing share price, when the security is *bought*. Similarly, the *dashed* line shows the change in investor's wealth, caused by a changing share price, when the security is *sold*.

Investing in shares

Fig. 13.10 *Buying and selling shares*

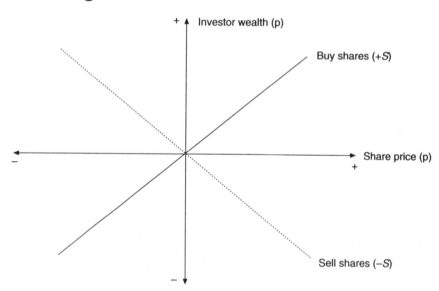

Obviously, if you buy the shares, every 1p increase in the share price leads to a 1p increase in the investor's wealth, and vice versa. Conversely, if you sell shares, then every subsequent 1p increase in the value of the shares is effectively a 1p loss in the investor's wealth (Fig. 13.10).

Investing in risk-free bonds

Technically, risk-free bonds are free of any risk of default and do not pay interest (Fig. 13.11). You earn a risk-free rate of return through a capital gain in the value of the bond. Thus if B is the nominal or par value of the bond which is to be repaid, its current value will be its discounted present value: $B(1 + r_F)^{-T}$. Example 8 helps to make this clear.

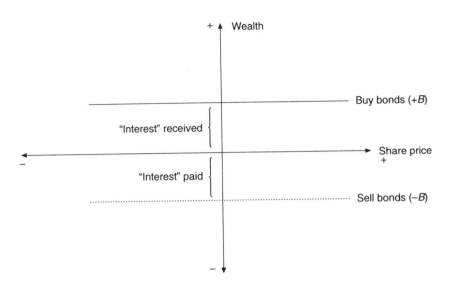

Fig. 13.11 *Buying and selling bonds*

The rate of return that you receive (r_F) if you buy bonds, or the rate of return that you pay (r_F) if you sell bonds is *entirely* unaffected by changes in the share price as its return is risk-free and so is certain.

Example 8

If you have a bond which is due to be repaid at 100p in one year's time and the risk-free interest rate is 10%, then its current value will be: 100p $(1 + 0.10)^{-1}$ = 90.9p. Buying the bond at 90.9p and being repaid at 100p gives a gain of: 9.1p (100p − 90.9p) which represents a return or 9.1p ÷ 90.9p ≈ 10%.

Investing in call options in the shares

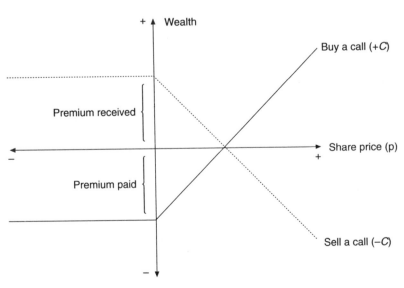

Fig. 13.12 *Buying and writing calls*

If you buy a call option, its cost, the premium you pay, is indicated on the vertical axis (Fig. 13.12). The value of the option increases if the share price rises: a 1p increase in the value of the shares leads to a 1p increase in the value of the option. Hence the positive-sloping 45° solid line on the graph. On the other hand, if the share price falls, options cannot have negative values – all you can lose is the premium paid. The reverse relationship holds if you sell a call option. You receive a premium (the option's price) when you sell the option which is your maximum gain. But if the share price then rises you (as an option seller) start to lose.

Investing in put options in the shares

Fig. 13.13 *Buying and writing puts*

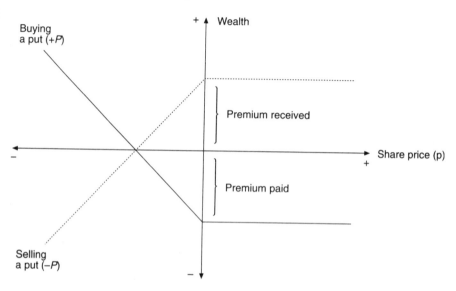

Puts are the opposite of calls. So if you buy a put, you gain if the share price falls. However, if the share price rises, then all you can lose is the option premium that you paid. Again, the reverse relationship holds for selling a put (Fig. 13.13).

The fundamental relationship

We can now state the fundamental relationship that exists between these four basic securities: $S + P = B + C$. That is, buying a share ($+S$) and buying a put option in the share ($+P$), is equivalent to buying a bond ($+B$) and buying a call option ($+C$) in the share (at the same exercise price and expiry date as the put).

This relationship can be seen to be true by combining the relevant figures. Figs 13.14 and 13.15 illustrate the left-hand and right-hand sides respectively of this fundamental equation.

In the situation shown in Fig. 13.14, if the share price *rises* there is *no change* in the value of the put, but every 1p increase in the share price increases wealth by 1p as a result of the investment in the shares.

Conversely, if the share price *falls*, each 1p fall in the share price *loses* 1p of wealth from the investment in the share but this is offset by 1p *gain* in wealth from the investment in the put option. So one cancels out the other.

Thus, if you buy a share and a put, you *gain* if the share price increases (less the option premium) but there is *no effect* on your wealth from a fall in the share price (again, except for the loss of the option premium that you paid).

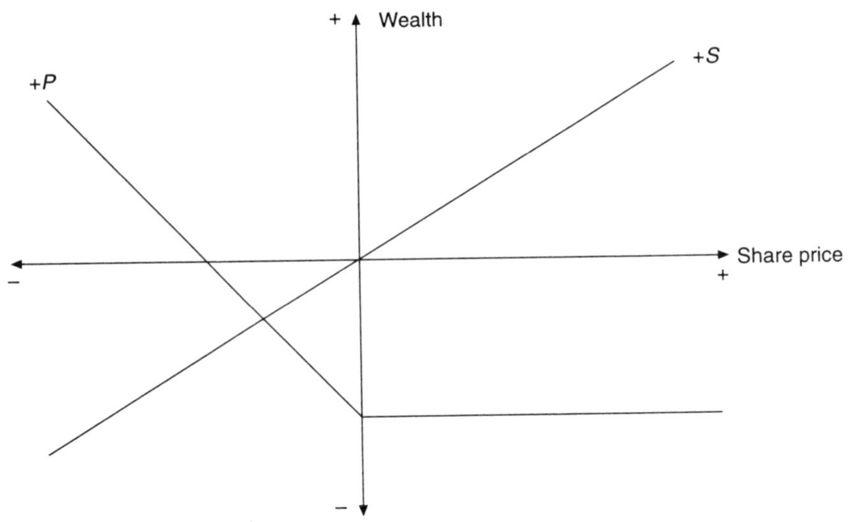

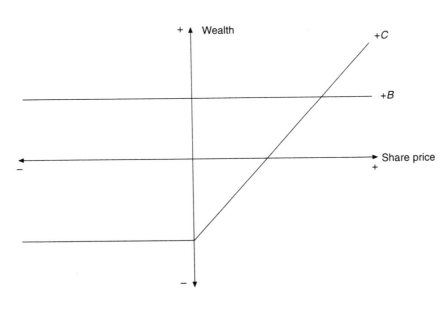

Fig. 13.14 *Buying a share and a put option*

From Fig. 13.15 we can see that the *net* outcome is identical to that arising from buying a share and a put option: if the share price rises there is no impact on the bond but each 1p increase in the share price leads to a 1p increase in the value of the call option and therefore in the investor's wealth. If the share price falls, there is no impact on the investor's wealth from either security.

Thus if you buy a bond and a call, you gain if the share price increases (less the option premium) but there is no effect on your wealth if the share price falls (except for the loss of the option premium that you have paid).

Fig. 13.15 *Buying a risk-free bond on a call option*

A risk-free investment portfolio

Having shown that $S + P = B + C$, it follows that the relationship should hold if we rearrange it.

For example, one important rearrangement is $S + P - C = B$.[4] In other words, if you buy a share $(+S)$ and a put option $(+P)$ and you also sell a call option $(-C)$, this is equivalent to an investment in a risk-free bond $(+B)$. Fig. 13.16 uses a graphical analysis to show this relationship.

Fig. 13.16 *A risk-free portfolio*

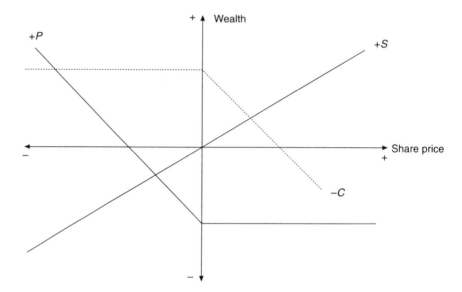

If the share price rises, there is no impact on the value of the put and the increased value of the shares is offset by the loss in value on the sold call. Hence there is a zero net effect on wealth. Similarly, if the share price falls there is no impact on the value of the call and the fall in the value of the share is offset by an increase in the value of the put. Once again, there is a zero net effect on wealth.

As we have seen previously, when investing in bonds, changes in the share price have a zero net effect on wealth. Therefore the portfolio strategy of buying a share, buying a put and selling a call is a risk-free investment which has an identical outcome to simply buying a risk-free bond.

Put–call parity theorem

We can now use the general relationships considered above to look at a *fixed* relationship that exists between the premiums of European put and call options, called the Put–Call Parity Theorem.

In order to develop this theorem, we first need to show that not only does $S + P - C = B$, but also that the net outcome from the portfolio investment of $S + P - C$ is equal to the exercise price of the options, which we will call X.

Suppose shares in the ABC company have a current market value of 100p and both the call and put options in the shares have an exercise price of 100p (so the options are 'at the money') and have two years to maturity.

Furthermore, suppose the annual risk-free rate of return is 6%. (We will see shortly why we need to know this.)

We arrange our portfolio of investments in the following way:

1. buy a share in ABC;
2. buy a put option in ABC shares;
3. sell a call option in ABC shares.

Let us now look at what the outcome would be under the two alternative scenarios: ABC's share price goes up (Example 9) and ABC's share price goes down (Example 10). However, before doing so, remember that if, at expiry, the share price is *below* the exercise price, *call* options are worthless. Similarly, if at expiry, the share price is *above* the exercise price, *put* options are worthless.

Example 9

Scenario 1: In two years' time ABC's share price has risen to, say, 140p

Value of the shares	140p
Value of put option	0
Value of call option	(40p)*
Net value of the investment portfolio =	100p = Exercise price of the options.

*Notice that you will lose 40p on the call options that you sold because on expiry they will be worth exercising, so the investor who bought the call from you will want to buy an ABC share which is now worth 140p for only 100p – the exercise price – thus you lose 40p on the option being exercised.

We can see algebraically that the net outcome of your investment portfolio must *always* be equal to an amount X, which is equal to the exercise price of the option, whatever the price of the shares on expiry:

$$\text{Net value of portfolio} = S + P - C,$$

Where: S = value of share;
P = value of put option;
C = loss on call option sold = $(S - X)$.

Again, remember that the value of the put option will be zero, $(P = 0)$, as a rising share price makes them worthless. Therefore

$$S + P - C = S + 0 - (S - X),$$

and so,

$$S + P - C = S + 0 - S + X = + X.$$

Example 10

Scenario 2: In two years' time ABC's share price has fallen to, say, 35p.

Value of shares	35p
Value of put option	65p*
Value of call option	0
Net value of the investment portfolio =	100p = Exercise price of the options.

We obtain exactly the same result from the second scenario, where the share price, on the expiry of the options, has fallen.

Once again, the predictability of this outcome can be seen algebraically:

Net value of portfolio: $S + P - C = S + (X - S) - 0 = + X$.

As the value of the portfolio at the expiry date, in all circumstances, will be equal to X – the exercise price of the options – then the *present value* of the portfolio's worth will be given by:

$$X(1 - r_F)^{-T},$$

(or, more strictly, Xe^{-r_FT} if we were to use continuous discounting). Notice that the risk-free interest rate is used for discounting because, as we know, the $S + P - C$ portfolio has an outcome equivalent to a risk-free bond investment:

$$S + P - C = B$$

The present value of the portfolio in our example, given r_F is 6%, is:

$$100p\,(1 + 0.06)^{-2} = 89p.$$

As a result, we are now able to take this general relationship:

$$S + P - C = X(1 + r_F)^{-T},$$

rearrange it:

$$S - X(1 + r_F)^{-T} = C - P$$

and insert the known *current* data: $S = 100p$

$$X(1 + r_F)^{-T} = 89p,$$

to give:

$$100p - 89p = C - P = 11p.$$

This indicates that the value of the *put* option should be 11p *less* than the value of the call.

Put–call parity equation

We have here an example of how we would use the put–call parity equation to identify the price differential between call and put options:

$$S - X(1 - r_F)^{-T} = C - P,$$

(or more strictly speaking, $S - Xe^{-r_FT} = C - P$).

If we were then to use the Black–Scholes model to value the ABC call options, we could simultaneously derive the value of the ABC put options as being worth 11p less.

Therefore we can state in general terms that the value of a put option with the same exercise price and expiry date as a corresponding call option is given by:

$$P = C + X(1 + r_F)^{-T} - S.$$

That is to say, the value of the put is equal to the value of the call, plus the present value of the exercise price, less the current share price.

If we return to Example 7, the ABC company call options, we used the Black–Scholes model to value them at 34.42p, where $S = 165p$, $X = 150p$, $r_F = 6\%$ and $T = 2$ years.

Therefore the value of ABC put options with an exercise price of 150p and an expiry date of two years would be:

$$P = 34.42p + 150p \times (1.06)^{-2} - 165p = 2.92p.$$

The puts are worth so little because they are a long way 'out of the money': $S > X$.

The problem of dividends

So far in this discussion we have ignored the problem of dividends. Why they are a problem, and how we can adjust the Black–Scholes model to take them into account, is what we examine next.

Companies pay dividends on shares; they do not pay dividends on share options. One immediate implication of this is that our earlier statement that holders of American call options would never (normally) exercise the option before the expiry date, will not always hold true. An investor in a company's call options may exercise the option and convert into shares before the expiry date, simply in order to be holding the shares when the dividend payment is made.

In addition, the payment of a dividend by a company affects the share price.[5] Therefore dividends will affect the valuation of share options. Dividend payments were explicitly excluded from the original Black–Scholes model, but the model can be adapted quite easily to take them (approximately) into account.

In order to see how the model can be adapted, we first have to examine the impact that dividends have on the market price of a share. Let us begin with the terminology. Just before a dividend is paid, the share price is quoted as being 'cum dividend'. That is to say, if you buy shares at the current price, you are buying with ('cum') the current dividend which will be paid shortly. Suppose the cum div. share price is 100p and the company is due to pay a 10p dividend shortly. If you buy the shares at 100p, then you will receive back a 10p dividend in the near future. (Thus your real acquisition cost is effectively only (100p − 10p = 90p).

After the dividend has been paid, the share price is quoted as being 'ex dividend'. This is because if you buy the shares at this point in time, you are buying them without ('ex') the current dividend which has just been paid to the previous owner of the share.

The difference between the cum div. and the ex div. share price is the amount of dividend that has been paid. Thus, in the above example, if the cum div. share price were 100p – with an expected dividend of 10p due to be paid shortly – once the dividend is paid, the share price will *fall* by the amount of the dividend, to 90p ex div. In this way, the payment of a dividend can affect the share price and so affect the value of the share option.

We can now turn to look at how the Black–Scholes model can be adjusted to take account of dividend payments. All that is required to get a reasonably accurate approximation of the impact of dividends is to subtract from the current share price the present value of the expected future dividends. This adjusted share price (rather than the actual share price) is then used in the Black–Scholes model to value the options. This procedure is illustrated in Example 11.

Example 11

The shares in Faro plc have a current market price of 190p. The company is due to pay a dividend in three months' time, which is expected to be 10p per share.

You have a call option that is due to expire in six months' time with an exercise price of 175p. The risk-free interest rate is 6% and the share price has a volatility of 24%.

Given that the shares are due to pay a dividend of 10p in three months' time, the present value of the dividend, (using continuous discounting[6]), is given by:

$$\text{Dividend} \times e^{-r_f T} = \text{PV of dividend}$$

That is,

$$10p \times e^{-0.06 \times 0.25} = 9.85p$$

(where $t = 3$ months (0.25 of a year)).

Thus the adjusted price for Faro's shares is:

$$190p - 9.85p = 180.15p.$$

This can now be used in the Black–Scholes model, where:

$S = 180.15$
$X = 175p$
$r_f = 0.06$
$T = 0.5$
$\sigma = 0.24$

Therefore

$$d_1 = \frac{\log(180.15 \div 175) + (0.06 \times 0.5)}{0.24 \times \sqrt{0.5}} + \frac{1}{2} \times 0.24 \times \sqrt{0.5}$$

$$d_1 = \frac{(\log 1.029) + 0.03}{0.1697} + 0.0848$$

$$d_1 = \frac{0.029 + 0.03}{0.1697} + 0.0848 = 0.29$$

$$\text{and } d_2 = 0.29 - (0.24 \times \sqrt{0.5}) = 0.12$$

These values for d_1 and d_2 give cumulative probabilities of:

$$N(d_1) = 0.50 + 0.1141 = 0.6141$$
$$N(d_2) = 0.50 + 0.0478 = 0.5478$$

Now using the Black–Scholes model:

$$C = (180.15 \times 0.6141) - 175 \times e^{-0.06 \times 0.5} \times 0.5478$$
$$C = 110.63 - 93.03 = 17.6p$$

Therefore, on this basis, the call options are currently worth 17.6p.

Notice what the value of the call options would have been calculated at, if we had ignored the dividend payment due in two months' time:

$$S = 190$$
$$X = 175$$
$$r_F = 0.06$$
$$T = 0.5$$
$$\sigma = 0.24$$

$$d_1 = \frac{\log(190 \div 175) + (0.06 \times 0.5)}{0.24 \times \sqrt{0.5}} + \frac{1}{2} \times 0.24 \times \sqrt{0.5}$$

$$d_1 = 0.75$$
$$d_2 = 0.75 - (0.24 \times \sqrt{0.5}) = 0.58$$
$$N(d_1) = 0.50 + 0.2734 = 0.7734$$
$$N(d_2) = 0.50 + 0.2190 = 0.7190$$
$$c = (190 \times 0.7734) - 175 \times e^{-0.06 \times 0.5} \times 0.7190$$
$$c = 146.95 - 122.11 = 24.84p$$

As can be seen, ignoring the possibility of a dividend payment on the underlying share during the time to expiry can introduce a substantial error in the valuation of the options.

The binomial model

Before we leave the valuation of share options, it is helpful to look at their valuation from a simpler – but much more limited – perspective than the Black–Scholes model. This alternative approach to option valuation is known as the binomial model because it deals with a situation where there are only two possible future outcomes for a share's market price. The model is demonstrated in Example 12.

Example 12

Suppose we have an investor who holds shares in the ABC company. They each have a current market value of 100p. The investor believes that, in twelve months' time, either the share price will have risen to 125p, or it will have fallen to 75p. (These are the only two possible future outcomes.)

ABC call options are available at an exercise price of 100p and with an expiry date of twelve months' time.

The risk-free rate of interest is 6% per annum.

As we know (from Figs 13.5 and 13.7), shares and call options can be combined so as to create a risk-free investment, called a *hedge portfolio*. Such an investment portfolio should, by definition, give the same return as that available from investing in risk-free bonds: 6%.

It is this latter observation which provides the key to being able to value the ABC call options. In order to do so, we need to be able to determine the number of shares our investor will need to hold and the number of call options he will need to buy or sell in order to provide a *certain* return of 6%, whichever one of the two future share price outcomes actually occurs.

If we purchase a share in the ABC company today for 100p, in twelve months' time the anticipated outcome will be that the share is sold for either 125p or 75p. This implies that if we purchase a call option in the ABC company's shares today, with an exercise price of 100p, the outcome in twelve months' time will be that either the share price rises to 125p and the option is exercised, resulting in a gain of 25p, or the share price falls to 75p and the option is allowed to lapse as worthless.

Now, how are we to create a risk-free portfolio for our investor? We know that if the share price goes *up*, he or she will *gain* on his or her shareholding. Conversely, if the share price *falls* he or she will *lose* on his or her shareholding. Therefore, in order to set up a risk-free position, we will require the call option to provide for the *opposite* result to this loss.

We know that call options increase in value if the share price rises, and vice versa. Therefore, to achieve the desired effect, our investor will need to *sell* call options in the ABC shares. So, if our investor buys ABC shares and sells ABC call options, the investment outcomes from the two possible future states of the world will be:

If the share price rises

1. We receive 125p from the sale of the shares.
2. We lose 25p on the exercise of the option by its purchaser.

If the share price falls

1. We receive only 75p from the sale of the shares.
2. The option buyer allows the option to lapse as it is worthless.

Let us suppose that our investor sells x ABC call options for every one ABC share that he holds. His net wealth at the end of the year will be:

If the share price rises

$$+125p - x \times 25p.$$

If the share price falls

$$+75p - 0p.$$

If the investment is to be risk-free, the investor must achieve the same net wealth outcome in both share price scenarios. Thus:

$$125p - x \times 25p = 75p - 0p.$$

Solving for x gives:

$$\frac{125p - 75p}{25p} = x = 2.$$

In other words, this analysis indicates that, in order to create a risk-free hedge, our investor needs to sell two ABC call options for every one ABC share held.

In Example 12, the inverse of $x - \frac{1}{2}$, or 0.50 – is known as the *hedge ratio*. It represents the ratio of shares to calls required to construct a risk-free hedge portfolio. Formally the hedge ratio is:

$$\frac{\text{Number of shares bought}}{\text{Number of calls sold}}.$$

In this case, for every one ABC share bought, the investor needs to sell two ABC call options. The resulting outcome is shown in Example 13.

Example 13

The 2:1 ratio of sold calls to bought shares will guarantee an investor the same net wealth position in twelve months' time, whatever the share price scenario.

If the share price rises to 125p, both the options that the investor sold will be exercised for 100p. Therefore, he will have to sell two shares, worth 250p (2 × 125p) for only 200p (2 × 100p), making a loss of 50p as a result. As his one share is now worth 125p, his net wealth will be 75p (125p − 50p).

If the share price falls to 75p, as this is below the 100p exercise price, both options will be allowed to lapse as worthless. Therefore the investor is simply left with his one ABC share worth 75p, which would represent his net wealth.

We can now use this hedge portfolio to place a value on the current market price of the ABC call options. This is done by comparing the hedge portfolio with a risk-free bond yielding a return of 6%.

Our risk-free hedge portfolio gives a *certain* outcome in twelve months' time of 75p. As this should represent an annual rate of return of 6% on the initial investment (I) the value of this initial investment can be found by solving:

$$I(1 + 0.06) = 75p$$

$$I = \frac{75p}{(1 + 0.06)} = 70.755p.$$

Therefore, the net cost of buying one ABC share less the proceeds from the sale of two ABC call options should be 70.755p. Given that the current price of ABC shares is 100p, this implies that the investor needs to sell the two call options for 29.245p (100p − 70.755p), or 14.6225p each. This represents the current market price of the ABC call options: 14.6225p.

We could now, if we wanted, use the put–call parity theorem to value the ABC put options.

Given:

$$P = C + X(1 + r_F)^{-T} - S.$$

Then:

$$P = 14.6225p + 100p(1 + 0.06)^{-1} - 100p = 8.96p.$$

Therefore, the ABC put options would have a market value of 8.96p each.

Obviously, this binomial valuation approach is very limited, as it only allows two possible future share price outcomes (although, it can be extended to look at more than just one time period forward). However, it is useful in that it introduces the idea of the hedge ratio: the ratio of sold calls to bought shares needed to construct a risk-free portfolio.

Delta risk and the hedge ratio

Finally, let us take another, intuitive, look at the Black–Scholes option valuation model. When we first started to look at options, we defined the intrinsic value of a call option as the difference between the current share price and the exercise price, referring to it as the gain that you would make if you had to exercise the option immediately because it was just about to expire. However, we then said that the market value of the option would be greater than this intrinsic value, because of the gamble element that exists between now and the future expiry date.

The Black–Scholes model takes an essentially similar approach in saying that the value of a call (C) is the difference between the current share price (S) and the present value of the future exercise price ($Xe^{-r_F T}$), but with some adjustments.

The current share price is adjusted by the factor $N(d_1)$ and the present value of the future exercise price is adjusted by $N(d_2)$:

$$C = S\,N(d_1) - Xe^{-r_F T}N(d_2).$$

Can we impute any meanings to these adjustment factors $N(d_1)$ and $N(d_2)$? The answer is that we can, although we are not going to go into their meanings in great detail here.

$N(d_1)$ is in fact the 'hedge ratio' or the 'delta risk' of the option. It is known as the delta risk of the option in that it measures the sensitivity in the value of the option to changes in the value of the shares. The higher the delta risk value (and $N(d_1)$ can never be greater than 1), the more the value of the option is affected by changes in the value of the underlying shares, and vice versa. The hedge ratio is the number of call options required to be sold to provide a risk-free hedge against a shareholding. It is calculated as follows:

$$N(d_1) = \frac{\text{Number of shares bought}}{\text{Number of calls sold}}.$$

In Example 7, where we used the Black–Scholes model to value the call options of the ABC company, we calculated a value for $N(d_1)$ of 0.8686. Therefore if we hold 5000 ABC shares, we can calculate how many ABC call options we need to sell to set up a risk-free hedge:

$$\frac{5000.0}{0.8686} \approx 5756 \text{ call options.}$$

This implies that by selling 5756 ABC call options and simultaneously holding 5000 ABC shares, an investment portfolio is constructed so as to give a return equal to the risk-free return.

Lastly, turning to the $N(d_2)$ factor by which the present value of the exercise price is adjusted, this indicates the probability that the option will be worthwhile exercising at expiry. In other words, it gives the probability that the option will be 'in the money' at expiry.

Summary

- Options confer a right, but not an obligation, on their holder to buy (or sell) a security, at a fixed price, on or before, a future specific date.

- An option's intrinsic value is the gain that would be made if it had to be exercised immediately. This value can never be negative. An option's market value will always be greater than its intrinsic value, except at the final expiry date, when the two values will be the same.

- From an investor's viewpoint options confer two fundamental benefits: they magnify the investor's exposure to a security's upside potential and they also limit the investor's exposure to the security's downside risk.

- Options can either be bought or written (sold). When buying an option, the investor's profit potential is unlimited; however the loss is limited to the option premium paid. An option writer, on the other hand, has the potential for unlimited loss, with the possible gain limited to the option premium received.

- The market value of an option is a combination of its intrinsic value and its time value. The intrinsic value is a function of the exercise price, the current share price, the risk-free rate of interest and the time to expiry. The time (or gamble) value is a function both of the option's time to expiry and the volatility (or variability) in the price of the shares to which the option relates. This market value can be found via the Black–Scholes option valuation model.

- There are four fundamental financial securities which form the building blocks of all investments: shares (S); risk-free bonds (B); call options (C); and put options (P). They can be combined into a fundamental equality relationship: $S + P = B + C$.

- Given this fundamental relationship, it follows that a risk-free investment can be artificially created by the combination: $S + P - C = B$.

- Furthermore, the fundamental relationship can also be used to develop a fixed relationship between the premiums on calls and puts: the put–call parity theorem: $S - X(1 + r_F)^{-T} = C - P$ or, using continuous discounting: $S - Xe^{-r_F T} = C - P$.

- The Black–Scholes model specifically excludes the possibility of dividends being paid on the underlying shares. However, the model can be easily adapted to allow approximately for the impact of dividends by adjusting the share price for the present value of the expected dividend, before inserting its value in the Black–Scholes model.

- The valuation of options can be looked at from a far simpler, but more limited perspective, using a binomial option valuation model. It is based on the fact that a risk-free investment – known as a hedge portfolio – can be constructed out of shares and options. This hedge portfolio can then be compared with the return on a risk-free bond to identify the implied value of the option.

Appendix: the area under the normal curve

In this appendix we quickly review the very basic elements of the area under the normal curve that we need to know in order to operate the Black–Scholes model.

A symmetrical probability distribution – we first came across these in Chapter 9 – can be completely described by two 'adjectives': its mean value and its standard deviation.

The normal probability distribution is the most common symmetrical distribution and is illustrated in Fig. 13.17. It is a perfectly symmetrical bell-shaped curve, distributed around its mean (or average) value of x.

Half the area under the normal curve is to the left of x and the other half is to the right of x. The properties of the area under the normal curve can be used to estimate the probabilities of particular events.

Fig. 13.17 *The normal distribution*

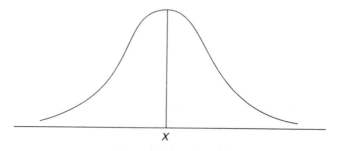

Suppose a machine manufactures metal rods which should all be of the same length but, because of the machine's imperfections, they vary slightly. Assume that the lengths of these rods are normally distributed with a mean length of 100 cm and a standard deviation of 15 cm.

We can use the properties of the area under the normal curve to find, for example, the percentage of rods that will be between 100 and 130 cm long. This is done by first calculating the 'Z value' – that is, the number of standard deviations represented by the distance between our two extreme values of 100 cm and 130 cm:

$$Z \text{ value} = \frac{130 \text{ cm} - 100 \text{ cm}}{15 \text{ cm}} = 2.0.$$

If we then look up a Z value of 2.0 in the normal distribution tables given at the end of the book, this gives the area under the normal curve represented in Fig. 13.18 by the shaded portion. This area represents the percentage of rods that will be between 100 cm and 130 cm long: 0.4772 or 47.72%.

Suppose we were to slightly alter our question and ask what percentage of the rods were *up to* 130 cm long (not just between 100 cm and 130 cm)?

This represents our existing shaded area *plus* the 50% of the area under the curve which lies to the *left* of 100 cm, as shown in Fig. 13.19.

Fig. 13.18 *Area under the normal curve*

Fig. 13.19
Cumulative probabilities.

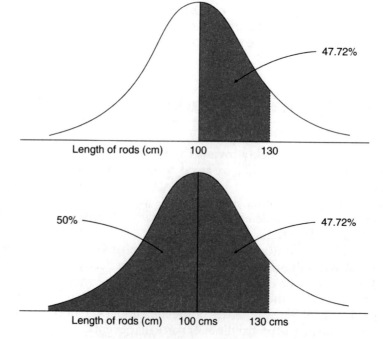

Therefore the proportion of rods up to 130 cm long will be: 0.50 + 0.4772, or 97.72%. This is known as the *cumulative* probability. It is this figure that we need to calculate for the Black–Scholes model where the 'Z values' are the d_1 and d_2 calculations.

Notes

1. The term 'hedging' really means 'avoiding'. Thus if risk is hedged, action is being taken to avoid it – or at least to reduce exposure to it.

2. This point may need to be made more clearly. In Fig. 13.1, if you were to buy the ABC call option (with an exercise price of 100p) for 40p, then you would start to make a net profit on your investment once the ABC share price went above 140p (100p + 40p). For example, if the share price went to 145p, you would make a net profit of 5p. You would do this by paying 100p to exercise your right to buy the share for 100p, then selling the share on the stock market for 145p – this would give you a profit of 45p less the 40p it cost you originally to purchase the option: a net profit of 5p.

3. Notice that you will only make a net profit once the ABC share price rises above the 105p. At a price of 105p you achieve a break-even position in that the gain that you have made from the rise in the share's price just offsets the cost of the options, (the cost of your insurance).

4. Think back to our earlier discussion, where we saw that simultaneously buying a call and selling a put is equivalent to buying the shares. Therefore, selling a call and buying a put is equivalent to selling the shares. Hence $+P - C = +S$. Thus on the left-hand side of the equation, $S + P - C = B$, shares are effectively being bought *and* sold.

5. We will look at this phenomenon in detail in Chapter 16, when we examine the process of share prices moving from cum dividend to ex dividend.

6. Notice that if non-continuous discounting is used, it makes very little difference:

$$10p(1 + 0.06)^{-0.25} = 9.855p.$$

Further reading

1. Much of the literature on options is very mathematical. For a general descriptive review see D.A. Ross and N.M. Cavalla, 'Options', in J. Rutherford and R.R. Montgomerie (eds), *Handbook of UK Corporate Finance*, Butterworths 1992 and F. Black, 'Fact and Fantasy in the Use of Options', *Financial Analysts Journal*, July–August 1975.
2. For a more difficult review of option pricing, see J.C. Cox, S.A. Ross and M. Rubinstein, 'Option Pricing: a simplified approach', *Journal of Financial Economics*, March 1979.
3. Finally a good, clear introduction to options is given by D.B. Hemmings, 'An Introduction to Options', *Managerial Finance*, Summer 1982.

1. What is a European put option?
2. What is an American call option?
3. When will an option's intrinsic value be the same as its market value?
4. It is known that a company is bidding for a very large and profitable contract. If they win the contract, the share price is likely to rise, if they lose the contract, then it will fall. How might you try to profit from such a situation using options?
5. If you simultaneously buy a call and sell an identical put, what is the effect?
6. The market value of an option can be said to consist of two elements. What are they?
7. The Black–Scholes option pricing model is a function of five variables. What are they?
8. What are the four basic financial securities? What is the fundamental equality relationship that exists between them?
9. What is the put–call parity equation?
10. What is a Delta risk?

Problems

1. The shares in Annat plc are currently priced at 415p and call options, with an exercise price of 400p and which are due to expire in three months' time, are priced at 25p. Given that the risk-free interest rate is 5% per year and Annat's share price has a standard deviation (volatility) of 22%, are the options worth buying? Assume that Annat is not due to pay any dividends over the next three months.
2. Value Annat plc's call options if the current share price was 380p. What would be the worth of the put options?
3. If Annat plc's share price was currently 408p and a 10p dividend was expected to be paid in two months' time, what value would you place on the company's call options?

14 Interest rate risk management

Introduction

Our analysis of portfolio theory illustrated how risk exposure could be reduced through diversification. However, as we saw in Chapter 11, the management of companies should not be concerned with internal diversification for its own sake. In other words, managers should not be concerned with the management of unsystematic risk – which their shareholders can eliminate quite easily for themselves. In practice there are many reasons why managers might wish to become involved in diversification but, from a theoretical viewpoint, we can ignore these. However, systematic risk is different and if there is any way that managers can reduce exposure to systematic risk without also reducing cash flows, this is likely to be of benefit to investors.

In the previous chapter we saw how a combination of risky securities (shares) and call and put options could be combined so as to bring about a risk-free position. In this chapter we consider the use of options – and a variety of other hedging techniques – to manage one particular type of systematic risk that faces company management: interest rate risk.

A definition

Risk, as we know, describes a situation where the outcome is uncertain. In the economy, interest rates vary as a result of the interplay of a whole variety of macro-economic factors and, as a result, the future direction and level of interest rates is uncertain.

Interest rate risk refers to the risk that is borne by companies of an adverse movement in interest rates. This adverse movement may be an *increase* in interest rates if the company wishes to *borrow* money. But, on the other hand, if the company has surplus cash that it intends to place on *deposit*, an adverse movement would be represented by a *fall* in interest rates.

The money markets

Before we look at some interest rate risk management techniques, we first need to set out some background information concerning the money markets. The 'money markets' can be used as a general term to describe the market-place where organizations can lend and borrow (relatively large) amounts of money for short periods of time. Typically, money can be lent and borrowed on the money markets for periods ranging from 'overnight' (which is from 3pm on one day to 3pm on the next day), to up to about twelve months.[1]

Money market interest rates are continuously changing in the light of supply and demand market forces (remember that interest rates are simply the 'price' of money and they respond to changes in demand in exactly the same way as does the price of anything else), and to the changing macro-economic situation.

At any one point in time, money market interest rates are quoted for a variety of time periods (or *maturities*). Typically, these are: overnight, seven days, one month, three months, six months and one year – although rates are also available for other maturities as well (e.g. five months).

These money market interest rates, although they refer to loans or deposits for periods of generally less than a year, are *always* quoted as an *annual* rate of interest. For example, you may see money market interest rates quoted as in Table 14.1.

Table 14.1[2]

Overnight	7%
Seven days	$6\frac{1}{2}$%
One month	6%
Three months	$5\frac{3}{4}$%
Six months	$5\frac{1}{2}$%
One year	5%

These rates are quoted in annual terms[3] to facilitate easy comparison. To calculate the actual interest rate over the specific time period, the annual rate has to be divided by the number of those time periods in the year. Table 14.2 shows the translation of the annual rates into the rate per time period.

Table 14.2

	Annual interest rate				Actual interest rate
Overnight	7%	÷	365	=	0.0192%/day
Seven days	$6\frac{1}{2}$%	÷	52	=	0.125%/day
One month	6%	÷	12	=	0.5%/month
Three months	$5\frac{3}{4}$%	÷	4	=	1.4375%/quarter
Six months	$5\frac{1}{2}$%	÷	2	=	2.75%/half year
One year	5%	÷	1	=	5%/year

Although money market interest rates are continually *changing*, once money is borrowed or deposited at a particular rate, then that rate is *fixed* for the time period concerned – irrespective of what subsequently happens to interest rates. Therefore, using the data in Table 14.2, if you place £10 million on deposit for six months in the money market at an (annual) interest rate of $5\frac{1}{2}\%$, then whatever happens to interest rates over the next six months, you are locked into receiving £10m × 0.055 × 6/12 = £275 000 interest for the deposit.

Finally, in these examples just a single interest rate for each maturity has been quoted. Given that money markets are where you can lend *and* borrow short term, for each maturity there will be two rates – one (the borrowing rate) higher than the other (the lending rate). Thus if the six-month money market interest rates were quoted at: $5\frac{1}{2}$–6%, this means that you could deposit money for six months at an annual interest rate of $5\frac{1}{2}\%$ and you could borrow money for six months at 6% per year.

Forward forward loans

Suppose that your company's cash flow forecast indicates that, in two months' time, it will need to borrow £50 million for a six-month period. The *current* six-month money market interest rates are $5\frac{1}{2}$–6%, but you fear that, over the next two months, interest rates will rise. As a result, when you come to borrow the £50 million in two months' time you fear that you'll have to pay a significantly higher rate of interest that the current rate of 6%.

In these circumstances the company is exposed to *interest rate risk*: the risk that there may be an adverse movement (i.e. a rise) in interest rates by the time the loan is required. One way to avoid this uncertainty about what rate of interest the company will actually pay on the loan would be for it to hedge the risk using a *forward forward loan*.

This is achieved very simply. Instead of waiting for two months, the company would borrow £50 million *now* for *eight* months, and immediately place the borrowed money on deposit for the next two months until it is required. The net outcome is shown in Example 1.

Example 1

Suppose the current money market interest rates are:

Two months: $5\frac{1}{4}$–$5\frac{3}{4}\%$
Six months: $5\frac{1}{2}$–6%
Eight months: $5\frac{5}{8}$–$6\frac{1}{8}\%$

The company borrows £50 million now for eight months at an annual rate of interest of $6\frac{1}{8}\%$. It then places £50 million on deposit for two months at an annual interest rate of $5\frac{1}{4}\%$. Therefore the company's net interest charge for having a £50 million loan available, for its own use, over the required six month time period is:

£50m × 0.06125 × $\frac{8}{12}$ = £2 041 667 interest payable
£50m × 0.0525 × $\frac{1}{12}$ = £ 437 500 interest received
Net interest payable   = £1 604 167

The amount of net interest payable represents an interest rate on the required loan of:

$$\frac{£1\ 604\ 175}{£50\text{m.}} = 3.20833\%/6\text{ mths or}$$

$$3.20833\% \times 2 = 6.4167\%/\text{year.}$$

By undertaking a forward forward loan arrangement, the company avoids any uncertainty about the actual rate of interest it will have to pay on its £50 million six-month loan which is required in two months' time: it will pay 6.4167%.

Notice that the *current* six-month loan rate is 6% per year. Therefore the extra 0.4167% annual rate of interest that the company pays though the use of a forward forward loan is, effectively, the cost of eliminating the risk. In a sense, the extra interest it pays on the loan, relative to the current interest rate, is like an insurance premium.

$$£50\text{m} \times 0.004167 \times \tfrac{6}{12} = £104\ 165$$

The company is paying a premium of £104 165 to be able to lock into today's interest rate for its future loan, thereby avoiding all uncertainty as to the loan's cost.

Forward rate agreements

Forward forward loans are relatively unusual nowadays, because more efficient ways have been developed to achieve the same effect. However, as we shall see, the concept of the forward forward loan interest rate is still important.

Taking the same example as before, an alternative strategy for the company to follow would be to approach its bank with the proposal: can we fix the rate of interest today that we will have to pay in two months' time on a £50 million six-month loan? Essentially, what is being requested is termed a forward rate agreement (an FRA). It is a mechanism by which a company can lock itself into a rate of interest today for a future loan.

The bank is likely to respond positively to this proposal and agree to an FRA on a £50 million six-month loan in two months' time at an annual rate of interest of 6.4167%. Why 6.4167%? Because the bank will have calculated what rate of interest the company *could* have locked into through a forward forward loan. It is this rate which mainly determines the rate at which an FRA is agreed.

Now although the *effect* of an FRA is as we have described it – the bank and the company are agreeing to the company being able to borrow £50 million for six months in two months' time at 6.4167% interest – the *actual* mechanics of the arrangement are somewhat different.

Having secured its FRA, the company then waits for two months before it borrows the £50 million it requires. Suppose it turns out that its original fears are justified, and during the intervening two months, six-month loan interest rates have moved up sharply from 6% to 8%. As a result, when the company borrows the £50 million it has to pay 8% interest – the going market interest rate. But, it will also receive *compensation* under its FRA, equal to the *extra* interest it has to pay: 8% − 6.4167% = 1.5833%. The net outcome is shown in Example 2.

Example 2

The company takes out an FRA on a £50 million six-month loan at 6.4167% interest.
   At the time when the loan is actually required interest rates have risen to 8%. As a result the company will *receive* 8% − 6.4167% − 1.5833% interest in compensation under its FRA agreement to bring its *net* interest cost back down to the agreed rate of 6.4167%:

£50m. × 0.08 $\quad\times \frac{6}{12}$ = £2 000 000 interest payable
£50m. × 0.015833 $\times \frac{6}{12}$ = £ 395 825 compensation received

Net interest payable = £1 604 175

This is equivalent to an annual rate of interest on the loan of 6.4167%, as agreed:

$$\frac{£1\ 604\ 175}{£50m} = 3.2083\%/6\ \text{mths} \times 2 = 6.4167\%/\text{year}.$$

Suppose, on the other hand, having taken out its FRA at 6.4167%, the company then finds that when it takes out its loan in two months' time, interest rates have actually *fallen* to 5%. Under these circumstances, the company has to *pay* compensation under its FRA, equivalent to 1.4167% in order to brings its effective interest charge on the loan up to the agreed rate. Example 3 illustrates this alternative situation.

One important thing to understand is that the forward rate agreement is a totally separate contractual agreement from the loan itself. Therefore the financial institution (typically a bank), from which the company obtains its FRA may or may not be the same institution which eventually supplies the company with the subsequent loan.

Example 3

The company takes out an FRA on a £50 million six-month loan at 6.4167% interest.
   At the time when the loan is actually taken out, interest rates have *fallen* to 5%. As a result the company will *pay* compensation under its FRA equivalent to 6.4167% − 5% = 1.4167% interest.

£50m. × 0.05 $\quad\times \frac{6}{12}$ $\quad$ = £1 125 000 interest payable
£50m. × 0.014167 $\times \frac{6}{12}$ $\quad$ = £ 354 175 compensation payable

Total effective loan cost = £1 604 175

This is equivalent to an annual rate of interest on the loan of 6.4167%, as agreed:

$$\frac{£1\ 604\ 175}{£50m} = 3.2083\%/6\ \text{mths} \times 2 = 6.4167\%/\text{year}.$$

This separation of the FRA contract from the loan contract is an important point, because it means that a company has the ability, if it so wishes, to enter into a forward rate agreement without any intention of borrowing money.

Other uses of FRAs

Forward rate agreements are normally supplied by banks. They are very widely used in practice and can extend up to about two years into the future. In our examples we have shown FRAs being used to hedge interest rate risk on a future loan. But this is by no means the only use of FRAs.

Many companies believe that their revenues, and hence their operating profits, are *inversely* correlated with interest rate movements. In other words, when interest rates go up, their revenues, and hence their operating profits, go down – and vice versa. The type of companies whose revenues are very sensitive to interest rate movements in this way are likely to be those whose products form part of consumers' *discretionary* (rather than necessary) expenditure.

A furniture retailer may well be in this situation. People don't *have* to buy new furniture, in the way that they do have to buy food, and so will not buy new furniture when times are tough and money is short. A furniture retailer may argue therefore as follows: most of our customers own their own homes, and they have borrowed money in order to buy them. When interest rates go up, they are required to pay more interest on the loans they have taken out to pay for their homes. As a result, they have less money available to spend on furniture and so our sales will decline. Conversely, when interest rates fall, they have more spare money and may well use some of that to buy new furniture; hence our sales go up. In other words our sales are negatively correlated with interest rates.

Such a company is therefore also exposed to interest rate risk – the risk to its operating profitability of an adverse impact on its customers' buying activity from an increase in interest rates. A company in this situation could reduce its risk exposure by using FRAs. This would enable the company to receive compensation when interest rates go up and thus help to maintain its profitability.[4] Conversely, when interest rates go down, the company has to pay compensation under the FRA, but this is offset by rising sales and profitability. Thus a series of FRAs can be used to smooth out the impact on the company's operating profit of interest rate movements. Fig. 14.1 illustrates this effect.

Fig. 14.1 *Using FRAs*

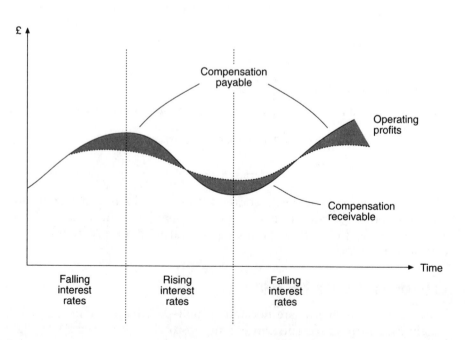

Another use of FRAs would be for a company with a high level of floating rate debt finance to use them in order to protect its level of profitability: if interest rates rose, the payments would be offset by compensation received under the FRAs, and vice versa.

The market in FRAs

The FRA market is very active and well developed on an inter-bank basis (i.e. with banks dealing between themselves). However, the market's development is relatively limited for non-bank users.

This slow development of FRAs by non-bank users is probably due to a combination of two factors. One is that the same hedging effect can be achieved by other means (e.g. see the later discussion on interest rate futures – although the use of FRAs avoids the 'margin' requirement of futures). The other reason is that banks will actually quote *forward* loan and deposit rates to their customers if requested. Therefore, returning to our original FRA example, a company wishing to borrow £50 million for six months in two months' time may well be able to get the bank to agree *in advance* an interest rate of 6.4167% for the loan that is required in two months' time. (Notice that by fixing this future loan rate now, the bank is exposing itself to interest rate risk – which it may well hedge by agreeing an FRA with another financial institution.)

A final point

There is a final point to notice about FRAs as a method of hedging a company's exposure to interest rate risk. In the previous chapter, we noted how options had the characteristic of hedging against an adverse movement (downside risk), while allowing advantage to be taken of a favourable movement (upside potential). Forward rate agreements do *not* have this characteristic. They hedge the company, as we saw in Examples 2 and 3 against both an adverse movement in interest rates *and* a favourable movement. What they do effectively is *lock* the company into a *specific* rate of interest.

Interest rate guarantees

Interest rate guarantees (or interest rate options – IROs), possess the characteristic that all options have: the ability to provide a hedge against adverse movements in interest rates, while also allowing advantage to be taken of any favourable movements.

If we return to the example used previously we can see that an IRG can be utilized to hedge interest rate risk exposure as an alternative to an FRA. For example, our company which wanted to borrow £50 million in two months' time for a six-month period could take out an *option* on such a loan – normally with a bank – at, say, an interest rate of 6.5% per annum.

If, in two months' time, interest rates have indeed risen as feared to 8%, then the company can *exercise* its option to borrow £50 million for six months at 6.5% interest. On the other hand, if interest rates fall over the next two months to 5%, then the company can allow its option to *lapse* and will, instead, borrow the £50 million on the money market at the current interest rate of 5%.

In this way it can be seen that interest rate guarantees – or options – can be used to hedge against adverse movements in interest rates; but they also allow the company to take advantage of any favourable movement in interest rates that may occur.

Pricing IRGs

Because of this additional advantage of IRGs – not only do they provide a hedge against a rise in interest rates, they also allow advantage to be taken of a fall in rates – they are more expensive to buy as a hedging instrument than FRAs. The reason for this is that with an FRA, *both* parties to the agreement (the company on one side and the bank on the other side) obtain a hedge – the company gains a hedge against rising interest rates and the bank gains a hedge against falling interest rates (because, in such circumstances, the company will pay compensation to the bank with which it has the FRA).

Having said that an interest rate option contract would be more expensive than a forward rate agreement, how would its price be set? The answer is by application of the Black–Scholes option valuation model which we examined in Chapter 13.

In that chapter we examined the general principles that underlie option valuation within the context of share options. Those same principles apply to all options, including interest rate guarantees. Thus the cost or value of an interest rate call option (an option to buy a loan at a fixed price/rate of interest) would be a function of five variables:

1. the current market rate of interest;
2. the exercise price interest rate of the option;
3. the length of time to expiry;
4. the volatility of interest rates;
5. the risk-free interest rate.

An illustration of applying the Black–Scholes model to an IRG is shown in Example 4.

Example 4

Nessa plc wishes to borrow £1 million for a year, in twelve months' time. The current rate of interest on such loans is 5% and the risk-free rate of interest is 3% per year. Interest rate volatility in the recent past has been represented by a standard deviation of 10%. What would be the expected cost of an interest rate guarantee on the loan at 4% interest?

At the current rate of interest, the interest charge on the loan would be: £1m × 0.05 = £50 000. The company wishes to buy an option with an interest rate exercise price of 4%, giving an interest charge on the loan of: £1m × 0.04 = £40 000. Therefore in terms of our usual Black–Scholes notation:

$$S = 50\ 000$$
$$X = 40\ 000$$
$$T = 1$$
$$\sigma = 0.10$$
$$r_F = 0.03$$

$$d_1 = \frac{\log(S \div N) + r_F T}{\sigma \times \sqrt{T}} + \frac{1}{2} \times \sigma \times \sqrt{T}$$

$$d_1 = \frac{\log(50\,000 \div 40\,000) + (0.03 \times 1)}{0.1 \times \sqrt{1}} + \frac{1}{2} \times 0.10 \times \sqrt{1}$$

$$d_1 = 2.58$$

$$d_2 = d_1 - \sigma\sqrt{t}$$

$$d_2 = 2.58 - (0.10 \times \sqrt{1}) = 2.48.$$

Using the tables of the area under the normal curve, this gives cumulative probabilities for the d_1 and d_2 values of:

$$N(d_1) = 0.4951 + 0.50 = 0.9951$$
$$N(d_2) = 0.4934 + 0.50 = 0.9934$$

and so C, the value of the option, can be found from the Black–Scholes model:

$$C = N(d_1) \times S - Xe^{-r_F t} \times N(d_2)$$
$$C = (0.9951 \times £50\,000) - (£40\,000 \times e^{-0.03 \times 1} \times 0.9934)$$
$$C = £11\,193$$

Therefore the interest rate guarantee would cost Nessa plc £11 193 to purchase.

FRAs versus IRGs

Under what circumstances might a company choose to use an FRA, and when might it prefer an IRG? In order to answer this question, first notice that *both* arrangements can hedge the company against an *adverse* movement in interest rates.

Therefore if a company wishes to borrow money at some time in the future and believes that between now and that future time interest rates will *rise*, it will hedge the risk using the cheapest means possible: it will hedge using an FRA.

However, suppose the company's management simply feel that market interest rates are *volatile*, and could go either up *or* down between now and when the loan will be required. Under these circumstances, the management may be willing to use the more expensive hedging instrument: an IRG – the obvious point at issue here being that if the company uses an FRA and interest rates then fall, the company will be unable to get the benefit of those lower rates. An IRG does not *lock* the company into paying a specific interest rate in the way that an FRA does.

Option contract markets

In the previous chapter we discussed the general ideas underlying option contracts. What we did not go into is *where* options can be purchased. The reason why this was not looked at was because it was not important to that discussion.

However, it is desirable that we touch upon this point now. Fundamentally there are two types of option 'markets' where options (of different sorts) are bought and sold. These are the 'over-the-counter' market (OTC) and the 'option exchange' market. Options that are bought on the OTC market are usually 'tailor-made' to the precise requirements of the purchaser. Because of their unique nature they are not readily tradable. In other words, having bought an OTC option, there is very little scope for being able to sell it on to a third party; all you can really do is hold it until you take a subsequent decision to exercise it or allow it to lapse. The interest rate option in Example 4 would have been an OTC option, tailor-made to the precise requirement of Nessa plc and the seller or writer of the OTC option would have been a bank.

In contrast, option contracts bought and sold on option exchanges are *not* tailor-made, but are *standardized* contracts. Therefore exchange traded share options are for a standard number of shares in the company per contract (usually 1000) at a set (*not* negotiated) exercise price and for a set (*not* negotiated) future expiry date (usually, nine months into the future). It is this standardization which makes them marketable. Therefore having bought an exchange traded option, apart from being able to hold the option and subsequently decide whether to exercise it or allow it to expire, you have also got the opportunity to sell it, unexpired and unexercised, to another investor. Share options, in particular, are usually in exchange traded form, but options exchanges – of which there are several throughout the world – will usually trade options on a range of underlying financial assets – shares, commodity prices, interest rates and foreign exchange rates, amongst others.

In addition, the traded options market often trades in another type of financial instrument, called 'futures contracts'. In the UK the trade option market is called the London International Financial Futures and Options Exchange – know as LIFFE for short. It deals in a range of different traded option contracts *and* futures contracts.

Interest rate futures

Of particular concern to us here is one specific type of futures contract: interest rate futures. Let us first have an informal look at them.

Futures contracts differ from options contracts in one fundamental way. As we know, options hedge against adverse events but allow you to take advantage of favourable events. By contrast, futures contracts have a 'locking-in' effect and so hedge you against both adverse *and* favourable movements in events.

We have just been discussing two types of option contracts: tailor-made OTC options and standardized exchange-traded options. In many ways we can make a similar distinction between forward rate agreements and interest rate futures contracts. FRAs are *tailor-made* contracts which hedge the company against both adverse and favourable movements in interest rates. In a similar way, as we shall see, interest rate futures are *standardized* contracts that hedge against both adverse and favourable interest rate movements.

Formally, a futures contract is a standardized, legally binding agreement to buy or sell a specific asset at a fixed time in the future at a specific price. With futures – unlike options – you cannot simply walk away from the contract and allow it to lapse. You take your profit or you accept your loss, depending on how prices move between when you took out the contract and its future expiry (or 'delivery') date. Interest rate futures can appear a little confusing at first, but we will come to realize that they are, in fact, very easy to handle. Initially, we need to describe their basic characteristics.

Interest rate futures contracts are available in a number of different currencies, principally the US dollar, Japanese yen, German mark and British pound sterling. For purpose of explanation we will use sterling futures contracts, but in practice you would use contracts in whichever currency you faced interest rate risk. Therefore, if you wanted to borrow some US dollars in the future and feared the risk of an increase in US dollar loan interest rates, then you would hedge with dollar futures contracts.

In addition, there are both short-term and long-term interest rate futures contracts. Naturally enough, short-term contracts are used to hedge against adverse movements in short-term interest rates, and long-term contracts are for movements in long-term interest rates. Given that, within the context of the present discussion, we are looking at relatively short-term interest rate risk – on money market loans and deposits – we will use short-term sterling interest rate futures for purposes of explanation.

A single sterling short-term interest rate futures contract relates to the *interest* that could be earned on a three-month deposit of £500 000. Thus the 'unit of trading' is £500 000. One feature of futures markets is that you can only trade in whole contracts. Therefore you can trade in short-term sterling interest rate contracts in £0.5 million 'steps' (i.e. £0.5 million, £1 million, £1.5 million, etc.).

If you buy or sell a sterling futures contract, you are in fact buying or selling the *interest* on a £0.5 million three-month deposit. The rate of interest[5] is given by the 'price' of the futures contract (called the quotation) which is expressed on an 'index basis'. What is meant by this is that the price = 100 – the annual interest rate. Thus if the annual interest rate on the £0.5 million deposit were $6\frac{3}{4}\%$, the price of the contracts would be quoted as : $100 - 6.75 = 93.25$.

Contracts are issued on a three-monthly cycle – typically, March, June, September and December. Each one matures or expires towards the end of the month in question, typically on the third Wednesday of the month. Therefore the June contracts expire on the third Wednesday in June and the September contracts expire on the third Wednesday in September. At any one time, dealers in the futures market are faced with a choice of three different expiry dates. For example, suppose we are currently in February. You would be faced with a choice of March, June or September contracts. By the time we reach the third Wednesday in March, the March contracts will expire and *new* December contracts are created. Thus, at the end of March, the choice would be between June, September and December contracts.

Profits and losses on futures contracts are measured in 'ticks'. With interest rate futures, one tick represents price movements of one-hundredth of 1%, (i.e. 0.0001), in the annual interest rate. Therefore, for example, a 1.5% movement in interest rates represents 150 ticks.

The *value* of a tick of profit or loss is calculated on the basis of the amount of interest it represents. On sterling three-month interest rate futures contracts, the value of a tick can be calculated as:

$$£500\,000 \times \tfrac{3}{12} \times 0.0001 = £12.50 = \text{Value of a tick}^6$$

Finally, you can hedge interest rate risk by either *buying* or *selling* futures contracts. Whether you buy or sell depends upon what represents an adverse movement in interest rates. For example, if you want to hedge against the chance of an *increase* in interest rates (because you wish to borrow money in the future) then you hedge by *selling* futures – called a 'short hedge'. However, if you want to hedge against a *fall* in interest rates (because you want to place money on deposit in the future) then you will hedge by *buying* futures – a 'long hedge'. (Incidentally, don't get concerned about a short hedge where you have – apparently – to 'sell' something you haven't already got. As we will see, this presents no problem in a futures market.)

We now know enough about interest rate futures to be able to look at an explanatory illustration of their use. This is shown in Example 5.

Example 5

It is now 1 June. In two months' time, on 1 August, Frog plc will need to borrow £3.9 million for three months. Frog can currently borrow money at 8% per annum interest, but Frog's treasurer fears that interest rates will have risen by August and so wishes to hedge using interest rate futures contracts. Currently sterling September three-month interest rate futures contracts are priced at 93.

We will look at the action required to hedge this risk in a number of steps. First though, we need to explain why we are considering September interest rate futures contracts. Remember that it is now 1 June and so Frog would have a choice of three contracts: June, September and December contracts. The June contracts are of no use to Frog, as they will have expired by the time Frog need to borrow the money on 1 August. This leaves a choice of either September or December contracts. Although either could be used, it is normal to use the contract with the *next* expiry date after the date when the loan is required. We require the loan on 1 August and so the futures contracts with the next expiry date after that would be the September contracts. The following steps would be necessary for the company to set up its hedged position:

1.   The first step is for the treasurer to set up a 'target' loan cost based on the *existing* interest rate. If there were *no* change in interest rates between now (1 June) and 1 August, then the loan would involve an interest charge of

$$£3.9m \times 0.08 \times \tfrac{3}{12} = £78\,000 \text{ interest target.}$$

As we shall see, Frog's futures hedge will result in the company paying an actual *net* interest charge which is very close to this targeted cost of £78 000. (It may end up paying a little more or a little less than £78 000, for reasons we shall see presently.) This outcome will occur *whatever* happens to interest rates between 1 June and 1 August, when the loan is taken out.

2.   The second step is to identify the number of futures contracts that are required to hedge the interest charge on the £3.9 million loan. Each contract is in respect of the interest on a deposit of £0.5 million and so Frog will require £3.9m ÷ £0.5m = 7.8 contracts.
Given that we can only deal in *whole* contracts, this means that Frog will round up to eight contracts. (Notice what this means – Frog are hedging the interest charges on a £3.9 million loan with futures contracts in respect of a total deposit of: 8 × £0.5m = £4m.)

3.   The third and final step in setting up the hedge position is for Frog to decide whether they need to *buy* or *sell* the futures contracts. Remember the rule: if you wish to hedge a loan against rising interest rates: sell futures: if you want to hedge a deposit against falling interest rates, buy futures. Here Frog want to hedge a loan and so they will *sell* eight sterling September interest rate futures contracts at a price of 93.

The reason for the buying and selling rule on futures contracts for deposits and loans respectively will become obvious as we proceed with the example. As we shall see, if Frog initially *sell* futures and then interest rates go *up*, they will end up making a *profit* on the futures which acts like compensation under an FRA, offsetting the higher interest charges on the loan. Similarly, if Frog initially *buy* futures and then interest rates *fall*, again they will make a *profit* on the futures which will compensate for the reduced interest earned on our deposited money as a result of the fall interest rates.

Therefore futures hedges work on a very simple basis, similar to the compensation that is paid or received under an FRA. With Frog's loan, if interest rates go *up*, they will make an offsetting *profit* on the futures, and if interest rates go *down*, they will make an offsetting *loss* on the futures. Thus, as was pointed out before, futures contracts hedge the company against *both* sides of risk: the risk of adverse *and* favourable movements in interest rates.

Having set up this hedged position on 1 June we can then move forward two months to 1 August. This is the day Frog plc will need to borrow £3.9 million for three months.

Suppose that on 1 August short-term interest rates have risen to 10.5% and sterling September interest rate futures contracts are now priced at 90.75:

1. The company has to borrow £3.9 million for three months at 10.5% interest. Thus the actual interest charge incurred by the company on the loan will be:

$$£3.9m \times 0.105 \times \tfrac{3}{12} = £102\ 375.$$

This can be compared against the *target* interest cost of £78 000 to show a 'loss' on target of: £102 375 − £78 000 = £24 375. In other words, because interest rates have risen by 2.5% over the two-month period from 1 June to 1 August, Frog plc is having to pay £24 375 more interest on the loan than it had hoped.

What we shall see is that the company will make a profit on its futures contracts which will approximately offset this extra interest cost.

2. On 1 August, as well as borrowing £3.9 million, the company needs to 'close out' its futures position. It does this by transacting a deal in the futures market which is the *reverse* of the original transaction undertaken on 1 June. In that original transaction the company *sold* eight sterling September contracts; and so – in order to close out its futures position – it now *buys* eight sterling September contracts, at their current price of 90.75.

What have these two sets of futures transactions achieved? Originally, the company sold eight sterling September contracts at 93. Remember that the 'price' of the contracts represents an interest rate quoted on an index basis. Thus 93 represents: 100 − 93 = 7% interest. Therefore what the company sold was the interest, at 7%, on eight three-month deposits of £500 000 each. This represents a total amount of interest of:

$$8 \times £0.5m = £4m \times 0.07 \times \tfrac{3}{12} = £70\ 000.$$

This interest was due to be delivered on the third Wednesday of September. However, futures contracts are very seldom left to 'mature' in this way. Instead, futures positions are usually 'closed out' before the delivery date by undertaking an offsetting transaction. This is just what the company did in buying eight September contracts at 90.75. What they were doing in this transaction was buying the interest of eight £0.5 million three-month deposits. Therefore how much interest had they bought? Remembering that 90.75 represents an interest rate of: 100 − 90.75 = 9.25%:

$$8 \times £0.5m = £4m \times 0.0925 \times \tfrac{3}{12} = £92\ 500.$$

In other words, through its futures transaction the company had *bought* £92 500 of interest and had *sold* £70 000 of interest. One set of futures contracts offsets (or cancels out) the other set of futures contracts and the company either *receives* the balance (if it has bought more interest than it has sold), or it has to *pay off* the balance (if it has sold more interest than it bought). In this way, it makes either a *profit* or a *loss* on its futures transactions.

In this example the company receives more interest than it sold and so it makes a profit on its futures transaction of: £92 500 − £70 000 = £22 500. However, recall that we said earlier that profits and losses on futures contracts are usually measured in ticks. Therefore, how this profit would normally be calculated is as follows:

Bought the contracts at:	90.75		
Sold the contracts at:	93		
Profit per contract	2.25%	=	225 ticks
Total profit = 8 contracts × 225 ticks/contract		=	1800 ticks
Value of the profit: 1800 × £12.50 = £22 500.			

Therefore once the company closes out its futures position on 1 August, it will receive a profit from the futures market of £22 500 which will largely (but not *precisely*) offset the extra interest charge on its £3.9 million loan.

Interest charge:	£102 375
less Profit on futures:	£22 500
Net interest cost:	£79 875
Target interest cost:	£78 000

Hedge efficiency

Notice in Example 5, how close the company's *actual* interest cost, net of the futures profit, is to the target cost set two months earlier of £78 000. How good a hedge this action has been is usually measured by the hedge efficiency ratio of profit (on the futures) over loss[7] (on target):

$$\frac{\text{Profit}}{\text{Loss}} = \frac{£22\ 500}{£24\ 375} = 0.923 \text{ or } 92.3\%.$$

The hedge efficiency ratio is calculated in such a way that if the net interest charge (£79 875) were *greater* than the target interest charge (£78 000) the hedge efficiency would be *less than* 100%. If the net interest charge were *less than* the target charge, the hedge efficiency would be *greater* than 100%, and if the net interest charge were exactly *equal* to the target charge, then the hedge efficiency ratio would be 100%: a 'perfect' hedge.

Futures will only provide a 100% efficient hedge through luck. There are two reasons for this. One is the fact that we can only deal in *whole* contracts. In Example 5, Frog plc would have *liked* to have hedged with 7.8 contracts, but had to round up to eight whole contracts. Thus one reason why a perfect hedge is unlikely is this standardized nature (rather than being tailor-made to the company's precise requirements) of futures contracts. We can only hedge sterling amounts in £0.5 million units.

The other reason for the imprecise nature of a futures hedge is that the price of futures contracts will only move *approximately* in line with changes in the interest rate faced by the company. This is referred to as 'basis risk'. In Example 5, the company's loan interest rate rose by 2.5% from 8% to 10.5%. However, the futures price only moved by 2.25% from 93 (i.e. 7%) to 90.75 (i.e. 9.25%).

For both these reasons, futures hedges are unlikely to be 100% efficient; even so, the actual efficiency is likely to be fairly close to 100%. The other thing to remember is that these futures contracts hedge the company against both adverse *and* favourable movements in interest rates. In Example 5 there was an *adverse* movement in interest rates and so the futures contracts provide an offsetting *profit*. In Example 6, the opposite situation is illustrated by changing the scenario on 1 August.

Example 6

In Example 5, on 1 June, the company had sold eight sterling September interest rate futures contracts at 93 in order to hedge its risk on a £3.9 million three-month loan required from 1 August.

Taking this same situation, but now suppose that on 1 August loan interest rates had fallen from 8% (on 1 June) to 6.5% and sterling futures are now quoted at 94.25. The following now occurs:

(a) The company borrows £3.9 million for three months at 6.5% incurring an interest charge of:

$$£3.9m \times 0.065 \times \tfrac{3}{12} \quad = \quad £63\ 375$$

Target interest charge	=	£78 000
'Profit' on target	=	£14 625

Because interest rates have *fallen* – they have moved in the company's favour – the actual interest charge is significantly below the target level.

(b) The company needs to 'close out' its futures position by reversing the earlier deal. Therefore it now *buys* eight sterling September contracts which are priced at 94.25.

(c) The outcome from the futures transactions is:

Contracts bought at	94.25		
Contracts sold at	93		
Loss per contract	1.25%	=	125 ticks
Total loss on futures: 8 × 125 × £12.50		=	£12 500

(d) Actual interest charge on £3.9m loan: £63 375
plus loss on futures contracts: £12 500

Total costs:	£75 875
Target cost of loan	£78 000

$$\text{Hedge efficiency:} \quad \frac{\text{Profit}}{\text{Loss}} = \frac{£14\ 625}{£12\ 500} = 1.17 \text{ or } 117\%.$$

In this case the hedge efficiency is over 100% because the net cost of the loan to the company is slightly *less* than the target amount. Here the standardization of the contracts and the basis risk have combined to act slightly in the company's favour.

Maturity mis-match

Examples 5 and 6 both involved *three-month* interest rate futures being used to hedge a *three-month* loan. What would have happened if the company had required a loan for more or less than three months? This situation is known as a 'maturity mis-match' and can be easily handled by adjusting the number of contracts dealt in.

Taking Example 6, suppose the company wanted to borrow £3.9 million for six months (rather than three). It can still hedge its exposure to interest rate risk using three-month interest rate futures, by *doubling* the number of contracts used from eight to sixteen. The idea here is that, as the duration of the loan is *twice* that of the futures contract, it will require *twice* the number of contracts to hedge the risk. If the loan was for nine months, then it would require three times the number of contracts: 8 × 3 = 24 contracts. Similarly, if the £3.9 million loan was required for only *one* month, (i.e. the duration of the loan was only *one-third* of the duration of the futures contract) then the number of contracts required to hedge would be:

$$\frac{£3.9m}{£0.5m} = 7.8 \times \tfrac{1}{3} = 2.6, \text{ round up to 3}.$$

Example 7 provides an illustration of a maturity mis-match on a short-term deposit.

Example 7

Fluff plc is based in the UK and imports from and exports to Germany. It is now early January. In April, Fluff is due to receive DM3.95 million from a German customer. Fluff's treasurer has decided that the money will then be placed on deposit for five months and then used to pay off an invoice, denominated in DM, which is due to be settled in September. The current interest rate available on short-term DM deposit is 6% per annum, but the treasurer fears that this will fall sharply in the next few weeks. As a result, the company decides to hedge its exposure to interest rate risk by using three-month DM interest rate futures. The contract size is DM1 million and June contracts are currently quoted at 94.

The treasurer's target interest income on the DM deposit, on the basis of current interest rates, would be: DM3.95m $\times$ 0.06 $\times \frac{5}{12}$ = DM98 750.

To set up the hedge the company will need to *buy* DM futures (as they are hedging a deposit and so fear *falling* DM interest rates). If there was *no* maturity mis-match, the number of contracts required would be DM3.95m ÷ DM1m = 3.95.

However, because there *is* a maturity mis-match (three-month futures and a five-month deposit), the required number of contracts has to be increased proportionally:

$$3.95 \times \frac{5}{3} = 6.58 = 7 \text{ contracts.}$$

Therefore Fluff plc will buy seven DM June futures contracts at a price of 94 in order to hedge its exposure to interest rate risk.

In April, when the company receives the DM3.9 million, it finds that DM short-term interest rates have fallen to 4.75% per annum and June DM futures are quoted at 95.25.

As a result, the company then places the DM3.95 million on five-month deposit to yield:

DM3.95m × 0.0475 × $\frac{5}{12}$	=	DM78 177
Target interest income	=	DM98 750
Loss on target	=	DM20 573

At the same time, the company will close out its position in the futures market by reversing the earlier deal and so it *sells* seven DM June contracts at 95.25.

The outcome of its futures trades is calculated as follows:

Contracts bought at:	94		
Contracts sold at:	95.25		
Profit per contract:	1.25%	=	125 ticks

Given the value of a DM tick is DM1m × 0.0001 × $\frac{3}{12}$ = DM25, then: total profit = 7 × 125 × DM25 = DM21 875.

This results in a hedge efficiency of

$$\frac{\text{Profit}}{\text{Loss}} = \frac{\text{DM21 875}}{\text{DM20 573}} = 1.063 \text{ or } 106.3\%.$$

Target interest income:	=	DM98 750
Actual interest income:	=	DM78 177
Profit on futures:	=	DM21 875
Total income:	=	DM100 052

A strip hedge

Suppose that a treasurer has £10 million of surplus finance available to invest for the next two years. Market conditions are such that interest rates on longer-term deposits are higher than on shorter-term deposits. (Technically, the 'yield curve' is rising – see the next chapter.) Therefore he or she knows that he or she can get a better rate of interest investing the money longer term, (say, in two-year bonds), but his or her liquidity preference dictates that he or she would prefer to invest it in a series of short-term (three-month) deposits in order to have easy access to the funds in an emergency. However, he or she would then run the risk of short-term interest falling over the next two years, and of being criticized for not taking the opportunity to lock into the higher longer-term rate.

There are a number of solutions available to solve the treasurer's problem. One would be to hedge the interest rate risk using a 'strip' of futures contracts.

On LIFFE, sterling three-month interest rate futures contracts now extend out twenty-four months. Suppose it is early January 1998. The treasurer is faced with the following futures prices (and their implied rates of interest):

	Quote	Implied interest rate (%)	
March 98	94.28	5.72	
June	94.44	5.56	
Sept	94.36	5.64	
Dec	94.16	5.84	Average
March 99	93.84	6.16	= 6.17125%
June	93.50	6.50	
Sept	93.15	6.85	
Dec	92.90	7.10	

The treasurer can place the £10 million on three-month deposit and buy twenty contracts (remember that he or she buys because when hedging a *deposit* the number of contracts required can be calculated as: £10m ÷ £0.5m = 20 contracts) in *each* of the eight contract expiry dates which are available. By doing this, the treasurer is maintaining easy access to the £10 million held on deposit while, at the same time locking himself into 6.17125% interest over the next two years and avoiding the possibility of falling short-term interest rates over this period.

(The treasurer would close out each set of futures contracts at their expiry. If interest rates have gone up he or she will receive a higher rate of interest on the deposited money to offset the loss on the futures. If interest rates go down, the profit on the futures will offset the lower level of interest earned on the deposited cash.)

Margin

Finally, we need to examine the concept of 'margin'. All futures deals (and traded option deals) are conducted though the futures market which effectively stands as a guarantor of the obligations of each party (the buyer and the seller of the contracts).

Futures contracts are 'zero sum games', in the sense that every deal has a buyer and a seller, and the profit made by one party equals the loss made by the other. The great fear of dealing in futures is that having made a profit on your futures, the other party (who has therefore made a loss) then defaults. This risk, (referred to as counter-party credit risk), is overcome by the futures market requirement that whenever a futures position is 'opened' (this would occur in our examples when we set up the hedge by selling futures – to hedge a loan – or buying futures – to hedge a deposit), a certain sum of money known as 'initial margin' must be placed on deposit with the futures market, to act as security against possible default. (The rules on margin amounts are quite complex and need not concern us here.)

Thereafter, at the end of every day until the company's futures position is closed out, the futures market calculates the profit or loss that has been made on the open futures position. This profit or loss is then added to or subtracted from the balance on the margin account. (This process of daily updating of profits and losses is known as being 'settled to market'.) If the company is making substantial losses on its open futures position, such that the balance on the margin account falls below some specified minimum, (remember the margin is there to act as security against default), then the company is required by the futures market to place further money on deposit to top up the margin account to its minimum required level. This additional margin is referred to as 'variation margin'.

Caps, collars and floors

Forward forward loans, forward rate agreements, interest rate guarantees or options and interest rate futures are all short-term hedging devices. They can only be used to hedge against adverse movements in interest rates in the relatively short-term future, up to a maximum of about twelve to eighteen months ahead.

However, both interest rate guarantees and forward rate agreements have equivalent, longer-term, hedging techniques. Interest rate *caps*, interest rate *floors* and interest rate *collar* agreements can all be considered longer-term versions of interest rate guarantees. They are hedging devices which are generally bought 'over the counter' from a bank and they can be used to limit a company's exposure on longer-term loans and deposits to *adverse* movements in interest rates, while at the same time allowing advantage to be taken of favourable movements.

Interest rate caps

For example, suppose Trebear plc wishes to raise a £15 million seven-year loan. The company's bank will only offer such a loan at a floating or variable rate of interest of LIBOR[8] plus 2%.

Trebear's treasurer is unwilling to agree to these terms because he believes that interest rates are likely to rise in the future. If this were to happen, then the interest rate on the company's loan would rise also, and it is thought that too sharp a rise in future interest rates could seriously damage the company's profitability and liquidity.

One obvious solution would be for the company to raise the loan at a fixed rate of interest. However, the bank is unwilling to agree to such an arrangement because it too believes interest rates will rise and so does not want to get locked into a lending agreement at the low current levels of interest.

The solution would be for the treasurer to accept the floating rate loan but, in addition, buy an *interest rate cap* agreement at, say, 15%. A cap agreement does what the name suggests – it places a 'cap' or 'limit' on how high an interest rate the company can be asked to pay for its floating rate loan. A cap of 13% means that if, during the term of the loan, LIBOR goes *above* 13% (at which rate the company pays: 13% + 2% = 15%), the interest rate on the loan sticks at 15%. If LIBOR subsequently falls below 13%, the company's loan rate will also fall.

It is in this way that a cap operates as an option – limiting the company's exposure to an adverse movement in interest rates, while allowing it to take advantage of falling interest rates. How much this option would cost to buy depends very much on the circumstances. In particular, the cost is a function of the level at which the cap was set – a cap at 20% would cost less than a cap at 13% – and the perceived risk of rising interest rates in future. However, essentially, its cost would be determined in line with the factors contained in the Black–Scholes model.

Interest rate collars

One way of reducing the cost of the cap – and effectively converting the variable rate loan into a semi-fixed rate loan – is to simultaneously buy a cap – say at 13% – and *sell* an interest rate *floor agreement* at, say, 6%. This combined arrangement is known as a *collar*. It places a limit on how high the interest rate can float up *and* on how low the interest rate can float down. In this example the treasurer would be fixing the interest rate on the floating rate loan so that it doesn't exceed 15%, nor does it go below 8%.

A collar arrangement will obviously cost less than a cap because it provides protection to the bank as well as the company. (In this example the bank is protected from receiving a rate of interest on their loan of less than 8%.) Nevertheless, just how much an interest rate collar agreement would cost again depends upon the cap and floor rates set and the outlook for future interest rate movements.

Interest rate floors

Interest rate floor agreements on their own, or combined with a cap into a collar agreement, can be used by companies to hedge interest rate risk on floating rate deposits. Thinking back to the example in our discussion of futures where we showed a treasurer hedging interest risk on a short-term deposit through a *strip hedge* of futures contracts, an alternative would be a collar or floor agreement related to the deposited sum.

Interest rate swaps

Just as caps, collars and floors are longer-term versions of interest rate guarantees/options, so interest rate swaps are longer-term version of FRAs.

The market in swap agreements is both large and important, and has developed rapidly over a relatively short period. There are a great many variations now available, but we will confine ourselves at this stage to looking at the basic type of interest rate swap agreement. (At a later stage, when we come to consider foreign exchange risk, we will return to the idea of interest rate swaps.)

The basic interest rate swap agreement is where one company swaps with another company a stream of *floating* rate interest obligations (on a notional loan) for a stream of *fixed* interest obligations. The companies involved in such an arrangement may deal directly with each other or, more typically, the deal would be arranged through an intermediary, such as a bank.

Suppose Company A has a £50 million five-year loan at LIBOR plus 1% and Company B has a £50 million five-year loan at a fixed rate of interest of 9%. If they arrange a swap, each of the companies (called the counter-parties) agrees to pay the other party's loan interest commitments. Thus the effect is that Company A has converted its floating rate loan into a fixed rate loan and Company B has done the reverse.

If the two companies are of different credit risk (e.g. suppose Company A had a better credit rating than Company B and could borrow at a fixed rate of, say, 8%), then an up-front payment is made by one party to the other to offset the difference.

Interest rate swaps can be used in many situations. One situation is of immediate concern here – using a swap agreement to hedge against an adverse movement in interest rates.

Suppose a company has a £100 million long-term loan at a floating rate of interest. The treasurer now believes, on an analysis of the macro-economic situation, that over the next three years, say, interest rates are likely to rise. What he or she can do is enter into a three-year swap agreement with a counter-party to swap into a fixed rate of interest for the next three years. At the end of this time, the company will revert back to paying a floating rate of interest, when hopefully interest rates will have started to fall back. Therefore, by this action, the treasurer is hedging the company against the possibility of an adverse movement in interest rate over the next three years.

Swaptions

Alternatively, a company with a fixed interest loan which believed that interest rates were likely to fall over the next few years could swap into a floating rate of interest with the intention of taking advantage of the anticipated fall in interest rates. However, such a move could backfire on the company if, having arranged a swap into a floating rate of interest, interest rates subsequently rise.

One way around this would be for the company to arrange a cap agreement with the swap intermediary. If the floating rate of interest went above the cap, the company would only have to make interest payments at the capped level and the intermediary would finance the difference out of its own resources to the swap counter-party. Such an arrangement is known as a swap option or 'swaption'.

Quality spread swaps

Although not strictly to do with interest rate risk, we will take this opportunity to look at another common reason for the existence of swap agreements. This is in order to take advantage of slight inefficiencies between different capital markets. This is illustrated in Example 8.

Example 8

Companies A and B both want to raise £100 million ten-year loans. Company A wishes to borrow at a fixed rate of interest, wanting to have a certainty about its future interest liabilities.

Company B wishes to borrow at a floating rate because its treasurer believes that interest rates are likely to fall in the future.

Company A has been offered a fixed interest loan at 12% and a floating rate loan at LIBOR +2.5%. Company B has a better credit rating than A. As a result, it has been offered a fixed interest loan at 10% and a floating rate loan at LIBOR +1 %. These facts are tabulated below:

	Fixed interest		Floating rate	
Company A	12%		LIBOR +2.5%	
Company B	10%		LIBOR +1%	
Quality spread differential:	2%	–	1.5%	= 0.5%

Because of B's superior credit rating, it is able to borrow money more cheaply than A – the so-called 'quality spread'. However, notice that the rate at which B can borrow below that of A is *not* consistent between the two types of loan. Company B can borrow 2% cheaper than A on fixed interest loans, but only 1.5% cheaper than A on floating rate loans. If the capital market were really efficient, we would expect B's superior credit standing to have the *same* impact on both types of loan.

In circumstances such as these, when there is a difference in the quality spreads between the two types of loan, it is possible for both parties to benefit from a swap arrangement. In this example, the quality spread differential is 0.5% and therefore a swap agreement will result in a *total* interest saving between the two parties equal to this amount (before any fee charged by an intermediary for putting the two counter-parties together). How this interest saving is split between the two parties is negotiable, but it is usually divided equally. If this were to be the case, then a swap agreement can be used which will result in each company getting the type of loan it wants at 0.25% less than the rate of interest it would normally have to pay. (You might think that 0.25% isn't much, but it represents a saving of £250 000 per year for ten years on each company's £100 million loan.)

Therefore A will achieve the fixed interest loan that it wants at 12% – 0.25% = 11.75%; and B will acquire a floating rate loan at LIBOR +1% – 0.25% = LIBOR + 0.75%.

The swap is put together on the following basis:

(a) The *largest* quality spread is first identified. The *type* of loan to which it applies is then borrowed by whichever company can borrow at the cheapest rate. This company is referred to as the 'lead' company. In this example the quality spread on fixed interest loans is the largest: 2% (the quality spread on floating rate loans being only 1.5%), and on this type of loan, Company B can get the best rate: 10%. Therefore Company B borrows £100 million at a fixed rate of interest of 10%.

(b) The counter-party company then borrows the *other* type of loan. Therefore Company A borrows £100 million at LIBOR + 2.5%.

(c) The counter-party to the lead company (that is, Company A) then pays the lead company the *normal* rate of interest that it would pay on the type of loan it really wants, *less* the agreed swap saving.

In this example we will assume that the total interest saving of 0.5% (the quality spread differential) will be split equally between the two parties. Company A wants a fixed interest loan and would *normally* pay 12%. Therefore Company A pays to Company B 12% – 0.25% = 11.75% interest.

(d) Finally, the lead company – Company B in our example – pays the interest on the loan that has been raised by the counter-party. Therefore Company B pays Company A interest equal to LIBOR +2.5%.

The outcome of this arrangement is as follows:

Company A:	Pays LIBOR + 2.5% on the loan raised
	Pays 11.75% interest to Company B
	Receives LIBOR + 2.5% from Company B
Net payment:	Pays 11.75% interest fixed.
Company B:	Pays 10% interest on loan raised
	Pays LIBOR + 2.5% to Company A
	Receives 11.75% interest from Company A
Net payments:	Pays LIBOR + 2.5% + 10% – 11.75% = LIBOR + 0.75%

Therefore each company achieves the type of loan it requires, with an interest rate saving of 0.25%.

Advantages and disadvantages

Swap arrangements have a number of advantages. Principal amongst these is their flexibility and their low transaction costs. In terms of flexibility, they can usually be arranged in respect of any amount of money (typically £5 million to £50 million) and over virtually any time period. Furthermore they can be reversed, if desired, before the planned maturity date by re-swapping with other counter-parties. Swap deals do not depend on being able to identify a suitable counter-party, as banks are often willing to act in this role themselves. (Indeed many large banks raise fixed interest debt with the express intention of using it to swap into floating rate debt with commercial organizations who do not have a sufficiently good credit standing to raise fixed interest loans directly.)

Transaction costs on swap are relatively modest. Standardized legal documentation is usually used which reduces legal costs and competitive market forces restrain the level of fees demanded by intermediaries.

The main problem with swaps, and one which is often ignored by the parties concerned, is 'counter-party' risk – that is, the risk that your swap partner may default on their obligations. Thus in Example 8, Company B relies on Company A, the less creditworthy company, to meet its obligations to pay 11.75% interest each year. If A does default, B can in turn stop paying LIBOR + 2.5% to A, but B is still left with a type of loan (fixed interest) that it does not want. Using an intermediary is one way of reducing this risk, with the intermediary (for a fee) agreeing to take over the swap in the event of one of the counter-parties defaulting.

Summary

- Interest rate risk can be defined as the risk of an adverse movement in interest rates.

- The basic hedging technique for interest rate risk is the forward forward loan, where the company borrows money before it is required, so as to lock itself into a particular rate of interest. This money is then placed on deposit to earn interest until the loan is actually required.

- Forward rate agreements represent a simpler and more convenient way of achieving the same hedging effect as that achieved with a forward forward loan. Under an FRA, the company either receives or pays compensation to offset an adverse or favourable movement in interest rates.

- Whereas FRAs hedge the company against both adverse *and* favourable movements in interest rates, interest rate guarantees are true options, in that they hedge the company against adverse interest rate movements, but allow it to take advantage of favourable movements.

- Another hedging instrument is the interest rate futures contract. Unlike FRAs, which are tailor-made to the firm's precise requirements, these are standardized hedging instruments which are traded on future markets. Like FRAs, they effectively lock the company into a specific rate of interest and so provide a hedge against both adverse and favourable interest rate movements.

- Interest rate caps, floors and collars are all longer-term versions of FRAs. Interest rate cap agreements place a limit on a company's exposure to the risk of rising interest rates on a floating rate loan. Floor agreements similarly place a limit to the risk of falling interest rates on a monetary deposit. Interest rate collar agreements can be used to effectively turn a floating rate loan into a semi-fixed rate loan by limiting interest rate movements in both directions.

- Interest rate swap agreements come in many forms. However, they are basically agreements to swap a stream of floating interest rate payments for a stream of future fixed interest rate payments.

Notes

1. Notice that there is not a *single* money market, but rather a series of different money markets, such as the inter-bank market, the certificate of deposit market, discount house market and the Treasury bill market. However, for our purpose, we can treat the money markets as a single entity without any loss of understanding.

2. Notice that whether money market interest rates increase or decrease over time depends upon circumstances and the shape of the yield curve.

3. Money market rates are quoted in terms of *nominal* annual interest rates. Thus the one month rate is, in the example in the text, $\frac{1}{2}\%$ per month. This gives a nominal annual rate of: $\frac{1}{2}\% \times 12 = 6\%$ per year. However, the *effective* annual interest rate – known as the APR, the annual percentage rate – is the compounded value of the monthly rate: $(1 + 0.005)^{12} - 1 = 0.06168$, or 6.168% per year.

4. It can be seen from this reasoning why banks are happy to enter into FRAs with commercial companies. Generally speaking, banks are more profitable when interest rates are high. Under an FRA, the bank receives compensation when interest rates fall – thus helping the bank to reduce its own risk exposure.

5. The interest rate on LIFFE short-term sterling futures reflects LIBOR – the London InterBank Offered Rate which is, effectively, the short-term rate that banks lend at between themselves.

6. The value of a tick depends on the type of contract. For example, three-month German Mark (DM) futures have a contract size of DM1 million and so the value of a tick on these contracts will be: $DM1m \times \frac{3}{12} \times 0.0001 = DM25$.

7. This 'loss' value of £24 375 is the difference between the actual loan interest paid (£102 375) and the target amount of interest (£78 000).

8. LIBOR is the London InterBank Offered Rate, a floating rate of interest which is widely used as a benchmark interest rate for floating rate commercial

loans. In this case, the company is offered a loan at an interest rate which is 2% higher than LIBOR.

Further reading

1. A good article on the general area of financial futures, including interest rate futures is K.R. French, 'Pricing Financial Futures Contracts: An Introduction', *Journal of Applied Corporate Finance*, Winter 1989.
2. For a specific examination of interest rate futures and option, see S.B. Block and T.J. Gallagher, 'The Use of Interest Rate Futures and Options by Corporate Financial Management', *Financial Management*, Autumn 1986.
3. Two interesting articles on swaps are: S.M. Turnbull, 'Swaps: A Zero Sum Game?', *Financial Management*, Spring 1987 and L.D. Wall and J.J. Pringle, 'Alternative Explanations of Interest Rate Swaps: A Theoretical and Empirical Analysis', *Financial Management*, Summer 1989.
4. Finally, a good general review article is: C.W. Smithson, 'A LEGO Approach to Financial Engineering: an Introduction to Forwards, Futures, Swaps and Options', *Midland Corporate Finance Journal*, Winter 1987.

Quickie questions

1. If the three-month money market interest rate is 8%, how much interest would you pay on a £1 million three-month loan?
2. You wish to borrow £5 million for three months in two months' time. How would you set up a forward forward loan hedge?
3. If you had an FRA on a £10 million six-month loan at 6.5% and, at the time the loan was taken out the market interest rate was 7%, would you pay or receive compensation, and how much?
4. What is the fundamental difference between an FRA and an interest rate guarantee or option?
5. If you wish to hedge against a rising rate of interest on a floating rate loan, would you set up a hedge position by buying or selling interest rate futures?
6. If interest rate futures are priced at 93.75, what rate of interest does this imply?
7. If a single US$ three-month interest rate futures contract is in respect of $1 million, what is the value of one tick of profit or loss?
8. What is 'basis risk'?
9. Why is it unlikely that a futures hedge will be 100% efficient?
10. Company A can borrow at a fixed rate of interest of 11% and also at LIBOR + 1%. Company B can borrow at a fixed rate of interest of 12.75% and at LIBOR + 2.75%. Is there an advantage to an interest rate swap?

Problems

1. Manling plc has £14 million of fixed rate loans at an interest rate of 12% per year which are due to mature in one year. The company's treasurer believes that interest rates are going to fall, but does not wish to redeem the loans because large penalties exist for early redemption. Manling's bank has offered to arrange an interest rate swap for one year with a company that has obtained

floating rate finance at London InterBank Offered Rate (LIBOR) plus $1\frac{1}{8}$%. The bank will charge each of the companies an arrangement fee of £20 000 and the proposed terms of the swap are that Manling will pay LIBOR plus $1\frac{1}{2}$% to the other company and receive from the company $11\frac{5}{8}$%.

Corporate tax is at 35% per year and the arrangement fee is a tax allowable expense. Manling could issue floating rate debt at LIBOR plus 2% and the other company could issue fixed rate debt at $11\frac{3}{4}$%. Assume that any tax relief is immediately available.

Required:
(a) Evaluate whether Manling plc would benefit from the interest rate swap:
  (i) if LIBOR remains at 10% for the whole year;
  (ii) if LIBOR falls to 9% after six months.
(b) If LIBOR remains at 10%, evaluate whether both companies could benefit from the interest rate swap if the terms of the swap were altered. Any benefit would be equally shared.

2. (a) It is now 31 December and the corporate treasurer of Omniown plc is concerned about the volatility of interest rates. His company needs in three months' time to borrow £5 million for a six-month period. Current interest rates are 14% per year for the type of loan Omniown would use, and the treasurer does not wish to pay more than this.
He is considering using either:
  (i) a forward rate agreement (FRA), or
  (ii) interest rate futures, or
  (iii) an interest rate guarantee.

Required:
Explain briefly how each of these three alternatives might be useful to Omniown plc.

(b) The corporate treasurer of Omniown plc expects interest rates to increase by 2% during the next three months and has decided to hedge the interest rate risk using interest rate futures.
March sterling three-month time deposit futures are currently priced at 86.25. The standard contract size is £500 000 and the minimum price movement is one tick (the value of one tick is 0.01% per year of the contract size).

Required:
Show the effect of using the futures market to hedge against interest rate movements:
  (i) If interest rates increase by 2% and the futures market price also moves by 2%.
  (ii) If interest rates increase by 2% and the futures market moves by 1.5%.
  (iii) If interest rates fall by 1% and the futures market moves by 0.75%.
  In each case, estimate the hedge efficiency.

(c) If, as an alternative to interest rate futures, the corporate treasurer had been able to purchase interest rate guarantees at 14% for a premium of 0.2% of the size of the loan to be guaranteed, calculate whether the total cost of the loan after hedging in each of situations (i) to (iii) in (b) above would have been less with the futures hedge or with the guarantee. The guarantee would be effective for the entire six-month period of the loan.

15 Market efficiency and the term structure of interest rates

Introduction

We now turn to look at some aspects of the company's *financing* decisions. More specifically, we shall be looking at how we can measure the economic (as opposed to the accounting) costs of the different types of finance which are available, in order to then begin consideration of the complex question concerning the company's capital structure decision.

However, before we turn to examine these topics, we first need to consider elements of the economic background against which financing decisions are made. In particular, in this chapter, we consider two important aspects of financial markets.

The first of these is a consideration of the extent to which the financial markets – and in particular, the stock market – can be said to be 'efficient' in the pricing of company securities. In other words, we need to look at the degree to which we can rely on the stock market being able to correctly value a company's shares.

The second aspect of financial markets that we look at in this chapter is referred to as the 'term structure' of interest rates. This is concerned with the relationship between long- and short-term interest rates and the messages, or otherwise, that the term structure might give to the corporate treasurer, when taking decisions about how the company's assets should be financed.

Market efficiency

A definition

The efficient markets hypothesis (EMH) holds that a stock market is efficient if the market price of a company's shares (or other financial securities, such as bonds), rapidly and correctly reflects all relevant information as it becomes available. In a truly efficient stock market, if all information turned out to be entirely reliable and complete, share prices could be relied upon to correctly reflect the true economic worth of the shares. In such a market, over- or under-valued shares would not exist. However, when we talk about market efficiency in the real world we have to recognize that we have no way of knowing what the future will bring and so we have to qualify our interpretation of the value of shares. We cannot claim that an efficient market means that share prices reflect true economic worth because that is determined by the future but we can say that share prices reflect fully and accurately all available information. We will discuss what this actually means below.

Importance of market efficiency

The concept of an efficient stock market, and the degree to which the market actually *is* efficient, is of prime importance to the financial manager for a number of reasons.

Perhaps the most fundamental of these reasons relates back to our discussions in Chapter 1 about financial objectives. There we said that the fundamental objective behind financial management decision making was the maximization of shareholder wealth. This was then 'translated' – in order to make it into an operational objective – into the maximization of the value of the company's shares.

With this in mind therefore, it is important that the financial manager can rely on the stock market to correctly value the company's shares. If the financial manager makes a decision that will increase shareholder wealth, then it is important that both the manager and the shareholders should have the implications of that decision correctly *signalled* to them through a rise in the company's share price. A similar argument would also hold in a situation where a manager makes a decision which *damages* shareholder wealth. It is important that the stock market price of the company's shares gives accurate feedback to both the principals and their agents.

However, apart from this fundamental reason for making stock market efficiency highly desirable, there are a number of other reasons of almost equal importance. In the forefront of these is the market's risk–return relationship, which we examined in Chapters 10, 11 and 12. Indeed, a fundamental assumption which underlies the concept of portfolio theory is a belief that the stock market is reasonably efficient. This is because, in an efficient market, share prices are valued so as to give the return that they *should* be expected to produce (on average), given their relative systematic risk exposure.

If the stock market were inefficient at pricing shares, then we could not rely on the risk–return messages given by the CAPM. Indeed, in such circumstances, the concept of the market portfolio as the optimal share portfolio loses credibility. If the stock market were really inefficient, then the optimal share portfolio would be one which consisted of holdings in undervalued 'bargain' shares. Diversification, in its own right, would not necessarily be a desirable objective to achieve in such circumstances; investing in bargain shares which gave higher returns than they should, given their level of risk, would be the best investment objective.

A further implication of an inefficient stock market is that the CAPM would no longer be able to provide the financial manager with an NPV discount rate for project appraisal purposes. In fact, in an inefficient stock market, it would be virtually impossible for managers to take rational capital investment decisions on behalf of the company's shareholders. In our earlier discussion on NPV we saw that the discount rate was an opportunity cost, reflecting the return available elsewhere on similar risk investments. In an inefficient market it would be effectively impossible to identify such a rate of return, as different investments with the same degree of risk as the project might give different returns and it would be impossible for managers to ensure that they had identified the *best available* forgone rate of return to use as the NPV discount rate.

Finally, another important implication of market efficiency for financial managers concerns the importance of *information disclosure*. The stock market can only be expected to value a company's shares correctly on the basis of the information that has been disclosed. Therefore if financial managers – and shareholders – want the stock market to correctly value the company's shares, they must ensure that they communicate sufficient information to the market to allow it to do so. In an efficient stock market, information disclosure is a key requirement.

Levels of market efficiency

Having discussed why the concept of market efficiency is important for financial managers, we now reach a crucial question. Is the stock market efficient in the pricing of shares? Do share prices quickly and correctly reflect the impact of new, relevant information?

It has become the norm to consider the efficiency of markets in terms of whether or not they are efficient at three different levels:

1. weak form efficiency;
2. semi-strong form efficiency;
3. strong form efficiency.

Although we should not get too bogged down in the definitions of these levels, they do have important implications for the ways in which it might be possible to 'beat the market' as we will see in the next section.

Weak form efficiency is the lowest level of efficiency. It implies no more than that share prices fully reflect any information that may be obtained from studying and analysing *past* movements in the share price. Thus if the market is weak form efficient, it will not be possible to identify mispriced securities by analysing their past prices.

Semi-strong form efficiency is the next level. If the market is semi-strong efficient, it will also be efficient in the weak sense. Semi-strong efficiency implies that share prices fully reflect all the relevant, *publicly* disclosed information that is known about the company and its circumstances. Thus if the market is semi-strong efficient, it will not be possible to identify mispriced securities by analysing publicly available information.

Finally, there is strong form efficiency. This is the most extreme form of market efficiency. If the stock market is strongly efficient, this implies that share prices reflect *all* relevant information about their value, even though some of that information may *not* have been publicly disclosed. Thus if the market is strong form efficient, it will not be possible to identify mispriced securities at all. This does not mean that share prices would never change but it does mean that share prices will respond to events inside companies so quickly that it will be the individuals holding the shares at the time of the event that will either gain or lose as a result of the event.

Market efficiency and share dealing

Most active stock market investors try to *beat* the market. What they try to do is to identify under-valued shares and buy them before their price rises; similarly, they also look for over-valued shares in order to sell them before their prices fall. In other words, such investors are backing their *own* judgement about what the shares are worth, against the *collective* judgement of the stock market as seen in the current price of the shares. Therefore they act as though the market were *inefficient*.

There are basically three forms of stock market *analysis* that investors use to help them try and identify over- or under-valued shares and these are linked to the levels of efficiency we have just discussed. They are technical analysis, fundamental analysis and the use of 'inside' information.

Technical analysts study charts of share price movements (and hence are often referred to as 'chartists'), with the intention of discovering particular patterns of share price movements which appear to recur. Once these patterns have been identified, then, in following the share price movements of a particular company, if they see one of these patterns *starting* to develop, they believe that they are then able to predict the share's future course of movement and so give buy or sell investment advice.

Technical analysts believe that they have discovered hundreds of these recurring patterns; an example of one – termed a 'head and shoulders' pattern – is given in Fig. 15.1. So, an analyst who is following the share price movement of the ABC company, as in Fig. 15.2, may conclude that the share price is currently reaching the top of a head and shoulders pattern, and so advises that the shares be sold now, before the share price falls.

Technical analysts do not know why, nor do they particularly want to know why, a particular share's price is predicted to rise or fall. All they know is that that is the movement implied by the developing pattern. However, it has to be said that if chartism is to work, it implies that there are patterns in the behaviour of investors since it is very difficult to see how there might be patterns in the real-world events driving the value of an individual company.

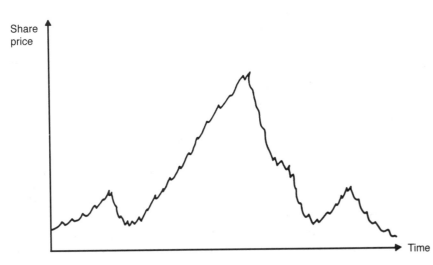

Fig. 15.1 *The 'head and shoulders' pattern*

Fig. 15.2 *ABC Co.*
shares

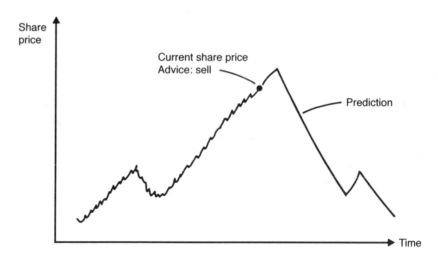

Fundamental analysis takes a completely different approach. Fundamental analysts tend to specialize in particular sectors of the stock market, about which they become *extremely* knowledgeable. They cast very wide information-capture nets and then, on the basis of this information, and with the use of a share valuation model, determine what they think the shares should be worth. This value is then compared with the current market price of the shares and, if the analyst thinks the shares are worth more than the current market price, 'buy' advice is given. Conversely, if the analyst believes the shares to be over-valued on the market, 'sell' advice is given.

These analysts are called *fundamental* analysts, because they look at the fundamental factors that lie behind a share's value: the revenues the company can be expected to generate, the costs that the company is expected to incur in the generation of those revenues, the uncertainty surrounding both the future costs and revenues and finally, the price (or return) of comparable investments. Logic suggests that it really should be possible to make profits from this type of activity and we might suggest that these profits are in fact justified as the result of the investment in information gathering and processing systems. Furthermore, it is reasonable to suggest that fundamental analysts provide the mechanism by which the market attains the level of efficiency that it does.

The third approach to stock exchange investment is of course in some forms illegal. But in many forms it is not. All investors are, in a sense, looking for 'inside information'. In other words they are looking for information, insights or connections which they believe are *not* yet fully reflected in the market price. It is in this sense – rather than in the illegal sense – that we refer to the use of *inside information* as the third approach to formulating stock exchange investment advice.

The efficient markets hypothesis (EMH) has implications for all three approaches. Quite simply, if the market is weakly efficient, technical analysis is worthless. If there is any information to be gained from looking at past share price movements, that information – according to the weak efficiency definition – is *already* reflected in the current share price. You would be *unable* to predict future share price movements on the basis of past share price movements.

If the market is semi-strong efficient, not only is technical analysis worthless, but so too is fundamental analysis. The implication of semi-strong efficiency is that, however wide the fundamental analyst's trawl for information, and however good his or her input of that information into his or her share valuation model, that information's implications are *already* impounded in the share's market price. Thus if the fundamental analyst believes the shares are over- or under-priced, it is unlikely that it is the analyst's valuation, rather than the market's valuation, which is incorrect.[1]

Finally, in a world of strong stock market efficiency, you would not even be able to expect to profit from inside information. This is because, with strong efficiency, the share price reflects *all* relevant information about the company, whether or not that information is in the public domain.

The empirical evidence of EMH

So, how efficient is the stock market? Can the market be relied upon to correctly value a company's shares, or is it possible to find shares which are being either over- or under-valued by the stock market?

The concept of market efficiency has been subject to more empirical testing than practically any other area in the theory of corporate finance (and indeed the social sciences more generally). This is not surprising since identification of inefficiencies might be expected to provide opportunities for substantial financial gains. For this reason we need to be a little circumspect about the results of empirical studies in this area. It may be that evidence of efficiency is disclosed whilst evidence of inefficiency is exploited! Even allowing for this, as so often happens with empirical evidence, the results do not always give a completely unambiguous and uncontroversial message.

However, it would be true to say that the tests of weak efficiency do overwhelmingly suggest that stock markets *are* efficient in the *weak* sense. The evidence on semi-strong efficiency is much more mixed – often as a result of difficulties in the testing procedures themselves. Nevertheless, it would be fair to conclude that the majority of the evidence does suggest that most stock markets *are* semi-strong efficient, most of the time. Finally, no one would really expect the stock market to be strongly efficient; in order for this to be so, share prices would need to reflect information that had not been disclosed. But despite this, there is evidence that stock markets may be efficient – to some extent – even in the strong sense.

Weak efficiency

So far as weak efficiency is concerned, empirical studies show that share prices tend to follow a 'random walk'. This term can be misleading, in that it gives the impression that share prices move at random, without any reason.

In fact random walk means almost the *opposite* of this commonsense interpretation. If share prices follow a random walk, the implication is that share prices *only* move in response to the disclosure of new information that is relevant to their value. This might be something like the disclosure of annual profits at an unexpected level, an oil strike in the North Sea, or the announcement of a major new customer. Given that new information like this arises in a random manner, share price movements should also occur in a random manner.

Therefore random walk implies that share prices only move when they have got *good reason* to move. If researchers can find evidence of *non-random* movements in share prices, this implies that the market is being *inefficient* because share prices are moving when they have not got a good reason to do so.

If share prices do follow a random walk, it then follows that technical analysis is worthless, in that it cannot have any predictive power: by definition, anything which moves at random cannot be predicted.

All sorts of different tests on random walk have been conducted by researchers, and the reading references at the end of this chapter indicate a selection of this work. However, virtually none of these tests have been able to discover evidence of significant non-randomness in share price movements, indicating that the market does pass the weak efficiency test.

There are, however, two interesting articles that go against the idea of weak efficiency. One is known as Schiller's volatility tests. Schiller argues that in an efficient market, you would expect share prices to be volatile; however, according to Schiller, share prices are *too* volatile to be truly random. In other words, Schiller is casting doubt on whether share price movements are always a justifiable response to the information that was being disclosed. The other article is by Matt Ridley who suggests that in some ways share prices are like the weather. Thus whilst the dryness or wetness of the weather compared to the average is fairly random over the long term (ignoring global warming and other long-term change factors) there do seem to be short-term patterns. There is a greater chance that it will be sunny tomorrow if it is sunny today than if it is raining today. There is similar evidence that it is more likely that share prices will rise tomorrow if they rise today rather than falling. However rises and falls in share prices are not at constant levels and betting on rises following rises does not seem to be a viable strategy.

Semi-strong efficiency

A large number of ingenious tests have been devised to examine semi-strong efficiency, and although the results have been mixed, the majority of the tests have tended to support the hypothesis that stock markets are semi-strong efficient.

A good example of a semi-strong test would be one of the very first that was carried out. It was undertaken in the USA by Fama, Fisher, Jensen and Roll and the results were published in 1969. They examined the price behaviour of shares where bonus or scrip issues were made (referred to as a stock split, in the USA).

In a one-for-one bonus issue, for instance, one new share is issued free of charge for every existing share. Thus the number of shares in issue is doubled. In such an exercise nothing has happened to alter the total worth of the company but, as the number of shares has doubled, the price *per share* can be expected to be halved.

Fama *et al.* looked at the 'abnormal returns' on the shares of such companies over the thirty months prior to the bonus issue and over the thirty months after the bonus issue. By 'abnormal return', what is meant is the return on the shares is greater (a positive abnormal return) or less (a negative abnormal return) than the return expected given the share's beta value.

What they found was that in the thirty months prior to the bonus issue announcement the shares gave a strong positive abnormal return (i.e. the price of the shares rose). Subsequent to the announcement, there was virtually no movement, on average, in the shares' return. Fig. 15.3 illustrates the situation.

The implications of this finding are as follows. A bonus issue should not really have any effect on the wealth of shareholders. The company remains exactly the same as before and all that happens is that the number of shares in issue is increased, but nothing has happened to change the value of those shares in aggregate. Therefore why should a share's price tend to rise prior to a bonus issue?

A very simple answer to this is that the bonus issue is actually a response to the rise in share prices that precedes it. Another possibility is that with bonus issues there is often an effective increase in dividends. For example, in our one-for-one bonus issue the dividend *per share* might have been maintained – thereby effectively doubling the level of dividends paid out. And, of course, an increase in dividends *would* seem to cause an increase in shareholder wealth. However, dividend payout rates are not the same thing as increased cash flows and it is difficult to see why the share's price should rise two and a half years prior to an announcement of a bonus issue in *anticipation* that this event would be accompanied by an effective increase in dividends (and probably before anybody had considered making the bonus issue).

However, Fama *et al.* went further with their analysis. They divided their sample of bonus-issuing companies into those which did and those which did not increase dividends at the time of the bonus issue. They then found that for those companies that *did* increase dividends there was, on average, no significant change in their returns *after* the bonus issue. In other words, the shares had risen in anticipation of the dividend increase and, once the increase had been announced, they maintained their new level.

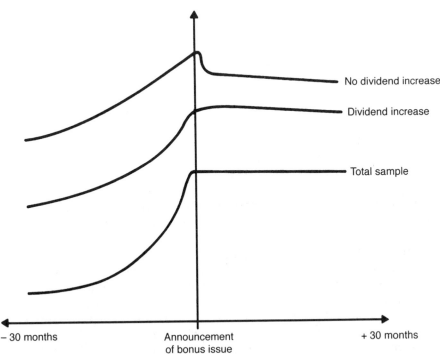

Fig. 15.3 *Impact of a share issue*

No dividend increase

Dividend increase

Total sample

− 30 months

Announcement
of bonus issue

+ 30 months

This supports the idea of the efficiency of the stock market. The share price rose in anticipation of the information and, once the information was publicly disclosed, the share price *already* reflected the impact of that information.

On the other hand, those companies making a bonus issue and *not* increasing dividends suffered, on average, *negative* abnormal returns after the bonus issue: again, evidence that the shares had originally risen in anticipation of new information (about a dividend increase) but, when that expectation subsequently was unfulfilled, the price fell back. Again, this situation is illustrated in Fig. 15.3. However, once again, it has to be said that the share price might have risen in anticipation of increased dividends rather than a bonus issue and that because this did not happen the price fell back again. Thus the bonus issue itself might be irrelevant.

The evidence on semi-strong efficiency, although very substantially in support of the concept, is less overwhelming than that for weak efficiency. Two examples of research which cast doubt on semi-strong efficiency are discussed here.

One of the implications of market efficiency is that the stock market should not be fooled by 'creative accounting'. In other words, the market should not be misled by companies artificially manipulating their reported profits by changing their accounting policies. Researchers have all tended to find this to be the situation, with one exception. A researcher in the USA, Professor Briloff, wrote an article in a US business magazine about the large amount of creative accounting that he found in the accounts of the McDonalds hamburger chain. On the day of the publication of the article, McDonalds' share price fell dramatically.

At first sight, this might be taken as evidence of the market being efficient. Here was a new piece of information about a company and, as a result, the share price fell. However, as was stated initially, an efficient stock market should *not* have been fooled by McDonald's creative accounting in the first place; yet for some reason, it is clear from the reaction of the share price, that the market *was* being fooled by creative accounting.

Whether or not this event is evidence of inefficiency is unclear – not least because, although Briloff has discovered and written about many other companies using creative accounting, none of his other disclosures has had any impact on the share price of the companies concerned. Therefore, the question remains: did the article cause McDonalds' share price to fall, or was that the result of other factors, the article's publication being just a coincidence?

Another implication of market efficiency is that share 'tip-sheets' should be worthless. Given that share tip-sheets try to identify under- and over-valued shares on the basis of analysing publicly disclosed information (it would be illegal to base their analysis on non-disclosed, 'inside' information) in a semi-strong efficient market, share prices should already *fully reflect* such information. Thus the 'buy' and 'sell' recommendations of such tip-sheets should be worthless.

This is exactly the conclusion reached by empirical research on tip-sheets, with one notable exception. One US tip-sheet called *Value Line does* appear to have some success in identifying under- and over-valued shares. *Value Line* has created much interest amongst researchers and has been the subject of a large amount of empirical research; although some researchers have claimed that abnormal returns cannot be earned on *Value Line*'s share tips, other researchers have argued strongly that *Value Line* really does appear to work. Just why *Value Line* should work, and other tip-sheets don't, and what it implies for market efficiency remains a controversial area.

Strong efficiency

Finally, there is strong market efficiency. As was stated earlier, no one really expects stock markets to be strongly efficient in the strict sense of the definition – if they were, share prices would have to reflect information of which the stock market was unaware – a rather unrealistic scenario. Furthermore, in such an efficient market, investors could not even profit from inside information, but we have the casual evidence – especially from US court cases – of cases where investors *have* made large profits from the use of inside information – and have subsequently ended up in court and in jail.

Formal research into strong efficiency has been hampered by the fact that researchers require knowledge of inside information in order to test whether or not it has affected share prices. Not suprisingly, they have met with difficulty in obtaining such information to use in testing. Nevertheless, some inventive approaches have been used, particularly concerning the performance of institutional investors such as unit trusts and pension funds.

The idea here is that institutional investment managers often have semi-private conversations with the top executives of the major companies in which they invest. In these meetings they are likely to gain insights and information about the company which is not available to investors generally.

If the market is *not* efficient in the strong sense, then unit trust managers should be able to profit from this additional information. The empirical evidence suggests that they cannot so do. For example, in another early study (1969) by Jensen which looked at the performance of 115 unit trusts, no evidence was found of superior performance or, where there was a positive abnormal return, it was so small as to be eliminated in the unit trust's management charges.

Conclusion

The evidence on market efficiency should not really be seen as surprising. It appears to indicate that new information divides itself up into that which is capable of being anticipated by the market (such as the level of profits for the year) and that which is *not* capable of being anticipated (such as a major factory fire).

The market appears to be very good at anticipating new information and the share price progressively reacts as these market 'guesses' become more confidently held. It is not surprising that this is the case, given the number of highly paid, intelligent people who are consistently striving to anticipate movements in share prices. It is equally unsurprising that no single analyst has been able to show that they can consistently act ahead of the rest.

In respect of that much smaller class of information, the information that is *not* capable of anticipation, the situation is different. Inside knowledge of this type of information (which is *not* the type likely to be obtained by unit trust managers) is likely to lead to an ability to 'beat' the stock market; though, of course, it is likely to be illegal to use the information in that way. In other words, it would appear logical that the market is not strongly efficient in the strictest sense of the definition.

On the other hand, the evidence also points to the fact that when unanticipated information does become publicly disclosed, share prices tend to react very rapidly as a result; again, too rapidly for most investors to react quickly enough to beat the share price movement. In this respect, the study by Neiderhoffer and Osborne (1973) is of particular interest.

Perhaps, then, instead of being concerned with whether or not markets are perfectly efficient in each form, we should be concerned with whether or not they are efficient enough so that the prices they set can be relied upon. An expert, fundamental analyst will have created an expensive information gathering and processing system. Through this system, information about a company is converted into a share price movement. We should not see this as meaning that markets are inefficient even if the strict definition would lead us to believe that they are.

Finally, it is worth stepping back from the evidence to reconsider the logic of market efficiency. An experiment was carried out in the USA some years ago that involved faculty members at a university predicting the results of football games week by week. They first predicted the results as individuals and then as a group. The group prediction was always in the top three (most accurate) but there was always somebody who beat it and it was never the same person twice. The implication of this is that on balance the group was the best predictor because it removed the bias of individual members. However, there are always unpredictable results in football – Everton might beat Liverpool whatever logic might suggest. These unlikely results will coincide with the bias of one of the individuals and thus in one week, that person outguesses the group. The stock market is very similar to this. The consensus view generated by the individuals in the market will tend to provide the most reliable indication of value but it will always be possible that your hunch will turn out to be true and you will beat the market. Mind you, it could be that your hunch turns out to be entirely wrong. Real inefficiency means that it is possible to beat the market consistently, or at least more often than not. This would require a valuation system that was superior to that used by the market as a whole. However, if such a system exists and it is known about, it will become part of the market's own valuation system. If such a system exists and only a few insiders know about it, to all intents and purposes it might as well not exist as far as the majority are concerned. The evidence seems to suggest that there is no known system (other than costly and high effort fundamental analysis) that can be shown to consistently beat the market. Thus we should accept that the market valuation is the best valuation we have.

So far as financial managers are concerned, the evidence is very substantially (but not entirely) in favour of semi-strong efficiency. Therefore managers should be aware of the fact that the results of their decisions will be reflected in the company's share price, once those decisions have been communicated to the stock market.

The term structure of interest rates

Let us now move on to examine another important aspect of financial markets. This is the relationship between short-term and long-term interest rates or rates of return, referred to as the 'term structure' of interest rates.

The yield to maturity

If you invest in corporate bonds,[2] the return that you receive is a combination of two elements: the rate of interest that the bond pays (termed the coupon rate), and the capital gain or loss that you may make on the bond when you come to sell it on to a third party,[3] or when the loan is repaid by the issuer.

With some bonds, the interest element is intended to be the main or only source of return; others have a balance between interest and capital gain, while still others pay no interest at all (zero coupon bonds), and are designed to provide their return purely in the form of a capital gain.

On all of these different types of bonds, the 'yield to maturity' is the annual rate of return that you would expect to get if you held the investment until the loan/bond was redeemed or repaid. The yield to maturity is calculated on the basis of the internal rate of return on the cash flow that the bond generates for an investor, if held up to the date when the loan is repaid (that is, until it 'matures').

Suppose a bond is currently priced in the market at £90.[4] It has a 10% coupon and is due to be redeemed for £100 in three years' time.[5] Its 'redemption yield' or 'yield to maturity' is represented by the IRR of the bond's future cash flow up to maturity:

$$-£90 + £10.A_{3\neg i} + £100 (1 + i)^{-3} = 0 \text{ NPV}$$

At a 10% discount rate, NPV = +£10
At a 12% discount rate, NPV = +£5.20

$$\text{IRR} = 10\% + \left(\frac{10}{10 - 5.20} \times 2\% \right) = 14.3\% = \text{Redemption yield.}$$

What we observe in the financial markets is that bonds with the same risk, but with *different* maturities, have different redemption yields. The relationship between the redemption yield and the length of time to maturity is known as the 'Term Structure of Interest Rates' and is described by the *yield curve*.

The yield curve

Generally speaking, we find that *shorter*-term maturity bonds have a *lower* yield, and *longer*-term maturity bonds have a *higher* yield, as shown in Fig. 15.4.

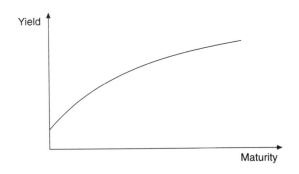

Fig. 15.4 *Rising, or normal yield curve*

However, the yield curve is not always rising in this way. It may be flat, or it may fall, as illustrated in Fig. 15.5.

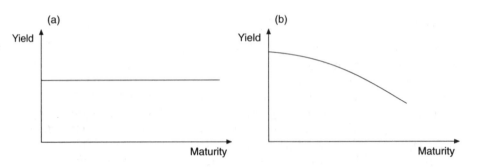

Fig. 15.5
(a) Flat yield curve
(b) Falling yield curve

We need to examine the factors which underlie the term structure of interest rates, as it is obviously important both to investors and to companies.

From an investor's point of view, suppose I have £100 000 that I want to invest for a total of ten years. Should I invest it in bonds which mature in ten years' time, or should I invest it in a sequence of one-year bonds over each of the next ten years? (There are of course many other strategies: I could invest the money in bonds which mature in five years' time and then, at that time, reinvest it in more five-year maturity bonds.)

What course of action I take may well be determined by the term structure of interest rates. If the yield curve is upward sloping, I may conclude that I would get a better return investing in longer-term (ten-year) bonds. But if the curve were downward sloping, I might conclude that I would do better with a sequence of one-year bond investments as one-year redemption yields are higher than the longer-term yield. A similar judgement would have to be made by a company treasurer who wished to borrow money for, say a ten-year period. He would have to decide between raising the finance with ten-year bonds or through a series of shorter-term bonds.

Spot interest rates

Before we start to examine the determinants of the term structure of interest rates more closely, we first have to look again at how the yield curve is calculated. In practice, the yield curve is constructed by calculating the annual redemption yield of similar-risk bonds, which each have a different future maturity date. This is illustrated in Table 15.1.

Table 15.1   Annual redemption yields

Years to redemption	Annual redemption yield (%)
1	4.0
2	4.2
3	4.7
4	4.9
5	5.4
6	5.5
7	5.9
8	6.3
9	6.6
10	6.9

Although this is how yield curves are *normally* constructed, *in theory* they should be constructed on the basis of future 'spot' interest rates. If we define a spot interest rate as the current rate of interest on a one-year bond, then the yield should really be composed of what will be the spot interest rate in each future time period.

The obvious difficulty with this – and the reason why we construct the yield curve on the basis of redemption yields – is that we do not know what these future spot rates will be. However, the important question is: does it matter? The answer is that yes, it may make a significant difference.

In our initial example, the redemption yield of our bond was estimated to be 14.3%. In other words:

$$£10(1.143)^{-1} + £10(1.143)^{-2} + £110(1.143)^{-3} = £90.$$

On the other hand, given that the spot interest rate for each time period, t, is given the notation S_t, then the true relationship should be:

$$£10(1 + S_1)^{-1} + £10(1 + S_1)^{-1} \times (1 + S_2)^{-1} + £110(1 + S_1)^{-1} \times (1 + S_2)^{-1} \times (1 + S_3)^{-1} = £90.$$

In particular, whereas with the redemption yield, the interest rate is assumed to be the same in each future time period, this is *not* necessarily the case with spot rates.

For example, suppose that we knew what the future spot interest rates were:

$S_1 = 10\%$
$S_2 = 12\%$
$S_3 = 22.66\%$

			(£)
Then:	$£10(1.10)^{-1}$	$=$	9.091
	$£10(1.10)^{-1}(1.12)^{-1}$	$=$	8.117
	$£110(1.10)^{-1}(1.12)^{-1}(1.2266)^{-1}$	$=$	72.792
			£90

This set of spot rates: 10%/12%/22.66% would represent the true term structure of interest rates over Years 1, 2 and 3. Therefore our estimated Year 3 rate of 14.3% (found from the redemption yield on a three-year bond), differs from the true Year 3 rate of 22.66%.

The point at issue is whether there is any difference between these two discounted cash flows:

$$£10(1.43)^{-1} + £10(1.143)^{-2} + £110(1.143)^{-3} = £90, \text{ and}$$

$$£10(1.1)^{-1} + £10(1.1)^{-1}(1.12)^{-1} + £110(1.1)^{-1}(1.12)^{-1}(1.2266)^{-1} = £90.$$

As such, there is not. But suppose we wish to value a new three-year bond with a coupon of, say, 4%. If we valued it on the basis of the redemption yield of 14.3%, or on the basis of the future spot rates of 10%/12%/22.66%, we would *not* get the same value, as Example 1 illustrates.

Is this difference important? It has the potential to be, especially with steeply rising or falling yield curves and significant differences in coupon rates. However, under most circumstances we can be reasonably satisfied that spot rates are fairly well approximated by the yield to maturity on bonds of differing maturity periods.

Present value of a three-year £100 bond with a 4% coupon rate at a 14.3%/year discount rate.[6]

$£4A_{3-0.143} + £100(1 + 0.143)^{-3} = £76.21$ PV.

The present value of this same bond using the following discount rates:

Year 1:   10%
Year 2:   12%
Year 3:   22.66%, is:

$$£4(1.10)^{-1} + £4(1.10)^{-1}(1.12)^{-1} + £104(1.10)^{-1}(1.12)^{-1}(1.2266)^{-1} = £75.70$$

Pure expectations hypothesis

Let us now turn to examine the factors which underlie the term structure of interest rates. What determines whether the yield curve is flat, rising or falling?

The fundamental theory of the yield curve's determination is the *pure expectations hypothesis*. This holds that what determines the yield curve is the market's expectations about future interest rates. If this hypothesis holds true, the term structure can be used to forecast future (spot) interest rates.

Suppose that the annual redemption yield on a one-year bond is 10% and is 12% on a two-year bond. Thus we have a rising yield curve. We can use these yield curve data to estimate the *expected* yield on a one-year bond, *twelve months from now*. This can be estimated on the basis that the expectation hypothesis says that you should be indifferent between investing in a single two-year bond (from Year 0 to Year 2) and investing in *two* one-year bonds (one from Year 0 to Year 1 and the other from Year 1 to Year 2).

Given that you can currently earn an annual rate of return of 12% investing for two years (in a two-year bond), and you can earn a rate of return of 10% investing over the next twelve months (in a one-year bond), we can therefore find what rate of return we expect to be able to earn over the subsequent twelve months. This is illustrated in Example 2.

Example 2

Suppose you have £1000 to invest for two years. Investing in a two-year bond will give:

$$£1000 \times (1 + 0.12)^2 = £1254.40.$$

If you invest £1000 in a one-year bond, at the end of twelve months you will have:

$$£1000 \times (1 + 0.10)^1 = £1100.$$

Therefore what rate of return will you then have to earn from investing that £1100 for a further year, to give exactly the same outcome from investing the £1000 in a two-year bond? This can be found as follows, where S_2 is the spot interest rate in the second year:

$$£1100 \times (1 + S_2)^1 = £1254.40$$

$$S_2 = \frac{£1254.40}{£1100} - 1 = 0.1404 \text{ or } 14.04\%.$$

Thus the current term structure of:

Years to maturity	Annual redemption yield (%)
1	10
2	12

implies that (spot) interest rates are expected to rise next year from their current level of 10% to 14.04%. This is why two-year bonds currently give an annual redemption yield of 12%.

This analytical approach can be extended as far into the future as data will allow. Suppose that the term structure was: 1 Year: 10%, 2 Year: 12% and 3 Year: 13%. We have already found the expected spot rate for next year: 14.04%. Therefore the expected spot rate for the *following* year can also be found. Example 3 provides the illustration.

Example 3

$$(1 + 0.10) \times (1 + 0.01404) \times (1 + S_3) = (1 + 0.13)^3.$$

In other words, the capital plus interest received from an investment in a three-year bond should be the same as the capital plus interest received from investing in three consecutive one-year bonds.[7]
Solving for S_3 gives:

$$S_3 = \frac{1.13^3}{1.10 \times 1.1404} - 1 = 0.1502.$$

Therefore our forecast spot one-year interest rates for the next three years are now:

Year 0	10%
Year 1	14.04%
Year 2	15.02%

Forward interest rates

These future spot interest rates that we estimated in Example 3, on the basis of the pure expectations hypothesis, are known as *forward* interest rates. In other words we have estimated the current, one-year forward and two-year forward spot interest rates as estimates of the *future* spot rates.

The pure expectation theory recommends forward rates as good predictors of future spot rates on the basis that, if they weren't, you could profit from the situation.

For instance, in our example, the one-year forward rate is 14.04%, but let us suppose that the *expected* spot rate in twelve months' time is higher than this – say 16%. This implies that you could borrow money for two years at 12% (remember, this is the current annual redemption yield on two-year bonds) and then invest it in two consecutive one-year bonds and so make a profit, as Example 4 illustrates.

Example 4

1. Borrow £1000 for two years at an annual rate of interest of 12%.

2. At the end of two years you will owe (capital, plus interest) $£1000 \times (1 + 0.12)^2 = £1254.40$,

3. The £1000 that you have borrowed is invested in a one-year bond with a 10% redemption yield, producing: $£1000 \times (1 + 0.10)^1 = £1100$ in one year's time.

4. In one year's time this £1100 is then reinvested for a further year at 16% (remember that this, we are assuming, is what the interest rate is expected to be in twelve months' time). This provides a total sum (capital plus interest) in two years' time of $£1100 \times (1 + 0.16) = £1276$.

5. This money can then be used to repay your £1000 two-year loan, plus interest, providing you with an 'arbitrage' profit of $£1276 - £1254.40 = £21.60$.

According to the expectations hypothesis, if such a profitable opportunity were to exist, lots of investors would like to take advantage of it. As a result there would be an increase in the demand to borrow two-year money (at 12%) and an increase in investors wishing to place money on deposit in one-year bonds. The supply and demand market forces arising out of this increased demand for two-year loans would force *up* two-year redemption yields, and the increased availability (i.e. supply) of people wishing to lend would push *down* one-year rates. These supply and demand market forces will stabilize interest rates at the point where no such profits are possible.

The transactions we have described here are referred to as 'arbitrage' (or 'interest' arbitrage) and the resulting profits are known as 'arbitrage profits'. Such situations – it is said – represent a disequilibrium in the market-place (making money is never normally so easy), and are usually eliminated rapidly by supply and demand market forces which rapidly restore equilibrium – which, in the present case is where the expected spot rate equals the forward rate.[8]

The Fisher Effect

Having looked at the pure expectations hypothesis, we can now turn to another question: what determines these forward rates/future spot rates? Why do people sometimes believe interest rates in the future will rise or fall (or stay the same)?

In order to answer this question, we need to return to the Fisher Effect which we first met in Chapter 7. This states that:

(1 + money interest rate) = (1 + real interest rate) × (1 + inflation).

Adapting this slightly to our present needs:

(1 + expected future spot interest rate) = (1 + expected future real interest rate) × (1 + expected rate of inflation).

If we assume that the real interest rate remains constant (a reasonable assumption, at least in the shorter term), the Fisher relationship implies that it is the expected rate of *inflation* that determines expected future interest rates. In our earlier example, the spot rate was expected to go up from its current level of 10% to 14.04% next year and to 15.02% the following year. The Fisher Effect implies that this rise in future interest rates arises from the fact that inflation is expected to increase from its current level.

Therefore, on the basis of the pure expectations hypothesis and the Fisher Effect, a rising yield curve would imply rising future inflation rates; a falling yield curve would imply falling inflation, and a flat yield curve would imply stable future inflation rates.

Taxes and transaction costs

There are a number of problems with the pure expectations theory, when it states that a long-term bond and a series of short-term bonds should be seen by investors as perfect substitutes for each other. Two obvious problems are taxes and transaction costs.

Suppose we have zero coupon bonds that deliver their annual rate of return in the form of a capital gain. Under these circumstances – and keeping in mind that capital gains are only taxed when they are realized – we would *not* be indifferent between the three-year bond and a series of three consecutive one-year bonds, referred to in Example 3.[9]

Returning to Example 3, we said that a 13% per annum yield to maturity on a three-year bond would be seen as being equivalent to a consecutive series of three one-year bonds yielding 10%, 14.04% and 15.02% respectively. However, they would not be equivalent if tax were taken into account.

There are two reasons for this. First, with the three-year bond, no tax would be payable until Year 3, when the total capital gain was realized, whereas with the series of one-year bonds a capital gain would be realized each year and so there would be a liability to pay tax on that capital gain each year. But not only would the *timing* of the tax payments be different, but so too would the *amount* of tax paid, both in absolute cash terms and in present value terms. Example 5 sets out these calculations.

Example 5

You have a choice between investing £1000 in a three-year zero coupon bond yielding an annual return of 13%, or investing in a series of three one-year zero coupon bonds. The first bond gives a return of 10%, the second 14.04% and the third 15.02%.

Income tax is paid on capital gains as soon as they arise, at a rate of 25%. Your time value of money is 10%.

Capital gain on the three-year bond:[10] $£1000(1 + 0.13)^3 - £1000 = £442.90$.

Income tax on the capital gain $= £442.90 \times 0.25 = £110.73$.

This is payable at Year 3 and so its present value cost is: $£110.73 \times (1 + 0.13)^{-3} = £76.74$. Repeating this analysis for the series of three one-year bonds:

1st Year Bond

$$£1000(1 + 0.10) = £1100 - £1000 = £100 \times 0.25 = £25 \text{ tax}$$
$$£1100 - £25 = £1075 \text{ available for reinvestment.}$$

2nd Year Bond

$$£1075(1 + 0.1404) = £1225.93 - £1075 = £150.93 \times 0.25 = £37.73 \text{ tax}$$
$$£1225.93 - £37.73 = £1188.20 \text{ available for reinvestment.}$$

Given a particular tax situation we *could* work out a series of three one-year spot rates of return that would be equivalent, after tax, to the return on a three-year bond. However, the problem is that not all investors face the same rates of tax on their capital gains and as a result you cannot achieve a generally agreed set of spot rates for financial markets.

A second difficulty for the pure expectations hypothesis is provided by transaction costs. The problem with transaction costs is that their presence in the process of buying bonds (in terms of commission payable to an intermediary) means that, once again, investors are not going to view a single longer-term bond and a consecutive series of shorter-term bonds as perfect substitutes: the latter is likely to incur greater transaction costs than the former.

Liquidity preference

Perhaps a more serious problem with the pure expectations hypothesis is that it is developed in a world of certainty. Once the fact that the future is *not* certain is taken into account, problems arise for the perfect substitutability criterion. According to the pure expectations hypothesis, both borrowers and investors should be indifferent between long-term bonds and a series of short-term bonds.

However the returns available on future short-term bonds are uncertain, and they may turn out to be above or below what the expectations hypothesis predicts. For instance, as we saw in an earlier example, suppose the annual yield to maturity on one- and two-year bonds is 10% and 12% respectively. This implies that the current spot interest rate is 10% and the one-year forward spot interest rate will be 14.04%, because this would make a series of two consecutive one-year bonds give the same yield as a two-year bond. The problem that an investor in one-year bonds faces (and, for that matter, a borrower via the issue of one-year bonds), is that there is *no certainty* that the yield on one-year bonds in twelve months' time *will be* 14.04%. The yield may turn out to be more or less (or equal to) 14.04%, whereas the investor knows with certainty that by investing in a two-year bond, he can lock into 12% per annum for certain.

On this basis it is generally thought that investors prefer liquidity: if interest rates do go up, they want to be able to take advantage of that rise, rather than being locked into a lower rate. Thus they will prefer bonds with shorter maturities and, indeed will be willing to take a lower return than they could get on longer-term bonds in order to retain this flexibility.

You might be inclined to argue that *other* investors may prefer longer-term bonds to avoid the risks of *falling* yields on shorter-term bonds. However, the argument in favour of short-term bonds is based on the relationship between bond yields and bond prices. If you have invested in the two-year bond used in our earlier example and it then transpired that the yield on one-year bonds in twelve months' time was not 14.04% but had *risen* to 15%, the impact on your bond would be that its price or value would *fall*. It is this potential loss in the capital value on longer-term bonds that investors are felt to particularly dislike.

On the other hand, it is thought that *borrowers* have the opposite preference to investors. In other words, they like to borrow via long-term bonds so that they know their borrowing liabilities and, furthermore, they avoid the risk of having to re-borrow short-term bonds under adverse conditions (i.e. rising interest rates). This therefore leads borrowers to be willing to pay more for long-term loans.

The conclusion of this analysis is that both borrowers and lenders have *liquidity* preferences. Investors are willing to take a lower yield on shorter-term bonds, and borrowers have to be offered a lower yield to persuade them to issue such debt. Conversely, borrowers are willing to pay a higher yield to obtain longer-term borrowing and investors have to be offered higher yields to persuade them to invest in longer-term bonds.

As a result, liquidity preference theory concludes that whatever is the term structure of interest rates arising out of the pure expectations hypothesis and the Fisher Effect, liquidity preferences of investors and borrowers will tend to bias longer-term bond yields *upwards*. This is why the 'normal' yield curve is upward sloping, as shown earlier in Fig. 15.4.

Segmented markets

Finally, there is a third argument at work, which is referred to as 'segmented markets'. This holds that the reason why the redemption yields of bonds differs for different maturities has little to do with future interest rate or inflation rate expectations, nor is it to do with liquidity premiums.

Instead, it is argued that markets for both lenders and borrowers are segmented. Some people *only* want to invest short term, other people *only* what to invest long term. Investing in a series of short-term bonds is held *not* to be an acceptable substitute for investing in a single long-term bond – an assumption which underpins the expectations hypothesis.

Similarly, some borrowers *only* want to borrow short term; other borrowers *only* want to borrow long term. In such circumstances borrowers and lenders prefer a *specific* maturity, irrespective of differences between long- and short-term interest rates, and therefore whether long-term interest rates are above or below or the same as short-term rates (in other words, whether the yield curve is rising, falling or is flat) is simply a function of supply and demand market forces in each segment of the market-place.

Conclusion

Which theory is correct: pure expectations, liquidity preference or market segmentation? The truth probably lies somewhere between all three, but generally speaking, the pure expectation hypothesis is seen as the bedrock factor in determining the term structure.

The term structure probably does contain liquidity premiums to compensate for risk but, at the same time, more and more techniques and mechanisms are becoming available to limit exposure to interest rate risk – as we have seen in the previous chapter – and its importance may, if anything, be diminishing.

Similarly, undoubtably there are lenders and borrowers who are only interested in specific maturities, and who will select those maturities irrespective of the term structure. But not all borrowers and lenders will ignore the substitutability of a sequence of short-term bonds and a long-term bond. Therefore if segmented supply and demand market forces have a significant impact on bonds of one particular maturity – for example, a shortage of supply may force up the long-term yield significantly above expected future spot rates – then at least some investors will seek to make arbitrage profits. Such arbitraging activities are then likely to bring the yield curve back down towards the configuration hypothesized by pure expectations.

Summary

This chapter has examined the efficient markets hypothesis and its implications and the term structure of interest rates. The main points covered were:

- The efficient markets hypothesis examines the degree to which the stock market is efficient in reflecting relevant information in share prices.

- Weak efficiency occurs when market prices follow a random walk, thereby limiting the usefulness of technical analysis.

- Semi-strong efficiency occurs when share prices quickly and correctly reflect any relevant information as it arises in the public domain. Its occurrence limits the usefulness of fundamental analysis of share prices.

- Strong efficiency occurs when share prices reflect *all* relevant information, whether or not it is in the public domain. In such circumstances investors could not even expect to profit from the possession of inside information.

- The empirical evidence overwhelmingly supports weak efficiency, and substantially supports semi-strong efficiency. On strong efficiency, the empirical evidence is less clear.

- The implications for financial managers of semi-strong efficiency, in particular, are important. It implies that project NPVs will be reflected in share prices; the timing of capital-raising exercises is unimportant from the viewpoint of whether a company's shares are currently 'cheap' or 'expensive' and this casts doubt on the take-over of a publicly-quoted company ever being expected to produce a positive NPV.

- The relationship between a bond's redemption yield and the length of time until its maturity is described by the term structure of interest rates, and is illustrated by the yield curve.

- The yield curve usually rises over time, but it may be flat or fall over time.

- There are a number of theories which attempt to explain the shape of the yield curve. The pure expectations hypothesis holds that the yield curve reflects expectations about future interest rates, which, in turn, reflect expectations about future inflation rates.

- Another explanation for the shape of the yield curve is given by the liquidity preference theory, which holds that, because the future is uncertain, lenders prefer to lend short term and borrowers like to borrow longer term. Hence lenders are willing to accept lower short-term interest rates because of their preference and borrowers are willing to offer higher long-term rates because of their preference. Hence the 'normal' shape of the yield curve.

- A third explanation is given by the market segmentation argument, which holds that the markets for long- and short-term bonds are unconnected. People do not see a series of short-term bonds as a substitute for a single longer-term bond. Thus long- and short-term bond maturity yields are simply a function of supply and demand market forces.

Notes

1. There is an interesting paradox here. Fundamental analysis is worthless in the sense that analysts are unable to identify under- or over-valued shares, except through luck. However, fundamental analysts have a value to the stock market *as a whole*, in that they help to keep the market 'on its toes' and efficient. In other words, their efforts to seek out bargains go towards ensuring that share prices react swiftly to the disclosure of new, relevant information. The paradox here is that an efficient market needs investors who think it is inefficient, in order to keep it efficient.

2. In other words, you are effectively lending a company money, in return for which you receive a certificate – the 'bond' – which acknowledges the loan.

3. These bonds are marketable securities and so can be bought and sold on financial markets, where their price will reflect supply and demand pressures.

4. We will look more closely at the pricing of bonds in Chapter 16.

5. Bonds are normally issued in £100 units. Therefore £100 is known as their 'par' or redemption value, and it represents the amount that will be repaid when the loan reaches maturity.

6. The annuity factor is calculated as:

$$A_{3\neg 0.143} = \frac{1 - (1.143)^{-3}}{0.143} = 2.31,$$

$$\text{and } (1 + 0.143)^{-3} = 0.67.$$

7. Or from an investment in a two-year bond followed by reinvestment of the proceeds in a one-year bond:

$$(1 + 0.12)^2 \times (1 + S_3)^1 = (1 + 0.13)^3.$$

8. Notice that you could also make an arbitrage gain if the expected spot rate were *less* than the forward rate, by borrowing short term and lending longer term.

9. This example is used for purposes of exposition, and is not intended to be realistic. The tax rules on zero-coupon bonds can be quite complex. This example is purely designed to show that tax does potentially provide a problem for the pure expectations theory.

10. The bond will cost £1000 to buy now. It does not provide any interest payments but, at the end of three years a total of £1442.90 is repaid, giving a total capital gain of £442.90, equivalent to an annual rate of return – before tax – of 13%.

Further reading

1. The reading on market efficiency is almost limitless. However a really good, classic introduction is B.G. Malkiel, *A Random Walk Down Wall Street*, Norton 1985.
2. A good review of the original research into EMH is given by E.F. Fama, 'Efficient Capital Markets: A Review of Theory and Empirical Work', *Journal of Finance*, May 1970.
3. The October 1987 stock market crash made many people stop and rethink their ideas of EMH. However, see: K. Brown and S. Tinic, 'How Rational Investors Deal with Uncertainty (or, Reports of the Death of Efficient Markets Theory are Greatly Exaggerated)', in J.M. Stern and D.H. Chew (eds), *The Revolution in Corporate Finance*, Blackwell 1992.
4. A really classic article on EMH research is that by R. Ball and P. Brown, 'An Empirical Evaluation of Accounting Income Numbers', *Journal of Accounting Research*, Autumn 1968. But this can be contrasted with E.F. Fama and K.R. French, 'Business Conditions and Expected Returns on Stocks and Bonds', *Journal of Financial Economics*, November 1989.
5. Of obvious interest, there is T.B. O'Keefe and S.Y. Soloman, 'Do Managers Believe the EMH?: Additional Evidence', *Accounting and Business Research*, Spring 1985.
6. Some interesting insights into short-term patterns in price movements can be found in Matt Ridley, 'On the Edge': Frontiers of Finance. Economist Special Survey. *The Economist* 9 October 1993.
7. There is also a considerable amount of interesting material in Adler and Adler, *The Social Dynamics of Financial Markets* J.A.I. Press 1984. As the title suggests, this book is concerned with the way that players in financial markets interact and the psychology of their decision making.
8. For a deeper analysis of the term structure of interest rates, see R. Roll, *The Behaviour of Interest Rates: An Application of the Efficient Market Model to US Treasury Bills*, Basic Books 1970.

Quickie questions

1. What are the three levels of market efficiency?
2. What are the implications of semi-strong market efficiency for financial managers?

3. What are the implications of EMH for stock exchange investment analysis?
4. Why do share prices follow a random walk?
5. What does a technical analyst attempt to do?
6. What is the shape of a 'normal' yield curve?
7. What is the pure expectations hypothesis?
8. What is the liquidity preference theory?
9. What does a falling yield curve imply about future inflation rates, according to the pure expectations hypothesis?
10. The yield on a one-year bond is 6% and on a two-year bond it is 7%. What is the implied one-year interest rate that is expected next year?

Problems

1. The following statement contains several errors. Explain what these errors are. 'According to the efficient market hypothesis all share prices are correct at all times. This is achieved by prices moving randomly when new information is publicly announced. New information from published accounts is the only determinant of the random movements in share price.

   'Fundamental and technical analysts of the stock market serve no function in making the market efficient and cannot predict future share prices. Corporate financial managers are also unable to predict future share prices.'

2. You are given the following annual redemption yields on corporate bonds of equal risk:

Years to redemption	Redemption yield (%)
1	6
2	5.75
3	5.50
4	5
5	4.5

   Required:
   (a) Estimate spot interest rates for the next five years.
   (b) Plot the yield curve.
   (c) If the real interest rate is expected to be 2% per annum, forecast inflation rates over the next five years.
   (d) If you expect the spot interest rate to be 7% next year (S_2) show why you would prefer to invest in two consecutive one-year bonds, rather than in one two-year bond.

16 The cost of company capital

The financing decision

So far, our analysis has been confined to an evaluation of project investment appraisal and the problem of risk. We have not considered how any particular project should be financed – or indeed, whether the method of finance makes any difference.

This exclusion of any consideration about the financing method has been assisted by the assumption of a perfect capital market, which implies that if a company can identify a project that has a non-negative NPV, when discounted at a rate that reflects its level of systematic risk, then the required finance will be made available by the capital market.[1] Thus the question of financing has appeared to be irrelevant.

In this chapter, and in the three that follow, we start to examine whether the question of project financing is irrelevant and, if it is not, then what factors should be considered when evaluating different methods or sources of finance.

It is perhaps wise at this point to make very much the same sort of observation that was made at the outset of our analysis of the handling of risk in decision making. Just as our knowledge of how we should take account of risk is still incomplete, this is also the case in terms of the financing decision, especially in terms of the decision concerning the 'optimal' capital structure of companies. Indeed, as we shall see, it is difficult to see how an optimal capital structure can be identified or, indeed, exists in any meaningful way.

In this chapter, we examine much the same area as we did in Chapter 12 on the CAPM – the rate of return on financial securities (e.g. the shares of companies) but, in one sense, from the other side of the coin. This is the area of the cost of company capital. We do this first, in order to begin to examine the decision itself. We shall see in the following chapter that the cost of capital concept can also provide us (under certain restrictive circumstances) with a capital investment appraisal discount rate.

Chapters 18 and 19 look directly at the implications for the firm and its owners of the financing decision. Chapter 21 then examines how capital investment decisions and financing decisions interact and how such interactions may be analysed.

Types of long-term finance

Generally speaking, capital investment projects are financed from three alternative (but not necessarily mutually exclusive) sources: finance directly supplied by the capital markets in the form of ordinary share capital; finance directly supplied by the capital markets in the form of interest-bearing medium and long-term loans; and finance internally generated by the firm in the form of retained profits. There are other sources of long-term finance – one important one may be government grants[2] – but in the main these three sources of finance predominate.

These various types of finance differ from each other in several ways. These include how they are issued, the obligations that they impose on a firm's management, and how they are affected by the tax system. They also differ significantly in terms of risk. Our analysis of the CAPM showed that the return required on *any* investment should reflect the systematic risk involved. Therefore if these different types of capital have different levels of systematic risk, then we can expect their returns to reflect these differences.

Finally, although we shall be examining the expected returns required by the *suppliers* of corporate finance, because we are interested in what these returns are from the viewpoint of management, they will be referred to as the *costs* of the various types of capital.

The cost of equity capital

Physical and financial investments

In our analysis, in Chapter 4, using the single-period investment–consumption model we distinguished between physical investment decisions and financial investment decisions. In fact the distinction between financial and physical investments is almost entirely artificial, so far as decision making is concerned.

A physical (or real) investment could be defined as involving cash (i.e. consumption power) being spent in order to combine and operate productive resources (the factors of production) so as to generate a saleable output (of either goods or services), which can be exchanged for cash. A financial investment still involves an outlay of cash – it is lent on the financial markets – but now a third party undertakes the physical investment.

Individuals or companies borrow money through the medium of the financial markets in order to undertake physical investments, with the hope that the investment will produce a sufficient cash return in the future, to allow a surplus to remain once the borrowed funds (capital plus interest) have been repaid. Obviously, this is a highly simplified view of the distinction between physical and financial investments, but it is essentially correct.

The required return on equity capital

There are many ways in which investors can 'lend' money on the capital market. One is to buy the ordinary shares issued by a company (either directly from the company or from a third party in the form of an existing shareholder) so that the *company*, rather than the investor personally, undertakes the physical investments.

An essential characteristic of an investment in ordinary shares or *equity capital*, which differentiates it from most other forms of capital market lending, is that the loan never comes to maturity, i.e. the loan is permanent and is never repaid.[3] (However, ordinary shares are *negotiable*: the permanent loan to a company can be sold on to another investor. These transactions form the bulk of stock exchange dealings.) Because of this characteristic of equity capital, the investors making such loans to a company are held to be the legal owners of the company.

To find what is the expected return required by ordinary shareholders on their capital, we shall return to our earlier discussion on the objective of financial management decision making. The objective, we said, could be stated as the maximization of the (current) market value of the company's ordinary share capital. This was a surrogate for maximizing the dividend flow to shareholders through time (which in itself was a surrogate for wealth maximization), because it is this *dividend flow* (including a terminal cash flow) that gives a share its market value.

We also know that cash flows are uncertain and that cash flows which arise at different points in time cannot be directly compared, but must first be converted to values at one point in time (usually, the present time is chosen). Thus the market value of an ordinary share represents the sum of its *expected* future dividend flow, *discounted* to present value.

This particular line of reasoning leads to the share valuation model known as the *dividend valuation model*: the market price of a company's shares equals the sum of its future expected dividend flow, to infinity, discounted to present value. In this model what is of particular interest to us is the *discount rate* implied by a particular stock market share price. The discount rate represents the return an investor can expect to obtain on the shares. This is illustrated in Example 1.

Example 1

Suppose that an ordinary share in a particular company is generally expected to produce a 10p dividend at the end of each year, in perpetuity. If the share has a market value of 80p, this represents the sum of the expected future discounted dividend stream:

$$80p = 10p(1 + i)^{-1} + 10p(1 + i)^{-2} \ldots + 10p(1 + i)^{-\infty}$$

As this is a perpetuity, the sum reduces to:

$$80p = \frac{10p}{i} \quad \text{and so } i = \frac{10p}{80p} = 0.125 \text{ or } 12.5\%.$$

Therefore *i*, the rate of discount implied, given the share's market value, is 12.5%. It is this interest or discount rate that reduces the sum of the future expected dividend flow to a present value of 80p.[4]

So, 12.5% must be the expected return that is required by ordinary shareholders in this company, taking into consideration the systematic riskiness of the future expected dividend flow. (This, in turn, depends upon the systematic riskiness of the expected returns from the physical investments which the company has undertaken.) In other words if an investor bought a share in the company for 80p and received a 10p dividend each year, then he would be getting a 12.5% annual return on his money.

The cost of equity capital

If equity capital were to be the only source of investment funds used by the company in Example 1 – and the shareholders require an expected return of 12.5% on their investment, then 12.5% could be taken by management as representing the discount rate to be used in the company's project appraisal NPV calculations.

The reasoning behind this is that investors have implicitly specified a 12.5% return through the price set on the shares in the market-place. The shares are priced at 80p because, on this basis, investors can expect a 12.5% return. Why is an expected 12.5% return required? Because this must be the going rate of return elsewhere on the stock market, for investments of the same level of systematic risk.

If shareholders can obtain a return of 12.5% elsewhere on the stock market for a similar level of risk, the inference is that the company's management must earn at least this rate of return on any physical investments they wish to undertake with shareholders' funds, providing, of course, that they are of a similar systematic risk class as the average for the company. If they cannot find projects yielding *at least* such expected returns (given the risk level) then they should not invest. They should give the money back to shareholders – perhaps in the form of a dividend – because shareholders *can* invest that money elsewhere to yield a 12.5% expected return. Thus 12.5% becomes – from the perspective of management – the cost of using equity capital to invest in projects. (Notice that this cost is, in fact, an *opportunity cost*.)

The discount rate that reduces the sum of a share's expected future dividend flow to a present value equal to its market price is called the *cost of equity capital*. It is the minimum expected return required by shareholders from the investment of their funds by the company's management. However, the cost of equity capital is an appropriate discount rate to use in NPV calculations *only* in circumstances where the project being appraised has the same level of systematic risk (i.e. the same beta value) as the systematic risk of the company's *existing* cash flows (i.e. those cash flows generated by capital investment projects that have already been undertaken).

This is a very important (and limiting) proviso, but it is obvious from our previous analysis. A rate of return is appropriate for a given risk level, and so a company's cost of equity capital is a required rate of return relative to its *existing* level of risk. Therefore, this will be appropriate to use as a discount rate for project evaluation only if the project has a similar level of risk as the existing company.

If the project has a *different* level of risk, then the company's existing cost of capital is not the appropriate discount rate. In these circumstances, we would have to rely upon a CAPM/beta type of analysis as discussed in Chapter 12, in order to identify the correct rate of discount.

Expected return, dividends and market price

Workings of the stock market

Before proceeding to consider further how the required expected return on equity is to be estimated, let us examine the nature of the relationship between expected return, dividends and market price. In order to do so we shall be taking a simplified but generally correct view of the workings of stock markets.

With the company used in Example 1 above, shareholders required an expected return (or yield) of 12.5%. On the basis of an expected annual dividend per share of 10p in perpetuity, this produced a market value of 80p per share. Now, in the following analysis, the *riskiness* of the expected future dividend flow will remain unchanged.

Suppose something happens which leads investors, in general, to believe that the company will now pay an annual dividend per share in future of 12p, instead of 10p. At the market price of 80p the share now yields a return of 12p/80p = 0.15. This 15% return is *above* the required return (of 12.5%) for this level of risk, and so investors will start to buy the company's shares because they represent a 'bargain' priced at only 80p.

Stock exchanges work through a supply and demand market mechanism, and therefore this increased demand for the company's ordinary shares will force up the market price. Suppose, in response to this increased demand, the market price rises to 85p per share. It is still yielding an excessively high return: 12p/85p = 0.141, and so demand will continue. In fact the price of the share should rise until its price equates with the required yield of 12.5%. So the market price will settle at 12p/0.125 = 96p per share. (Any *further* increase in share price will cause the share to have too *low* an expected return, investors will wish to sell, and so the reverse process will start, with the share price falling until it produces the required yield of 12.5%.)

A changing required return

The foregoing example illustrates the *positive* relationship between the dividend expectations of a share and its market price. Increases or decreases in the expected dividend flow will cause a respective rise or fall in market value, with the linchpin of the mechanism being the required expected return.

Similarly, suppose an event occurs which causes investors to change the level of a share's required rate of return. For example, because a company's expected future dividend flow is viewed, for some reason, as becoming more or less risky than before; or because *alternative* investments have become more or less attractive in terms of their risk–return. Then a consequent change in market price will occur until the revised required yield has established itself. There is an *inverse* relationship between required return and market price.

As an example, suppose that we return to the original situation of a market price of 80p per share, a constant annual expected dividend of 10p and hence an expected return of 12.5%. Suppose that, for some reason, rates of return throughout the economy rise. (One possible reason might be that the government has increased the return it gives on government stock and so this has pushed up *all* rates of return in the economy.) As a result, investments with a similar level of systematic risk to that of our company whose share price we are considering, rise to (say) 15%.

This means that our shares are no longer giving a sufficient return at 12.5%. In consequence, investors will start to sell the shares, and this selling pressure will cause the share price to fall. How *far* the share price will fall is determined by what is the new level of required expected return.

In this case, the shares will fall in price until they reach 66⅔p, at which point they too now produce a return of 15% – as do comparable risk investments. Hence the share price has *fallen*, but the expected return has *risen*.

The share price–return relationship

At first sight these relationships between the market price of a share and its return can appear confusing. If the share price *rises*, then the return *falls*, and vice versa.

If we return to the figures in Example 1, suppose you buy shares in the company when they are 80p each. You get an annual dividend of 10p, and so you earn an annual rate of return on your investment of: 10p/80p = 12.5%.

Consider a situation where, assuming that nothing is happening to change the level of the expected annual dividend – it remains at 10p – but that, for some reason, the share price now *rises* to 100p. We know that the return on the shares will now have *fallen* to: 10p/100p = 10%.

However notice what this means. It does *not* mean that *your* return has fallen to 10%. By buying the shares at 80p, you have effectively locked yourself in to receiving a 12.5% return on your investment for as long as you continue to hold the shares. This is because you only paid 80p a share and you continue to receive an annual dividend of 10p, giving a 12.5% rate of return on your investment.

The rise in the share price means that *new* investors in the shares receive the lower return of 10% because they have to pay 100p a share in order to get the annual dividend of 10p. Thus not only does the rising share price not lower your own return, it also makes you better off relative to new investors. Your 'better-offness' manifests itself in the fact that you've made a capital gain on your shares: their price has risen from 80p to 100p.

What does this 20p capital gain represent? Suppose that you had originally spent £100 buying 125 shares in the company at 80p each. Thus you receive a total annual dividend of £12.50(125 × 10p). Once the share price has risen to 100p, new investors investing £100 could only buy 100 shares and would receive an annual dividend of £10(100 × 10p). Therefore you receive £2.50 *more* dividend than they get. The sum of these extra dividends, to infinity, discounted back to present value at the new cost of equity capital is: £2.50 ÷ 0.10 = £25. Which is the capital gain you've made on your shares:

Purchase cost:	125 × 80p	=	£100
Current value:	125 × 100p	=	£125
Capital gain		=	£25

Therefore, what does the 20p per share capital represent? It represents the present value of your additional dividends.

The shareholder and the market

The individual investor has to decide whether to buy, hold or sell a particular share. It is not the individual shareholder's actions, but those of the market as a whole (i.e. all investors collectively) that determines a share's expected yield. Therefore the individual investor has to estimate a share's future expected dividend flow and from this, together with the share's market price, he will be able to derive its expected yield or return.

What action he then takes (buy, sell or hold) depends upon his own personal attitude to risk and the return he requires for bearing varying amounts of it. Other things being equal, if he believes that the share's expected yield is *at least* sufficient compensation for the risk that owning the share involves then he will buy; if *just* sufficient he will hold; if *less than* sufficient he will sell. The individual shareholder's actions will not have much *direct* effect on the market price. However, if investors in general have a similar attitude to the required 'risk–expected return' trade-off, then they are *all*[5] likely to undertake similar action and the share's market price will adjust accordingly. Hence the position of market equilibrium is achieved, as was referred to in our discussion of the market portfolio and the CML.

Applying the dividend valuation model

Introduction

At first sight, the dividend valuation model may appear to be a rather naive and incomplete model of share price behaviour. It implies that share prices are only determined by the expected future level of dividends and the systematic risk of the future dividend flow.[6]

If we think back to how we defined the return on a share for purposes of portfolio theory, we said that the return was composed of two elements: the dividend and the capital gain (or loss) on the share price. The dividend valuation model appears to be ignoring this second element of return – the capital gain.

However, the dividend valuation model does *not* ignore the idea of capital gains and losses on the share price. Instead, what the model implies is that what *causes* a capital gain (or loss) is *changed expectations* as to the future level (or riskiness) of the expected dividends.

In addition, notice how the underlying logic of the dividend valuation model fits in with the general assertion made earlier in this book: that values are applied to objects (including shares) in order to allow decisions to be made about them, and an object's current value, on the assumption of a rational, economic man, is based on the net stream of future benefits it will produce (or, rather more correctly, that it is *expected* to produce). Furthermore, we have already recognized the importance of cash and cash flow in economic wealth-maximizing decisions, and the dividend valuation model, being a cash flow valuation model, is therefore in close accord with this reasoning.

The model

If we make use of the following notation:

P_E = market price per share;
V_E = total market value of equity = $P_E \times$ number of shares in issue;
d_t = dividend per share paid in time t;
D_t = total dividend paid to equity holders at time $t = d_t \times$ number of shares in issue;
K_E = cost of equity capital (expected return on equity);

then the dividend valuation model can be expressed in general terms as:

$$\text{either } V_E = \sum_{t=1}^{\infty} \frac{D_t}{(1+K_E)^t} \text{ or } P_E = \sum_{t=1}^{\infty} \frac{d_t}{(1+K_E)^t}.$$

The only difference between the two expressions is that the first displays the model in terms of the *total* market value of the equity, whereas the second displays the model in terms of the market value *per share*.

If we assume that the future expected dividend flow will remain at a *constant* level for all future time periods (i.e. a level perpetuity), then the model can be simplified into the form we used in the earlier example that explained the relationship between expected return, dividend flow and market price:

$$V_E = \frac{D}{K_E} \text{ or } P_E = \frac{d}{K_E}.$$

Bid and offer prices

There are several additional points to be made in connection with this model. The first concerns the value of P_E (and consequently V_E) that is to be used.

Shares are normally given *two* prices: a bid (selling) price and an offer (buying) price. The former will be greater than the latter, with the difference being known as the 'jobber's turn'.[7] However, we are retaining the assumption of a perfect capital market, and one of the sub-assumptions of this is that there are no transaction costs involved in buying and selling shares. As the jobber's turn is a type of transaction cost, this assumption allows us neatly to side-step the problem and instead assume that there is no difference between the bid and offer price. Therefore we will use what is referred to as the share's 'middle price'. This is usually the price seen quoted in the pages of the financial press.

Cum dividend and ex dividend

The second point to be made concerns the fact that market prices of ordinary shares can sometimes be quoted either 'cum div' (with dividend), or 'ex div' (without dividend). When a dividend is proposed there has to be cut-off point in terms of who has rights to receive the dividend. Say the cut-off point is close of trading on 5 March. If a share is sold before close of trading on that day it is sold 'cum div' which is to say that the person buying the share buys the right to the dividend. If a share is sold after close of trading on 5 March it is sold without the transfer of rights to the dividend, in other words the vendor still gets the dividend. Other things being equal, we would expect the price of the share to fall by the after-tax value of the dividend at the point at which it goes ex div (at close of trading on 5 March in our example)

Suppose a company is generally expected to pay a 10p dividend per share in perpetuity and shareholders require an expected return of 10%. The dividend valuation model can be used to estimate the share's market value: $P_E = 10p/0.10 = 100p$. This is the *ex div* market value of the equity (i.e. it is the market value of the share at that point in the company's year when the *next* 10p dividend is due to be paid in approximately twelve months' time), because the dividend valuation model is based on the arithmetic of an *immediate* annuity, and so it automatically assumes that the first/next dividend payment will occur in twelve months' time.[8]

Assuming that there are no changes in investors' expectations and that all expectations are fulfilled, a share's market price will follow a 'dogs-tooth' pattern over time. Using the example above, the share's market price will rise steadily over the year from the ex div market price of 100p until, just prior to the payment of the next dividend, it will have a price of 110p (100p plus the forthcoming dividend of 10p, ignoring any tax implications). This latter figure is the share's *cum div* price. Once the dividend has gone ex div the market price falls back to the ex div price of 100p and so restarts the slow rise over the year towards the next dividend.

Fig. 16.1 illustrates this highly simplified, account of a share's market price movements over time in a perfect market with unchanging and fulfilled expectations about the future.

Fig. 16.1 *Ex and cum dividend*

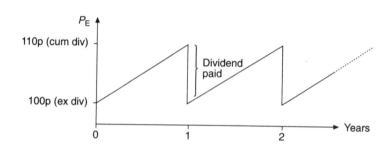

As the dividend valuation model employs ex dividend market prices, so cum dividend prices have to be adjusted accordingly. For example, if a share was expected to yield a constant annual dividend of 22p and it had a current market price of £1.59½ cum div, then its equivalent ex div price would be the cum div price, less the expected forthcoming dividend: 159½p − 22p = 137½p. The share's required return would thus be: 22p/137½p = 0.16. From now on we shall use P_E (and, consequently, V_E) to represent the ex div market price of equity.[9]

The dividend growth model

Up to this point we have made use of a simplified version of the dividend valuation model which assumes a constant, level flow of expected dividends through time. This may well be quite realistic.[10] There are several examples of companies that have been observed to pay (approximately) constant dividends per share over relatively long periods of time. However, it is important to realize that such an assumption is not an assumption of the general dividend valuation model, but of just the simplified version of it, which we have been using as an example.

If it is believed that a company's flow of future dividends is likely to be a more complex pattern than the one we have assumed, then that more complex pattern can be taken account of within the more general model. We are using the simplified model purely for reasons of arithmetic convenience.

An alternative simplifying assumption about the future pattern of a share's dividends is not that they are constant, but that they *grow* at a constant annual rate, in perpetuity. Table 16.1 shows how this 'dividend growth' model can be derived as:[11]

$$P_E = \frac{d_1}{K_E - g} \text{ or as} : P_E = \frac{d_0(1+g)}{K_E - g},$$

where d_0 = current dividend per share (i.e. at t_0)
d_1 = expected dividend per share in twelve months' time (i.e. t_1)
K_E = cost of equity capital
P_E = ex div market price per share
g = constant annual growth rate of dividends

Notice that both versions of the model are equivalent, because $d_1 = d_0(1 + g)$. In other words, next year's dividend equals this year's dividend, times one plus the growth rate.

Table 16.1

$$P_E = \frac{d_1}{(1+K_E)} + \frac{d_1(1+g)}{(1+K_E)^2} + \frac{d_1(1+g)^2}{(1+K_E)^3} \cdots + \frac{d_1(1+g)^{N-1}}{(1+K_E)^N} \tag{1}$$

multiplying each side by $(1 + g)/(1 + K_E)$ gives,

$$\frac{P_E(1+g)}{(1+K_E)} = \frac{d_1(1+g)}{(1+K_E)^2} + \frac{d_1(1+g^2)}{(1+K_E)^3} \cdots + \frac{d_1(1+g)^N}{(1+K_E)^{N+1}} \tag{2}$$

subtracting equation (2) from equation (1) gives,

$$P_E - \frac{P_E(1+g)}{(1+K_E)} = \frac{d_1}{(1+K_E)} - \frac{d_1(1+g)^N}{(1+K_E)^{N+1}} \tag{3}$$

as long as $K_E > g$ then, as N approaches infinity so $d_1(1 + g)^N/(1 + K_E)^{N+1}$ approaches zero and therefore,

$$P_E - \frac{P_E(1+g)}{(1+K_E)} = \frac{d_1}{(1+K_E)} \tag{4}$$

multiplying equation (4) by $(1 + K_E)$ gives,

$$P_E(1 + K_E) - P_E(1 + g) = d_1 \tag{5}$$

$$P_E(K_E - g) = d_1$$

$$\therefore P_E = \frac{d_1}{K_F - g} \tag{6}$$

Just as the constant dividend model can be rearranged to give the cost of equity capital:

$$K_E = \frac{d}{P_E},$$

so too can the dividend growth model:

$$K_E = \frac{d_1}{P_E} + g \text{ or } K_E = \frac{d_0(1+g)}{P_E} + g.$$

Therefore if a company's equity has an ex dividend market price per share of 70p and a constant expected annual dividend growth rate of 5%, and a dividend of 10p has just been paid, the cost of equity capital or expected return on equity would be:

$$K_E = \frac{10p(1+0.05)}{70p} + 0.05 = \frac{10.5p}{70p} + 0.05 = 0.20 \text{ or } 20\%.$$

The dividend growth rate

There are two main approaches to estimating g – the constant expected dividend growth rate – in practice. One is to take the average *past* rate of growth of dividends and assume that this rate will continue unchanged in the future. If need be, this rate can be adjusted to take account of any additional information that leads to the belief that the past growth rate will not be approximately reflected in the future growth rate.

As an example, suppose the past patterns of dividends per share is given by:

Year	Dividends per share (p)
t_{-4}	8.0
t_{-3}	9.0
t_{-2}	9.5
t_{-1}	10.5
t_0	12.0

The dividends per share have grown over a *four*-year period (i.e. five items of data produce four years of growth), from 8p to 12p. This represents an average annual rate of growth (g) of:

$$8p(1+g)^4 = 12p$$

$$1+g = \left(\frac{12p}{8p}\right)^{\frac{1}{4}} = 1.1067$$

$$g = 1.1067 - 1 = 0.1067 \text{ or } 10\tfrac{2}{3}\%$$

The other approach, originally put forward by the American economist Myron Gordon, examines the basis of dividend growth and attempts to derive a future growth rate rather than just to extrapolate a past growth rate.

Gordon started from the idea that a company cannot pay out a growing level of dividends each year without a growing level of profitability/earnings. Nor can a company be expected to generate a growing level of annual earnings without a growing investment in the company's fixed asset base.

Therefore, on the basis of a number of limiting assumptions which are listed below, Gordon argued that if the company retained a constant proportion of earnings each year – b – and reinvested them, (the growing investment base) to earn an annual rate of return of r (the growing level of earnings), then the company would be able to sustain an annual dividend growth rate – g – equal to the product of r and b.

Table 16.2

$$g = rb$$

Assuming a constant proportion (b) of each year's earnings (E_t) are reinvested to earn a constant annual rate of return (r), then the annual earnings pattern is:

$$
\begin{aligned}
E_1 \\
E_2 &= E_1 + rbE_1 = E_1(1 + rb) \\
E_3 &= E_2 + rbE_2 = E_1(1 + rb) + rbE_1(1 + rb) \\
&= E_1(1 + rb)(1 + rb) \\
&= E_1(1 + rb)^2 \\
&\;\;\vdots \\
E_N \quad &= E_1(1 + rb)^{N-1}
\end{aligned}
$$

The annual dividend pattern is therefore:

$$
\begin{aligned}
D_1 &= (1 - b)E_1 \\
D_2 &= (1 - b)E_2 = (1 - b)E_1(1 + rb) \\
D_3 &= (1 - b)E_3 = (1 - b)E_1(1 + rb)^2 \\
&\;\;\vdots \\
D_N &= (1 - b)E_N = (1 - b)E_1(1 + rb)^{N-1}
\end{aligned}
$$

Therefore each year the annual dividends grow by an amount equal to $(1 + rb)$ times the previous year's dividends: an annual rate of dividend growth of rb. In practice, given the validity of the assumptions, b and r would be estimated as follows:

$$b = \frac{\text{Earnings} - \text{Dividends}}{\text{Earnings}}$$

$$r = \frac{\text{Earnings}}{\text{Book value of capital employed}}$$

and the dividend growth model (which is often known as the Gordon growth model in this form) becomes:

$$P_E = \frac{d_0(1 + rb)}{K_E - rb}.$$

The derivation of this approach to estimating the dividend growth rate – g – is given in Table 16.2. The assumptions which underlie it are as follows:

1. an all-equity company;
2. retained profits (earnings) are the only source of additional investment capital;
3. a constant proportion of net profits is retained each year for reinvestment;
4. projects financed through retained profits produce a constant annual return.

Notice that this particular version of the dividend valuation model is only applicable to companies which have an all-equity capital structure, because if debt capital is involved (a case examined in the next section), then it causes problems in keeping r and b, and hence g, constant. Obviously, Gordon's variant of the dividend growth model is very naive, but it may well be a self-fulfilling predictor of share market values if investors generally believe that g can be estimated as rb and so partly base their market actions on such calculations.

A changing dividend growth rate

We can modify the model to allow for changing growth rates (although it has to be said that it would be unusual to know that growth rates would change in three, five or however many years' time). Suppose we were given the following information about the ABC Company. The company has just paid an annual dividend of 5p per share. Dividends per share are expected to grow at 10% per year for the next three years, and then will only grow by 5% per year thereafter. Shares in other companies with a similar level of systematic risk to ABC yield a 15% return on equity. We can adopt the dividend growth model, which assumes a *single*, constant rate of dividend growth to handle this type of situation where there are *two* rates of dividend growth. Example 2 takes this information to estimate the current, ex div value of ABC shares.

Example 2

The ABC Company

$d_0 = 5p$

The dividend per share will grow at 10% per year until Year 3. Thereafter it will grow at 5% per year. A discount rate of 15% is thought to reflect the systematic risk involved.

The current value of ABC shares will equal the sum of the future expected dividends (to infinity), discounted back to present value:

Year			
0	5p	=	5p
1	$5p (1.10)^1$	=	5.5p
2	$5p (1.10)^2$	=	6.05p
3	$5p (1.10)^3$	=	6.655p
4			
5			
6			From Year 3,
7			dividends now grow
⋮			at 5% per year.

Notice that the dividend valuation model's assumption of a constant divided growth rate *does* hold true from Year 3 onwards. Therefore the standard model can be adapted to value ABC shares at Year 3:

Standard model

$$P_{E0} = \frac{d_0 \times (1 + g)}{K_E - g}$$

Adapted model

$$P_{E3} = \frac{d_3 \times (1 + g)}{K_E - g}.$$

In terms of the adapted model:

$d_3 = 6.655p$
$g = 0.05$
$K_E = 0.15$

and so: $P_{E3} = \dfrac{6.655 \times (1 + 0.05)}{0.15 - 0.05} = 69.88p.$

Notice what this represents. It is the sum of the future expected dividends from Year 4 onwards, (remember $d_3(1 + g) = d_4$), discounted back to Year 3.

We can now find the current ex div value of ABC shares based on the present value sum of the future dividend flow:

$$
\begin{array}{llll}
\text{Year}^{12} \\
1 & 5.5\text{p} & \times\,(1+0.15)^{-1} & = & 4.78\text{p} \\
2 & 6.05\text{p} & \times\,(1+0.15)^{-2} & = & 4.57\text{p} \\
3 & (6.655\text{p}+69.88\text{p}) & \times\,(1+0.15)^{-3} & = & 50.32\text{p} \\
& \uparrow & P_{EO} & = & \underline{\underline{59.67\text{p}}} \\
\end{array}
$$

Sum of the dividends
from Year 4 onwards,
discounted back to
Year 3

Therefore the current ex dividend value of the ABC shares is approximately 59⅔p.

Chapter 22 discusses the nature of the dividend decision in companies but we should emphasize at this point that the valuation models we have just developed assume that the rate of growth is related to the real performance of the company. The dividends paid out by companies are, to an extent, discretionary and the rate of growth (at least in the short term) might not be linked to real growth in cash flows.

The cost of retained earnings

One of the most important sources of corporate long-term investment capital is retained earnings, i.e. that part of net cash flow generated by a company's past investment projects which, at the time it arises, is retained within the firm rather than being distributed to shareholders as part of the dividend flow. Because retained earnings arise from sources internal to the company, rather than externally (such as a new equity issue), there is a temptation to believe that this source of capital is somehow 'costless'.

In fact, both from a legal and an economic standpoint, retained earnings belong to the ordinary shareholders of a company and so the 'cost' of retained earnings, or the minimum expected return that their use in investment projects should generate, is *exactly the same* as the expected return required by shareholders on new equity: the cost of equity capital. Retained earnings form part of the equity capital of a company and their cost is therefore a reflection of this fact.

This has already been implicitly taken into account in that the *market* value of equity was used in the specification of K_E, and the market value reflects *both* the nominal value of a company's equity capital *and* the value of the retained earnings. (In practice retained earnings are a slightly cheaper source of capital than a new issue of equity because of the issue costs incurred with the latter, but this rather minor point will be dealt with in Chapter 21.)

CAPM and the cost of equity capital

We have now looked at how we can estimate the cost of equity capital using the dividend valuation model (DVM). However, if we pick up on a point made right at the start of this chapter, we said that the *cost* of equity capital is really the *return* on equity capital. Whether it is called a 'cost' or a 'return' depends upon whose point of view we are taking.

From management's viewpoint, it is a *cost* of capital. In fact, it represents an *opportunity* cost of capital: the minimum return that they must seek to earn when investing shareholders' funds. However, from the investors' viewpoint, it represents the rate of *return* they can expect to receive if they were to invest in the company's shares. If we think of the *cost* of equity capital as the *return* on equity, we have already seen in Chapter 12 how this may be identified – by using the CAPM.

This means that a company's cost of equity capital can be estimated in *two* different ways. Either the dividend valuation model can be used to find K_E – as we have seen – or the CAPM can be used to estimate $E(r_{SHARES})$. Essentially K_E and $E(r_{SHARES})$ can be seen as two different sets of notation representing the same thing: the cost or return on equity capital.

Example 4 illustrates the use of both models in this way.

Example 3

Portimao plc is a long-established, stock exchange quoted, ship repairing company. Its current balance sheet, in summarized form, is as follows:

	(£m)
Fixed assets (net)	40
Net current assets	25
Total assets	65
Financed by:	
Share capital	35
Reserves	30
Total liabilities	65

The company's shares currently stand at 130p cum div on the stock market. In the current year the company produced earnings after tax of £10 million from which the stock market is expecting a total net dividend pay-out of £6 million or 12p net per share.

The dividend per share record of the company, over the last six years, is as follows:

Year	Div./share (pence)
t_{-5}	9.0
t_{-4}	9.5
t_{-3}	10.0
t_{-2}	10.5
t_{-1}	11.0
(expected) t_0	12.0

The current return on government stock is 10%, the market return is around 18% and Portimao plc has an equity beta of 0.90.

The company wishes to estimate its cost of equity capital. Given the available information, this can be found both from using the capital asset pricing model *and* from using the dividend valuation model:

USING THE CAPM:

$$E(r_{Portimao}) = 10\% + (18\% - 10\%) \times 0.90 = 17.2\%.$$

USING THE DIVIDEND VALUATION MODEL:
From the information on the historical dividend record, it would appear that the dividend growth version of the model is most appropriate. There are two possible approaches to estimating the *future* dividend growth rate:

(a)   On the basis of the past dividend growth rate.
(b)   On the basis of the Gordon model: *rb*.

(a)   Past dividend growth rate:

$$9p(1 + g)^5 = 12p$$
$$(1 + g)^5 = 12 \div 9$$
$$1 + g = (1\tfrac{1}{3})^{1/5}$$
$$g = (1\tfrac{1}{3})^{1/5} - 1 = 0.059 \text{ or } 5.9\%$$

(b)   Gordon rb:

$$b = \frac{£10m - £6m}{£10m} = 0.40$$

$$r = \frac{£10m}{£65m} = 0.154$$

$$g = 0.40 \times 0.154 = 0.062 \text{ or } 6.2\%$$

As both give an estimate of the dividend growth rate of *approximately* 6%, that figure will be used in the dividend valuation model:

$$d_0 = 12p$$
$$P_E = 130p - 12p = 118p$$
$$g = 0.06$$
$$K_E = \frac{12(1 + 0.06)}{118} + 0.06 = 0.168 \text{ or } 16.8\%$$

Therefore given the estimates of the two share valuation models of 17.2% and 16.8%, Portimao plc should use 17% as its estimated cost of equity capital.

CAPM versus the DVM

Given, as we have seen in Example 4, that there are two ways in which we can estimate the cost of equity capital, does it matter which approach we use? Putting this question more directly: will the dividend valuation model (DVM) provide the same estimate as the CAPM? The answer is that, in the real world, they probably will *not* do so.

There are four main reasons for this conclusion. The first is that the two models are significantly different, in that the CAPM is a *normative* model and the DVM is a *positive* model. What is meant by a normative model is that CAPM gives the return that *should be* expected from the shares given their relative systematic risk. In contrast, the DVM as a positive model indicates what *is* the return on the share, given its current market price and dividend, and its expected dividend growth rate. Therefore the two models may give significantly different estimates of K_E because 'what should be' is not always 'what actually is'.

For example, suppose that CAPM estimates that the expected return on the shares should be 20%. Sometimes it will be more than 20%, sometimes less; but *on average* it should be 20%. Therefore when, at a particular moment in time, we use the DVM to calculate the cost of equity capital, the shares may not be priced at that time to give the average rate of return that CAPM suggests we should expect.

A second reason why the two models may not provide similar estimates of the cost of equity capital is that the CAPM is a *single* time period model; while the DVM is a *multi* time period model.

The CAPM is a single time period model in that – as we saw – the rate of return is calculated over just a single time period. (See, for example, Chapter 10 and the Introduction to Portfolio Theory.) On the other hand, the DVM is very much a multi time period model, with the share price being the sum of the *future* expected dividend, to infinity. The CAPM therefore provides just a *single* time period rate of return, while the DVM provides an average *multi* time period rate of return. The one will not always be the same as the other.

A third reason for possible differences between the two models is that the CAPM (as was noted in the brief discussion of the Arbitrage Pricing Model in Chapter 12) is a single-*factor* model. As such, CAPM may not be capturing *all* the determinants of return and so the model may be 'incomplete'. For example, there is some evidence to suggest that company size plays a part in determining return, with small companies apparently providing a slightly greater return than larger companies of the same beta value. Incidentally, the problem of whether or not the model is 'complete' is only one that affects normative models. This is never a problem of positive models. The DVM is not saying what actually determines K_E. All it is saying is that given P_E, d_0 and g, then it follows that the return on the share is K_E.

The final reason for the two models not giving the same estimate of the cost of equity capital concerns inaccuracies in the input data (of the garbage in, garbage out variety). The DVM requires three items of data, as was noted in the preceding paragraph, and there are potential problems with each of them.

We have discussed the fact that we input into the model the ex dividend share price. The problem here is that share prices are quoted ex div for approximately five to six weeks; if, during this time period, the share price has been volatile, then we are faced with the problem of deciding on the best representative value of the ex div share price.

Finally, the third data input problem is the most serious. This concerns the estimation of the future rate of growth of dividends – g. We have seen two possible ways of estimating g; one from the past rate of growth of dividends, and one on the basis of rb. *Neither* method is satisfactory. Trying to estimate the future on the basis of the past is never a good forecasting technique unless there are positive reasons to believe that the past will be replicated in the future. No such justification exists here. On the other hand, we have already commented upon the fact that the estimation of g using rb relies on assumptions which are wholly unrealistic.

It is not only the DVM which suffers from problems of accurate data input; so too does the CAPM. Like the DVM, the CAPM requires three items of data: r_F, $E(r_M) - r_F$ and b.

Two problems arise with the risk-free rate of return, r_F. The first is that we use the return on Treasury bills as the measure of r_F, but this return is only risk-free/certain in terms of its *money* return. What is still uncertain is the *purchasing power* of that money return, because the future rate of inflation is unknown.

For example, suppose the annual rate of return on Treasury bills is 8%. All this means is that if you invest £100 now in Treasury bills, you are *certain* to receive back £108 in twelve months' time. What is *uncertain* is the purchasing power of that £108 in twelve months' time, because we don't know what the rate of price inflation over the next twelve months will be. What is needed is a *real* risk-free return – that is a risk-free return in terms of purchasing power; however, such a number cannot be satisfactorily identified.

The second problem with r_F concerns taxation. The CAPM, as we know, is developed within a framework of no tax. But if we are going to use it in the real world, allowance must be made for tax. What is required here is the value of the risk-free return after payment of *personal* tax. The problem is to identify what personal tax rate to use because, potentially, investors could have a range of personal tax rates from being tax exempt, up to being a higher-rate taxpayer.

The second data problem concerns the average market risk premium: $E(r_M) - r_F$. Once again, what we require is the after-tax risk premium, but we have difficulty in identifying the correct tax rates to use. The other problem is that this average risk premium is extremely volatile. In recent years, it has been as great as 13% and as low as 4%. Indeed, it is so volatile that researchers are usually forced to use a long-run (fifty years) average of this figure in order to get a reasonably stable estimate. Having done this, it is then somewhat uncomfortable to have to assume that over the *next* time period the market risk premium will be the same as this very long-run average figure.

The final piece of data that is required is beta. The problem here lies in how beta values are estimated in the real world. We saw that normally betas are estimated using regression analysis. What we require in order to use CAPM is a *forward-looking* beta, but we estimate this by looking *backwards* at the *past* relationship between the return on the shares and the return on the market portfolio.

As such, there would be no problem with this as long as we could rely on beta values remaining fairly stable over time. This prompts the question: do beta values remain stable over time? The answer depends – to some extent – on how you wish to interpret the evidence. Beta values certainly do move over time, as companies change their exposure to systematic risk. But, on the other hand, they tend to move relatively slowly. However, it remains a far from ideal situation.

Therefore, on the basis of all these reasons, we would not necessarily expect the dividend valuation model and the capital asset pricing model to produce the same estimates of the cost of equity capital. However, of the two, we can probably conclude that the CAPM is *likely* to provide the more reliable figure. The reason for reaching this conclusion is the fact that the dividend valuation model – in its practical application – really does have an almost insurmountable problem with regard to identifying a *reliable* estimate of the future rate of growth of dividends.

The cost of debt capital

We came across the idea of the cost of debt capital in Chapter 15, when discussing the term structure of interest rates, although we referred to it then as the 'redemption yield'. In our foregoing discussion on the cost of equity capital, we said that the cost of equity and the return on equity were essentially the same thing. The former term was used when looking at things from management's viewpoint and the latter term was used when looking at things from the shareholder's viewpoint. In a similar way, the term 'redemption yield' looks at the calculation from the investor's or lender's viewpoint, while the 'cost of debt capital' takes the management's viewpoint.

However, as we shall see, the redemption yield on bonds and the cost of debt capital are *not* the same in one important respect. When looking at the cost of debt capital from the company's point of view, we need to take into account the fact that companies normally receive *tax relief* on debt interest. However we will come to this point later. Let us now start to look at the cost of debt capital from the beginning.

Debt versus equity capital

So far we have examined the cost of equity capital. We now turn our attention to the other[13] major source of finance: loan finance. This comes in a great variety of forms, and so we will assign it the generic term of 'debt capital'.

Debt capital can be defined as a *loan* made to a company which is normally repaid at some future date. Debt capital differs from ordinary share capital in two fundamental ways.

First, subscribers to debt capital do not become part-owners of the company but are merely creditors, because they are only lending money to the company for a fixed period.[14] On the elapse of this period, the loan is repaid: the debt capital is said to be redeemed. In contrast, equity capital represents a permanent loan which is never repaid except in very special circumstances (such as company liquidation).

Second, the holders or suppliers of debt capital usually receive a contractually *fixed* annual percentage return on their loan, which is specified when the debt capital is issued and which is known as the *coupon rate*. Again, this contrasts with the situation of the suppliers of equity capital whose annual return – the dividend – is *not* contractually fixed and the exact level is set at the discretion of the directors.

In addition to these two fundamental differences between debt and equity capital, debt capital is ranked ahead of equity for payment of the annual return. In other words, legally, interest on debt capital *must* be paid in full before any dividend may be paid to the suppliers of equity. Thus, if there is any shortfall in company earnings in any year, it is the ordinary shareholders who are more likely to suffer than the debt holders.

Debt capital therefore represents a loan with a contractually fixed rate of return, a contractually fixed time of repayment and preferential payment treatment over equity capital. In an uncertain world, all three factors combine to make the debt capital of any given company a substantially *less risky* investment for a supplier of capital than that company's ordinary share capital.

As debt can be viewed as less risky than ordinary shares, it follows that the required expected return on a company's debt[15] will be *less than* that required on its equity capital. In a *certain* world, debt and equity capital would logically require the same return from any given company; but in an uncertain world the required returns differ.

The interest valuation model

We know that sometimes shares are *quoted* (i.e. they are traded on a stock market), and sometimes they are *unquoted*. The point was made in the introductory chapter that, for convenience, we shall normally be dealing with a stock exchange quoted company in our development of the theory of financial management.

Debt capital is similar to equity capital in that some debt capital is quoted whilst other debt capital (in fact, the majority) is unquoted. Again, for convenience we shall deal initially with *quoted* debt capital, although we will return later to the problem with *unquoted* debt. For clarity, we will refer to quoted debt capital as 'bonds'.

In order to examine the cost of debt capital we shall use the principles upon which the dividend valuation model was based in order to develop a bond valuation model. Therefore we shall postulate that the market value of a bond is determined by the summation of the future cash flows it will produce, discounted to present value. These future cash flows usually consist of the expected future interest flow and (if they are redeemable bonds) their redemption value.

'Plain vanilla' bonds

In the UK, bonds are normally issued in units of £100. Thus each bond represents £100 of loan or debt capital and the £100 is termed the bond's 'nominal' or 'par' value.

Attached to each unit are details of the interest rate that will be paid by the borrower, expressed as a percentage of the nominal value. This interest rate is referred to as the 'nominal' interest rate or 'coupon' rate.[16] In addition, the bond will contain details of when it is to be repaid, (its redemption date) and the value at which it will be redeemed (normally, its par value).

A company might issue £25 million worth of (£100) bonds with a coupon rate of 8% and redemption due in five years' time at par value (i.e. £100 per bond is due to be repaid). This is the standard form of bond and is sometimes known as a 'plain vanilla' bond. There are many variations on this basic type, as we shall see.

Pricing bonds

Bonds, like shares, are traded in supply and demand markets. As a result, the market price of a bond depends upon supply and demand market forces. Essentially, what drives these market forces is the difference between the *current* market interest rate for investments of the same risk level as the bond, and the bond's own *coupon* rate. Thus if a bond has a coupon rate *below* current market interest rates, its market value will be *below* its nominal value of £100, and vice versa. This relationship is demonstrated in Example 4.

Example 4

To see why the foregoing would be so, let us look at an example using – for simplicity – an irredeemable bond, (i.e. a bond which is never due to be repaid), with a coupon rate of 5%. It is therefore expected to produce an annual cash flow of £5 of interest, in perpetuity (i.e. £100 × 0.05 = £5).

Suppose that the current market interest rate (for similar risk investments) is 8%. If the bond's perpetuity stream of interest payments is discounted back to present value at this current interest rate, its present value sum is: £5 ÷ 0.08 = £62.50. This represents the bond's current *market* value.

The bond has a market value of only £62.50, against a nominal value of £100, because that is how much would be needed to be invested today, at the current interest rate of 8%, to produce annual interest of £5: £62.50 × 0.08 = £5.

Using a similar form of analysis, if market interest rates then *fell* to 4%, the value of the bond would *rise* to: £5 ÷ 0.04 = £125. Finally, if market interest rates were the *same* as the bond's coupon rate, then the bond would have a market value equal to its nominal value: £5 ÷ 0.05 = £100.

The opportunity cost of debt capital

It is at this point that an important fact emerges. We are concerned with finding the 'cost' to a company of the various types of capital it might use to finance an investment project, in order to use this cost as a possible discount or cut-off rate in the appraisal process. For such a use we might easily believe that the Bond's *coupon rate*, rather than the current market interest rate (assuming they differ), reflects the cost to the firm of using this source of capital. However, such a belief would be incorrect.

This possible misunderstanding really arises from an incorrect interpretation of the word 'cost'. Cost of capital does not refer to *how much* the capital costs the firm to buy – in other words, the interest rate – but refers to the best available return, at that risk level, available elsewhere that the firm forgoes when it applies the capital to a particular project: the *opportunity* cost of debt capital is the thing that matters.

Therefore, as far as the investment appraisal and the cost of debt capital is concerned, it is the *current* market interest rate that is important; *not* the *coupon* rate. An example can easily show the logic behind this statement.

Suppose a company undertook an issue of bonds some years ago at a coupon rate of 5%. (At the time of issue, 5% would have been the current market interest rate for debt capital of that risk level.) Now the current market interest rate (for a similar risk level) is 8%.

The company has now discovered an investment project which requires an outlay of £1000 and which is expected to produce a net cash flow of £290 per year for four years. It proposes to finance the investment by using part of the proceeds of the bond issue. Therefore it calculates the project's NPV using the bond's *coupon* rate of 5% as the discount rate. This is shown in Table 16.3. As a result, the project has a positive NPV of £28.34 and so the company undertakes the investment.

However, if we recall our analysis of the logic of the NPV decision rule, we can see that such a discount rate is *incorrect*. In discounting a project's cash flows to produce a positive or negative NPV, an implicit comparison is automatically being made between the returns from investing in the project and the returns that could be achieved by investing the project's outlay on the capital market. Hence we use the *market* interest rate as the discount rate.

Therefore, discounting the project by 5% means that an *incorrect* comparison is being carried out: in fact, as an alternative to the project, an interest rate of 8% can be earned for the same level of risk. We can see that when discounting the project at 8% it yields a negative NPV, indicating rejection – a better return could be earned by investing the £1000 on the capital markets.

Table 16.3

Project cash flows

Year	0	1	2	3	4
	−1000	+290	+290	+290	+290

At a 5% discount rate:

$$NPV = -1000 + 290A_{4\neg0.05} = +\pounds28.34$$

At an 8% discount rate:

$$NPV = -1000 + 290A_{4\neg0.08} = -\pounds39.48$$

As the project has a negative NPV at the current market rate of discount, it should not be undertaken. The £1000 required outlay could be better employed deposited on the money market at 8% where it could, for example, produce the following flows:

Year	0	1	2	3	4
	−1000	+301.92	+301.92	+301.92	+301.92

Compare this flow with that expected from the project. (In other words, given an 8% interest rate, £1000 now can produce an annuity of £301.92 a year for four years.)

The cost of irredeemable debt capital

We will now turn to look systematically at how to go about estimating the company's (opportunity) cost of debt capital. To start, we will examine the simplest type of debt capital: irredeemable or undated bonds. These are bonds which are not expected to be repaid and whose interest payments form a perpetuity cash flow.

We will make use of the following notation:

P_B = market price per bond, ex interest;[17]
V_B = total market value of the bonds = P_B × number of bonds issued;
i = annual interest paid per bond;
I = total annual interest = i × number of bonds issued.

The general valuation model for irredeemable bonds is:

$$V_B = \frac{I}{K_D} \text{ or, on a per unit basis, } P_B = \frac{i}{K_D}.$$

Where K_D is the current market rate of interest (for similar risk securities). In other words, K_D is the (opportunity) cost of debt capital. Therefore, the models can be switched around to provide this cost of debt directly:

$$K_D = \frac{I}{V_B} \text{ or, similarly, } K_D = \frac{i}{P_B}.$$

For example, a company has issued irredeemable bonds at a coupon rate of $7\frac{1}{2}$% and each bond currently has a market value of £93.75, ex interest. The company's cost of debt capital can then be estimated as: K_D = £7.50 ÷ £93.75 = 0.08 or 8%. We can conclude from this that, for an investment of the bond's risk level, the current market interest rate is 8%.

Because we are dealing with an uncertain world, just as we talked in terms of K_E being the *expected* return on equity, so we should talk in terms of the *expected* return to bond holders. Although a company's debt is less risky than their ordinary shares, it is not riskless.[18] Sometimes bonds can be a very risky investment, for instance in cases where there is a substantial probability that the issuing company will be unable to meet the future interest and redemption payments (if the bond is redeemable).

In calculating the cost of debt capital by means of the formula $K_D = I/V_B$ (or i/P_B) we are calculating what is called the bond's *yield to maturity*, or *redemption yield*. This is the maximum yield (as opposed to the expected yield) that the bond will produce at its current market price, as it assumes that all future contractual payments attached to the bond will be met by the issuing company.

However, working on the normal basis of viewing companies as going concerns, then K_D, or the yield to maturity, is likely to be a fairly accurate estimate of the cost of debt capital for investment appraisal purposes. If the going concern concept is *not* thought applicable to a particular company, its marginal cost of debt capital should be based on the alternative cash flow which its debt is expected to yield.

The cost of redeemable debt

The cost of redeemable debt is found by estimating the internal rate of return of the bond's cash flow. This can be found by using the linear interpolation method that was used in the earlier discussion about the IRR. Example 5 illustrates the approach.[19]

Example 5

Lagoa plc issued £10 million worth of 5% bonds seven years ago. They are due to be redeemed at par in three years' time. The bonds have a current market price of £101 *per cent* (i.e. per £100 unit), cum interest.

The company's cost of debt capital can be estimated as follows. First, the equivalent ex interest price of the bonds would be: £101 − £5 (i.e. the annual amount of interest payable) = £96. Then, if the company were to issue an identical bond now, its cash flow would be:

Year	0	1	2	3
	+£96	−£5	−£5	−£105

The company would be able to sell the bond for £96 but it would then have to pay out £5 of interest at the end of each of the next three years. In addition, in three years' time, the bond would have to be repaid at its £100 par value.

Using linear interpolation to find the IRR of this cash flow:

At a 5% discount rate:

$$+96 - 5A_{3-0.05} - 100\,(1.05)^{-3} = -4.0 \text{ NPV.}$$

At a 15% discount rate:

$$+96 - 5A_{3-0.15} - 100\,(1.15)^{-3} = +18.83 \text{ NPV.}$$

Therefore K_D, the IRR, can be estimated as:

$$K_D = 5\% + \left[\frac{-4.0}{-4.0 - (+18.83)} \times (15\% - 5\%) \right] = 6.75\%.^{[20]}$$

Furthermore, the total market value, ex interest, of the company's bonds can be calculated as:

$$V_B = £10m \times \frac{£96}{£100} = £10m \times 0.96 = £9.6m.$$

Finally, notice that a very rough approximation to the cost of redeemable debt can be obtained as follows:

$$K_D = \text{coupon rate} + \text{average annual capital gain.}$$

The bonds issued by Lagoa have a 5% coupon. As the current ex interest price is £96 and they are redeemable at £100, then the capital gain is approximately 4%. As this capital gain is made when the bonds are redeemed in three years' time, the average annual capital gain is: $4\% \div 3 = 1\frac{1}{3}\%$. Thus Lagoa's cost of debt capital could be roughly approximated as:

$$= 5\% + 1\frac{1}{3}\% = 6\frac{1}{3}\%.$$

Semi-annual interest payments

In our examples so far, we have assumed the bonds pay their interest annually. However, in practice, semi-annual payments of interest are more usual. For example, suppose a bond had a coupon rate of 10%, with interest paid semi-annually. Each year, £10 of interest in total would be paid, with £5 being paid mid-year and the other £5 being paid at year end. In these more realistic circumstances, calculating the cost of debt capital, is a little more complicated. Example 6 illustrates such a situation.

Example 6

A company has issued 12% bonds with interest due to be paid semi-annually. The bonds have a current market value of £114 ex interest and are due to be repaid at their £100 par value in three years' time. What is their annual cost of debt capital?

Each year £12 of interest is paid in two instalments of £6. Therefore on the basis of half-year time periods, the bond's cash flow is:

Year	0	1 to 6	6
	£114	−£6 per time period	−£100

The IRR of this cash flow can be estimated using linear interpolation, as usual:

At a 4% discount rate:

$$+114 - 6.A_{6-0.04} - 100\,(1.04)^{-6} = +3.52 \text{ NPV.}$$

At a 6% discount rate:

$$+114 - 6.A_{6-0.06} - 100\,(1.06)^{-6} = +14 \text{ NPV.}$$

$$\text{IRR of the cash flow} = 4\% + \left(\frac{352}{3.52 - 14} \times 2\% \right) = 3.33\%.$$

Notice that this IRR relates to a *half-yearly* cash flow. And so it has to be adjusted on to an *annual* basis in order to estimate the annual cost of debt capital:

$$(1 + 0.0333)^2 - 1 = 0.0677 \text{ or } 6.77\%/\text{year.}$$

Discount or zero-coupon bonds

All the examples used so far have been of 'plain vanilla' bonds. In other words, the bonds are issued and redeemed by the company at their nominal value and the company pays a specified rate of interest to the investor.

Although there are, as was mentioned earlier, a *great* number of variations on this standard type of debt capital it is convenient at this stage to look at one important type of bond which is significantly different. This is the discount bond or zero-coupon bond. These differ from plain vanillas in that they are not issued by the company at their nominal value, but at a *discount* on this value. For example, some bonds may be issued at £75 for every £100 of nominal value. Therefore when the company issues one of these bonds with a £100 nominal value, they only receive £75 from the lender.

The other way in which these bonds differ from plain vanillas is that they *don't* pay any interest. The investor obtains a return in the form of a capital gain only, because the bonds are redeemed at their nominal value. Example 7 illustrates the circumstances in which a company might issue discount or zero-coupon bonds, and the procedure that we follow to calculate their cost of debt capital.

Example 7

Silves plc wishes to raise a three-year loan in order to buy a vacant plot of land on which to build an office block. The cost of the land, together with the construction costs, will amount to £150 million. Therefore the company plan to borrow this amount and repay the loan in three years' time, when they hope to sell the building for £250 million. Because this investment will not generate any cash inflow until the building is sold, the company decide not to issue plain vanilla bonds, which would require interest to be paid each year (for which the company would have no cash inflow available) but instead issue discount/zero coupon bonds.

Suppose the company decide to issue zero coupon bonds with a total *nominal* value of £200 million. These will be issued at a 25% discount on their nominal value, they will carry a zero coupon rate and will be redeemed at their nominal value in three years' time. What would be the cost of this debt capital?

First of all notice that the issue will raise the £150 million required: £200m $(1 - 0.25) = £150$m. This means that each bond with a nominal value of £100 (but paying no interest) will be issued in return for a loan of £75 from investors.

As usual, the cost of debt capital is the internal rate of return of the bond's cash flow:

Year	0	3
Cash flow	+75	−£100

NPV at 6% = −£8.96

NPV at 12% = +£3.82

Using linear interpolation:

$$IRR = 6\% + \left(\frac{-8.96}{-8.96 - 3.82} \times (12\% - 6\%) \right) = 10.2\%.$$

The cost of debt capital on these discount bonds is 10.2%.

Low-coupon bonds

One obvious variation are bonds which lie midway between the two 'extremes' of plain vanilla bonds and discount/zero-coupon bonds. Such bonds *do* pay a rate of interest, but at a *lower* level than a plain vanilla would pay. In order to compensate investors for this lower rate of interest, they are also issued at a discount to their nominal value – but at a smaller discount than zero-coupon bonds would be issued at. Such bonds are usually termed low-coupon bonds.

A plain vanilla bond is usually issued by a company at its £100 nominal value, with a coupon rate that reflects the current market interest rate at the time of issue. Subsequent changes in the market interest rate then cause the market value of the plain vanilla bond to rise above or fall below its nominal value of £100. An investor who buys a plain vanilla bond at its time of issue (and so pays £100 for it) and who then holds it until maturity when the £100 is repaid, receives an annual rate of return equal to the coupon rate. Thus the return received is purely in terms of the interest payments.

On the other hand, as we have just seen in Example 7, an investor in a discount bond receives no interest, but derives a return in the form of a capital gain.

Low-coupon bonds fall somewhere between these two extremes where an investor who buys a bond at the point of issue will get part of their return in the form of interest payments and part of their return in the form of a capital gain on redemption. Example 8 illustrates this case.

Example 8

A company wishes to raise a £100 million five-year loan at a coupon rate of 3%. The current annual rate of return on similar risk securities is 8%. Show that the company will therefore have to sell the bonds at a 20% discount on their nominal value in order to give investors (approximately) their required rate of return.

At a 20% discount, each £100 nominal bond will be issued at £80. (And so the company will have to issue bonds with a total nominal value of £100m × 100/80 = £125m in order to raise the £100 million required.) Therefore the yield to maturity can be found from the IRR of the bond's cash flow:

Year	0	1 to 5	5
	+ £80	− £3	−£100

NPV at 6%   =   − £7.37

NPV at 10%   =   + £6.54

Using linear interpolation:

$$IRR = 6\% + \left(\frac{-7.37}{-7.37 - 6.54} \times (10\% - 6\%) \right) = 8.1\%.$$

Thus when priced at £80 and with a 3% coupon rate, these bonds will give a rate of return or redemption yield of approximately 8.1%, which is similar to the yield on securities with the same level of risk.

The impact of corporation tax

The company requires knowledge of its cost of debt capital for investment appraisal purposes and so, from this viewpoint, the expected return which the *supplier* of debt capital receives – the redemption yield – is not the main focus of attention. The point of importance is the cash flow which the *company* must pay out in order to service the debt.

In this respect, taxation has an important effect when the tax regime (as most tax regimes, including the UK's, usually do) allows companies to offset debt interest (but not redemption payments) against their corporation tax liability. Therefore, as far as company investment appraisal is concerned, it is the *after* corporation tax receipt cost of debt capital which is important.

So far, we have ignored taxation in the calculation of K_D, and so we have, in effect, been calculating a before-tax cost of debt capital: $K_{D_{BT}}$. If T represents the current rate of corporation tax – and assuming it is expected to remain a constant over the life of the debt – then the after-tax cost of irredeemable bonds can be found as:

$$K_{D_{AT}} = \frac{i(1 - T)}{P_B} \text{ or } K_{D_{AT}} = K_{D_{BT}}(1 - T).$$

For redeemable bonds, their after-tax cost can be found by solving the internal rate of return of the following cash flow:

$$P_B - i(1 - T)A_{N \neg K_{D_{AT}}} - R(1 + K_D)^{-n} = 0.$$

where n equals the number of years to redemption and R represents the redemption value of the bonds. Example 9 illustrates the calculations required.

Example 9

Cinta plc issued £25 million of 15% irredeemable bonds some years ago. Their current market price is £116.50 ex interest. Corporation tax is charged at 35%. Therefore the company's after-tax cost of debt capital is:

$$K_{D_{AT}} = \frac{£15(1 - 0.35)}{£116.50} = 0.084 \text{ or } 8.4\%.$$

The total market value of the bonds is:

$$V_B = £25m \times 1.1650 = £29.125m.$$

Luvas plc has issued £5 million of 13% bonds. They are due to be redeemed in four years' time at par. Their current market value is £104 ex interest. Corporation tax is charged at 35%. The company's current cost of debt capital is found by solving the IRR of the following cash flow:

$$+£104 - £13(1 - 0.35)A_{4 \neg K_{D_{AT}}} - £100(1 + K_{D_{AT}})^{-4} = 0 \text{ NPV.}$$

At 5%, the cash flow's NPV is: −8.23 NPV

At 15%, the cash flow's NPV is: +43.21 NPV

Using linear interpolation, the after-tax cost of debt capital can be estimated as:

$$K_{D_{AT}} = 5\% + \left(\frac{-8.23}{-8.23 - 43.21} \times (15\% - 5\%) \right) = 6.6\%.$$

And the total market value of the bonds would be:

$$V_B = £5m \times 1.04 = £5.2m.$$

Notice that, again, the after-tax cost of debt could be *very* roughly approximated as:

Coupon rate $(1 - T)$ + Average annual capital gain

So: Coupon rate $(1 - T) = 13\% (1 - 0.35) = 8.45\%$
and: Average annual capital *loss* = −4% ÷ 4 = −1%

Therefore $K_{D_{AT}} = 7.45\%$.

This adjustment to take account of tax *must* be made, as the following example shows. If a company issues bonds with a 10% coupon rate and pays corporation tax at 35%, then the company does not *actually* pay £10 interest per bond per year (although the bond holder actually receives £10 of interest per year). As interest is allowable against corporation tax, the company only pays £10(1 − 0.35) = £6.50. The balance of interest of £3.50 can be viewed as being paid by the tax authorities. This obviously causes the *effective* cost of debt (to the company) to fall substantially below the before-tax rate.

There are two further points worth noting. First, the after-tax K_D is only applicable on the assumption that a company has sufficient tax liability to take advantage of tax relief on debt interest. Second, the $K_{D_{AT}}$ computations in the examples are an approximation because corporation tax (and hence the reduction in corporation tax which comes about through offsetting debt interest) is paid approximately 12 months in arrears. This fact has not been taken into account in the discounting calculations. The calculation *could* be adjusted to allow for this, but such exactness is probably not really justified, especially as K_D is, in itself, only an estimate of the *expected* K_D.

Unquoted debt

So far, we have only considered debt capital which has been quoted on a stock exchange (referred to as a *public* issue of debt) and so has a market price. However, most debt capital – such as bank loans – is unquoted (or termed a *private* issue). It is possible to estimate the cost of unquoted debt, but only if the cost of similar-risk quoted debt is known. We cannot obtain the cost of unquoted debt directly because – as we have seen in the previous examples – in order to find a cost of debt we need a *market* value. However, if we have some similar-risk quoted debt, its cost can be used as an estimate of the unquoted debt's cost, on the basis that similar risk securities should yield the same return. Example 10 illustrates this situation.

Example 10

Lagost plc has issued £12 million of 8% bonds which are redeemable at par in three years' time. Each bond currently has a market price of £92 ex interest. In addition the company has a £6 million three-year bank loan at 14% interest.

As both the quoted and unquoted debt (i.e. the bank loan) rank equally for payment purposes, they can be assumed to be of similar risk. The corporation tax rate is 33%.

The after-tax cost of the quoted debt capital (i.e. the bonds) is given by the internal rate of return of its cash flow:

Year	0	1 to 3	3
	+£92	−£8 (1 − 0.33)	−£100

NPV at 4% = −£11.77

NPV at 6% = −£6.29

Interpolating:

$$IRR = 4\% + \left(\frac{-11.77}{-11.77 - (-6.29)} \times (6\% - 4\%) \right) = 8.29\%.$$

Therefore the after-tax cost of debt capital of the company's quoted bonds is: $K_{DQ} = 8.29\%$ and their total market value is: $V_{BQ} = £12m \times 0.92 = £11.04m$.

As the unquoted bank loan is thought to be of similar risk, then:

$$K_{DVQ} = K_{DQ} = 8.29\%.$$

Floating debt rate

Up to this point, all our examples have involved debt capital which paid a *fixed* rate of interest. However, a great deal of debt capital raised by companies pays a rate of interest which is not fixed, but which varies with movements in current market interest rates.

This type of debt capital is known as floating or variable rate debt. Typically, the debt will pay interest at a fixed 'margin' (or 'spread') over a *floating benchmark* interest rate.

The term 'benchmark interest rate' is used to describe a widely recognized rate of interest which varies over time in response to supply and demand market pressures and other macro-economic forces. Two well-known benchmark interest rates are Bank Base Rate and LIBOR (the London InterBank Offered Rate). Bank Base Rate is the minimum rate of interest at which banks will lend money to their customers; LIBOR represents the interest rate at which banks lend money to each other.

If a company raises a loan at 'LIBOR + 3%', the company will be paying a rate of interest on its loan equal to whatever rate LIBOR is, *plus* an extra 3%. (This 3% is the fixed margin or spread.) And so, if LIBOR is 6%, the company pays 9% interest on its loan; if LIBOR falls to 5%, the company's loan interest rate will fall to 8%.

How often a company's loan interest rate is altered in this way is known as the 'rollover' period. LIBOR is *continually* changing (usually only by very small amounts), and it would cause obvious administrative problems if a company's loan interest rate moved continually as well. Therefore, to avoid this problem, loans with floating rates of interest have their interest rate reset periodically.

In practice, one of the most common rollover periods is three months. If we take our example of a loan at LIBOR + 3% with a three-month rollover, this means that every three months the interest rate that the company will pay on its loan over the following three months is reset.

Suppose the company has interest rollover dates of 1 January, 1 April, 1 July and 1 October each year. If on 1 January LIBOR is 6%, the company pays 9% (6% + 3%) interest on its loan over the next three months. If by 1 April LIBOR has now risen to 7.5%, the company will then pay 10.5% interest on its loan over the next three-month time period, and so on.

However, notice that these interest rates in this example would be *annual* rates of interest. Thus the *actual* rate of interest paid over the three months 1 January–1 April would have been: $9\% \times 3/12 = 2.25\%$. Similarly, in the next three-month period, they would pay $10.5\% \times 3/12 = 2.625\%$.

As far as calculating the after-tax cost of debt capital is concerned, floating rate debt causes very little problem. In such circumstances K_D is simply the current interest rate that is payable on the debt and the total *market* value of the debt will always be equal to its total *nominal* value. This is because, as we have already noted, what causes the market price of fixed interest debt to move is changes in the difference between the fixed coupon rate on the debt and the current market interest rate. With floating rate debt this situation does not occur because the interest rate paid moves in line with market interest rates. Hence the market value and the nominal value of floating rate debt will always be the same. Example 11 illustrates the situation with the most common type of floating rate debt, a bank loan.

Example 11

Podia plc has a £10 million bank loan, repayable in seven years' time. The interest rate payable is 3% over bank base rate. The company pays corporation tax at 35%. Bank base rate is currently 11%. It wishes to calculate its after-tax cost of the bank loan. This can be done as follows:

The company currently pays an interest rate of: 11% + 3% = 14%.

Therefore: $K_{D_{AT}} = 14\% (1 - 0.35) = 9.1\%$.

The 'market value' of the bank loan is equal to its nominal value of £10 million.

Implicit and explicit costs of debt capital

It is important to remember that financial decisions are principally made on behalf of and for the benefit of ordinary shareholders, the legal owners of a company. As far as debt holders are concerned, management's only wish is to fulfil their contractual obligations to them in terms of interest and redemption payments.

In this respect, we have only considered here the *explicit* cost of debt capital, but there is also an *implicit* cost which company managements must take into account. This implicit cost of debt arises from risk considerations that directly affect the ordinary shareholders. We shall examine this aspect in detail later, in Chapter 18 on capital structure, but it is as well to be aware at this stage that debt capital does have a cost which is additional to its explicit cost which is what we have been calculating.

Cost of preference shares

There is a wide variety of types of long-term capital, apart from debt and equity. One of these is preference capital or preference shares. Typically, preference share capital is similar to fixed interest debt, with one very important difference from the viewpoint of the calculation of its cost.

Preference shares are similar to redeemable fixed interest debt capital, in that the holders receive an annual preference 'dividend' which is expressed as a fixed percentage of their nominal value. This annual dividend, unlike normal debt interest, is *not* an allowable expense against corporation tax.

However, other than for this, calculating the cost of preference capital is virtually identical to the calculation of the cost of debt. Example 12 provides an illustration.

Example 12

Sangres plc has £25 million of 4% preference shares in issue, each with a nominal value of £1. They are each currently quoted on the stock exchange at 72p ex div and are due for redemption at par value in five years' time.

The cost of this preference capital can be identified (as with the cost of debt) as the internal rate of return of the security's cash flow:

Year	0	1 to 5	5
	−72p	−4p	−100p

Therefore:

$$\text{NPV at 4\%} \quad = \quad -28p$$

$$\text{NPV at 16\%} \quad = \quad +11.29p$$

Interpolating:

$$IRR = 4\% + \left(\frac{-28}{-28-(+11.29)} \times (16\% - 4\%) \right) = 12.55\%.$$

Therefore our estimate of the cost of the preference capital (K_p) is 12.55%.

We can also calculate the total market value of the preference capital. Its total nominal value is £25 million and as each £1 unit has a market value of 72p, the total market value is:

$$\text{£25m} \times 0.72 = \text{£18m}.$$

Convertible debt

Convertible debt is a really interesting type of long-term capital because it is a 'hybrid' – it is part debt capital and part equity capital. Another way of viewing it would be as *deferred* equity capital.

Typically, convertible debt capital is similar to fixed interest redeemable debt capital, with one important exception. This is that, at the redemption date, the holders have an *option*: they can either have the loan repaid (usually at its nominal/par value), or they can convert the debt's redemption value into the company's shares, at a fixed price per share.

Therefore convertible debt is debt capital with a *call* option attached in respect of the company's shares. It is the presence of this option that makes valuing convertible debt, and calculating its cost, a difficult area.

Some definitions

Let us begin with some definitions. Suppose that a company has issued £50 million worth of convertible bonds paying a fixed rate of interest (coupon) of 5% and which are redeemable at par in four years' time, or convertible into twenty-five ordinary shares. The company's shares are currently priced at 250p each.

The *conversion ratio* is the number of shares into which each unit of debt can be converted. Therefore, in this example, the conversion ratio is 25:100, i.e. each £100 bond can be converted into twenty-five shares. The *conversion price* is effectively the *exercise price of the option*. In this case as each £100 bond can be converted into twenty-five shares, this gives a conversion price or exercise price of: £100 ÷ 25 = £4 per share.

The *conversion premium* is the percentage by which the conversion price exceeds the current share price. Therefore in our example, the conversion premium is:

$$\frac{400p - 250p}{250p} = 0.60 \text{ or } 60\%.$$

Advantages of convertibles

Convertibles can be attractive securities, both from the viewpoint of the company and for the investor. As we saw with low-coupon bonds, investors are willing to accept a lower rate of interest as long as it is compensated with the possibility of a capital gain. With low-coupon bonds, the capital gain element was provided by the company selling the bonds at a discount to their nominal value.

The investor also has the potential to make a capital gain with convertible debt out of the option element. If, at the time of conversion, the market price of the company's shares is *above* the conversion price, the investor will be able to make a capital gain upon exercising the option to convert. Therefore, just as with low-coupon bonds, the investor is willing to accept a lower than normal interest rate on convertible debt because they offer this prospect of a compensating capital gain in the future. Thus the potential saving in interest costs make them attractive securities from the company's viewpoint – and we have discussed in Chapter 13 how desirable options are from an investor's viewpoint.

There is of course a further advantage to convertible debt from a company's point of view. Normal (or 'straight') debt usually has to be repaid at some future point in time, with the consequent negative impact on the company's cash resources. In contrast, with luck, convertible debt will *not* have to be repaid, because investors will convert into shares instead.

The downside to this advantage, of course, is that if investors do convert into shares in the future, then that may lead to a reduction in the company's earnings per share (i.e. diluting the EPS) at that time.

Cost of convertible debt

Let us now turn to the question of the *valuation* of convertible debt and their *cost* of capital. As was stated previously, convertible debt can be viewed as a combination of a plain vanilla bond *plus* a call option in the company's shares. As such, it would appear relatively simple to value each of these components individually and then combine them to find the value of the convertible.

Finding the value of the bond element *is* straightforward: it is simply the sum of the future expected cash flow discounted to present value at a rate which reflects its risk. The real problem lies in the valuation of the option element.

The Black–Scholes valuation model can only be of partial help, for two reasons. One is that the model assumes that the company's shares do not pay out any dividends, when in reality they will do. The other is that convertible debt normally is 'callable' by the company.

What this means can be seen if we return to our earlier example of convertible debt with an option to convert or redeem in four years' time. Usually, the company will give itself the right to *force* investors to convert earlier than four years' time if it wishes. This is what is meant by the term 'callable'.

An investor who buys convertible debt is buying a straight bond plus a call option on the company's share and simultaneously *selling* a call option to the company. The arithmetic of even a simplified example is really too complex for us to investigate within the context of this book. However, what we can do is look at what would be the *minimum* value of a convertible bond. This minimum value must be the *greater* of its value as straight debt and its current conversion value. Example 13 illustrates this situation. It is important to realize that the bond's *actual* value will always be *greater* than this *minimum* value, in much the same way that we saw that the actual value of an option is always greater than its intrinsic value (except on expiry).

Example 13

Lisboa plc has issued some convertible bonds with a coupon rate of 6%. Each bond has a £100 nominal value and is redeemable at par in three years' time or convertible into forty shares. The company's current share price is 210p and similar-risk debt securities are expected to produce a 14% redemption yield. Place a minimum value on these convertible bonds.

The value of the bond as straight debt can be found from the sum of the future interest and redemption cash flow, discounted to present value at 14%:

$$\text{Value of bond: } £6.A_{3-0.14} + £100(1.14)^{-3} = £81.43.$$

The current conversion value of the bond, given its conversion ratio of 40, is:

$$\text{Conversion value: } 40 \times 210p = £84.$$

Therefore the convertible bond's minimum value will be £84.

Finally, we will conclude with a simple example of how we might attempt to identify the after-tax cost of convertible debt. This is shown in Example 14. You will quickly notice that the validity of the calculation rests entirely on the assumption that the firm is able to estimate the worth of the shares at the future redemption/conversion date.

Example 14

Amarra plc has issued £50 million of 6% bonds which are either repayable at par in three years' time, or convertible into shares at 250p each. The bonds are currently priced at £102.97 ex interest.

The company's shares have a market price of 220p ex div, this year's dividend of 10p having just been paid. Dividends are expected to grow in the future at 10% per year. Corporation tax is at 33%.

In order to find the after-tax cost of capital of these convertible bonds, the first thing to do is to determine whether bond holders are likely to redeem or convert their bonds in three years' time. In order to do this we have to estimate what will be the worth of the shares in three years' time.

The company's cost of equity capital can be found from using the dividend growth model:

$$K_E = \frac{10 \times (1 + 0.10)}{220p} + 0.10 = 0.15 \text{ or } 15\%.$$

If dividends are to grow at 10% per year, then the dividend in three years' time will be:

$$10p \times (1 + 0.10)^3 = 13.31p.$$

And so the estimated market price of the shares in three years' time can be found from a further application of the dividend valuation model:

$$P_{E_3} = \frac{13.31p \times (1 + 0.10)}{0.15 - 0.10} = 292.82p.$$

As the conversion price of the shares is 250p and the estimated value of the shares at the time of conversion is 292.82p, it will be worthwhile for bond holders to convert: the share price (292.82p) is expected to be above the call option exercise price (250p).

At a conversion price of 250p, the conversion ratio is:

$$£100 \div 250p = 40,$$

and so the shares are expected to be worth:

$$40 \times 292.82p = £117.13,$$

which, of course, is greater than the bond's redemption value of £100.

Finally, the after-tax cost of the convertible bonds can be estimated from the IRR of the bond's cash flow:

Year	0	1 to 3	3
	+£102.97	−£6(1 − 0.33)	−£117.13

NPV at 4% discount rate: −£12.31

NPV at 16% discount rate: +£18.90

Interpolating:

$$IRR = 4\% + \left(\frac{-12.31}{-12.31 - (+18.90)} \times (16\% - 4\%) \right) = 8.73\%.$$

Therefore the after-tax cost of the company's convertible bonds is estimated to be 8.73%.

Summary

This chapter has examined the costs of equity and debt capital. The main points covered were:

- The dividend valuation model states that the share price is equal to the present value sum of the future expected dividends, discounted to present value.

- The discount rate in such an analysis reflects the current rate of return on similar systematic risk investments. This rate of return is known as the cost of equity capital and represents the opportunity cost, to management, of using shareholders' funds to undertake capital investment projects.

- Normally two, alternative, simplifying assumptions are used about the future flow of dividends represented in the model:

either dividends per share are assumed to remain at a constant level in the future, or they are expected to grow at a constant annual rate.

- Assuming dividend growth, the growth rate can either be estimated on the basis of the past rate of growth of dividends; or by using the Gordon approach. This states that the dividend growth rate – under certain assumptions – is the product of the earnings retention rate and the company's return on capital.

- A company's cost of equity capital can also be estimated using the capital asset pricing model. However, there are a number of significant differences between the two models, which cannot be expected to produce similar estimates.

- In a similar way to shares, debt capital is also valued on the present value sum of the future expected interest and redemption cash flow.

- The discount rate in such an analysis reflects the current rate of return on similar risk investments. As such, it again represents the opportunity cost, to management, of using debt capital to finance projects.

- In other words, if managers wish to maximize shareholder wealth they should not invest debt capital to earn a lower rate of return than could be earned elsewhere in the capital market from a similar risk investment.

- Debt capital is issued by companies in many different forms. It may be issued privately or through a public issue. It may be at a fixed or floating rate of interest. With fixed interest debt, there are again many possible variations from 'plain vanilla' bonds to 'zero-coupon' bonds.

- Finally there is convertible debt which can be seen as a hybrid: part equity and part debt. From a cost of capital point of view, such a type of capital poses particular problems because of the option element that it contains.

Appendix

With the current imputation system in the UK, for the basic rate taxpayer who receives relatively little income in the form of dividends (unearned income) there is *effectively* no tax on dividends (although basic rate tax is *imputed* to have been paid). However, from the company's viewpoint, dividend payments have the effect of bringing forward (by one year under the assumption below) the payment of part of the total corporation tax liability. This advanced corporation tax is calculated as the amount of tax that would have been payable on the dividends paid, if they were taxed at the lower rate of income tax.

As an example, suppose a company has a constant annual taxable profit of 100. Corporation tax is levied at 33%, assumed payable twelve months in arrears. The company propose to pay a net dividend this year of 10, increasing at a compound annual rate of 10%. Income tax is at 20% and there is an imputation system. The current market value of the company's equity is 550 ex div.

Unadjusted to allow for the effects of corporation tax, the dividend growth model yields:

$$K_E = \frac{10(1+0.1)}{550} + 0.10 = 0.12.$$

However, this is only an approximation. Taking account of tax the ACT payable on the net dividend of 10p is: $10p \times \frac{20}{80} = 2.5p$ and K_E is:

$$K_{E_{AT}} = \frac{10(1+0.1)+(0.10\times2.5)}{550} + 0.1 = 0.12045.$$

Hence the management must earn a return on equity slightly over 12% (12.045%) in order to provide the 12% return expected by shareholders.

Calculations are shown in the tables below. As a result of a policy of increasing dividends by 10%, a small proportion of corporation tax is brought forward in time and this also increases at 10% per annum; but in terms of the required expected return, this is raised slightly to allow for this tax effect.

Year	0	1	2	3
Net dividend (10% growth rate)	10	11	12.10	13.31
ACT ($\frac{20}{80}$ of div.)	2.5	2.75	3.03	3.33
Gross dividend	12.5	13.75	15.13	16.64

Year	0	1	2	3
Corporation tax liability	33	33	33	33
− ACT paid in previous year	2.27[a]	2.5	2.75	3.03
Corporation tax payable	30.73	30.50	30.25	29.97
+ ACT payable	2.50	2.75	3.03	3.33
Total CT payable	33.23	33.25	33.28	33.30
Extra CT payable (i.e. > 33)	0.23	0.25	0.28	0.30
Dividend	10.00	11.00	12.10	13.31
Cash outflow from dividends	10.23	11.25	12.38	13.61

[a]This is calculated on the assumption that the dividend at time $t - 1$ was:

$$\frac{100}{110} \times 10 = 9.1 \text{ (approx)}.$$

And so the ACT payable on the dividend of 9.1 is given by: $9.1 \times \frac{20}{80} = 2.27$. It should be noted that ACT is in the process of being phased out.

Notes

1. The exception to this was our discussion as to how our DCF appraisal techniques coped with the problem of capital rationing.

2. Another source is lease finance. This will be explicitly considered at a later stage.

3. Except under very exceptional circumstances, such as liquidation.

4. This is assuming that the rate of discount remains a constant at 12.5% in perpetuity. Alternatively, we could view the 12.5% as the average rate of discount over this time period.

5. Or, if not all, at least a sufficient number to move the market price.

6. It should be pointed out that the dividend valuation model does not, itself, make any distinction between systematic and unsystematic risk. However, from our knowledge of portfolio theory and the CAPM we can infer that the dividend valuation model implies a consideration of systematic rather than total risk.

7. The middleman who makes the market for shares on the London Stock Exchange is called a jobber or market maker. The difference between the bid and offer price represents his profit or 'turn'.

8. For a detailed explanation of immediate annuities, see the earlier appendix on compounding and discounting. Remember that the key characteristic of such annuities is that the first cash flow (i.e. the first dividend) arises in twelve months' time.

9. We have only examined the situation where a single annual dividend is paid. Where, say, dividends are paid twice a year (an interim and a final dividend) there are, in effect, two ex/cum dividend situations. For example, suppose a 5p per share dividend is paid half-yearly on a share with an ex div market value of 100p. We cannot say that $K_E = 10/100 = 0.10$ as this only represents the share's nominal annual return. The effective annual return would be given by:

$$5p \div 100p = 5\%/\text{half-year}$$
$$K_E = (1 + 0.05)^2 - 1 = 0.1025 \text{ or } 10.25\%/\text{year}.$$

10. This assumption could be relaxed so that dividends through time, *on average*, are assumed to be a constant, but to do so can lead to problems, where the discount rate changes over time.

11. Obviously the model can also be presented in terms of total market values: $V_E = D_1/(K_E - g)$.

12. We have left the Year 0 dividend out of the calculation at this stage because we want the current *ex div* share price. The current cum div share price would be: $59\frac{2}{3}p + 5p = 64\frac{2}{3}p$.

13. The reader should remember that in analysing the cost of equity capital we have covered the 'cost' both of directly raised equity capital and the 'cost' of retained earnings.

14. Irredeemable or undated debt capital does exist, where the loan is never repaid (except in liquidation), but is very rare.

15. Just like ordinary shares, loans are not homogeneous in terms of risk. The riskiness of any particular loan depends upon a number of factors including the riskiness of the company raising the loan, the security (if any) attached to the loan and how it ranks for payment with other debt capital issued by the company.

16. The term 'coupon' rate is used because on some bonds there is a strip of perforated coupons. Each year the bond holder detaches one of these coupons and sends it in to the company in order to claim the interest payment date.

17. Debt market values follow a dog's-tooth pattern similar to those of equity market values. Just as we only dealt with ex div equity market values – adjusting a cum div value if necessary to an equivalent ex-dividend basis – so similarly the debt valuation model only deals with ex interest bond values.

18. However, the amount of risk they involve may be very small.

19. It is worthwhile noting that if redeemable bonds have an ex interest market price of £100 and they are redeemable at par value, then their cost of debt capital *does* equal their coupon rate.

20. Notice that when calculating the IRR we obtained a negative NPV at the low discount rate and a positive NPV at the higher discount rate. This is the opposite of our previous experience with project IRRs. This is because the cash flow – an inflow followed by a series of outflows – is the opposite of a normal project's cash flow.

Further reading

1. The two most interesting original articles on the cost of capital are: D. Durand, 'Growth Stocks and the St. Petersburg Paradox', *Journal of Finance*, September 1957, and M.J. Gordon, 'Dividends, Earnings and Stock Prices', *Review of Economics and Statistics*, May 1959.
2. Some more recent contributions of interest are: M.J. Gordon and L.I. Gould, 'The Cost of Equity Capital: a Reconsideration', *Journal of Finance*, June 1978; A. Chen, 'Recent Developments in the Cost of Debt Capital', *Journal of Finance*, June 1978; R.S. Pindyck, 'Risk Inflation and the Stock Market', *American Economic Review*, June 1984.
3. For some practical attempts to measure cost of capital, see: L.J. Gitman and V.A. Mercurio, 'Cost of Capital Techniques Used by Major US Firms', *Financial Management*, Winter 1982; J.J. Siegal, 'The Application of the DCF Methodology for Determining the Cost of Equity Capital', *Financial Management*, Spring 1985; R. Harris, 'Using Analysts' Forecasts to Estimate Shareholders' Required Returns', *Financial Management*, Spring 1986; and D.F. Scott and J.W. Petty, 'Determining the Cost of Common Equity Capital: The Direct Method', *Journal of Business Research*, March 1980.
4. Finally, an interesting companion to Gitman and Mercurio, noted above is: J.A. Frankel, 'The Japanese Cost of Finance: A Survey', *Financial Management*, Winter 1991.

Quickie questions

1. Given the following information, estimate the company's cost of equity capital:

		Div/share record		
P_E	=	£1.47 cum div	t_{-3}	$11\frac{1}{4}p$
d_0	=	13p net	t_{-2}	12p
			t_{-1}	$12\frac{1}{2}p$
			t_0	13p

2. What are the assumptions behind the $g = rb$ model?
3. Estimate the company's after-tax cost of debt capital and the total market value of the debt capital ex interest:
£12 million 15% bonds. Redeemable in four years at £110 per cent. Current market price is £128 cum interest. Corporation tax is at 33%.
4. If a company had issued £10 million of 12% unquoted debt, redeemable in three years at par and similar in risk to those in question 3, estimate their total market worth.
5. What is the after-tax cost of debt capital of an issue of 18% bonds which is redeemable at par in 7 years' time and whose current market price is £118 cum interest? Corporation tax is charged at 33%.
6. A company has issued £50 million of zero-coupon bonds, due for repayment in three years' time at par. Their current market price is £87. What is the company's cost of debt capital?
7. Define the following:
   (a) plain vanilla bonds;
   (b) discount bonds;
   (c) conversion ratio;
   (d) conversion price;
   (e) conversion premium.
8. What are the advantages of convertible debt?
9. A company has issued £25 million of 5% convertible bonds, redeemable in four years' time or convertible into 50 shares. The current price of the bonds is £88 ex interest and the current market price of the company's shares is 165p ex div. If the share price is expected to rise by 8% per year in future, calculate the after-tax cost of the convertibles. The corporation tax rate is 33%.
10. What is the minimum value of a convertible?

Problems

1. Thamos plc is a successful food retailing company. Over the last five years it has increased its share of the UK food retail market by 30%. Thamos plc makes no use of debt and has financed its operations entirely from retained earnings. Thamos plc has a current price/earnings ratio of 28 compared with the food retailing sector average of 19. Other financial data over the last five years are shown below.

	t_{-4}	t_{-3}	t_{-2}	t_{-1}	Current year
Earnings per share (p)	16.1	19.3	24.7	30.5	35.8
Net dividend per share (p)	4.86	5.86	7.5	9.0	11.0
Book value of equity per share (p)	103	124	142	165	190

Required:
(a) Estimate the cost of equity capital for Thamos plc using the following:
   (i) dividend growth model;
   (ii) Gordon model;
   (iii) capital asset pricing model (you should assume a risk-free rate of interest of 10%, a beta of 0.8 and a market return of 19%).
(b) Discuss whether the assumptions underlying the models used in part (a) are realistic and explain how the effects of using these assumptions are reflected in the results obtained.
(c) Explain why managers need to know the cost of the equity capital of their companies.

2. (a) A colleague has been taken ill. Your managing director has asked you to take over from the colleague and to provide urgently needed estimates of the discount rate to be used in appraising a large new capital investment. You have been given your colleague's working notes, which you believe to be numerically accurate.

Working notes
Estimates for the next 5 years (annual averages)

Stock market total return on equity	16%
Own company dividend yield	7%
Own company share price rise	14%
Standard deviation of total stock market return on equity	10%
Standard deviation of own company total return on equity	20%
Correlation coefficient between total own company return on equity and total stock market return on equity	+0.7
Correlation coefficient between total return on the new capital investment and total market return on equity	+0.5
Growth rate of own company earnings	12%
Growth rate of own company dividends	11%
Growth rate of own company sales	13%
Treasury bill yield	12%

The after-tax earnings available to ordinary shareholders in the most recent year were £5 400 000, of which £2 140 000 was distributed as ordinary dividends. The company has 10 million issued ordinary shares which are currently trading on the stock exchange at 321 pence. The company pays corporation tax at 35%.

Required:
Estimate the company's cost of equity capital using:
(i) The dividend valuation model.
(ii) The capital asset pricing model.
(b) Why might you not expect these two models to produce similar values for the cost of equity capital?

3. Bolar plc currently has three types of marketable debt in its capital structure.
(a) Unsecured 14% bonds, redemption date 30 June 1998, with interest payable annually on 31 December. The current market price is £95 ex interest.
(b) 10% secured debentures, redemption 31 December 1997–99 with £5 interest payable per debenture six monthly on 30 June and 31 December. The current market price is £91.50 ex interest.
(c) 8% unsecured convertible debentures, convertible on either 1 January, 1997 into 40 ordinary shares, or on 1 January 1999 into 30 ordinary shares. The redemption date is 1 January 2005. Interest is payable annually on 1 January and the current market price is £93 cum interest.
The debt all has a unit par value of £100. All of Bolar's marketable debt is redeemable at its par value.
Assume that it is now 31 December 1994. Taxation may be ignored.

Required:
(a) Calculate the annual redemption yields for each of the three types of debt. For the convertible debenture estimate the annual yield if the company's share price, currently 190 pence, increases by
(i) 5% per year,
(ii) 10% per year.
Assume that, if conversion occurs, the shares would immediately be sold, and that the ex-interest value of convertible debentures is expected to be £88.50 on 1 January 1997 and £92 on 1 January 1999.

(b) Explain briefly why the redemption yields in your answer to (a) above differ.

17 The weighted average cost of capital

The project discount rate

At the outset of the previous chapter it was stated that – apart from other uses principally concerned with the capital structure decision – the cost of capital analysis could possibly provide another way (as an alternative to the CAPM) of identifying a discount rate/cut-off rate for DCF investment appraisal. It is to this that we now turn our attention.

The capital structures of companies can be separated into two types. Companies can have either a capital structure which consists *entirely* of equity capital, or they can have a *mixed* capital structure, where debt capital and equity capital are held in varying proportions. In addition there are some organizations that have capital structures that cause a certain amount of difficulty in terms of their exact nature. In particular mutuals have rather ambiguous ownership bases and a very good example of the sort of problem that might arise from this could be seen when the Trustee Savings Bank demutualized in 1985 and a court ruling was necessary. However, we shall limit our analysis to the more usual commercial capital structure. Of these, the mixed capital structure is the more common in practice (especially amongst stock exchange quoted companies) but the equity financed company provides us with a much less complex situation, and so initially we shall examine the question of the investment appraisal discount rate in terms of an all-equity financed company.

All-equity financed companies

Suppose that a company has an all-equity capital structure and intends to remain as such (at least up to the horizon of its current planning). *Under a number of limiting assumptions*, we can state that its current cost of equity capital could properly be used as the discount rate for investment appraisal.

This rate, the expected return required by the ordinary shareholders, could be used because it represents the minimum acceptable return for a project undertaken by the company, in opportunity cost terms. The cost of equity capital represents the opportunity cost of the shareholders' capital, in that it reflects the return that they could earn elsewhere (for a similar level of risk). Therefore their capital should be applied to a particular capital investment project undertaken by the company's management, *only* if it is expected to yield this return, as a minimum.

This condition applies whether the project is being financed by a new equity issue (ignoring any issue costs), or by funds from an equity issue made in the past, or by using retained net earnings. In all cases, the investment capital being used represents shareholders' funds, and the company should only use such funds if each project to which they are applied is expected to earn at least this minimum return. Use of the NPV decision rule, with the cost of equity capital as the discount rate, will ensure that this is the case.

Two limiting assumptions

There are two important limiting assumptions to this advice. The first is that the company is assumed to be evaluating projects which, if they were accepted, would not cause any significant change in the company's overall level of risk. That is, the acceptance of the project would not cause investors generally to view the company's expected future cash flows as having changed in their level of uncertainty. The reason for this assumption is obvious. The market-derived cost of equity capital is the required return relevant *only* to the company's existing level of risk and so would be an inappropriate rate to apply to a project which had a different level of risk.

The second limiting assumption is that the project being appraised is small, relative to the overall size of the company, i.e. the project represents a *marginal* investment. The reason for this assumption is as follows. The company's cost of equity capital is a marginal cost; it refers to the minimum expected return required from a relatively small (i.e. marginal) investment in the shares of the company. This is so because the current share price that is used in the cost of equity calculation is the price at which a relatively small quantity of the company's shares can be currently bought or sold – if a large quantity of shares were involved, then a separate price would have to be negotiated. Therefore, the cost of equity capital is only appropriate for the evaluation of a project which represents a marginal change in the company's total investment.

If either of these assumptions is violated, then the company's cost of equity capital does *not* provide an appropriate rate of discount for project investment appraisal. Of the two, it is the first one which is the most important and which is likely to cause the most problems in practice: projects will often have a level of risk which is not the same as the company's current average risk level.

Mixed capital structure companies

Where a company's capital structure is composed of both debt and equity capital, with their differing opportunity costs, what discount rate should be used for investment appraisal purposes? The short answer to this question, which we shall expand upon and attempt to justify, is that a *weighted average* of the costs of all the individual components of the capital structure should be used: the company's weighted average cost of capital.

On the surface this can appear to be strange advice. Assume a company possesses a capital structure of which (measured in current stock market values) half is equity with a cost of (say) 20% and half is debt with a cost of (say) 10%. Using the proportion of each type of capital in the overall structure as the weights, we find that the company's weighted average cost of capital (which we shall call K_0) is given by:

$$(0.5 \times 20\%) + (0.5 \times 10\%) = 15\%.$$

Now, suppose an investment project is identified by the company which requires a cash outlay of £1 million and the company proposes to raise the capital through a bond issue at the current market rate of interest of 10%. The cost – in the everyday sense of the word – of the capital put into the project would be 10%, and so it would appear logical to use this as the NPV discount rate: if the project yields a return greater than 10%, (i.e. it has a positive NPV at a 10% discount rate), the company must find the project beneficial.

In contrast to this, we have stated that the company's weighted average cost of capital *should* be the discount rate used for project evaluation: 15%.[1] But why should the company require a minimum return of 15%, when it appears that the project would be worthwhile as long as it yields a return in excess of 10%?

For instance, if the project were found to have a yield (i.e. an IRR) of 14%, evaluating it using K_0 as the discount rate would lead to its rejection, on the grounds of having a negative NPV, even though it appears to produce a return 4% above its cost. To use K_0 as the discount rate *appears to be* nonsensical.

For another view of things suppose the same company later has *another* investment opportunity which it is proposed to finance through an issue of equity capital (whose cost is 20%). If the project yields a return of 17% (say), it would have a positive NPV when discounted by K_0 and so would be accepted. Once again, the use of K_0 *appears* to lead to a nonsensical decision: acceptance of a project which does not generate sufficient return to cover the cost (20%) of the capital outlay required.

A constant capital structure

What lies behind the advice that the company's weighted average cost of capital (WACC) should be used as the NPV discount rate, rather than the cost of the specific type of capital which is being used to finance the project? The fundamental reason is that it is assumed that the company intends to maintain its *existing* capital structure of debt and equity capital. (Just *why* a company should wish to do so will be dealt with in the following chapter on the capital structure decision. However, for the moment, let us accept that management believe that the company's existing capital structure is somehow *ideal* and so wish to retain it.)

This implies, therefore, a belief that how any individual project is financed is purely a function of *chance circumstances*. Sometimes it may be more convenient for a company to raise debt, sometimes equity. However, using our example above, if the company intends to maintain its existing 50:50 debt–equity mix in the medium to longer term, (although it may fluctuate a little in the short term as first debt is raised and then equity is raised), then the *average* cost of its capital is 15%. It therefore follows that projects should not be accepted which generate *less than* this average, overall required rate of return.

In the example above, the really nonsensical decision would be for the company to use the cost of the specific source of finance as the NPV discount rate. It could then find itself *accepting* the first project which gave a 14% return, and then *rejecting* a second project which would have given a 17% return.

Using the company's WACC as the NPV discount rate avoids the possibility of such an erroneous sequence of decisions: use of the WACC would *reject* the 14% project and would *accept* the 17% project. Given the company's average cost of capital is 15%, this now seems a sensible sequence of decisions.

'Pool of funds' concept

The above line of argument is often referred to as the 'pool of funds' concept. The argument runs as follows. It is neither practical nor especially sensible, to try to identify a particular source of investment cash, physically, with a particular project. Once cash enters a company, it enters the general *pool* of capital within that company, and it is out of this pool that investment funds are drawn, in order to be applied to particular investment projects.

Not unnaturally, the cost involved in using funds out of this pool of capital is the weighted average of all the individual capital inputs. Therefore, on the assumption that a company's capital structure (and hence the make-up of its capital pool) remains stable in the medium to longer term, it is the weighted average of these capital costs that must be the minimum acceptable return for any investment project. Neither the cost of what appears to be the individual source of capital used, nor the K_0 of the *short-term* capital structure fluctuation are appropriate for designating a minimum acceptable return in opportunity cost terms.

The arguments for the use of the weighted average cost of capital as the investment appraisal discount rate are not perfect, and they are made under a number of assumptions which may or may not be borne out in practice. We have already noted these when examining the all-equity company case: unchanging capital structure, unchanging company risk, marginal projects. But if we return to the example we used previously, we can see that using K_0 produces the most *sensible* long-term investment decision advice. As we are assuming that the projects are similarly risky, the first (yielding a 14% return) *should* be rejected as it does not generate the expected return required by the company in the medium to longer term, whereas it is correct to accept the second project (yielding 17%) because it does meet this requirement.

The calculation of K_0

Let us now turn to examine how the weighted average cost of capital (WACC) is calculated and how a company's capital structure is measured. The two questions are to some extent interlinked, but we shall start with the calculation of K_0.

The formal derivation

A company's WACC is derived in a way that is analogous to other costs of company capital. It is the linchpin of the relationship between the expected *total* future net cash flow of the company (i.e. dividends plus interest) and the current *total* market value of the company (i.e. debt capital plus equity).

In other words, using as a basis the logic which underpins the dividend valuation model, a company's *total* market value must be based on the sum of the expected future *total* net cash flow, discounted to present value. This cash flow can be split into two separate streams: interest payments (and loan capital repayments) and dividend payments. Assuming that a company has not issued redeemable debt capital, then the WACC could be found by solving the following equation for K_0 (i.e. K_0 is given by the internal rate of return of the cash flow):

$$V_E + V_B - \sum_{t=1}^{\infty} \frac{D_t}{(1+K_0)^t} - \sum_{t=1}^{\infty} \frac{I_t}{(1+K_0)^t} = 0,$$

where V_E and V_B are the current total market values of equity and bonds, (i.e. debt), and D_t and I_t are the total dividend and interest payments made at time t.

If the assumption of only irredeemable debt is joined by an assumption of a constant annual dividend flow in perpetuity,[2] then the expression for K_0 simplifies, as shown in Table 17.1

Table 17.1

$$V_E + V_B - \frac{D}{K_0} - \frac{I}{K_0} = 0$$

Multiplying both sides by K_0 and rearranging, gives:

$$V_E K_0 + V_B K_0 - D - I = 0$$

$$K_0(V_E + V_B) = D + I$$

$$K_0 = \frac{D+I}{V_E + V_B}$$

On the basis that, under the cash flow assumptions made, $V_E = D/K_E$ and so $D = V_E \times K_E$ and similarly $I = V_B \times K_D$:

$$K_0 = \frac{(V_E \times K_E) + (V_B \times K_D)}{V_E + V_B} \quad \text{or}$$

$$K_0 = K_E \times \left(\frac{V_E}{V_E + V_B} \right) + K_D \times \left(\frac{V_B}{V_E + V_B} \right)$$

From Table 17.1 we can see why the discount rate to be used in project appraisal is the WACC and that the weights to be applied to the individual costs of capital are the market values of each capital source, as a proportion of the company's total market value.

In this derivation of K_0, we have ignored the presence of corporation tax and the fact that the company receives tax relief on its interest payments. If tax is to be included – as indeed it should be given that in an NPV analysis we require the *after-tax* discount rate to be applied to the *after-tax* project cash flows – then the *after-tax relief* cost of debt capital should be used in the calculation of K_0:

$$K_0 = K_E \times \left(\frac{V_E}{V_E + V_B} \right) + K_{D_{AT}} \times \left(\frac{V_B}{V_E + V_B} \right).$$

The assumptions behind the use of the WACC

Given this formal derivation of the weighted average cost of capital, we can now see that there are in fact four assumptions that have to be complied with if it is to be used as an NPV discount rate.

1. The project should be marginal. That is, the project should be small relative to the size of the firm.
2. The project should be financed in such a way as not to change the company's existing capital structure.
3. The project should have the same degree of systematic risk as the existing average systematic risk level of the company.
4. All cash flows (i.e. dividends, interest and project cash flows) should be level perpetuities.

The first assumption is required because both K_E and K_D represent marginal costs of capital. That is, they represent the return available on relatively small investments in the equity and debt securities of the company. Therefore K_0, in turn, also represents a marginal cost of capital: the *overall* return on a relatively small investment in the company. It therefore follows that, strictly speaking, the WACC should only be used as an NPV discount rate on projects which are themselves relatively small.

The second assumption is required because, if the project is financed in such a way that the capital structure of the company *is* changed, then obviously the *weights* in the WACC calculation will change. This, we would expect, would lead to a change in the value of K_0.

However, there is also another reason why K_0 might be expected to change if the company's capital structure is changed. It was pointed out in Chapter 16 that a company's debt capital is a less risky investment than a company's equity capital. This is because, legally, a company *must* pay its debt interest in full before equity dividends can be paid. In bad years, there is a chance that equity holders will miss out on their dividends whilst debt holders will have a legal right to their interest. Should a company be unable to pay interest to its debt holders it will have to come to some sort of arrangement with them (e.g. the Channel Tunnel) or the likelihood is that it will find itself going into liquidation.

Because equity is more risky than debt (for the provider of the funds rather than the company), the expected return on a company's equity capital is *greater* than is the expected return on its debt. This extra return that equity holders receive is compensation for the risk that arises from being at the back of the pay-out queue (both in terms of income and in terms of getting back their money should the company be liquidated), and is termed the *financial risk* premium.

Obviously, other things being equal, the more debt interest the company has to pay, the greater is the risk for equity holders that the firm will have insufficient cash flow to pay them their dividend, all the cash flow having gone to paying interest charges. Therefore, the more debt interest the company has to pay out, the greater will be the financial risk premium demanded by equity holders – that is, the greater will be K_E. Therefore, unless projects are financed so as *not* to change the capital structure, K_0 would also be expected to change because of the resulting change in K_E.

In these circumstances the question would then appear to be: which K_0 should be used: the company's *existing* K_0 or the *new* K_0 that applies once the capital structure is changed? The answer, in fact, is that neither would be correct.

Why this is so will be explained more fully in Chapter 21. For now, all we will say is that if the company is thinking of undertaking a project and wants to finance it in such a way that the capital structure *will* change, then two decisions are involved. The company is making a capital investment decision *and* a capital structure decision. The NPV technique is a capital investment appraisal technique *only*. It cannot cope with a simultaneous capital structure decision as well. Therefore, if we are to use a company's WACC as an NPV discount rate, we need to assume that the capital structure will remain unchanged.

The third assumption is required because – as we know – the NPV discount rate should reflect the systematic risk of the project. The company's WACC is its *overall* rate of return. Like any other market-derived rate of return it reflects the systematic risk involved – the systematic risk of the overall company. Therefore K_0 would only be a suitable NPV discount rate if the project had a similar level of systematic risk.

Finally, there is the fourth assumption. From the formal derivation of the WACC calculation it can be seen that, strictly speaking, the WACC model is a level perpetuity cash flow model. Therefore the company's K_0, calculated on the basis of that model, should really only be applied to projects which themselves have perpetuity cash flows.

How much of a problem will these assumptions cause in practice? The first and last assumptions will cause little difficulty. Most projects evaluated *are* relatively small when compared to the size of the company. Even if they were not, the violation of the first assumption is unlikely to lead to a serious distortion of the investment appraisal.

A similar conclusion can be reached over the last of these four assumptions. The fact that the company may have redeemable debt (and so a non-perpetuity dividend flow) is likely to make little difference in practice. The WACC can still be calculated as an average of the costs of equity and debt, weighted by their market value proportions. Similarly, the fact that the project is almost certainly not going to have perpetuity cash flows is unlikely to bias the investment appraisal unduly, when using K_0 as the discount rate.

The second assumption does cause problems. These are normally avoided by accepting that the capital structure *may* change in the short run, but is likely to be maintained in the medium to long term, and so K_0 should be calculated on the company's longer-run (or target) capital structure. However, if financing the project causes a significant change in capital structure, then an NPV-WACC approach to the investment appraisal is not appropriate. What is an appropriate approach will be discussed in Chapter 21.

That leaves the third assumption about risk. It is here that we run into real difficulties.

The WACC and project risk

If the company is a single-product company (such as a cement manufacturer), and the project under consideration is a general expansion of its existing business, then it may well be safe to assume that the project *does* have the same degree of systematic risk as the existing risk of the company. However, if the project represents a move into a *new* area of business, then the existing WACC would *not* be an appropriate discount rate to use.

However, very few companies are single-product companies. Most companies are, to some extent, diversified. In such circumstances the company's WACC does not reflect the systematic risk of *any one* particular area of its business. It reflects its *average* level of systematic risk throughout all its areas of business.

Therefore, for a diversified company, its WACC is going to be an unsuitable discount rate for project appraisal purposes. Its WACC is unlikely to reflect the systematic risk of any particular project, except by chance. Example 1 is an illustration of this problem. As can be seen, the company's WACC is estimated to be 17.5% but notice the different ways in which the WACC can be calculated.

Example 1

Rocha PLC has two main divisions. One operates a chain of supermarkets while the other manufactures office furniture. The company is financed by both debt and equity capital.

The total market value of the company's equity is £30.3 million ex dividend. The company has recently paid this year's dividend which totalled £4 million. This was in line with the company's policy of increasing dividends by 6% per year. In addition, Rocha has issued £12.625 million of 8% irredeemable bonds. They are currently quoted at £80 per cent, ex interest.

The company's equity has a beta value of 1.71 and its debt beta[3] is estimated at 0.29. The supermarket industry has an average beta of 0.80 while office furniture manufacturers have an average beta of 1.92. Rocha's business is roughly divided equally between its two divisions.

The risk-free return is 8% and the return on the FTSE stock market index is 15%. Ignore tax.

Rocha currently uses its weighted average cost of capital to evaluate *all* projects, but is now thinking of using a different discount rate for each one of its divisions.

WACC calculation
This can be arrived at through three different routes:

1. Cost of equity capital: $K_E = \dfrac{£4m(1.06)}{£30.3m} + 0.06 = 0.20 \text{ or } 20\%$

   Total market value of equity = V_E = £30.3m

   Cost of debt capital: $K_D = \dfrac{£8}{£80} = 0.10 \text{ or } 10\%$

   Total market value of bonds: V_B = £12.625m × 0.80 = £10.1m

   Total market value of company: $V_0 = V_E + V_B$ = £40.4m

Weighted average cost of capital: $K_0 = \left(20\% \times \dfrac{30.3}{40.4}\right) + \left(10\% \times \dfrac{10.1}{40.4}\right) = 17\frac{1}{2}\%.$

2. Cost of equity capital:

$K_E = 8\% + (15\% - 8\%) \times 1.71 = 20\%$ (approx.)

Cost of debt capital: $K_D = 8\% + (15\% - 8\%) \times 0.29 = 10\%$ (approx.)

Weighted average cost of capital: $K_0 = \left(20\% \times \dfrac{30.3}{40.4}\right) + \left(10\% \times \dfrac{10.1}{40.4}\right) = 17\frac{1}{2}\%.$

3.

$$\beta_{ROCHA} = \left(\beta_{EQUITY} \times \dfrac{V_E}{V_0}\right) + \left(\beta_{DEBT} \times \dfrac{V_B}{V_0}\right)$$

$$\beta_{ROCHA} = \left(1.72 \times \dfrac{30.3}{40.4}\right) + \left(0.29 \times \dfrac{10.1}{40.4}\right) = 1.355$$

$$K_{0_{ROCHA}} = 8\% + (15\% - 8\%) \times 0.80 = 13.6\%$$

Divisional discount rates
Supermarket division:

Required return = $8\% + (15\% - 8\%) \times 0.80 = 13.6\%$

Office Furniture manufacture division:

Required return = $8\% + (15\% - 8\%) \times 1.92 = 21.4\%$

(Notice that: $(21.4\% \times 0.50) + (13.6\% \times 0.50) = 17.5\%$.[4])

The *third* of the three WACC calculations in Example 1 shows that WACC reflects the company's *average* systematic risk level, which is represented by its weighted average beta value of 1.355.

The CAPM can be used to calculate specific discount rates for each division, based on the beta value of their industry groups. Therefore, the minimum required rate of return from the supermarket division should only be 13.6%, given its relatively low systematic risk. On the other hand, the minimum required rate of return from the office furniture division is 21.4%, reflecting its relatively high degree of systematic risk.

On this basis, we can see that if Rocha were to evaluate all its capital invesments using its WACC as the NPV discount rate, it would be using too *high* a discount rate for projects in the low-risk supermarket division (17.5% > 13.6%), and it would be using too *low* a discount rate for projects in the higher-risk office furniture division (17.5% < 21.4%)

Example 1 highlights the dangers of companies using a single required rate of return (i.e. their WACC) across the whole of their business, without taking into account the specific level of systematic risk of individual divisions. Furthermore, this situation is diagrammatically illustrated in Fig. 17.1.

If the company simply applies its WACC to all projects, then it will incorrectly *accept* the high-risk projects whose risk and expected return characteristics locate in shaded area A. Conversely, it will incorrectly *reject* low-risk projects whose risk and return characteristics locate in shaded area B.

With projects whose risk and return characteristics locate in either areas C or D, there is no problem. Area C projects will be correctly accepted by the WACC. Area D projects will be correctly rejected. However, the danger lies with area A and B projects.

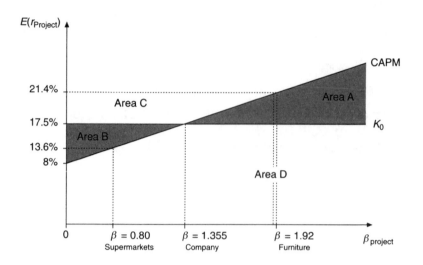

Fig. 17.1 *The dangers of WACC*

Returning to Example 1, the company's supermarket division could be quite needlessly rejecting what are perfectly acceptable (area B) projects because too high a minimum return is being specified. But, even worse, the furniture manufacturing division may be accepting projects, thinking they will produce a positive NPV, when in reality, they can be expected to generate negative NPVs. The mistake arises because too low a discount rate is being used for the risk involved.

For project appraisal purposes, what is always required is an NPV discount rate which is *tailor-made* to reflect the individual systematic risk level of that particular project. The company's WACC does *not* provide this (except, as was mentioned before, if the company is in a single area of business and the project represents a simple expansion of that existing business), but the CAPM *can* provide it.

The absence of tax

We will pick up on this analysis in Chapter 21. However, it is very important to note that Example 1 did not include tax. Tax makes a significant difference to the analysis, as we shall see.

Conclusion

The conclusion of our analysis, to this point, is as follows. The company's weighted average cost of capital represents its overall rate of return, (and hence the notation of K_0 for the WACC), and reflects its overall level of systematic risk.

Traditionally, the WACC is used as an NPV discount rate for project appraisal purposes.[5] However, we have seen that four assumptions need to hold good if an NPV/WACC analysis is to be correct. Although three out of those four assumptions may be thought to cause little *real* difficulty, one of the assumptions does have the potential to cause *real* problems: that of risk differences.

We have seen in Example 1 how this problem may be overcome by using a discount rate calculated specifically to reflect an individual project's systematic risk, rather than using the company's WACC. However, we have not yet finished with this analysis and will return to it in Chapter 21, where we will also address two other related problems: what happens if the project is *non*-marginal and what happens if the project is to be financed in such a way that the company *does* significantly change its capital structure?

For the remainder of this chapter, and in the three chapters which follow, we will put the issue of the NPV discount rate to one side. Instead, we shall turn to look directly at the financing decision and try to answer two questions: does it matter whether individual projects are financed with debt or equity capital (or some mixture of the two), and does it matter what overall capital structure or gearing ratio[6] the company uses to finance its assets?

Differing corporate and private costs of debt

Financing via debt capital

Through the single-period investment–consumption model, we developed the important Hirshleifer separation theorem. The essence of the theorem is that investment and consumption decisions can be effectively separated and analysed in isolation. Thus company managements can make decisions about physical investment opportunities without reference to the indifference curve maps of individual owners/shareholders.

On receipt of the dividend from the company, each shareholder can decide, with reference to his own indifference map, whether or not to use the capital market to borrow or lend money. In this way, the theory of investment decision making is able neatly to side-step one of the great stumbling-blocks of the practical application of economic theory: the identification of individuals' indifference maps and the need to make an interpersonal comparison of utility, when the preferences of individuals differ.

The reader may well have wondered at the ease with which the separation theorem conclusion gave way to a seemingly different analysis. The theorem would appear to suggest that companies need be financed only by equity share capital and retained cash earnings, and that money market borrowing and lending at fixed interest rates can be left to individual shareholders, in their personal manipulation of the pattern of their received dividend flows.

But, having dealt with the conclusion of this theorem, the analysis turned later to examine the costs of a *variety* of sources of company finance and the way in which these costs may be combined into a weighted average, and possibly then be used as a discount rate for investment appraisal.

Therefore, the idea of using debt capital to finance a company was introduced without either giving any reason *why* a company should raise debt capital (when the separation theorem implies that this decision can be left to the individual shareholder), or analysing the alterations it makes, if any, to the conclusions of the investment–consumption model. In fact, under the initial assumptions of the single-period model, the answers to both questions are relatively straightforward.

Introducing tax

There is really *no* reason why a company should borrow money in a perfect capital market (i.e. raise debt capital), because individual shareholders are perfectly capable of taking such action if they wish. But, even where a company does raise debt capital, it does not really disturb the conclusions of the model. The debt can be viewed as just another investment undertaken by management, which can be fitted into the logic of the physical investment line with little difficulty.

However, in the real world, companies raise debt capital as well as equity capital for many reasons. Principal among these is the disturbances in the capital market caused by taxation: companies can offset interest payments against taxation, whereas individuals normally cannot.

Therefore, assuming that a company and an individual are seen as equally risky by the capital markets, the company can effectively borrow at a lower rate of interest (after tax) than can individual shareholders. So let us now analyse this situation, in terms of the single-period investment–consumption model, where the company's effective cost of borrowing on the capital market is less than that of the individual shareholder.

Debt capital in the perfect market case

First of all, assuming the existence of a perfect capital market in which individuals and companies borrow at effectively the *same* rate of interest, let us examine in what circumstances a company may raise debt capital, i.e. borrow.

Figure 17.2(a) shows the physical investment opportunities discovered by a company which have been ranked in order of decreasing rate of return. Under our previous analysis, we know that in order to help maximize shareholder wealth, the company will move along its physical investment line (PIL) until a point of tangency is reached with the financial investment line (FIL). This tangency occurs at point Q.

Moving to Fig. 17.2(b), where the vertical axis is superimposed on the previous figure, this shows that the shareholders' current resources in the company, OA, are not sufficient to achieve the point of optimality on the physical investment line. Additional cash resources, to the value of OB, are required.

To reach the point of physical investment optimality, the company is faced with two possible alternatives. It can either request its shareholders to subscribe additional equity capital (thus causing the vertical axis to shift to the left so as to intersect the horizontal axis at point B, rather than at point O). Alternatively, the company can itself borrow amount OB on the capital market and repay CD (capital plus interest) at time t_1.

With this latter course of action, the present value of the company's equity capital would be OE, and the gain in shareholders' wealth arising out of the physical capital investments would be AE. If instead, the company had simply invested the existing cash resources of shareholders up to point R on the physical investment line, then the current value of the equity would only be OF and the gain in shareholders' wealth would also have been smaller at AF.

That additional gain in shareholders' wealth of EF would also arise if, instead, the company undertook the former course of action and asked its shareholders to subscribe an amount OB of new equity. The resulting present value of the equity would now be even greater at BE, but the gain in shareholder wealth would be the same as previously: AE. In other words, the gain in wealth is found from the current value of the equity (BE), less the newly subscribed equity (OB) and less the original equity (OA).

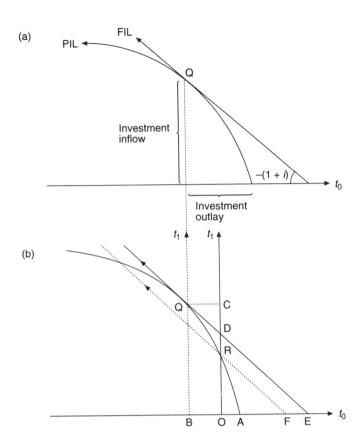

Fig. 17.2 *Financing investments*

(a)

FIL

PIL

Q

Investment
inflow

$-(1 + i)$

t_0

Investment
outlay

t_1 t_1

(b)

Q C

D

R

B O A F E t_0

The important result which follows from this analysis is that, in a perfect capital market, a company that wishes to maximize its shareholders' wealth should make physical investments until the return on the marginal investment becomes equal to the market interest rate; and it makes no difference to shareholders' wealth how these investments are financed, whether it be by equity capital or debt capital or by some combination of equity and debt. In the example used above, the company can maximize its shareholders' wealth either by using all equity investment capital (i.e. raise OB of additional equity) or by a mixture of both equity and debt (i.e. raise OB on the debt capital market).

Debt capital in the imperfect market case

So much for the perfect market case. Let us now examine the effects of debt capital financing when we have the particular type of capital market imperfection described earlier, which enables companies to borrow on the capital market at lower *effective* interest rates than can shareholders. In this analysis we shall assume that the company's interest rate and individual shareholders' interest rate, represented both the borrowing and the lending rate for each.

Fig. 17.3 sets up a situation similar to that of the previous analysis, except that there are now two points of tangency between the physical investment line and the *two* financial investment lines (one reflecting the company's interest rate and the other the shareholders' interest rate). These two points of tangency are at Y and Z respectively. Just as in the previous analysis, we shall assume that both points represent a capital investment requirement which is in excess of the company's existing resources. Thus both tangency points occur in the graph's northwest quadrant.

In this situation, the company is faced with a number of alternative courses of action, of which we shall initially specify and examine the effects of four:

1. raise no additional capital;
2. raise equity capital only;
3. raise both debt and equity capital;
4. raise debt capital only.

With the first of these four alternatives, the company would invest the whole of its capital resources (OA) available in time t_0 in physical investments, so as to reach point D on the physical investment line. The effect of this would be to give the company's equity capital a present value of OM.

Taking the second alternative of raising additional equity capital only, the maximum amount which the company could raise would be ON, thus allowing the company to move around the physical investment line to point Z. At this point, any further investment – which would necessitate raising further amounts of equity capital – would reduce the gain in the equity's current value; as it is, moving to point Z would cause the current total value of the equity to increase from OM to NB, which represents a gain in shareholder wealth – over the previous alternative course of action – of MB.

It is important to notice that with the first alternative (where no additional cash is raised), it would not matter which cost of capital (i.e. the company's interest rate or the shareholders' interest rate) was used to evaluate investment opportunities, because both would effectively move the company to point D. However, with the second alternative, the company must use the shareholders' cost of capital as the evaluation rate to ensure its location at point Z (which in Fig. 17.3 equals shareholders' market interest rate).

The third alternative would be for the company to raise amount ON in new equity capital and amount NE in debt capital. In order to do so investment opportunities would first be appraised with the shareholders' cost of capital as

Fig. 17.3 *Using corporate debt*

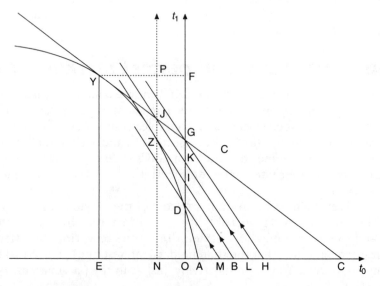

the discount rate. The total investment capital required for acceptable projects at this discount rate would specify the amount required to be raised in the form of new equity.

Those investment opportunities which remained unaccepted would then be appraised by the *company's* cost of capital. The total capital outlay required for the acceptable projects at this lower rate would then specify the amount of debt capital to be raised.

The overall effect of raising capital from these two sources and investing it in the accepted opportunities would locate the company at point Y on the physical investment line. This level of investment allows the company to generate cash of amount NP at time t_1, of which PJ represents interest and debt capital repayment and the remainder, NJ, is available for payment of dividend at t_1, which, at the shareholders' cost of capital, has a present value of NL. Thus this third alternative raises shareholders' wealth by a *further* amount: BL.

The fourth alternative requires that all investment opportunities are appraised with the *company's* cost of capital as the discount rate. The total amount of capital required to undertake the investments appraised as acceptable at this rate (AE), less the existing capital resources of the company (AO), specifies the amount of debt capital to be raised (OE). Once again, the combined effect is to move the company around its physical investment line to point Y and so generate a cash inflow of NP at time t_1. Of this cash inflow, amount FG represents the interest and capital repayment, and the remainder, amount OG is available for dividend. The present value of this dividend (and hence of the company's equity) is OH. Thus this fourth alternative has resulted in yet a further increase in the shareholders' wealth by amount LH.

The extreme use of debt capital

The logical conclusion of the foregoing analysis is fairly obvious. It is fully developed in Fig. 17.4, where it is assumed that at time t_0 the company has available capital resources (all equity) of amount OA.

Facing the physical investment line of AF and using the shareholders' cost of capital as the investment appraisal discount rate, the company would move to point Z, producing a time t_0 dividend of OD and a time t_1 dividend of OG. The present value of this dividend pattern represents the company's current value of OH.

If the company then appraises all the unaccepted projects at the *corporate* discount rate and borrows amount CD to undertake those which are acceptable, the company is moved further around the physical investment line to point Y. This would result in a revised amount of the market value of the equity of OJ, and an increase in shareholder wealth of HJ.

However, to *maximize* the increase in the company's equity value from its existing level of OA and hence bring greatest benefit to the shareholders, the company should pay a dividend at time t_0 of virtually *all* of OA (this dividend amount is labelled on Fig. 17.4 as OB, where AB represents a minute fraction of the existing equity[7]) and borrow amount BC.

This would result in paying lenders an amount in time t_1 of KL, which represents interest and capital repayment, whilst leaving BK as dividend. The combined dividend flow of OB in time t_0 and KB in time t_1 has the effect of maximizing the current value of the company (given the investment

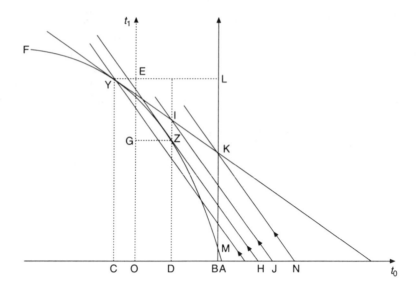

Fig. 17.4 *The extreme use of debt*

opportunities available and the market interest rates) from its existing value of OA to that of ON, which represents an increase in shareholders' wealth of AN.

Therefore, accepting all our previous assumptions and also assuming that the nature of business risk remains the same no matter how much is borrowed, we arrive at a surprising finding. When faced with an ability to borrow money at a rate *below* that charged to individual shareholders, because of the corporate tax relief on debt interest, the company should evaluate its physical investment opportunities using the *corporate* interest rate as the NPV discount rate, and should raise as much as possible of the resulting required investment capital in the form of debt rather than equity (i.e. the company's capital structure should be composed of virtually *all* debt capital and virtually no equity capital).

In practice this does not happen and the issues related to this are further developed in the following chapter.

The role of the WACC

The foregoing analysis has led us to conclude that, in order to locate correctly on the physical investment line, a company should use its own borrowing and lending interest rate as the discount rate for investment appraisal. In the model used, this rate had the appearance of being the company's after-tax cost of debt capital ($K_{D_{AT}}$), and so how can this be reconciled with our earlier conclusion that a company should use a weighted average of its own (K_D) and its shareholders' (K_E) interest rate: the weighted average cost of capital K_0?

The conclusion that a company's WACC was the appropriate rate to use for investment appraisal was made on the important assumption that the company intended to retain (at least in the medium to longer term) a given capital structure mix of debt and equity. On this basis, therefore, the company's financial investment line is not determined by the cost of debt capital but by the weighted average cost of *all* the types or sources of capital contained within its existing capital structure. So, the decision as to what is the appropriate mix of debt and equity is a separate decision from applying the resulting cost of capital to investment decisions. Thus, in concluding that the company should use its own market interest rate for investment appraisal purposes, this rate actually is its weighted average cost of capital.

We must remember that the Hirshleifer single-period investment–consumption analysis ignores risk. In particular, it ignores different *levels* of risk and so we need to recognize how suspect this conclusion is in terms of the use of the WACC.

However, of more interest is the conclusion of the analysis as far as capital structure is concerned. It appears to be saying that, in a taxed world where companies get tax relief on debt interest, but individual investors do not, then companies should use as much debt capital as possible, if they wish to maximize shareholder wealth.

Therefore, up until this point, we have only considered financial managers improving shareholder wealth through good *capital investment* decisions. This analysis now tends to suggest that financial managers can *also* improve shareholder wealth through good *financing* or *capital structure* decisions. This is the subject of the next three chapters.

Summary

The main points made are as follows:

- A company's overall cost of capital can be calculated on the basis of an average of the costs of the individual sources of capital, weighted by the market-valued proportions of those individual sources of capital: the WACC.

- The cost of a specific source of capital should never be used as an NPV discount rate. Instead, the company's overall weighted average cost of capital should be used.

- The WACC provides a suitable discount rate, given the validity of four assumptions: the project is marginal; no change in capital structure; no change in systematic risk level and all level-perpetuity cash flows.

- Of the four assumptions, the second and third are crucial. If a project is financed so as to cause a change in capital structure then an NPV/WACC analysis appears inappropriate. NPV is an investment appraisal technique and it cannot adequately handle a simultaneous capital structure decision.

- The third assumption is crucial because of the logic of NPV: the discount rate reflects the return available elsewhere on an investment with similar systematic risk to the project under appraisal.

- A company's WACC reflects its existing systematic risk level. Therefore to provide a suitable discount rate the project must have that level of risk also. In the real world such an assumption is likely to be very suspect.

- It was concluded that, in most circumstances it was likely to be safer to generate a discount rate from CAPM which was tailor-made to the project's systematic risk level, rather than to use WACC.

- Finally, returning to the Hirshleifer single-period investment–consumption analysis, this appeared to indicate that given the real-world situation where the effective after-corporation tax cost of company debt capital was less than the cost of capital market borrowing, companies should use as much debt capital as possible if shareholder wealth was to be maximized.

Notes

1.   We are deliberately ignoring the fact here that the issue of bonds might affect the company's capital structure and so affect the weights and hence the value of K_0. The effect of this change, and whether or not the company's existing K_0 or new K_0 should be used as the discount rate, will be dealt with later.

2.   Therefore both the interest cash flow and the dividend cash flow are level perpetuity cash flows.

3.   Although so far we have only talked about the beta value of shares, debt capital also possesses systematic risk and so will have a beta value.

4.   Weights of 50% (i.e. 0.50) are used in this calculation as we are told that Rocha's business is divided roughly equally between its two divisions.

5.   The WACC can also be used as the minimum required IRR.

6.   The word 'leverage' is used in the USA.

7.   It is necessary to leave a minute amount so as not to liquidate the company totally.

Further reading

1.   There are a number of interesting articles which are, in the main, critical of the use of the WACC as an NPV discount rate. For example, see: F.D. Arditti, 'The Weighted Average Cost of Capital: Some Questions on its Definition, Interpretation and Use', *Journal of Finance*, September 1973, and M.J. Brennan, 'A New Look at the Weighted Average Cost of Capital', *Journal of Business Finance*, Summer 1973.
2.   Particularly good, in this context, are: S.M. Keane, 'The Cost of Capital as a Financial Decision Tool', *Journal of Business Finance and Accounting*, Autumn 1978; H.P. Lanser, 'Valuation, Gains from Leverage and the Weighted Average Cost of Capital as a Cut-off Rate', *Engineering Economist*, Fall 1983; and E.F. Brigham and T.C. Tapley, 'Financial Leverage and the Use of the NPV Criterion: A Re-examination', *Financial Management*, Summer 1985.

Quickie questions

1.   Given the following information, what is the company's weighted average cost of capital?

$$d_0 = 5p \qquad P_E = 88p \text{ cum div}$$
$$g = 0.07 \qquad 24 \text{ million shares in issue.}$$

£25 million 15% irredeemable debt. $P_B = £110$ ex int.
£10 million 12% irredeemable debt, unquoted.
£3 million 7-year term loan at 4% over base.
Bank base rate = 10%.
Corporation tax = 35%.

2. What is the argument for why the cost of a *specific* source of capital should not be used as the NPV discount rate?
3. What are the assumptions behind the use of the WACC as an NPV discount rate?
4. What is the problem faced by a diversified company wishing to use its WACC as an NPV discount rate?
5. Why is the CAPM likely to produce a superior NPV discount rate than WACC?
6. Why is the company's effective cost of debt capital likely to be less than the rate available to investors, given similar risk?
7. If the company can borrow more cheaply than can investors, what implications does this have for the company's capital structure?
8. How is a company's capital structure measured?

Problems

1. The directors of Osmin plc are considering opening a factory to manufacture a new product. Detailed forecasts of the product's expected cash flows have been made, and it is estimated that an initial capital investment of £2.5 million is required. The company's current (t_0) authorized share capital consists of 4 million ordinary shares, each with a nominal value of 25p. During the last five years the number of shares in issue has remained constant at 3 million, and the market price per share is 135p ex div. The dividends for the last five years have been as follows:

Year	t_{-4}	t_{-3}	t_{-2}	t_{-1}	t_0
Dividend per share (pence)	10.0	10.8	11.6	13.6	13.6

Osmin plc currently has in issue 800 000 8% debentures redeemable in four years' time. The current market price of these debentures is £82.5 ex interest. The company also has outstanding a £900 000 bank loan repayable in eight years' time. The rate of interest on this loan is variable, being fixed at $1\frac{1}{2}\%$ above the bank's base rate which is currently 15%.

Required:
(a) Calculate the weighted average cost of capital (WACC) for Osmin plc.
(b) Explain briefly to the directors of Osmin plc what assumptions they are making if the WACC calculated in (a) above is used to discount the expected cash flows of the project.
(c) Describe the practical problems that might be encountered when attempting to compute the WACC for a large UK listed company.
Ignore taxation.

2. Redskins plc is a holding company owning shares in various subsidiary companies. Its directors are currently considering several projects which will increase the range of the business activities undertaken by Redskins plc and its subsidiaries. The directors would like to use discounted cash flow techniques in their evaluation of these projects but as yet no weighted average cost of capital has been calculated.

Redskins plc has an authorized share capital of 10 million 25p ordinary shares, of which 8 million have been issued. The current ex div market price per ordinary share is £1.10, a dividend of 10p per share having been paid recently. The company's project analyst has calculated that 18% is the most appropriate after-tax cost of equity capital. Extracts from the latest balance sheets for the group are given below:

Redskins plc

	(£000s)
Issued share capital	2000
Share premium	1960
Reserves	3745
Shareholders' funds	7705
Minority interests	895
3% irredeemable debentures	1400
9% redeemable debentures	1500
6% loan stock	2000
Bank loans	1540
Total long-term liabilities	6440

All debt interest is payable annually and all the current year's payments will be made shortly. The current cum interest market prices for £100 nominal value stock are £31.60 and £103.26 for the 3% and 9% debentures respectively. Both the 9% debentures and the 6% loan stock are redeemable at par in ten years' time. The 6% loan stock is not traded on the open market, but the analyst estimates that its effective pre-tax cost is 10% per annum. The bank loans bear interest at 2% above base rate (which is currently 11%) and are repayable in six years. The effective corporation tax rate of Redskins plc is 35%.

Required:
(a) Calculate the effective after-tax weighted average cost of capital as required by the directors.
(b) Discuss the problems that are encountered in the estimation of a company's weighted average cost of capital when the following are used as sources of long-term finance:
  (i) bank overdraft
  (ii) convertible loan stock.
(c) Outline the fundamental assumptions that are made whenever the weighted average cost of capital of a company is used as the discount rate in net present value calculations.

3. Bonzo plc is a divisionalized company, quoted on the London Stock Exchange. Two of its divisions are currently evaluating investment proposals and have submitted them to Head Office for approval.
The project cash flows are as follows:

Cement division	(£000s)	Timber division	(£000s)
Year: 0	−200	Year: 0	−150
1	+100	1	+ 75
2	+100	2	+ 48.36
3	+ 79.3	3	+ 75

The following information about the company is available:
Current balance sheet (summarized):

		(£000s)
Assets:	Net fixed assets	7500
	Net current assets	2460
		9960
Finance:	30m 10p Ordinary shares	3000
	Reserves	6960
		9960

Dividend/share and earnings/share record

Year	Dividend (p)	Earnings (p)
t_{-4}	5.12	6.19
t_{-3}	5.32	6.44
t_{-2}	5.53	6.69
t_{-1}	5.76	6.90
t_0 (current year)	5.99	7.31

The current total market value of the company's shares is £13.35 million, ex div. Bonzo plc has a beta of 1.16. The cement industry has a beta of 1.50 and the timber industry has a beta of 0.50. The annual return on three-year government stock is currently 11% and the expected return on the FT All-Share Index is 17%. Ignore tax.

Required:
(a) The company usually evaluate all investment proposals with NPV, using the cost of company capital as the discount rate. Estimate this discount rate and evaluate both projects.
(b) Advise the company as to why they should evaluate projects using risk-adjusted discount rates. Estimate an appropriate rate for each project and re-evaluate them both.
(c) Comment and explain, with the help of a diagram, the implications of your answers to parts (a) and (b).
Assume all-equity financing throughout.

18 The capital structure decision in a no-tax world

Introduction

The analysis in the previous chapter led us to an interesting provisional conclusion. Management who wish to maximize their company's shareholders' wealth should gear the company up to such an extent that its capital structure would consist almost entirely of debt capital, with the very minimum of equity capital. This conclusion does not seem to match with practice,[1] where companies' capital structures rarely contain more than 50% debt capital and the average level of gearing is around 25% debt capital and 75% equity capital.

An optimal capital structure

To take a closer look at the problem, let us begin by posing the question: can any particular ratio of debt to equity in a company's capital structure be said to be optimal in terms of helping to increase the wealth of ordinary shareholders? This is an important question for several reasons.

First and most importantly, up to this stage we have assumed that management could increase the wealth of ordinary shareholders *only* by the decisions they made about physical investment projects. If, however, an optimal gearing ratio exists, then it would appear that management could also increase shareholder wealth by manipulating the company's capital structure through the selection of particular types (e.g. debt and equity) of project finance. In other words, not only can the *investment* decision enhance shareholders' wealth, but so too can the *financing* decision.

A second reason for the importance of the question about the existence of an optimal capital structure is the implications that it has for the approach which we have developed to investment decision making. Hitherto, we have assumed that the question of *how* a particular investment project is to be financed (the financing decision) can be taken separately from the investment decision itself (as a direct result of the separation theorem). The investment decision has therefore been examined in isolation. If the financing decision can be shown to be important for the company – in terms of the desired capital structure – then we may have to revise our approach to investment appraisal.

A third reason could also be proposed. In suggesting the possible use of the weighted average cost of capital for discounting and appraisal purposes we assumed that a company's capital structure would remain constant. This assumption would obviously gain support if it could be shown that an optimal capital structure does exist for a company. Because then, management would wish to attain, and *remain* at, that particular gearing ratio.

The capital structure decision was first rigorously analysed by two American economists, Modigliani and Miller (universally known in the abbreviated form of M and M), in a justly famous article that appeared in 1958. Much of our analysis in this section will be based upon the approach that they took.

Initially we will assume that there is *no* tax. This is known formally as the Modigliani and Miller, no tax, capital structure hypothesis.

The total market value model

We introduced the term 'gearing' or 'leverage' when examining the costs of the various sources of capital which are available to a company. We can define the term as the ratio of the total market value of a company's debt capital to the total market value of its equity capital.[2] The distinction between debt and equity was important because each type of capital bore a different level of risk: debt capital was a less risky investment in a company than an equity capital investment in that same company.

This risk differential resulted from the fact that debt capital interest had first claim on a company's annual net earnings, ahead of equity dividends. In addition, debt capital had repayment preference over equity capital in circumstances of company liquidation. As a result of this risk differential, the suppliers of debt capital to a company would require a lower return than the suppliers of equity, because they bore less risk.

In order to calculate the costs of the different capital sources, two valuation models were constructed, both based on the premise that an object's value is determined by the flow of future net benefits which it produces. Therefore, a company's equity capital derived its value from the future (discounted) flow of dividends which it was expected to produce. Similarly, debt capital was valued on the basis of the summation of the future expected (discounted) interest flow and the redemption payment.

From these two valuation models, it follows that the total market value of a company (debt plus equity), V_0, must be derived from its expected future (discounted) net cash flow – which consists of its future dividend flow and its future interest and redemption flow. It will be helpful, for later analysis, to restate this in terms of the notation used earlier when analysing a company's cost of capital.

Table 18.1 gives this restatement (ignoring taxation for the present), under the assumption of constant annual dividends in perpetuity and irredeemable debentures. If we let $V_E K_E + V_B K_D = Y$, and if we assume that none of a company's net cash flow is retained but is paid out in full each year as dividends and interest, then Y is a constant and so a company's total market value is given by:

$$V_0 = \frac{Y}{K_0}.$$

Table 18.1

If Y is the company's total annual cash flow which is assumed to be a level perpetuity that is paid out each year as dividends and interest:

$$V_E = \frac{Y - V_B \times K_D}{K_E} \tag{1}$$

$$V_E \times K_E = Y - V_B \times K_D \tag{2}$$

Taking expression (2) and factoring out V_0:

$$\frac{V_0 \times V_E \times K_E}{V_0} = Y - \frac{V_B \times K_D \times V_0}{V_0} \tag{3}$$

$$\frac{V_0 \times V_E \times K_E}{V_0} + \frac{V_B \times K_D \times V_0}{V_0} = Y \tag{4}$$

$$V_0 \left[\frac{V_E \times K_E}{V_0} + \frac{V_B \times K_D}{V_0} \right] = Y \tag{5}$$

$$V_0 = \frac{Y}{\dfrac{V_E \times K_E}{V_G} + \dfrac{V_B \times K_D}{V_0}} = \frac{Y}{K_0} \tag{6}$$

where $V_E \times K_E = D$ and $V_B \times K_D = I$.

Gearing and V_0 in a no-tax world

The question that we wish to examine is whether or not a company's gearing ratio (i.e. its capital structure) can affect its total market value.[3] From the above it should be clear that changing a company's gearing ratio will affect its total market value (V_0) *only* if it causes a change in either the company's annual net cash flow (Y) or its weighted average cost of capital (K_0). We can argue that changing the gearing ratio of a company will *not* affect either of these factors, as follows.

Changing the gearing ratio cannot have any effect on the company's annual cash flow (Y), as that is determined by the assets in which the company has invested, and not by how those assets are financed. The only effect that changing the gearing has on the firm's annual cash flow is that it changes the *proportions* of the cash flow that are paid out as dividends and interest. The more highly geared the firm, the greater is the proportion of its annual cash flow paid out as interest and the smaller the proportion paid out as dividends. However, changing the level of gearing will *not* change the level of the annual cash flow, but just how it is *split* between debt and equity holders.

Changing the gearing ratio will also not affect the value of K_0. The company's weighted average cost of capital reflects the average return required by the suppliers of the capital. Its level is determined (as in any rate of return) by the degree of systematic risk in the *company's* overall cash flow. There is no reason why changing the gearing ratio should affect the systematic risk of the cash flow being generated by the company's assets, and hence changing the gearing ratio will not affect K_0.[4]

From this analysis we can draw two important conclusions. The first is that simply changing a company's capital structure cannot (by itself) change the company's total market value. Thus companies can only enhance their shareholders' wealth by making good *investment* decisions. The financing decision (through which a company's capital structure or gearing ratio can be changed) *cannot* affect shareholder wealth.

The second conclusion is that companies whose *assets* display the same degree of systematic risk can be expected to have the same weighted average cost of capital, *even though* they may have entirely different gearing ratios. This is because it is the systematic risk of the company's collection of assets which determines its overall return of K_0.

The assumptions

Before proceeding further with this analysis, we should first make explicit the very important assumptions upon which it is based. These are:

1. At any given level of risk, individuals and companies can all borrow at the same rate of interest, which remains constant regardless of the gearing.
2. There are no costs attached to market transactions, the supply of information or the process of bankruptcy.[5]
3. There is no difference between corporate borrowing and personal borrowing in terms of risk (e.g. there is no limited liability advantage for companies).
4. There is no taxation.

An example

Suppose we are considering setting up a company which would operate a set of machines that would cost £100 000 in total. These machines involve a given level of systematic risk which requires the expectation of an annual return of 15%. Therefore they are expected to produce an annual net cash flow of £15 000 in perpetuity. This cash flow will be paid out in its entirety each year, to the suppliers of capital.

Three different financing packages are being considered:

1. The machines are financed entirely by equity capital.
2. £50 000 of 10% debt (the current market cost of debt capital) is raised with the remaining £50 000 supplied via equity capital.
3. £80 000 of 10% debt is raised, with the balance provided by equity capital.

Table 18.2 illustrates the returns to equity and debt, and the weighted average cost of capital that would result from each of these three financing options.

It should be noted that this example does nothing to prove or disprove the relationship between a company's gearing ratio and its weighted average cost of capital that was argued in the previous section. Rather, it is *based* upon that relationship, in that it assumes that K_0 remains unchanged, despite the different gearing ratios. As a result of that assumption (and the four assumptions listed above), the rest follows.

Table 18.2

	Option 1	Option 2	Option 3
Machine annual cash flow	15 000	15 000	15 000
Less interest payment	–	5 000	8 000
Dividend payments	15 000	10 000	7 000
Return on equity (D/V_E)	15%	20%	35%
Return on debt (I/V_B)	–	10%	10%
WACC (Y/V_0)	15%	15%	15%
Total value of company (Y/K_0)	100 000	100 000	100 000

This example does serve a very useful purpose in that it highlights the fact that although K_0 remains unchanged as gearing changes, the cost of equity capital does change. It is the relationship between gearing and K_E that is now examined.

Business and financial risk

In the earlier discussion of portfolio theory and the CAPM we saw that total risk could be split up into two components: systematic (or undiversifiable) risk and unsystematic (or diversifiable) risk. Further, we saw that it was only an investment's systematic risk that determined its expected return. We can now split a *company's* systematic risk into two components: *business risk* and *financial risk*.

The business risk of a company refers to the *operating* cash flows. In other words, business risk relates to the systematic risk of the net cash flows that result from the operation of the company's *assets*. Both the equity and the debt holders in a company bear this risk.

However, financial risk refers to some *additional* systematic risk which is borne only by the equity holders of a geared company.[6]

In Chapter 16, when we discussed the cost of debt capital, it was pointed out that K_D was only the *explicit* cost of debt capital and that there was another cost, an *implicit* (or hidden) cost. This implicit cost is caused by the presence of financial risk.

Financial risk arises directly out of the gearing process and is borne by the equity shareholders in a geared company. It is caused through debt capital having priority over equity capital in both the distribution of the company's annual net cash flow (as interest and dividends) and in any final liquidation distribution. As interest payments to debt holders must legally be paid in full by the company before any dividend payments can be made, the greater the proportion of debt capital within a company's capital structure, the greater the probability that the company will have no cash remaining with which to pay a dividend. This risk of a reduced or zero dividend, which is borne by ordinary shareholders, is termed financial risk, and its severity is likely to increase as a company increases its level of gearing.

Diagrammatically, a company's expected annual net operating cash flow can be portrayed as a probability distribution. In an all-equity company (on the assumption of no retention by the company of this net cash flow), the probability distribution of the net operating cash flow also represents the probability distribution of the dividend flow. Gearing up has the effect of imposing a fixed annual charge on this distribution (the interest payments), so shifting the *dividend payment* probability distribution to the left (see Fig. 18.1). The greater the proportion of debt in the capital structure, the further will be the leftward movement and the greater will be the proportion of the dividend probability distribution falling within the negative portion of the horizontal axis. Thus the greater is the risk of a reduced or zero dividend as gearing is increased.

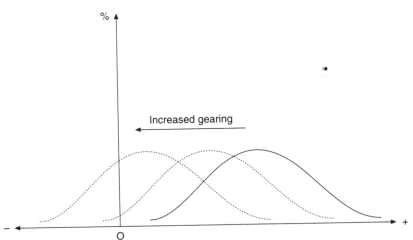

Fig. 18.1 *Probability distribution of dividends*

Thus financial risk arises from the fact that equity holders are always at the back of the annual 'pay-out queue'. The more highly geared the company, the greater the amount of interest that has to be paid before dividends can be paid (i.e. the longer the queue in front of the equity holders), and hence the greater amount of financial risk borne by ordinary shareholders.

This financial risk is *systematic* risk, in that it cannot be diversified away. As a result, shareholders will require a higher expected return on their capital for bearing increased amounts of financial risk. Therefore as a company increases its gearing, the amount of financial risk borne by ordinary shareholders increases and, in consequence, the cost of equity capital rises.

This effect was seen in the example in Table 18.2. As the gearing ratio increases, the return on equity rises from 15% to 35%. In option 1, the 15% return on equity simply reflects the business risk of the assets. However, the 20% return in option 2 reflects a 15% return for holding the business risk of the assets, *plus* a 5% return for holding the financial risk represented by the level of gearing involved. Further, it is important to note that the shareholders have *not* gained in moving (say) from option 1 to option 2. The higher return on equity simply reflects the higher risks involved in holding equity capital.

Asset betas and gearing

Given that beta values are used as an index of systematic risk, it follows from the above that we can distinguish between the beta value of a geared company's equity and the beta value of its assets. The reason for this is that the assets will only contain *business* systematic risk, whereas the equity will contain both *business* and *financial* systematic risk.

We know from our discussion of the CAPM in Chapter 12 that the beta value of a collection of securities is a *weighted average* of the beta values of the individual securities. This allows us to conclude therefore that the beta value of an asset is a weighted average of the beta values of the collection of securities that finance that asset. (In reality this relationship is determined the other way around. The betas of the financing securities will be determined by the systematic risk of the asset they are financing.)

Hence:

$$\beta_{\text{company assets}} = \beta_{\text{equity}} \times \frac{V_E}{V_0} + \beta_{\text{debt}} \times \frac{V_B}{V_0}.$$

Further, if we assume that a company's debt capital is virtually riskless, then $\beta_{\text{debt}} \approx 0$ and so the relationship reduces to:

$$\beta_{\text{company assets}} = \beta_{\text{equity}} \times \frac{V_E}{V_0}$$

$$\text{and } \beta_{\text{equity}} = \beta_{\text{company assets}} \times \frac{V_0}{V_E}.$$

Thus, for an all-equity company, the asset beta and the equity beta will be identical, but for a geared company the equity beta will be *greater than* the asset beta. The equity capital contains more systematic risk than the assets because it involves both business *and* financial risk.

Table 18.3

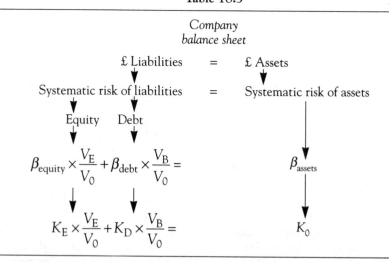

This distinction between asset betas and equity betas is important in relation to the use of beta values in determining a project discount rate. We shall return to examine this in the following chapter. Table 18.3 develops the relationship further.[7] The key points to keep in mind are that the *equity* beta measures the systematic business risk *and* the systematic financial risk of the shares, while the *asset* beta measures the company's systematic business risk *only*.

Gearing and K_E

We shall turn now to examine the exact nature of the relationship between gearing and the cost of equity capital, but all the while retaining our set of specified assumptions. The relationship can be derived from the dividend valuation model, as is shown in Table 18.4.

Table 18.4

Given the relationship:
$$V_0 = \frac{Y}{K_0} \tag{1}$$

then
$$Y = V_0 K_0 \equiv V_E K_0 + V_B K_0 \tag{2}$$

The dividend valuation model can be expressed as

$$K_E = \frac{D}{V_E} \equiv \frac{Y - V_B K_D}{V_E} \tag{3}$$

Substituting the definition of Y given in (2):

$$K_E = \frac{V_E K_0}{V_E} + \frac{V_B K_0}{V_E} - \frac{V_B K_D}{V_E} \tag{4}$$

Cancelling and simplifying:

$$K_E = K_0 + (K_0 - K_D)\frac{V_B}{V_E}$$

From Table 18.4 it can be seen that the cost of equity capital of a company consists of two elements, K_0 (which reflects the expected return required for the business risk of the company's assets), plus $(K_0 - K_D) V_B/V_E$. This latter element represents the *financial risk* premium and is a *positive* linear function of the gearing ratio.

Therefore, returning to the table used in Example 1, option 3 involved the following data:

$$
\begin{aligned}
K_0 &= 15\% \\
K_D &= 10\% \\
V_B &= £80\,000 \\
V_E &= £20\,000
\end{aligned}
$$

Hence:

$$K_E = 15\% + (15\% - 10\%) \times \frac{80\,000}{20\,000} = 35\%.$$

Earlier, we concluded that companies with assets that had the same degree of business risk (the same asset betas) would have the same weighted average costs of capital, whatever their gearing ratios. Therefore a slightly different (but equivalent) way of expressing the relationship between gearing and the cost of equity capital can be given:

$$K_{E_g} = K_{E_{ug}} + (K_{E_{ug}} - K_D)\frac{V_B}{V_E},$$

---

where K_{E_g} = cost of equity capital of a geared company;

and $\quad K_{E_{ug}}$ = cost of equity capital of a *similar business risk*, but *all-equity financed* company.

The graphical relationship

The relationship between a company's gearing ratio and the costs of its various types of capital is shown in Fig. 18.2. The lower diagram illustrates the fact that the total worth of a company's assets (and hence the total worth of the company) remains constant, *however* the assets are financed. Although, once again, it should be pointed out that this set of relationships – often referred to as the 'M and M No Tax Case' – was developed under the four sets of assumptions specified earlier.

Fig. 18.2 M and M *without tax*

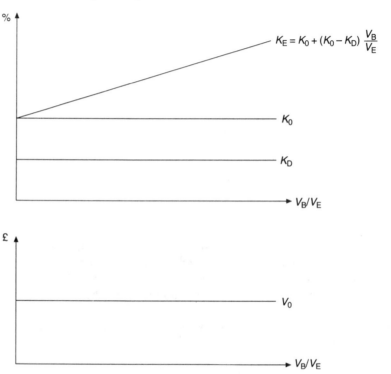

$$K_E = K_0 + (K_0 - K_D)\frac{V_B}{V_E}$$

The arbitrage proof

All the conclusions that we have drawn from the foregoing analysis are based on the initial premise that a company's gearing ratio does not itself determine or affect either its WACC or its total market value; but what reason do we have for believing this initial premise to be correct? Modigliani and Miller showed that if this was found *not* to hold true in practice (for example, if two companies with the same degree of business risk were found to have *different* WACCs) then that would represent a short-lived *disequilibrium* situation.

In such circumstances, *arbitragers* would move into the market, *selling* shares in the company with the lower-valued K_0 and *buying* shares in the company with the higher valued K_0. They would do so because they could profit from such transactions.

Investors would continue to trade until the WACCs of the two companies equated. This equating of the weighted average costs of capital would be brought about through normal market supply and demand forces (selling shares causing the price to fall, and vice versa). Once this position was reached, no further gains could be made, and equilibrium would have been restored.

The word 'arbitrage' is a technical term referring to a situation where two identical goods are selling in the same market for different prices. If such a situation arises, then it will not persist for long as dealers will start to buy at the lower price and sell at the higher price, thereby making a profit. Buying pressure (increased demand) will force up the price of the lower priced goods and selling pressure (increased supply) will force down the price of the higher priced goods.

Although stockbrokers do not often refer to this process in the share market by the term arbitrage, many of their transactions are arbitrage deals. The same is true of many commodity transactions on the commodity exchanges – but there they *do* refer to them by the technical name of arbitrage, as do foreign exchange dealers. In fact arbitrage is a very common form of transaction in many different markets.

An arbitrage example

Suppose that there are two companies, A and B, with identical levels of business risk, although their annual net cash flows are of different magnitudes. Data on the two companies are given in Table 18.5.

Because these two companies have identical levels of business risk, their WACCs *should* be the same. As they are not, an arbitrage opportunity exists: specifically for shareholders in company B (the company with the lower K_0) to move out of B and into company A.

Consider an investor who owns shares in B that have a current market value of £30 000. Those shares can be expected to produce an annual dividend of £30 000 × 0.166 = £5000. For this expected annual dividend flow the shareholder is bearing two types of risk: he holds the business risk of the company, and he also holds financial risk, as company B is geared.

Table 18.5

	Company	
	A	B
Year	$1 \rightarrow \infty$	$1 \rightarrow \infty$
	(£000s)	(£000s)
Annual dividends (D)	1000	2000
Annual interest (I)		400
Annual cash flow (Y)	1000	2400
Equity market value (V_E)	6250	12 000
Debt market value (V_B)		4000
Total market value (V_0)	6250	16 000
Equity cost of capital ($K_E = D/V_E$)	0.16	0.166
Debt cost of capital ($K_D = I/V_B$)	–	0.10
Weighted average cost of capital ($K_0 = Y/V_0$)	0.16	0.15
Number of shares in issue	6.5m.	10m.
Market price per share (P_E)	50p	120p

If he were to sell his £30 000 shareholding and simply invest the proceeds in the shares of company A, the two investments (shares in A, compared with shares in B) would *not* be comparable, as company A has an all-equity capital structure; thus although the business risk of the two investments would be the same, the shareholding in A would result in no financial risk being held.

To be able to compare 'like with like' would require the investor to maintain the *same* level of financial risk in company A as that held as a shareholder in company B. To do so, he substitutes home-made gearing (or home-made financial risk) for the corporate gearing that was borne as a shareholder in B.

Company B has borrowed (at the market rate of interest, K_D) £1 for every £3 of its shareholders' capital (i.e. the debt–equity ratio is 1:3), and so the investor should similarly borrow £1 (at the market interest rate of 10%) for every £3 of his own cash. Hence he borrows £10 000 and, by so doing, maintains his existing level of financial risk.

The investor has now amassed a total of £40 000 (£10 000 borrowed and £30 000 of his own) and *all* of this is now invested in the shares of company A. He or she thereby maintains both the business and the financial risk levels he or she held as a shareholder in company B.

This shareholding in A can be expected to produce an annual dividend of £40 000 × 0.16 = £6400. Out of this the investor has to pay an annual interest charge on his or her loan of £10 000 × 0.10 = £1000, leaving him or her a net annual expected cash flow of £5400. Thus the investor – through this arbitrage transaction – has increased his or her annual income by £400 with *no change* in either his or her business or financial risk levels.

Table 18.6

In equilibrium the WACC of company B will be 16% (that is, equal to the WACC of company A). Therefore the equilibrium total market value of company B is (£000s).

$$V_0 = \frac{£2400}{0.16} = £15\,000.$$

Given that company B's debt is correctly valued at £4000, then the equilibrium value of company B's equity will be:

$$V_E = £15\,000 - £4000 = £11\,000.$$

At which point $K_E = \dfrac{£2000}{£11\,000} = 0.182$ (approx.) which is exactly what is predicted by our M and M expression for the cost of equity capital:

$$K_E = 0.16 + (0.16 - 0.10)\frac{£4000}{£11\,000} = 0.182 \text{ (approx.)}.$$

However notice that this expression will only provide K_E when *equilibrium* values of K_0 (or $K_{E_{ug}}$), K_D, V_E and V_B are used.

Other shareholders in company B will also see this opportunity to make an arbitrage gain and will undertake similar transactions. The net result will be that selling pressure on B's shares will force the market price down to a point at which the WACCs of the two companies equate. Once this point is reached, there will be no further gains to be made from arbitrage dealings and so the price will stabilize: equilibrium will have been attained.

If the (not too unreasonable) assumption is made that the market *correctly* prices company A's equity and company B's debt, then the foregoing analysis suggests that the market value of B's equity will fall sufficiently far to raise the company's WACC to 16% (i.e. equal to that of company A). The equilibrium value of B's equity can then be calculated, as is shown in Table 18.6.

Thus the market value of company B's equity capital will fall from £12 million to £11 million. In other words, the shares will fall in price from 120p each to 110p each.

Reverse arbitrage

Now suppose that the stock market got things slightly wrong and over-reacted to the arbitrage transactions taking place, with the result that company B's shares fell in price to 104p per share. The situation would be as follows (figures in £000s).

$$\text{Company B:} \quad \begin{aligned} K_E &= £2000/£10\,400 &= 0.1923 \\ K_D &= £400/£4000 &= 0.10 \\ K_0 &= £2400/£14\,400 &= 0.166 \end{aligned}$$

As the company's WACC is now *above* that of company A, there would be an arbitrage opportunity in a move from the shares in company A into company B. However, notice that such a move, unlike the previous example, would involve going *from* an all-equity company *to* a geared company. This situation is sometimes referred to as *reverse* arbitrage, but it is rather misleading to do so as it is simply another arbitrage transaction, but now the *mechanics* of the move differ.

For example, suppose that there is an investor who holds £5000 worth of shares in company A. He or she presently expects to receive an annual dividend of £5000 × 0.16 = £800. This is in exchange for holding just the business risk of company A. As the company is all-equity, the shareholder bears no financial risk. Thus the problem is now how does the shareholder sell his or her shares in A and move into B – to take advantage of the temporary disequilibrium price of B's equity – while maintaining his or her current level of *zero* financial risk?

One approach is to buy *both* the debt and equity of company B in the same proportion as B's debt–equity ratio. Therefore the shareholder would sell his shares in A for £5000 and buy £4 of B's debt for every £10.40 of B's equity that was bought (B's debt–equity ratio is now £4m:£10.4m.). Thus he would buy £3611.11 of B's equity and £1388.89 of B's debt.

This process by which the investor maintains his zero financial risk level can be explained in several ways. Perhaps the most intuitively appealing is to argue that although he takes on a *positive* amount of financial risk through his equity holding in B, he also takes on a *negative* amount of financial risk through his debt holding. The net effect of holding both securities, in a combination equal to the gearing ratio, is that the financial risk is cancelled out.[8]

The effect of this reverse arbitrage transaction would be to give the investor an annual expected dividend of £3611.11 × 0.1923 = £694.42 and annual interest of £1388.89 × 0.1 = £138.89. Thus a total annual income of

£833.31 would be expected, which represents a gain of £33.31 over the original investment in company A, with no change in the risk borne.

Once again, other investors are likely to spot the opportunity to make this arbitrage gain and will act in a similar fashion. Their combined effect will be to bring about an equilibrium position and the equating of the WACCs of the two companies.

Two further points

In both the example of 'normal arbitrage' and of 'reverse arbitrage' there has been a concern to maintain a particular level of financial risk in order to allow investment returns to be comparable. However, in both cases, this was done on the basis of B's gearing ratio when in *disequilibrium*. Company B's equilibrium debt–equity ratio is 4:11. Therefore a more precise approach to holding financial risk at a given level would be to utilize this equilibrium ratio.

Thus in the normal arbitrage example, the investor would have substituted home-made for corporate gearing by borrowing £10 909.09 and the resulting arbitrage gain would have been slightly higher at £454.54. Similarly, in the reverse arbitrage example, the investor would have brought £1333.33 of company B's debt and £3666.67 of its equity. This again would result in a slightly increased arbitrage gain of £838.43.

Finally, what if an investor identifies the possibility for gain by arbitraging between two *geared* companies? In these circumstances, both mechanisms have to be employed. For example suppose company C had a debt–equity ratio of 1:3 whereas company D had a debt–equity ratio of 2:1. A shareholder in C wishes to move to D in order to take an arbitrage gain but also wishes to maintain his existing level of financial risk. This can be achieved by selling his shareholding in C, borrowing £1 for every £3 of sale proceeds and then applying the whole amount (borrowings plus own cash) to buying both the debt and equity of D in the proportion of £2 of debt for every £1 of equity.

Conclusions

The analysis up to this point allows three important conclusions to be made. The first is that companies with this same level of business risk should, in equilibrium, have the same weighted expected cost of capital.

Secondly, changes in a company's gearing ratio should leave its WACC unchanged. The increased return required by ordinary shareholders that arises out of an increase in gearing represents the compensation required for bearing additional financial risk. It is determined by the expression: $K_E = K_0 + (K_0 - K_D) V_B/V_E$.

Finally, and perhaps most importantly, the analysis leads us to conclude that the financing decision is relatively unimportant. It can have no bearing on the value of the company and so does not affect the wealth of ordinary shareholders.

In respect of the second of these three conclusions, the Modigliani and Miller analysis can be couched in very simple terms: as a company increases its gearing, two effects occur.

The first is that the company gains an *advantage* in that debt capital is cheaper than equity capital. The reason for this is that debt is a lower risk security than equity as debt holders get preferential 'pay-out' treatment, hence debt requires a lower expected return.

The second effect is that the company incurs a *disadvantage* in that the expected return required by equity capital increases. This is because increasing the gearing increases the financial risk held by equity and so forces up the required expected return, by way of compensation.

These two effects – the advantage and the disadvantage – are two different sides of the same coin. They both arise through the same phenomenon: debt holders are paid before equity holders. Therefore it is not surprising that the two effects exactly cancel each other out, so that the net effect is zero: changing the gearing leaves the company's total market value and its WACC unaltered.

The assumptions

Having outlined the basic M and M capital structure hypothesis, and before proceeding to examine alternative theories about the relationship between a company's gearing ratio and the cost of its equity capital, let us now take a closer look at the many assumptions upon which the hypothesis is based. In particular, we shall look at the assumptions underlying the arbitrage process which helps to restore the M and M equilibrium position in the presence of short-run disequilibrium stock market prices and which is held up as proof of their capital structure theory.

Arbitrage, as we know, is a technical term to describe a supply and demand market process which prevents perfect substitutes from selling at different prices in the same market. The key phrase here is 'perfect substitutes' and so, for the arbitrage process to act as a proof of the M and M hypothesis, ordinary shares in an all-equity company must be seen as (or must be able to be made) a perfect substitute for shares in a geared company.

We know from the valuation principles, which were defined originally, that value results from the future flow of net benefits and the certainty (or otherwise) attached to that future flow. Therefore, if we take two companies with the same expected annual cash flow and the same level of business risk, it follows that they should have identical total market values. However, we also know that if one company is all-equity and one company is geared, their ordinary shares are not perfect substitutes for each other, because the shares in the geared company include an additional risk element: financial risk.

In order to make the ordinary shares in the two companies perfect substitutes in terms of the risk borne in holding them, the investors in the geared company must be able to substitute home-made gearing (i.e. personally gear themselves) for corporate gearing. (We saw this process being undertaken in the first example used above.) To be able to do so, there must be no difference between the cost and risk of corporate borrowing (and hence gearing) and individual borrowing (gearing). This requires two assumptions of highly questionable real-world validity: individuals and companies must be able to borrow at the same rate of interest and the facility of limited liability for companies either must not exist, or must also extend to individuals.

In practice, individuals almost invariably have to pay a higher rate of interest on borrowed money than do companies, and in that borrowing their liability is unlimited, whereas companies have the protection of limited liability. Therefore, quite plainly, corporate and individual borrowing differs both in terms of cost and of risk, and so this requirement of the arbitrage process, as far as share dealings are concerned, appears to be unfulfilled.

However, the discrepancy between theory and practice can be resolved to some extent by the fact that for share prices to regain an equilibrium position, not *all* investors have to arbitrage in order to cause the necessary price changes through the supply and demand market mechanism. Just sufficient share transactions are required to 'move the market'. There are many limited liability companies with substantial holdings of shares in other companies, who could themselves undertake arbitrage transactions (and thereby avoid the problems outlined above), and so bring about market equilibrium.

This counter-argument, against the real-world invalidity of the two assumptions required for effective stock market arbitraging, appears reasonably sound – at least in theory – although it should be pointed out that there is some evidence to suggest that many institutional investors do not readily indulge in arbitrage transactions. However, there is another assumption involved in the arbitrage process which in practice does not hold, and so causes frictional problems: the assumption that all market transactions are undertaken at no cost (i.e. no stockbrokers' fees or commissions).

In practice, market transaction costs can be relatively expensive. Such a cost is likely to interfere with the smooth and efficient operation of arbitraging (e.g. the gain that might accrue to an investor from arbitraging may be completely offset by the transaction costs involved, and so these costs could be expected to interfere with the equilibrium producing mechanism). However, it could be claimed that transaction costs will only outweigh arbitrage gains either in very small share transactions or at the 'fine-tuning' stage, when the amount of disequilibrium remaining (and hence the level of arbitrage gains) is small.

Thus, although transaction costs will (as always) interfere with the economic mechanism, the degree of interference may well be relatively unimportant. We shall return to this assumption later, for it contains another, implicit assumption, that bankruptcy costs are zero. But before doing so, we shall examine the effects of two other assumptions within the hypothesis: that the cost of debt capital remains constant whatever the level of gearing, and that there is no taxation.

A rising cost of debt

It is difficult to see how M and M's analysis as originally presented can apply once really high levels of debt are reached. Logically, as a company gears up, the cost of debt should increase, so that K_D approaches what would have been the cost of equity capital, if the company had remained ungeared. This is because, at the extreme of 100% gearing (if such a thing is possible), the risks borne by the suppliers of debt capital would be the same as the risks borne by equity capital if the company were ungeared.

Fig. 18.3 shows how the required rate of return on both debt and equity increases as gearing increases. In this particular case it has been assumed that the cost of debt rises consistently from 8% risk free to the 15% return required to accept all the risk of the business. In other words the debt providers are accepting an increasing level of risk and the associated rewards. However any relationship between gearing and the riskiness of debt can be accommodated by the model.

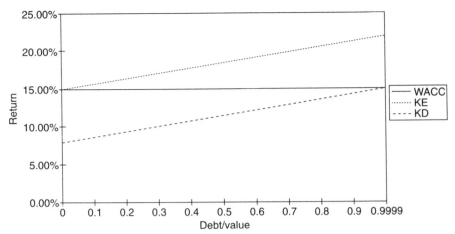

Fig. 18.3 A *rising cost of debt*

There is an inescapable logic here. We have seen that the return required by an investor is directly related to the amount of risk to which investors are exposed. If we ignore the fact that different types of risk might emerge as a company becomes very highly geared, we can see that the required return on the business as a whole must remain constant and so all we are doing in our analysis of the returns on debt and equity is deciding just how the risks, and hence the returns, are shared out between investors.

Summary

- This chapter has developed the M and M *no-tax* capital structure hypothesis. Its basic conclusion is that the capital structure decision cannot affect shareholder wealth and so is irrelevant.

- The analysis is presented in two stages. The first concerns the firm valuation model: $V_0 = Y \div K_0$ and the fact that K_0 is determined by the *risk* of Y. Gearing determines how Y is divided up between dividends and interest, but has no effect on the risk of Y and so has no effect on K_0. It is from this analysis that the basic conclusion follows.

- Further, assuming K_D remains a constant, then it is shown that K_E is a positive, linear function of the gearing ratio, given by the expansion:

$$K_E = K_0 + [K_0 - K_D]\frac{V_B}{V_E}.$$

- Thus the first stage of the analysis gives a constant K_0 at all levels of gearing and the second stage gives a constant K_D and a linearly increasing K_E. Finally, given the *overall* firm valuation model, as neither Y nor K_0 changes with gearing, nor will V_0. Graphically this is seen in Fig. 18.2.

- A secondary conclusion of the M and M analysis is that what determines a company's *overall* return (K_0) is its business risk – that is, the general uncertainty surrounding its net operating cash flow. As this is unaffected by gearing it therefore follows that companies with the same degree of business risk (that is, the same asset betas) will all have the same K_0, even though they might have different capital structures.

- Finally, M and M show that this conclusion *must* hold in an equilibrium capital market. If not, and companies in the same business risk class had different WACCs, then this would represent an arbitrage opportunity.

- If such arbitrage opportunities arise then investors will move in quickly to take advantage – and so make a profit – and the effect will be to re-establish the market equilibrium position.

Notes

1. A not entirely surprising result, in view of the rather unrealistic assumptions made in order to reach the conclusions of the analysis.

2. There are numerous definitions of gearing in use, perhaps the most common of which is the ratio of the total market value of debt capital to total market value of the company (i.e. debt plus equity). In those circumstances, the proportion of debt can be quoted as a percentage of a firm's total capital.

3. In fact, remembering the objective function we have assigned to management decision making, we really want to know whether the gearing ratio can affect the market value of a company's *equity* capital. We shall later reconcile changes in total market value and equity market value.

4. As a result, the assumption of an unchanging capital structure as a condition for the use of the weighted average cost of capital as an investment appraisal discount rate would appear to be no longer necessary.

5. In other words, it is assumed that if the company becomes bankrupt it will be possible to liquidate its assets and distribute them amongst the various claimants without cost.

6. The equity holders of an all-equity financed company only hold business risk. They do *not* hold any financial risk.

7. The reader may like to refer back to Example 1 of the previous chapter to see this relationship in action.

8. It should be noticed that this cancelling-out process does not mean that the financial risk has been eliminated in a diversification sense. Financial risk is systematic and therefore non-diversifiable.

Further reading

At the end of this chapter we have only really reached the half-way point in our analysis of the capital structure decision. However, obviously M and M's original article, together with some contemporary observations, are well worthwhile: F. Modigliani and M. Miller, 'The Cost of Capital Corporation Finance and the Theory of Investment', *American Economic Review*, June 1958; J.F. Weston, 'A Test of Cost of Capital Propositions', *Southern Economic Journal*, October 1963; and R.F. Wippern, 'Financial Structure and the Value of the Firm', *Journal of Finance*, December 1966.

Quickie questions

1. If a company had a cost of equity capital of 20% and a cost of debt of 10% and a 1:4 debt/equity ratio, what would the company's cost of capital be if it was all-equity financed?
2. Given the information in question 1, if the company were to change its gearing ratio from 1:4 to 3:5 what would be the change in its K_E and its K_0?
3. Two companies, A and B, are in the same business risk class. A is all-equity and B has a gearing ratio of 1:3. You have £100 worth of shares in company A. Show how you would arbitrage into company B.
4. In an arbitrage transaction, what is the purpose of home-made gearing?
5. What is financial risk and who bears it?
6. A company has a gearing ratio of 1:2. Its cost of equity capital is 20% and its cost of debt is 10%. If $E(r_M) = 15\%$ and $r_F = 10\%$ what is the company's asset beta?
7. Given the information in question 6, if the company were to change its gearing from 1:2 to 2:5, what would be the company's revised equity beta? (Assume K_D remains at 10%.)
8. Given the information in question 6, another company also has a cost of equity of 20% and a cost of debt of 10%. However it has a debt/equity ratio of 2:5. Are they in the same business risk class?

Problems

1. Alpha plc and Beta plc are two publicly quoted companies whose assets have the same level of systematic risk. Each has a constant annual earnings flow (before dividends and interest) of £5 million. This level of earnings is expected to be maintained by both companies in the future.

    Alpha has issued £8 million of 9% irredeemable debentures; each £100 debenture is currently quoted at £50, ex interest. Beta has no debt. Each of Alpha's 17.2 million ordinary shares is currently quoted at £1, ex div, while Beta has issued 46.4 million shares each of which has a market price of 50p, ex div. Both companies pay out the entire earnings flow each year as dividends and interest.

    Jill Gamma holds 464 000 shares in Beta as part of her well-diversified investment portfolio. Her market analysis leads her to believe that Alpha shares are currently under-priced, because of a temporary disequilibrium in the market. As a result, she is considering selling her Beta holding and investing in Alpha instead.

    Required:
    (a) Suggest how Ms Gamma could undertake the arbitrage deal so as to maintain her current level of financial risk. Explain briefly why you think your suggested approach will maintain her financial risk level. What would be her resulting gains?
    (b) What would be the equilibrium share price of Alpha's equity if other investors also undertook arbitrage deals?
    Assume that the market prices of Alpha's debentures and Beta's shares are in equilibrium. Assume no taxation.

2. Cabernet plc and Chardonnay Ltd, are two companies in the same business risk class. Cabernet is a quoted company with a debt:equity ratio of 1:3. The company's equity has a beta of 1.6 and the debt capital can be assumed to be riskless. Chardonnay is an unquoted, all-equity financed company.

The expected return on the FT All-Share Index is 16%. The return on government stock (and also the return on Cabernet's debt) is 10%.

Assume that both Cabernet and Chardonnay pay out constant annual dividends. Cabernet's debt is irredeemable. Ignore taxation.

Required:
(a) Explain precisely what is meant by the term 'same business risk class'. Estimate the beta value of Chardonnay's equity.
(b) Estimate the weighted average cost of capital of each company and comment briefly on the significance of your figures in respect of the Modigliani and Miller (no-tax) capital structure hypothesis.
(c) A small shareholder in Chardonnay has just received his regular dividend of £150. The shareholder has now been offered £1000 for his shareholding. However, he does not know whether or not to sell his shares as he relies heavily on his annual dividend from the company.

Explain how the shareholder can make himself better off with no change in risk by selling his shares in Chardonnay and investing in Cabernet. What would be his resulting gain?
(d) Assuming Cabernet's debt and equity capital are at their equilibrium value, estimate the equilibrium value of the investor's shareholding in Chardonnay.

3. Ekwitty Ltd has an all-equity capital structure. Geer Ltd is very highly geared. Both companies come within the same business risk class. You are given the following information:

	Geer Ltd Yrs 1–∞	Ekwitty Ltd Yrs 1–∞
Annual dividends	100 000	180 000
Annual interest	80 000	–
Total annual cash earnings	180 000	180 000
Total market value of equity	400 000	1 800 000
Total market value of debt	1 000 000	–

There is a perfect capital market, no taxation, no transaction costs and no difference between corporate and private gearing.

Required:
(a) What would you conclude from the above information?
(b) Draw a diagram or diagrams (not to scale), to illustrate the current situation and to show what would happen if arbitragers entered the market.
(c) Illustrate the gain to be made from arbitrage by an individual currently holding £1000 worth of shares in one of the above companies (i.e. there are only arbitrage gains to be made from trading one way; therefore, you have to specify initially the direction of arbitrage).

Assume that the ordinary shares of Ekwitty Ltd and the debentures of Geer Ltd are in equilibrium.

19 Capital structure in a world with tax

Taxation and capital structure

In Chapter 18 we examined the M and M *no-tax* capital structure hypothesis. In this chapter we will look at the M and M *with-tax* analysis and we shall see that, as a result, the conclusion that we reached in Chapter 18 will be radically changed. However, we need to be aware that the analysis carried out by M and M refers to what is know as a *classical* tax system whereas the system in the UK and other European countries is an *imputation* system. In the case of a classical system, the company pays tax on its profits after paying interest on debt and the shareholders then pay tax on all of the dividends they receive. However, in the case of the imputation system, whilst the company still pays tax on its profits after interest, the shareholders are deemed to have already paid income tax, normally at the standard rate, when they receive a dividend. This makes the application of M and M's ideas much more complex. We will explain the analysis carried out by M and M because it offers a useful insight into the factors that might determine an optimal capital structure for a company but it should not be seen as offering a straightforward analytical tool that can be simply applied to calculate the optimal gearing position.

In the analysis of the capital structure problem in Chapter 18 (under the set of simplifying assumptions used) we stated that the total market value of a company could be defined as: $V_0 = Y/K_0$. Therefore, a company's gearing ratio could only affect its total market value (V_0) if it affected either the company's expected annual net cash flow (Y) or its weighted average cost of capital (K_0). With the introduction of a taxation regime which allows debt capital interest to be set off against tax liability, a company *will* be able to increase its expected annual net *after-tax* cash flow (Y) by gearing up.

This is effectively the same situation as was examined by means of the single-period investment–consumption model in the last section of Chapter 17.

Table 19.1 shows that a geared company's total *after-tax* cash flow can now be split into two elements: the after-tax cash flow that would arise if it were all equity financed, *plus* the tax relief it receives on the debt interest payments.[1] Therefore the total after-tax cash flow of the company will increase as it increases its gearing. This is because the more highly geared the company becomes, the more debt interest it pays, the greater the amount of tax relief it obtains and hence the smaller is the amount of tax paid. In such circumstances, the company would theoretically maximize its total market value by gearing up so that its capital structure consists of virtually all debt and just a token amount of equity to determine ownership.

In other words, taking the final expression for V_0 in Table 19.1:

$$V_0 = \frac{X(1-T)}{K_{E_{ug}}} + V_B T \tag{5}$$

Table 19.1

The dividend and interest valuation models indicate that the total value of a company is equal to the present value sum of the future expected dividend and interest cash flow streams. Still assuming all-level perpetuity cash flow streams, where X represents the annual operating net cash flow *before* interest and taxes:

$$V_E = \frac{(X - V_B K_D)(1-T)}{K_{E_g}} \tag{1}$$

$$V_B = \frac{V_B \times K_D}{K_D} \tag{2}$$

$$V_0 = \frac{(X - V_B K_D)(1-T)}{K_{E_g}} + \frac{V_B K_D}{K_D} \tag{3}$$

Looking at the total cash flow

$$(X - V_B K_D)(1 - T) + V_B K_D,$$

and expanding the terms:

$$X - XT - V_B K_D + V_B K_D T + V_B K_D.$$

Cancelling and simplifying:

$$X(1 - T) + V_B K_D T.$$

Thus the company's after-tax cash flow is what it would be if it were all-equity financed ($X(1 - T)$), *plus* the value of the interest tax relief ($V_B K_D T$). The total value of the company is found by discounting these annual cash flows to present value. The discount rate to be applied to $X(1 - T)$ is the cost of equity capital that *would* apply to the company *if* it were all-equity financed ($K_{E_{ug}}$). The discount rate to be applied to $V_B K_D T$ (i.e. the interest rate that reflects the risk involved) is K_D. Thus:

$$V_0 = \frac{X(1-T)}{K_{E_{ug}}} + \frac{V_B K_D T}{K_D} \tag{4}$$

$$V_0 = \frac{X(1-T)}{K_{E_{ug}}} + V_B T \tag{5}$$

Hence, the more highly geared the company becomes, the larger becomes the second term (the first term remains unchanged) and so the greater becomes the value of the company.

this can be interpreted as follows: The total market value of a geared company (V_0) is equal to what it *would be worth* if it was all-equity financed,

$$\left(\frac{X(1-T)}{K_{E_{ug}}} \right),$$

plus the present value of tax relief on debt interest – $V_B T$.

Expression (5) can be rewritten as:

$$V_{0g} = V_{E_{ug}} + V_B T,$$

where V_{0g} is the total market value of a geared company and $V_{E_{ug}}$ represents what the company would be worth if it were all-equity financed. $V_B T$ represents the present value worth of the tax relief on debt interest, and is often referred to as the 'tax shield'.

Therefore under the assumption of tax relief being available on debt interest, the total market value of the company is an *increasing* function of the level of gearing. What effect does gearing now have on both a company's cost of equity capital and its weighted average cost of capital? To answer that question we must once again examine the relationships involved.

Taxation and the WACC

The revised relationship between the gearing ratio and WACC can be derived both intuitively and analytically. Let us start with the intuitive explanation.

We saw in a world *without* tax that there was both an advantage $(K_D < K_E)$ and a disadvantage (financial risk $\rightarrow$ increased K_E) to gearing up. However, these two effects exactly offset each other and so the net effect was zero: K_0 remained unaffected by gearing changes.

With the introduction of tax, there is now an additional *advantage* to gearing up: the tax relief obtained on the debt interest. Further, this advantage is *cumulative* – the more highly geared a company becomes, the more tax relief it obtains and the smaller its tax liability becomes. Thus we could intuitively argue that in a world where there was tax relief on debt interest, we would expect a company's *after-tax* WACC to be progressively lowered as it increased its level of gearing.

Indeed, this conclusion can also be inferred from the WACC expression. In this expression, the cost of debt capital is *after tax* and as a company gears up, a progressively greater weight is given to this 'cheap' capital:

$$K_0 = K_E \times \frac{V_E}{V_0} + K_D(1-T) \times \frac{V_B}{V_0}.$$

A more analytical derivation of the relationship between the WACC and gearing is given in Table 19.2 (where $K_{E_{ug}}$ represents the cost of equity capital of a similar business risk, but all-equity financed company).

The derivation of the WACC in Table 19.2 shows that, (as we intuitively reasoned), as a company increases the proportion of debt in its capital structure, so the WACC declines. In fact, the WACC is a *negative* linear function of the ratio V_B/V_0.

The cost of equity capital

The cost of equity capital's relationship with the gearing ratio can also be intuitively derived. We know that the expected return required by equity rises (in a world of no taxes) as gearing is increased, because of the increasing

Table 19.2

Starting with the company valuation expression derived in Table 19.1:

$$V_0 = \frac{X(1-T)}{K_{E_{ug}}} + V_B T \tag{1}$$

Multiplying through by $K_{E_{ug}}$

$$V_0 K_{E_{ug}} = X(1-T) + V_B T K_{E_{ug}}. \tag{2}$$

Rearranging and factoring out V_0

$$V_0 K_{E_{ug}} - V_B T K_{E_{ug}} = X(1-T) \tag{3}$$

$$V_0 K_{E_{ug}} - \frac{V_0 V_B T K_{E_{ug}}}{V_0} = X(1-T) \tag{4}$$

$$V_0 \left(K_{E_{ug}} - \frac{V_B T K_{E_{ug}}}{V_0} \right) = X(1-T) \tag{5}$$

$$V_0 \frac{X(1-T)}{K_{E_{ug}}[1-(V_B T/V_0)]} \tag{6}$$

Given that $\qquad V_0 = X(1-T)/K_0.$

Then $\qquad K_0 = K_{E_{ug}}[1-(V_B T/V_0)]. \tag{7}$

Table 19.3

The WACC can be calculated either as:

$$K_0 = \frac{V_E}{V_0} \times K_{E_g} + \frac{V_B}{V_0} \times K_D(1-T)$$

or

$$K_0 = K_{E_{ug}} \left(1 - \frac{V_B T}{V_0} \right)$$

Therefore:

$$\frac{V_E}{V_0} \times K_{E_g} + \frac{V_B}{V_0} \times K_D(1-T) = K_{E_{ug}} \left(1 - \frac{V_B T}{V_0} \right) \tag{1}$$

Multiplying through by V_0 and rearranging:

$$K_{E_g} = \frac{K_{E_{ug}}(V_0 - TV_B)}{V_E} - \frac{V_B K_D}{V_E} + \frac{V_B K_D T}{V_E}$$

$$= \frac{K_{E_{ug}} V_E}{V_E} + \frac{K_{E_{ug}} V_B}{V_E} - \frac{K_{E_{ug}} TV_B}{V_E} - \frac{V_B K_D}{V_E} + \frac{V_B K_D T}{V_E} \tag{2}$$

$$= K_{E_{ug}} + \frac{K_{E_{ug}} V_B}{V_E}(1-T) - \frac{K_D V_B}{V_E}(1-T)$$

$$K_{E_g} = K_{E_{ug}} + (K_{E_{ug}} - K_D) - \frac{V_B(1-T)}{V_E} \tag{3}$$

burden of financial risk. The financial risk arises because debt interest has to be paid in full, before any dividends can be paid.

In a taxed world, debt interest payments are, effectively, subsidized by the tax authorities. Thus if the company had interest of £100 to pay and corporation tax was at 33%, then £33 out of the £100 of interest payable would be provided for through a reduced tax liability. Therefore, in a taxed world, although the cost of equity capital would still be expected to increase with increased gearing because of the presence of financial risk, it would do so at a slower rate than in a tax-free world. The presence of subsidized interest payments effectively *reduces* gearing ratios from the viewpoint of shareholders and their financing risk.

Once again, this intuitive argument can be shown, analytically, to hold good. Table 19.3 illustrates the relationship. What we derive is an expression that is very similar to the cost of equity capital function in an untaxed world, except that the effect of the gearing ratio is *dampened down* by the presence of taxation. As a result, the amount of debt in the gearing ratio is measured as $V_B(1 - T)$, rather than just V_B.

The graphical relationship

The relationship between the various costs of capital and the gearing ratio is shown graphically in Fig. 19.1. (Note that although the WACC is a *linear* function of V_B/V_0, it is an *asymptotic* function of V_B/V_E.)

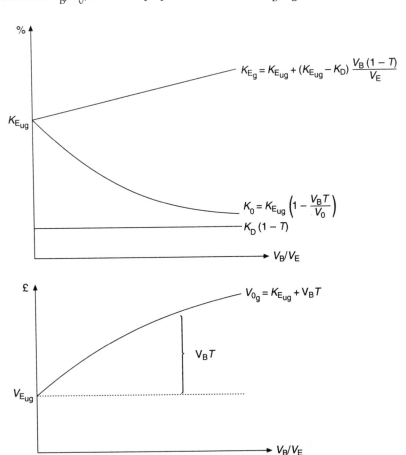

Fig. 19.1 M and M with tax

$$K_{E_g} = K_{E_{ug}} + (K_{E_{ug}} - K_D)\frac{V_B(1-T)}{V_E}$$

$$K_0 = K_{E_{ug}}\left(1 - \frac{V_B T}{V_0}\right)$$

$$K_D(1-T)$$

$$V_{0_g} = K_{E_{ug}} + V_B T$$

Therefore we can reiterate the conclusion of the M and M with-tax capital structure hypothesis: companies should try to gear themselves up (by issuing debt capital) as high as possible. The more highly geared the company, the lower will be K_0, the higher will be V_0 and the greater will be shareholder wealth. This increase in shareholder wealth comes about through the *tax shield*, for it is the shareholders who gain the benefit of the company, receiving tax relief on debt interest and so paying less tax.

In the last chapter we saw how we could allow for increased required returns on debt and it is possible to carry out a similar exercise allowing for the effects of taxation. In Fig. 19.1 we assume that $K_{E_{ug}}$ is 15%, that the riskless cost of debt is 8% and that the tax rate is 31%. This illustrates how, given the assumptions under which we are operating, the WACC decreases from 15% with no debt to 10.35% with 100% debt. 10.35% is, of course, $15\% \times (1 - 31\%)$ since at this point we have to assume that the required return would be 15% but that interest would be a tax allowable expense.

Using the M and M equations

The M and M with-tax analysis produces three fundamental equations, as we have seen:

$$K_{E_g} = K_{E_{ug}} + (K_{E_{ug}} - K_D) - \frac{V_B \times (1-T)}{V_E} \tag{1}$$

$$K_0 = K_{E_{ug}} \left(1 - \frac{V_B.T}{V_0}\right) \tag{2}$$

$$V_{0_g} = V_{E_{ug}} + V_B.T \tag{3}$$

These equations can be utilized to illustrate the impact on the company's total market value, its various costs of capital and on shareholder wealth, of changes in the company's capital structure.

We will use two examples. In Example 1, a company undertakes an 'artificial' change to its capital structure by issuing new equity capital and using the money to 'repay' debt. Thus the new finance is not increasing the assets of the company, but is being used to simply change the company's capital structure (to *reduce* its level of gearing). In Example 2, a company is issuing debt capital in order to finance a capital investment. In this case the finance *is* increasing the assets of the company, as well as changing its capital structure.

Example 1

Dongo Plc has a geared capital structure, with details as follows:

V_E	=	£80 million	V_B	=	£35 million
K_{E_g}	=	20%	K_D	=	12% before tax
			T	=	33%

The management propose to issue £10 million of new equity and to use the money raised to repay £10 million of the company's bonds (which can be assumed to be undated).

Dongo's current weighted average cost of capital can be calculated as:

$$K_0 = K_{E_g} \times \frac{V_E}{V_0} + K_D \times (1 - T) \times \frac{V_B}{V_0}$$

$$K_0 = 20\% \times \frac{£80m}{£115m} + 12\%(1 - 0.33) \times \frac{£35m}{£115m} = 16.36\%.$$

We will now examine the impact of the management's proposal on:

1. the company's total market value;
2. the shareholders' wealth;
3. the company's WACC;
4. the company's cost of equity capital.

However, before doing so, we can *anticipate* the effect on all four factors on the basis of Fig. 19.1. Dongo's management propose to *reduce* the company's gearing level and so:

1. the company's total market value (V_0) will *fall*;
2. shareholder wealth will fall because of a reduction in the size of the *tax shield*;
3. the company's WACC will *rise*;
4. the company's K_{E_g} will *fall*.

Let us now look at the precise effects of Dongo's proposed change in capital structure, taking each of those four impacts in order.

1. Using the *current* data, on the M and M equation:

$$V_0 = V_{E_{ug}} + V_B.T$$

to solve for $V_{E_{ug}}$

$$£115m = V_{E_{ug}} + £35m \times 0.33$$

$$£115m - £11.55m = V_{E_{ug}} = £103.45m.$$

Therefore if Dongo's assets were all-equity financed, the company's total market value would be £103.45 million. Its total market value is currently £115 million because of the tax shield – the tax relief that Dongo receives because of its interest liabilities.

If Dongo now raises £10 million of new equity and uses the finance to reduce its outstanding debt from £35 million to £25 million then, again using:

$$V_0 = V_{E_{ug}} + V_B.T,$$

we can find the new total market value of the company:

$$V_0 = £103.45m + £25m \times 0.33 = £111.7m.$$

Dongo's total market value has been reduced from £115 million to £111.7 million (a reduction of £3.3 million), because it has lost the tax shield on the £10 million of repaid debt equal to £10m × 0.33 = £3.3m (remember, the value of the tax shield is given by: $V_B.T$)

2. The change in the company's capital structure will lead to a fall in shareholder wealth equal to the lost tax shield of £3.3 million. This can be demonstrated as follows:

Currently:	V_E =	£80m.
Given:	V_0 =	$V_E + V_B$
Therefore:	V_E =	$V_0 - V_B$

and so after the change in capital structure:

$$V_E = £111.7m - £25m = £86.7m.$$

Therefore the total market value of the equity has risen from £80 million to £86.7 million but, remember, shareholders have invested an *extra* £10 million in the company. As the value of their shares has only gone up by £6.7 million, there has been a loss in their wealth of: £10m − £6.7m = £3.3m.

3. Using the current data in the M and M equation:

$$K_0 = K_{E_{ug}} \times \left(1 - \frac{V_B.T}{V_0}\right),$$

we can solve for $K_{E_{ug}}$:

$$16.36\% = K_{E_{ug}} \times \left(1 - \frac{£35m \times 0.33}{£115m}\right)$$

$$\frac{16.36\%}{0.90} = K_{E_{ug}} = 18.22\%.$$

This would be Dongo's cost of equity capital, if the company were all-equity financed. Therefore 18.22% represents the return required for just Dongo's *business* risk. At present Dongo's shareholders receive a return (K_E) of 20% because they also bear financial risk from Dongo's current level of gearing.

If Dongo now issues an extra £10 million of equity and repays £10 million of debt, then again using:

$$K_0 = K_{E_{ug}} \times \left(1 - \frac{V_B.T}{V_0}\right),$$

we can find the new WACC:

$$K_0 = 18.22\% \times \left(1 - \frac{£25m \times 0.33}{111.7m}\right) = 16.87\%.$$

Therefore the change in capital structure has *increased* Dongo's WACC from its existing level of 16.36% to 16.87%.

4. Finally, the M and M equation for K_E, together with our calculation of $K_{E_{ug}} = 18.22\%$ can be used to identify the company's new cost of equity capital:

$$K_{E_g} = K_{E_{ug}} + (K_{E_{ug}} - K_{DBT}) \times \frac{V_B \times (1-T)}{V_E}$$

$$K_{E_g} = 18.22\% + (18.22\% - 12\%) \times \frac{£25m \times (1-0.33)}{£86.7m} = 19.42\%.$$

Thus, the company's cost of equity capital will fall from 20% to 19.42% with the proposed reduction in the company's gearing ratio.

Example 2

Bertie Plc is an all-equity financed company with a total worth of £12 million and a cost of equity capital of 18%. Bertie intends to invest in a £3 million capital investment to expand the company's existing manufacturing capacity. The investment has a +£1m NPV.

The company intends to finance the project with a £3 million irredeemable bond issue at the current market interest rate of 10%. The corporation tax rate is 33%. What is the impact of the project and its finance on Bertie's:

1. total market value, V_0;
2. shareholders' wealth;
3. WACC; and
4. cost of equity capital?

Taking each of these in turn:

1. At present, because Bertie is all-equity financed:

$$V_0 = V_E = V_{E_{ug}} = £12m.$$

The new V_0 arising out of the change in capital structure can be found from the M and M equation:

$$V_0 = V_{E_{ug}} + V_B.T$$

therefore

$$V_0 = £12m + £3m \times 0.33 = £12.99m.$$

However, we must not forget that, in this example, £3 million of *additional* assets are being added to the company, *plus* the project's positive NPV. Thus the new total market value of the company, after taking into account not only the change in capital structure, but also the £3 million of newly added assets (i.e. the capital investment) and the project's NPV is given by:

$$V_0 = £12.99m + £3m + £1m = £16.99m.$$

This is made up as follows:

Existing total market value of company:	£12m
+ Extra tax shield:	£0.99m
+ Extra capital investment:	£3m
+ Project's NPV:	£1m
= New total market value of the company:	£16.99m

2. Given that $V_0 = V_E + V_B$, then the post-investment total market value of the equity will be:

$$V_E = V_0 - V_B$$

$$V_E = £16.99m - £3m = £13.99m.$$

Therefore shareholder wealth, represented by the total market value of the equity, has increased by £1.99 million. This is composed of two separate elements: the NPV of the project (£1 million) and the tax shield on the debt interest (£0.99 million).

3. Given the fact that Bertie is currently all-equity financed, then:

$$K_0 = K_E = K_{E_{ug}} = 18\%.$$

Using the M and M equation, the new WACC can be calculated:

$$K_0 = K_{E_{ug}} \times \left(1 - \frac{V_B.T}{V_0}\right)$$

$$K_0 = 18\% \times \left(1 - \frac{£3m \times 0.33}{£16.99m}\right) = 16.95\%.$$

Thus the increase in Bertie's gearing will cause its WACC to fall from 18% (its K_E) to 16.95%.

4. Using the M and M equation:

$$K_{E_g} = K_{E_{ug}} + (K_{E_{ug}} - K_{DBT}) \times \frac{V_B(1-T)}{V_E},$$

the new cost of equity capital can be estimated:

$$K_{E_g} = 18\% + (18\% - 10\%) \times \frac{£3m(1-0.33)}{£13.99m} = 19.15\%.$$

Therefore the change in Bertie's capital structure causes its cost of equity capital to increase from 18% to 19.15%. This is because, before the capital structure change, Bertie's shareholders only bore the company's *business* risk, as it was all-equity financed. However, after the issue of £3 million of debt, the company's shareholders are starting to bear *financial* risk as well, and so their return rises by 1.15% (the financial risk premium) to 19.15%.

Arbitrage in a taxed world

Before we leave the M and M analysis, it is worthwhile to point out that the arbitrage analysis that we looked at in Chapter 18 can be adapted to a taxed world. To show how we can do so, we will refer back to the two examples that were used in Chapter 18.

In the first arbitrage example, which was set out in Table 18.5, our investor was moving from a *geared* company (company B) to an *all-equity* financed company (company A). In order to be able to compare like with like, our investor had to substitute home-made or personal gearing for corporate gearing. This was done by the arbitrager borrowing money, at an interest rate equal to K_D, such that:

$$\left(\begin{array}{lll} \text{Borrowed} & & \text{Share} \\ \text{funds} & : & \text{sale} \\ & & \text{proceeds} \end{array} \right) = V_B : V_E \text{ of company B.}$$

With *tax* in the analysis, the procedure remains exactly the same, except that the arbitrager borrows money in the ratio:

$$\left(\begin{array}{lll} \text{Borrowed} & & \text{Share} \\ \text{funds} & : & \text{sale} \\ & & \text{proceeds} \end{array} \right) = V_B \times (1 - T) : V_E \text{ of company B.}$$

Therefore, in that example, given that $V_B : V_E$ of company B was 1:3, and now assuming a corporation tax rate of 33%, our arbitrager would borrow money in the ratio: $1 \times (1 - 0.33){:}3$, or 0.67:3. In other words, the arbitrager would borrow 67p for every £3 of share sale proceeds in order to maintain his existing level of financial risk.

A similar adjustment is made in the 'reverse arbitrage' situation. In that example, in the previous chapter, our arbitrager bought both debt *and* equity in the geared company in the same ratio as the company's gearing ratio. This now changes so that both debt and equity is bought in the ratio $V_B \times (1 - T){:}V_E$.

In our reverse arbitrage example the $V_B{:}V_E$ ratio was 4:10.40. Assuming a corporate tax rate of 33%, the arbitrager, instead of buying £4 of debt for every £10.40 of equity would buy debt and equity in the ratio of $4 \times (1 - 0.33){:}10.40$, or £2.68 of debt for every £10.40 of equity.

M and M in the real world

The previous analysis suggests that companies should gear themselves up to the maximum possible extent. However, in the real world, it is unlikely that companies will be able to fund themselves with 100% debt for legal and taxation reasons. Even allowing for this, the evidence is that companies generally do not borrow at anything like the levels that M and M's analysis suggests should happen. So far as UK companies are concerned, the average level of gearing is such that debt capital represents about 25% of total capital. This fact suggests that our model is too simple – it must be excluding some important aspects about the financing decision and its effects.

Agency costs

One possible reason why we do not find companies gearing up to the high levels suggested by the previous analysis is that there are some 'hidden' costs of debt capital that we have so far ignored. One particular group of these is referred to as agency costs.

Agency costs arise out of what is known as the principal–agent problem.[2] This problem is concerned with how the instructions or objectives, and the rewards, given to agents (i.e. management) can be formulated so that the agents, acting in their own interests, also act in the interest of the principals (i.e. the suppliers of company capital). In other words, the principal–agent problem is the problem of external financial control of managements by the suppliers of company finance.

In respect of debt finance, the suppliers of debt finance are concerned that they are not fooled or misled by a company's management. For example, a situation could occur where a management raise finance for a supposed investment in a low-risk project but, once the debt is issued, they use the money to invest in a high-risk project. Despite what we have seen concerning the sharing of risks between shareholders and debt holders, in such circumstances the debt holders might suffer simply because there is insufficient equity capital to carry the risk. Thus the expected rate of return for the debt holders would not properly reflect the risk of their investment.

In order to try to avoid this sort of situation we find that debt suppliers often impose very restrictive conditions (or covenants) on loan agreements that constrain management's freedom of action. For example, debt covenants may restrict the level of dividends that may be paid (to prevent shareholders stripping the firm of cash, to the detriment of debt holders); or they may restrict the level of additional debt finance that can be raised (in order to maintain a given degree of security); or they may restrict management from disposing of major fixed assets without the debt holders' agreement.

All of these examples represent *constraints* on management – they constrain their freedom of action – and are known as *agency costs*. All agents realize that they are going to be controlled or constrained by their principals, but that does not mean that agents actually *like* these costs they are forced to bear. They do not, and will often try to minimize them.

The more money the suppliers of debt capital lend to a company – that is the more highly geared the company becomes – then the more constraints they are likely to impose on the management in order to secure their investment. Hence it could be argued that management may well limit the level of a company's gearing in order to avoid the more onerous of these agency costs. As a result we do not find, in practice, companies gearing up to the high levels suggested by the M and M analysis.

Bankruptcy costs

Another cost which may be viewed as a part of the general agency costs is that of bankruptcy. In the previous analysis it was always assumed, implicitly, that companies could go bankrupt costlessly, but what happens when the possibility and the associated costs of corporate bankruptcy are introduced?

The probability of bankruptcy is likely to be (amongst other things) an increasing function of a company's gearing ratio but, as far as the capital structure problem is concerned, the important factor is the substantial cost which may be involved in a company's liquidation or bankruptcy. If a company that was forced into bankruptcy could be liquidated costlessly (i.e. if its assets could be sold off at their 'correct' market values and if there were no legal or administrative costs), then the fact that the probability of bankruptcy is an increasing function of the gearing ratio would not have any adverse effect on the total market value of a company.

Unfortunately, in the real world, the costs of bankruptcy are considerable. As well as very substantial administrative and legal costs, the company's specialized assets may have to be disposed of at less than their operational values, because they have lost their going-concern/synergy value and because their sale has to take place hurriedly in an imperfect market. These costs (in whole or in part) will come out of the liquidated pool of funds which is destined to be returned to shareholders. Therefore, bankruptcy involves a company's shareholders in a cost they would otherwise not have incurred and so it is effectively responsible for causing a reduction in their level of wealth.

All shareholders, whether they be shareholders in geared or all-equity companies, face the (hopefully small) probability that their company may be forced into bankruptcy. This fact is just one component of the concept of business risk and, as such, is allowed for in the expected value of the future dividend flow and the required expected return on equity capital. However, the act of gearing up by a company has the effect of positively *adding* to the probability of its bankruptcy, due to the fact that if a company is unable to meet its fixed debt interest payments, then the debt holders have the legal right to liquidate the company in order to repossess their capital and unpaid interest.

Therefore, as a company increases its level of gearing, an increasing proportion of its expected annual cash flow is likely to be paid out as interest. But, as the future is uncertain, these annual cash flows are variable while debt interest represents a fixed, contractual obligation, and so there is also an increasing chance that the company's cash flows will not be sufficient to meet these debt interest payments. A succession of such years for a geared company will almost certainly lead to bankruptcy and the incursion of its associated costs.

Thus, as gearing increases, so too does the probability of bankruptcy and hence the *expected* cost of bankruptcy. (Expected cost of bankruptcy = cost of bankruptcy × probability of bankruptcy.) Given this analysis, the M and M expression for the total market value of a geared company might be altered to:

$$V_{0_g} = V_{E_{ug}} + V_B T - E_{[\text{BANKRUPTCY}]}$$

where $E_{[\text{BANKRUPTCY}]}$ represents the expected cost of bankruptcy. As a result, it could be argued that management restrict the company's level of gearing because V_{0_g} – and so shareholder wealth – *reduces* at very high levels of gearing. Fig. 19.2 illustrates the possible situation.

Therefore bankruptcy costs would appear to provide yet another reason why we do not find companies with very high gearing ratios: there is this additional implicit cost which is borne by shareholders. However, these expected costs may not be the most important element in the role that the possibility of bankruptcy plays in limiting gearing ratios.

Shareholders can generally be expected to hold well-diversified portfolios. Therefore, if one particular company within an investment portfolio goes into liquidation, the associated costs will be incurred by the investor, but they are likely to be relatively small. In contrast the management of a company hold *undiversified* portfolios as far as their labour is concerned (i.e.

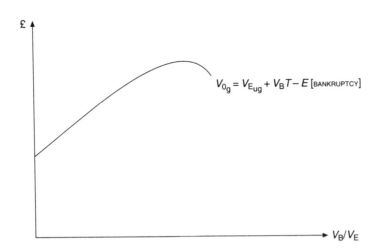

Fig. 19.2 *Bankruptcy costs*

$$V_{0_g} = V_{E_{ug}} + V_B T - E \text{ [BANKRUPTCY]}$$

V_B/V_E

they only work for the one company) and so, to them, the cost of bankruptcy is *very* substantial – they lose their employment. Therefore we can conclude that management – for their *own* reasons – are also likely to want to restrict the level of gearing, in order to restrict the *probability* of bankruptcy and hence avoid the very substantial *personal* costs involved.

Debt capacity

A further reason for explaining why companies do not gear up to high levels to take advantage of debt interest tax relief is *debt capacity*. In fact it could be argued that debt capacity may play the *most* important role in the determination of real-world capital structures.

Most debt capital lent to companies by banks and other debt suppliers is *secured* against the assets of the company. Relatively little debt capital is unsecured. The idea behind securing a loan against the company's assets is obvious. If the company defaults on the loan agreement, the bank can step in, seize the assets against which the loan was secured, sell them off and recover their loan (and any unpaid interest) out of the sale proceeds.

From the foregoing, it will be clear that some assets provide better security for a loan than other assets. Perhaps the two most important characteristics of an asset in determining its suitability to act as security against a loan are:

1. the 'quality' of the second-hand market in the asset;
2. the asset's rate of depreciation.

The quality of the second-hand market refers to the ease (or otherwise) with which a seized asset could be sold. Thus the better the quality of the second-hand market, the more suitable is the asset as loan security. Similarly an asset which depreciates rapidly (in reality rather than accounting terms) is going to offer poor security. The value of the asset may then be worth significantly less than the outstanding value of the loan – particularly in the latter years of a loan's terms.

Therefore it is not surprising that if a company wishes to acquire a piece of property costing £1 million, the bank may be willing to loan £900 000 against the security of the asset. The property would be said to have a 90% *debt capacity*. However, if a company wished to purchase £1 million worth of specialized industrial equipment, the bank may only be willing to lend, say, £300 000 against the security of that asset. The asset only has a debt capacity of 30%.

Property could be expected to have a high debt capacity because of its active second-hand market and its slow rate of depreciation (it could even appreciate). Specialized industrial machinery, on the other hand, is likely to have a relatively low debt capacity because it probably has a poor second-hand market and a high rate of depreciation.

A further interesting issue concerns the intangible assets that a company owns and more especially goodwill. Goodwill is simply the difference between the value of a company as a whole and the sum of the values of its separate assets. We have already seen that a company will make investment decisions so as to increase the present value of its cash flows. Say that it invests £1 million in plant because this will produce cash flows with a PV of £2 million and that the market recognizes this fact. The value of the company will increase by £1 million but this is not reflected by any increase in tangible assets in its balance sheet. The cost of the plant is simply transferred from one asset (cash) to another (plant) and does not lead to an increase in assets. There are very few companies whose market value is close to the value of their separate assets and an interesting exercise is to compare the balance sheet (accounting) value of a company with its market capitalization, which is, as we know, based on expected cash flows. The way to find out the accounting value of a company's equity is to add together the figures shown for ordinary share capital and reserves in its annual report (balance sheet). The market capitalization is simply the number of ordinary shares in issue multiplied by the share price on the day in question. This difference is partly due to the company's assets not reflecting their separate market values (because of changing prices) but it is also because the company has other assets that are impossible to either value or sell separately. These include reputation, customer loyalty, the quality of the workforce, the quality of management, know-how and all the other things that go to make a company more than the sum of its parts. These cannot really be offered as security for borrowing.

Therefore, from this discussion on debt capacity, we may conclude that high levels of corporate gearing are unusual, not because of a positive management decision to limit the gearing level, but simply because the company has run out of debt capacity. In other words the capital structure decision may be determined more by the *suppliers* of debt capital, than by the managers of the company.

There is remarkably little research into how executives actually make decisions about the amount that their company will borrow but there is some evidence that there is a belief that debt is generally a cheaper option than raising new equity and that the upper level of debt a company takes on is often determined using judgement as to how much risk new debt poses to the company. This judgement may be exercised by either the company or its potential lenders.

Tax exhaustion

A final reason that we will mention for observed gearing levels is tax exhaustion. Debt financing gained its attractions from the tax relief allowable on the interest payments. As a company increases its gearing, so it increases its annual interest payments and it also increases the amount of tax relief that it gains. The term 'tax exhaustion' refers to the situation where a company does not have a sufficient tax *liability* to be able to take advantage of all the tax *relief* that it has available.

At the point of tax exhaustion the *effective* cost of debt capital rises significantly from $K_D(1 - T)$ to simply K_D. Therefore, once this position is reached, debt capital loses its attraction for the company, and so we have a fourth possible reason for the observed levels of corporate gearing.

Further views on capital structure

The Modigliani and Miller analysis of the capital structure problem, whether in a taxed or a tax-free world, is based upon a number of assumptions about the environment, including the tax regime, and the working of the capital markets. On the basis of these assumptions, their analysis produces rigorous conclusions about the nature of the trade-off between financial risk and gearing and about the behaviour of a company's cost of equity capital, its weighted average cost of capital and also its total market value, as the gearing ratio changes.

In addition, an important conclusion arising from the discussion, as far as company managements and shareholders are concerned, is that gearing up (i.e. increasing the proportion of debt in a company's capital structure) enhances the total market value of the company – and hence increases shareholders' wealth – through the tax relief that is allowable on corporate debt interest.

However, when we examine the real world we find that companies do not follow this conclusion to its logical extreme and gear up so that 99%+ of capital is debt. We then concluded that there must be some relevant factors that were missing from the analysis, of which we considered four possibilities: agency costs, bankruptcy costs, debt capacity and tax exhaustion. What can we conclude from this discussion? Perhaps the safest conclusion that we can make is that the capital structure decision (and hence the financing decision) is both complex and difficult. In particular the costs of increased gearing cause identification problems that prevent any general decision advice being formulated.

In this section we will examine two further views of the capital structure decision faced by companies. The first is referred to as the 'traditional' view, as it is a view that is often casually subscribed to, without much rigorous analysis being applied. The second is a further development by Miller (of M and M) who had some additional thoughts on the matter.

The traditional view of capital structure

It is often held that the generally accepted wisdom of investors, analysts and company managements alike (hence the term 'traditional' view) is that there are both advantages and disadvantages, as far as the maximization of shareholders' wealth is concerned, to corporate gearing. It is believed that at relatively low levels of gearing the advantages outweigh the disadvantages and so the market value of the company gradually rises but that, after a while, the relationship reverses and the disadvantages start to outweigh the advantages, so that further increases in gearing cause the company's market value to decline. Fig. 19.3 sketches the various relationships involved in this traditional view of capital structure.

The main advantage of gearing is seen to be that, because corporate debt interest is allowable against taxation, a company is able to raise capital at an effective cost which is substantially below the market rate (i.e. debt capital is held to be 'cheap' capital because of tax relief). The main disadvantage arises from the fact that increased gearing results in an increased level of financial risk being borne by the company's shareholders. This, in turn, leads the shareholders to require a higher expected return on their capital (i.e. an increased K_E), by way of compensation.

A *further* disadvantage is also postulated. This is that, at very high gearing ratios, debt holders also start to bear their own version of financial risk – due to the quantity of debt issued and so the amount of interest required to be paid out of cash flow. As a result, K_D *also* starts to rise in order to provide compensation for this additional risk.

In contrast to this traditional view of capital structure, the M and M hypothesis was that, in a tax-free environment, the advantages and disadvantages of gearing *exactly* offset each other at all gearing ratios; whereas in a taxed world, the advantages consistently *outweigh* the disadvantages at all levels of gearing. However, the real point of difference between the M and M and traditional views is the exact nature of the relationship between the cost of equity capital and the gearing ratio.

Whereas in the M and M hypothesis the increased return required by equity capital as compensation for bearing financial risk rises at a *constant* rate as the gearing level increases, the traditional view is that this required expected return rises at an *increasing* rate, i.e. at a rate which is, at relatively low levels of gearing, below that hypothesized by M and M, but which increases above the return required by equity in the M and M model, at higher gearing ratios.

Fig. 19.3 *The traditional view*

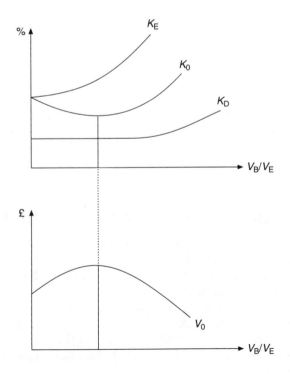

In this respect it is interesting to note that as financial risk is systematic, the CAPM analysis would probably lead us to expect a positive *linear* relationship between the cost of equity and the gearing ratio (if it is only financial risk that is causing the cost of equity to rise). Thus CAPM would support the M and M hypothesis.

As far as the rising cost of debt argument is concerned, the M and M analysis simply assumes that K_D remains a constant at all gearing levels. Whether K_D would actually *rise* at a high gearing level is debatable. Our discussion on debt capacity would suggest that as long as the company can provide suitable security for its debt, then debt holders are not likely to bear their own version of financial risk as gearing increases. Thus the assumption of a constant K_D may well be realistic – up to the level of gearing at which the firm's overall debt capacity is reached.

The traditional view of capital structure is just that: a view or reflection of what is traditionally believed to be the relationship between a company's various costs of capital and the gearing ratio, and it has never rested on a rigorous theoretical model as does the M and M hypothesis. Several writers have expressed the traditional view of capital structure in algebraic form, but none has been able to show satisfactorily, in the way in which M and M used the existence of arbitrage transactions, *why* the cost of equity capital should have a non-linear relationship with the gearing ratio, as argued by the traditionalist view.

The most notable feature about the traditionalist view of capital structure (which follows on from the assumed nature of the K_E function) is the U-shaped weighted average cost of capital curve and the corresponding inverted-U total market value curve. At low gearing levels, the advantages outweigh the disadvantages, and so K_0 is pulled down; and as a result V_0 rises. But, as the company continues to gear up, the advantages now start to become outweighed by the disadvantages, K_0 rises and consequently V_0 falls.

This leads firmly to the conclusion that each company has an optimal capital structure which minimizes its weighted average cost of capital and so maximizes its total market value. Company managements must search for this particular gearing ratio (which is likely to vary from company to company and may well vary over time for any one particular company) and so the financing decision is elevated to a position of importance almost on a par with the investment decision itself.

Corporate and personal taxes

The Modigliani and Miller analysis of the capital structure decision in a taxed world implies that tax relief on debt interest would encourage companies to gear up to as high a level as possible. The greater the level of gearing, the greater would be the tax subsidy on debt financing accruing to the company. However M and M only considered *corporate* taxes. It was left to a subsequent analysis by Miller (1977) to include the effects of *personal* as well as corporate taxes. Miller's arguments, although they can be developed intuitively, are complex and they are briefly outlined below.

Miller showed that when personal as well as corporate taxes are taken into account, then the expression for the value of the tax shield (the present value of the tax relief on corporate debt) changes. Thus the M and M expression:

$$V_{0_g} = V_{E_{ug}} + V_B T,$$

changes to:

$$V_{0_g} = V_{E_{ug}} + V_B \left[1 - \frac{(1-T_C)(1-T_E)}{1-T_D} \right]$$

where T_C = corporate tax rate;
        T_E = personal tax rate on equity income;
        T_D = personal tax rate on debt income.

In a homogeneous personal tax regime where all personal income is taxed at the same rate, then $T_E = T_D$ and so Miller's expression for V_{0_g} reduces back to:

$$V_{0_g} = V_{E_{ug}} + V_B T_C.$$

In other words, homogeneous personal taxes were an implicit assumption of the M and M with tax analysis.

However in the real world the personal tax regime is heterogeneous where $T_E \neq T_D$. Here Miller argued that, effectively, $T_E = 0$ as shareholders can avoid taxes on dividends by taking dividends as capital gains (i.e. selling cum div and repurchasing at ex div) for which there is a large annual tax-free allowance.[3] In addition he put forward a macro-economic argument that, in an equilibrium market for corporate debt $T_D = T_C$.

It is this latter argument that lies at the heart of Miller's analysis and it is the most controversial part of his thesis. He argued that the existence of tax relief on debt interest – but not on equity dividends – would make debt capital more attractive than equity capital to companies. However, given that the market for corporate debt capital operates under the laws of supply and demand, companies would have to offer a higher return on debt (K_D) in order to generate a greater supply of debt.

Assuming a certain world in which investors hold either debt or equity, to persuade an equity supplier to switch over to become a *debt* supplier (because the company would prefer debt), the company must offer an after-personal tax return on debt at least equal to the after-personal tax return on equity. Then, remembering that $T_E = 0$, the after-personal tax return on debt must, at a *minimum* be:

$$K_D(1 - T_D) = K_E.$$

Therefore, the minimum interest rate the company must pay on debt capital is:

$$K_D = \frac{K_E}{1-T_D}.$$

If the previous expression gives the minimum debt interest rate the company must offer to persuade equity investors to switch to debt, what then is the *maximum* interest rate the company would be willing to pay? This would be where the after-corporate tax cost of debt equalled the cost of equity:

$$K_D(1 - T_C) = K_E.$$

At that point, the company would be indifferent between equity and debt finance as the effective cost of each would be the same. In other words, the highest interest rate they would be willing to pay would be:

$$K_D = \frac{K_E}{1 - T_C}.$$

Given a supply and demand market for corporate debt, as long as the interest rate: $K_D < K_E/(1 - T_C)$ companies would want to issue debt. And as long as $K_D \geq K_E/(1 - T_D)$, investors would be willing to supply debt. Thus an equilibrium position in the corporate debt market – where supply and demand equated – would occur where:

$$\frac{K_E}{1 - T_C} = K_D = \frac{K_E}{1 - T_D}.$$

In other words, equilibrium would occur where $T_C = T_D$; where the corporate tax rate equals the personal tax rate of marginal (or incremental) investors in debt capital. This is shown graphically in Fig. 19.4.

From this analysis, the conclusion can be drawn that, from the viewpoint of an individual company, it will be indifferent between raising debt or equity as the effective cost of each will be the same. (Obviously a non-tax paying company would strongly prefer equity finance because $K_D > K_E$.) All the *advantages* of the tax relief on debt interest will go to the *suppliers* of debt capital whose own personal T_D is less than T_C. This is represented by the shaded area on Fig. 19.4.

This conclusion can be seen from the fact that Miller's expression for V_{0_g}:

$$V_{0_g} = V_{E_{ug}} + V_B\left[1 - \frac{(1 - T_C)(1 - T_E)}{1 - T_D}\right]$$

reduces, when $T_E = 0$ and $T_D = T_C$, to:

$$V_0 = V_{Eug}.$$

The value of the tax shield now becomes zero. There is no advantage to gearing and one capital structure is therefore as good as another. (Notice

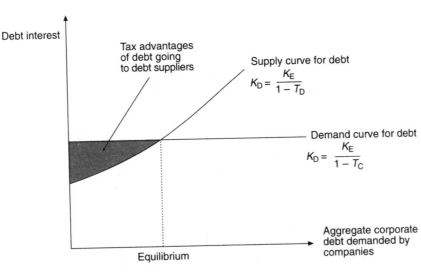

Fig. 19.4 Miller's analysis

Debt interest

Tax advantages of debt going to debt suppliers

Supply curve for debt
$K_D = \dfrac{K_E}{1 - T_D}$

Demand curve for debt
$K_D = \dfrac{K_E}{1 - T_C}$

Aggregate corporate debt demanded by companies

Equilibrium

Corporate and personal taxes

that this conclusion is, rather ironically, identical to that of the original M and M no-tax capital structure hypothesis.) Hence the financing/capital structure decision is relegated to being a matter of little importance for corporate financial management.

Whether Miller's argument holds true in practice is unclear. As supportive evidence he draws attention to the fact that if debt *does* possess a net advantage due to tax relief on interest, then companies would be expected to move to higher gearing ratios at times of high rates of corporation tax and vice versa. (In other words, the higher the rate of corporation tax, the greater the tax advantage of debt.) However, he claims that there is little evidence to suggest that this does occur, which therefore supports his argument. Miller's evidence has been subject to criticism and hence there are some doubts about the empirical validity of his hypothesis. Nevertheless, his argument does caution against over-exaggerating the tax advantages of debt capital, and it provides another way of explaining observed gearing ratios: companies do not gear up to high levels not only because there are hidden costs involved in doing so, but also because the gains are themselves rather small.

In conclusion

In concluding our examination of the capital structure problem, all we can say is that it would appear that the financing decision may be of some importance, in so far as a company's capital structure can have both beneficial and detrimental effects on its total market value and, consequently, on the market value of the ordinary shares. However, the exact nature of the relationship in real life between a company's gearing level, its total market value and the costs of its various types of capital, remains unclear. What we have seen is that gearing can be a double-edged sword and hence should always be treated with caution. We must also recognize that because the market valuation of equity is constantly changing, so will be the gearing of the company. This probably means that there can be no optimal long-term target gearing ratio for companies and aiming to remain within a range is more likely to provide a workable approach to the problem.

Summary

- This chapter has discussed the M and M with-tax capital structure hypothesis, the traditional view of capital structure, Miller's 1977 analysis of debt and taxes and the 'real world' determinants of capital structure.

- The M and M with-tax analysis shows that as a company increases its gearing there are three effects: the advantage that debt costs less than equity ($K_D < K_E$); the disadvantage that gearing increases financial risk and so the cost of equity rises and the advantage that gearing brings further tax relief and so reduces the tax liability of the firm.

- The M and M no-tax analysis shows how the first two effects exactly offset each other (not surprisingly, because they both arise from the same source: the ordering of the 'pay-out queue' of debt and equity holders). This leaves a net advantage. As gearing increases, the after-tax WACC declines and V_0 rises.

- Assuming a constant cost of debt, then it follows that K_{E_g} is a positive linear function of the gearing ratio.

- Therefore the conclusion of the analysis is that companies should attempt to gear up as much as possible: the higher the gearing, the lower is K_0, the higher is V_0 and the greater is the increase in shareholder wealth.

- However, against this view is the traditional view which, like the M and M analysis, sees that there are both advantages and disadvantages to gearing. However, the traditional view holds that at low gearing levels the advantages outweigh the disadvantages and so the WACC is lowered. However at high gearing the reverse relationship holds and so the WACC rises.

- As a result, the company's WACC is U-shaped and the optimal gearing ratio is located where K_0 is minimized and V_0 is maximized. At that point shareholder wealth is also maximized.

- The empirical evidence does very little to solve the conflict between the two approaches because of a lack of company data for high gearing levels, which is where the two theories seriously diverge.

- However, empirically we find that companies tend *not* to gear up to the high levels the M and M analysis would lead us to expect suggesting either that the WACC curve *is* U-shaped or that the M and M analysis excludes some important variables.

- There is no reason – either of an analytical or of an empirical nature – to suggest that the WACC function is *really* U-shaped. Therefore this leads us to conclude that the M and M analysis excludes some important factors in the real-world capital structure decision.

- These important real-world determinants are thought to be: bankruptcy costs, agency costs, debt capacity and tax exhaustion.

- Finally, the Miller analysis suggests that when personal taxes are included in the analysis and given two somewhat contentious arguments about personal tax rates, then it can be shown that the value of the tax shield on corporate debt interest reduces to zero. This is not to say that companies do not get tax relief on debt interest. Rather it implies that even allowing for tax relief on debt interest, the use of debt capital confers no benefits on shareholders' wealth.

Notes

1. From this point on, K_D will refer to the *before-tax* cost of debt capital. References to the after-tax cost of debt will be designated $K_{D_{AT}}$, as before, or $K_D(1 - T)$, where T is the rate of corporation tax.

2. Which we encountered in Chapter 1.

3. There are other ways as well by which investors can avoid personal taxes on equity investment, such as investing through pension fund schemes and personal equity plans (PEPs).

Further reading

1. There are many articles on this area that are of interest. The basic ones of course are the two by M and M: F. Modigliani and M. Miller, 'The Cost of Capital, Corporation Finance and the Theory of Investment', *American Economic Review*, June 1958, and 'Corporation Income Taxes and the Cost of Capital', *American Economic Review*, June 1963, and, in addition, the later analysis by Miller: M.H. Miller, 'Debt and Taxes', *Journal of Finance*, May 1977. There is also Miller's Nobel Prize lecture: M.H. Miller, 'Leverage', *Journal of Finance*, June 1991.

2. A good overview is provided in: S.C. Myers, 'The Capital Structure Puzzle', *Journal of Finance*, July 1984 and this is extended in J. Rutterford, 'An International Perspective on the Capital Structure Puzzle', *Midland Corporate Finance Journal*, Autumn 1985. Another good overview is to be found in J. Board, 'Modigliani and Miller', in M. Firth and S.M. Keane (eds), *Issues in Finance*, Philip Allen 1986. An interesting article which looks at M and M from a UK tax perspective is: D.J. Ashton, 'Textbook Formulae and UK Taxation: M and M Revisited', *Accounting and Business Research*, Summer 1989.

3. In terms of Miller's analysis there have been some thoughtful articles: H. de Angelo and R.W. Mausulis, 'Leverage and Dividend Irrelevancy under Corporate and Personal Taxation', *Journal of Finance*, May 1980; V.A. Aivazain and J.L. Callen, 'Miller's Irrelevance Mechanism', *Journal of Finance*, March 1987; J. Cordes and S. Sheffrin, 'Estimating the Tax Advantage of Corporate Debt', *Journal of Finance*, March 1983; and A. Kane, A.J. Marcus and R.L. McDonald, 'How Big is the Tax Advantage of Debt?', *Journal of Finance*, July 1984.

4. On the real-world factors behind the capital structure decision, articles of interest include: A. Barnea, R.A Haugen and L.W. Senbet, 'Market Imperfections, Agency Problems and Capital Structure: A Review', *Financial Management*, Summer 1981; J.S. Ang and J.H. Chua, 'Corporate Bankruptcy and Job Losses Among Top Level Managers' *Financial Management*, Winter 1981; S.G. Rhee and F.L. McCarthy, 'Corporate Debt Capacity and Capital Budgeting Analysis', *Financial Management*, Summer 1982; and A. Agrawal and G.N. Mandelher, 'Managerial Incentives and Corporate Investment and Financing Decisions', *Journal of Finance*, September 1987.

5. Finally, there has been some interesting empirical work published: C.S. Patterson, 'The Financing Objectives of Large US Electric Utilities', *Financial Management*, Summer 1984; P. Marsh, 'The Choice Between Equity and Debt: An Empirical Study', *Journal of Finance*, March 1982; M. Bradley, G.A Jarrel and E.H. Kim, 'On the Existence of an Optimal Capital Structure: Theory and Evidence', *Journal of Finance*, July 1984; and M. Long and I. Malitz, 'The Investment-Financing Nexus: Some Empirical Evidence', *Midland Corporate Finance Journal*, Autumn 1985.

Quickie questions

1. Given the following facts about a company:

$$K_E = 25\%$$
$$K_D = 10\% \text{ pre-tax}$$
$$V_B{:}V_E = 1{:}3$$
$$T_C = 35\%$$

What is the cost of equity capital of a similar business risk, all-equity financed, company?

2. Given the information in question 1, what would be its K_0 if it moved its gearing ratio from 1:3 to 1:2?

3. An all-equity financed company is presently worth £40 million. It is thinking of issuing £10 million of 14% irredeemable debt to repurchase £10 million of equity. Given a corporate tax rate of 35%, what would be the effect on shareholder wealth?

4. What is the M and M expression for K_0 in a taxed world?

5. What does the 'tax shield' represent?

6. What is meant by debt capacity?

7. Given a company which has issued £10 million of debt (i.e. its current market value), a gearing ratio of 1:3, a probability of going bankrupt of 5% and estimated bankruptcy costs of £1 million; what would the company be worth if it was all-equity financed assuming a corporate tax rate of 35%?

8. What is Miller's expression for the total market value of a geared company?

Problems

1. Mandina plc and Clarice plc are two companies operating in different industries. Mandina plc operates in an industry for which the average asset beta (i.e. the ungeared beta after removing the impact of financial risk) is 0.5; the corresponding beta is 1.5 for the industry of Clarice plc. Both industries are homogeneous, and the industry asset betas are appropriate to the degree of business risk experienced by both companies. The current earnings before interest and tax for Mandina plc are £500 000 and for Clarice plc £1 200 000. These levels of earnings are expected to be maintained for the indefinite future, as neither company retains any earnings. The rate of return on riskless lending and borrowing opportunities is 7% per annum, and the return on the market portfolio is 15%. Both rates are expected to remain constant indefinitely.

   Mandina plc and Clarice plc each have 8% irredeemable debentures with a market value of £1 000 000 in their capital structures. At these levels of gearing there is an 8% chance of Mandina plc becoming bankrupt, and a 10% chance of Clarice plc becoming bankrupt. In both cases, the present value of the associated after-tax costs of bankruptcy will be £500 000.

   The rate of corporation tax will be 35% for the foreseeable future and all debenture interest is expected to be tax deductible. You may assume the markets are perfect apart from the existence of corporate taxes and bankruptcy costs.

   Required:
   (a) Calculate the total market values and debt/equity ratios of Mandina plc and Clarice plc.
   (b) Discuss why the directors of some UK-listed companies may choose high gearing ratios, whereas others may choose to have negligible debt in the capital structures.

2. Given below are extracts from the annual account of four UK listed companies, together with information concerning their stock market performance. Companies A and B are from the brewing sector and have as their principal business activities: brewing beer, wholesale and retail selling of

beers, wines, spirits and soft drinks and the ownership and management of public houses. The principal activities of companies C and D are the distribution and service of electronic components, microprocessor systems and related equipment. Company D is also involved in the manufacture of steel products such as partitions and lintels.

	Company			
	A	B	C	D
Latest annual report extracts:				
Ordinary shareholders' funds (£m)	90.4	65.4	5.9	33.3
Long-term loans (£m)	1.1	0.2	–	0.4
Bank overdraft (£m)	1.7	5.6	1.1	0.7
Net dividend per share (p)	4.3	8.2	2.4	9.9
Annual dividend growth since 1990	12%	10%	19%	22%
Current stock market details:				
Equity market value (£m)	68.0	63.2	68.8	123.4
Market value of long-term loans (£m)	0.6	0.1	–	0.3
Equity beta value	0.75	0.88	1.24	1.26
Share price (£)	1.64	2.80	3.03	4.70

You should assume that the return on short-dated government securities is 11% and that the equivalent return on all long-term loans is 12%. The market premium for risk (i.e. the difference between the return on the Financial Times All-Share Index and the return on short-dated government securities) should be assumed to be 9%.

Required:
(a) Calculate the weighted average cost of capital for each of the four companies, assuming a corporation tax rate of 35% and ignoring bank overdrafts.
(b) Using both the information given in the question, and the results of your calculations in part (a), explain why the weighted average costs of capital differ between the four companies.
(c) Discuss the proposition that under the present UK system of personal and corporate taxation, a company's capital structure does not affect its total market value.

3. The government of Despina has used a number of different corporation tax systems in recent years. In t_{-3} corporate profits were not taxable; however, in t_{-2} a corporate income tax at 50% of taxable profits was introduced. Under this tax regime debt interest was not allowed as a charge against taxable profits. In t_{-1} the government modified the tax system, allowing interest on corporate borrowings as a charge against taxable profits. Finally, in t_0, capital allowances and debt interest were allowed as charges against taxable profits. The magnitudes of these allowances were such as to shield fully earnings before interest from corporate taxes for all companies in Despina.
    The market capitalization of the equity of two companies, Dora and Bella and the market capitalization of the debentures in Bella at the end of each of the four years are:

		t_{-3} ($000)	t_{-2} ($000)	t_{-1} ($000)	t_0 ($000)
Dora	Equity	1000	510	520	980
Bella	Equity	800	370	440	790
	Debentures	200	140	160	190

Both companies were believed to have had identical earnings streams over the four-year period; to have had identical business risk characteristics; and to have paid out all their earnings as dividends at the end of each year. Neither company was expected to exhibit any growth during the four-year period, although the levels of earnings expectations and the rates of return on corporate shares varied between years.

You are required to explain the relative values of Dora and Bella in the light of the differing tax systems in Despina over the past four years.

20 The capital structure decision in practice

The gearing ratio calculation

At the start of this book we stated that we would examine how companies *should* make financial decisions. Thus we were looking at the 'normative' theory of financial decision making. We then went on to say that a normative theory cannot be developed in isolation from what actually happens in practice and that therefore we would also have to examine the *practice* of financial management decision making. Nowhere is this more important than in the area of capital structure.

As the previous two chapters have shown, the theory of the capital structure decision does not give company managements any clear advice. The Modigliani and Miller with-tax analysis concludes that companies should gear up as much as possible. The traditional view concludes that *some* gearing will be advantageous, but not too much – and just what is the optimal gearing ratio for any particular company is a matter of trial and error. Finally, Miller's analysis concludes – under specific assumptions about the personal tax regime, which may or may not be valid – that the capital structure decision has no impact on the value of a company and so is an irrelevance from the viewpoint of shareholder wealth.

Real-world considerations

Suppose a financial manager is faced with the problem of needing to raise additional long-term capital. The immediate decision is, should just equity capital be raised, and so lower the company's gearing, or should just debt capital be raised, and so increase the company's gearing; or should a mixture of both debt and equity be raised so as to approximately maintain the company's existing gearing ratio?

As we know, the theory of capital structure gives very little guidance to the manager and, in such circumstances, managers tend to take comfort from the idea that there is 'safety in numbers'. In other words, when the theory gives you no clear indication as to what you should do, the safest thing is to do what everybody else does. Thus one of the most important considerations in the capital structure decision in the real world will be, what is the average level of gearing for the industry group? Therefore, generally speaking, companies will tend to be rather cautious about moving their gearing ratios too far away from their industry average level of gearing.

Example 1

The following is the summarized balance sheet of Costa plc:

			(£)
Net fixed assets			400 000
Stocks	150 000		
Debtors	100 000		
Cash	50 000	300 000	
Creditors	80 000		
Bank overdraft	100 000	180 000	
Net current assets			120 000
Net total assets			520 000
Financed by:			
Issued share capital			50 000
Reserves			300 000
Shareholders' funds			350 000
12% debentures			170 000
			520 000

Its gearing ratio can be measured as:

$$\frac{\text{Long-term debt} + \text{Short-term debt} - \text{Cash balances}}{\text{Shareholders' funds}}.$$

This gives:

$$\frac{170\,000 + 100\,000 - 50\,000}{350\,000} = 0.629 \text{ or } 62.9\%.$$

Whilst in the theory of capital structure, gearing has always been measured in terms of *market* values (i.e. V_B/V_E), in the real world gearing tends to be measured in terms of *accounting balance sheet* values. Thus instead of V_E being used, the balance sheet value of 'shareholders' funds' (issued share capital plus all reserves) is used. Similarly, instead of the total market value of debt, V_B, being used, the balance sheet value (i.e. nominal value) of debt is used. Example 1 shows such an approach in more detail.

When we move away from the theory and look at the real world, accounting balance sheet values are used rather than market values for reasons of practicality. Whereas, for a quoted company, it is easy to calculate the total market value of the equity (V_E), this is not the case with the total market value of the debt (V_B).

The vast majority of corporate debt capital is issued privately and so is unquoted. Therefore it does not have a market value that can be observed. Rather than go to the trouble and difficulty of trying to estimate what its market value might be, nominal balance sheet values of debt are used.

Consequently, if the *balance sheet* value of debt is to be used, the view is that it would be inconsistent if *market* values of equity were used. As a result gearing ratios tend to be calculated on the basis shown in Example 1. However, as we have seen in the previous chapter, many assets are not represented in the balance sheet at all and those that are represented are shown at historic cost and not value. Accountants seem to accept historic cost (generally unadjusted for changing prices) because they claim it to be more objective than other values. In truth this is not so and all that can really be said in favour of historic cost is that it is more easily verifiable than the alternatives. (There are many accounting textbooks that deal with this issue and a list of appropriate references is included at the end of this chapter.)

Earnings per share and gearing

Risk and return

In making the capital structure decision in practice the financial manager will be aware of the relationship between risk and return. Therefore he will know that if the company's level of gearing is increased that will, in turn, lead to an increase in the amount of risk – financial risk – borne by the shareholders. As a result, shareholders will require some additional reward in compensation.

In finance theory (and in practice) the reward for risk-taking is the return on the investment which, in terms of equity capital, is a combination of dividend yield plus percentage capital gain. However, the financial manager requires a more direct and immediate measure of the reward for risk-taking when trying to assess whether he should, for example, increase the gearing of the company. In other words, he needs to be able to assess whether the company will be able to generate sufficient extra return to compensate the shareholders for an increased level of financial risk.

This more direct and immediate measure of reward for risk-taking is provided by the accounting profit (or earnings) concept in terms of *earnings per share* (EPS). In practice, the financial manager will tend to make capital structure decisions on the basis of the gearing ratio measured in terms of accounting balance sheet values and the subsequent impact on earnings per share, the final decision being, of course, a matter of judgement. Example 2 illustrates such an approach.

Example 2

Cerveja plc wishes to undertake a project which will cost £5 million. The project has already been evaluated and is thought to have a positive NPV.

The decision now facing management is how to finance the project. Two alternative financing 'packages' are under consideration:

1. issue 2.5 million new shares at 200p each, or
2. issue £5 million long-term debentures at a fixed rate of interest of 15%.

The project is expected to generate an extra £1 million of earnings (before tax and interest) each year. The company pays corporation tax at 35% and follows a policy of paying a constant dividend per share.

The current profit and loss account and balance sheet are as follows:

Profit and loss account	(£m)
Earnings before interest and tax	4.4
Interest	1.2
Taxable earnings	3.2
Taxation	1.12
Earnings available for shareholders	2.08
Dividends	0.4
Retained earnings	1.68

Balance sheet	(£m)
Net fixed assets	14.0
Net current assets*	10.0
Total assets	24.00
Financed by:	
Issued share capital (25p shares)	1.0
Reserves	15.5
Shareholder funds	16.5
12% long-term loan	7.5
	24.0

*Includes £2 million bank overdraft. Cash balances are zero.

The current gearing and the current EPS can be calculated as follows:

$$\text{Gearing}: \frac{£7.5m + £2m}{£16.5m} = 0.576 \text{ or } 57.6\%.$$

$$\text{EPS}: \frac{\text{Earnings available for shareholders}}{\text{Number of shares in issue}} = \frac{£2.08m}{4m} = £0.52 \text{ or } 52p.$$

Each financing package can be evaluated, in turn, by looking at what will be its impact on the gearing ratio and EPS:

Finance Package 1	(£m)
Earnings before interest and tax	4.4
Additional earnings from project	1.0
	5.4
Interest on existing loans	1.2
Taxable earnings	4.2
Taxation	1.47
Earnings available for shareholders	2.73
Dividends*	0.65
Retained earnings	2.08

*Currently £0.4 million of dividends are paid on 4 million shares. This represents a dividend per share of 10p. This financing package requires the issue of 2.5 million extra shares making a total of 6.5 million shares in total. If the company's policy of a constant dividend per share is to be maintained then the total amount of dividends paid will rise to £0.65 million.

$$\text{Gearing}: \frac{£7.5m + £2m}{£16.5m + £5m^* + £0.4m^{**}} = 0.434 \text{ or } 43.4\%.$$

$$\text{EPS}: \frac{£2.73m}{6.5m} = £0.42 \text{ or } 42p.$$

*This is the extra £5 million of shareholders' funds arising from the issue of £5 million of extra equity capital.

**In the existing balance sheet, the £1.68 million of retained earnings from the existing profit and loss account will already be included in the reserves figure of £15.5 million. The project, financed by Package 1, would raise the retained earnings figure by £0.4 million from £1.68 million to £2.08 million. Thus this *extra* retained earnings has to be added to the value of shareholders' funds.

Finance Package 2	(£m)
Earnings before interest and tax	4.4
Additional earnings from project	1.0
	5.4
Interest on existing loans	1.2
Interest on new loan	0.75
Taxable earnings	3.45
Taxation	1.21
Earnings available for shareholders	2.24
Dividends	0.4
Retained earnings	1.84

$$\text{Gearing}: \frac{£7.5m + £2m + £5m}{£16.5m + £0.16m} = 0.87 \text{ or } 87\%.$$

$$\text{EPS}: \frac{£2.24m}{4m} = £0.56 \text{ or } 56p.$$

Summary	Gearing	EPS
Existing situation	57.6%	52p
Finance Package 1	43.4%	42p
Finance Package 2	87.0%	56p

The use of judgement

It is far from clear, as the summary in Example 2 shows, just what would be the correct judgement to make in practice between the two financing packages. The first package produces a fall in gearing – and so a reduction in financial risk – but at the cost of a rather large fall in EPS. On the other hand, the second financing package leads to a sharp increase in gearing with only a relatively small rise in EPS.

It is up to the financial manager to judge whether shareholders would be willing to bear the 'cost' (in terms of a lower EPS) of the reduced exposure to financial risk provided by Finance Package 1; or whether they would be willing to bear the cost of increased financial risk (as measured by the rise in the gearing ratio) in order to gain the reward of an increase in EPS provided by Finance Package 2.

Although the impact of the change in capital structure on 'reward' can be quite directly related to changes in EPS, the impact on financial risk is more difficult to judge through the measure of gearing alone. However, the quality of this latter measure could be improved by knowing what the *average* level of gearing is for Cerveja's industry group.

Thus if the average gearing level of Cerveja's industry group was 90%, then the financial manager might well feel that the second package should be preferred to the first. The second package improves EPS while still leaving shareholders with a less than average exposure to financial risk. In contrast, the first package reduces still further the shareholders' already (relatively) low exposure to financial risk, at a significant cost in terms of EPS.

However, if the industry average gearing was only 25%, then the conclusion reached in the judgement of the financial manager might well be different.

Interest cover ratio

An additional way of judging the impact of gearing on financial risk exposure is through the interest cover ratio. This can be defined as:

$$\frac{\text{Earnings before interest and tax}}{\text{Interest liabilities}}.$$

The idea here is that the *lower* the ratio, the *greater* the probability that the company may default on interest payments and be forced into bankruptcy.

Using the data from Example 2, the interest cover ratios can be calculated as follows:

Existing situation: £4.4m/£1.2m = 3.67
Financing Package 1: £5.4m/£1.2m = 4.5
Financing Package 2: £5.4m/£1.95m = 2.77

This ratio can therefore be used to highlight the significance of the changes in gearing and to give some insight of the significance of a move from a gearing ratio of 57.6% to 87.0%. But of course, as was commented upon previously, knowledge of Cerveja's industry group average interest cover would bring a greater depth of understanding to the interpretation of these data.

Degree of operating gearing

In the discussion in the previous section on EPS and gearing, what was being examined was the risk and return relationship of just one type of systematic risk: systematic *financial* risk. That discussion therefore raises an additional question: how, in practice, are financial managers going to make a judgement concerning changes in systematic *business* risk?

Business and financial risk

In Chapter 12 we looked at the determinants of systematic and unsystematic risk, while in Chapter 18 we introduced the concept of business and financial risk. This present discussion provides a good opportunity to make clear the relationship between these different types of risk.

Portfolio theory teaches that a share's total risk is divided up into systematic and unsystematic risk. Modigliani and Miller's capital structure theory teaches that a share's total risk is divided into business and financial risk.

Unsystematic risk, as we know, arises from company-specific factors that have an impact on the level and variability of a firm's cash flow. Such factors as the ability of a company's senior management team, the state of its labour relations and the quality of its research and development work would all be examples.

On the other hand, systematic risk arises from the impact upon the firm of other factors which are *not* specific to the individual company, but which affect all companies (to a greater or lesser extent) throughout the stock market. These market-wide, macro-economic-type factors include things like the rate of national economic growth, interest rate levels and exchange rate volatility. Such factors do *not* just affect the individual company, but affect all companies throughout the stock market.

In Chapter 12, when discussing the determinants of an individual company's exposure to these systematic risk factors (and hence its beta value), we state that, apart from gearing there are two main determinants:

1. The sensitivity of a company's revenues to the general level of economic activity in the economy and other macro-economic factors.
2. The proportion of fixed to variable costs, both in terms of operating costs (e.g. wages, materials, energy costs) and financing costs (e.g. interest and dividend payments).

The greater the revenue sensitivity and the greater the proportion of fixed costs, then the greater the company's exposure to systematic risk (and the higher its beta value as a result).

Given all these different strands, the relationship between business and financial risk, and between systematic and unsystematic risk can now be explored.

Financial risk is really concerned with the proportion of fixed financing costs (interest payments that *must* be made), to variable financing costs (dividend payments which need not necessarily be made). Thus financial risk is part of a share's systematic risk.

Just as financial risk arises out of how a firm is financed, so business risk arises out of the risky nature and characteristics of a firm's business. Thus business risk encompasses not only systematic risk – in terms of the revenue sensitivity of the business and the proportion of fixed to variable operating costs that the nature of the business involves – but also unsystematic risk in terms of the ability of the senior management team, the labour relations and other company-specific factors which affect the business. Fig. 20.1 attempts to show these interrelationships more clearly.

We can now return to the problem of deriving a *practical* measure of systematic business risk. What is required is a way of measuring systematic business risk, in the same way that the gearing ratio (and, to some extent, the interest cover ratio) can be seen as a practical attempt to measure changes in systematic financial risk.

Fig. 20.1 M and M and the CAPM

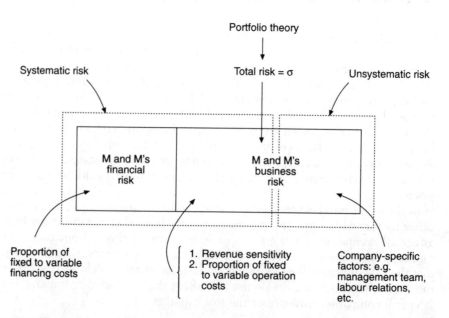

Systematic business risk can be approached through the concept of the degree of operating gearing (DOG). This can be defined as:

$$\frac{\text{revenues} - \text{variable operating costs}}{\text{earnings before interest and tax}}.$$

The DOG measure indicates the percentage change in earnings before interest and tax (EBIT) for every 1% change in revenues. Example 3 illustrates the calculation.

Example 3

Obrigado Ltd has the following, simplified, profit and loss account:

		(£000)
Revenues		500
Wages	150	
Materials	120	
Variable overheads	55	
		(325)
Fixed overheads		(75)
Earnings before interest and tax		100

$$DOG = \frac{£500\,000 - £325\,000}{£100\,000} = 1.75.$$

The degree of operating gearing is 1.75 which indicates that for every 1% change in Obrigado's revenues, there will be a 1.75% change in the company's earnings before interest and tax. For example, if revenue increased by 10%, then EBIT should increase by 17.5% – from £100 000 to £117 500. Conversely, if revenues, for example, fell by 5%, then EBIT should fall by 5% × 1.75 = 8.75% – from £100 000 to £91 250.

This can be seen to be the case as follows (notice the assumption that the percentage change in revenues will be reflected in the variable – but not the fixed – operating costs):

10% Increase in revenues

		(£000)
Revenues		550
Wages	165	
Materials	132	
Variable overheads	60.5	
		(357.5)
Fixed overheads		(75)
EBIT		117.5

5% Fall in revenues

Revenues		475
Wages	142.5	
Materials	114	
Variable overheads	52.25	
		(308.75)
Fixed overheads		(75)
		91.25

The meaning of DOG

The degree of operating gearing can be taken as a practical measure of systematic business risk, in the sense that it focuses on the proportion of fixed to variable operating costs and the impact that that proportion has on earnings, given changes to the company's revenues.

The greater the proportion of fixed to variable operating costs, the larger will be the DOG value. The larger the DOG value, the greater the impact on EBIT of changes in revenues. Thus the DOG value links revenue sensitivity to the subsequent variability of earnings.

Just as with the gearing ratio, so the DOG value is far from being a perfect measure of systematic business risk. It is limited in a number of important ways.

Certainly, if the value of the DOG increases for a particular company, then it is relatively safe to conclude that its business risk has also increased (and vice versa). However the DOG must be used with care when trying to compare the business risk of one company with that of another. If the two companies are in the same area of business, and therefore have got comparable degrees of revenue sensitivity, then it would be safe to conclude that the company with the larger DOG value has the greater exposure to systematic risk.

However, the DOG is of very little use for comparing the relative business risk of two companies with significantly different revenue sensitivities. A *high* DOG value may not mean that a company has a high degree of business risk, if that company has a very *low* degree of revenue sensitivity. Similarly, a company may well have a high level of systematic business risk – even though it has a low DOG value – because it has such a high degree of revenue sensitivity.

Thus the DOG value, like the gearing ratio, must be used with care in order to make judgements about risk. However, it *can* be helpful to financial managers who are faced with the practicalities of decisions involving trade-offs between systematic business risk and return. Example 4 illustrates such a case.

Example 4

Fiambre plc is considering the acquisition of a new machine. It has already been evaluated and has been shown to have a positive NPV. However, it is expected to affect the firm's proportion of fixed to variable operating costs.

The relevant part of the company's existing profit and loss account is as follows:

		(£000)
Revenues		800
Wage costs	180	
Material costs	200	
Energy costs	150	
Variable overheads	100	(630)
Fixed overheads		(70)
Earnings before interest and tax		100

The new machine will not affect revenues but it will lower the wages cost of the company by 10%, the material costs by 5% and the energy costs by 20%. However, fixed overheads will increase by 50%.

The company's existing DOG value is:

$$\frac{£800\,000 - £630\,000}{£100\,000} = 1.70.$$

With the new machine, the company's profit and loss account would be revised as follows:

		(£000)
Revenues		800
Wage costs	162	
Material costs	190	
Energy costs	120	
Variable overheads	100	(572)
Fixed overheads		(105)
Earnings before interest and tax		123

$$DOG = \frac{£800\,000 - £572\,000}{£123\,000} = 1.85.$$

The new machine would increase the company's exposure to systematic business risk – the DOG value has increased from 1.70 to 1.85. However, this is compensated for by the fact that EBIT rises by £23 000 from £100 000 to £123 000. Whether the additional earnings justifies the additional risk is a matter of judgement on the part of management.

In practice, the final decision could not be taken on these data alone. Information on Fiambre's revenue sensitivity and the DOG values of its competitors would also be required.

Summary

This chapter has looked at how financial management approach the capital structure decision in practice. The main points covered were as follows:

- In practice gearing is usually measured in terms of accounting balance sheet values rather than market values.

- The risk and return trade-off in the capital structure decision is viewed in terms of the impact on the gearing ratio and on earnings per share.

- In practice the capital structure decision is a matter of judgement rather than arithmetic calculation.

- Financial risk is totally systematic and is the risk that is measured through the gearing ratio in the capital structure decision.

- Business risk is partially systematic and partially unsystematic. In practice, an attempt can be made to measure systematic business risk through the degree of operating gearing (DOG) ratio.

Further reading

The areas covered in this chapter are essentially very practical and have not really been explored in the academic literature. However the type of textbooks that provide coverage of what values might be shown in company balance sheets include:

Financial Reporting, D. Alexander and A. Britton 4th edn, Thomson Business Press.

Accounting Theory and Practice, M. Glautier and B. Underdown 6th edn, Pitman Publishing.

Advanced Financial Accounting, R. Lewis and D. Pendrill 5th edn, Pitman Publishing.

and for a fuller discussion of the issue

Income and Value Measurement, T.A. Lee, Van Nostrand Reinhold.

Quickie questions

1. How would the gearing ratio of a company be calculated in practice?
2. How is earnings per share calculated?
3. If a company had a gearing ratio of 50% would that be considered a high or low level of gearing?
4. Is financial risk unsystematic?
5. What determines the systematic part of business risk?
6. How is DOG calculated?
7. What information does DOG provide?
8. If one company had a DOG of 1.50 and another company in the same industry had a DOG of 2.50, what conclusion could you draw?

Problems

1. Latost plc wishes to raise £10 million in external finance by issuing either ordinary shares, or 14% (nominal rate) preference shares or a 12% unsecured loan stock.

   Summarized profit and loss account

	(£000)
Turnover	45 320
Operating profit	11 170
Interest	2 280
Profit before tax	8 890
Tax	3 112
Earnings available to ordinary shareholders	5 778
Dividend	3 467
Retained earnings	2 311

   Summarized balance sheet

	(£000)	(£000)
Fixed assets (net)		24 260
Current assets	28 130	
Less: Current liabilities*	18 370	9 760
		34 020
13% debentures		12 000
Net assets		22 020
Shareholders' funds		
Ordinary shares (50p par value)		5 000
Share premium		4 960
Other reserves		12 060
		22 020

   *Including a bank overdraft of £6 million.
   The share price is 350p.

   Required:
   Prepare a brief report, with supporting evidence, recommending which of these three financing sources the company should use. State clearly any assumptions that you make. Issue costs may be ignored.

2. (a) What is meant by business risk?

Outline the major factors that determine a company's business risk and comment upon how controllable these factors are by a company.

(b) Discuss to what extent business risk is of relevance to an investor owning a well-diversified portfolio.

(c) Huckbul Ltd plans to purchase a new machine in the near future which will reduce the company's direct labour costs, but will increase fixed costs by £85 000 per year. Direct labour costs are expected to fall by 20% per unit of production. The new machine will cost £820 000 and will be financed by a five-year fixed rate term loan at an interest cost of 15% per year, with the principal repayable at the maturity of the loan. The company normally pays half of after-tax earnings as dividends, subject to the constant that if after-tax earnings fall the dividend per share is kept constant.

Huckbul expects its volume of sales to increase by 15% during the current financial year. Ignore inflation. Summarized extracts from the company's most recent financial accounts are detailed below.

	(£000)	(£000)
Profit and loss account		
Turnover		3381
Operating expenses		
Wages and salaries	1220	
Raw materials	873	
Direct selling expenses	100	
General administration (all fixed)	346	
Other costs (all fixed)	380	2919
Profit before interest and tax		462
Interest		84
Profit before tax		378
Corporation tax		151
Profit available to ordinary shareholders		227
Balance sheet	(£000)	(£000)
Fixed assets (net)		1480
Current assets	1720	
Less current liabilities	1120	600
Net assets		1510
Ordinary shares (25p)		800
Share premium account		320
Other reserves		390
		1510

The company is subject to taxation at a rate of 40%.

Required:
State clearly any assumptions that you make.

(a) Evaluate the effect of the purchase of the machine on both the degree of operating gearing and the financial gearing of Huckbul Ltd, comparing the position at the start of the current financial year with the expected position at the end of the current financial year.

(b) What are the implications for the ordinary shareholders of Huckbul as a result of the purchase of the machine

    (i)   if turnover increases by the expected 15%;

    (ii)   if turnover falls by 10%?

3. Bestlodge plc is planning to build production facilities to introduce a major new product, at a cost of £12 million.

The board of directors has already approved the project on the basis that it will yield a positive net present value when discounted, over a ten-year period, at the company's market weighted average cost of capital. The investment is expected to increase profit before interest and tax by approximately 25%.

No internally generated funds are available.

The finance director has suggested three possible sources of finance:

1. A five-year £12 million floating rate term loan from a clearing bank, at an initial interest rate of 10%.
2. A ten-year 46 million Deutsche mark fixed rate loan from the Eurocurrency market at an interest rate of 7%.
3. A rights issue at a discount of 10% on the current market price.

The company's share price is 170p and debenture price £108.
The current summarized financial statements are shown below.:

Bestlodge Plc

Summarized balance sheet

	(£000)	(£000)
Fixed assets at cost less depreciation		38 857
Current assets	18 286	
Current liabilities	(16 914)	
Net current assets		1 372
		40 229

Financed by:

	(£000)
Share capital	
Ordinary shares of 25p each	7 200
Reserves	19 863
Loan capital	
11% Debenture stock 2010	13 166
	40 229

Summarized profit and loss account for the year

	(£000)
Sales	57 922
Profit before interest and taxation	7 744
Debenture interest	1 448
	6 296
Taxation	3 148
Profit available for ordinary shareholders	3 148
Ordinary dividend	2 250
Retained profits	898

Corporation tax is at 50%

Exchange rates

	DM/£
Spot	3.7017
1 year forward	3.4775

Required:
(a) Acting as a consultant to Bestlodge prepare a report discussing the advantages and disadvantages of each of the three suggested sources of finance. Illustrate how the utilization of each source might affect the various providers of finance.
(b) Discuss whether the board of Bestlodge is likely to be correct in evaluating the investment on the basis of the net present value produced by discounting at the market weighted average cost of capital.

21 Investment and financing decision interactions

Company valuation and investment appraisal

The Hirshleifer separation theorem that was developed in Chapter 4 led to the conclusion that decision makers could appraise capital investment opportunities *without* reference to how they are to be financed. However, that model was developed under a very restrictive set of assumptions, including that of a perfect capital market.

In Chapter 19, we saw that when we allow for some real-world capital market imperfections (in particular, taxation, agency and bankruptcy costs) the separation theorem starts to break down. As a result, there are likely to be some significant interactions between capital investment and financing decisions.

The question of concern in this chapter is how are we to take account of such interactions? As a starting point, we are going to examine the relationship between different company valuation models and alternative approaches to investment appraisal. Before doing so, however, we must set out the assumptions upon which the analysis is based. There are five in total:

1. All cash flows represent level perpetuities.
2. Investors are rational, risk-averse and base decisions on expected return and variance of returns.
3. Capital markets are perfect and in equilibrium.
4. Bankruptcy is costless.
5. Companies are each located at a 'target' gearing ratio at which they wish to remain.

It is worth considering these assumptions briefly before moving on with our analysis. Assumption 1 is merely to allow fairly straightforward calculations and does not present any problems. We have already seen that assumption 2 should hold (approximately at least) and small numbers of irrational investors should not invalidate our findings. Assumption 3 is more contentious but it is difficult to see how we can hope to prove that it is not true – indeed, if we did know it to be untrue, we could make significant amounts of money and 'beat the market'! Assumption 4 is clearly untrue but relaxing this later will provide us with insights into how decisions might be made. Finally assumption 5 is unlikely to hold true since real gearing (i.e. that based on market values) fluctuates constantly with market prices but, again, it is reasonable to carry out our analysis based on this assumption and then consider what the effects might be if it were not true.

We start our analysis by briefly considering the different approaches to the valuation of companies that have been developed. There are four models that are of interest but, as we will demonstrate, they are basically consistent with each other. The models are:

1. the dividend and interest valuation model;
2. the adjusted present value model;
3. Modigliani and Miller's valuation models;
4. the traditional valuation model.

The dividend and interest valuation model

The dividend valuation model states that the total market value of a company's equity reflects the sum of the future expected dividend flow, discounted to present value. A similar statement can be made about the total market value of debt capital. Thus – using our usual notation – the total market value of the firm is given by the sum of the equity and the debt market values:

$$V_0 = \frac{(X - V_B K_D)(1 - T)}{K_{E_g}} + \frac{V_B K_D}{K_D}.$$

If the company's annual cash flow is taken as its dividend plus interest flow:

$$(X - V_B K_D)(1 - T) = \text{Annual dividend flow}$$

$$V_B K_D = \text{Annual interest flow}$$

then the total annual cash flow can be expressed as follows:

$$(X - V_B K_D)(1 - T) + V_B K_D = X - XT - V_B K_D T + V_B K_D T + V_B K_D$$
$$= X(1 - T) + V_B K_D T$$

where $X(1 - T)$ represents the annual after-tax cash flow that would occur if the company had been all-equity financed, and where $V_B K_D T$ represents the annual amount of tax relief the company gains from having to pay debt interest.

Adjusted present value model

Taking the two annual cash flow streams as given above, and discounting each to present value, we arrive at an alternative expression for valuing the total market value of the company:

$$V_0 = \frac{X(1-T)}{K_{E_{ug}}} + \frac{V_B K_D T}{K_D} = \frac{X(1-T)}{K_{E_{ug}}} + V_B T.$$

Notice that each cash flow is discounted at a rate that best reflects its risk. Thus $X(1-T)$ is discounted by what would have been the company's cost of equity capital if it were all equity financed and $V_B K_D T$ is discounted at the cost of debt capital.

This company valuation model is termed the *adjusted* present value (APV) model, as the company is *first* valued as if it were all-equity financed, and then this value is *adjusted* to allow for the tax relief on debt capital.

The M and M valuation model

If the APV model is multiplied through by $K_{E_{ug}}$ and V_0 is factored out, then a third valuation model is arrived at:

$$K_{E_{ug}} V_0 - V_B T K_{E_{ug}} = X(1-T)$$

$$K_{E_{ug}} V_0 - \frac{V_0 V_B T K_{E_{ug}}}{V_0} = X(1-T)$$

$$V_0 = \frac{X(1-T)}{K_{E_{ug}}[1-(TV_B/V_0)]}.$$

This values the firm as the present value of the future expected after-tax cash flow. Here the discount rate is the M and M weighted average cost of capital, and this implicitly takes the tax relief on debt interest into account. Hence it is applied simply to the after-tax cash flows that would arise if the firm were all-equity financed.

The traditional valuation model

Finally, returning to the dividend valuation model, but now factoring out V_0, a fourth company valuation model is derived:

$$V_E = \frac{(X - V_B K_D)(1-T)}{K_{E_g}}$$

$$V_E K_{E_g} = X(1-T) - K_D V_B(1-T)$$

$$\frac{V_0 V_E K_{E_g}}{V_0} + \frac{K_D V_B V_0(1-T)}{V_0} = X(1-T)$$

$$V_0 = \frac{X(1-T)}{\dfrac{V_E}{V_0} K_{E_g} + \dfrac{V_B}{V_0} K_D(1-T)}.$$

Here the numerator is the same as with the previous model, but now the denominator is the traditional expression for the WACC. Once again, the effect of the tax relief on debt interest is implicitly allowed for in the discount rate.

Approaches to investment appraisal

All four models of company valuation are equivalent, as long as the set of five assumptions, specified initially, all hold good. However, it should be noted that each model implicitly reflects a different approach to investment appraisal. The dividend and interest valuation model reflects a dividend flow approach; the APV valuation model reflects a risk adjusted present value approach and the M and M and traditional valuation models each reflect the standard net present value approach.

Maintaining the gearing ratio

An example may help to illustrate these different approaches.

Suppose we have the following data about a company (remember that we have the assumption of all level perpetuity cash flows):

$$V_E = £400\,000$$
$$V_B = £100\,000$$
$$D = £\ 73\,500$$
$$I = £\ 10\,000$$
$$T = 35\%$$

therefore

$$K_E = 18.375\%$$
$$K_D = 10\%$$
$$K_0 = 16\%$$

The company is considering a project requiring an outlay of £100 000, which is expected to produce an annual after-tax net cash flow of £28 000 in perpetuity (£43 077 per year, pre-tax). It would not involve any change in risk.

Given that the company wishes to remain at its current (target) gearing ratio of 1:4 (debt–equity), how is the investment to be financed? It would not be correct to simply finance the project with £20 000 of debt and £80 000 of equity, as this ignores the project's NPV which would accrue to the equity holders. Instead a somewhat more lengthy analysis is required.

If the company is going to maintain its current gearing ratio (and there is no change in risk caused by the project's acceptance), then K_0 will remain at 16%. Hence the project's annual net cash inflows will have a present value of:

$$\frac{£28\,000}{0.16} = £175\,000.$$

If there is to be no change in the gearing ratio, this increase in company value must be split between debt and equity in the ratio 1:4. Therefore, as a result of the project the market value of the debt should increase by £35 000 and the market value of the equity should rise by £140 000.

The increase in the market value of the debt issued by the company implies that £35 000 of new debt is raised in order to undertake the project. The remaining £65 000 of the £100 000 required outlay would therefore come from the equity holders.

The total value of the company's equity would rise by £140 000 because the equity holders have subscribed an extra £65 000 and, in addition, they will receive the benefit of the project's NPV:

$$-£100\,000 + \frac{28\,000}{0.16} = +£75\,000\,\text{NPV}.$$

Thus the total market value of the equity capital will rise by: £65 000 + £75 000 = £140 000.

Having decided that the project will be financed by £35 000 of debt capital (at a K_D of 10%) and £65 000 of equity capital, in order to maintain the existing gearing ratio, let us now examine the application of each of the possible approaches to investment appraisal.

Dividend flow approach

This approach evaluates the project on the basis of examining the total market value of the equity *before* (V_E) and *after* (V_E^*) the investment is undertaken. The decision rule is to accept the project as long as it does not cause a reduction in shareholder wealth:

$$V_E^* - (V_E + \text{newly issued equity}) \geqslant 0$$

where $V_E^* = D^*/K_E^*$ (the asterisk refers to the situation *post* investment).

As there is to be no change in the gearing ratio (and hence no change in financial risk: $K_E^* = K_E = 18.375\%$. But what about the post-investment annual dividend flow? This can be found as follows:

		(£)
Project cash flow	=	43 077
Less interest payable on new debt	=	3 500
Taxable cash flow	=	39 577
Less tax at 35%	=	13 852
Additional dividends	=	25 725
Existing dividends	=	73 500
Post-investment dividends = D^*	=	99 225

$$\text{Hence } V_E^* = \frac{£99\,225}{0.18375} = £540\,000$$

and £540 000 − (£400 000 + £65 000)   = +75 000

The project should be accepted, as it will increase shareholder wealth by £75 000.

APV approach

The second approach uses the APV. Here, the project's net cash flow is evaluated as if it were all-equity financed and then the benefits of the tax relief from the new debt capital are added on. The decision rule is to accept the project as long as its total worth is greater than the outlay required:

$$(V_{\text{project}} - \text{Outlay}) \geqslant 0$$

$$\text{where } V_{\text{project}} = \frac{X(1-T)}{K_{E_{ug}}} + V_B T.$$

The first task here is to identify what *would be* the discount rate if all-equity financing where involved. For this, use can be made of the M and M expression:

$$K_{E_{ug}} = K_{E_{ug}} + (K_{E_{ug}} - K_D)\frac{V_B(1-T)}{V_E}.$$

This can be switched around to solve for $K_{E_{ug}}$:

$$K_{E_{ug}} = \frac{V_E K_{E_g} + V_B K_D (1-T)}{V_E + V_B (1-T)},$$

which in the case of the present example gives a value for $K_{E_{ug}}$ of:

$$\frac{(£400\ 000 \times 0.18375) + (£100\ 000 \times 0.10)(1-0.35)}{£400\ 000 + £100\ 000(1-0.35)} = 0.172.$$

Therefore the value of the investment opportunity can now be found:

$$V_{project} = \frac{£28\ 000}{0.172} + £35\ 000 \times 0.35$$

$$= £162\ 750 + £12\ 250 = £175\ 000.$$

As the value of the project is £75 000 more than the required outlay, it should be accepted.

NPV approach

With this approach either the M and M or traditional expressions can be used for calculating the company's weighted average cost of capital of 16%. The decision rule is to accept the project as long as it has a non-negative NPV:

$$-£100\ 000 + \frac{£28\ 000}{0.16} = +£75\ 000\ \text{NPV}.$$

Therefore the project should be accepted. It will increase shareholders' wealth by £75 000.

A changing capital structure

The equivalence of all three approaches (and all four company valuation models) is obvious from the above example. However, it should also be noted that in order to determine how the project should be financed in order to maintain the existing gearing ratio, *the project's worth had first to be found*. In other words, the whole analysis smacks of a 'cart-before-the-horse' approach.

To highlight this problem and the difficulties it causes we now examine a situation where the company finances the investment in such a way that it does *not* maintain the existing gearing ratio. For example, suppose the company intended to finance the project with an £80 000 issue of 10% debt capital and £20 000 of equity.

In order to utilize the dividend flow approach, we need to find V_E^*. This is given by $V_E^* = D^* / K_E^*$.

The post-investment dividend flow is easy enough to find (£96 300), but we *cannot* identify what will be the post-investment cost of equity capital. This can only be found by first knowing what will be the post-investment gearing ratio which, in turn, we cannot identify until we know the worth of the project.

If we are prevented from using the dividend flow approach, what about the NPV/WACC approach? Again we face a difficulty. We cannot use the *existing* WACC for obvious reasons: it reflects the *existing* capital structure, which will change if the project is accepted. Further – even if we wished to use it – we could not identify the post-investment WACC for the same reasons as we could not use the dividend flow approach.

One possible way around the difficulty is as follows. The M and M capital structure analysis shows that there are three effects directly arising from an increase in corporate gearing. Two of these, the advantage of debt being 'cheaper' than equity and the disadvantage of the cost of equity rising because of increased financial risk, exactly offset each other. This leaves one net advantage: the tax relief on debt interest.

We know that behind the use of the WACC as the NPV discount rate is the assumption of an unchanging capital structure. In using the WACC, the net advantage of debt capital is taken into account by using the *after-tax* cost of debt capital. Thus if the project were appraised using the company's *existing* WACC, the implicit assumption would be that it was being financed with £35 000 of debt (because it is this amount of debt that will maintain the existing gearing).

In this example, it is proposed to finance the project using £80 000 of debt. The advantage to the company that accrues from using the £45 000 extra debt (i.e. £80 000 − £35 000) is given by the present value of the tax relief:

$$V_B T = £45\ 000 \times 0.35 = £15\ 750.$$

If the project were to be financed with the existing gearing ratio, then K_0 would remain unchanged at 16% and the NPV of the project would be:

$$-£100\ 000 + \frac{£28\ 000}{0.16} = +£75\ 000.$$

Hence the total benefits of the project are given by its worth if there were no change in capital structure (£75 000), *plus* the worth of the change in capital structure (£15 750). This represents a total of £90 750. However, once more notice the cart-before-the-horse element of the analysis. It can only be accurate if we know how the project should be financed in order to maintain the existing gearing ratio (i.e. £35 000:£65 000 debt:equity ratio).

That brings us to the APV approach. Given the company's existing gearing ratio and its existing cost of equity capital, we have previously calculated that – if the company were all-equity financed – its cost of equity capital would be 17.2% approx. Hence the 'pure' value of the investment opportunity under consideration –which can be referred to as the *base-case present value* – is (as before):

$$-£100\ 000 + \frac{£28\ 000}{0.172} = +£62\ 750\ \text{NPV}.$$

The present value of the tax relief on the £80 000 of debt used to finance the investment is:

$$£80\ 000 \times 0.35 = £28\ 000.$$

Therefore the *adjusted* present value of the investment proposal is given by:

$$£62\ 750 + £28\ 000 = £90\ 750.$$

Adjusted present value

Of all three approaches to the appraisal of the project used in the example above only the adjusted present value (APV) approach was capable of handling the situation where the company's existing gearing ratio was not being maintained. Furthermore, in that example, we also saw that it is not as straightforward as it might initially appear for a company to finance a project in such a way as not to change the existing capital structure. (Where we had a gearing ratio of 1:4 the £100 000 project in question had to be financed by a 35:65 debt:equity mix and not simply 1:4.)

From that example we must conclude that, unless a project is going to be financed in such a way as to leave the capital structure unchanged (or if we have an M and M *no-tax* world, where capital structure is irrelevant), APV is the only safe way of *ensuring* that all the effects of a project – together with its financing method – are going to be captured in the appraisal.

However, before we examine the use of the APV technique in greater detail, let us first clarify the basic approach that it uses. Adjusted present value essentially uses a *divide and conquer* approach to capital investment appraisal. As we saw in the previous example, it first evaluates the project *assuming* that it is all-equity financed. This is referred to as the project's base-case present value. Then this figure is adjusted to take into account any *side-effects* that arise through the financing method used. Although these side-effects can be numerous, the principal one, again as we saw in the example, is likely to be the tax relief on the interest paid on the debt capital used.

The base-case discount rate

In the example used to illustrate the basic mechanics of the APV technique the base-case discount rate was calculated by taking the geared company's K_E and then using a rearranged version of the M and M expression for the cost of equity capital in a taxed world:

$$K_{E_g} = K_{E_{ug}} + (K_{E_{ug}} - K_D)\frac{V_B(1-T)}{V_E}$$

was rearranged to find $K_{E_{ug}}$, the all-equity cost of equity capital:

$$K_{E_{ug}} = \frac{V_E K_{E_g} + V_B K_D(1-T)}{V_E + V_B(1-T)}.$$

This approach is a perfectly acceptable means of identifying the base-case discount rate ($K_{E_{ug}}$), but *only* in one set of circumstances.

In the example used in the previous section, we assumed that the project had the *same* degree of systematic risk as the company's *existing* average systematic risk level. Given this assumption, the approach used for calculating the base-case discount rate is satisfactory. However, as we have already discussed at an earlier stage when criticizing the use of the WACC as an NPV discount rate, such an assumption is likely to be highly unrealistic in practice.

Therefore, if we wish to use the APV technique but feel that we cannot legitimately assume that the project's systematic risk reflects the company's average systematic risk, how are we go to about calculating a suitable base-case discount rate? The answer is – as it was before in our discussion about the use of the WACC – to use the capital asset pricing model.

Asset betas and gearing

In Chapter 12 we discussed the possible use of the CAPM to generate an NPV discount rate that was *tailor-made* to reflect the systematic risk level of the project under evaluation. This could be achieved by using an appropriate beta generated by reference to outside sources as a surrogate for the project's beta. This might be the beta value of the project's *industry* group or it might be based on the beta of a quoted company specializing in a business similar to the project being considered. In the example that follows we will use the beta from the industry group that corresponds to the project.

Example 1

For simplicity, assume that a debt beta is zero. Therefore[1]

$$\beta_{assets} = \beta_{equity} \times \frac{V_E}{V_0}.$$

Suppose a project is to be financed using a 1:3 gearing ratio (i.e. debt:equity) and the project's industry group has an equity beta of 1:2 and an average gearing ratio of 1:4. The industry's equity beta could be *ungeared* and then *regeared* to reflect how the project is financed as follows:

$$\beta_{industry\ assets} = 1.2 \times \frac{4}{5} = 0.96,$$

$$\beta_{industry\ assets + project\ gearing} = 0.96 \times \frac{4}{3} = 1.28.$$

The beta value of 1.28 could then be put into the CAPM to provide a value for the *project's* cost of equity capital. This, together with the cost of debt used to finance the project and the project's gearing ratio, could then be used to calculate a 'weighted average cost of capital' for the project and used as an NPV discount rate.

The industry beta would simply be the average equity beta value of all the quoted companies within that industry.

Later, in Chapter 18, we saw how capital structure caused financial risk and that financial risk formed part of the total systematic risk borne by the equity capital in a company. This therefore implies that if we are to use an *industry* beta to act as a surrogate for a *project's* beta, then account must be taken of any difference between the industry's gearing ratio and the gearing ratio used to finance the project.

This could be done through the expression we developed in Chapter 18:

$$\beta_{assets} = \beta_{equity} \times \frac{V_E}{V_0} + \beta_{debt} \times \frac{V_B}{V_0},$$

where the industry's asset beta could be regeared to reflect how the project is financed. Example 1 illustrates a possible situation. We will develop a more complex example of the calculation of a risk-adjusted weighted average cost of capital at a later point in this chapter.

We must be careful with Example 1, because it is only applicable in a *no-tax* situation.[2] This is because the expression used for identifying the asset beta does not take into account the fact that tax relief on debt capital effectively reduces the financial risk borne by equity at any particular gearing level.

Asset betas and tax

Let us now look at the identification of an asset beta in a taxed world. Taking the M and M expression for the total market value of a geared company in a taxed world:

$$V_{0_g} = V_{E_{ug}} + V_{B_g} T$$

where V_{0_g} = total market value of a geared company;
$V_{E_{ug}}$ = what the company would be worth if it was all equity financed;
$V_{B_g} T$ = present value of the tax relief on debt interest.

This expression can be restated as follows:

$$V_{E_g} + V_B = V_{E_{ug}} + V_{B_g} T$$
$$V_{E_{ug}} = V_{E_g} + V_{B_g} - V_{B_g} T$$
$$V_{E_{ug}} = V_{E_g} + V_{B_g}(1 - T).$$

And, on the basis that the beta value of a company's assets reflects a weighted averaged of the beta values of the securities that finance those assets, then we can formulate the expression in terms of beta values:

$$\beta_{assets} = \beta_{equity} \times \frac{V_E}{V_E + V_B(1-T)} + \beta_{debt} \times \frac{V_B(1-T)}{V_E + V_B(1-T)}.$$

This is therefore our revised expression for calculating asset betas in a *taxed* world.

However, before we now start to apply this expression, two words of caution have to be sounded. One assumption that has been maintained throughout this analysis is of perpetuity cash flows. This is *not a necessary* assumption of the APV technique, but it *is* an assumption of the expression we have developed for estimating an asset beta in a *taxed* world.

Therefore if this expression is used in a situation where the cash flows are *not* perpetuities, then it should be recognized that there will be some degree of error. However, when estimating an industry's asset beta, this assumption's lack of validity may not be substantial and so the error would be relatively minor.

The second problem is more profound. As we have already seen, the simple expression of the value of tax benefit from borrowing as shown above is not really adequate to describe the situation that holds in the real world were individuals pay taxes on income and capital gains and also receive tax credits with dividends.

Applying the APV technique

Example 2 illustrates the use of the APV technique in a relatively simple situation. However, it should be noted that, even here, a traditional NPV/WACC approach would have great difficulty in arriving at a satisfactory evaluation of the project.

Example 2

The problem

Tento plc is an industrial holding company. It is currently considering diversifying into the construction industry. The particular project under evaluation would require capital expenditure of £100 000 and would have a zero scrap value at the end of its three-year life. It is estimated that the project would generate an annual net cash flow (revenues less operating cash costs) of £50 000.

The proposal is to finance the project with an £80 000 three-year term loan from Tento's bank. The project would have sufficient debt capacity to support such a loan and the annual interest rate would be 14%. There would be an arrangement fee on the loan of £1500. In addition, the company would utilize £20 000 of retained earnings.

The construction industry has an average equity beta of 2.43 and its debt capital can be considered to be virtually risk-free and so can be assumed to have a zero beta value. The average gearing (debt:equity) ratio in the industry is 3:4.

Tento plc pays corporation tax at 35%, twelve months after year-end. Capital expenditure attracts a 25% writing-down allowance calculated on the reducing balance and tax relief is available on debt interest. The project would be bought on the first day of the company's financial year and the loan taken out accordingly.

The return on government stock with a three-year maturity is 10.2% per annum. The market return is 16.2% per annum.

The company wishes to evaluate the proposed investment using an adjusted present value analysis.

The solution

The starting point is to identify the NPV of the project as if it were all-equity financed – that is the base-case present value:

1. *Base-case discount rate*

$$\beta_{industryassets} = 2.43 \times \frac{4}{4 + 3(1 - 0.35)} = 1.634.$$

Using CAPM: 10.2% + (16.2% − 10%) × 1.634 = 20% = base-case discount rate.

This is the return required from the project due to its systematic business risk (principally, its revenue sensitivity and its proportion of fixed to variable operating costs).

2. *Writing-down allowances*

(£)			WDA			Tax relief	Timing
100 000	×	0.25	= £25 000	×	0.35 =	£8 750	Yr 2
−25 000							
= 75 000	×	0.25	= 18 750	×	0.35 =	6 562	Yr 3
−18 750							
= 56 250	−	0	= 56 250	×	0.35 =	19 688	Yr 4

3. *Base-case present value*

Year	0	1	2	3	4
Outlay	(100 000)				
WDA tax relief		8 750	6 562	19 688	
Net cash flow		50 000	50 000	50 000	
Tax on cash flow			(17 500)	(17 500)	(17 500)
After-tax cash flow	(100 000)	50 000	41 250	39 062	2 188
20% discount factor	× 1	× .8333	× .6944	× .5787	× .4 823
PV cash flow	(100 000)	41 665	28 644	22 605	1 055

Base-case present value: (£6031)

4. **Present value of the financing side-effects**

   (i) *Present value of the tax shield*

   Annual interest: $£80\,000 \times 0.14 = £11\,200$
   Annual tax relief: $£11\,200 \times 0.35 = £3920$
   PV of tax relief: $£3920\,A_{3-0.14}(1.14)^{-1} = £8009$

Notice that the pre-tax cost of debt capital is used as the discount rate. This rate is used as the best rate to reflect the low-risk nature of the tax relief cash flow. (The after-tax cost of debt is not used as this would represent 'double counting' of the debt interest tax relief.)

   (ii) *Present value of capital issue costs*

   Arrangement fee: (£1500)
   Tax relief on arrangement fee: $£1500 \times 0.35 = £525$
   PV of the tax relief: $£525(1.14)^{-2} = £404$

5. **Adjusted present value**

		(£)
Base-case present value	:	(6031)
Present value of tax shield	:	8009
Arrangement fee	:	(1500)
PV of arrangement fee tax relief	:	404
Adjusted present value	:	+£882

Although the project would have been rejected if it had been all-equity financed (NPV: −£6031), it *is* worthwhile accepting the project because of its proposed financing method: its overall APV is positive. Therefore, if the project is accepted it will increase shareholder wealth by £882.

Two further points

There are two further points to be made about Example 2. The first concerns the reference to debt capacity.

It can be seen from the analysis used in the example that debt capacity is valuable. A project's debt capacity indicates its ability to act as security for a loan. It is the tax relief available from such a loan which gives debt capacity its value.

This then raises a potential problem. Some projects may be undertaken where the amount of debt finance that is used effectively *undergears* the project, leaving *spare* debt capacity. Alternatively, a project might be financed by more debt capital than the project itself can support. In other words, the project might be *overgeared*, because of the availability of *unused* debt capacity elsewhere in the company.

The problem here concerns how the project should be evaluated via APV. Should the PV of the tax shield be based on the *actual* amount of debt financing used, or on the theoretical amount of debt financing the project's own debt capacity would allow it to raise?

The answer is that the tax shield should be based on the *theoretical* level of financing, as to do otherwise would lead to the danger of *cross-subsidization*. Example 3 shows two possible situations.

Example 3

Suppose a company is considering Project A. It costs £100 000 and has an infinitely long life. It has a debt capacity of 80%. The management decide to finance the project with £50 000 of equity and £50 000 of irredeemable bonds at 10% interest. The corporation tax is 35% and there are no other costs involved.

Projects A's base-case PV is negative: −£25 000. If the PV of the tax shield is based on *actual* level of debt financing its value is:

$$\frac{£50\,000 \times 0.10 \times 0.35}{0.10}(1.10)^{-1} = £15\,909.$$

However, based on the *theoretical* amount of debt the project could support the tax shield is then valued at:

$$\frac{£80\,000 \times 0.10 \times 0.35}{0.10}(1.10)^{-1} = £25\,455.$$

Therefore, in the former case the APV would be negative and the project – incorrectly – rejected. In the latter case the project should, quite properly, be accepted, because of its positive APV. This latter analysis is correct because although the project is not utilizing the whole of its debt capacity, the company has got the ability to raise debt finance *in the future*, secured against this project's unused debt capacity. Hence, its value should be credited to the project.

Suppose the company decided to undertake Project A. Some time later, Project Z was discovered. This requires £80 000 of capital expenditure and it has a 50% debt capacity. However, instead of just using £40 000 of 10% debt, the company proposes to use £60 000 of 10% debt – £40 000 of which is secured against the project's own assets, in line with its debt capacity, and £20 000 secured against the unused debt capacity arising from the earlier acceptance of Project A.

If Project Z has a negative base-case present value of £18 000 and it could be financed with irredeemable debt (for simplicity), then its APV might be either positive or negative, depending on the tax shield chosen.

On the basis of debt financing of £60 000, the PV of the tax shield is:

$$\frac{£60\,000 \times 0.10 \times 0.35}{0.10}(1.10)^{-1} = £19\,091.$$

Thus the project would be accepted with an APV of: −£18 000 + £19 091 = +£1091.

However, on the basis of the debt financing which the project can support in its own right – £40 000 – the PV of the tax shield is:

$$\frac{£40\,000 \times 0.10 \times 0.35}{0.10}(1.10)^{-1} = £12\,727.$$

In this case the project's APV is negative: −£18 000 + £12 727 = −£5273 and so should be rejected.

The latter analysis is, of course, correct. In the former analysis, the PV of the tax shield contains a *subsidy* from project A equal to the value of A's unused debt capacity:

$$\frac{£20\,000 \times 0.10 \times 0.35}{0.10}(1.10)^{-1} = £6364.$$

Quite simply, to be acceptable, a project should be capable of generating a positive APV *in its own right*. Logically, we should not cross-subsidize between projects in the evaluation process.

The second point to be made is as follows. The logic behind the APV technique is simple: different risk cash flows should be evaluated separately using discount rates which specifically reflect the systematic risk level involved. For this reason, the technique is sometimes referred to as the 'valuation of components rule' (VCR).

In a more sophisticated analysis of a large project, more than one discount rate may be used to calculate the base-case PV. For example, it may be thought that a project's revenues are significantly more (systematic) risky than its cost cash flows. Therefore the present value of the revenues may be calculated separately from the present value of its costs, using a different discount rate in each case. Alternatively, it could be legitimately argued that the WDA tax relief cash flows are particularly low risk and so should have a separate discount rate applied to them which specifically reflects their low-risk nature.

A more complex example

A more complex problem is illustrated in Example 4. Here the APV analysis takes account not only of the tax relief on debt interest, but also of a cheap loan and capital issue costs. Any number of side-effects can be included in the analysis by just adding them on to the base-case present value.

The problem

The project that a company is considering consists of the purchase and operation of two machines, A and B. Machine A costs £60 000 and Machine B £40 000. The project is expected to produce a net annual revenue, before tax, of £66 000 and is expected to have a life of three years. At the end of its life the two machines will be worthless.

For this type of asset the company would normally expect to finance 75% of the capital expenditure with debt capital with a maturity equal to that of the project's life. Thus they expect to raise £45 000 of debt to purchase machine A and £30 000 of debt to purchase machine B. The balance, in each case, would be met from an issue of equity. Issue costs are expected to be 7½% of the amount raised in the case of debt.

Because the government wishes to promote the purchase and operation of Machine B, they will make a loan available (repayable at the end of three years) for 100% of machine B's cost, at a subsidized rate of interest of only 6%. This is in contrast to the current market cost of debt of 10%. However, as a result of this facility, the company will only raise £35 000 of debt to finance machine A, so that the overall debt ratio of the project remains at around 75%.

The project falls within an industry category having an equity beta value of 1.363 and an average debt–equity ratio of 1:3. The risk-free return and market return are 6% and 13.5%, respectively. Corporation tax is 35%. For simplicity, assume that tax is paid at each year-end without delay and that there is no tax relief available on either capital expenditure or issue costs. Also assume that debt betas are zero.

The solution

Base-case PV of the project

$$\beta_{project} = 1.363 \times \frac{3}{3 + 1(1 - 0.35)} = 1.12$$

$$E(r_{project}) = 6\% + (13.5\% - 6\%) \times 1.12 = 15\%$$

$$-£100\ 000 + £66\ 000(1 - 0.35)\ A_{3-0.15} = -£2038$$

Financing side-effects

(i) PV of tax relief on debt interest
  Machine A
  £35 000 × 0.10 × 0.35 $A_{3-0.10}$ = £3046
  Machine B
  £40 000 × 0.06 × 0.35 $A_{3-0.10}$ = £2089
  _____
  + £5135

(ii) PV of cheap loan

Interesting saving after tax $£40\,000 \times (0.10 - 0.06)(1 - 0.35)A_{3-0.10}$	£3979
(iii) Issue costs: $£25\,000 \times 0.075$	$-£(1875)$
Base PV of project	$-£(2038)$
plus PV of tax relief on interest	$+£5135$
plus PV of cheap loan	$+£2586$
less issue costs	$-£(1875)$
APV	$+£3808$

Therefore the project should be accepted; it has a positive APV of $+£3808$.

In conclusion

In conclusion, what can be said about investment and financing interactions? It should be noted that, in most cases (except for such situations as found in Example 4), the major financing side-effect arises from the tax shield. However, in this respect, we should not ignore the conclusion of Miller's 1977 analysis that the *true* worth of the tax shield may be zero.

Whether or not Miller's analysis holds good in the real world is still subject to empirical testing. However, it may well be realistic to suggest that the value of the tax shield, even if it is not zero, is substantially less than the value placed upon it by the M and M with-tax analysis.

In such a case, an APV analysis – although technically more correct in most circumstances than a 'traditional' WACC/NPV analysis – may add very little to the project evaluation. In other words, given all the general uncertainties surrounding any investment appraisal, an NPV/WACC analysis may be thought to be sufficiently accurate.

However, in contrast to the above comment, it should also be pointed out that in *very* major projects (sometimes referred to as 'giant' projects) the financing package attached to the project plays a crucial role. In such circumstances an APV analysis would be *strongly* desirable.

Risk-adjusted WACC

If we accept that an NPV/WACC analysis will be sufficiently accurate, we have a fairly accessible method of making our decision.

As we have already noted, the most problematic assumption lying behind an NPV/WACC analysis is that the project has the same systematic risk as the company. Where this is *not* the case, but where the project is relatively small and the company is intending to maintain its existing capital structure, it is still reasonable to use an NPV/WACC analysis if the WACC is *adjusted* to take into account the different systematic risk.

Example 1 gave a very simple illustration of this approach. In Example 5, we now give a full-scale illustration of the calculation of a risk-adjusted weighted average cost of capital to be used as an NPV discount rate in the type of situation described in the previous paragraph.

Example 5

The problem

Lagoon plc is a cement manufacturer with a debt:equity ratio of 1:4 and a pre-tax cost of debt capital of 12%. It is considering whether to undertake a project that involves the manufacture of ice-cream. The company realizes that it cannot use its WACC as an NPV discount rate in order to evaluate the project, as the systematic risk of cement manufacturing is unlikely to be the same as that of ice-cream manufacturing.

In order to solve this problem, Lagoon has identified a quoted ice-cream manufacturer, Icecold plc, about which it has obtained the following information:

$$\beta_{equity} = 1.40 \qquad \beta_{debt} = 0.15$$
$$V_B : V_E = 2:3$$

In addition, the current return on government stocks is 10% and the return on the market portfolio is estimated to be 17%. Corporation tax is at 33%.

The company wishes to use this information to generate a risk-adjusted WACC: an NPV discount rate which will reflect both the systematic *business risk* of the ice-cream project and the systematic *financial risk* of the cement manufacturing company which intends to undertake the project.

The solution

There are two possible approaches to the generation of a suitable discount rate. Both are shown here for purposes of illustration:

Approach 1:
This is completed in four stages.
1. The data concerning Icecold plc can be used to estimate *an asset* beta for ice-cream manufacturing.

$$\text{Using}: \beta_{asset} = \beta_{equity} \times \frac{V_E}{V_E + V_B(1-T)} + \beta_{debt} \times \frac{V_B(1-T)}{V_E + V_B(1-T)}$$

$$\beta_{asset} \atop icecold\,plc = 1.40 \times \frac{3}{3 + 2(1-0.33)} + 0.15 \times \frac{2(1-0.33)}{3 + 2(1-0.33)}$$

$$\beta_{asset} \atop icecold\,plc = 0.968 + 0.046 = 1.014.$$

This asset beta reflects Icecold's systematic business risk of ice-cream manufacturing and therefore can be used as an estimate for the asset beta of Lagoon's ice-cream project:

$$\beta_{asset} \atop project = \beta_{asset} \atop Icecold = 1.014$$

2. The second stage of the analysis is to 'regear' this asset beta with Lagoon's capital structure to estimate an equity beta for Lagoon's ice-cream project. Before doing so, however, we need to estimate a debt beta for the project. Given that Lagoon has a pre-tax cost of debt of 12%, the debt beta can be estimated from the CAPM:

$$K_D = r_F + (E(r_M) - r_F) \times \beta_{debt}$$

therefore: $12\% = 10\% + (17\% - 10\%) \times \beta_{debt}$

$$\frac{12\% - 10\%}{(17\% - 10\%)} = \beta_{debt} = 0.286.$$

An equity beta for the project can now be estimated, again using:

$$\beta_{\substack{asset \\ project}} = \beta_{\substack{equity \\ project}} \times \frac{V_E}{V_E + V_B(1-T)} + \beta_{\substack{debt \\ project}} \times \frac{V_B(1-T)}{V_E + V_B(1-T)}$$

where:

$$1.014 = \beta_{\substack{equity \\ project}} \times \frac{4}{4 + 1(1-0.33)} + 0.286 \times \frac{1.(1-0.33)}{4 + 1(1-0.33)}$$

$$1.014 = \beta_{\substack{equity \\ project}} \times 0.854 + 0.041$$

$$\frac{1.014 - 0.041}{0.856} = \beta_{\substack{equity \\ project}} = 1.137.$$

This equity beta reflects the systematic risk of the shareholders' funds invested by Lagoon plc in the ice-cream project: it reflects the systematic *business* risk of the project, *and* the systematic *financial* risk of Lagoon's capital structure.

3. The third stage is to take the project's equity beta and use CAPM to generate a cost of equity capital for the project. Therefore, using the CAPM:

$$K_{E_{project}} = r_F + (E(r_M) - r_F) \times \beta_{\substack{equity \\ project}}$$

$$K_{E_{project}} = 10\% + (17\% - 10\%) \times 1.137 = 17.96\%.$$

Thus this estimates that Lagoon's shareholders will require a 17.96% return on their funds that are to be invested in the ice-cream project, to reward them for the project's systematic business risk and the company's financial risk.

4. The final stage of the analysis is to use Lagoon plc's capital structure to calculate a risk-adjusted weighted average cost of capital for the project, using:

$$K_{0_{project}} = K_{E_{project}} \times \frac{V_E}{V_0} + K_D(1-T) \times \frac{V_B}{V_0}$$

$$K_{0_{project}} = 17.96\% \times \frac{4}{4+1} + 12\%(1-0.33) \times \frac{1}{4+1} = 15.97\%.$$

Approach 2:

This is more direct and makes use of the fact that the asset beta, when inputted into the CAPM, generates $K_{E_{ug}}$. This is on the basis that the asset beta measures systematic business risk only and so, when put into CAPM, it generates the return required for the systematic business risk. As we know from the capital structure analysis in Chapter 19, $K_{E_{ug}}$ is the cost of equity capital in an *all-equity* financed company: such a company *only* has systematic business risk.

1. The first stage is exactly the same as in the previous approach: the project's asset beta is estimated on the basis of Icecold's asset beta.
   Therefore:

$$\beta_{\substack{asset \\ project}} = 1.014$$

2. This can be input into the CAPM to estimate $K_{E_{ug}}$ for the project;

$$K_{E_{ug}} = r_F + (E(r_M) - r_F) \times \beta_{\substack{asset \\ project}}$$

$$K_{E_{ug}} = 10\% + (17\% - 10\%) \times 1.014 = 17.1\%.$$

This represents the expected return required on the project, given its systematic business risk.

3. Finally, the M and M equation for the weighted average cost of capital can be used – using Lagoon's capital structure – to provide an estimate of a risk-adjusted weighted average cost of capital for the project:

$$K_{0_{\text{project}}} = K_{E_{ug}} \times \left(1 - \frac{V_B \times T}{V_0}\right)$$

$$K_{0_{\text{project}}} = 17.1\% \times \left(1 - \frac{1 \times 0.33}{4+1}\right) = 15.97\%$$

Notice that both approaches produce exactly the same result; a risk-adjusted, after-tax weighted average cost of capital of 15.97%, which could then be used in an NPV analysis of Lagoon plc's ice-cream project.

Lease or purchase decision

Financial and operating leases

Many companies use leasing to obtain the services of an asset, as an alternative to outright purchase. Therefore it can be seen as a source of finance and hence the 'lease or purchase' decision can be classed as a financing decision.[3]

The evaluation of the lease or purchase decision has been problematic mainly because it cannot really be viewed as a *pure* financing decision, as it also involves interactions with the investment decision.[4] In this section, we will examine how the lease or purchase decision should be evaluated, in the light of our development of the APV technique.

The process of leasing involves one party (the lessor) purchasing an asset and renting out the use of that asset to another party (the lessee). Thus the lessee is able to operate the asset without actually being the legal owner.

It is usual for lease contracts to be classified into either *financial* or *operating* leases. The main characteristics of a financial lease are as follows. The lessor will lease the machine to the lessee, with the intention of receiving the full purchase price of the leased asset, plus a rate of return on capital, through the lease payments. For this reason, a financial lease cannot usually be cancelled or terminated by either party. Therefore with this type of lease, the lessee – although not the legal owner – holds all the risks of asset ownership (e.g. the risk of technological obsolescence and the risk that the demand for the asset's services will be below expectations). The lessor holds no risk, other than the risk of the lessee's default on the lease payments. Hence a financial lease is virtually indistinguishable from more normal debt capital – both in theory and in practice.

Operating leases are very different. They are generally short-term and usually represent the rental of an asset to carry out a particular job. Characteristically, the asset will be used by many lessees over its life. The lessor does not necessarily expect to recover the full cost of the asset, plus a return on capital, out of the lease payments, but will also take account of the expected second-hand value of the asset at the termination of the leasing agreement. Therefore, with an operating lease, the lessee does not bear any of the risks of ownership – these are borne instead by the lessor – because of the option to cancel the agreement at short notice. Where such a lease is entered into on a longer-term basis, it can be viewed, not so much as a form of finance (although that is what it is), but more of a marketing device. In other words the *manufacturer* of an asset may offer the asset's services through an operating lease as a marketing device to encourage 'sales' (e.g. photocopiers are often 'sold' on operating leases).

The evaluation of an operating lease is relatively straightforward. Because the lease is terminable at short notice, the lease payments are treated as just another operating cost of the asset involved. Hence a straightforward NPV analysis can be used, where the (after tax) lease payment cash flows are included along with all the other cash flows involved, and which are then discounted to present value by a discount rate that reflects the asset's systematic risk.

Evaluating a financial lease

We stated earlier that a financial lease is effectively the equivalent of debt capital in that, from a gearing viewpoint, the present value of a lease contract liability would be seen in the same terms as the liability on straightforward debt finance. However, the APV analysis of lease finance differs somewhat from that involving debt finance.

Example 6 illustrates the APV technique being applied to a lease versus loan-purchase decision. This can then be contrasted with the evaluation of the same project in Example 7, but which is done along the lines of a more *traditional* lease versus purchase analysis. The anomalies in this second example should be fairly obvious – given what we know about risk and return relationships. (The fact that the two analyses produce the same conclusion is, of course, fortuitous.)

Example 6

The problem

A company is considering undertaking a project which consists of the acquisition and operation of a machine. The machine would cost £1000 and would have a zero scrap value at the end of its three-year life.

It is expected to produce the following net cash flows (i.e. revenues less operating costs), pre-tax:

Year	Cash flow
1	+600
2	+500
3	+200

The machine could either be bought outright or acquired via a financial lease. Purchase would be made through a £600 three-year term loan at 14% interest, secured against the machine (which has a 60% debt capacity), together with £400 of retained earnings. The lease agreement requires three payments of £320, paid annually in advance.

Assume that all initial transactions are made on the last day of the previous accounting year and the company expects to have a corporate tax liability throughout the next three years.

It is thought that the project is required to produce an after-tax return of at least 20% to make it acceptable. This can be assumed to represent an adequate base-case discount rate.

Corporation tax is charged at 35%, payable twelve months in arrears. Writing-down allowances of 25% on the reducing balance are available on capital expenditure.

The analysis

In this type of situation, an APV analysis has to be undertaken on the basis of a pair of mutually exclusive alternatives: the project purchased and the project leased.

(a) *Project purchased*

Base-case PV:

Year	0	1	2	3	4
Outlay	(1000)				
Net cash flow		600	500	200	
Tax charge			(210)	(175)	(70)
After-tax c/f	(1000)	600	290	25	(70)
20% discount	×1	×.8333	×.6944	×.5787	×.4823
	(1000)	499.98	201.38	14.47	(33.76)

Base-case PV: −£317.93

PV of financing side-effects

(i) PV of WDA tax relief

Tax relief:

			WDA				Tax relief	Timing
1000	×	0.25	=	250	×	0.35	=	87.50	Yr 1
− 250									
= 750	×	0.25	=	187.5	×	0.35	=	65.63	Yr 2
− 187.5									
= 562.5	×	0.25	=	140.63	×	0.35	=	49.22	Yr 3
− 140.63									
= 421.87	−	0	=	421.87	×	0.35	=	147.65	Yr 4

PV calculation using K_D (14%) to reflect the low-risk nature of the cash flow:

Year	Tax relief		14% discount		
1	+ 87.50	×	0.8772	=	+ 76.76
2	+ 65.63	×	0.7695	=	+ 50.50
3	+ 49.22	×	0.6750	=	+ 33.22
4	+147.65	×	0.5921	=	+ 87.42
					+247.90 PV of tax relief

(ii) PV of tax shield

Annual interest   : £600 × 0.14 = £84
Annual tax relief : £84 × 0.35 = £29.40
PV of tax relief   : £29.40 $A_{3-0.14}(1.14)^{-1}$ = + £59.87

Adjusted present value

Base-case PV	:	−£317.93
PV of WDA tax relief	:	+£247.90
PV of tax shield	:	+£ 59.87
APV		−£ 10.16

Therefore the project is not worthwhile if loan-purchased.

(b) *Project leased*

Base-case PV: −£317.93

PV of financing side-effects

(i) PV of lease payments: −320 − 320$A_{2-0.14}$ = −£846.94

(ii) PV of tax relief on lease payments:
(+320 × 0.35)$A_{3-0.14}$ = +£260.02

(iii) PV of capital expenditure saved = +£1000

Adjusted present value

Base-case PV	:	−£ 317.93
PV of lease payments	:	+£ 846.94
PV of tax relief	:	+£ 260.02
PV of saved capital expenditure	:	+£1000
APV		+£ 95.15

Therefore the project *is* worthwhile if leased.

Example 7

A more traditional approach to lease versus purchase decisions (although there are many variations) is to treat it as a two-stage decision. The first is to compare the PV cost of leasing against purchase. The second is to then evaluate the project using the least-cost method of acquisition as the 'outlay'. In the first stage of the decision the after-tax cost of debt is used to reflect the low-risk nature of the cash flows and to take into account the tax-deductibility of debt. In the second stage, a discount rate is used which reflects the project's own systematic risk level.

Stage One

After-tax cost of debt: 14% $(1 - 0.35) = 9.1\%$ = discount factor.

PV of lease cash flows:

Year	Lease	Tax relief		Discount factor		
0	−320		×	1	=	−320
1	−320	+112	×	0.9166	=	−190.65
2	−320	+112	×	0.8401	=	−174.74
3		+112	×	0.7701	=	+ 86.25
				PV of lease payments	=	£−599.14

PV of purchase cash flows

Year	Outlay	WDA		Discount factor		
0	−1000		×	1	=	−1000
1		+87.50	×	0.9166	=	− 80.20
2		+65.63	×	0.8401	=	− 55.14
3		49.22	×	0.7701	=	+ 37.90
4		147.65	×	0.7058	=	+ 104.21
				PV of purchase	=	−£722.55

Therefore, it is cheaper to acquire the machine with a lease rather than purchase.

Stage Two

Project's NPV analysis

Year	PV cost	Net cash flow	Tax charge		20% discount factor		
0	−599.14			×	1	=	−599.14
1		+600		×	0.8333	=	+499.98
2		+500	−210	×	0.6944	=	+201.38
3		+200	−175	×	0.5787	=	+ 14.47
4			− 70	×	0.4823	=	− 33.76
					NPV	=	£+ 82.93

Therefore the project is worth undertaking via a financial lease agreement.

There is a final point concerning leases that we need to consider. Given that a finance lease is effectively a form of borrowing, should it be taken into account when calculating gearing? The answer to the question is yes. Many companies using leases hid their effective debt levels from the outside world. (This was referred to as 'off-balance sheet' financing). Eventually a UK accounting standard on this issue was produced (SSAP 21, 1984), requiring the disclosure of finance leases. This is important as it has been shown that companies required to disclose this information for the first time suffer a fall in share prices – because investors see the company as having higher gearing than was previously disclosed. Information is given in financial statements that allows for the lease to be treated as any other form of debt by interested parties.

Summary

This chapter has investigated the investment and financing decision interactions.

- Four different valuation models were analysed. All four were found to be equivalent, given a set of restrictive assumptions which included a fixed or unchanging gearing ratio.

- Given these assumptions, all four valuation models were capable of correctly evaluating a capital investment proposal.

- However, when the assumption of an unchanging gearing ratio is relaxed, all become, effectively, unworkable – with the exception of the adjusted present value model.

- The APV model is a very general model and, because it takes a 'divide and conquer' approach – evaluating each different risk cash flow separately – it can handle highly complex capital investment appraisals, together with the associated financing implications.

- In circumstances where an NPV/WACC analysis would be satisfactory, if it were not for the fact that the project's systematic risk is not the same as that of the company, then a risk-adjusted WACC can be estimated to reflect the project's systematic business risk *specifically*, together with the financial risk of the company's capital structure.

- Finally, the lease versus purchase decision was analysed using an APV/valuation by components rule approach. Here it was seen that the analysis had to be conducted on the basis of a mutually exclusive investment decision. It is also recognized that a finance lease is really just the same as any other company borrowing and should be treated as such.

Notes

1. An alternative, equivalent expression, after Hamada (1972), which is widely used is:

$$\beta_{assets} = \beta_{equity} / \left(1 + \frac{V_D}{V_E}\right),$$

but notice this expression assumes $\beta_{debt} = 0$.

2. Because of this, in Example 1, there is really no need to regear the industry's asset beta of 0.96. This could be used in CAPM to generate a suitable discount rate for the project, which would be equal to the project's WACC. This is because, in a no-tax world, capital structure – although it does affect K_E – does not affect the overall return required.

3. Some approaches treat the decision as an investment decision.

4. For a survey of the different approaches, see Bower (1973).

Further reading

1. Two excellent articles which look at the whole area of investment and financing decisions, their interactions and the use of CAPM are: M.E. Rubinstein, 'A Mean-Variance Synthesis of Corporate Financial Theory', *Journal of Finance*, March 1973, and R.S. Hamada, 'The Effect of the Firm's Capital Structure on the Systematic Risks of Common Stocks', *Journal of Finance*, May 1972. In addition, a worthwhile reference on debt betas is: M. Weinstein, 'The Systematic Risk of Corporate Bonds', *Journal of Financial and Quantitative Analysis*, September 1981.

2. In addition, the following articles are of interest in providing a general overview: A.K. Makhaya and H.E. Thompson, 'Comparison of Alternative Models for Estimating the Cost of Equity Capital for Electric Utilities', *Journal of Economics and Business*, February 1984; and I.E. Brick and D.G. Weaver, 'A Comparison of Capital Budgeting Techniques in Identifying Profitable Investments', *Financial Management*, Winter 1984.

3. As far as APV is concerned, the original article is: S.C. Myers, 'Interactions of Corporate Financing and Investment Decisions – Implications for Capital Budgeting', *Journal of Finance*, March 1974. However, a good introductory article is to be found in R. Taggart, 'Capital Budgeting and the Financing Decision: An Exposition', *Financial Management*, Summer 1977.

4. Other articles of interest include: D.R. Chamber, R.S. Harris and J.J. Pringle, 'Treatment of Financing Mix in Analysing Investment Opportunities', *Financial Management*, Summer 1982; R.C. Greenfield, M.R. Randall and J.D. Woods, 'Financial Leverage and the Use of the NPV Investment Criterion', *Financial Management*, Autumn 1983; and I. Cooper and J.R. Franks, 'The Interaction of Investment and Financing Decisions when a Firm has Unused Tax Credits', *Journal of Finance*, May 1983.

5. A good introductory article on the lease decision is R.S. Bower, 'Issues in Lease Financing', *Financing Management*, Winter 1973. In addition, three other articles worth reading are: L.D. Schall, 'Evaluation of Lease Financing Contracts', *Midland Corporate Finance Journal*, Spring 1985; J. Ang and P.P. Peterson, 'The Leasing Puzzle', *Journal of Finance*, September 1984; and H.H. Weingartner, 'Leasing, Asset Lives and Uncertainty: Guide to Decision Making', *Financial Management*, Summer 1987. Finally an interesting perspective is given by J.C. Drury and S. Braund, 'The Leasing Decision: A Comparison of Theory and Practice', *Accounting and Business Research*, Summer 1990.

Quickie questions

1. If a company has a gearing ratio of 1:3 why will financing a £1000 project with £250 of debt and £750 of equity not necessarily maintain the firm's existing capital structure?
2. What does the base-case discount rate represent?
3. What does the base-case present value of a project represent?
4. Distinguish between an operating lease and a financial lease.
5. If an industry's equity beta is 1.45 and its debt beta is 0.25 with an average gearing rate of 2:5, what is its assets beta, given a 35% corporate tax rate?
6. Given the information in question 5, estimate the beta value for the industry's average level of *financial* risk.
7. What is debt capacity?
8. A project costs £5000. It will be financed with a £3000 five-year loan at 10% interest. The corporation tax rate is 35%, paid twelve months in arrears and the project has a 50% debt capacity. What is the PV of its tax shield?

Problems

1. Arthur plc, an industrial conglomerate, is currently evaluating a project to produce a new electronic lock mechanism recently developed by the company. The project will require an immediate outlay of £10 000 on production machinery. This would have a zero scrap value at all times and would not be an allowable expense against tax. The project is expected to have a three-year life and produce a net annual cash flow of £6700 in each year. The amount would be subject to corporation tax.

   Although the project only has a debt capacity of 30% of cost, the company has unused debt capacity elsewhere and so proposes to finance the project with a £4000 three-year loan, with an annual interest charge of 14%, together with a £3000 rights issue of equity and £3000 of retained earnings. The rights issue will incur issue costs amounting to 2% of the money raised and the debt capital will incur issue costs of 1%. Both sets of issue costs are allowable against tax.

   The electronics sector has an equity beta of 1.26 and an average gearing ratio of 1:3 (debt:equity). The industry's debt can be assumed to have a beta of 0.10. The after-tax return on government stock is 7% and the after-tax return on the FT index is 15.5% Corporation tax is charged at a rate of 35% at each year-end without delay.

   Required:
   (a) Evaluate the project for the management of Arthur plc.
   (b) How would your evaluation change if the manufacturer of the production machinery offered you a three-year £10 000 interest-free loan (with an issue cost of 1%)?

2. Alpacca Products plc is a widely diversified industrial company. It has recently acquired the rights to manufacture a special type of mechanical folding widget patented by a German company. The rights – which last for five years – were bought by Alpacca's marketing director shortly before he was dismissed for incompetence.

   The company's production director has now been given the task of assessing whether manufacture is likely to be a worthwhile investment for Alpacca. His decision, already presented to the Board, is to reject the project on the basis of an indicated negative NPV.

   However, the chairman of Alpacca Products is uneasy about the production director's analysis and has called you in as a consultant for advice. From the production director's report, you establish the following facts:

Cash flows

	Capital £000	Sales £000	Operating expenses £000	Tax £000	Net cash flow £000
Immediately	(1300)				(1300)
End year 1–5		1800	(1450)	(140)	210
End year 5	600				600

NPV calculation:

	Net cash flow £000	Discount factor (10%)	Present value £000
Immediately	(1300)	1	(1300)
End year 1–5	210	3.9708	834
End year 5	600	0.6209	372
Total NPV			(94)

The production director's analysis is based on the following:

(a) The company's market research department have estimated sales of 100 000 units per annum at £11 per unit.

(b) The estimate of annual operating expenses consists of the following:

	£000
Direct materials @ £2.50 per unit	250
Direct labour @ £3.20 per unit	320
Production overhead @ £3.80 per unit	380
Interest @ 10%	120
Administration, selling and distribution expenses	380
Total	1450

The labour rate is based on a time allocation of workers on a fixed rate. Each worker costs the company £15 000 per annum, and this contract would necessitate employing eleven new ones. The company would need to spend £270 000 training these new employees in the first year, but this is not included specifically above as such costs are incorporated in production overhead expenses.

Production overhead is calculated on an allocated rate per labour hour of which 20% relates to variable overhead. Specific items of fixed overhead incurred as a result of this contract are:

Depreciation	£80 000 per annum
Supervisory labour	£56 000 per annum
Rent of additional property	£12 000 per annum

Interest is based on the latest interest rate information, and it is the company's intention to finance this project with a £1.2 million five-year term loan at 10% interest, plus £0.1 million of retained earnings.

Administration, selling and distribution expenses are charged on the basis of a fixed rate on sales, 25% of these expenses are variable.

(c) The tax charge is based on a rate of 40%, which is the company's current marginal rate of corporation tax.

(d) The project is discounted at the anticipated interest rate.

(e) The capital cost of £1.3 million represents £1 million for plant and machinery, and £300 000 for working capital. It is anticipated that the plant and machinery will have a resale value of £600 000 at the end of five years.

In addition to the above you ascertain the following:

(i) The company's marginal tax rate will fall to 35% after year 1.

(ii) The company will claim capital allowances at the rate of 25% on the reducing balance.

(iii) On average, tax is payable one year after the relevant profits arise.

(iv) The production machinery is estimated to have a 50% debt capacity. Working capital only has a 10% debt capacity. However, the company is, at present, all-equity financed and so has a considerable amount of unused debt capacity.

(v) Manufacturing companies with similar characteristics to the proposed project have average equity and debt betas of 2.29 and 0.15 respectively. Their average gearing ratio is 2:3 and their average marginal rate of corporation tax is 35%.

(vi) The current after-tax risk-free return on government stock is estimated at 8.5%. The average return on the FTSE stock market index is 15.5%.

(vii) The capital expenditure on the machinery would take place (at year 0) on the last day of the company's previous financial year for maximum tax efficiency.

Required:

Draft a report to the chairman of Alpacca Products plc:

(a)   presenting a revised assessment to assist them in their decision making;

(b)   discussing any differences between your assessment and that of the production director;

(c)   briefly discussing the basis of adjusted present value as a decision-making criterion.

22 The dividend decision

Dividend policy in perfect capital markets

The dividend decision is the third major category of corporate long-term financial decisions that we shall investigate. In a similar vein to both the capital investment decision and the capital structure decision, we shall pursue the question: can management affect shareholder wealth through the dividend decision?

The dividend decision is, perhaps, the least analysed and most elusive and controversial of the three areas of financial decision making. Indeed, one of the most celebrated academic articles on the area is entitled 'The Dividend Puzzle' (Black, 1976).

Consequently, the theory in this area is the least complete. The complications and confusions surrounding the dividend decision arise principally because it is the linchpin to both the investment and financing decisions. As such, it therefore becomes difficult to abstract it from these influences so that it may be examined, initially at least, in isolation.

The problem of the dividend decision can be stated in the form of two questions: does the *pattern* of the dividend flow through time to shareholders affect the market value of the equity capital? If it does, can one *particular* pattern of dividends then be identified which would maximize the equity's market value? However, the meaning of these two questions can appear ambiguous, and so we shall start by clarifying the nature of our enquiry into the dividend decision.

The fundamental valuation model that we have used tells us that the market value of a company's equity capital is given by the summation of the expected future dividend stream, discounted to present value. In this sense, dividends (including any cash on winding up or sale) can clearly be said to affect the market value of a company's ordinary shares – in fact, they can be said to be the final determinant of all company values. However, the question that we shall explore is whether or not the *pattern* of the expected dividend flow is a determinant of equity market value rather than the *magnitude* of the summated present value of the expected flow.

As far as a company's management is concerned, the dividend decision problem is one of *allocation*. How, at the end of each accounting period (for simplicity we shall assume this to be a twelve-month period, although in practice the dividend decision is usually made twice-yearly in the UK and quarterly in the USA), should the company's net after-tax cash flow be allocated amongst the competing ends?

There is a possible three-way split to be made: interest payments to the suppliers of debt capital,[1] dividend payments to shareholders, and retention within the company for application to investment opportunities. As it is the capital structure decision which largely determines the level of interest payments, we are left with the question as to how the annual net of tax and interest cash flow (we could call it the distributable cash earnings) should be divided up between dividend payments and retention within the company for reinvestment.

Dividends as a residual

We can start the analysis by recalling the basic single-period investment–consumption model which existed in a world of perfect capital markets and no taxation. We shall also assume that there are no sources of capital available to management which are external to the company. Fig. 22.1 illustrates the model.

In terms of the dividend decision, the company management must decide at time t_0 what proportion of the company's wealth OA (this could be viewed as being equivalent to the distributable cash earnings referred to above) should be invested and what proportion should be paid out as a dividend. We know that for optimality (i.e. for the maximization of shareholder wealth) the company should retain amount AB and distribute amount OB.

Therefore, notice that the decision on the division of amount OA was taken only with reference to the physical investment opportunities available and the perfect capital market rate of interest. The amount OB distributed as dividend to the company owners at time t_0 was purely the cash *residual* that was left after the investment decision had been made.

Fig. 22.1 *The dividend decision*

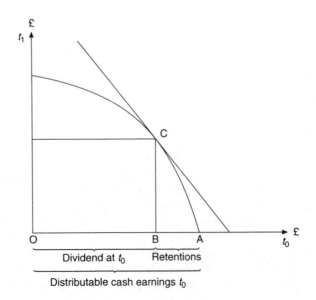

From this, we can derive a rather obvious dividend decision rule, which states that the distributable cash earnings should be retained within the company for reinvestment, as long as there are investment opportunities available which satisfy the NPV decision rule. Once this supply of investment opportunities has been exhausted (i.e. the company has moved to point C in Fig. 22.1) any distributable cash earnings remaining uninvested should be paid out to shareholders as a dividend.

This is the so-called 'dividend irrelevancy hypothesis' which was first explicitly formulated by Modigliani and Miller, but the name of the hypothesis – at this stage – is somewhat misleading: dividends themselves are not irrelevant (as we know from the dividend valuation model), it is the *pattern* of dividends which is irrelevant. They should be treated purely as a residual which arises once the investment decision is made.

In reaching this conclusion, M and M approached the problem of the dividend decision from a different, but equivalent, viewpoint. We shall illustrate this by means of an example, the data for which is illustrated in Table 22.1.

Suppose an all-equity financed company normally pays out its entire net cash flow each year as dividend. The company has previously undertaken investments which will generate an annual perpetuity net cash flow of £1000. The current market value of the company would be given by the present value sum of this future expected dividend flow (V_E).

The management have now discovered a project which they wish to undertake at t_1. The project costs £1000 and, rather than raise an extra £1000 from shareholders (by selling them some new shares), they decide to retain the dividend that was due to be paid at t_1. The project will produce a

Table 22.1

		t_1	t_2	t_3	t_n
$V_E = \sum_{t=1}^{n} \dfrac{D_t}{(1+K_E)^t}$	=	+1000	+1000	+1000 ...	+1000
$NPV = \sum_{t=1}^{2} \dfrac{A_t}{(1+K_E)^t}$	=	−1000	+1500		
$V_E^* = \sum_{t=1}^{n} \dfrac{D_t^*}{(1+K_E)^t}$	=	0	+2500	+1000 ...	+1000

Where V_E = current market value of the equity;
D_t = existing dividend flow;
V_E^* = post-investment market value of the equity;
D_t^* = post-investment dividend flow;
NPV = net present value of the proposed investment.

Therefore: $$V_E^* = V_E + NPV$$

or $$\sum_{t=1}^{n} \frac{D_t^*}{(1+K_E)^t} = \sum_{t=1}^{n} \frac{D_t^*}{(1+K_E)^t} + \sum_{t=1}^{2} \frac{A_t}{(1+K_E)^t}$$

To undertake the proposed investment: $V_E^* > V_E$ therefore: $NPV_p > 0$.

net cash inflow of £1300 at t_2 and the management propose to pay this out as *additional* dividend at that time.

Thus the *new*-market value of the equity (V_E^*) would be given by the present value sum of the *revised* expected dividend flow. This revised flow can be seen as consisting of two components: the original dividend flow (V_E) plus the project's cash flow (NPV_p).

The company would only undertake the proposed investment if the revised market value of the equity was greater than (or at least equal to) the existing market value of the equity: $V_E^* > V_E$. To ensure this, the NPV of the project must be greater than or equal to zero. The conclusion that can be drawn from this is that what has enhanced shareholder wealth was the investment decision alone. The decision on dividend policy was irrelevant. The dividend decision was purely a *residual* of the investment decision.[2]

However it must be remembered that the M and M argument is set in the perfect no-tax world of their initial capital structure hypothesis. As a counter to this view, we now turn to examine the more traditional view of dividend policy which holds that the pattern of dividend flow *is* relevant and *does* affect the market value of the ordinary shares.

Dividend patterns and the valuation model

Suppose that a company with an all-equity capital structure has made sufficient investments in the past to generate an annual net cash inflow of Y, in perpetuity. A constant proportion of this cash flow, b, is reinvested each year in projects which yield an average rate of return of r, whilst the remainder of each year's cash flow is paid out as dividends. As a result, Gordon's version of the basic dividend valuation growth model[3] can be applied to estimate the current market value of the company's equity capital:

$$V_E = \frac{Y(1-b)(1+rb)}{K_E - rb}.$$

Assuming a given value for Y and for K_E, we can see that the value for V_E produced by the model is dependent on the values given to r and b. It is the effect of different values of b that is of interest, because it is this that reflects the dividend decision: different values of b produce different dividend flow patterns over time.

The effect of the retention proportion on the market value of the equity depends upon the value of r relative to K_E. Where $r > K_E$, then V_E increases as b increases: where $r < K_E$, the reverse relationship holds, and where $r = K_E$, then V_E is unaffected by changes in b.

(But notice that what remains unaffected in such a situation is the *wealth* of ordinary shareholders. For example, if $Y = £100$ and $K_E = r = 0.20$ then, when $b = 0$, $V_E = £500$ and when $b = 0.1$, $V_E = £510$. Shareholder wealth can be seen to be unaffected by changes in b by the fact that when $b = 0$, they received a dividend of £100 and their shares had a market value of £500. Total wealth was therefore £600. When $b = 0.1$, they received a dividend of £90, £10 being reinvested, and their shares had a market value of £510. Total wealth is unchanged at $£90 + £510 = £600$.)

At first sight, therefore, it may well appear that the dividend decision can affect the market value of the equity (because it determines b), but *how* the dividend decision affects V_E depends upon the relationship of r to K_E. But really, it is not the dividend decision which is causing the market value of the equity to change, but the investment decisions which follow, i.e. it is the investment of the retained earnings which causes fluctuations in the equity market value.

We are seeing here, once again, confirmation of the NPV investment appraisal rule: increasing b will lead to an enhancement of equity market value *only* if the retained cash flows are being invested in projects yielding positive NPVs when discounted by K_E (i.e. when the project's yield or IRR $> K_E$). Retention of distributable cash flow for investment in projects yielding negative NPVs (i.e. $r < K_E$) serves merely to reduce the current market value of the company's equity capital.

Traditional view of the dividend decision

Notwithstanding the foregoing analysis, the traditional view[4] of the dividend decision is that at any particular point of time £1 of dividends (i.e. distributed cash flow) is somehow more valuable than £1 of retained cash flow – even though the cash flow may have been retained for investment in a project yielding a substantial positive NPV. This is sometimes referred to as the 'bird in the hand' argument (and sometimes the *bird in the hand fallacy*).

Proponents of this traditional view use the dividend growth model to support their argument in the following way. So far in this analysis, in using the dividend growth model, we have held K_E constant as b was varied. The traditionalists argue that this cannot be done, because K_E is partly a function of the value of b, because of the presence of risk. The cost of equity capital, as we have calculated it, is really no more than an average of a whole family of discount rates, each of which is related to a cash flow in a specific period. Therefore a company, by retaining a part of its current period cash flow, is replacing a *certain* cash flow 'now' with an *uncertain* future cash flow (i.e. the future dividends generated by the investment financed by the cash retention). This increased uncertainty will effectively raise the discount rate used against these future flows and so will cause K_E (the average discount rate) also to rise.

Thus, increasing the value of b is likely to lead to an increase in the value of K_E and so equity market values can be said to be affected by dividend policy itself and not simply through the effects of the investment undertaken with the retention, because dividend policy can alter the riskiness of the expected dividend flow. The optimal dividend–retention policy must be that which trades off the beneficial effects of retention and profitable reinvestment (i.e. an increased value for b on the assumption that $r > K_E$), against the detrimental effects of increased risk, so as to maximize the market value of the equity.

The traditional view can be put in an alternative and simpler way. The early payment of dividends may not actually change a company's business risk level, but it can favourably alter an investor's *perception* of the level of risk. Thus current dividends are viewed as more valuable than retained earnings because the investor's perception of risk is imperfect and this may lead him to under-value the future dividend stream that the retained earnings will generate.

An arbitrage criticism

The arguments of the traditionalists do not really stand up to a close theoretical examination, if the existence of a perfect capital market is assumed. The main counter-argument that can be put forward is that if two companies are identical in every respect except that their dividend–retention ratios differ, and if the market values retained earnings differently from dividends, the market prices of the two companies will be in disequilibrium (i.e. two identical goods will be selling at different prices in the same market). This will allow investors to undertake profitable arbitrage transactions, substituting home-made dividends for corporate dividends by selling part of their shareholding.

The following analysis illustrates this substitution in showing the irrelevance of dividend pattern and the opportunities which exist for arbitraging if a traditional view of dividend retention persists in the stock market.

We will assume that we have a perfect capital market in which there are no taxes or transaction costs and that the market interest rate of return is 10%. An all-equity company has made previous investments which are sufficient, in total, to generate an annual cash flow of £1000 in perpetuity. All this cash flow is paid out each year as dividends. Thus the company has a total market value of £1000/0.10 = £10 000. Each of the company's 1000 ordinary shares therefore has a market value of £10 and receives an annual dividend of £1.

An investor owns 100 of the company's shares. Thus the market value of his shareholding is £1000, from which he receives an annual dividend of £100.

The company has just paid the current year's dividend and has informed shareholders that next year's dividend (at time t_1) will be withheld so as to invest in a project that will yield a net cash inflow of £2000 at time t_2. The project's cash inflow will be paid out, at that time, as an additional dividend. The company's revised dividend flow, and hence its revised market value, at t_0 is as follows:

	t_1	t_2	$t_3 \ldots$
Existing cash flow	+1000	+1000	+1000
Project cash flow	−1000	+2000	
Revised dividend flow	0	+3000	+1000

$$V_E = \sum_{t=0}^{\infty} \frac{D_t}{(1+0.1)^t} = £10\,743.80.$$

As a result of its intentions, the company's market value has risen by £743.80: the NPV of the project. Our investor's shareholding will have risen in value by £74.38 to £1074.38.

However, suppose he or she relies upon his or her £100 per year dividend from the company for consumption purposes and is therefore alarmed at the news that there will be no dividend payout next year (t_1). There are two main alternative courses of action which may be taken to replace the withheld dividend, neither of which will reduce the current level of the investor's wealth of £1074.38. He or she can either sell part of the shareholding to generate sufficient cash to replace the dividend missed at t_1 (i.e. £100), or he or she can borrow the money at the perfect market rate of interest of 10%.[5] Let us examine the mechanics of this first alternative.

At time t_1, the company's total market value is the sum of the discounted future dividend flow:

Dividend flow	t_1	t_2	t_3	$t_4 \ldots$
	0	+3000	+1000	+1000 \ldots

$$V_{E_{t1}} = \sum_{t=0}^{\infty} \frac{D_t}{(1+0.1)^t} = £11\,818.18.$$

Therefore each share has an approximate market value of £11.82, and our investor's shareholding is worth £1181.82. If he or she now sells sufficient shares to produce £100 in cash as a substitute for the forgone dividend, he or she will sell £100/£11.82 = 8.46 shares,[6] leaving a shareholding of 91.54 shares in the company.

At time t_2 the company has £3000 to be distributed as dividends so each share receives a dividend of £3 and our investor receives a total dividend of: 91.54 × £3 = £274.62. Of this, £100 is required for consumption, leaving a balance of £174.62 available to repurchase shares in the company and so recover the original shareholding position. The ex div market value of the company at time t_2 will be £10 000 (the discounted sum of the future dividend flow) and so the individual share price is £10. Our investor can now buy back the 8.46 shares previously sold at a cost of £84.60, leaving him or her with additional cash at time t_2 of £174.62 − £84.60 = £90.02. Thus our shareholder has effectively used 'home-made' dividends as a substitute for the company dividends which the management decided to retain. In doing so, his or her wealth position remains unchanged as the present value (i.e. at time t_0) of £90.02 at t_2 is £74.38 – the amount by which his or her shareholding increased in value at time t_0 when the company's decision was announced.

A similar analysis could be undertaken where the investor borrows £100 at t_1 (at the market interest rate), and repays capital and interest at t_2, using his or her increased dividend payment at that time. The net outcome will be exactly the same as before.

It should be clear from this example that if stock markets valued retained earnings less favourably than dividends, there would be opportunities for profitable arbitrage transactions to take place (with investors either buying shares in companies which are increasing their cash flow retention proportions – as they will be under-valued – or selling shares in companies which are reducing their retention proportions – as they are likely to be over-valued). These transactions should rapidly produce 'correct' market valuations. Such an exercise is left to the reader to undertake.

The possibility of external finance

Up to this point in our consideration of the dividend decision, we have only considered situations in which the sole source of investment capital has been retained earnings. If we now widen the analysis to include the opportunity for companies to raise external finance for investment, what now becomes of the dividend decision?

When the possibility of external finance was excluded, the decision rule for company managements wishing to maximize shareholder wealth was to apply each year's cash earnings to investment in projects with positive NPVs. If the source of such projects dried up before all the net cash earnings had been allocated, then the remaining earnings could be paid out as a dividend. Thus the dividend 'policy' was to treat dividends as a residual to the investment decision.

Dividends cannot be said to be *irrelevant* in such circumstances. They are *very* relevant because, unless they are treated as a residual of the investment decision, they will be preventing 'profitable' investment from being undertaken and so will result in the shareholders' wealth failing to achieve the maximum.

Once the possibility of raising external finance is allowed, dividends no longer need to act as a residual but become *truly* irrelevant. This is because the payment of a dividend can no longer be held to prevent profitable investment from being undertaken, because the required finance can always be raised externally.

However, the raising of external finance in such circumstances – be it either debt or equity – is also likely (but not necessarily) to change a company's gearing ratio, and so the dividend decision can be said to be truly irrelevant only if, at the same time, it is accepted that changes in a company's gearing ratio leave its market value unaffected. If not, then dividend policy may well indirectly affect equity market values. As we are assuming a tax-free world of perfect capital markets, we can also assume that the conclusions of the initial M and M capital structure hypothesis will hold.

It is worthwhile noticing that this interdependence of the two M and M hypotheses works in both directions: not only does dividend irrelevancy depend on the capital structure hypothesis, but in turn the capital structure hypothesis holds true only if a company's dividend–retention ratio leaves its market value unaffected. For example, suppose that the greater the proportion of cash earnings paid out as dividends, the higher would be the market value of a company's equity capital. In such circumstances capital structure could not be said to be independent of market values because, other things being equal, the smaller the proportion of retained earnings the higher would be the company's market value, and vice versa.

The introduction of the possibility of external finance also leaves the traditional view largely unaffected. Dividend policy still retains its importance on the basis that current dividends are more highly valued than future dividends generated by retained earnings. But in addition, just as the two M and M hypotheses are in tandem, so too are the traditional views of dividends and capital structure. Therefore a company's dividend policy also gains importance from the fact that it is a partial determinant of the level of retained earnings and so can affect the company's market value through changing the gearing ratio. The exact effects of a company's dividend policy through such influences are not certain, but are dependent on its location on the U-shaped weighted average cost of capital curve.

Dividend policy in an imperfect market

'Clientele' effect

Once we move away from the assumption of a perfect capital market and a tax-free world, the dividend decision becomes much more problematical. In particular, there are a number of different capital market imperfections which are likely to interfere seriously with the hypothesis of dividend irrelevancy.

The dividend irrelevancy argument has been founded on the perfect capital market approach/separation theorem of our initial single-period investment–consumption analysis. The pattern of cash flows that the company provides the shareholder through the dividend policy is irrelevant because, each individual shareholder can adjust this dividend pattern to fit his or her desired consumption pattern by use of the capital market. It was this characteristic which allowed company managements to avoid the problem of having to identify the indifference curves of individual shareholders, when making investment decisions on their behalf.

However, capital market imperfections such as transaction costs (which in practice can be very substantial especially at the individual shareholder level), differential interest rates, and the presence of absolute capital rationing for the individual shareholder, all interfere with this process.

Quite simply, these capital market imperfections mean that an individual cannot *costlessly* adjust his dividend pattern to fit his preferred consumption pattern; indeed the cost of doing so may be relatively high. (In the case of absolute capital rationing for the individual, the cost of some consumption patterns can be seen as infinitely high.) In such circumstances, simple wealth maximization (i.e. in terms of the current market value of the equity) may not be a unique desire of shareholders, as the *pattern* of wealth receipt also becomes important.

In these circumstances, the company's dividend policy takes on a new dimension. Shareholders may positively prefer companies to supply them with a dividend pattern which matches fairly closely with their desired consumption pattern, thereby relieving them of having to adjust this cash flow themselves.

In practice companies often do this by following a stable and easily identifiable dividend policy, but whether it is done explicitly for these reasons is open to argument. As an example, many companies strongly follow a policy in which dividend reduction is regarded as a sign of weakness and an increased dividend will be declared only if management are convinced that the new dividend level can be at least sustained, if not improved upon, in future years. In this way, shareholders whose own consumption pattern closely follows the dividend pattern of the company will be attracted by the knowledge that they are unlikely to need to resort to the imperfect capital market in order to make dividend/consumption pattern adjustments.

Unfortunately, the fact that an easily identifiable dividend pattern may mean that shareholders avoid the costs of adjustment, does not mean that such advantage is necessarily gained costlessly. Indeed, the cost which is directly saved by the shareholder may be more than offset by the consequential cost to the company (which will, in turn, rebound on to the shareholders).

This consequential cost may come about in that, by paying a dividend, the company is left with insufficient finance to undertake a profitable investment (i.e. one with a positive NPV) and so the investment opportunity is missed. Alternatively, because a dividend has been paid, the company has to raise finance for an investment from an external source which involves the incurrence of issue costs.

It may be thought that the dividend decision in this situation resolves into a straightforward cost minimization trade-off, but a problem arises with the identification and quantification of the costs incurred or avoided by the shareholders and the fact that they are unlikely to be the same for each individual shareholder. So we are reduced to concluding that in an imperfect capital market, probably the best approach that a company can hope to take is to follow a consistent dividend policy[7] and hope that the particular policy chosen does not incur too heavy cost penalties, relative to the transaction and opportunity cost savings made by shareholders. Such a policy is often referred to as arising from the 'clientele' effect. By following a consistent dividend policy, the company attracts to it a clientele of shareholders whose consumption pattern accords with the dividend pattern.

Dividends as signals

Another capital market imperfection which bears on the dividend decision concerns the need for information in an uncertain world. Capital markets are imperfect in the sense that information is neither costless nor universally available, and so decisions have often to be made by stock market investors on the basis of imperfect and incomplete information.

In such circumstances, a company's dividend declaration – a free and universally available piece of data – is often thought to signal information about its future performance. In fact, given that information about a company's future performance prospects is fairly sparse – especially to the individual investor – any information that becomes available is seized upon and embodied with a measure of importance which may often be in excess of its real value.

In these terms, the dividend decision once again gains in importance. If the stock market places such an (albeit maybe unjustified) informational content on the dividend declaration, then a company will not be acting so as to maximize its shareholders' wealth if it ignores this fact. It is most likely for this reason that many publicly quoted companies follow the dividend policy referred to earlier, where a dividend is reduced or passed completely only in the most dire financial circumstances.

This signalling effect of the dividend declaration is an important issue for companies. Several studies have shown that an increase or decrease over the *expected* level of dividends does precipitate a rise or fall (respectively) in the market share price. Hence the dividend declaration effect on the share price may be a major (if not *the* major) consideration in the decision. However, there is also evidence that where a company has a good reason for reducing its dividend rate (e.g. an exceptional investment opportunity) *and* can adequately transmit information about this to shareholders, it is unlikely to suffer as the result of reducing its payout.

Tax considerations

Taxation and especially differential rates of personal income tax, a taxation distinction between income and capital gains, and the fact that a company might have both private and corporate shareholders who are taxed under different tax regimes, form a serious capital market imperfection which interferes with the dividend irrelevancy approach. The major problem with the presence of taxation is that it can interfere with the value equivalence between dividends and retained earnings. As a result, some shareholders may prefer 'home-made' dividends (generated through selling part of their shareholding) because the rate of capital gains tax may be lower than their marginal income tax rate, which would be imposed upon company-distributed dividends. In contrast, other shareholders may prefer company-distributed dividends because their marginal tax rate results in less tax being paid than the combined effect of capital gains tax and transactions costs incurred in the process of providing home-made dividends.

Once again, in the face of different taxation rates and different taxation regimes, we must conclude by saying that if a company follows a widely recognized, consistent dividend policy, then it can be expected to attract that class of shareholders on whom the particular dividend policy chosen has the most favourable (or least harmful) taxation effects.

In reaching this conclusion, there still remains the problem of what action the company should take in the face of significant changes in the taxation regime, as far as dividends are concerned. Should it try to adjust its dividend policy so as to bring about the most favourable outcome to its existing shareholders, or should it continue with its existing policy in the hope that new shareholders, to whom the company's dividend policy is now favourable in terms of taxation, will be attracted and so replace some of the existing shareholders?

The optimal decision in such circumstances requires an accurate evaluation of the cost trade-off concerned (on the basis that the objective of financial management is to benefit *existing* shareholders) between the cost to the company of changing its dividend policy[8] and the cost to its shareholders of *not* changing its policy. Both costs will be difficult to quantify in precise terms, but both may possibly be substantial and so should not be ignored.

The empirical evidence

Much of the empirical work on dividend policy has been carried out in the USA. Therefore some of these results must be interpreted with care as they will reflect the specifics of the US, 'classical' tax system which is very different from the 'imputation' system we have in the UK. However, the empirical evidence does appear to confirm the view that companies believe that the dividend decision is important and cannot be treated simply as a by-product of investment and financing decisions. For example Lintner (1956) in a survey of companies found that many did try to pay out an approximately constant proportion of earnings each year. At the same time there was a reluctance to match dividend growth with earnings growth and as a result dividend growth lagged behind earnings growth. These results were confirmed in a later study by Fama and Babiak (1968) which estimated that dividend growth lagged two to three years behind earnings growth.

This evidence does seem to support the signalling effect of dividends. Management appear to go to some lengths to ensure that dividends are only raised when they are fairly certain that they will be able to maintain at least that new level of dividends in the future. The fear is that, if they were forced to *reduce* dividends after an over-optimistic increase in the previous year, the market would read into the dividend decision unfavourable information. It is interesting to note that many leading British companies such as Sainsbury's appear to adopt the policy of steady dividend growth.

If dividends are really seen by investors as a means of sending signals then we would expect share prices to react to *unexpected* changes in dividend policy. Pettit's 1972 study found exactly this reaction and these results were confirmed by two later studies: Aharony and Swary (1980) and Asquith and Mullins (1983). Indeed the Asquith and Mullins' study seemed to suggest that, if anything, the information content effect of dividends was even stronger than that shown up in Pettit's original analysis.

As far as clienteles are concerned, the most well-known empirical evidence is that of Elton and Gruber (1970). They were particularly concerned about tax clienteles and the fact that some investors would strongly prefer to receive their returns in the form of capital gains rather than dividends, whilst other investors would prefer the reverse. Their evidence suggests that tax clienteles do exist: that shareholders in high dividend paying companies have lower tax rates than shareholders in low dividend paying companies.

However, later work by Miller and Scholes (1978) has cast doubt on Elton and Gruber's evidence. They essentially use an arbitrage argument based on earlier work by Brennan (1970). If tax clienteles do really exist, as evidenced by Elton and Gruber's results, this *should* present arbitrage opportunities: low rate taxpayers should be able to profit from the higher rate taxpayers' preference for capital gains and vice versa.

Conclusion

In truth, we really do not know whether dividend policy can affect shareholders' wealth. Whilst the bulk of the empirical evidence tends to suggest that either dividend policy *is* important, or is *seen to be* important much of the research needs to be treated with great caution. It is very difficult to research the thinking behind the dividend decision of companies and much of the research that has been published looks at cum and ex div share prices. The logic is that it should be possible to infer the value of dividends from the price movement that takes place when shares go ex div. Say a dividend of 10p per share is to be paid out and that the share price falls by 8p when the share goes ex div. This infers that the value of £1 worth of dividend is, on average, 80 pence. Conclusions have been drawn from findings such as these, including that dividends should not be paid out because there is a cost to the recipient (presumably 20 pence tax) and also that this will have an effect on the decisions of investors. However, they have generally failed to recognize that this is a very short-term phenomenon. Clearly it will be worthwhile for an investor to take into account the taxation on dividends around the time of the investment decision but this does not necessarily mean that this will be of great importance over the longer term.

However difficult it might be to carry out meaningful research in this area, it does seem that the dividend decision should be taken with care, given the imperfections of the real-world capital market. The benefit or otherwise of a particular dividend decision depends to a great extent upon how the individual shareholders are personally affected by the various market imperfections. It is likely, given a random selection of stock market investors, that the market imperfections with respect to dividends will affect individual shareholders in a number of conflicting ways, thus making a consensus dividend policy an unlikely possibility. The only escape from this dilemma for a company that intends to maximize the wealth of its shareholders is to follow a consistent dividend policy, which then allows the individual shareholder to judge its desirability in relation to his or her own personal circumstances.

Summary

- This chapter has looked at the dividend decision. However, it is difficult to reach any firm conclusions.

- In a perfect capital market world of no taxes, the dividend decision can be seen to be irrelevant. A shareholder receives his annual return in two elements: the dividend and the capital gain. The decision about what proportion of a firm's net distributable cash flow to retain and what proportion to pay out as dividends is therefore simply a decision as to how the overall return on the shares should be packaged. How large should be the capital gain package and how large should be the dividend package? However, the overall return itself is left unaffected by the decision.

- When capital market imperfections such as taxes, transaction costs and imperfect information are introduced, then it is possible for the dividend decision to begin to take on importance.

- Where dividends and capital gains are treated differently from the viewpoint of personal taxes and capital gains cannot be costlessly converted into income (nor dividends reinvested) without incurring transaction costs, it can be argued that companies should follow a stable and consistent dividend policy so as to attract to them a clientele of investors whose own personal tax position, and need (or otherwise) for income, suits that particular dividend policy.

- In addition to the clientele effect, the dividend decision may also be held to have an information content which it signals to the market. If this is so, then dividend policy is important in that management should ensure that their company's dividend decision does not give the wrong signal to the market.

- Although the empirical evidence is mixed and although some findings have been disputed, it does appear that the evidence points to the dividend decision being important both from a clientele and a signalling effect viewpoint.

Notes

1. Including preference share capital.

2. The reader may find it worthwhile to reflect how the M and M dividend irrelevancy hypothesis is also just a natural continuation of their capital structure hypothesis.

3. The model's numerator is slightly more fully defined than when it was first introduced.

4. So-called because it is one which is widely held amongst both stock market investors and analysts.

5. A third possible alternative is a combination of the two courses of action.

6. For simplicity, we are assuming here that shares are divisible. The fact that this is not true in practice can be viewed as a slight market imperfection.

7. It is important to notice that it is not constant dividends that are being advocated, but a constant policy. This *policy* may be to treat dividends as a residual of the investment decision, and hence may result in a highly erratic dividend flow, but a constant policy.

8. A cost which will ultimately be felt by the shareholders.

Further reading

1. The basic reading on dividend policy must be: M.H. Miller and F. Modigliani, 'Dividend Policy, Growth and the Valuation of Shares', *Journal of Business*, October 1961, and F. Black, 'The Dividend Puzzle', *Journal of Portfolio Management*, Winter 1976. For general empirical evidence on dividend policy, see J. Lintner, 'Distribution of Incomes of Corporations among Dividends, Retained Earnings and Taxes', *American Economic Review*, May 1956, and E.F. Fama and H. Babiak, 'Divided Policy: An Empirical Analysis', *Journal of the American Statistical Association*, December 1968.

2. In addition, an interesting more recent test of dividend irrelevancy is: G. Richardson, S.E. Sefcik and R. Thompson, 'A Test of Dividend Irrelevancy using Volume Reactions to a Change in Dividend Policy', *Journal of Financial Economics*, December 1986.

3. For evidence on the information content of dividends, see T.W. Foster and D. Vickrey, 'The Information Content of Stock Dividend Announcements', *Accounting Review*, April 1978; R.R. Pettit, 'Dividend Announcements, Security Performance and Capital Market Efficiency', *Journal of Finance*, December 1972; J. Aharony and I. Swary, 'Quarterly Dividends and Earnings Announcements and Stockholders Returns', *Journal of Finance*, March 1980; P. Asquith and D.W. Mullins, 'The Impact of Initiating Dividend Payments on Shareholder Wealth', *Journal of Business*, January 1983; J.R. Woolridge and C. Ghosh, 'Dividend Cuts: Do They Always Signal Bad News?', *Midland Corporate Finance Journal*, Summer 1985; and A.R. Ofer and D.R. Siegal, 'Corporate Financial Policy, Information and Market Expectations: An Empirical Investigation of Dividends', *Journal of Finance*, September 1987. Finally, in relation to investor rationality, see C. Ghosh and J. Woolridge, 'Stock Market Reaction to Growth-Induced Dividend Cuts: Are Investors Myopic?', *Management and Decision Economics*, March 1989.

4. On dividend policy, taxes and the clientele effect see: E.J. Elton and M.J. Gruber, 'Marginal Stockholders Tax Rates and the Clientele Effect', *Review of Economics and Statistics*, February 1970; D. Farrar and L. Selwyn, 'Taxes, Corporate Financial Policy and Returns to Investors', *National Tax Journal (US)*, December 1967; M. Brennan, 'Taxes, Market Valuation and Corporate, Financial Policy', *National Tax Journal*, December 1970; M. Miller and M. Scholes, 'Dividends and Taxes: Some Empirical Evidence', *Journal of Financial Economics*, December 1978; R.H. Litzenberger and K. Ramaswamy, 'The Effect on Dividends on Common Stock Prices: Tax Effects or Information Effects?', *Journal of Finance*, May 1982; and J.R. Woolridge, 'Dividend Changes and Security Prices', *Journal of Finance*, December 1983.

5. Finally, two further, interesting articles are: H.K. Barker, G.E. Farrelly and R.B. Edelman, 'A Survey of Management Views on Dividend Policy', *Financial Management*, Autumn 1985; and M.H. Miller, 'Behaviour Rationality in Finance: The Case of Dividends', *Journal of Business*, October 1986.

Quickie questions

1. Why might the dividend decision be said to be irrelevant?
2. What is the argument about dividends being a residual to investment decision?
3. What is the link between dividend irrelevancy and capital structure irrelevancy?
4. What is the bird-in-the-hand argument?
5. Which investors prefer capital gains to dividends?
6. If a clientele effect exists, what does it imply for dividend policy?
7. What empirical evidence is there to support the signalling effect of dividends?
8. In the real world, would it be wise for a company to retain a dividend which shareholders were expecting, in order to invest in a positive NPV project?

Problems

1. Pulini plc is currently financed entirely by 1 million ordinary shares with a nominal value of 75p per share which were issued at par. The dividends paid by Pulini plc have remained constant at £150 000 per annum and the market generally believes that dividends will continue at this level indefinitely, given the information presently available. The current dividend of Pulini plc is about to be declared and the current market price per share is £1.40.

The company has recently signed a contract to service factory equipment for an annual fee of £80 000, receivable in advance. The first annual fee has just been received. The contract, which is to commence immediately, will entail the annual purchase of specialized materials costing £22 400 payable at the end of each year, and will incur no other incremental costs. The contract will continue indefinitely and will have the same risk as the existing operators of Pulini plc. No details of the contract have been communicated or leaked to the stock market.

You may assume, for calculation purposes only, that there is no time delay between the dates of declaration and payment of the dividend.

Required:
(a) Estimate the cum div market value of Pulini plc in each of the three following situations:
   (i) the details of the contract are not communicated to the market, and the dividends are declared to be £150 000;
   (ii) the details of the contract are communicated and believed by the market, but the dividends declared remain at £150 000; and
   (iii) the details of the contract are not communicated to the market, but the dividends declared fully reflect the incremental annual cash flows from the contract.
(b) Discuss whether a company can affect its market price by altering its dividend policy.
(c) Outline the factors which might influence company management when deciding on the level of dividends to be declared.

Ignore taxation in part (a), but not in parts (b) and (c).

2. In the mid 1980s Chartwell Leasing plc ran into severe financial difficulties due to mistakes its management had made in the computer leasing business in which it operated. Between 1985 and 1989 it made large operating losses and had to stop paying dividends. However, late in 1989 a new management team was installed in the company – at the instigation of the institutional shareholders and non-executive directors. This new management turned the company around by restructuring its business and focusing on the international leasing of construction equipment and the company is once again profitable.

   As a result, at the board meeting held recently at the end of the company's financial year – which had seen a further increase in profits – the directors discussed whether or not the company should resume paying dividends. However opinions were divided. The chairman thought that a stable dividend policy should be introduced as quickly as possible. The finance director thought that dividend policy was unimportant as he remembered quite clearly from his MBA finance course that dividends are irrelevant. Finally, the treasurer (who also acted as the chief accountant) was of the opinion that the company should only pay an annual dividend if there were not sufficient profitable projects available to absorb all the company's earnings. Thus the amount paid out in dividends should purely be this residual.

   Required:
   Discuss dividend policy with special reference to the comments made by the board members of Chartwell Leasing plc.

3. Charles and Lupin Pooter each own 50% of the issued ordinary share capital of Charles Pooter (Contractors) Ltd, but neither plays any part in its management. The company presently has £3000 available on bank current account which it is proposing to invest in a project which is expected to produce cash inflows of £800 in Year 1, £1000 in Year 2, and £1700 after three years. No other cash flows are expected to be associated with the project. If the £3000 is not used on this project it will be paid out as a dividend to Charles and Lupin. If the project is accepted the cash inflows it produces will be paid out in full as dividends as they arise.

   Lupin is in agreement with the company investing in the proposed project, but Charles wishes to take his wife, Carrie, on a world cruise and claims that the company is not acting in his best interests if it fails to pay the money as dividend to enable him to do so. Charles Pooter (Contractors) Ltd is able both to lend and borrow funds freely at 4%.

   Required:
   (a) Calculate the net present value of the proposed project to Charles Pooter (Contractors) Ltd.
   (b) Explain whether the company is acting in the best interests of *both* its shareholders by accepting the project if:
   (i) Charles and Lupin may both borrow freely at 4%;
   (ii) Charles and Lupin may both borrow freely at 10%.
   (c) Comment briefly on the implications of your answers to (a) and (b) above for capital investment theory.

   Ignore taxation.

23 Foreign exchange markets and rates

Introduction

In the three final chapters of this book, we turn to look at some aspects of international financial management. In this chapter we look at the background to international financial management in terms of foreign exchange markets and the causes of movements in foreign exchange rates.

Then, in Chapter 24, we look at how importers and exporters may hedge their exposure to the risk of adverse movements in exchange rates. In that discussion, we will see a number of risk management techniques which parallel the techniques examined in Chapter 14 on interest rate risk management.

Finally, in Chapter 25, we look at an area of considerable importance and complexity: the overseas capital investment decision. This topic helps to bring together much of what has been discussed through the earlier part of the book.

In this chapter we look in detail at the basics of foreign exchange. We will find that although it does not contain anything that is difficult, there is a certain degree of complexity. A study of foreign exchange rewards a reader's attention to detail. It is these details that we address in this chapter.

Exchange rates

Foreign exchange 'rates' are simply the price of one currency in terms of another currency. Therefore if the exchange rate between the US$ and the £ is US$2 = £1, then this indicates that £1 will cost $2 and conversely, $1 will cost £0.50 (or 50p).

Given the above exchange rate, suppose we want to buy $1000. Given that the cost of $1 is 50p, $1000 will cost $1000 × 50p = £500. Therefore, in these circumstances, we could say that we were buying $($1000) and selling

£(£500). In other words, in any foreign exchange deal you are buying one currency and selling another.

If we were to look again at this $/£ exchange rate, it would be quoted as: $/£ : 2.0000. There are a number of points to be noted about this:

1. In any exchange rate there is a *pair* of currencies involved. In this example, $ and £.

2. Notice that the *first* of this pair of currencies quoted is the $ and the *second* is the £. In foreign exchange (FX), there are a large number of little rules and virtually all those rules are given in terms of the *first* of the pair of currencies. Therefore, whenever you are dealing with FX rates, always be sure to identify which currency is the *first* and which is given as the *second* in the pair of currencies.

3. The third point to note is in two parts:
   (a) Exchange rates are always given in terms of the *first* of the pair of currencies and so $/£ : 2.0000 means $2.0000.
   (b) Exchange rates are always given in terms of the *number* of units of the *first* currency per *single* unit of the *second* currency; and so $/£ : 2.0000 means that the exchange rate is $2.0000 = £1.

4. The final point to note is that exchange rates are *normally* given to four decimal places – but not necessarily. How many decimal places are used depends upon the size of the number before the decimal point. If the number is quite large, there may be only two decimal places: ¥/£ : 225.40; (where ¥ represents the Japanese yen). If the number is very large, there may be no decimal places at all: IL/£ : 3345; (where IL represents the Italian lira). Furthermore, exchange rates may be given in a variety of different forms, for example $/£ : 1.8525 may be given as $1.85\frac{1}{4}$.

Buying rates and selling rates

Suppose the $/£ exchange rate is given at $/£ 1.8525. This means that $1.8525 = £1. In other words, there is one dollar and 85¼ cents to the pound. The ¼ cent is known as '25 basis points'. In much the same way as cents represent one-hundredths of a dollar, so basis points represent one-hundredths of a cent. Therefore if the $/£ exchange rate is: $/£ 1.8645, the exchange rate is referred to as one–eighty-six–forty-five and it means 1 dollar, 86 cents and 45 basis points to £1.

When a single exchange rate is quoted, e.g. $/£ 1.8645, it is known as a 'middle rate' and you can assume that you – the financial manager – can both buy and sell at that rate of exchange. Therefore, if you want to *buy* $1000, the cost is: $1000 ÷ 1.8645 = £536.34. (You are selling £536.34.) And if you want to *sell* $1000, (and so buy £), your receipt will be exactly the same: $1000 ÷ 1.8645 = £536.34.

Normally, however, you are given two exchange rates: $/£ 1.8630–1.8660. The first rate is the rate at which you can *buy* the first of your pair of currencies and the second is the rate at which you can *sell* the first of your pair of currencies. Therefore if you want to buy $1000, the cost will be: $1000 ÷ 1.8630 = £536.77. And if you wish to sell $1000, your receipt will be: $1000 ÷ 1.8660 = £535.91.

The foreign exchange markets (i.e. the market-place where you can buy and sell currencies) are operated by the banks. They make their profit on these FX deals in two ways. One is that you will be charged commission on your transaction (which varies depending on how much currency is involved, but may be around ¼% – 0.0025 – of the amount of money involved), and the other way in which they take a profit is in the difference between the buying and selling exchange rates. Notice in the above example that to buy $1000 would cost you £536.77; if you then immediately sold those $1000 you would only receive £535.91 back. The difference, 86p, is the second part of the bank's profit.

Given that we say that the first rate is the buying rate and the second rate is the selling rate, be careful not to be misled next time you go into a bank, because what you might see is:

	Bank sells	Bank buys
$/£	1.8630	1.8660

The reason why the bank calls the first rate the selling rate and we call the first rate the buying rate is that the bank is looking at it from its own point of view, while we are looking at it from *our* point of view – from the point of view of the financial manager in a company. Therefore the financial manager can *buy* $ (from the bank) at $1.8630 = £1 and the bank will sell $ (to the financial manager) at $1.8630 = £1. We are always interested in looking at FX from the financial manager's viewpoint and so the rule is: the first rate is the *buying* rate, the second rate is the *selling* rate.

Finally, when we talk about the buying and selling rate, it is always in terms of the *first* of the pair of currencies. Therefore, given that $/£1.8630−1.8660:

1. The cost of buying $1000 is:

    $$\$1000 \div 1.8630 = £536.77 \text{ and}$$

2. The receipt from the sale of $1000 is:

    $$\$1000 \div 1.8660 = £535.91.$$

Notice in this example that, in each case we are doing something in terms of the *first* of the pair of currencies: buying $1000 and selling $1000. In each case we identified the correct exchange rate and *divided* it into the amount of currency involved.

The approach changes if you are asked to do something in terms of the *second* of the pair of currencies. First, to identify the correct exchange rate think what you are doing with the *first* of the pair of currencies; second, we now *multiply*, rather than divide, by this exchange rate.

As an example: $/£ 1.8630−1.8660 and you are asked what is the cost of buying £1000. As you are asked to do something (buy £1000) in terms of the second (£) of your pair of currencies ($/£), think what you must be doing in terms of the first currency ($): if we are buying £, then we are *selling* $ and so we require the selling $ exchange rate of: 1.8660. And so the cost of buying £1000 is: £1000 × 1.8660 = $1866.

Similarly, if asked for the receipt from the *sale* of £1000 the thought processes are:

1. We are being asked to do something in terms of the second of the pair of currencies.
2. Given that we are selling £, we are *buying* $ and so we want the buying $ exchange rate of 1.8630.

3. Given that we are doing something in terms of the second of our pair of currencies, we multiply by the exchange rate: £1000 × 1.8630 = $1863 receipt.

These basic elements of FX are so important that we shall stop for a quick test. Answer the questions in Table 23.1 on the basis that the DM/$ exchange rate is 2.0345–2.0365 (DM represents the German mark).

Table 23.1

---

1. What is the cost of buying DM100 000?
2. What is the cost of purchasing $1 million?
3. How much do we receive from selling $150 000?
4. How much do we receive from the sale of DM10 million?

Answers:

1.	DM100 000 ÷ 2.0345	=	$49 152 cost.
2.	$1m × 2.0365	=	DM2.0365m cost.
3.	$150 000 × 2.0345	=	DM305 175 receipt.
4.	DM10m ÷ 2.0365	=	$4 910 385 receipt.

If you have *not* got all four answers correct, reread the chapter so far until you can do the calculations correctly. Once you are confident in your understanding of these calculations, then it is safe to proceed.

Inverting exchange rates

If you are given a middle rate: $/£ 1.5385, this indicates that $1.5385 = £1. The £/$ exchange rate can be found from the *inverse* of the $/£ exchange rate, thus:

$$£/\$ = \frac{1}{1.5385} = 0.6500. \text{ In other words £0.6500 (or 65p)} = \$1.$$

However, be careful if you wish to turn exchange rates around in this way and you are given a buying and selling rate. Not only should you take the inverse of each, you should also switch each around as follows:

$$\$/£ \quad = \quad \frac{1.4820}{1} \quad - \quad \frac{1.4850}{1}$$
$$\frac{1}{1.4850} \qquad \frac{1}{1.4820}$$

$$£/\$ \quad = \quad 0.6734 \quad - \quad 0.6748$$

Cross rates

Suppose you are given the $/£ rate and the ¥/£ rate, and we wish to find the ¥/$ rate – the 'cross rate'. For example:

$$\$/£ = 1.5240$$
$$¥/£ = 235.20$$

The ¥/$ cross rate is going to be one of these two exchange rates divided by the other. But which divided by which?

$$\frac{1.5240}{235.20} \quad \text{or} \quad \frac{235.20}{1.5240}?$$

There are a number of ways to get to the correct answer but one of the easiest is a simple rule to decide which of the two exchange rates should be the numerator in the fraction. The rule is one of *opposites* and proceeds as follows:

1. Look at the two exchange rates given: $/£ and ¥/£; what currency is common to both? The answer here is that £ is the common currency, it occurs in both exchange rates.
2. Look to see whether this common currency is the *first* or the *second* currency in each of the two exchange rates. In this example, the common currency – £ – comes second in each of the two exchange rates ($/£ and ¥/£).
3. Where the common currency comes *second*, it is the exchange rate involving the *first* currency of our cross rate that is the numerator of the fraction. In this example, the cross rate we require is ¥/$ and the first of these two currencies is the ¥; and so it is the exchange rate involving the ¥ – the ¥/£ rate – which goes on top of our fraction, with the other being the denominator:

$$¥/\$ = \frac{¥/£}{\$/£} = \frac{235.20}{1.5240} = 154.33.$$

Example 1

Suppose you want the £/$ cross rate and you are given:

$$¥/\$ = 154.33$$
$$¥/£ = 235.20$$

The procedure is as follows:

1. The common currency is the ¥.
2. The common currency comes *first* in each of our given exchange rates.
3. Using a rule of opposites, the *second* currency of our cross rate (£/$) is $ and so –
4. The exchange rate involving the $, (the ¥/$ rate) goes on top:

$$\frac{154.33}{235.20} = £/\$ = 0.6562.$$

Finally, you can have a situation as follows, where the common currency between the two given exchange rates does not consistently come first or second. Example 2 demonstrates this situation.

Example 2

Suppose you require the ¥/£ rate, and you are given the following rates:

$$£/\$ = 0.6562$$
$$¥/£ = 235.20$$

Here the common currency between the two exchange rates is £, but it is the *first* currency in the £/$ exchange rate and the *second* currency in the ¥/£ exchange rate. The solution to this problem is to remember that you can always 'turn exchange rates around' by taking the inverse. Therefore, given we have the £/$ exchange rate at 0.6562, the $/£ rate is:

$$\frac{1}{0.6562} = 1.5240 \text{ and so we now have: } \$/\pounds = 1.5240 \text{ and}$$
$$\yen/\pounds = 235.20$$

As the common currency now comes *second* in both exchange rates, the exchange rate involving the first of our cross-rate currencies (¥/$) goes on top:

$$\frac{235.20}{1.5240} = 154.33.$$

Once again, a quick test might be helpful. This is provided in Table 23.2.

Table 23.2

Answer the following questions:

1. Given

DM/£	=	2.5150
Esc/£	=	205.80 (Esc is the Portuguese escudo)

What is the Esc/DM exchange rate?

2. Given

SFr/£	=	4.3510
$/SFr	=	0.4450 (SFr is the Swiss franc)

What is $/£ exchange rate?

Answers:

1. $\dfrac{205.80}{2.5150}$ = Esc/DM = 81.83

2. SFr/$ = $\dfrac{1}{0.4450}$ = 2.2472

   SFr/£   = 4.3510

   $/£   = $\dfrac{4.3510}{2.2472}$ = 1.9362

Foreign exchange markets

We can identify two FX markets, both of which are run by the international banks. These are the 'Spot' FX market and the 'Forward' FX market. The spot market is where you can buy and sell currencies for immediate (i.e. on the spot) exchange or delivery. (In practice, exchange of currencies takes place two days later.) The forward market is where you can arrange a deal now to buy or sell a specific amount of currency at a specific rate of exchange (the forward rate) for exchange/delivery on a specific future date (the forward date).

Foreign exchange markets are like any other market, in that they exist only if there is sufficient demand. Therefore although spot markets exist for most of the world's currencies, for many of the more minor, (called 'exotic'), currencies there is no forward market, because there is insufficient demand.

Where a forward market exists, just how far forward in time you can deal again depends upon the level of demand. The four major trading currencies in the world are the American dollar, pound sterling, Japanese yen and German mark, and the forward market amongst these currencies can stretch up to ten years forward. Thus, for example, you could arrange a deal now to buy $5 million, say, in ten years' time at a $/£ exchange rate of, say, 1.4000. More normally, most forward market rates extend up to about six months into the future; but some only extend three months forward, or less.

The point about the 'depth' of the forward market is made because sometimes you might be faced with an FX problem where your suggested solution is to use the forward market. Be careful: the forward market in your required currency may not exist and, even if it does, it may not extend far enough forward in time for your purposes.

Nevertheless, given the depth of any particular forward market, you can arrange a deal for *any* time period forward you desire, up to its maximum depth. Therefore suppose it is 1 July and you want to buy FF10 million (French francs) for delivery on 23 September – that is in 84 days' time – then you can arrange a deal to buy FF10 million, 84 days forward.

This means that, unlike the spot market where there is a *single* pair of exchange rates (the buying and selling rates) at which you can deal for immediate delivery of currencies, on the forward market there are a whole range of pairs of exchange rates – one pair for each possible future date. Therefore, in the FF example, you would be quoted the 84 days forward rate for FF/£.

'Standard' periods of time forward are one month and three months and these rates – together with the spot rate – are instantly available. Other forward rates, such as an 84-day forward rate, have to be specifically quoted by the banks.

Discounts and premiums

You may find that spot and forward rates may be given as follows:

$/£ spot	1.5840 – 1.5860
$/£ 1 month forward	1.6290 – 1.6335
$/£ 3 months forward	1.6525 – 1.6560

However, it is more likely that instead of the forward rates being expressed like this, they are given as a rate of 'discount' on the spot rate:

$/£ spot	1.5840 – 1.5860	
1 month forward	4.50¢ – 4.75¢	discount
3 months forward	6.85¢ – 7.00¢	discount

To obtain the actual forward rate, you *add* the discount to the spot rate. Notice that these rates of discount are always very small amounts of money. For example 4.50¢ is *not* $4.50, but is $4\frac{1}{2}$ cents, or 4 cents and 50 basis points. Therefore:

Spot		1.5840	–	1.5860
+		450	–	475
1 month forward	=	1.6290	–	1.6335

and

Spot		1.5840 –	1.5860
+		685 –	700
3 months forward	=	1.6525 –	1.6560

Also, notice that when forward rates are larger numbers than spot rates, (e.g. $/£ spot 1.5840, three months forward 1.6525), the forward rates are at a discount to the spot rate. To see what this means, look at the situation in the example above. If you wanted to buy $/£ spot, for every £1 you would receive $1.5840; but if you bought dollars for three months/forward delivery you get *more* dollars to the pound: $1.6525 for every £1. Thus, in the forward markets, the dollar is becoming cheaper to buy. Putting this more technically, the markets expect the dollar to weaken or *depreciate* against sterling – it expects it to become less valuable. (And sterling therefore is appreciating, or becoming more valuable against the dollar.) More generally, if forward rates are at a *discount*, the *first* currency is *depreciating* against the second currency in your pair of currencies.

The opposite of rates of discount are *premiums*. When forward rates are quoted at a premium, we *subtract* the premium from the spot rate to find the forward rate. Therefore whenever forward rates are smaller numbers than spot rates, the forward rates are at a premium and this signifies that the first currency is *appreciating* against the second of the pair of currencies.

For example:	$/£ spot	1.8240 –	1.8260
	1 month forward	0.85¢ –	0.75¢ premium
and so:	Spot	1.8240 –	1.8260
	– Premium	85 –	75
	1 month forward =	1.8155 –	1.8185

Here the dollar is becoming more valuable – it is appreciating against sterling. Every £1 buys you $1.8240 at spot, but only buys you $1.8155 in one month's time.

Rates of depreciation and appreciation

Suppose we have a situation where the $/£ buying rates are given as:

Spot	$1.5210
12 months forward	8.65¢ disc.

The forward rate, as we know, can be found by adding the discount to the spot rate:

Spot $/£	$1.5210
+ discount	865
12 months forward	$1.6075

Notice that we could also express the amount of discount as a percentage of the spot rate:

$$\frac{8.65¢}{\$1.5210} = 0.0569 \text{ or } 5.69\%$$

which indicates (as it is a discount) that the forward rate represents a 5.69% depreciation of the $ on the spot rate. As a result, the forward rate can be calculated as: spot × (1 + rate of depreciation):

Spot: $1.5210. (1 + 0.0569) = $1.6075 12 months forward.

Similarly, if the $/£ forward rate was at a *premium*, then expressing the premium as a percentage of the spot rate would represent the percentage rate of appreciation of the dollar. In these circumstances: spot $/£ × (1 − rate of appreciation) = forward $/£. Example 3 illustrates some applications of these results.

Example 3

Suppose we have the following information:

$/£ spot	1.6580	
12 months forward	5¢	premium

Then: 5¢ ÷ $1.6580 = 0.03 or 3%.

Therefore the forward rate represents a 3% appreciation in the dollar, giving:

Spot: $1.6580 × (1 − 0.03) = $1.6083 12 months forward.

Therefore you can calculate forward rates on the basis of annual rates of appreciation or depreciation. For example, suppose you are told that $/£ spot is $1.5345 and the $ is expected to depreciate by 5% per year over the next two years and thereafter appreciate by 7% per year. The forward rates for the next five years can be calculated as follows:

Spot:	$1.5345 × (1 + 0.05)	=	$1.6112	one year fwd
	$1.6112 × (1 + 0.05)	=	$1.6918	two years fwd
	$1.6918 × (1 − 0.07)	=	$1.5734	three years fwd
	$1.5734 × (1 − 0.07)	=	$1.4632	four years fwd
	$1.4632 × (1 − 0.07)	=	$1.3608	five years fwd

Exchange/delivery of currencies

Note that with forward market deals, no money changes hands now, but only at the future agreed date. Therefore if you agree a deal *now* to buy $1 million three months forward at 1.4875, in three months' time you must give the bank: $1m ÷ 1.4875 = £672 270, and they will give you $1 million in exchange.

We can distinguish between two types of FX forward contract: *fixed* forward contracts (normally simply referred to as forward contracts), and *time option* forward contracts (normally known as option forward contracts). The former are by far the most common; the latter are used only infrequently.

With a fixed forward contract, exchange of currencies must take place on the agreed future date. Thus if you sell $10 million three months forward, in three months' time (to the very day) you must hand over $10 million to the bank and they will give you the sterling amount as specified at the agreed rate of exchange. In contrast, an option forward contract allows you – the financial manager (and not the bank) – to exchange dollars for sterling at *any* time *between* two specified future dates. Therefore, if you sold $10 million, three to five months forward, you could exchange dollars for sterling at any time you wanted during that period. (You could not exchange *before* three months or *after* five months, but could exchange at any time between the two dates.)

When might a financial manager use such contracts? Suppose you had a UK company exporting to the USA and it invoices its US customer for $500 000 on three months' credit. If we could rely on the US customer paying *precisely* on time in three months (for example we could arrange for payment to be made via a three-month bill of exchange, which is essentially a cheque for $500 000 post-dated for three months' time), then we could arrange a deal now with the bank to sell $500 000 three months forward.

However, suppose we couldn't rely on our customer paying the invoice on time, and past experience with the customer indicated that they could be up to four weeks late in payment. In such circumstances we could use an option forward contract to arrange a deal with the bank to sell $500 000 three to four months forward. In this way, whenever the customer does actually pay up within three to four months' time, we can activate our deal with the bank to sell the $500 000 at the agreed rate of exchange.

The problem with option forward contracts is that we get a poor deal as far as the forward exchange rate is concerned. Taking the previous example, suppose we tell the bank that we wanted to sell $500 000 three to four months forward, the bank would look at the three months and the four months forward rates and would only agree to the deal at whichever was the *worst* rate of exchange from our point of view.

Suppose: $/£   three months forward   1.6380 – 1.6420
                     four months forward   1.6470 – 1.6515

then between the two selling $ rates of 1.6420 and 1.6515 we would prefer to deal at 1.6420, but the bank will only agree to the deal at 1.6515. (At 1.6420 we would receive: $500 000 ÷ 1.6420 = £304 507. At 1.6515, we only receive: $500 000 ÷ 1.6515 = £302 755.) Therefore, whenever we do exchange between three and four months' time, the deal is done at 1.6515 and we receive £302 755 in exchange for $500 000.

It is for this reason that option forward contracts are unusual in practice – they are seen as being rather unprofessional in the FX markets. Consequently, exporters go to great trouble to ensure that their customers do pay up on time.

Using the same example, what would happen if we arranged to sell our $500 000 through a fixed forward contract, three months forward and then shortly before payment is due, we hear that it will be delayed for a further month? In such circumstances we can arrange to have the $500 000 sale contract 'rolled forward' for a further month. However, such a situation is undesirable because it could turn out to be very expensive. Example 4 makes this clear.

Example 4

You are due to receive $500 000 from your customer on 1 March and arrange a forward sale at an exchange rate of $/£1.5860. (Therefore you are due to receive $500 000 ÷ 1.5860 = £315 258.) Suppose you hear on 1 March that payment will be delayed one month until 1 April. The spot $/£ rate on 1 March is $1.6210–1.6240 and the one-month forward $/£ rate is $1.6330–1.6365. The bank will roll your deal forward until 1 April, but will charge you an amount effectively equal to the cost of *purchasing* $500 000 to be able to meet your sale obligation on 1 March and roll the forward sale of $500 000 to the new date of 1 April:

1.	Purchase of spot $	:	$500 000 ÷ 1.6210	=	£(308 452)	Cost
2.	Original fwd sale	:	$500 000 ÷ 1.5860	=	£315 258	Receipt
3.	New fwd sale	:	$500 000 ÷ 1.6365	=	£305 530	Receipt
	Net revised receipts			=	£312 336	
	Original planned fwd sale receipts			=	£315 258	
	Fee charged by bank to 'roll forward'				£ 2 922	

Therefore the one-month delay in the receipt of the $500 000 will cost the exporter £2922, plus the time value of money (one month's lost interest on the invoice's proceeds).

Exchange rate systems – from Bretton Woods to EMU

We now need to look a little more closely at foreign exchange markets. To do so, we will first look at some history.

In 1944 there was a historic meeting in the USA, at a place called Bretton Woods, where all the world's leading trading countries agreed on a system of *fixed* exchange rates. Each country's currency was set at a fixed rate of exchange against the US dollar. The reason for this agreement was that it was generally recognized that the Second World War was coming to an end and that moves would have to be made to resume international trade and so expand the world's economy. In order to help this process they wanted to make it just as easy for, say, a UK company to sell to a customer in Miami as it was for it to sell to a customer in Manchester. With fixed exchange rates (the $/£ rate was fixed at $4 = £1) this process can be helped in that if some goods are sold to a Manchester customer for £250 000, those same goods can just as easily be sold to a Miami customer for $1 million. UK exporters invoicing their US customer for $1 million would know *precisely* what they would receive in sterling terms because the exchange rate was fixed.

However, although a system of fixed exchange rates is good for importers and exporters and for the promotion of international trade, such a system is inherently unstable, as it tries to deny the power and influence of supply and demand market forces. The result is that every so often these market forces become overpowering and the fixed exchange rate has to be reset at a new level. (Currencies are said to be devalued or revalued at such times.)

This system of fixed exchange rates lasted a surprisingly long time – up until 1971–2. It was able to do so because the centrepiece was the US dollar, (which was backed/guaranteed by gold), and during this time the US economy was so strong and so dominated the world economy that the supply and demand market forces were generally kept in check.

The Bretton Woods system fell apart in the early 1970s under two influences. One was the cost of the Vietnam War, which began to seriously damage the strength of the US economy in the late 1960s. The other, in the early 1970s, was the first of several oil price 'shocks', in which the oil producing countries sharply increased the price of oil through the OPEC cartel. As a result, since around 1971–2, world trade has carried on with a system of 'floating' exchange rates, where exchange rates have been allowed to move in response to supply and demand market forces.

Clean and dirty floats

In such a system we find two types of foreign exchange regime. One is called a 'clean' float and the other a 'dirty' or 'managed' float. Where a currency is allowed to float clean, the government of the country concerned is indicating that they are willing to allow the exchange rate to go in whatever direction market forces push it. Thus, in the early 1980s, the British government stated that sterling was in a clean float and so if there were a demand to buy sterling it would be allowed to appreciate; if there were selling pressure, then it would be allowed to depreciate.

Few governments are willing to leave their currencies at the mercy of market forces in this way; more commonly, governments operate a dirty or managed float. This represents a policy on the range of movement within which they are willing to allow their currency to float. If the currency appreciates beyond this range, then the country's central bank starts selling the currency on the foreign exchange markets to counter the buying pressure and, hopefully, to force the exchange rate back to a politically more acceptable level. Similarly, if market forces depreciate the exchange rate below an acceptable level, the central bank begins buying the currency to push the exchange rate back up to a more acceptable level. Thus the government attempts to 'manage' its currency's exchange rate.

The problem with a floating exchange rate is that it causes difficulties for international trade because it exposes companies to foreign exchange risk – that is the risk of an adverse movement in exchange rates and uncertainty as to what will be the cost or receipt, in their own currency, of an import or export deal. For example, say the \$/£ exchange rate is currently \$2.0000 = £1 and a UK company exports goods to the USA, invoicing their customer for \$1 million on three months' credit. The company is *expecting* to receive the equivalent of £500 000, but is uncertain just what \$1 million will be worth in terms of sterling in three months' time, because they don't know what the exchange rate will be then. The possibility exists that it could move to, say, \$2.5000 = £1 and so instead of receiving the expected £500 000, they will only receive £400 000 (\$1m ÷ 2.5000).

The ERM and EMU

It was because of the foreign exchange risk problem that the European Union developed the Exchange Rate Mechanism – the ERM. The ERM is essentially a system of *semi-fixed* exchange rates between the currencies of member countries and is an attempt to gain the best of both worlds of fixed and floating exchange rate systems.

In this system, the currency of each member country has a fixed ('central') rate of exchange against the currencies of each of the other members. The exchange rate is allowed to move, within certain boundaries, in response to the forces of supply and demand.

The benefit of such a system is that companies with import/export trade between member countries have the near certainty of the worth, in their own currency, of invoices payable in the currency of another member country. Therefore, given the DM/FF exchange rate has a central fix of, say, 0.3000, then a French exporter to Germany who invoices their customer for DM600 000 on three months' credit will be fairly confident of receiving around DM600 000 ÷ 0.30 = FF2m.

At the same time as providing a fairly secure framework for importing/ exporting between companies in EU member countries, the ERM also tries to allow – to a limited extent – for the forces of supply and demand. If these market forces result in one of the exchange rates being pushed up against its appreciation ceiling or down to its depreciation floor, there is an agreement whereby the central banks of all member countries take collective action to buy or sell the currency (as appropriate), to force it back towards its central fixed rate.

There are two further points to note about the ERM. One is that, from time to time, supply and demand market forces have overwhelmed the system and exchange rates have had to be reset (or 'realigned') to new central rates in much the same ways as devaluations and revaluations used to occur occasionally under the 1944–1971/2 Bretton Woods system. The other point is that obviously, under the ERM, the currencies of member countries are only fixed in relation to the currencies of other member countries and continue to float as normal (in – usually – a managed float) against other world currencies.

One of the problems with ERM was the levels at which currencies stood at the time that they joined the system and the situation that arose when those levels were realized to be inappropriate. In late 1993, the ERM came under enormous pressure as speculators backed their view that the pound sterling and the Italian lira would be forced to devalue. The pressure was such that the two currencies had to come out of the system to float freely against the other ERM currencies. In addition, virtually all the other EU currencies within the ERM were permitted to float by up to 15% around their central rate. Such a wide fluctuation band – which was introduced to relieve supply and demand market pressures – effectively destroys the purpose of the system in terms of the benefits it had been intended to bring in terms of promoting import and export activities between EU member countries.

Since 1993 the European Union has been working on European Monetary Union (EMU) and the introduction of the single European currency – the Euro. At the time of writing it would appear that eleven nations will join EMU even though there is a belief that for some at least this is more political than straightforwardly economic. The UK is expected to join some time around 2003. It remains to be seen what the effect of EMU will be but the belief is that the increasing integration of Europe will mean that it is much easier to sustain the relationships dictated by EMU. Also, because it is to be a single currency, it will not be possible to speculate against individual currencies and it will be extremely difficult for a member to leave once they have joined.

Determinants of FX rates

We now turn to investigate the answers to three questions:

1. What causes foreign exchange rates to move?
2. What determines forward exchange rates?
3. What determines *future* spot rates?

Although we will deal with each of these questions individually, the answers to all three are interrelated (as we shall see), in that the answer to each question also affects the answer to the other two questions. The complexity means that, in practice, although we know the answers to all three questions, it is difficult (if not impossible) to *predict* future exchange rates because of these interactions.

Supply and demand

As noted earlier, exchange rates are simply the *price* of one currency in terms of another. Therefore if the $/£ spot middle rate is 1.5580, this indicates that pounds cost $1.5580 each and dollars cost 64.18p each. The prices of currencies are just like the prices of anything else, in that they respond to supply and demand market forces. Therefore if lots of people want to *buy* dollars then the price of dollars will *rise* – the dollar will appreciate in value. Conversely, if lots of people want to sell dollars, this selling pressure will force *down* the price of the dollar – it will depreciate.

Therefore the simple answer to the question: what causes foreign exchange rates to move, is supply and demand market forces. These market forces come from two principal sources. The first is speculators and speculation (so-called Hot Money) and the second is international trade and 'real' investment. Some estimates suggest that as much as 90% of these market forces arise out of currency speculation, and only 10% arise out of the buying and selling of foreign exchange for purposes of international trade.[1]

Individuals and financial institutions speculate on exchange rates in much the same way as they might speculate on stock markets. If you think the shares of XYZ plc look cheap, you might buy them in anticipation of their price rising as soon as their true worth becomes more generally recognized. (You might also like to invest in XYZ because it pays out a high level of dividends.) Similarly, if the spot DM/£ exchange rate is 2.5000–2.5040 and you think that the DM is under-valued at only 40p each (i.e. 1 ÷ 2.5000), you might want to buy DM in anticipation of the currency appreciating. (Alternatively, if you think that German interest rates might go up in the future you might want to buy DM in order to place them on deposit and so benefit from the higher rate of interest.) In this way speculation market forces play a major role in the movement of exchange rates.

Market supply and demand forces also arise from the needs of international trade and investment. A Japanese company exports to the USA and receives dollars in payment. That company will wish to sell those dollar receipts in order to buy their own currency – the yen. Similarly, a UK company may import goods from Germany and be invoiced in DM. As a result that UK company will need to sell pounds in order to buy marks with which to pay the invoice.

These demands to buy and sell currencies arising out of import/export transactions also play their part in moving exchange rates in one way or another. So too will another form of international trade: international investment in assets. Suppose a UK company wishes to build a factory in Australia. It will need to sell pounds in order to buy Australian dollars in order to pay for the cost of building the factory in Australia.

Finally, there are also the supply and demand market forces arising out of international finance. A German company may wish to borrow money and decides to borrow Swiss francs to take advantage of lower interest rates in Switzerland than in Germany. Once that loan is raised, it will want to sell the francs in order to buy the marks that it requires. Over the life of the loan, it will periodically have to sell marks in order to buy Swiss francs in order to pay interest on the loan and repay the principal.

Thus the forces of supply and demand, both from speculators and from companies involved with international trade, financing and investment (as well as from governments engaged in the management of their floating exchange rates) are the factors lying behind movements in exchange rates.

Interest rates

Let us now turn to answer the second question. If the current $/£ spot rate (as determined by supply and demand market forces) is 1.5840–1.5860, what, for instance, determines why the twelve-month forward rate is at a 4.70¢–4.60¢ premium?

The answer lies with the Interest Rate Parity Theorem (IRPT), which effectively works on the principle that international financial markets are efficient. There are no bargain rates of interest to be had on loans/deposits in one currency rather than another. What you might seek to gain from a more favourable rate of interest in one currency rather than another, you are likely to lose in an adverse movement in exchange rates. Quite literally, exchange rates move to effectively bring about interest rate parity amongst different currencies. This process is illustrated in Example 5.

Example 5

In our example, spot $/£ is 1.5840–1.5860 and twelve-month forward $/£ is 1.5370–1.5400. Suppose that the rate of interest on UK Treasury bills[2] is 8% and on US Treasury bills 5%. You wish to place £10 000 on deposit, risk-free, for one year. Should you invest in UK T-bills and get 8%, or in US T-bills and get only 5%? IRPT says that it doesn't matter – either investment will yield exactly the same return.

If you were to invest £10 000 in UK T-bills for a year, you would receive back £10 800 in twelve months' time. However, suppose you invested in US T-bills. Selling your £10 000 spot would yield £10 000 × 1.5840 = $15 840. These could be placed on deposit at 5% interest for a year to produce $15 840 × (1 + 0.05) = $16 632. To avoid any uncertainty over the worth of these dollars in twelve months' time, (remember, you want no risk) you can arrange to sell them for pounds at the twelve-month forward rate of 1.5400 to yield $16 632 ÷ 1.5400 = £10 800. This is *exactly* how much you would have received if you had kept your money on sterling deposit, because forward exchange rates are set so as to effectively bring about parity between interest rates in different currencies.

Therefore we can conclude from the IRPT that forward rates are determined by the differential between interest rates in the different countries. The forward rates of the currency of the country with the *lower* rate of interest will *appreciate* against the currency of the country with the higher rate of interest by *approximately* the interest differential. In this example: 8% – 5% = 3%.

The precise rate of change is given by the following formula (given here in terms of $/£; but notice that the $ is the 'first' currency and £, the 'second' currency):

$$\frac{\$ \text{ interest rate} - \pounds \text{ interest rate}}{1 + \pounds \text{ interest rate}} = \% \text{ change in the } \$.$$

Therefore, in our example:

$$\frac{0.05 - 0.08}{1.08} = 20.0278 \text{ or a } 2.78\% \text{ appreciation in the } \$ \left(\begin{array}{l} - = \text{appreciation} \\ + = \text{depreciation} \end{array} \right)$$

Spot $/£: 1.5840. (1 – 0.0278) = 1.5400: twelve-month forward $/£.

Finally, there is an important point which is often misunderstood. This is that this twelve-month forward rate is technically called an 'unbiased estimator' of what *will be* the $/£ spot rate in twelve months' time. Although this may well hold true in the longer run, generally speaking, forward rates are rather poor estimates of future spot rates. What determines actual future spot rates is the subject of our third question.

Inflation

The main determinant of future exchange rates is given by another theorem, the Purchasing Power Parity Theorem (PPPT). This states that exchange rates move to effectively bring about purchasing power parity between the currencies of different countries.

The PPPT as such is not as robust a theorem as IRPT, in that IRPT determines forward rates almost precisely. In contrast, PPPT will be a major influence behind future exchange rates, but is not the only influence (as we know from our discussion on supply and demand market forces).

The rationale behind the PPPT begins with the 'Law of One Price'. This law (given here in terms of $/£) states that the pound sterling price of a good, multiplied by the exchange rate, equals the dollar price of the same good. For example, suppose that a particular make of lap-top PC costs £3000 in the UK and the $/£ spot rate is 1.7000. The 'law of one price' suggests that the US price of that same lap-top PC will be: £3000 × 1.7000 = $5100.

The reasoning behind the law is arbitrage. Suppose that the lap-top could be bought in the USA for only $4250. This would mean that you could buy them in the USA for the sterling equivalent of $4250 ÷ 1.70000 = £2500 and export them to the UK where you could sell them for £3000, making an (arbitrage) profit of £500. If this were to occur, the situation would not last long. The increased demand for lap-tops in the USA (by potential exporters) would force up their dollar price and the increased supply of the lap-tops in the UK (from importers) would force down the sterling price. These supply and demand market forces would continue until the law (and so equilibrium) re-established itself.

Like the PPPT itself, the Law of One Price is not a very robust or powerful law, because it does not apply to *all* goods, for two fairly obvious reasons. The first is that to operate efficiently, the transportation cost of the goods concerned must be small relative to the good's value. Thus the law will not work for such things as toothpaste or cornflakes. However, it does work for things such as gold and other precious metals, commodities (tea, coffee, tin, rubber, etc.) and industrial machinery. Of course this is not quite the case for the final consumer and the late nineties has seen quite a heated debate about the fact that it has been difficult for UK residents to buy right-hand drive cars in Europe for the same price that left-hand drive cars sell for. There have also been cases of motor manufacturers making it difficult for other nationals to buy cars in EU countries where they are typically sold at a lower price.

The second limitation on the working of the law is that it does not operate unless the goods are *physically* capable of being traded internationally. This requirement therefore excludes one very important group of assets from the law's influence: land and buildings. (You cannot buy a factory in the USA and physically transport it to the UK.)

Assuming that the Law of One Price does tend to work for the majority of goods, let us continue with the example of the lap-top PC and assume that the expected annual rates of inflation over the next twelve months in the UK and in the USA are 4% and 6% respectively.

As a result, we would expect the lap-top to cost £3000 × (1 + 0.04) = £3120 in the UK in twelve months' time, and to cost $5100 × (1 + 0.06) = $5406 in the USA. Therefore, in order to maintain the law of one price, this implies that the $/£ spot rate in twelve months' time will be 1.7327, (i.e. 5406 ÷ 3120), so that £3120 × 1.7327 = $5406.

This is what is meant by the Purchasing Power Parity Theorem. Exchange rates move to maintain purchasing power parity between different currencies – that is, they move to maintain the Law of One Price. Therefore, the answer to the question as to what determines future spot rates is *inflation differentials* between different countries: the currency of the country with the higher rate of inflation will depreciate against the currency of the country with the lower rate of inflation by *approximately* the inflation differential. In our example, this differential is: 6% − 4% = 2% and so the dollar will depreciate by approximately 2% against sterling over the year.

The precise rate of change in the exchange, in terms of $/£ (again note which is the first and which is the second currency) is given by a formula which is very similar to that for IRPT:

$$\frac{\text{US inflation} - \text{UK inflation}}{1 + \text{UK inflation}} = \text{percentage change in the \$}$$

$$\left(\begin{array}{l} + = \text{depreciation} \\ - = \text{appreciation} \end{array} \right)$$

Using the data in our example, the percentage rate of change in the $/£ exchange rate is:

$$\frac{0.06 - 0.04}{1 + 0.04} = +0.01923 \text{ or a } 1.923\% \text{ rate of depreciation in the \$.}$$

Therefore our estimate of the $/£ spot rate in twelve months' time is:

current spot: $1.7000 \times (1 + 0.01923) = 1.7323$: estimated future spot.

Forecasting exchange rates

In this way, we can use estimates of future rates of inflation to estimate future spot exchange rates. Example 6 shows how this process works.

Example 6

Suppose the current ¥/£ spot rate for buying ¥ is 224.20 and estimates of UK and Japanese inflation rates over the next three years are as follows:

	Inflation rates	
	UK	Japan
Year 1	3%	5%
Year 2	4½%	2%
Year 3	3%	3%

1. At Year 1:

$$\frac{0.05 - 0.03}{1.03} \quad = \quad +0.0194 \quad : \quad \text{¥ will depreciate by 1.94\%}$$

$$\text{¥ }224.20\,(1 + 0.0194) \quad = \quad \text{¥}228.55 \text{ Year 1 spot.}$$

2. At Year 2:

$$\frac{0.02 - 0.045}{1.045} \quad = \quad -0.023 \quad : \quad \text{¥ will appreciate by 2.3\%}$$

$$\text{¥ }228.55\,(1 - 0.023) \quad = \quad \text{¥}223.81 \text{ Year 2 spot.}$$

3. At Year 3:

$$\frac{0.03 - 0.03}{1.03} \quad = \quad 0 \quad : \quad \text{No change in the ¥/£ spot rate}$$

$$\text{¥}223.81 \text{ Year 3 spot.}$$

The calculations in Example 6 are very imprecise estimates of future ¥/£ spot rates for two reasons. The first is that the inflation differentials are themselves only estimates. The second reason is that at Years 1, 2 and 3 the *actual* spot rate will also be affected by supply and demand market forces *at that time*.

The next step

That ends our review of foreign exchange markets and foreign exchange rates. In doing so, we are now in a position to turn to look at the management of a company's exposure to foreign exchange risk. This we do in Chapter 24.

Summary

- Exchange rates are really currency prices, of which there is a buying and a selling price (or rate).

- Exchange rates can either be quoted as 'spot' or 'forward' rates. Spot rates are for the immediate delivery (exchange) of currencies. Forward rates are for the delivery of currencies at specific future dates.

- Forward rates are normally quoted as a 'discount' or 'premium' to the spot rate. A discount is added to the spot rate; a premium is subtracted from the spot rate. A discount signals that the 'first' of the pair of currencies is depreciating; a premium signals that it is appreciating.

- There are two types of forward FX contract: 'fixed' forward contracts and 'time option' forward contracts. Fixed forward contracts are for the exchange of currencies at a specific future date. Time option forward contracts are for the exchange of currencies at any time between two future dates.

- Exchange rate systems can either be fixed, floating or semi-fixed. Since 1972, most of the world's currencies have been in a system of floating exchange rates. However, since 1979, most of the EU currencies have been in a semi-fixed system, referred to as the Exchange Rate Mechanism (ERM).

- Finally, within a system of floating exchange rates, there are three factors which cause exchange rates to move: the forces of supply and demand; interest differentials between countries, and inflation differentials between countries.

Notes

1. It was this type of speculation which led to the difficulties for the ERM that were referred to earlier.

2. Treasury bills are similar to government stocks and represent risk-free investments.

Further reading

1. At this stage we are only half-way through our examination of foreign exchange risk management. However, there are a number of good books which give a deeper analysis of the foreign exchange markets and the causes of exchange rate movements.
2. From a UK perspective, see J.A. Donaldson, *Corporate Currency Risk*, Financial Times Business Information, 1984 and Chapters 1–6 of A. Buckley, *Multinational Finance*, Prentice-Hall, 1992.
3. Although it is written from a US perspective, another excellent book is D.K. Eiteman, A.I. Stonehill and M.H. Moffett, *Multinational Business Finance*, Addison-Wesley, 1992. See especially Chapters 2 and 4.

Quickie questions

If ¥/DM spot 85.10–85.90
1 month forward 1.20–1.10 premium
1. What are the ¥/DM forward rates?
2. Is the Deutsche Mark appreciating or depreciating against the yen?
3. What is the cost of selling DM350 000 spot?
4. What is the receipt from the one-month forward sale of ¥3.5 million?
5. If the £/DM spot rate is 0.3946–0.3956, what is the ¥/£ cross spot rate?
6. Given the ¥/DM spot buying rate, and if you are told that the pound is expected to depreciate by 3% per year for the next four years and then is likely to appreciate by 10% per year thereafter, estimate the six-year forward ¥/DM buying rate.
7. If $/£ spot is 1.5210 and $/£ 12-month forward is 1.5815 and the yield on UK Treasury bills is 5%, what is the yield on US Treasury bills?
8. US inflation is expected to be 5% next year and UK inflation 3%. If the current $/£ spot rate is 1.4550, forecast the spot rate in 12 months' time.
9. The current $/£ spot rate is 1.5835. Inflation forecasts for the next three years are:

USA	UK	Year
5%	6%	1
7%	7%	2
9%	5%	3

Forecast the spot rates over the next three years.

Problems

1. What causes exchange rates to move?
2. Describe the different types of exchange rate system.

24 Foreign exchange risk management

Definitions

Risk, as we know, means uncertainty of outcome and so foreign exchange (FX) risk refers to the uncertainty of outcome that arises because exchange rates move unpredictably.

Three types of FX risk can be identified:

1. transaction risk;
2. translation risk;
3. economic risk.

Formally, we can define *transaction risk* as the risk that movements in exchange rates will affect the sterling value of future foreign currency cash flows arising out of transactions already entered into by a company in the UK. It arises mainly from import and export trade and occurs when the company has short-term assets (i.e. debtors) or liabilities (i.e. creditors) denominated in a foreign currency.

Companies are also exposed to transaction risk if they undertake 'real' investment (i.e. building a factory) in a foreign country. That real investment will be expected to generate a future stream of positive net cash flows denominated in the foreign currency.

Finally, companies are also exposed to transaction risk if they borrow money denominated in a foreign currency. On such loans, they have future foreign currency interest and capital repayment liabilities on which they are exposed to the risk of movements in exchange rates.

The second type of FX risk, *translation risk*, arises when foreign currency assets and liabilities have to be translated into sterling terms to be included in the UK company's balance sheet. Many people would argue that although *transaction* risk can have a real impact on the value of the firm and shareholder wealth, this is *not* the case with translation risk. Translation risk is seen here as an accounting problem, and not one which affects the real worth of companies, in that it has no *cash flow* impact. If we assume that markets are efficient then it follows that accounting problems such as this do not represent a real risk at all. The only real (as opposed to perceived) problem arising from translation of foreign currency items would thus be one resulting from market inefficiencies relating to the interpretation of financial data.

The exposure of companies to translation risk arises principally from having medium- to long-term assets (such as projects) or liabilities (loans) denominated in foreign currencies which have to be translated at each year end into sterling terms to be included in the balance sheet.

Finally, *economic exposure* to FX risk arises from the possibility that the present value in sterling terms of the company's future expected foreign currency cash flows may alter through changes in exchange rates. By this definition, economic FX risk can be viewed as a longer-term version of transaction risk. Thus future export sales that the company may hope to achieve and future net foreign currency cash flows that it is hoped will arise from a foreign project will all generate exposure to economic FX risk.

For our present purposes, our attention is focused on the problem of FX transaction risk, and particularly the risk faced by importers and exports.

Transaction risk hedging

Suppose a UK company exports goods worth £1 million to a customer in the USA and, because the current $/£ spot selling rate is 1.5000, they invoice their US customer for $1.5 million on the normal terms of trade of three months' credit. That UK exporter is faced with FX risk: they are uncertain what will be the sterling revenues generated from the export deal. Although they know that they are going to receive $1.5 million in three months' time, they don't know how much sterling those $1.5 million will buy when they come to sell them in three months' time, because they don't know what the $/£ spot rate will be in three months' time. (Remember, exchange rates float.)

What can be done about this FX risk? One answer is simple. Instead of invoicing the customer for $1.5 million, invoice the customer for £1 million. The exporter will then have no uncertainty as to the sterling revenues from the export sale: £1 million.

The only problem with this course of action is that the FX risk does not disappear. Instead, the exporter is simply *pushing* the risk onto the customer, who now faces uncertainty about the *dollar* cost of paying for those imported goods because they don't know what will be the $/£ spot rate in three months' time when the £1 million will have to be purchased in order to pay the invoice.

Pushing the FX risk onto the customer in this way is perfectly acceptable as a solution to the exporter's FX risk problem *if* the customer allows them to do so. In other words, if the exporter has some sort of monopoly power and there is no other source of supply for the goods, then the customer may well simply have to accept the FX risk being pushed onto them in this way.

However, in most circumstances, export markets are highly competitive and so exporters are unable to operate in that way, for fear of losing the business to a rival who is willing to invoice the customer in the customer's own currency. Thus this solution to the exporter's FX risk problem is often unrealistic or unavailable.

Do nothing

An alternative would be for the exporter to invoice their customer for $1.5 million and then to do nothing about the FX risk, but just accept the chance that there may be an adverse movement in FX rates over the credit period. This course of action may be perfectly acceptable, provided two conditions apply:

1. the amount of money involved is relatively small (in relation to the company's business);
2. the company does not expect exchange rates to move significantly in an adverse direction.

On this latter condition, how is the company able to predict how future exchange rates will move? One way is to look at the *forward* rates. If the $/£ three-month forward rate is at a *premium*, this indicates an *appreciation* in the value of the $, relative to £. Such a movement in FX rates would be in the exporter's favour – they are owed money, $1.5 million, in a currency that is becoming more valuable over time. In such circumstances, the exporter may be tempted not to do anything about its exposure to FX risk, in the hope that, if anything, exchange rates may move in its favour.

However, the problem with this is that, as we know, forward rates are *not* very good predictors of future spot rates. Forward rates are determined by IRPT, while actual future spot rates are determined by PPPT and supply and demand market forces at that future point in time. Therefore the fact that three-month forward rates are at a premium is no guarantee that in three months' time the dollar will have appreciated from its current spot exchange rate. As a result, and given that a large amount of money – $1.5 million – is involved, the exporter would be foolish to take a chance on FX risk, doing nothing to reduce or eliminate it. Therefore how can the exporter avoid – 'hedge' – its potential exposure to FX risk?

Natural hedging or netting

There are a number of hedging techniques. The first that we can look at is the easiest and most obvious: foreign currency 'netting' or 'natural hedging'. The opportunity for this arises when a company is both an importer and an exporter and so has assets and liabilities in the same foreign currency *and* with the same maturity date.

For example, suppose a UK company exports to the USA and has invoiced a customer for $1 million payable in three months' time. In addition, they have also imported some goods on three months' credit and have been invoiced for $0.8 million. Effectively, the $0.8 million liability can be paid by partially utilizing the $1 million due to be received in three months' time. Therefore one amount can be netted off against the other, leaving the balancing $0.2 million asset to be hedged by other means.

Swaps

Currency swaps have grown from an insignificant to a fairly major market involving many $billions in a relatively short time. They involve two companies from different countries coming to a mutually beneficial arrangement so that both receive or pay cash in their own currency. For example a

US company would swap payments denominated in £s with payments in $s due by a UK company. The swap is arranged through a bank which will take a relatively small commission and this can provide a relatively low-cost method of guaranteeing a given exchange rate

Forward market hedging

A second hedging device – and the most widely used in practice – is the forward market hedge. In the above example, the company could hedge the net $0.2 million that is due to be received by the company in three months' time by using a forward contract: it could arrange to sell $0.2 million three months forward. In so doing, the company will contract to sell the $0.2 million in three months' time in exchange for sterling at a fixed rate of exchange (the three-month forward rate), and so there will be no uncertainty as to the sterling value of $0.2 million receivable in three months' time.

An example will make this clear, but now using the case of an *importer*.

Example 1

A German company imports goods from Japan and is invoiced for ¥10 million payable in six months' time. The current FX rates are as follows:

¥/DM spot	122.10–125.80
6-mth fwd	10.20–9.50 premium.

The first thing to notice is that the forward rate here is at a premium, indicating that the exchange rate is likely to move *adversely* from the German company's point of view: they owe money in a currency (¥) which is expected to appreciate against their own (DM). Therefore, it would be unwise not to hedge their exposure to FX risk.

To hedge in the forward market, the company would buy ¥10 million six months forward (remember, they need to buy ¥ in order to be able to pay the invoice), at ¥122.10 − 10.20 = ¥111.90. Therefore the DM cost of buying ¥10 million six months forward is: ¥10m. ÷ 111.90 = DM 89 365. By using this forward market hedge, the German company has no uncertainty about the cost in its *own* currency (DM 89 365) of having to pay off the ¥10 million invoice in six months' time.

Money market hedging

A third hedging technique is called a 'money market' or 'financial' hedge. Although at first sight this will look more complicated than a forward market hedge, it has a very simple underlying logic.

Suppose a UK company exports to the USA and invoices its customer for $0.5 million on three months' credit. Current data are given in Table 24.1.

The money market[1] is where companies (and individuals) can lend and borrow money for a *short* period of time. This time period can be as short as 'overnight' (which means from 3pm one afternoon to 3pm the next day) or as long as twelve months. Each time period in the money market has its own interest rate and in this example we are given the interest rates for lending and borrowing for a three-month time period. It is vital to remember that money market interest rates, for whatever time period, are *always* given in nominal *annual* terms. Thus the loan and deposit rates for sterling do *not* represent the actual amount of interest that is payable or paid on a three months' loan or deposit. To get the actual rate of interest over three months, each interest rate has to be divided by 4. Thus the three-month sterling loan rate is actually: 8% ÷ 4 = 2% and the deposit rate is 5% ÷ 4 = 1.25%. Finally, and fairly obviously, note that the dollar rates are the rates applicable for dollar loans and dollar deposits and the sterling rates are for sterling loans and sterling deposits.

Table 24.1

$/£ Spot	1.5580 – 1.5620
3-mth. fwd.	1.5840 – 1.5880

Three-month money market interest rates:

	Deposit	*Loan*
$	7%	9%
£	5%	8%

The 'money market hedge' uses what is termed the 'matching principle'. The UK company has a $0.5 million asset which is due to mature in three months' time. It hedges its risk exposure on these dollars by creating a *matching* $0.5 million *liability*, which also matures in three months' time.

This liability is created by taking out a three-month dollar loan. The company will borrow $x for three months, at an interest rate of (9% ÷ 4) = 2.25% so that capital ($x), plus accumulated interest will amount to $0.5 *million* at the end of three months. Therefore, the size of the loan can be calculated as follows:

$$\$x \times (1 + 0.0225) = \$0.5m$$
$$\$x = \$0.5m \div 1.0225 = \$488\ 998.$$

How the money market hedge works is as follows: the company invoices its customer for $0.5 million on three months' credit. Simultaneously, it borrows $488 998 from its bank for three months and immediately sells those dollars at spot to turn them into $488 998 ÷ 1.5620 = £313 059. This sterling amount represents their receipt from the export deal. And, in three months' time when they receive $0.5 million from the customer in settlement of the invoice, they then use these dollars to repay their dollar loan which by now has accumulated (capital plus interest) to $0.5 million.

Therefore, in this example, by using a money market hedge the exporter receives £313 059 *now*. An alternative would have been for the company to use a forward market hedge and sell the $0.5 million three months forward, to yield $0.5m ÷ 1.5880 = £314 861, which would be received in three months' time.

Comparing hedges

If we contrast these two possible hedges, we can determine which one would be best: the money market hedge, where the company received £313 059 immediately, or the forward market hedge where it receives £314 861 in three months' time.

These two amounts *cannot* be compared directly, because of the time value of money. Either we have to *compound* the £313 059 forward for three months, or we have to discount the £314 861 back three months. Normally, we compound forward the sterling received from the money market hedge. The interest rate we would use would be the sterling three-month deposit rate: $5\% \div 4 = 1.25\%$ on the assumption that by using the money market hedge the company could actually place the money on deposit if it so wished. The result is shown in Table 24.2.

Table 24.2

	Now	Three months' time
Forward market hedge:		£314 861
Money market hedge:	£313 059 (1 + 0.0125)	= £317 510

We can now compare like with like and as £317 510 is more than £314 861, the company's best hedge strategy in this example is to use the money market hedge.

Leading hedge

In this last example, the case of an exporter was used; but it will be helpful also to look at an example using an importer. However, before doing so, we can continue to use the existing example to look at another hedging strategy: 'leading the payment'.

In this context, 'leading' refers simply to asking the customer to forgo the three-month credit period and to pay the invoice immediately. As a result, the exporter will receive dollars immediately and can then sell them at spot for sterling, and so has no FX risk.

Obviously, the customer is unlikely to be willing to forgo the credit period without being given some sort of discount on the full invoiced amount. The *maximum* discount that the exporter would be willing to give would be where the sterling outcome resulting from the customer leading the payment was the *same* as the sterling outcome from the best hedge: in this case, the money market hedge where £313 059 is received immediately. The identification of the discount is given in Table 24.3.

Table 24.3

If $x represents the $ received now from the customer leading the payment:

$$\$x \div 1.5620 = £313\ 059$$
$$\$x = £313\ 059 \times 1.5620 = \$488\ 998$$

If the customer were to pay $488 998 immediately and forgo the credit period this would imply a discount of:

$$\frac{\$500\ 000 - \$488\ 998}{\$500\ 000} = 0.022 \text{ or } 2.2\%$$

Therefore 2.2% would be the maximum discount the exporter would be willing to offer to get the customer to lead the payment. Offering a greater discount than this would mean that the exporter would receive less sterling than they would from using a money market hedge and the customer paying the invoice in full after three months.

Another money market hedge

Let us now return to another example of using a money market hedge, but now with an *importer* facing FX risk. This is given in Example 2.

Example 2

A UK importer has been invoiced for \$280 000 payable in six months' time.

\$/£ spot	1.5240 – 1.5260
6 mth forward	1.4980 – 1.5030
6 mth money market:	\$5% – 7%
	£7% – 9%

Once again, the matching principle is used but here the importer has a dollar *liability* (which matures in six months' time), and so needs to create a matching dollar *asset* in order to hedge.

The dollar asset is created by the importer buying \$x at spot and placing them on six-month dollar deposit at an interest rate of: 5% ÷ 2 = 2.5% so that capital and interest accumulate to \$280 000 at the end of six months. At that time, the contents of the dollar deposit account are then used to pay off the \$280 000 invoice.

The amount of dollars needed to be placed on deposit can be calculated as:

$$\$x \times (1 + 0.025) = \$280\ 000$$
$$\$x = \$280\ 000 \div 1.025 = \$273\ 171.$$

The cost of buying \$273 171 spot will be:

$$\$273\ 171 \div 1.5240 = £179\ 246.$$

This is the cost *now*, in sterling, of the UK company's import deal.

Once again, this hedging device could be compared with the alternative of a forward market hedge.

FX futures contracts

We can now turn to yet another hedging device using 'FX futures' contracts.[2] In *effect*, there is very little difference between a company hedging on the FX forward market and hedging on the FX futures market, except that on the forward market the FX deal is *tailor-made* to the company's precise requirements: forward deals can be conducted for any amount of money, for (virtually) any currency and for (virtually) any time period forward. In contrast, futures deals are in the form of *standardized* contracts of a fixed amount of money and are available in only a limited range of currencies and for a limited range of forward time periods.

Because of the standardized nature of futures contracts, as opposed to the tailor-made nature of forward contracts, the transaction costs (e.g. commission payments) on futures are likely to be lower than on forward contracts for *small* FX hedging transactions (say, less than \$500 000); and so it is in these circumstances that futures hedges are often used.

A single futures contract is in respect of a fixed, standard amount of one currency being exchanged for a given amount of another currency for delivery/exchange on a specific, standard future date. Futures contracts are only available in a limited range of currencies, including: \$/£, \$/¥ and \$/DM. Futures contracts always have the US\$ on one side of the deal and so \$/£ contracts are simply known as sterling contracts, \$/¥ contracts are known as yen contracts, etc.

Each contract is in respect of a fixed amount of currency. Therefore sterling contracts are for £25 000 each; yen contracts are for ¥1 million each and DM contracts are for DM 80 000 each. Deals can be done in *whole* contracts only. For example, sterling amounts can only be dealt in £25 000 steps: £25 000 (one sterling contract), £50 000 (two sterling contracts), etc.

Futures contracts can be either bought or sold in the futures market, and the 'price' of the contract is effectively the exchange rate at which the deal is done. Therefore if you buy one sterling contract priced at $1.50, you are buying £25 000 in exchange for: £25 000 × 1.50 = $37 500. Similarly, if you sold ten sterling contracts at $1.60, you would be selling: 10 × £25 000 = £250 000 in exchange for: £250 000 × 1.60 = $400 000.

Finally, contracts are issued on a three-monthly cycle, (typically: March, June, September and December) with three different contracts available at any one time. For example, suppose that it is early February; at that time you would have a choice available to you of March, June and September contracts. Each of these contracts would be due to expire towards the end of the month concerned (typically, the third Wednesday of the month). Therefore, if you bought one sterling March futures contract priced at $1.50, you would be buying £25 000 in exchange for £25 000 × 1.50 = £37 500, with exchange of currencies being due on the third Wednesday in March.

Example 3

It is now January. Duck plc, a UK company invoices its US customer, Drake Inc, for $120 000 payable in April. Current spot $/£ is 1.5240 – 1.5260 and June sterling futures contracts are currently priced at $1.52½. (Notice, the price of the contract will normally be roughly equal to the exchange rate.) The futures contract size is £25 000.

Target outcome

Duck is due to receive $120 000 in April. If exchange rates do not move between now and April, they will be able to sell the dollars and receive:

$$\$120\ 000 \div 1.5260 = £78\ 637.$$

This amount therefore represents what can be called the 'target outcome', in that the company will hope to be able to arrange hedge protection that will result in them actually receiving an amount in sterling as close as possible to this figure of £78 637.

Number of contracts

In order to set up the hedge, the first thing is to determine how many contracts will be needed. The amount of money needed to be hedged is $120 000 and as the futures are in sterling units (£25 000) the dollars will have to be converted to find their equivalent sterling value. In order to convert the dollars, the futures price is usually used as the exchange rate. Therefore: $120 000 ÷ 1.52½ = £78 688 and so the number of contracts required are:

$$£78\ 688 \div £25\ 000 = 3.15 \text{ contracts}$$

However, remember, only *whole* contracts can be dealt with on the futures market and we normally round *up* to the nearest whole number of contracts – in this case four contracts.

To buy or sell futures?

The next thing to decide is whether Duck needs to buy or to sell four sterling June futures contracts in order to hedge its FX risk exposure. The answer to this can be found through the following process: in April the UK company will receive $120 000 cash from its customer; they will then want to sell these dollars (at spot) in order to *buy sterling*. Therefore in this transaction, (called a 'cash market' transaction), as they will want to *buy sterling*, then in order to hedge they will similarly *buy sterling futures contracts*. Therefore, to hedge, the company will buy four sterling June futures contracts at their current price of $1.52½.

There are two further points to notice here. The first is, why is Duck hedging with *June* contracts? Why not, for example, use March or September contracts? The answer is that the company will need to hedge with a contract which has still not expired by the time the invoiced amount is received in April. In this case, the March contract would not be suitable, as it would have expired on the third Wednesday in March. The September contract would have been suitable for hedging, but normally we hedge with those contracts which have the first expiry date after payment is due to be received. The first futures contracts to expire after April are the June contracts and so that is why they are used.

The second point is that if, in the cash market, Duck would have *sold sterling*, then to hedge they would also *sell sterling futures contracts*. For example suppose a US company exports goods to the UK and invoices its customer in sterling. As the US company is due to receive sterling it will want to *sell* that sterling in order to buy dollars. Therefore, if it wished to hedge its FX risk using futures, the US company would need to *sell* sterling futures.

Returning now to our example of Duck plc, we have seen how the hedge is put into place by buying four sterling June futures contracts at $1.52½. The contracts would be bought, through a dealer, from the futures market.[3]

'Profit' or 'loss' on target

No further action is then taken until April, when Duck receives $120 000 from Drake Inc. Suppose, at that time, we find:

$/£ spot	1.5875 – 1.5910
June sterling futures contracts	$1.59

Duck will then sell the $120 000 for sterling on the spot market to yield:

$$\$120\,000 \div 1.5910 = £75\,424$$

The target outcome was £78 637 and so there has been a shortfall of: £78 637 − £75 424 = £3213 caused by the depreciation in the dollar between January (when the exchange rate for selling $ was 1.5260) and April (when the exchange rate has moved to 1.5910). However, as we shall see, this shortfall will be offset by a profit on the futures contracts that were bought in January.

Closing out the futures position

What Duck now needs to do is 'close out' its futures position. It does this by *reversing* the earlier deal. In that earlier futures deal it *bought* four sterling June contracts and so now, in order to close out its futures position it *sells* four sterling June contracts at their current price of $1.59.

Profits or loss on futures

To see the profit that Duck has made on its futures dealings, we need to understand what its two futures transactions really imply.

It originally bought four sterling June contracts at $1.52½. Therefore it was buying 4 × £25 000 = £100 000 for delivery in June at a cost of £100 000 × 1.52½ = $152 500.

The company then sold four sterling June contracts at $1.59. Therefore it was arranging to sell 4 × £25 000 = £100 000 for delivery in June. It is in this way that the company closes out its futures position: it has got contracts to both buy *and* sell £100 000 for June delivery and so one set of contracts cancels out the other.

However, in the second futures deal, the £100 000 was sold for June delivery in exchange for £100 000 × 1.59 = $159 000. As the dollar receipt from the sterling sale was greater than the dollar cost of the original sterling purchase, the company receives the difference as the profit on its futures deal: $159 000 − $152 500 = $6500. This is shown more clearly below:

First Futures Transaction:	Bought	£100 000	Cost:	$152 500
Second Futures Transaction:	Sold	£100 000	Receipt:	$159 000
		—	Profit:	$ 6 500

The company can then sell these dollars spot to yield $6500 ÷ 1.5910 = £4085.

Hedge efficiency

As a result, the net sterling outcome for Duck plc – in comparison to its 'target outcome' – is:

Receipt from spot sale of $120 000	£75 424
Profit from futures transaction	£4085
Total £ outcome	£79 509
Target £ outcome	£78 637

The success of the company's hedging can be measured by the 'hedge efficiency' ratio. This is given by profit ÷ loss where the 'profit' is that made on the futures transaction and the 'loss' is the shortfall in the cash market against the target outcome caused by the adverse movement in exchange rates. Therefore the hedge efficiency is:

$$\frac{£4085}{£3213} = 1.27 \text{ or } 127\%.[4]$$

As soon as the third Wednesday in March is reached, the March contracts expire (i.e. they are no longer available to be bought and sold) and a new contract is created: December contracts, to ensure that a choice of three different dated contracts are available.

A futures hedge

At first sight, futures contracts can be confusing, but their mechanics are really quite simple and can be seen through the use of an example.

Perfect hedges

In Example 3, the hedge efficiency was 127%. Where the 'profit' exactly matches the 'loss', then we shall get 100% hedge efficiency. In practice 100% efficiency is unlikely to occur, except by chance – it is likely to be a little above (as in this example) or a little below 100%.

There are two reasons why a perfect hedge is unlikely. One is that we can only deal in *whole* contracts. In Example 3, Duck plc would have *liked* to have dealt in 3.15 futures contracts, but instead had to deal in four contracts. The second reason why a perfect hedge is unlikely is because futures contract prices are not precisely in line with exchange rates (this is referred to as 'basis risk'). For both these reasons, future hedges, unlike tailor-made forward market hedges, are unlikely to be perfectly efficient.

An important characteristic

We saw that with a *forward market* hedge, the company effectively 'locks itself in' to a specific rate of exchange and so is effectively hedged not only against an adverse movement in exchange rates, but is also hedged against a favourable movement.

For example, suppose a UK exporter invoices a customer for $10 million on three months' credit and hedges by selling $10 million forward for three months at 1.6000. This means that the exporter will receive $10m ÷ 1.6000 = £6.25m in three months' time, *whatever* happens to the $/£ exchange rate over the next three months. Therefore if in three months' time spot $/£ is 1.7500, they will be very glad that they hedged the $10 million at 1.6000. But, on the other hand, if spot $/£ in three months' time moved to 1.5000, they would be rather sorry about having hedged, because selling the $10 million spot would have yielded $10m ÷ 1.5000 = £6.67m.

However, the whole point in hedging is to avoid uncertainty of outcome – not to look back regretfully with the benefit of hindsight. (I insure my house against fire; at the end of the year I don't regret having done so just because it hasn't burnt down.) The purpose of this example is to emphasize the point that a forward market hedge has the effect of hedging against both adverse *and* favourable movements in exchange rates. In other words, the company selling goods overseas makes its profit from selling those goods rather than speculating in currency movements.

This characteristic of a forward market hedge is also a characteristic of a futures market hedge. In Example 3, we saw that an adverse movement in exchange rates (the $/£ rate moved from 1.5260 in January to 1.5910 in April) caused a shortfall of £3213 to be made in the cash market in April when compared against the target outcome. However, this shortfall was then offset by a profit on the futures trades.

We would also find that the *reverse* situation holds: if there had been a favourable movement in exchange rates so that a *surplus* was made in April on the cash market when compared against the target outcome, then this surplus would, once again, have been offset – but this time by a *loss* on the futures trades.

Margin

As was mentioned previously, companies deal in futures via futures markets. In London, the main market in futures is called LIFFE, but there are futures markets – of varying sizes – in most financial centres internationally. LIFFE is the largest European futures market.

One important element of futures trading is the concept of 'margin'. Margin is essentially a deposit held by LIFFE on behalf of futures traders as security against the trader defaulting upon their trading obligations. Therefore, in our futures example, when the company set up its hedge position in January, (by buying four sterling June contracts), it would have had to deposit some cash (or government securities) with LIFFE for as long as its futures position remained 'open', (remember, the company in our example did not 'close out' its position until April). This initial deposit is called 'initial margin'; the rules about how much money would need to be placed on deposit need not concern us, except to note that the margin requirement is relatively small.

Whilst the company's futures position remains open, LIFFE monitors the situation on a daily basis and if the company is making significant losses on its futures position, then they may be required to place additional money on deposit – called variation margin. One potential disadvantage of a futures hedge is uncertainty as to the demands for variation margin.

An interesting footnote concerning foreign currency futures arises from the Barings Bank debacle. Effectively Barings, through their Singapore dealer, Nick Leeson, bet against the yen falling. As the yen fell, so the bank needed to provide the variation margin, which it did. Eventually the losing bet grew to such an extent that the bank collapsed. This illustrates the possibility for speculation provided by futures in that the only money required 'up front' is the margin and thus the speculative 'bet' can be very large without the speculator necessarily having the financial resources to cover the possible loss.

Forward vs. futures

It is interesting to compare the advantages of forward market hedging to futures market hedging. In this respect, futures have two advantages over forward hedges for *smaller* users of the FX markets:

1. The initial margin required is often considerably less than the deposit that is required by banks from small companies wishing to use forward contracts.
2. The relatively small unit size of individual futures contracts (e.g. sterling futures are for £25 000 per contract) means that small importers and exporters can use the futures market and so avoid the relatively high commissions charged by banks on small FX deals.

For larger companies, in particular, the forward markets have many benefits:

1. Forward FX rates are, to some extent, negotiable and so a large company can use its market power with a bank to negotiate a favourable forward market rate. In contrast, futures prices are simply market determined and are non-negotiable.
2. The banking system is open twenty-four hours a day, seven days a week (on an international basis) and so companies can deal on the forward markets at any time. In contrast, futures markets are shut overnight, at weekends and on public holidays.
3. Futures markets are relatively small and so a company wishing to hedge a very large amount of foreign exchange may find that the market is not liquid enough for their needs (i.e. their future deals may be large enough to actually move the market prices against them).
4. Variation margin requirements are assessed on a daily basis and so a company which hedges using futures faces the possibility of an unpredictable and uncontrollable cash flow while their futures position remains open.
5. Finally, and as has been mentioned before, futures, unlike forward contracts, are only available in a limited range of major currencies and for only a restricted forward time period.

FX options contracts

We can now turn to look at a final foreign exchange hedging instrument: foreign exchange option contracts.

As has already been pointed out, futures and forward contracts hedge the company against both adverse *and* favourable movements in FX rates. It is in this respect that FX options differ. An FX option can be used to hedge the company against an adverse movement in FX rates whilst, at the same time, allowing the company to take advantage of a favourable movement in exchange rates.

Because of this advantage, hedging with options is more expensive than hedging with either futures or forward contracts. Consequently, companies will tend to hedge with futures/forward contracts if they are confident of an adverse movement in exchange rates, because this would be the cheapest way of hedging. However, if exchange rates are simply volatile and it is thought that the rate movement could just as easily be favourable as adverse, then companies may choose to use options to hedge – even though the cost is greater – so as to be able to take advantage of a possible favourable FX movement, should one occur.

The way in which options differ from forward and futures contracts is that with a forward contract the agreed exchange of currencies *must* take place; similarly, a company must close out its futures position. However, with an option contract, the company has a *choice* (or option): either it can exchange currencies as agreed (that is, it is said to *exercise* the option) or it can simply walk away from the whole arrangement if it is better off so doing (that is, it allows the option to *lapse*).

Example 4

Suppose a UK company is due to pay $10 million in three months' time to an overseas supplier. In order to hedge its FX risk, it has bought an FX option contract to buy $10 million in three months' time at an exchange rate of $/£: 1.8000. If, in three months' time, spot $/£ is 1.5000 the company will choose to exercise the option and buy $10 million through the option contract at $/£1.8000. To do so costs: $10m ÷ 1.8000 = £5.55m, whereas to buy $10 million spot would cost $10m ÷ 1.5000 = £6.67m. However, if in three months' time $/£ spot was 2.0000, the company would choose to allow the option to lapse and instead, buy $10 million on the spot market at a cost of only:$10m ÷ 2.0000 = £5m.

Thus, in the first scenario, the company was protected against the adverse movement in exchange rates, while in the second scenario, the company was able to take advantage of the favourable movement in exchange rates. What the option was effectively doing was fixing the *maximum* sterling cost of buying the required $10m: £5.55m; if the $10 million could have been bought at a lower cost on the spot market, then the company was allowed to walk away from the option contract.

Over-the-counter options

There are two basic types of FX option contract: over-the-counter (OTC) options and traded currency options. These are analogous to the tailor-made forward contracts and the standardized futures contracts, respectively.

Just as the banks operate the FX forward markets, they also deal in OTC FX options. These OTC options are available for any amount of money, in virtually any currency and for virtually any time period forward. Thus the OTC option contract is tailor-made to the firm's precise requirements. An illustration of a tailor-made OTC option is shown in Example 5.

Suppose a UK exporter invoices a customer for $9 million on three months' credit. The three-month forward rate for selling sterling is 1.8000. Thus the company could hedge by selling the $9 million three months forward and, as a result, the company would receive $9m ÷ 1.8000 = £5m in three months' time, whatever happens to the $/£ exchange rate in the meantime.

Alternatively, they could hedge their exposure to FX risk by buying an option to sell $9 million three months forward at, say, $1.8000. Then, in three months' time if $/£ spot is above 1.8000, say 2.000, they will choose to exercise the option to sell $9 million for £5 million. However, if the $/£ spot is below 1.8000, say 1.5000, then they will allow the option to lapse and sell the $9 million on the spot market to yield, in this example, $9m ÷ 1.5000 = £6m.

Traded currency options[5]

Traded currency option contracts are, in many ways, similar to futures contracts. They are available from LIFFE, (futures markets usually deal in option contracts as well as futures) in a limited range of currencies, with a standard amount of money per contract and with a limited range of time periods forward.

Just as with futures, traded currency options are normally issued on a three-month cycle – typically: March, June, September and December – with three contract dates available at any one time. Thus, in February, you could deal in either March, June or September contracts. Once the March contracts expire, (at the end of March), a new series of contracts, for December, will be created.

Calls and puts

There are two basic types of traded currency options: 'call' options and 'put' options. A call option is an option to buy a particular currency and a put option is an option to sell a particular currency.

Again, like futures, traded currency options always involve the US$ on one side of the contract. Therefore, there are $/£, $/DM, $/¥, etc., option contracts. Because the dollar is *always* one of the two currencies involved, $/£ options are simply known as 'sterling options', $/DM options are known as 'DM options', etc.

This is as far as the similarities go between futures and options contracts. Option contracts, for hedging purposes, can *only* be bought. But, a company can either buy call options, (options to buy a particular currency), or it can buy put options, (options to sell a particular currency). Therefore if a company bought a *sterling* put option they would be buying a contract to *sell sterling* in exchange for dollars. Similarly, if they bought a *yen call*, they would be buying a contract to *buy yen* in exchange for dollars.

Exercise price

Finally, the financial manager is usually faced with a choice of three different exchange rates (the 'exercise' or 'strike' price) with traded currency options. Typically, one is approximately equal to the spot rate, one is a little below and the other is a little above.

Suppose a UK exporter was due to be paid in $US in April. June sterling option contracts (remember, these are really $/£ contracts) – as with futures, we would usually hedge with the contracts with the next expiry date after we were due to receive payment – are available at the following $/£ rates: 1.40, 1.50 and 1.60. How is the exporter to decide on the choice of option exchange rate?

Obviously an exchange rate of $1.40 = £1 is more attractive to the exporter than an exchange rate at $1.60 = £1, because at $/£ 1.40 they are ensuring that they will receive a greater minimum amount of sterling than they will receive at $/£1.60. However, there is a cost trade-off problem here. As we shall see, the more favourable is the option exchange rate (the exercise price), the more expensive is the option cost, and vice versa.

Therefore the decision about what exchange rate the option should be taken at is a matter of managerial judgement. If the management believe that there is a strong possibility of a significant adverse movement in the spot rates, then they may judge that it is worth the higher cost to ensure a higher minimum sterling outcome. On the other hand, if management feel that a favourable movement in exchange rates is the most likely outcome (but they will want to hedge the risk that their expectations may be wrong) then they may decide to select the less favourable – and hence cheaper – option exchange rate.

Setting up an option hedge

We will now make use of an illustration. This is given in Example 6.

Example 6

Suppose it is June. Ding plc, a UK company has invoiced Dong Inc, an overseas customer for $240 000, payable on 31 December. Data is as follows:

Current $/£ spot	1.4780 – 1.4830
Money market interest rates:	$6%–8½%
	£5%–7%

December sterling option contracts (contract size £25 000):

Exercise price	December options	
	Calls	Puts
$1.45	11.60	1.24
$1.50	8.45	4.44
$1.55	3.20	7.30
Premiums in cents/£		

Suppose Ding plc wishes to hedge the FX risk using options with an exercise price of $1.50 = £1 so as to ensure a minimum sterling receipt from the export deal of: $240 000 ÷ 1.50 = £160 000.

Number of contracts

The first task is to decide how many options need to be bought in order to hedge the $240 000. The contract size is £25 000 and so we first need to convert the dollar invoiced amount into sterling at the exchange rate given by the exercise price chosen:

$$\$240\,000 \div 1.50 = \pounds160\,000 \div \pounds25\,000 = 6.4 \text{ contracts}$$

As we can only deal in whole contracts, we would normally round this number *up* to seven option contracts.

Calls or puts?

The next task is to decide whether Ding needs to buy sterling call options or sterling put options in order to hedge its FX risk exposure. The rule used is similar to that used with futures contracts: look to see what the company wishes to do to the 'currency of the option' in the cash market. In this example, the currency of the option is sterling – we are involved with sterling options (remember, these are *really* $/£ options) – and in the cash market the firm will be receiving $240 000 which it will wish to sell in order to buy sterling. Therefore, in the cash market the firm will want to *buy sterling* and so it hedges its FX risk by *buying options to buy sterling*: sterling call options. Thus the company buys seven sterling December call option contracts at an exercise price of $1.50.

Contract cost

Finally, what is the cost of these option contracts? The cost is given by the option 'premium' data given in the table above. December sterling calls at an exercise price of $1.50 cost 8.45 *cents per pound sterling* of option value. Therefore the total cost of the seven option contracts can be calculated as:

$$7 \times \pounds25\,000 = \pounds175\,000 \times 8.45\cent = \$14\,787.50.$$

This cost will be payable immediately, at a sterling spot cost of $14 787.50 ÷ 1.4780 = £10 005.

The operation of the hedge

The next stage of the example is to see the effect of Ding's hedged position. Suppose that on 31 December when the company receives the $240 000 from its export customer the following is the situation in the FX markets:

Scenario A: $/£ Spot: 1.4620 – 1.4650
Scenario B: $/£ Spot: 1.5880 – 1.5910

Scenario A:

Ding plc faces a choice. It can either sell its $240 000 through the exercise of the options at an exchange rate of $1.50 = £1 or it can allow the options to lapse and sell the $240 000 on the spot market at an exchange rate of $1.4650 = £1.

Obviously, the best course of action is to sell the dollars spot, as this gives a more favourable exchange rate, and so allow the options to lapse, yielding a sterling outcome of:

$$\$240\,000 \div 1.4650 = \pounds163\,822.53.$$

In so doing, Ding is taking advantage of the favourable movement in the exchange rate away from the option exercise price of $1.50.

Scenario B:

Again, Ding plc has a choice of either exercising the options at an exchange rate of $1.50 = £1 or allowing the options to lapse and selling the dollar spot at an exchange rate of $1.5910.

In this scenario, exercise of the options provide the company with a more favourable exchange rate than that obtainable from a spot rate of exchange.

The seven sterling call options with an exercise price of $1.50 give Ding the right to buy (call) 7 × £25 000 = £175 000 in exchange for dollars at an exchange rate of $1.50 = £1. Therefore, in order to exercise the options, the company will have to pay over: £175 000 × 1.50 = $262 500. This required quantity of dollars can be partially met from the $240 000 just received from the export customer, leaving a balance of: $262 500 – $240 000 = $22 500 to be bought at spot costing: $22 500 ÷ 1.5880 = £14 169.

Therefore the net outcome of exercising the options is as follows:

£ receipt from the exercise of the options:	£175 000
less: £ cost of the spot purchase of $22 500:	£(14 169)
Net £ receipt:	£160 831

This net figure could be compared with the sterling receipt from the spot sale of $240 000:

$$\$240\ 000 \div 1.5910 = £150\ 848.$$

Therefore, in Scenario B we have an example where the options are exercised so as to protect the company from the adverse movement in the $/£ spot exchange rate, away from the option exercise price of $1.50.

An importer case

The previous example used an exporting scenario. Let us now consider the case of an importer.

Bell plc has imported goods from the USA and has been invoiced for $470 000 payable on 30 June. Current data are:

Current $/£ spot	1.5210 – 1.5240
June £ option contracts	(size £25 000)

Exercise price	June options	
	Calls	Puts
£1.50	7.15	3.50
£1.55	4.10	5.85
£1.60	1.25	9.20
Premiums in cents/£		

The company decides to hedge using options with an exercise price of $1.50.

Number of contracts

$470 000 ÷ 1.50 = £313 333. Contract size £25 000 = 12.53 rounded to 13 contracts.

Calls or puts?

In the cash market, the company will need to buy $ (and thus sell £) in order to pay the invoice. Thus, in order to hedge they will want the option to sell £: i.e. sterling puts.

Hedge

To hedge the company will buy 13 sterling June put options at an exercise price of $1.50.

Premium cost

$$13 \times £25\ 000 = £325\ 000 \text{ at } 3.5 \text{ cents} = \$11\ 375.$$

This would be bought spot to pay the option premium, i.e. $11 375 ÷ 1.5210 = £7479.

On 30 June

Let us assume that on 30 June the $/£ spot rate is now 1.4680 – 1.4725.

The company faces a choice. If it allows the option to lapse and buys spot this would cost:

	(£)
$470 000 ÷ 1.4680	320 163
plus £ cost option premium	7 479
Total cost	327 642

The alternative is to buy the $ through the exercise of the options. The company holds 13 options totalling £325 000. These are put options with an exercise price of £1.50. This gives the company the right to sell £325 000 at $1.50, i.e. for $487 500. However, only $470 000 is required to pay off the invoice and the surplus of $17 500 can be sold spot to return $17 500 ÷ 1.4725 = £11 885.
  Thus the result of exercising the option is:

	(£)
Cost of exercise	325 000
less £ receipt from sale of $ surplus	(11 885)
plus £ cost option premium	7 479
Total cost	320 594

In this case it is in the interests of the company to exercise the options as this produces a lower total cost than allowing them to lapse.

An important variation

In both of the examples above, Ding plc and Bell plc, the foreign exchange was due to be received or paid on the very day that the options were due to expire. However, this type of situation is a very special case and the analysis would be different if, for example, Bell plc had to pay the $470 000 on a date before 30 June (say 1 June).

Options are a little like an insurance policy. Thus June sterling puts with an exercise price of $1.50 ensure that you will be able to buy a specific quantity of US dollars at an exchange rate that will not be worse than $1.50/£. If the spot market provides a better exchange rate, use the spot market, if it provides a worse exchange rate, exercise the option. So the choice faced by Bell plc on 30 June was to buy $470 000 either on the spot market or by exercising the options at £1.50. It turned out to be better to exercise the option. Had circumstances been different and the spot rate had been advantageous, the option would not have been exercised and it would have been discarded as worthless.

However, what would have happened if the $470 000 was due on 1 June and on that day it could get a better spot rate than the option exercise rate of $1.50? Although the option was not exercised on 1 June, it is not worthless and it is not discarded. It still has a month to run and it could be sold on (or even kept as a speculative investment in case it should it turn out to be worthwhile exercising it at a later date).

Thus the choice facing the company on 1 June is not simply to exercise the options or let them lapse. It is rather:

1. buy the $ through exercise of the options;
2. buy the $ spot and sell on the options;
3. buy the $ spot and hold onto the options.

Suppose we return to the case of Bell plc on the assumption that the invoice is going to be paid on 1 June but that the 30 June options in the original example were purchased. On 1 June we find:

Current $/£ spot   1.4450 – 1.4480
June £ option contracts   (size £25 000)

Exercise price	June options	
	Calls	Puts
£1.50	5.15	6.25
£1.55	1.80	8.40
£1.60	0.95	11.10
Premiums in cents/£		

The company holds 13 options totalling £325 000. These are put options with an exercise price of £1.50. This gives the company the right to sell £325 000 at $1.50, i.e. for $487 500 of which $470 000 is required to pay off the invoice and the surplus of $17 500 can be sold spot to return $17 500 ÷ 1.4480 = £12 086.
   Thus the result of exercising the option is:

	(£)
Cost of exercise	325 000
less £ receipt from sale of $ surplus	(12 086)
plus £ cost option premium	7 479
Total cost	320 393

The most likely alternative would be to buy the $ spot and sell on the options.
   The cost of buying the $470 000 spot would be $470 000 ÷ 1.4450 = £325 259. The receipt from the sale of the unexercised options would be 13 options × £25 000 × 6.25 cents = $20 312. This could be sold spot at 1.4480 to give £14 028. The net cost of this alternative would be:

	(£)
Cost of buying spot	325 259
less £ receipt from sale of options	(14 028)
plus £ cost option premium	7479
Total cost	318 710

Thus it is better to buy $ spot and sell on the unexercised options than it is to exercise the options.

Valuation of options

We noted above that, in circumstances where foreign exchange is due to be paid or received on a date before the option's expiry date there was the following set of alternatives open to the company:

1. exercise the options;
2. use the spot market and sell on the options;
3. use the spot market and hold onto the options as a speculative investment.

We will discount the third option on the grounds that our company is not in business to speculate and so we will concentrate on the first two.

In practice we will find that under normal circumstances, alternative 2 will always produce a better outcome than alternative 1. The reason for this lies in the fact that options will always be worth more to another investor unexercised than the benefit gained by early exercise. There will (almost certainly) be an option premium.

The Black–Scholes option valuation model indicates that the market price of an option (the premium) consists of two elements:

$$\text{Market price of option} = \text{Intrinsic value} + \text{Time (or gamble) value.}$$

The intrinsic value of an option is the gain that could be made from immediate exercise (this cannot be negative). Thus in the case of Bell plc, on 1 June this would arise out of the difference between the option price of $1.50/£ and the spot price of $1.4450/£. By exercising the option, Bell receives £135 000 × 1.50 = $202 500 whilst the spot rate would provide £135 000 × 1.445 = $195 075 for the same sterling investment.

The gamble element is also valuable. It is referred to as the 'time' value of the option because the value of the gamble is largely a function of time: the longer the option has to run, the greater is the chance that the gamble will be successful. (This is nothing to do with discounting and should not be confused with the 'time value of money'.)

If we reduce the intrinsic value of Bell's option to £1 we find the following: on 1 June, £1 call option with an exercise price of $1.50/£ produces a profit of $1.50 − $1.445 i.e. 4.5 cents per £. However, on that date we are told that the premium on puts is 6.25 cents per £. This tells us that investors are prepared to pay a premium of 6.25 − 4.5 cents or .75 of a cent per £ for the gamble element of the options.

As a result we have the rule that options should *never* be exercised early, i.e. before their expiry date. Early exercise merely provides the intrinsic value whereas the sale of the option provides its market value which is made up of the intrinsic value *plus* the gamble value.

Contingent exposure to FX risk

Importers and exporters do use FX options as an alternative to hedging with either forward or future contracts – even though to do so incurs greater costs – in order to be able to take advantage of any favourable movement in exchange rates that might occur. However, there is one set of circumstances where using options is the *only* feasible hedging method and futures and forward market hedges are inappropriate. This occurs when a company has a contingent exposure to foreign exchange risk.

Suppose a UK civil engineering contractor is bidding to undertake an overseas contract. The bid (and payment) must be made in dollars and be submitted by, say, 1 March. The winning bid will be awarded the contract on, say, 1 June with payment being made on completion of the contract on 1 September.

If the UK company decides it is willing to undertake the contract for payment of £5 million and given that the spot $/£ rate on 1 March is 1.5000, it enters a bid of $7.5 million.

The problem that the company faces is that as soon as it makes its bid to undertake the contract for a payment of $7.5 million it is exposed to the risk of an adverse movement in exchange rates between 1 March and 1 September, when payment would be eventually received. However, the company *cannot* simply hedge its FX risk by selling $7.5 million forward to 1 September (or by using the futures market), because with such contracts *exchange of currencies must take place*. The company may not end up winning the contract and so will not receive the $7.5 million it would have contracted to sell forward on 1 September. This is because its exposure to FX risk on 1 March is *contingent* on another event occurring: it is contingent on winning the contract.

In such circumstances, an option hedge is ideal. On 1 March the company could buy an *option* to sell $7.5 million forward to 1 September at an exercise price of $1.50 = £1. Then, if it won the contract it would be assured of receiving at least: $7.5m ÷ 1.50 = £5m. If it lost the contract and the dollar rate is no higher than 1.5 on the exercise date, then it could simply allow its option to lapse.

Thus it is in the face of contingent exposures to FX risk that we are more likely to see companies hedging through the options market.

Traded options vs. OTC options

To round off our look at FX options, let us contrast the advantages and disadvantages of traded versus over-the-counter (OTC) options.

There are seven specific points to be made:

1. OTC options are available in a wide range of currencies, while traded currency options are only available in a narrow range of major trading currencies.
2. OTC options are available in 'cross currencies' (e.g. £/FF), while trade options are only available in currencies against the US$.
3. OTC options are available for any exercise date up to a year forward (or even longer). Traded options do not usually extended more than nine months forward.
4. OTC option prices/'premiums' are determined by the bank which sells them, whereas traded option premiums are market determined (and so are non-negotiable). This means that a large company may be able to use its financial strength to negotiate a more favourable deal on OTC options. Conversely, small companies may find that they get a more favourable premium quoted on the traded market where their lack of financial muscle does not affect the cost of the deal.
5. OTC options may be more suitable for very large transactions which may be more difficult to arrange on a traded option exchange because of the danger of such a large single 'trade' moving the market price.

6. The banking system which deals in OTC options is a global, twenty-four hour, 365 day a year market which is never closed. Traded option markets have only very limited facilities for trading 'out of hours' (e.g. evenings, weekends and public holidays).

7. Traded options are freely marketable because of their uniform/standardized nature and so are liquid. In contrast, OTC options are not readily saleable and hence are essentially illiquid securities.

Summary

- There are three 'types' of foreign exchange risk: transaction risk; translation risk and economic risk. At this stage, we focus on transaction risk – the risk to which importers and exporters are exposed.

- Many exporters try to avoid exposure to FX risk by invoicing in their own currency. However, this simply transfers the FX risk to the customer. In competitive export markets customers are unlikely to be willing to have FX risk imposed upon them in this way and will demand that they be invoiced in their own currency, not the currency of the exporter.

- Other exporters, although exposed to FX risk, undertake no hedging and so leave their exposure open. In many circumstances this action is unwise as exchange rates can move significantly over short time periods and so turn a potentially profitable export sale into a loss-making sale.

- The basic hedging technique is netting, where assets and liabilities in the same currency and with the same maturity can be offset against each other.

- Cash flows in one currency can be swapped for cash flows in another currency as this is likely to be in the interests of both parties.

- Another hedging technique which is very widely used is to forward market hedge, where foreign currency is bought or sold forward in time, thus locking the company into a specific rate of exchange and so avoiding the uncertainty of a possible adverse movement in exchange rates.

- A money market hedge achieves the same effect as a forward market hedge, but involves the creation of a matching foreign currency asset or liability. The nature of this hedging technique is such that it is only likely to be used if a forward market hedge is not available (because there is no forward market or its depth forward is insufficient).

- Forward market and money market hedges are tailor-made to the precise requirements of the company suffering the FX exposure. In contrast, a futures market hedge provides standardized hedging contracts which, while providing roughly the same hedge effect as either a forward or money market hedge, will not provide the company with 100% hedge efficiency.

- Finally, FX risk can be hedged through the use of foreign currency options. The key difference that exists between FX options and all other hedging devices is that options protect the firm from an adverse movement in interest rates, while allowing advantage to be taken of favourable movements. All other hedging techniques lock the firm into a specific exchange rate and so hedge against both adverse and favourable FX movements.

Notes

1. As we have seen in Chapter 14, when discussing interest-rate risk management.

2. Once again, futures contracts were first encountered in our discussion on interest rate risk in Chapter 14.

3. There are futures (and options) markets throughout the world. In London, the futures market is known as the London International Financial Futures and Options Exchange (LIFFE).

4. Notice how the hedge efficiency is calculated. If the profit is greater than the loss, the hedge efficiency is greater than 100%. If the profit is less than the loss, the hedge efficiency is less than 100%.

5. Of course options have been encountered before in Chapters 13 and 14.

Further reading

1. Both books referred to as further reading for Chapter 23 – Buckley (1992) and Eiteman, Stonehill and Moffett (1992) – contain good coverage of FX risk.
2. Two good articles are D.P. Walker, 'What is Foreign Exchange Risk', *Managerial Finance*, Summer 1982 and P.A. Beck and M. Glaum, 'The Management of Foreign Exchange Risk in UK Multinationals', *Accounting and Business Research*, Winter 1990.

Quickie questions

1. Spot DM/$ 2.3440 – 2.3460
   1 mth fwd   1.80f – 1.65f premium
   What is the DM cost of buying $1000 one month forward?
2. What causes FX rates to move?
3. Given the data in (1), a US company exports to Germany and invoices for DM10 000 on one month's credit. One-month DM interest rates are 8%–10%. One-month $ interest rates are 11%–13%.

   (a)   show the forward market hedge;
   (b)   show the money market hedge;
   (c)   what is the maximum discount the US exporter would offer for immediate payment?

4. FF/\$ Spot = 5.1020
   FF/£ Spot = 9.8040
   \$/£ Spot cross rate = ?

5. A company has put in a bid for a contract in the USA. In order to hedge the FX risk exposure they have bought an OTC put option in respect of \$100 000, six months forward at an exercise price of \$1.80. What action will they take in six months' time if:

   (a) They win the contract and:
       (i)   FX spot is \$1.95;
       (ii) FX spot is \$1.70?
   (b) They lose the contract and:
       (i)   FX spot is \$1.95;
       (ii) FX spot is \$1.70?

6. \$/£ 5-month forward 1.7460, 6-month forward 1.7650. A company wishes to hedge via a five- to six-month time option forward dollar sale contract. What will be the contract's exchange rate?

7. What advantages do over-the-counter options have over traded currency options?

8. A German company exports goods to the USA and invoices their customer for \$526 000 payable in August. It is now June.

Spot \$/DM	0.4070 – 0.4090
August forward	0.4130 – 0.4150

   September DM futures contracts are priced at \$0.41. (One DM futures contract represents DM80 000.)

   Required:
   (a) Set up a hedge position.
   (b) Calculate hedge efficiency if, in August:

   $$\text{\$/DM spot } 0.4150 – 0.4170$$

   and September DM futures are priced at \$0.41$\frac{1}{2}$.

9. A UK company imports from the USA and is invoiced for \$297 500 payable in October.

\$/£ Spot rate	1.7500 – 1.7520
October forward	1.7000 – 1.7015

   (a) Show how a forward market hedge would be carried out.
   (b) Show how a futures market hedge would be carried out. (One £ futures contract represents £12 500 and December sterling futures are priced at \$1.70.)
   (c) What would be the result if the futures market hedge in \$/£ spot turned out to be 1.7800–1.7820 in October and December sterling futures were priced at \$1.78?

Problems

1. Oxlake plc has export orders from a company in Singapore for 250 000 china cups, and from a company in Indonesia for 100 000 china cups. The unit variable cost to Oxlake of producing china cups is 55 pence, and unit sales price to Singapore is S\$2.862 and to Indonesia, 2246 rupiahs. Both orders are subject to credit terms of 60 days, and are payable in the currency of the importers. Past experience suggests that there is 50% chance of the customer

in Singapore paying 30 days late. The Indonesian customer has offered to Oxlake the alternative of being paid US$125 000 in three months' time instead of payment in the Indonesian currency. The Indonesian currency is forecast by Oxlake's bank to depreciate in value during the next year by 30% (from an Indonesian viewpoint) relative to the US dollar.

Whenever appropriate, Oxlake uses time option forward foreign exchange contracts.

Foreign exchange rates (mid rates)

	$ Singapore/$US	$US/£	Rupiahs/£
Spot	2.1378	1.4875	2481
1 month forward	2.1132	1.4963	No forward
2 months forward	2.0964	1.5047	market exists
3 months forward	2.0915	1.5105	

Assume that in the United Kingdom any foreign currency holding must be immediately converted into sterling.

Money market rates (% per year)

	Deposit	Borrowing
UK clearing bank	6.5	10.5
Singapore bank	4	7
Indonesian bank	15	Not available
US domestic bank	8	12

These interest rates are fixed rates for either immediate deposits or borrowing over a period of two or three months, but the rates are subject to future movement according to economic pressures.

Required:
(a) Using what you consider to be the most suitable way of protecting against foreign exchange risk, evaluate the sterling receipts that Oxlake can expect from its sales to Singapore and to Indonesia, without taking any risks.
All contracts, including foreign exchange and money market contracts, may be assumed to be free from the risk of default. Transaction costs may be ignored.
(b) If the Indonesian customer offered another form of payment to Oxlake, immediate payment in US dollars of the full amount owed, in return for a 5% discount on the rupiah unit sales price, calculate whether Oxlake would be likely to benefit from this form of payment.
(c) Discuss the advantages and disadvantages to a company of invoicing an export sale in a foreign currency.

2. (a) Discuss briefly four techniques a company might use to hedge against the foreign exchange risk involved in foreign trade.
(b) Fidden is a medium-sized UK company with export and import trade with the USA. The following transactions are due within the next six months. Transactions are in the currency specified.
(i) Purchases of components, cash payment due in three months: £116 000.
(ii) Sale of finished goods, cash receipt due in three months: $197 000.
(iii) Purchase of finished goods for resale, cash payment due in six months: $447 000.
(iv) Sale of finished goods, cash receipt due in six months: $154 000.

Exchange rates (London market)
($/£)

Spot	1.7106 – 1.7140
Three months forward	0.82 – 0.77 cents premium
Six months forward	1.39 – 1.34 cents premium

Three months or six months	Borrowing	Lending
Sterling	12.5%	9.5%
Dollars	9%	6%

Foreign currency option prices (New York market)
(Prices are cents per £, contract size £12 500)

		Calls			Puts	
Exercise price ($)	March	June	Sept	March	June	Sept
1.60	–	15.20	–	–	–	2.75
1.70	5.65	7.75	–	–	3.45	6.40
1.80	1.70	3.60	7.90	–	9.32	15.35

Assume that it is now December, with three months to expiry of the March contract.

Required:
(a) Calculate the net sterling receipts/payments that Fidden might expect for both its three- and six-month transactions if the company hedges foreign exchange risk on:
   (i)   the forward foreign exchange market;
   (ii) the money market.
(b) If the actual spot rate in six months' time was with hindsight exactly the present six months forward rate, calculate whether Fidden would have been better to hedge through foreign currency options rather than the forward market or money market.
(c) Explain briefly what you consider to be the main advantage of foreign currency options.

3. Differn Inc. is a US-based medium-sized import-export company. It is now 1 December and the following transactions have been contractually agreed:

(i)   Sale of sprogets, cash receipt due 1 February of £197 000.
(ii) Purchase of raw materials, invoice payable 1 May, for £447 000.
(iii) Sale of sprogets, £154 000 cash receipt due 1 May.

$/£ FX rates

Spot	1.7106	–	1.7140	
Forward 1 February	0.82	–	0.77¢ premium	
Forward 1 May	1.39	–	1.34¢ premium	

£ FX futures prices (contract size £25 000)
£ March contracts $1.71¼
£ June contracts $1.71

Money market interest rates

£	12.6%	–	10.8%
$	9%	–	6%

Required:
(a) Hedge Differn's FX risk exposure on the forward markets.
(b) Hedge Differn's FX risk exposure on the money markets.
(c) Ignoring transaction costs, but not the time value of money, compare the forward market hedge outcome to that of the money market hedge.
(d) Calculate the hedge efficiency that Differn could achieve on its FX risk exposure using an FX futures market hedge, if:
   (i)   1 February spot $/£   1.7020 – 1.7055
         March £ contracts $1.70¼
   (ii) 1 May spot $/£   1.6280 – 1.6320
         June £ contracts $1.63
(e) Briefly state why hedging using currency futures is not likely to be 100% efficient (i.e. not a 'perfect' hedge).

25 Overseas capital investments

Introduction

Domestic versus foreign projects

The appraisal of capital investments in foreign countries involves several difficulties not present in domestic project appraisal. Principal among these difficulties are the following:

1. Foreign exchange (FX) rates fluctuate over time in an essentially unpredictable way. Therefore an overseas project's cash flows are exposed to the risk of adverse FX movements.

2. There are a variety of ways in which an overseas government (the 'host' government) might take action which adversely discriminates against an overseas project once the investment has been undertaken. Such actions might range from the imposition of a penal rate of taxation, and/or restrictions on the remittance of project net cash flows back to the parent, to confiscation of the project's assets without compensation. These possibilities are referred to as 'country risk'.

3. There is the problem of correctly evaluating the systematic risk and required expected rate of return on the project within an international, rather than domestic, context.

4. Finally, there is the problem of the correct project appraisal procedure. In particular, should the analysis be undertaken from the viewpoint of the project itself, or from the viewpoint of the parent company? This problem arises because of differences that can occur between a project's net cash flows, and a project's net cash flows which are available for repatriation back to the parent company.

This chapter examines these difficulties and the way in which they might be overcome. It builds on the previous two chapters which looked at the FX markets and the way that managements can hedge FX risk.

The basic approach

A project in a foreign country generates a stream of net cash flows in the currency of its host country. How is the parent to evaluate those cash flows in an NPV analysis? We can formulate two possible approaches to the problem which should provide exactly the same expected result.

Using as an example a UK company investing in the USA, the two alternative approaches are:

1. The project's dollar cash flows are discounted at the dollar discount rate to generate a $NPV. This can then be converted at the $/£ spot rate to give a sterling NPV.
2. The project's dollar cash flows are converted to sterling cash flows. These sterling cash flows are then discounted at the sterling discount rate to generate a sterling NPV.

Notice how each approach starts off at exactly the same point (the project's dollar cash flows), and ends up at exactly the same point (the sterling NPV). Both approaches are illustrated in Example 1.

As both approaches provide exactly the same results, given our estimates and given that the IRPT holds, which approach should be used in practice is likely to depend on what information is available, and how difficult it might be to forecast the information that may *not* be available. Generally, it may be assumed that management might be more uneasy about forecasting future FX rates than they would be about forecasting the required dollar return. Therefore approach 1 may be the more likely one to be found in practice. There is, however, a lack of empirical evidence on the matter.

Example 1

US project's net cash flows:	Year	$m.
	0	−10
	1	+ 5
	2	+ 6
	3	+ 4

The $/£ spot rate is 1.8050 and the dollar is expected to depreciate by 5% per year. A similar-risk UK-based project would be expected to earn a minimum return of 20%.

Calculations:
Given the spot rate and the expected rate of annual depreciation, the future exchange rates can be estimated:

$$1.8050(1.05)^1 \quad = \quad 1.8952 \quad : \quad \text{Year 1}$$
$$1.8050(1.05)^2 \quad = \quad 1.9900 \quad : \quad \text{Year 2}$$
$$1.8050(1.05)^3 \quad = \quad 2.0895 \quad : \quad \text{Year 3}$$

Adapting the IRPT, the dollar discount rate can be estimated:

$$\frac{\text{US discount rate} - \text{UK discount rate}}{1 + \text{UK discount rate}} = \% \text{ change in US\$}$$

$$\frac{\text{US discount rate} - 0.20}{1 + 0.02} = +0.05$$

US discount rate = $(0.05 \times 1.20) - 0.20 = 0.26$ or 26%

Approach 1:

Year	$m	26% discount factors		$ PV c/fs
0	−10	1	=	−10
1	+ 5	0.7936	=	+ 3.968
2	+ 6	0.6299	=	+ 3.779
3	+ 4	0.4999	=	+ 2.000
				$− 0.253m NPV

$$-\$0.253m \div 1.8050 = -\£0.14m \text{ NPV}$$

Approach 2:

Year	$m		$/£ rate		£m		20% discount factors		£ PV c/fs
0	−10	÷	1.8050	=	−5.540	×	1	=	−5.540
1	+ 5	÷	1.8952	=	+2.638	×	0.8333	=	+2.198
2	+ 6	÷	1.9900	=	+3.015	×	0.6944	=	+2.094
3	+ 4	÷	2.0895	=	+1.914	×	0.5787	=	+1.108
									£−0.14m NPV

The project cash flows

Whichever approach to the appraisal of overseas projects is used, both take as their starting point the project's net cash flows denominated in the host country's currency. It is here that some controversy is found.

The point of dispute is whether the project's net cash flows should be viewed from the standpoint of the project itself, or from the standpoint of the parent. In other words should the year-by-year net operating cash flows of the project be evaluated, or should the project's net cash flows *available to be remitted back to the parent be evaluated?*

Example 2

Rush plc is thinking of undertaking a capital investment in an overseas country whose currency is the dollar. The project's net cash flows are:

Year	$m
0	−10
1	+ 8
2	+ 4
3	+ 3.5

At the current $/£ spot rate of 2.50, the project will require an outlay of £4 million. The company intends to finance the whole of this out of retained earnings. Given the systematic risk involved, it is thought that 20% is a suitable required rate of return in dollar terms. The company follows a policy of paying out all of each year's net cash flow as a dividend.

The host country's laws permit foreign projects to remit back to their parents a maximum annual cash flow equal to 10% of the project's cost. Any surplus (or blocked) cash flows have to be placed on special deposit at an interest rate of 5%. All blocked funds can be remitted back to the parent at the end of the project's life. From the viewpoint of the project, it produces a positive NPV and so is acceptable:

Year	$m	×	20% discount		
0	−10	×	1	=	−10
1	+ 8	×	0.8333	=	+ 6.67
2	+ 4	×	0.6944	=	+ 2.78
3	+ 3.5	×	0.5787	=	+ 2.02
					$+ 1.47m NPV

+$1.47m ÷ 2.50 = +£0.588m NPV

However, from the viewpoint of the *parent* the project is undesirable, as it has a *negative* NPV:

Year	1	2	3
+ project cash flow	+8	+ 4	+ 3.5
Blocked funds		7	10.35
interest		+ 0.35	+ 0.52
Total cash flow	+8	+11.35	+ 14.37
Repatriated c/f	−1	−1	− 14.37
Blocked funds	+7	+10.35	−

Year	$m	×	20% disc.		
0	−10	×	1	=	−10
1	+ 1	×	0.8333	=	+ 0.83
2	+ 1	×	0.6944	=	+ 0.69
3	+14.37	×	0.5787	=	+ 8.32
					$− 0.16m NPV

−$0.16m ÷ 2.50 = −£64 000 NPV

With foreign country projects these two cash flows can often be significantly different because of host country restrictions on the repatriation of project net cash flows. Example 2 shows how crucial the difference might be.

Although there has been some controversy over this matter, it is difficult to understand why. It should appear obvious that, as it is the parent which is investing in the project, the project *must* be evaluated from the parent's viewpoint.

That is to say, what is important is the NPV of the project's cash flows that are available to be remitted back to the parent. The fact that the project used in Example 2 has a positive NPV when viewed in its own right must be irrelevant. However good an investment might appear to be, there is little point in undertaking that investment if the investor cannot enjoy its benefits. Thus Rush plc, acting on its shareholders' behalf, are not going to be interested in undertaking the project if it does not represent a positive NPV investment from their point of view.

Overseas currency finance

The conclusion reached above then raises an interesting point as far as financing is concerned. One of the fundamental principles of capital investment appraisal is that the financing decision can be kept separate from the investment decision. This then leads us always to exclude *financing* cash flows in calculating a project's NPV. (Notice that this approach even held in an APV analysis. The base case present value did not include any financing cash flows.)

The reason for this is *not* that the financing cash flows are being *ignored*, but that their present value is always *equal* to the amount of finance involved. Therefore the outlay on a project at 'Year 0' reflects the present value of the financing cash flows involved with the outlay. Example 3 simply illustrates this point, which has been made in earlier chapters, but which is of particular importance as far as overseas project appraisal is concerned.

Example 3

A company wishes to buy a machine for £1000. It has a net operating cash flow of £450 per year for each of the three years of its life and a zero scrap value. Given the systematic risk of the project, a 15% discount rate is thought suitable for evaluation purposes.

The machine is to be financed by a three-year £1000 term loan at 10% interest. Ignoring tax (which would just be a complication, but which would not change the conclusions drawn), the approach used is to calculate the project's NPV, without *apparently* taking either the loan interest payments or loan repayment into account:

$$(-1000 + 450A_{3-0.15} = +27.44 \text{ NPV})$$

However, the loan cash flows are *not* being ignored. They involve the following cash flows.

Year	£
0	
1	− 100
2	− 100
3	−1000

Applying the principle that the discount rate should always reflect the risk of the cash flow, the discount rate that would best reflect the risk of the loan cash flow would be the loan interest rate itself; and so:

Year	£		10% discount			
0						
1	− 100	×	0.9091	=	−	90.91
2	− 100	×	0.8264	=	−	82.64
3	−1000	×	0.7513	=	−	836.43
					PV	−1000^2

Therefore, in entering the project's outlay of £1000 in the NPV analysis we are implicitly entering the *present value* of the financing cash flows involved with the project.

However, problems can arise as far as this principle is concerned when part or all of a foreign project's finance is raised in the foreign country rather than – what has been implicitly assumed so far – via the export of sterling. This is because the foreign financing can affect the amount of the project's cash flows available to be remitted back to the parent. To illustrate this, let us return to Rush plc and the project dealt with in Example 2, but now involve some foreign currency financing. Example 4 gives the details.

Example 4

Rush plc now propose to finance the foreign project (referred to in Example 2) as a joint venture with investors in the host country. Foreign investors will buy $5 million of equity and Rush plc will export £2 million for the remaining 50% of the equity. The company plans to follow its normal policy of paying out each year's entire net cash flow as dividends.

Under these circumstances, from the *project's* viewpoint, its NPV remains at +£0.588 million. However, from the *parent's* viewpoint, the revised financing plans alter their analysis:

Year	1	2	3
+ project cash flow	+8	+4	+3.5
− foreign dividends	−4	−2	−1.75
+ blocked funds		+3	+4.15
+ interest		+0.15	+0.21
Total cash flow	+4	+5.15	+6.11
Repatriated c/f	−1	−1	−6.11
Blocked funds	+3	+4.15	−

Year	$m	×	20% discount		
0	−5²	×	1	=	− 5
1	+1	×	0.8333	=	+ 0.83
2	+1	×	0.6944	=	+ 0.69
3	+6.11	×	0.5787	=	+ 3.54
					$+ 0.06m

$$+\$0.06m \div 2.50 = +\pounds24\ 000\ NPV$$

As a result the foreign project which formerly produced a negative NPV now produces a positive NPV.

In Example 4 it can be seen that because of the change in the source of the finance (dollars rather than sterling for 50% of the financing requirement) the resulting impact on the cash flows available to the parent now makes this particular project worthwhile.

Example 4 contains a very important conclusion as far as foreign project appraisal is concerned: the cash flows of any finance raised in the host country *must* be included in the NPV evaluation of the project, if there are restrictions imposed on the repatriation of the project's cash flows back to the parent. If there are no restrictions on net cash flow remittance back to the parent, then the project should be appraised in the same way as any domestic project – excluding all the financing cash flows.

The project discount rate

The conclusion reached in the above section then leads on to the problem of identifying the correct discount rate to use (whether Approach 1 is applied and a dollar discount rate is required, or Approach 2 is applied and a sterling discount rate is needed). With the Rush plc example used in Examples 2 and 4 the problem was deliberately avoided by using all-equity financing. In such a case the discount rate simply has to reflect the systematic business risk of the project.

The all-equity financing used in the two Rush plc examples also helped avoid having to make a distinction between taxed and no-tax cases. Therefore the analysis to date applies equally to both situations. However, we know from previous chapters that as soon as we start to look seriously at the choice and identification of the discount rate, we *must* distinguish between taxed and no-tax situations. For the moment, we will proceed on the assumption that there are no taxes.

What would happen in the Rush plc example if the company had originally intended to finance the project by exporting £4 million, of which £2 million would be in the form of retained earnings and the other £2 million would be raised via a three-year term loan? In these circumstances, the sterling discount rate would have been the project's weighted average cost of capital.

However, what if Rush then decided to raise the three-year term loan in the US in dollars? In these circumstances, as far as the project appraisal from the parent's viewpoint is concerned, what would be evaluated would be the project's cash flows available for repatriation back to the parent. The point here is that these cash flows would be the ones that were available for equity only (the debt interest having been paid in dollars). As a result, the discount rate to apply to these cash flows would be one which reflected the project's business risk *plus* the financial risk that arises from the gearing – in other words the cost of equity capital. Example 5 illustrates the situation, making use of the Rush plc data.

Example 5

Rush plc *had* decided to use a 20% discount rate in dollar terms because they had identified the project's asset beta to be 1.6. In the US, the current return on government stocks is 12% and the return on the New York Stock Exchange index is 17%. Therefore, using the CAPM:

$$20\% = 12\% + (17\% - 12\%) \times 1.6$$

The company now propose to finance the $10 million project by exporting sterling to finance half the project and then raise a three-year $5 million term loan in the US for the remainder. The interest rate on the loan would be 12% as it would be viewed in the US as being virtually risk-free.

$$\text{Given the relationship: } \beta_{assets} = \beta_{equity} \times \frac{V_E}{V_0}$$

$$\text{then } \beta_{equity} = \beta_{assets} \times \frac{V_0}{V_E} = 1.6 \times \frac{2}{1} = 3.2$$

and the dollar return required on the project, from the *equity's* viewpoint, can be estimated via the CAPM:

$$28\% = 12\% + (17\% - 12\%) \times 3.2$$

The project appraisal analysis is now as follows:

Year	1	2	3
Project cash flows	+8	+ 4	+3.5
– interest payments	–0.6	– 0.6	–0.6
– loan			–5.0
+ blocked funds		+ 6.4	+9.12
+ interest		+ 0.32	+0.46
Total cash flow	+7.4	+10.12	+7.48
Repatriated c/f	–1	– 1	–7.48
Blocked funds	+6.4	+ 9.12	–

Year	$m	×	28% discount		
0	–5	×	1	=	– 5.
1	+1	×	0.7812	=	+ 0.78
2	+1	×	0.6103	=	+ 0.61
3	+7.48	×	0.4768	=	+ 3.57
					$– 0.04m

$$-\$0.04m \div 2.50 = -\pounds16\,000 \text{ NPV}$$

From the parent company's viewpoint, the project is *not* worthwhile.

Foreign projects in a taxed world

Just as with domestic projects, so it is that with overseas projects: the only really satisfactory approach to use in a taxed world is an APV analysis. But with such an analysis, because of the importance of having to look at the project's cash flows from the parent's viewpoint, a greater *decomposition* of the various elements is required than we have so far used with APV. As a result, the analysis becomes more complex. Example 6 illustrates an application.

Example 6

Visa plc is a highly profitable UK conglomerate. It is thinking of undertaking a capital investment in an overseas country whose currency is the dollar. The following information is available:

Project:	Cost: $12m. Life: three years Scrap value: $3.4m. Operating cash flow $8m year, pre-tax
Finance:	$4m three-year term loan at 15% £3m three-year term loan at 9.5% £1m retained earnings These financing arrangements fully utilize the project's debt capacity.
Risk:	The project is in an area that the company knows well as far as UK investment is concerned and an asset beta of 1.40 is usually applied.
Market data:	In the UK, the risk-free rate of return is 6% and the return on the FTSE market index is 16%.
Tax and other data:	The UK corporate tax rate is 35%, paid twelve months in arrears. The corporate tax rate of the host country is 40%, payable at each year-end without delay. In the host country, straight-line depreciation on cost, and interest charges, are both allowable expenses against tax. Overseas investors are allowed only to remit 50% of each year's pre-tax, but after interest, accounting profits back to the parent. All blocked funds earn 5% tax free in a special government account and can only be repatriated at the end of the project's life. The project is not expected to attract any UK tax on the remitted cash flow. The current spot exchange rate is $2.00 = £1. The dollar is expected to depreciate against sterling by 5% per year, for the foreseeable future.

Calculations:
The estimated FX rate in twelve months' time is: $2.00\,(1.05)^1 = 2.10$.
The £ base-case discount rate can be found from the CAPM:

$$6\% + (16\% - 6\%)\,1.40 = 20\%.$$

Using the IRPT, the dollar base-case discount rate can now be estimated:

$$\$ \text{ required return} = (0.05 \times 1.20) + 0.20 = 0.26 \text{ or } 26\%$$

The project can now be evaluated, as if it were all-equity financed:

	($m)
Annual operating cash flow	+8
less depreciation	−4
Annual accounting profit	+4

Tax charge: $4m × 0.40 = $1.6m/year
Remittable cash flow: $4m × 0.50 = $2m/year

Parent cash flow analysis:

Year		1	2 ($m)	3
Operating cash flow	:	+8	+ 8	+ 8
Tax charge	:	−1.6	− 1.6	− 1.6
Scrap value	:			+ 3.4
Tax charge on scrap	:			− 1.36
Blocked funds	:		+ 4.4	+ 9.02
Interest at 5%	:		+ 0.22	+ 0.45
Net cash flow	:	+6.4	+11.02	+ 17.91
Remittable cash flow	:	−2.0	− 2.0	− 17.91
Blocked cash flow	:	+4.4	+ 9.2	−

Base-case PV calculation:

Year	$m		26% discount[3]		
0	− 12	×	1	=	−12
1	+ 2	×	0.7936	=	+ 1.59
2	+ 2	×	0.6299	=	+ 1.26
3	+ 17.91	×	0.4999	=	+ 8.95
					$− 0.20m

−$0.2m ÷ 2.00 = −£0.1m base-case present value

Present value of the financing side-effects:

(i) *Tax relief on $ loan*

$4m × 0.15 = $0.6m/year interest
$0.6m × 0.40 = $0.24m/year tax relief

None of this tax relief can be remitted back to the parent until Year 3 and will be reinvested up to that time at 5% interest. Thus the PV of the additional Year 3 cash flow is:

$$\left.\begin{array}{l}\$0.24\text{m} \times S_{3\neg 0.05}(1.15)^{-3} \\ \$0.24\text{m} \times 3.1525 \times 0.6575\end{array}\right\} = +\$0.50\text{m} \div 2.00 = +£0.25\text{m}$$

(ii) *PV of increase in blocked funds:*

The debt interest charges will reduce the company's accounting profit, and so will reduce the level of remittable cash flows:

$0.6m/year interest = reduction in accounting profit
$0.6m × 0.50 = $0.3m/year increase in blocked funds

$$\left.\begin{array}{l}\$0.3\text{m} \times A_{3\neg 0.15} \\ \$0.3\text{m} \times 2.2832\end{array}\right\} = -\$0.68\text{m} \div 2.00 = -£0.34\text{m}$$

(iii) *PV of the increased terminal cash flow to parent*

The additional blocked funds are invested to yield 5% and are remitted at Year 3:

$$\left.\begin{array}{l}\$0.3\text{m} \times S_{3\neg 0.05}(1.15)^{-3} \\ \$0.3\text{m} \times 3.1525 \times 0.6575\end{array}\right\} = +\$0.62\text{m} \div 2.00 = +£0.31\text{m}$$

(iv) *Tax relief on £ loan*

£3m × 0.095 = £0.285m/year interest
£0.285m × 0.35 = £0.1m/year tax relief

$$\left.\begin{array}{l} \text{\pounds}0.1m \times A_{3-0.095}(1 + 0.095)^{-1} \\ 30.1m \times 2.5089 \times 0.9132 \end{array}\right\} = +\text{\pounds}0.23m$$

Adjusted present value:

	($m)
Base-case PV	: − 0.10
PV $ loan tax shield	: + 0.25
PV of increase in blocked funds	: − 0.34
PV of increase in terminal c/f	: + 0.31
PV £ loan tax shield	: + 0.23
APV	: £+ 0.35m

The project is worthwhile. From the parent company's viewpoint it is expected to have a positive APV of £350 000 approximately.

A simpler approach

A simpler approach to that of Example 6 which should still produce an analysis with an acceptable degree of accuracy, can be suggested. This would involve using the approach used in Example 5 to produce a modified base-case present value and then allowing for just the UK-based financing side-effects.

In this approach, the base-case cash flows would be the project cash flows remittable to the parent and the base-case discount rate would, effectively, be the cost of equity capital which reflected the combined business and financial risk of this cash flow. Example 7 takes the same Visa plc problem as used in Example 6, but applies this simpler analysis.

Example 7

Accounting profit:

		($m)
Annual operating cash flow	:	+8
less depreciation	:	−4
less interest	:	−0.6
Accounting profit		−3.4

Annual tax charge: $3.4m × 0.40 = $1.36m
Annual remittable cash flow: $3.4m × 0.50 = $1.7m

Project's remittable cash flows to parent:

Year	1	2	3
		($m)	
Operating cash flow	+8	+ 8	+ 8
Tax charge	−1.36	− 1.36	− 1.36
Interest payments	−0.6	− 0.6	− 0.6
Loan repayment			− 4.0
Scrap value			+ 3.4
Scrap tax charge			− 1.36
Blocked funds		+ 4.34	+ 8.9
Interest at 5%		+ 0.22	+ 0.44
Net cash flow	+6.04	+10.6	+13.42
Remittable cash flow	−1.7	− 1.7	−13.42
Blocked funds	+4.34	+ 8.9	−

Thus the revised 'base-case cash flow' is:

Year	($m)
0	− 8
1	+ 1.7
2	+ 1.7
3	+13.42

The 'base-case discount rate' can be calculated via the equity beta found from the following expression:

$$\beta_{assets} = \beta_{equity} \times \frac{V_E}{V_E + V_B(1 - T_C)} + \beta_{debt} \times \frac{V_B(1 - T_C)}{V_E + V_B(1 - T_C)}$$

Assuming (for convenience) that the debt beta is zero, then:

$$\beta_{equity} = \beta_{assets} \times \frac{V_E + V_B(1 - T_C)}{V_E}$$

where β_{assets} = 1.40 (given)
V_E = £4m (exported £: loan plus retained earnings)
V_B = £2m (overseas currency loan)
T_C = overseas corporate tax rate

$$\beta_{equity} = 1.40 \times \frac{4 + 2(1 - 0.40)}{4} = 1.82$$

and using the CAPM, a £ discount rate can be generated:

$$6\% + (16\% - 6\%) \times 1.82 = 24.2\%$$

Using the IRPT, a $ discount rate can then be calculated:

$$(0.05 \times 1.242) + 0.242 = 0.304 \text{ or } 30.4\%$$

'Base-case present value':

Year	$m		30.4% disc		
0	− 8	×	1	=	−8
1	+ 1.7	×	0.7669	=	+1.30
2	+ 1.7	×	0.5881	=	+1.00
3	+13.42	×	0.4510	=	+6.05
					$+0.35m ÷ 2.00
				=	£+0.17m

Present value of the financing side-effects:

£ loan tax shield:

£3m × 0.095 = £0.285m/year interest
£0.285m × 0.35 = £0.1m/year tax relief

$$\left. \begin{array}{l} £0.1m \times A_{3\text{--}0.095}(1 + 0.095)^{-1} \\ £0.1m \times 2.5089 \times 0.9132 \end{array} \right\} = +£0.23m$$

Adjusted present value:

	($m)
Base-case present value	+0.17
PV of £ loan tax shield	+0.23
	£+0.40m

This analysis also indicates acceptance: the project is expected to have a positive APV of £400 000.

Translation risk

Translation risk can be defined as the risk a company is exposed to through movements in FX rates when it holds medium- to long-term assets and liabilities in an overseas currency. The concept specifically refers to the fact that, with such assets and liabilities, at each year-end their values have to be *translated* into sterling terms for inclusion in the parent company's balance sheet. Example 8 illustrates the problems that might arise.

Example 8

A UK company undertakes a project in the US, costing $10 million. It is financed through the export of sterling via a £5 million loan. The $/£ exchange rate is 2.00.
The parent company's opening balance sheet will show:

Balance sheet

£ Loan: £5m	$ Assets: £5m

Suppose twelve months go by and the $/£ exchange rate has now moved to 3.00. The company's balance sheet now shows up an FX loss:[4]

Balance sheet

£ Loan: £5m less FX loss: (£1.67m)	$ Assets: £3.33m
£3.33m	

The reason for the loss is that the $10 million worth of assets are now only worth £3.33 million in sterling terms because the dollar has depreciated against sterling.[5]

Overcoming the firm's exposure to translation risk is quite simple – if it is possible. The solution is to finance the project through a *dollar loan* rather than a *sterling loan*. In such circumstances, the company is protected against FX risk through the *matching* principle: the foreign currency asset is matched with a foreign currency liability. Therefore a fall in the value of one – through a movement in the FX rate – will be countered (or matched) through a corresponding fall in the other. Example 9 illustrates the situation.

Example 9

Using the data from Example 8, if the UK company financed the project with a $10 million loan, then the opening balance sheet would show:

Balance sheet

$ Loan: £5m	$ Assets: £5m

Twelve months later when the FX rate has moved to $3.00, the balance sheet now becomes:

Balance sheet

$ Loan: £3.33m	$ Assets: £3.33m

> Although the sterling value of the assets has declined, this decline has been matched by the sterling worth of the dollar loan. As a result there is no net FX loss.

The difficulty with the solution to the problem of translation risk as advocated in Example 9 is that such a financing method is usually unavailable or inadvisable. For example, many governments insist that a minimum proportion of a project's outlay is financed directly by the parent company. Even where such a requirement is not legally stipulated, it is probably not a very good idea, from a public relations viewpoint, for the parent not to put in any of its *own* money into the project.

Indeed, there is a third reason why 100% foreign currency financing might not be possible. Quite simply the host country's capital market may not be sufficiently developed to provide the financing levels required.

Given, therefore, that it is unrealistic to suppose that 100% foreign currency financing is possible, the standard financing advice for overseas projects is:

1. the project's *property fixed assets*: finance with a foreign currency loan;
2. the project's *non-property fixed assets*: finance via the export of sterling;
3. the project's *working capital requirements*: finance with a foreign currency loan.

This advice means that the firm will be protected from FX risk as far as property fixed assets and working capital are concerned, through the matching principle. But what about the non-property fixed assets?

It is with the non-property fixed assets that the Law of One Price (referred to in Chapter 23) comes to the rescue. The idea here is that non-property fixed assets (such as industrial machinery) obey, to some extent, the workings of the Law of One Price because they are capable of being traded internationally. Neither property fixed assets nor working capital are capable of being physically traded internationally, and so do not follow the law and need to be protected against FX risk through matching.

We will use what appears to be a highly specific example to illustrate how the law of one price can give protection against FX risk. However, the example is only as specific as it appears to ease the explanation. It will *tend* to hold generally, whatever the circumstances, given that the assets in question can be traded internationally (and that the transportation costs do not form too significant an element in its total value). Example 10 gives the details.

Example 10

Suppose that the $10 million US project referred to in Example 8 was composed of the following elements:

Property:	$2m
Machinery:	$7m
Working Capital:	$1m

The suggested financing scheme would be a $3 million loan and $7 million worth of exported sterling.

The fall in the $/£ FX rate from 2.00 to 3.00 from one year-end to the next will cause the sterling worth of the US property and working capital to decline, but this will be matched by a corresponding decline in the sterling worth of the dollar loan. But in these circumstances what happens as far as the US machinery is concerned?

Support (for the purpose of easing the explanation) that the machinery in question is manufactured in the UK and is normally sold for £3.5 million. At an opening $/£ FX rate of 2.00, this is why it cost $7 million to purchase it for the US project.

After an elapse of twelve months, the machinery still costs £3.5 million but, because the dollar has depreciated against sterling, the US cost of the machinery now becomes: £3.5m × 3.00 = $10.5m. (What is seen here is the working through of the Law of One Price: the sterling price of a good × $/£ FX rate = dollar price of the good.)

Therefore (ignoring the problem of depreciation which is just a complication and does not change the basis of the argument), we would be justified in valuing the machinery of our US project at the end of the first year at $10.5 million rather than $7 million on a *replacement cost* basis. (And the company's UK auditors are likely to accept such an argument.)

As a result the company's balance sheets would appear as follows:

Opening balance sheet: $/£ = 2.00

$ loan	:	£1.5m	$2m property	:	£1m
£ funding	:	£3.5m	$7m machinery	:	£3.5m
		£5.0m	$1m work. capt.	:	£0.5m
					£5.0m

Balance sheet at Year 1: $/£ = 3.00

$ loan	:	£1m	$2m property	:	£0.67m
£ funding	:	£3.5m	$7m machinery	:	£3.5m
		£4.5m	$1m work. capt.	:	£0.33m
					£4.5m

The company has managed to hedge its exposure to FX translation risk through a combination of the matching principle and the operation of the Law of One Price.

It is not suggested that the Law of One Price will work as *perfectly* in practice as is the case in Example 10. But, given that the dollar depreciates against sterling and given that industrial machinery is traded internationally, then there will be a definite tendency for the dollar worth of the machine to rise as the value of the dollar declines. Thus, at the very least, companies can expect to get *some* protection (if not perfect protection) against FX risk through the workings of the law.

In summary therefore, the general principle behind financing foreign projects is to raise as much finance as possible in the overseas currency so as to get the maximum protection from translation risk through matching. Where 100% foreign currency financing is not possible, then the company should try to ensure that at least those assets which are not going to be responsive to the operation of the Law of One Price are financed in the overseas currency.

However, we should remind you that it is debatable whether or not translation represents a real risk. It really all depends on the significance placed on the numbers used in financial statements.

Economic risk

The previous discussion on translation risk also touches upon another FX risk of foreign investments which could be called *economic* risk. This is the risk of *unexpected* changes in FX rates.

For example, a proper investment appraisal evaluation might have been undertaken which had indicated that a project would bring about an increase in parent shareholders' wealth. The project then performs perfectly to plan but, because of unexpected and adverse FX movements, in hindsight, it leads to a reduction in parent company shareholders' wealth.

The possible presence of this risk causes real difficulties. The first question it raises is whether the risk is systematic or unsystematic. The second is, if it is systematic, how should it be taken into account in the appraisal process? There is, of course, an even more fundamental question here: does this type of risk exist at all? Example 11 illustrates what is behind this latter question.

Example 11

A US project costs $1 million. It has a life of three years and results in an annual production output of 1000 units. The net after-tax cash flow resulting from the production is expected to be $0.5 million in *current* terms. This cash amount is expected to increase in line with the average US inflation rate which is expected to remain constant at 8% per year.

The project will be entirely financed with sterling and there are no restrictions on net cash flow remittance to the UK parent. A similar-risk UK project would be expected to produce a minimum annual return of 16%.

The current $/£ spot exchange rate is 1.9000 and UK general inflation rate is expected to remain constant at 5% per year.

On the basis of this information, the dollar discount rate can be estimated via the IRPT. First though, the $/£ FX rate of change has to be estimated. This can be done through the PPPT:

$$\frac{0.08 - 0.05}{1.05} = +0.0286$$

and so, using the IRPT:

$$\$ \text{ discount rate} = (0.0286 \times 1.16) + 0.16 = 0.193 \text{ or } 19.3\%$$

The project can now be evaluated:

Year	$m		19.3% discount		
0	−1.0	×	1	=	−1.00
1	+0.54	×	0.8382	=	+0.453
2	+0.583	×	0.7026	=	+0.410
3	+0.630	×	0.5889	=	+0.371
					$+0.234m NPV

$$\$+ 0.234m \div 1.90 = £+0.123m \text{ NPV}$$

The project is worthwhile and should be accepted.

If the firm then undertakes the project, the $/£ FX rates that they are expecting over the next three years can be found from the PPPT:

Spot:	1.9000 (given)
Year 1:	1.9000 (1 + 0.0286) = 1.9543
Year 2:	1.9543 (1 + 0.0286) = 2.0102
Year 3:	2.0102 (1 + 0.0286) = 2.0677

Therefore, they are expecting the following sterling cash flow from the project:

Year	$m	÷	$/£	=	£m
0	−1	÷	1.9000	=	−0.526
1	+0.54	÷	1.9543	=	+0.276
2	+0.583	÷	2.0102	=	+0.290
3	+0.630	÷	2.0677	=	+0.305

(And this cash flow will, of course, have a + NPV of £123 000 when discounted at 16% (ignoring rounding errors).)

However, suppose that US inflation turns out to be higher than expected, say 12% rather than 8%. It means that the future exchange rates will also differ.

$$\text{Rate of change in \$:} \quad \frac{0.12 - 0.05}{1.05} = +0.067$$

Year 1:	1.9000 (1 + 0.067) = 2.0273
Year 2:	2.0273 (1 + 0.067) = 2.1631
Year 3:	2.1631 (1 + 0.067) = 2.3081

Will the UK parent suffer as a result of this unexpected, adverse movement in the $/£ FX rates? They should not, if the project performs as expected and produces 1000 units per year; the reason being that the *increased* US inflation rate *should* result in *increased* dollar cash flows from the project which will now inflate up at 12% rather than 8%:

Year	$m	÷	$/£	=	£m
0	−1	÷	1.9000	=	−0.526
1	+0.56	÷	2.0273	=	+0.276
2	+0.627	÷	2.1631	=	+0.290
3	+0.702	÷	2.3081	=	+0.304

Therefore the parent will receive exactly the same sterling cash flow, whose NPV will remain at +£123 000.

The problem with Example 11 is that life does not work quite so perfectly. Remember, although the IRPT tends to work well, the PPPT tends to be more approximate because of the imperfections in the workings of the Law of One Price. Therefore the FX rates may not turn out as predicted at a 12% inflation level and, indeed, the project's net after-tax cash flow may not respond, in the perfect way illustrated, to the rise in US inflation. Thus it is fairly safe to conclude that, in the real world, the risk of unexpected FX movements *does* exist for firms in investing overseas.

This then brings us back to the first question posed: is this risk wholly systematic or unsystematic or partly both? The answer is highly uncertain, but probably some of it is capable of being diversified away through international diversification.

The uncertainty arises because economists cannot agree whether individual country capital markets are *segmented* (and so largely independent of each other) or *integrated*. But, despite this, there is a relatively simple solution (although this is not always possible to apply and it is far from a perfect answer). That solution is to eliminate the risk of unexpected FX rate movements by using the forward markets to sell forward a project's expected foreign currency net cash flow.

This solution may not be possible to apply in practice because forward markets only extend substantial periods of time forward in the world's major currencies. If the project were in Egypt, for example, we would have difficulties trying to apply this solution. Even when suitably extended forward markets do exist (such as with $/£), forward contracts are for *certain* amounts of currency, while the project's cash flow is only *expected*. Thus a perfect hedge against the FX risk is unlikely to be achieved.

Alternatives to the forward sale of currencies also exist through the matching principle. For example an overseas currency loan extending over the life of the project could be raised. This loan could be converted immediately into sterling and capital and interest could be repaid out of the project's net cash flow. Again, this would not give a perfect hedge, but it would provide a significant degree of protection. A further alternative would be to use the overseas project's net cash flow to purchase exportable goods from the host country; thereby converting the project's FX risk-exposed cash flow into a non-exposed (or, less exposed) goods flow.

Country/political risk

The final risk attached to foreign projects is country or political risk. There is an academic debate as to whether or not there is a difference between country risk and political risk but we will treat them as though they are one and the same. This is the risk that, once a project has been undertaken, something of a political or serious economic nature will happen to inhibit the ability of the company to remit the cash flows expected from the project. This may be because of war or revolution or it may simply be that the host government adversely changes the 'rules of the game' for either political or economic reasons. Whilst there is evidence that there is little systematic, quantitative analysis by companies of this type of risk, simply because it is so unpredictable, it is fair to say that it is generally possible to judge if a partner country is high or low risk. We hesitate to mention high-risk countries on the grounds that this could be taken as an insult but it is safe to suggest that countries such as the USA, Canada, Australia and our European partners would generally be seen as low risk, along with many other politically stable countries. Demirag and Goddard (page 273) provide details of a political risk ranking exercise carried out by *Euromoney* in 1992 and also discuss a number of other ranking systems. Whilst these rankings are better than nothing, they are bound to remain more or less subjective.

It is unusual for governments to seize the assets of overseas companies, if only because it is likely to be counterproductive in the longer term. Multinational companies exercise considerable power in terms of the control of both production and markets. There are also international bodies that might be expected to exert pressure on countries that act in an unreasonable way. Thus whilst assets might be lost or destroyed as the result of war or expropriation, the most likely problems concern changes to the rules on the transfer of cash out of the host country.

As far as the risks of restrictions being imposed unexpectedly on net cash flow repatriation, the simple rule is to try and minimize its possible impact by using as many different remittance channels as are available. Thus a project's net cash flows may be remitted back to the parent in the form of dividend payments or interest payments. If the overseas project undertakes any process for which the parent has royalty rights, then royalty payments may be another possible channel.

Although an overseas project's lower and middle management are drawn from the host country itself, the top management are normally seconded from the parent. The parent might then charge the foreign project for the services of these top management, effectively using the management charge as a further means of remitting back the project's net cash flow.

Finally, if there is any transfer of goods between the parent and the overseas project, then the transfer pricing mechanism can be employed as yet another channel for remitting back the project's net cash flows. This is covered in the next section.

Obviously, national governments are aware of all these different possible channels and so if they *really* want to restrict the repatriation of a project's net cash flows to an overseas parent, then they are perfectly capable of doing so. However, sometimes a government might want to be *seen* to be doing something about restricting foreign project cash flows, without wishing to restrict them absolutely. Thus they might enforce restrictions on, for example, dividends as this is seen as a politically sensitive area linked directly to profits. At the same time, however, such things as interest and royalty payments may be seen as much more legitimate business expenses and so remain unrestricted.

As far as the other elements of country risk are concerned there are two main possible courses of action that can be taken to reduce them. The first would be to tie-in host country investors or even the host government, through such things as joint ventures. This sort of arrangement is likely to discourage any host government from taking such adverse action against the project that the overseas parent pulls out, if this would then cause the project to fail. Such action would not only hurt the overseas parent, but would also hurt host country investors.

The second course of action is insurance. It is possible to insure an overseas project against the most extreme forms of country risk such as expropriation. In such circumstances, the cost of the insurance should be included as part of the overall cost of undertaking the project in any financial appraisal.

Management charges and transfer pricing

Management charges and transfer prices are both normal parts of business activity that can be manipulated to circumvent restrictions on the tranfer of funds through dividends.

Management charges are simply a way of charging a division or a subsidiary company for services provided by other parts of the company. This might include the cost of computer facilities, a share of world-wide marketing costs or part of the central managment costs including all kinds of head office costs. Generally speaking these might be expected to reflect the real cost of the services being provided to the subsidiary or division but this is not always the case even when there is no international dimension. Increasing the charge represents one way of transferring profit and (possibly) cash from one country to another. However, it is likely that the authorities of the host country will look closely at really significant management charges if they are serious about controlling overseas remittances.

Transfer prices pose more of a problem in terms of government control. Goods and services will often pass from one group company or division to another. There are a number of ways of deciding on the prices to be charged for transfer (transfer prices) and in general these are designed to achieve overall corporate objectives, in particular (we assume) maximization of shareholder wealth. Thus good transfer prices will encourage divisional and subsidiary managers to act in the best interests of the company. It is beyond the scope of this book to go into the detail of the setting of transfer prices and the interested reader can refer to any good management accounting text such as Drury for an analysis of this. However, the manipulation of transfer prices offers a relatively simple way of moving profit from one country to another. Let us assume that we have a company based in the UK – St George plc, with subsidiary companies in Urbanaland, a country with high taxes and restrictions on dividend payments, and also Alpland, a very stable country with very low corporate taxes and no retriction on dividend payments. St George buys goods from and sell goods to its subsidiary in Urbanaland. It also sells finished goods to a retailing subsidiary in Alpland. By setting the price for goods sold to Urbanaland artificially high and that for goods bought from Urbanaland artificially low, St George can move its profits out of Urbanaland and into the UK. Furthermore, by setting the transfer price for goods sold from the UK to Alpland artificially low, the profits can be moved again to Alpland with its advantageous tax regime. This type of manipulation has long been recognized and some states in the USA have sought to put a stop to it by passing laws that specify that tax will be paid on the higher of the profit declared in the state or the world-wide profit of the company multiplied by the proportion of world-wide turnover accounted for by the state. The fact that such a crude device is seen as being justifiable is an indication of the difficulties outside bodies might have in assessing the appropriateness or otherwise of the transfer prices being used. One of the most notorious cases of manipulation of transfer prices involved the sale of the drugs librium and valium in the late 1960s and early 1970s by the Swiss company Hoffman-La Roche to its UK subsidiary at vastly inflated prices at a time when taxation was high in the UK and low in Switzerland.

Summary

This chapter has provided a fairly brief overview of a highly complex area which contains many still unresolved difficulties. The main points covered were as follows:

- As far as foreign project appraisal is concerned, there are two equivalent approaches: the project's overseas currency cash flows can be converted to sterling cash flows and a sterling discount rate applied; alternatively, the project's overseas currency cash flows can be discounted at the overseas currency discount rate to produce an NPV. This can then be converted at spot into a sterling NPV.

- A major difference between domestic and foreign project evaluation arises when the latter suffers from cash flow remittance restrictions. In such circumstances the project must be evaluated from the viewpoint of the cash flows that are available to be remitted back to the parent. In particular, this means including in the project's cash flows any foreign currency financing cash flows.

- Once taxation is brought into consideration, then an APV analysis becomes appropriate. However, such an approach can be complex and a simplified approach can be utilized by modifying APV.

- Foreign project financing can play a significant role in reducing the parent's exposure to translation risk. Here, the standard advice is to finance the project requirement for property and working capital in the overseas currency, while the non-property fixed assets can be financed via the export of sterling.

- Economic and country/political risk were examined and ways by which exposure to both may be reduced were discussed.

- Finally management charges and transfer prices were considered as a way of moving profits and cash around on an international basis.

Notes

1.   The rounding error is just two pence.

2.   Notice, the parent only has to contribute $5 million to the project, in terms of sterling.

3.   These discount factors are not included in the tables supplied and have been calculated separately.

4.   For simplicity, these examples ignore depreciation. The conclusions of the analysis remain unchanged in a more realistic setting.

5.   The dollar *could* equally have appreciated, and an FX gain would have been made.

Further reading

1.   International aspects of investment appraisal and financing decisions are complex and form the subject matter of specialist books. The three books referred to in Chapters 23 and 24 – Buckley (1992), Eiteman, Stonehill and Moffet (1992) and I. Demirag and S. Goddard *Financial Management for International Business*, McGraw Hill 1994 – provide good coverage.

2.   Good introductory articles on the subject matter include: A.C. Shapiro, 'Capital Budgeting for the Multinational Corporation', *Financial Management*, Spring 1978, and, by the same author, 'International Capital Budgeting', *Midland Corporate Finance Journal*, Spring 1983; A. Buckley, 'Evaluating Overseas Projects', *Accountancy*, May 1987; J.B. Holland, 'Overseas Capital Investment', in Firth and Keane (eds), *Issues in Finance*, Philip Allen 1986; and M. Wilson, 'Capital Budgeting for Foreign Direct Investment', *Managerial Finance*, Summer 1990.

3.   On the use of APV in an international context, see: D.R. Lessard, 'Evaluating Foreign Projects – an Adjusted Present Value Approach', in D. Lessard (ed.), *International Financial Management*, Warren, Gorham and Lamont 1979.

4.   On the financing problem see: M.R. Eaher, 'Denomination Decision for Multinational Transactions', *Financial Management*, Autumn 1980 and A. Buckley, 'Financing Overseas Subsidiaries', *Accountancy*, August 1987.

5.   Other articles of interest include: R.C. Hechman, 'Foreign Exchange Exposure: Accounting Measures and Economic Reality', *Journal of Cash Management*, February–March 1983; S.H. Goodman, 'Foreign Exchange Rate Forecasting Techniques', *Journal of Finance*, May 1979; and D.J. Oblack and

R.J. Helm, 'Survey and Analysis of Capital Budgeting Methods Used by Multinationals', *Financial Management*, Winter 1980.

Quickie questions

1. What is the PPT formula?
2. If a project requires a 25% return in the UK and the $/£ exchange rate is: 1.9050 spot and 1.8420 twelve months forward, what is the project's dollar required return?
3. The current $/£ spot rate is 1.9280. The dollar is expected to appreciate against sterling by 7% per year. Estimate the $/£ FX rate in three years' time.
4. The $/£ spot rate is 1.7940, the two-month forward rate is at 1.50 cent premium. What is the forward rate?
5. What are the two basic approaches by which a UK company can evaluate a US project?
6. Why should foreign financing flows be included in an overseas project's appraisal?
7. What is the standard advice for financing overseas projects?
8. What possible channels might a company use to remit back a foreign project's cash flows?
9. What is country risk?
10. What is economic risk?

Problems

1. Blue Grass Distillery Inc., a North Carolina based manufacturer of rye whiskey, is evaluating its position with respect to the UK market.

   The EU has just announced a five-year 25% common external tariff on rye whiskey, to protect Scottish and Irish distillers. Blue Grass believes that this tariff will reduce the profits on its exports to the UK to negligible levels. The company is therefore considering whether to establish a subsidiary in a Welsh Development Area in order to avoid the tariff, or to pull out of the UK market completely.

   If the company immediately stops exporting to the UK market some production could be diverted to the non-EU European market, yielding an annual after-tax net cash flow of $1.5 million for the foreseeable future. The company is currently working at full capacity and has no plans to expand production in the USA.

   The proposed UK subsidiary would cost £15 million to establish, 20% of which would be met by a grant from the EU. A suitable factory has already been located in South Wales and production could commence quickly. The company's marketing department forecast possible sales of 20 000 gallons in the first year and 50 000 gallons a year for the following four years. Blue Grass evaluate all projects on the basis of a five-year planning horizon.

   The rye whiskey would be sold to off-licences at a price of £300 per gallon in the first year. Subsequently this price is expected to rise in line with the rate of UK inflation. The distilling and bottling costs in the UK have been estimated at £140 per gallon plus £2 million of fixed costs in the first year. These too are expected to rise in line with inflation. In addition a royalty of $50 per gallon will be charged by Blue Grass. The realizable value of the factory at the end of five years is expected to be £10 million.

It is the company policy of Blue Grass Distillery to remit to the USA all possible funds from its foreign subsidiaries at the end of each year. Corporate taxes, payable one year in arrears, are levied at a rate of 30% in the USA and 35% in the UK. A bilateral tax agreement exists between the two countries.

A 25% writing-down allowance is available on the whole of the £15 million outlay.

Exchange rates ($/£):	Spot	$1.5500
	12 mths. fwd	$1.4725

Sterling is expected to depreciate against the dollar by 5% per year.

UK inflation rate forecasts for the next five years have been published by the UK Treasury, as follows:

Year	RPI increase (%)
1	4
2	4
3	3
4	3
5	4
6	5

Return on UK government stock (5-year maturity): 8% per annum.
UK market return: 13%
Standard deviation of returns on the UK market portfolio: 0.48
Standard deviation of returns on the proposed investment: 0.65
Correlation coefficient of returns between the UK market portfolio and the proposed investment: +0.885

Required:
(a) Evaluate the project using NPV and advise management on the proposal to set up a UK subsidiary.
(b) How would you advise the management of Blue Grass Distilleries Inc. about the financing of the UK subsidiary?

2. Polycalc plc is an internationally diversified company. It is presently considering undertaking a capital investment in Australia to manufacture agricultural fertilizers. The project would require immediate capital expenditure of A$15 million plus A$5 million of working capital which would be recovered at the end of the project's four-year life. It is estimated that an annual revenue of A$18 million would be generated by the project, with annual operating costs of A$5 million. Straight-line depreciation over the life of the project is an allowable expense against company tax in Australia which is charged at a rate of 50%, payable at each year-end without delay. The project can be assumed to have a zero scrap value.

Polycalc plans to finance the project with a £5 million four-year loan at 10% from the Euro-sterling market, plus £5 million of retained earnings. The proposed financing scheme reflects the belief that the project would have a debt capacity of two-thirds of *capital* cost. Issue costs on the Euro debt will be $2\frac{1}{2}$% and are tax deductible.

In the UK the fertilizer industry has an equity beta of 1.40 and an average debt:equity gearing ratio of 1:4. Debt capital can be assumed to be virtually risk-free. The current return on UK government stock is 7.1% and the market return is 17.85%.

Corporate tax in the UK is at 35% and can be assumed to be payable at each year-end without delay. Because of a double-taxation agreement, Polycalc will not have to pay any UK tax on the project. The company is expected to have a substantial UK tax liability from its other operations for the foreseeable future.

The current A$/£ spot rate is 2.0000 and the A$ is expected to depreciate against the £ at an annual rate of 10%.

Required:
(a) Using the adjusted present value technique, advise the management of Polycalc on the project's desirability.
(b) Comment briefly on the company's intended financing plans for the Australian project. Suggest, with reasons, a more sensible alternative.

3. Scouse plc is a successful manufacturing company based in the north of England. As a result of the changing relationship between the EU and Eastern European countries an opportunity has arisen to invest in Glumrovia. The directors of Scouse plc have decided that because of the risky nature of investments in this part of the world, they will require a return of at least 20% after tax on the project.

The government of Glumrovia is prepared to grant Scouse plc a five-year licence to operate and market research suggests that cash flows from the project will be as follows (in 000s of Glumrovian $):

Year	1	2	3	4	5
	250	400	500	600	700

However much of the increase is because of expected rates of inflation and the G$/sterling exchange rate is expected to be:

Year	1	2	3	4	5
	4	5	6	7	8

as compared with the current rate of 3G$ to the £1.

The project will cost G$600 000 to set up but the present Glumrovian government will pay G$600 000 to Scouse plc for the business (not including working capital) at the end of the five-year period. They will also lend Scouse plc the G$250 000 required for working capital at the advantageous rate of 6% to be repaid at the end of the five-year period. Scouse plc will pay Glumrovian tax on profits after interest at the rate of 20% at the end of each year at which time the balance of profits can be remitted to the UK. There is a tax arrangement between the governments of Glumrovia and the UK so that any Glumrovian tax paid can be offset against UK tax. UK tax is payable at the rate of 30% and you should assume that it is payable at the time that the cash is remitted to the UK. As yet there is no stock exchange in Glumrovia as the Christian Democrats who replaced the Communist regime that ran the country from 1948 to 1993 have not had time to get around to all of the economic reforms required. An article in the *Guardian* dated 28 February 1998 reveals that the people of Glumrovia are disappointed with the pace of reform and that the elections in 2000 might well see a big upswing in Communist influence.

Assume all cash flows take place at the end of periods.

(a) Prepare a report for the management of Scouse plc that analyses the data available and makes argued recommendations as to whether or not the project should be taken on.
(b) Discuss the possible problems that might confront a company making the type of decision facing Scouse plc.

Tables

Compounding and discounting tables

Table A   Compound interest factor $(1 + i)^N$

i N	0.04	0.06	0.08	0.10	0.12	0.14	0.16	0.18	0.20
1	1.0400	1.0600	1.0800	1.1000	1.1200	1.1400	1.1600	1.1800	1.2000
2	1.0816	1.1236	1.1664	1.2100	1.2544	1.2996	1.3456	1.3924	1.4400
3	1.1249	1.1910	1.2597	1.3310	1.4049	1.4815	1.5609	1.6430	1.7280
4	1.1699	1.2625	1.3605	1.4641	1.5735	1.6890	1.8106	1.9338	2.0736
5	1.2167	1.3382	1.4693	1.6105	1.7623	1.9254	2.1003	2.2878	2.4883
6	1.2653	1.4185	1.5869	1.7716	1.9738	2.1950	2.4364	2.6996	2.9860
7	1.3159	1.5036	1.7138	1.9487	2.2107	2.5023	2.8262	3.1855	3.5832
8	1.3686	1.5939	1.8509	2.1436	2.4760	2.8526	3.2784	3.7589	4.2998
9	1.4233	1.6895	1.9990	2.3580	2.7731	3.2519	3.8030	4.4335	5.1598
10	1.4802	1.7909	2.1589	2.5937	3.1058	3.7072	4.4114	5.2338	6.1917
11	1.5395	1.8983	2.3316	2.8531	3.4785	4.2262	5.1173	6.1759	7.4301
12	1.6010	2.0122	2.5182	3.1384	3.8960	4.8179	5.9360	7.2876	8.9161
13	1.6651	2.1329	2.7196	3.4523	4.3635	5.4924	6.8858	8.5994	10.6993
14	1.7317	2.2609	2.9372	3.7975	4.8871	6.2613	7.9875	10.1472	12.8392
15	1.8009	2.3966	3.1722	4.1773	5.4736	7.1379	9.2655	11.9737	15.4070

Table B   Present value factor $(1 + i)^{-N}$

i N	0.04	0.06	0.08	0.10	0.12	0.14	0.16	0.18	0.20
1	0.9615	0.9434	0.9259	0.9091	0.8929	0.8772	0.8621	0.8475	0.8333
2	0.9246	0.8900	0.8573	0.8264	0.7972	0.7695	0.7432	0.7182	0.6944
3	0.8890	0.8396	0.7938	0.7513	0.7118	0.6750	0.6407	0.6086	0.5787
4	0.8548	0.7921	0.7350	0.6830	0.6355	0.5921	0.5523	0.5158	0.4823
5	0.8219	0.7473	0.6806	0.6209	0.5674	0.5194	0.4761	0.4371	0.4019
6	0.7903	0.7050	0.6302	0.5645	0.5066	0.4556	0.4014	0.3704	0.3349
7	0.7599	0.6651	0.5835	0.5132	0.4532	0.3996	0.3538	0.3139	0.2791
8	0.7307	0.6274	0.5403	0.4665	0.4039	0.3506	0.3050	0.2660	0.2326
9	0.7026	0.5919	0.5002	0.4241	0.3606	0.3075	0.2630	0.2255	0.1938
10	0.6756	0.5584	0.4632	0.3855	0.3220	0.2697	0.2267	0.1911	0.1615
11	0.6496	0.5268	0.4289	0.3505	0.2875	0.2366	0.1954	0.1619	0.1346
12	0.6246	0.4970	0.3971	0.3186	0.2567	0.2076	0.1685	0.1372	0.1122
13	0.6006	0.4686	0.3677	0.2897	0.2292	0.1821	0.1452	0.1163	0.0935
14	0.5775	0.4423	0.3405	0.2633	0.2046	0.1597	0.1252	0.0985	0.0779
15	0.5553	0.4173	0.3152	0.2394	0.1827	0.1401	0.1079	0.0835	0.0649

Table C   Present value of an annuity $A_{N\neg i}$

i / N	0.04	0.06	0.08	0.10	0.12	0.14	0.16	0.18	0.20
1	0.9615	0.9434	0.9259	0.9091	0.8929	0.8772	0.8621	0.8475	0.8333
2	1.8861	1.8334	1.7833	1.7355	1.6901	1.6467	1.6052	1.5656	1.5278
3	2.7751	2.6730	2.5771	2.4869	2.4018	2.3216	2.2459	2.1743	2.1065
4	3.6299	3.,4651	3.3121	3.1699	3.0373	2.9137	2.7982	2.6901	2.5887
5	4.4518	4.2124	3.9927	3.7908	3.6048	3.4331	3.2743	3.1272	2.9906
6	5.2421	4.9173	4.6229	4.3553	4.1114	3.8887	3.6847	3.4976	3.3255
7	6.0021	5.5824	5.2064	4.8684	4.5638	4.2883	4.0386	3.8115	3.6046
8	6.7327	6.2098	5.7466	5.3349	4.9676	4.6389	4.3436	4.0776	3.8372
9	7.4353	6.8017	6.2469	5.7590	5.3282	4.9464	4.6065	4.3030	4.0310
10	8.1109	7.3601	6.7101	6.1446	5.6502	5.2161	4.8332	4.4941	4.1925
11	8.7605	7.8869	7.1390	6.4951	5.9377	5.4527	5.0286	4.6560	4.3271
12	9.3851	8.3838	7.5361	6.8137	6.1944	5.6603	5.1971	4.7932	4.4392
13	9.9856	8.8527	7.9038	7.1034	6.4235	5.8424	5.3423	4.9095	4.5327
14	10.5631	9.2950	8.2442	7.3667	6.6282	6.0021	5.4675	5.0081	4.6106
15	11.1184	9.7122	8.5595	7.6061	6.8109	6.1422	5.5755	5.0916	4.6755

Table D   Terminal value of an annuity $S_{N\neg i}$

i / N	0.04	0.06	0.08	0.10	0.12	0.14	0.16	0.18	0.20
1	1.0000	1.0000	1.0000	1.0000	1.0000	1.0000	1.0000	1.0000	1.0000
2	2.0400	2.0600	2.0800	2.1000	2.1200	2.1400	2.1600	2.1800	2.2000
3	3.1216	3.1836	3.2464	3.3100	3.3744	3.4396	3.5056	3.5724	3.6400
4	4.2465	4.3746	4.5061	4.6410	4.7793	4.9211	5.0665	5.2154	5.3680
5	5.4163	5.6371	5.8666	6.1051	6.3528	6.6101	6.8771	7.1542	7.4416
6	6.6330	6.9753	7.3359	7.7156	8.1152	8.5355	8.9775	9.4420	9.9299
7	7.8983	8.3938	8.9228	9.4872	10.0890	10.7305	11.4139	12.1415	12.9159
8	9.2142	9.8975	10.6366	11.4359	12.2997	13.2328	14.2401	15.3270	16.4991
9	10.5828	11.4913	12.4876	13.5795	14.7757	16.0853	17.5185	19.0859	20.7989
10	12.0061	13.1808	14.4866	15.9374	17.5487	19.3373	21.3215	23.5213	25.9587
11	13.4864	14.9716	16.6455	18.5312	20.6546	23.0445	25.7329	28.7551	32.1504
12	15.0258	16.8699	18.9771	21.3843	24.1331	27.2707	30.8502	34.9311	39.5805
13	16.6268	18.8821	21.4953	24.5227	28.0291	32.0887	36.7862	42.2187	48.4966
14	18.2919	21.0151	24.2149	27.9750	32.3926	37.5811	43.6720	50.8180	59.1959
15	20.0236	23.2760	27.1521	31.7725	37.2797	43.8424	51.6595	60.9653	72.0351

Table E Annual equivalent factor $A^{-1}_{N\neg i}$

i	0.04	0.06	0.08	0.10	0.12	0.14	0.16	0.18	0.20
N 1	1.0400	1.0600	1.0800	1.1000	1.1200	1.1400	1.1600	1.1800	1.2000
2	0.5302	0.5454	0.5608	0.5762	0.5917	0.6073	0.6230	0.6387	0.6545
3	0.3603	0.3741	0.3880	0.4021	0.4163	0.4307	0.4453	0.4599	0.4747
4	0.2755	0.2886	0.3019	0.3155	0.3292	0.3432	0.3574	0.3717	0.3863
5	0.2446	0.2374	0.2505	0.2638	0.2774	0.2913	0.3054	0.3198	0.3344
6	0.1908	0.2034	0.2163	0.2296	0.2432	0.2572	0.2714	0.2859	0.3007
7	0.1666	0.1791	0.1921	0.2054	0.2191	0.2332	0.2476	0.2624	0.2774
8	0.1485	0.1610	0.1740	0.1874	0.2013	0.2156	0.2302	0.2452	0.2606
9	0.1345	0.1470	0.1601	0.1736	0.1877	0.2022	0.2171	0.2324	0.2481
10	0.1233	0.1359	0.1490	0.1627	0.1770	0.1917	0.2069	0.2225	0.2385
11	0.1141	0.1268	0.1401	0.1540	0.1684	0.1834	0.1989	0.2148	0.2311
12	0.1066	0.1193	0.1327	0.1468	0.1614	0.1767	0.1924	0.2086	0.2253
13	0.1001	0.1130	0.1265	0.1408	0.1557	0.1712	0.1872	0.2037	0.2206
14	0.0947	0.1076	0.1213	0.1357	0.1509	0.1666	0.1829	0.1997	0.2169
15	0.0899	0.1030	0.1168	0.1315	0.1468	0.1628	0.1794	0.1964	0.2139

Table F Sinking fund factor $S^{-1}_{N\neg i}$

i	0.04	0.06	0.08	0.10	0.12	0.14	0.16	0.18	0.20
N 1	1.0000	1.0000	1.0000	1.0000	1.0000	1.0000	1.0000	1.0000	1.0000
2	0.4902	0.4854	0.4808	0.4762	0.4717	0.4673	0.4630	0.4587	0.4545
3	0.3203	0.3141	0.3080	0.3021	0.2963	0.2907	0.2853	0.2799	0.2747
4	0.2355	0.2286	0.2219	0.2155	0.2092	0.2032	0.1974	0.1917	0.1863
5	0.1846	0.1774	0.1705	0.1638	0.1574	0.1513	0.1454	0.1398	0.1344
6	0.1508	0.1343	0.1363	0.1296	0.1232	0.1172	0.1114	0.1059	0.1007
7	0.1266	0.1191	0.1121	0.1054	0.0991	0.0932	0.0876	0.0824	0.0774
8	0.1085	0.1010	0.0940	0.0874	0.0813	0.0756	0.0702	0.0652	0.0606
9	0.0945	0.0870	0.0801	0.0736	0.0677	0.0622	0.0571	0.0524	0.0481
10	0.0833	0.0759	0.0690	0.0627	0.0570	0.0517	0.0469	0.0425	0.0385
11	0.0741	0.0668	0.0601	0.0540	0.0484	0.0434	0.0389	0.0348	0.0311
12	0.0666	0.0593	0.0527	0.0468	0.0414	0.0367	0.0324	0.0286	0.0253
13	0.0601	0.0530	0.0465	0.0408	0.0357	0.0312	0.0272	0.0237	0.0206
14	0.0547	0.0476	0.0413	0.0357	0.0309	0.0266	0.0229	0.0197	0.0169
15	0.0499	0.0430	0.0368	0.0315	0.0268	0.0228	0.0194	0.0164	0.0139

Table G Compound interest factor $(1 + i)^{N-0.5}$
Present value of £1 received evenly through year

i	0.04	0.06	0.08	0.10	0.12	0.14	0.16	0.18	0.20
N									
1	0.9806	0.9713	0.9623	0.9535	0.9449	0.9366	0.9285	0.9206	0.9129
2	0.9429	0.9163	0.8910	0.8668	0.8437	0.8216	0.8004	0.7801	0.7607
3	0.9066	0.8644	0.8250	0.7880	0.7533	0.7207	0.6900	0.6611	0.6339
4	0.8717	0.8155	0.7639	0.7164	0.6726	0.6322	0.5948	0.5603	0.5283
5	0.8382	0.7693	0.7073	0.6512	0.6005	0.5545	0.5128	0.4748	0.4402
6	0.8060	0.7258	0.6549	0.5920	0.5362	0.4864	0.4421	0.4024	0.3669
7	0.7750	0.6847	0.6064	0.5382	0.4787	0.4267	0.3811	0.3410	0.3057
8	0.7452	0.6460	0.5615	0.4893	0.4274	0.3743	0.3285	0.2890	0.2548
9	0.7165	0.6094	0.5199	0.4448	0.3816	0.3283	0.2832	0.2449	0.2123
10	0.6889	0.5749	0.4814	0.4044	0.3407	0.2880	0.2441	0.2075	0.1769
11	0.6624	0.5424	0.4457	0.3676	0.3042	0.2526	0.2105	0.1759	0.1474
12	0.6370	0.5117	0.4127	0.3342	0.2716	0.2216	0.1814	0.1491	0.1229
13	0.6125	0.4827	0.3821	0.3038	0.2425	0.1944	0.1564	0.1263	0.1024
14	0.5889	0.4554	0.3538	0.2762	0.2165	0.1705	0.1348	0.1071	0.0853
15	0.5663	0.4296	0.3276	0.2511	0.1933	0.1496	0.1162	0.0907	0.0711

Using this discount factor actually assumes that the cash flows take place in the middle of the year. However this is a very good approximation for cash flows that are spread evenly during the year.

Table H Present value of an annuity $A_{N-.05 \neg i}$
Present value of £1 received each year evenly throughout the year

i	2%	4%	6%	8%	10%	12%	14%	16%	18%	20%
N										
1	0.9901	0.9806	0.9713	0.9623	0.9535	0.9449	0.9366	0.9285	0.9206	0.9129
2	1.9609	1.9234	1.8876	1.8532	1.8202	1.7886	1.7582	1.7289	1.7007	1.6736
3	2.9126	2.8300	2.7520	2.6782	2.6082	2.5419	2.4788	2.4189	2.3619	2.3075
4	3.8456	3.7018	3.5675	3.4421	3.3246	3.2144	3.1110	3.0137	2.9222	2.8358
5	4.7604	4.5400	4.3369	4.1493	3.9758	3.8149	3.6655	3.5265	3.3970	3.2761
6	5.6572	5.3460	5.0627	4.8042	4.5678	4.3511	4.1520	3.9686	3.7994	3.6429
7	6.5364	6.1209	5.7474	5.4106	5.1060	4.8298	4.5787	4.3497	4.1404	3.9486
8	7.3984	6.8661	6.3934	5.9721	5.5953	5.2573	4.9530	4.6782	4.4294	4.2034
9	8.2435	7.5826	7.0028	6.4920	6.0401	5.6389	5.2813	4.9614	4.6743	4.4157
10	9.0720	8.2715	7.5777	6.9733	6.4445	5.9796	5.5693	5.2055	4.8818	4.5926
11	9.8842	8.9340	8.1200	7.4190	6.8121	6.2839	5.8219	5.4160	5.0577	4.7401
12	10.6806	9.5709	8.6317	7.8317	7.1463	6.5555	6.0435	5.5975	5.2068	4.8629
13	11.4613	10.1834	9.1144	8.2138	7.4501	6.7980	6.2379	5.7539	5.3331	4.9653
14	12.2267	10.7723	9.5698	8.5677	7.7262	7.0146	6.4085	5.8887	5.4401	5.0506
15	12.9771	11.3386	9.9994	8.8953	7.9773	7.2079	6.5580	6.0050	5.5309	5.1217

Using this discount factor actually assumes that the cash flows take place in the middle of each year. However this is a very good approximation for cash flows that are spread evenly during each year. It will be noticed that at 10% over 10 years, the annuity factor is 6.4445 whilst using the year end cash flow assumption (table C) produces a factor of 6.1446. It is a matter of judgement as to whether or not this difference (of 5%) is seen as being significant.

Area under the normal curve

Table I Areas under the normal distribution

z	0.00	0.01	0.02	0.03	0.04	0.05	0.06	0.07	0.08	0.09
0.0	.0000	.0040	.0080	.0120	.0160	.0199	.0239	.0279	.0319	.0359
0.1	.0398	.0438	.0478	.0517	.0557	.0596	.0636	.0675	.0714	.0753
0.2	.0793	.0832	.0871	.0910	.0948	.0987	.1026	.1064	.1103	.1141
0.3	.1179	.1217	.1255	.1293	.1331	.1368	.1406	.1443	.1480	.1517
0.4	.1554	.1591	.1628	.1664	.1700	.1736	.1772	.1808	.1844	.1879
0.5	.1915	.1950	.1985	.2019	.2054	.2088	.2123	.2157	.2190	.2224
0.6	.2257	.2291	.2324	.2357	.2389	.2422	.2454	.2486	.2517	.2549
0.7	.2580	.2611	.2642	.2673	.2704	.2734	.2764	.2794	.2823	.2852
0.8	.2881	.2910	.2939	.2967	.2995	.3023	.3051	.3078	.3106	.3133
0.9	.3159	.3186	.3212	.3238	.3264	.3289	.3315	.3340	.3365	.3389
1.0	.3413	.3438	.3461	.3485	.3508	.3531	.3554	.3577	.3599	.3621
1.1	.3643	.3665	.3686	.3708	.3729	.3749	.3770	.3790	.3810	.3830
1.2	.3849	.3869	.3888	.3907	.3925	.3944	.3962	.3980	.3997	.4015
1.3	.4032	.4049	.4066	.4082	.4099	.4115	.4131	.4147	.4162	.4177
1.4	.4192	.4207	.4222	.4236	.4251	.4265	.4279	.4292	.4306	.4319
1.5	.4332	.4345	.4357	.4370	.4382	.4394	.4406	.4418	.4429	.4441
1.6	.4452	.4463	.4474	.4484	.4495	.4505	.4515	.4525	.4535	.4545
1.7	.4554	.4564	.4573	.4582	.4591	.4599	.4608	.4616	.4625	.4633
1.8	.4641	.4649	.4656	.4664	.4671	.4678	.4686	.4693	.4699	.4706
1.9	.4713	.4719	.4726	.4732	.4738	.4744	.4750	.4756	.4761	.4767
2.0	.4773	.4778	.4783	.4788	.4793	.4798	.4803	.4808	.4812	.4817
2.1	.4821	.4826	.4830	.4834	.4838	.4842	.4846	.4850	.4854	.4857
2.2	.4861	.4864	.4868	.4871	.4875	.4878	.4881	.4884	.4887	.4890
2.3	.4893	.4896	.4898	.4901	.4904	.4906	.4909	.4911	.4913	.4916
2.4	.4918	.4920	.4922	.4925	.4927	.4929	.4931	.4932	.4934	.4936
2.5	.4938	.4940	.4941	.4943	.4945	.4946	.4948	.4949	.4951	.4952
2.6	.4953	.4955	.4956	.4957	.4959	.4960	.4961	.4962	.4963	.4964
2.7	.4965	.4966	.4967	.4968	.4969	.4970	.4971	.4972	.4973	.4974
2.8	.4974	.4975	.4976	.4977	.4977	.4978	.4979	.4979	.4980	.4981
2.9	.4981	.4982	.4982	.4982	.4984	.4984	.4985	.4985	.4986	.4986
3.0	.4987	.4987	.4987	.4988	.4988	.4989	.4989	.4989	.4990	.4990

Natural logarithms

Table J

N	0	1	2	3	4	5	6	7	8	9
1.0	0.0000	.0099	.0198	.0295	.0392	.0487	.0582	.0676	.0769	.0861
.1	.0953	.1043	.1133	.1222	.1310	.1397	.1484	.1570	.1655	.1739
.2	.1823	.1906	.1988	.2070	.2151	.2231	.2311	.2390	.2468	.2546
.3	.2623	.2700	.2776	.2851	.2926	.3001	.3074	.3148	.3220	.3293
.4	.3364	.3435	.3506	.3576	.3646	.3715	.3784	.3852	.3920	.3987
.5	.4054	.4121	.4187	.4252	.4317	.4382	.4446	.4510	.4574	.4637
.6	.4700	.4762	.4824	.4885	.4947	.5007	.5068	.5128	.5187	.5247
.7	.5306	.5364	.5423	.5481	.5538	.5596	.5653	.5709	.5766	.5822
.8	.5877	.5933	.5988	.6043	.6097	.6151	.6205	.6259	.6312	.6365
.9	.6418	.6471	.6523	.6575	.6626	.6678	.6729	.6780	.6831	.6881
2.0	0.6931	.6981	.7031	.7080	.7129	.7178	.7227	.7275	.7323	.7371
.1	.7419	.7466	.7514	.7561	.7608	.7654	.7701	.7747	.7793	.7839
.2	.7884	.7929	.7975	.8020	.8064	.8109	.8153	.8197	.8241	.8285
.3	.8329	.8372	.8415	.8458	.8501	.8542	.8586	.8628	.8671	.8712
.4	.8754	.8796	.8837	.8878	.8920	.8960	.9001	.9042	.9082	.9122
.5	.9162	.9202	.9242	.9282	.9321	.9360	.9400	.0439	.9477	.9516
.6	.9555	.9593	.9631	.9669	.9707	.9745	.9783	.9820	.9858	.9895
.7	.9932	.9969	.0006[a]	.0043[a]	.0079[a]	.0116[a]	.0152[a]	.0188[a]	.0224[a]	.0260[a]
.8	1.0296	.0331[a]	.0367	.0402	.0438	.0473	.0508	.0543	.0577	.0612
.9	.0647	.0681	.0715	.0750	.0784	.0818	.0851	.0885	.0919	.0952
3.0	1.0986	.1019	.1052	.1085	.1118	.1151	.1184	.1216	.1249	.1281
.1	.1314	.1346	.1378	.1410	.1442	.1474	.1505	.1537	.1568	.1600
.2	.1631	.1662	.1693	.1724	.1755	.1786	.1817	.1847	.1878	.1908
.3	.1939	.1969	.1999	.2029	.2059	.2089	.2119	.2149	.2178	.2208
.4	.2237	.2267	.2296	.2325	.2354	.2383	.2412	.2441	.2470	.2499
.5	.2527	.2556	.2584	.2613	.2641	.2669	.2697	.2725	.2753	.2781
.6	.2809	.2837	.2864	.2892	.2919	.2947	.2974	.3001	.3029	.3056
.7	.3083	.3110	.3137	.3164	.3190	.3217	.3244	.3270	.3297	.3323
.8	.3350	.3376	.3402	.3428	.3454	.3480	.3506	.3532	.3558	.3584
.9	.3609	.3635	.3660	.3686	.3711	.3737	.3762	.3787	.3812	.3837
4.0	1.3862	.3887	.3912	.3937	.3962	.3987	.4011	.4036	.4061	.4085
.1	.4109	.4134	.4158	.4182	.4207	.4231	.4255	.4279	.4303	.4327
.2	.4350	.4374	.4398	.4422	.4445	.4469	.4492	.4516	.4539	.4562
.3	.4586	.4609	.4632	.4655	.4678	.4701	.4724	.4747	.4770	.4793
.4	.4816	.4838	.4861	.4884	.4906	.4929	.4951	.4973	.4996	.5018
.5	.5040	.5063	.5085	.5107	.5129	.5151	.5173	.5195	.5217	.5238
.6	.5260	.5282	.5303	.5325	.5347	.5368	.5390	.5411	.5433	.5454
.7	.5475	.5496	.5518	.5539	.5560	.5581	.5602	.5623	.5644	.5665
.8	.5686	.5707	.5727	.5748	.5769	.5789	.5810	.5830	.5851	.5871
.9	.5892	.5912	.5933	.5953	.5973	.5993	.6014	.6034	.6054	.6074

a. Add 1.0 to indicated figure.

Answers to quickie questions

Introduction

1. (a) The capital investment decision.
   (b) The financing and capital structure decision.
   (c) The dividend decision.

2. The process by which the company seeks out alternative courses of action, alternative projects, etc.

3. The assumed objective of financial decision making is maximization of shareholder wealth. Whilst recognizing that this is a simplification of the real world, it is reasonable to accept that this should be the main objective, other things being equal.

4. It is a *reporting* concept, not a decision-making concept. Its use is to report on the success or failure of decisions taken. It has only a secondary role in the decision-making process itself. Accounting profit is also based on historic cost whereas financial management is concerned with value. The two things are very different. Finally, profit as reported is subject to the judgement of the accountant and cannot be regarded as entirely reliable.

5. On the basis of the expected flow of dividends they will generate in the future.

Chapter 1

1. The problem is one of control. How does the principal control the agent to ensure that the agent acts in the principal's best interests?

2. Fiduciary responsibilities; independent external audit; Stock Exchange Yellow Book listing rules; Stock Exchange's 'model code' for directors'

share dealings; Companies Act regulations on directors' transaction and Cadbury Committee 'code of best practice'.

3. Reward managerial ability, not luck; rewards should have a significant impact on managerial remuneration; reward system should work two ways; concept of risk should be taken into account; the shareholder's time horizon should be taken into account; scheme should be simple, inexpensive and difficult to manipulate.

Chapter 2

1. (a) Where are we now?
   (b) Where do we want to be?
   (c) How are we going to get there?

2. SWOT analysis helps to answer the question: where are we now? SWOT stands for: S = strengths; W = weaknesses; O = opportunities and T = threats.

3. The 'Boston Box' is a form of matrix analysis used to try to identify answers to the second question: where does the firm want to go in the future?

4. The idea of 'value drivers' arises out of Porter's work. Value drivers are: buyer power, supplier power, entry opportunities, substitute possibilities and competitor rivalry.

5. This again arises out of Porter's ideas on competitive strategy. There are four alternative strategic approaches that companies can follow:

   (a) broad product differentiation;
   (b) narrow product differentiation;
   (c) broad-based cost leadership;
   (d) narrow-based cost leadership.

6. In order to achieve the objective of maximizing shareholder wealth, management need to devise a strategy as to how this objective is to be achieved. Thus a strategy – based on an understanding of the business 'value drivers' – is a vital first stage in the achievement of the company's objective.

7. The responsibilities of the chief accountant would include:

   (a) preparation of internal and external financial reports;
   (b) responsibility for all aspects of the company's management information system;
   (c) all budgetary control procedures;
   (d) pricing policies;
   (e) capital investment appraisal and working capital management.

8. See Fig. 2.4 in the text.

9. It allows highly *illiquid* securities (e.g. shares) that are issued by companies to be held as highly *liquid* investments by investors, as it provides a market-place where such investments can be easily bought and sold.

10. Investors are generally assumed to be risk-averse. The idea of an individual being anything other than risk-averse is somewhat illogical and it is difficult to imagine why anybody would actively seek risk without reward. This dislike of risk does not mean that investors will not take on risky investments, but that they have to be rewarded for doing so. The reward is given in terms of a higher expected return on the investment: the higher the risk, the higher must be its expected return.

Chapter 3

1. Stage one: The best of the alternative projects has the shortest payback.
   Stage two: Accept the best project as long as its payback period satisfies the decision criterion.

2. Working capital is excluded from the analysis. Net cash flow:

0	−11 000	
1	+ 4 000	Payback = 2.75 years
2	+ 4 000	
3	+ 4 000	
4	+ 3 000	
5	+ 3 000	

3. (a) Quick and simple to calculate.
   (b) Thought to automatically select less-risky projects in mutually exclusive decision situations.
   (c) Saves management the trouble of having to estimate project cash flows beyond the maximum payback time-period.
   (d) Convenient method to use in capital rationing.

4. The payback criterion is reduced until total capital expenditure equates with the amount of finance available.

5. (a) Management's experience of successful projects within the firm.
   (b) Industry practice.
   (c) Reflects the limit of management's forecasting skills.

   However, none of these can be seen as being really objective.

6. The payback decision rule, adjusted to take account of the time value of money.

7. Ignores cash flows outside the payback time period. (The fact that 'normal' payback ignores the time value of money is equally important but this criticism can, of course, be easily overcome through the use of discounted payback.)

8. Money has a time value because it can earn a rate of interest/a rate of return. This has nothing to do with inflation although that might have an effect on the levels of return expected.

9. The question does not specify which ARR/ROCE to calculate, so *both* are given:

Annual depreciation: (£11 000 − £1000) ÷ 5 = £2000.

Profit:					
£4000	−	£2000	=	£2000	Yr 1
4000	−	2000	=	2000	Yr 2
4000	−	2000	=	2000	Yr 3
3000	−	2000	=	1000	Yr 4
2000	−	2000	=	0	Yr 5

Total profit = $\overline{£7000} \div 5 = £1400$

= Av. ann. profit

Average capital employed:

$$\frac{£11\ 000 - £1000}{2} + £1000 + £4000 = £10\ 000$$

Return on initial capital employed = £1400 ÷ £15 000 = $9\frac{1}{3}$%
Return on average capital employed = £1400 ÷ £10 000 = 14%

10. (a) Evaluates via a percentage rate of return.
    (b) Evaluates on the basis of profitability.
    (c) Appears logical to evaluate projects on the same basis as management have their own performance evaluated by shareholders.

11. (a) Ignores the time value of money.
    (b) Evaluates on the basis of profit, not cash, flow.

Chapter 4

1. This is an example of the economic concept of diminishing marginal utility. Each additional £1 of t_0 consumption forgone, through investment, is likely to be of increasing value in terms of consumption benefits forgone. Each additional £1 of future consumption gained is likely to be of decreasing value. Hence, the time value of money rises.

2. The complete range of maximum consumption combinations that the firm owner can obtain at t_0 and t_1.

3. The marginal return on the investment opportunity at any particular point.

4. A curve of constant utility. All combinations of consumption at t_0 and t_1 that lie along a single indifference curve would provide the same level of utility or satisfaction.

5. It invests until the return on the marginal investment equates with the owner's marginal time value of money.

6. Lending at t_0 would reduce the amount of money available for consumption at t_0 and increase the amount available at t_1, hence the move would be *up* the financial investment line.

7. The firm should continue to invest in projects as long as the marginal rate of return is not less than the market rate of interest. This rule is, of course, obvious. There would be little point in investing money in a project which gave a lower return than what could be obtained by lending the money on the capital market.

The cash (dividend) distribution to shareholders in t_0 and t_1 that arises out of the firm's investment decision can then be redistributed by shareholders, using the capital markets, to suit their own set of indifference curves.

8. A risky investment is one where the outcome is uncertain.

9. Ensure that any project earns at least the capital market rate of return that is available for investments of equivalent risk to the project.

10. (a) Single time horizon.
    (b) Infinitely divisible projects.
    (c) All independent projects.
    (d) Rational investors.

11. Investors dislike risk: they are said to be risk-averse. Hence they require a reward for taking on a risk, which is the expectation (but, of course, not the certainty) of a higher return.

12. In these circumstances, the market rate of return offers you greater compensation than you require to forgo current consumption. Therefore you would want to lend money.

Chapter 5

1.

0	-1000	×	1	=	-1000
1	$+ 500$	×	0.8772	=	$+ 438.60$
2	$+ 600$	×	0.7695	=	$+ 461.70$
3	$+ 400$	×	0.6750	=	$+ 270$
					$+ \overline{170.30}$ NPV

2. There are several interpretations:

   (a) It produces a return > 10%.
   (b) It produces £120 more (in t_0 terms) than a £1000 capital market investment of similar risk.
   (c) The project would produce a sufficient cash flow to repay its outlay, pay its financing charges *and* provide an additional £120 in t_0 terms.
   (d) If accepted, shareholder wealth would increase by £120.

3. At 4% discount rate: NPV = +147.48
   At 20% discount rate: NPV = −9.28

   $$\text{Therefore IRR} = 4\% + \left[\frac{147.48}{147.48 - (-9.28)} \times (20\% - 4\%) \right]$$

   $$= 19.05\% \text{ approx.}$$

   With any problem like this it is a good idea to use a computer to arrive at an answer. In this case the solution, using the IRR function of a spreadsheet is 18.825%.

4.

Year	Cash flow		Discount factor		
0	−500	×	1	=	−500
1	+200	×	0.9091	=	+181.82
2	+300	×	0.8264	=	+247.92
3	+200	×	0.7513	=	+150.26

$$500 - 181.82 - 247.92 = 70.26 \div 150.26 = 0.47$$
$$\therefore \text{ payback is 2.47 years approx.}$$

5. The return available elsewhere on the capital market on a similar risk investment.

6. For the same project they should be identical. In both cases they are the opportunity cost return referred to in the answer above to question five.

7. $+350 \, A_{4 \neg 0.10} = 350 \times 3.1699 = +1109.47$.

8. (a) Annuity due.
   (b) Immediate annuity.
   (c) Deferred annuity.

9. Given the PV of a perpetuity is: $\dfrac{\text{Annual amount}}{\text{Discount rate}}$, then:

$$\text{IRR} = \frac{£100}{£1000} = 0.10 \text{ or } 10\%$$

$$\text{because: } -£1000 + \frac{£100}{0.10} = 0 \text{ NPV}$$

10. $-1000 + 200 \, A_{2 \neg 0.16} + 500 \, A_{3 \neg 0.16} (1 + 0.16)^{-2} = \text{NPV}$
    $-1000 + (200 \times 1.6052) + (500 \times 2.2459 \times 0.7432) = +£155.62$

Chapter 6

1. The NPV rule is to accept whichever project has the largest positive NPV. Differences in magnitude, duration and risk can be ignored. Hence project A should be accepted.

2. The assumptions made are:

   (a) There is a perfect capital market so that the firm can finance the large project just as easily as it can finance the small project.
   (b) The projects represent independent decisions in that they are not part of a continuous replacement chain.
   (c) The discount rates used do correctly reflect the risk of each project.

3. NPV and IRR both make assumptions about the rate of return at which project-generated cash flows are reinvested. NPV assumes that the rate is the market discount rate, while IRR assumes that it is equal to the IRP of the project generating those cash flows. Given a perfect capital market, the NPV method is making the correct assumption.

4. Non-conventional cash flows, where there is more than one change in sign. The problem can be avoided by using the 'extended yield technique' or the 'modified IRR'.

5. Using the extended yield technique:

$$\text{Year 3: } -20 \, (1 + 0.10)^{-3} = -15.02 \text{ at Year 0}$$

Therefore the revised cash flow is:

0	−115.02
1	+ 60
2	+ 80

At a 4% discount rate: +16.64 NPV
At a 20% discount rate: −9.46 NPV

$$\therefore \text{IRR} = 4\% + \left[\frac{16.64}{16.64 - (-9.46)} \times (20\% - 4\%) \right] = 14.2\%.$$

6.

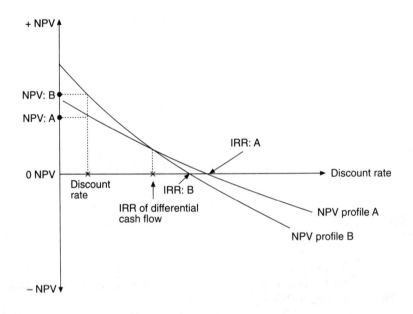

7. If IRR diff. c/f > hurdle rate: accept project smallest IRR.
   If IRR diff. c/f < hurdle rate: accept project largest IRR.

8.

			(£)
1	$+ 40 \, (1.10)^2$	=	+ 60.5
2	$+ 80 \, (1.10)^1$	=	+ 88
3	−30	=	−30
Year 3 Terminal value			+118.50

Modified cash flow of the project:

Year	(£)
0	− 80
3	+118.50

Estimating the IRR using linear interpolation:

NPV at 5% = +22.36

NPV at 20% = −11.42

$$\text{IRR} = 5\% + \left[\frac{22.36}{22.36 - (-11.42)} \times (20\% - 5\%) \right] = 14.9\%.$$

Chapter 7

1. $\dfrac{(1.13)}{(1.04)} - 1 = 0.086$ or 8.6%

2. Either: Project money cash flows discounted at the market discount rate to NPV.

   or: Project money cash flows discounted at the general rate of inflation and then at the real discount rate to NPV.

3. The money cash flow, deflated (discounted) by the general rate of inflation.

4. $\dfrac{1.155}{1.05} - 1 = 0.10 = $ real discount rate

   (a) £10 000 $(1.05)^2 = $ £11 025
   (b) £10 000
   (a) £11 025 $(1.155)^{-2} = $ £11 025 $(1.10)^{-2} (1.05)^{-2} = $ £8263.73
   (b) £10 000 $(1.155)^{-2} = $ £10 000 $(1.10)^{-2} (1.05)^{-2} = $ £7495.45

5.

	WDA					Tax relief	Timing
500	×	0.25	= +125	× 0.35	=	+43.75	Year 2
$\dfrac{125}{375}$	×	0.25	= + 93.75	× 0.35	=	+32.81	Year 3
$\dfrac{93.75}{281.25}$	−	0	= +281.25	× 0.35	=	+98.44	Year 4

6. Historic cost: £60 000 – irrelevant, sunk cost.
   Written-down book value: £10 000 – irrelevant non-economic figure.
   Scrap now: £3000
   Rent and then scrap: £2500 + £800 = £3300.

   Therefore, if the machine is used to undertake the project, the best opportunity forgone is the 'rent and then scrap' alternative. So this is the opportunity cost of using the machine on the project: −£3300.

7. Discount the after-tax cash flows by the after-tax discount rate.

8. They are non-incremental.

9. Market price of factory space: £2 per m^2 (external opportunity cost)
   Contribution £15 per m^2 (internal opportunity cost)
   Cost to project: 150 × (£15 + £2) = £2550.

Chapter 8

1. Hard and soft capital rationing.

2. The firm cannot necessarily accept a project just because it has a positive NPV, nor can it necessarily reject a project just because it has a negative NPV. Hence the standard NPV decision rule breaks down. In theory capital rationing should not exist because we assume that cash will be available for investments at an appropriate rate of return. In another sense it causes no problem for NPV because we could assume that the appropriate discount rate is the return on the alternative investments (i.e. opportunity cost of capital).

3. The benefit–cost ratios are:

$$
\begin{array}{llll}
A: & +60 \div 100 = & +0.60 & (1) \\
B: & +90 \div 200 = & +0.45 & (3) \\
C: & +20 \div 40 = & +0.50 & (2) \\
D: & -10 \div 100 = & -0.10 & (-)
\end{array}
$$

200	available		
−100	invest in A, producing	:	+ 60 NPV
100			
− 40	invest in C, producing	:	+ 20 NPV
60			
− 60	invest in 30% B, producing	:	+ 27 NPV
−			+107 Total NPV

4. The benefit–cost ratios are:

$$
\begin{array}{llll}
A: & +60 \div 50 = & +1.20 & (1) \\
B: & +90 \div 200 = & +0.45 & (2) \\
C: & +20 \div 150 = & +0.133 & (3) \\
D: & -10 \div - = & - &
\end{array}
$$

240	available		
−50	invest in A, producing	:	+ 60 NPV
190			
−190	invest in 95% of B, producing:		+ 85.5 NPV
0			+145.5 Total NPV

As D has a *cost–benefit* ratio of: $-10 \div 20 = -0.50$
and B, the marginal project, has a benefit–cost ratio of 0.45, further investment is not worthwhile.

5. Benefit–cost ratios:

$$
\begin{array}{llll}
A: & 40 \div 100 = & 0.40 & (1) \\
*B: & 30 \div 100 = & 0.30 & (2) \\
*C: & 50 \div 200 = & 0.25 & (3) \\
D: & 10 \div 100 = & 0.10 & (4) \\
E: & 4 \div 50 = & 0.08 & (5)
\end{array}
$$

```
  300    available
 -100    invest in A, producing          :  +40 NPV
 ────
  200
 -100    invest in B, producing          :  +30 NPV
 ────
  100
 -100    invest in D, producing          :  +10 NPV
 ────
    0                                        +80 Total NPV
 ────
```

alternatively:

```
  300  available
 -100    invest in A, producing          :  +40 NPV
 ────
  200
 -200    invest in C, producing          :  +50 NPV
 ────
    0                                        +90 Total NPV
 ────
```

Therefore, the best alternative is to undertake projects A and C.

6. $40a - 20b + 50c$ Max.

$$100a + 150b + 200c \leqslant 190$$
$$200a + 120c \leqslant 110 + 70b$$
$$30c \leqslant 50a + 70b$$
$$a, b, c \leqslant 1$$
$$a, b, c \geqslant 0$$

7. *Dual values* + *10% discount factor* = *Total opportunity cost of cash*

1.86	+	1	=	2.86	t_0
0.73	+	0.9091	=	1.6391	t_1
0.64	+	0.8264	=	1.4664	t_2
1.21	+	0.7513	=	1.9613	t_3

Gain from an extra £1 at t_1:

$$£1 \times 1.6391 = £1.6391$$

Loss from repayment of £1, plus interest (i) at t_2

$$£(1 + i) \times 1.4664 = £1.4664 + 1.4664i$$

The maximum interest rate would occur at the point where the gain equals the loss:

$$1.6391 = 1.4664 + 1.4664i$$
$$1.6391 - 1.4664 = 1.4664i$$
$$\frac{1.6391 - 1.4664}{1.4664} = i = 0.118 \text{ or } 11.8\% \text{ max.}$$

8. NPV:

```
   -100  × 1      =  -100
   + 40  × 0.9091 =  + 36.36
   + 90  × 0.8264 =  + 74.38
                     ────────
                     + 10.74 NPV
                     ════════
```

Internal opportunity cost:

$$
\begin{aligned}
-100 &\times 1.86 &=& -186 \\
+\ 40 &\times 0.73 &=& +\ 29.2 \\
+\ 90 &\times 0.64 &=& +\ 57.6 \\
&&& \overline{-\ 99.2}
\end{aligned}
$$

Total opportunity cost:

$$
\begin{aligned}
+10.74 &\quad \text{NPV} \\
-99.20 &\quad \text{Internal opportunity cost} \\
\overline{-88.46} &\quad \text{Net total opportunity cost}
\end{aligned}
$$

As this net figure is negative, the additional project will not be a worthwhile investment, reject.

Chapter 9

1. Success: $-1000 + 500\,A_{3\to 0.10} = +243$ NPV
   Failure: $-1000 + 350\,A_{3\to 0.10} = -130$ NPV

State	Prob.		NPV		
I	0.45	×	+243	=	+109
II	0.55	×	−130	=	− 72
					+ 37 ENPV

2.
Survey indicates	Action	Prob.		Outcome		
State I	Accept	0.45	×	+243 NPV	=	+109
State II	Reject	0.55	×	0 NPV	=	0
						+109 ENPV

ENPV with survey	:	+109
ENPV without survey	:	+37
Max. worth of survey	:	+72

3.
Survey indicates	Probability			State
State I correctly	0.45×0.75	=	0.3375	A
State I incorrectly	0.45×0.25	=	0.1125	B
State II correctly	0.55×0.75	=	0.4125	C
State II incorrectly	0.55×0.25	=	0.1375	D

State	Action	Prob.		Outcome		
A	Accept	0.3375	×	+ 243 NPV	=	+82
B	Accept	0.1125	×	− 72 NPV	=	− 8
C	Reject	0.4125	×	0 NPV	=	0
D	Reject	0.1375	×	−243 NPV	=	−33
				ENPV		+41

$$
\begin{array}{lll}
\text{ENPV with survey} & : & +41 \\
\text{ENPV without survey} & : & +37 \\
\hline
\text{Max. worth of survey} & : & +\;4 \\
\end{array}
$$

4.

State	Prob.		NPV		
I	0.3	×	+ 100	=	+ 30
II	0.5	×	+ 50	=	+ 25
III	0.2	×	− 300	=	− 60
			ENPV		− 5

Therefore, without the survey we would *not* accept the project and so incur a zero NPV.

Survey indicates	Action	Prob.		Outcome		
I	Accept	0.3	×	+100	=	+30
II	Accept	0.5	×	+ 50	=	+25
III	Reject	0.2	×	0	=	0
				ENPV		+55

$$
\begin{array}{lll}
\text{ENPV with survey} & : & +55 \\
\text{ENPV without survey} & : & 0 \\
\hline
\text{Max. worth of survey} & : & +55 \\
\end{array}
$$

5. If the machine is bought and, at the end of Yr 1, the decision is taken *not* to abandon the project, then the outcome will be:

State	Yr 1	Yr 2	NPV	Decision
I	−60	+100	+ 23.43	Don't abandon
II	−60	+ 60	− 6.81	Abandon
III	−60	+ 40	−21.93	Abandon

The investment decision is therefore:

State	Yr 0	Yr 1	Yr 2	NPV		Prob.	
I	−140	+100	+100	+22.57	×	0.70	= + 15.80
II	−140	+ 60		−35.65	×	0.10	= − 3.56
		+ 60					
III	−140	+ 40		−53.04	×	0.20	= −10.61
		+ 60					
				ENPV			+ 1.63

The complete decision is that the company should purchase the machine but, if either states II or III occur, then the machine should be sold off at the end of the first year.

6. $-1000 + 280\,A_{5\neg 0.10} = +61.42$ NPV

Life = x At 5 year life: +61.42 NPV
At 4 year life:
$-1000 + 280\,A_{4\neg 0.10} = -112.40$ NPV

Using linear interpolation:

$$x = 4 + \left[\frac{112.40}{61.42 + 112.40} \times (5 - 4) \right] = 4.65 \text{ yrs.}$$

Thus the life of the project can be reduced by up to 0.35 of a year (approx $4\frac{1}{4}$ months) before the original decision advice is incorrect. This represents a maximum change of $0.35 \div 5 = 7\%$.

Net cash flow $= x$

$$-1000 + x \, A_{5 \neg 0.10} = 0 \text{ NPV}$$

$$x = 1000 \div A_{5 \neg 0.10} = 264$$

Thus the annual net cash flow can fall by up to 16 per year, or $16 \div 280 = 5.7\%$ before the original decision advice is incorrect.

Chapter 10

1. (a) How to measure the project's risk.
   (b) How to find the return available on the capital market for that level of risk.

2. Transitivity means that choice between alternatives is consistent: if X is preferred to Y and Y is preferred to Z then X must be preferred to Z if the choice is to exhibit transitivity.

3. It is the guaranteed outcome that is regarded as being of equal value to the expected value of an uncertain investment. The guaranteed outcome will be smaller in cash terms than the equivalent uncertain outcome with the same perceived value so long as the investor is risk-averse.

4. $U (+10\,000) = 1$
   $U (-5000) = 0$
   $U (C - E) = pU (+10\,000) + (1 - p) U (-5000)$
   $U (3500) = (0.60 \times 1) + (0.40 \times 0) = 0.60$

5. Risk aversion.

6. Linear. However, it is likely that any individual will be risk-averse.

7. Certainty-equivalent $<$ expected outcome.

8. $\dfrac{(\text{Selling price} - \text{Purchase price}) + \text{Dividends received}}{\text{Purchase price}} = \text{Return}$

9.
State of world	Prob.		Return		
I	0.20	$\times$	+40%	=	+ 8%
II	0.60	$\times$	+15%	=	+ 9%
III	0.20	$\times$	−10%	=	− 2%
					+15% $= E(r)$

(Return)^2		Prob.		
(40%)^2	$\times$	0.20	=	320

$$\begin{array}{rcll}(15\%)^2 & \times & 0.60 & = & 135 \\ (-10\%)^2 & \times & 0.20 & = & 20 \\ & & & & \overline{475} = E(r^2)\end{array}$$

$$\sigma^2 = E(r^2) - E(r)^2 = 475 - (15\%)^2 = 475 - 225 = 250$$
$$\sigma = \sqrt{\sigma^2} = \sqrt{250} = 15.81\%$$

Solution: Expected return: 15%
Risk (std. dev.): 15.81%

10. Downside risk is concerned with the possibility that an investment might do worse than expected.

11. In this situation the variance or standard deviation of the returns are not adequate descriptors of risk. An investment with a lower variance might also be the investment that bears the greater chance of a loss.

Chapter 11

1. The correlation coefficient. The further away it is from +1, the greater the degree of risk-reduction effect.

2. $$\sigma_p = \sqrt{[x^2\sigma_A^2 + (1-x)^2\,\sigma_B^2 + 2x(1-x)\text{Cov}(r_A, r_B)]},$$
   or
   $$\sigma_p = \sqrt{[x^2\sigma_A^2 + (1-x)^2\,\sigma_B^2 + 2x(1-x)\sigma_A\,\sigma_B\,\rho_{A,B}]}.$$

3. A: $\begin{array}{rcl} 0.3 \times 28\% & = & 8.4\% \\ 0.4 \times 18\% & = & 7.2\% \\ 0.3 \times 6\% & = & 1.8\% \\ E(r_A) & = & \overline{17.4\%} \end{array}$ B: $\begin{array}{rcl} 0.3 \times 35\% & = & 10.5\% \\ 0.4 \times 15\% & = & 6\% \\ 0.3 \times 20\% & = & 6\% \\ E(r_B) & = & \overline{22.5\%} \end{array}$

$$\begin{array}{lcllll} (28\% - 17.4\%) & \times & (35\% - 22.5\%) & \times & 0.3 & = & +39.75 \\ (18\% - 17.4\%) & \times & (15\% - 22.5\%) & \times & 0.4 & = & -1.80 \\ (6\% - 17.4\%) & \times & (20\% - 22.5\%) & \times & 0.3 & = & +8.55 \\ & & & & \text{Cov}(r_A, r_B) & & \overline{+46.50} \end{array}$$

A: $\begin{array}{rcl} 0.3 \times (28\%)^2 & = & 235.2 \\ 0.4 \times (18\%)^2 & = & 129.6 \\ 0.3 \times (6\%)^2 & = & 10.8 \\ E(r_A^2) & = & \overline{375.6} \end{array}$ B: $\begin{array}{rcl} 0.3 \times (35\%)^2 & = & 367.5 \\ 0.4 \times (15\%)^2 & = & 90.0 \\ 0.3 \times (20\%)^2 & = & 120.0 \\ E(r_B^2) & = & \overline{577.5} \end{array}$

$$\sigma_A = \sqrt{[E(r_A^2) - E(r_A)^2]} \qquad \sigma_B = \sqrt{[E(r_B^2) - E(r_B)^2]}$$
$$\sigma_A = \sqrt{(375.6 - 17.4^2)} = 8.5\% \quad \sigma_B = \sqrt{(577.5 - 22.5^2)} = 8.4\%$$
$$\rho_{A,B} = \frac{\text{Cov.}(r_A, r_B)}{\sigma_A \times \sigma_B} = \frac{+46.50}{8.5 \times 8.4} = +0.65$$

4. $E(r_p) = xE(r_A) + (1 - x)\,E(r_B)$
$$\begin{array}{rcl} 20\% & = & x \times 17.4\% + (1 - x)\,22.5\% \\ 20 & = & 17.4x + 22.5 - 22.5x \\ 20 - 22.5 & = & 17.4x - 22.5x \end{array}$$

$$-2.5 = -5.1x$$

$$\frac{-2.5}{-5.1} = x = 0.49.$$

Therefore invest 49% of the funds in investment A, and the remaining 51% in B.

$$20\% = (0.49 \times 17.4\%) + (0.51 \times 22.5\%).$$

5.
$$E(r_i) = \sum_{i=1}^{N} x_i \rho_i.$$

$$\sigma_p = \sqrt{\sum_{i=1}^{N}\sum_{j=1}^{N} x_i x_j \sigma_i \sigma_j \rho_{ij}}.$$

6. A portfolio which lies along the capital market line (CML). It provides either (a) the maximum level of expected return for a given level of risk;

or   (b) the minimum level of risk for a given level of return.

7.
$$E(r_j) = r_F + \lambda \sigma_j \text{ or } E(r_j) = r_F + \frac{E(r_M) - r_F}{\sigma_M}\sigma_j.$$

8. An efficient portfolio consists of investing in the market portfolio and government stock (or borowing at the risk-free interest rate).

Thus, using:

$$
\begin{aligned}
E(r_p) &= xE(r_M) + (1 - x)r_F \\
15\% &= x \times 16\% + (1 - x)\,10\% \\
15 &= 16x + 10 - 10x \\
15 - 10 &= 16x - 10x \\
\tfrac{5}{6} &= x
\end{aligned}
$$

Therefore $83\tfrac{1}{3}\%$ of the funds should be placed in the market portfolio and the balance, $16\tfrac{2}{3}\%$, should be invested in government stock. The resulting portfolio's risk can be calculated from:

$$E(r_p) = r_F + \frac{E(r_M) - r_F}{\sigma_M}\sigma_p$$

$$15\% = 10\% = \frac{16\% - 10\%}{3\%}\sigma_p$$

$$\frac{15\% - 10\%}{2\%} = \sigma_p = 2.5\%.$$

9.
$$
\begin{aligned}
20\% &= x \times 16\% + (1 - x)\,10\% \\
20 &= 16x + 10 - 10x \\
20 - 10 &= 16x - 10x \\
10 &= 6x \\
\frac{10}{6} &= x = 1.66.
\end{aligned}
$$

Therefore borrow $66\frac{2}{3}$% of own personal funds at the risk-free interest rate of 10%:

$$\text{Borrow } £1000 \times 0.66 = £666.67.$$

Invest your own funds (£1000) *plus* the borrowed funds (£666.67) in the market portfolio.

Risk of the portfolio would be:

$$20\% = 10\% + \frac{16\% - 10\%}{3\%}\sigma_p$$

$$\frac{20\% - 10\%}{2\%} = \sigma_p = 5\%.$$

10. The market portfolio is the ultimate diversified portfolio and so contains *only* non-diversifiable risk. It consists of shares in *all* companies quoted on the stock exchange, held in proportion to the companies' total market values.

Chapter 12

1. $r_A = r_F + [E(r_M) - r_F]\,\beta_A.$

   The market portfolio has a beta of 1 so a portfolio with a beta of 0.5 would only be half as risky as the market portfolio.

2. The *systematic* risk of an investment, *relative* to the risk of the market portfolio.

3. Unsystematic risk is that part of an investment's total risk that can be diversified away. Its sources are those factors that are specific to the investment, such as its management's ability and the quality of its research and development activities.

4. There are three principal factors:
   (a) the sensitivity of the firm's revenues to the level of economic activity in the economy;
   (b) the proportion of fixed to variable costs;
   (c) the amount of debt finance (gearing).

5. $20\% \times 0.6 = 12\% = $ systematic risk
   $\underline{8\% = }$ unsystematic risk
   $\overline{20\%} = $ total risk

   $$\beta_B = \frac{20\% \times 0.6}{10\%} = \frac{12\%}{10\%} = 1.20.$$

6. $\beta_C = \text{Cov}\,(r_C, r_M) \div \sigma_M^2 = 73.5 \div [7\% \times 7\%] = 73.5 \div 49 = 1.5.$

7. $\beta_{\text{company + project}} = (1.20 \times 0.90) + (1.70 \times 0.10) = 1.25.$

8. If a share is over-valued, it is giving an expected return of less than it should. Hence, it would lie below the CAPM.

9. The CAPM is a single-factor model: expected return is determined by a single factor – systematic risk or beta. The arbitrage pricing model is a multi-factor model: expected return is determined by more than a single factor.

10. $E(r_{project}) = 8\% + (12\% - 8\%) \times 1.75 = 15\%$

$$
\begin{array}{lll}
- & 100\,(1.15)^0 & = -100 \\
+ & 60(1.15)^{-1} & = + \ 52.18 \\
+ & 50(1.15)^{-2} & = + \ 37.80 \\
& & \overline{-\ 10.02} \ \ \text{NPV}
\end{array}
$$

The project has a negative NPV when discounted at 15%. Thus it produces a return of less than 15%. As the CAPM indicates that the minimum return from an investment with this level of systematic risk (estimated by the beta value of the industry group into which the project can be classified) is 15%, the project should be rejected.

Chapter 13

1. An option to sell shares which can only be exercised on the expiry date.

2. An option to buy shares which can be exercised at any time up to the expiry date.

3. At expiry.

4. Use a straddle. Simultaneously buy both call options and put options at the same exercise price and expiry date.

5. The effect is the same as if the underlying shares had been bought: if the share price goes up, you gain; if the share price falls you make a loss. However, buying a call and selling a put is significantly cheaper than buying the underlying shares instead.

6. The intrinsic value of the option and the time value of the option.

7. The B–S model is a function of:
   (a) the current share price;
   (b) the future exercise price;
   (c) the risk-free rate of interest;
   (d) the time to expiry;
   (e) the volatility of the market price of the underlying shares.

8. Shares, risk-free bonds, call options on the shares and put options on the shares. The fundamental equality relationship is:

$$S + P = B + C.$$

9. $S - X(1 + r_F)^{-T} = C - P$ or $S - Xe^{-r_{ET}} = C - P$.

10. Delta risk is the hedge ratio of the option. It measures the sensitivity in the value of the option to changes in the value of the shares. It is given by $N(d_1)$. The greater the delta risk, the greater the sensitivity of the option's value to changes in the underlying share price, and vice versa.

Chapter 14

1. $8\% \div 4 = 2\%$ per three months. £1m $\times 0.02 = $ £20 000.

2. Borrow £5 million now for five months and place the money on deposit for the next two months until it is required.

3. You would receive compensation equal to:
$$£10m \times 6/12 \times (0.07 - 0.065) = £25\ 000.$$

4. FRAs provide a hedge against adverse and favourable interest rate movements. IRGs provide a hedge against adverse movements, but allow advantage to be taken of a favourable movement in interest rates.

5. You require a short hedge: you would sell futures.

6. Futures are priced on an indexed basis and so this implies: $100 - 92.75 = 7.25\%$.

7. $\$1m \times 3/12 \times 0.0001 = \$25$.

8. It is the risk that the futures price will not move precisely in line with interest rate movements.

9. Because of basis risk and because only *whole* contracts can be traded.

10. No. For there to be an advantage to an interest rate swap there must be a quality spread differential. Here, the QSD is zero. Fixed interest: $12.75\% - 11\% = 1.75\%$; LIBOR: $2.75\% - 1\% = 1.75\%$; QSD $= 1.75\% - 1.75\% = 0$.

Chapter 15

1. (a) Weak efficiency.
   (b) Semi-strong efficiency.
   (c) Strong efficiency.

2. (a) Share prices will reflect management decisions as long as they are communicated to the stock market.
   (b) Shares are never over- or under-valued from the point of view of the timing of capital raising.

(c) A take-over of a quoted company is unlikely to represent a positive NPV investment.

3. With weak efficiency, technical analysis is worthless; with semi-strong efficiency, so too is fundamental analysis and with strong efficiency investors cannot even expect to gain from inside information.

4. Share prices react to the disclosure of new, relevant information. New information arises at random intervals of time and can be randomly either good or bad. Hence share price movements themselves occur at random.

5. A technical analyst tries to identify patterns that recur in past share price movements. Then if one of those patterns is observed starting to develop, the technical analyst hopes that this will provide an ability to predict the future share price movement as the pattern develops more fully.

6. Update sloping. See Fig. 15.4 in the text.

7. This states that the shape of the yield curve is determined by expected future interest rates.

8. This states that the normal yield curve is upward sloping because investors prefer short-term bonds – they have a preference for liquidity. Thus they are willing to accept a low interest rate on short-term bonds, but have to be offered a higher interest rate to attract them to the less-preferred long-term bonds.

9. According to the Fisher Effect, market interest rates are determined by inflation rates. Thus if the market expects future interest rates to be lower – based on the pure expectations hypothesis and a falling yield curve – this implies that inflation rates are also expected to fall in future.

10. Suppose you invest £100 in a two-year bond. At the end of two years you will have: £100 $(1.07)^2 = £114.49$. If you invest £100 in a one-year bond, at the end of one year you will have: $£100.(1.06)^1 = £106$. This implies that the market expects the yield on one-year bonds next year to be: $(£114.49 \div £106) - 1 = 0.08$ or 8%, so that $£106.(1.08)^1 = £114.49$ (approx.).

Chapter 16

1. $P_E = 147 - 13 = 134$p ex div

$11\frac{1}{4}(1 + g)^3 = 13$

$$g = (13 \div 11\frac{1}{4})^{\frac{1}{3}} - 1 = 0.049$$

$$K_E = \frac{13(1 + 0.049)}{130} + 0.049 = 0.154 \text{ or } 15.4\%.$$

2. (a) Both r and b remain constant values.
    (b) All-equity financed company.
    (c) All projects financed out of retained earnings.

3. $P_B = £128 - £15 = £113$ ex int.

$$+ 113 - 15(1 - 0.35) A_{4 \neg K_{D_{AT}}} + 110 (1 + K_{D_{AT}})^{-4} = 0 \text{ NPV}$$
At 5%, NPV $= -12.07$
At 15%, NPV $= +22.28$

$$K_D = 5\% + \left[\frac{12.07}{22.28 + 12.07} \times (15\% - 5\%) \right] = 8.5\%$$

$$V_B = £12m \times 1.13 = £13.56m.$$

4. $\left. \begin{array}{l} 12(1 - 0.35) A_{3 \neg 0.085} + 100(1.085)^{-3} \\ (7.8 \times 2.5540) + (100 \times 0.7216) \end{array} \right\} = £92.08 = P_B$

$$£10m \times 0.9208 = £9.208m = V_B.$$

5. Given note 19 and the fact that:

$$P_B = £118 - £18 = £100 \text{ ex int.}$$

and the debt is redeemable at par then the coupon rate equals K_D and so

$$K_{D_{AT}} = 18\% (1 - 0.35) = 11.7\%.$$

6. $87 = 100 (1 + K_D)^{-3}$

$$\frac{87}{100} = (1 + K_D)^{-3} = 0.87$$

$$(1 + K_D)^3 = \frac{1}{0.87} = 1.149$$

$$K_D = 1.149^{\frac{1}{3}} - 1 = 0.0475 \text{ or } 4.75\%.$$

7. (a) The bonds are issued at par and are redeemable at par and carry a conform rate reflecting as market interest rate at the time of issue.
    (b) The bonds are issued at a substantial discount on par but are redeemed at par value. They pay zero interest. Thus the investor receives a return purely in the form of a capital gain.
    (c) The conversion ratio is the number of shares into which each unit of convertible debt can be converted.
    (d) The conversion price is effectively the exercise price of the call options on the company's shares which is contained in an issue of convertible debt.
    (e) The conversion premium is the percentage by which the conversion price exceeds the current share price (normally, at the time of issue).

8. Convertibles have advantages from both the investor's and the company's viewpoint. From the investor's viewpoint they offer the security of a fixed rate of interest, plus the possibility of making a

significant capital gain on conversion, together with the security of being able to have the debt redeemed if they so wish. From the company's viewpoint convertibles have the twin advantages of paying a lower coupon than straight debt and, with luck, never having to repay the loan (as investors will convert).

9. In four years' time, the share price is likely to be: 165p $(1.08)^4 =$ 224.5p. Thus 50 shares will be worth: $50 \times 224.5p = £112.25$. Therefore we would expect investors to convert.

The coupon rate is 5% and so the after-tax interest payments payable by the company are: $£5 \times (1 - 0.33) = £3.35$.

The after-tax cost of the convertible debt is given by the internal rate of return on the following cash flow:

Year:	0	1	$\rightarrow$	4	4
	88	(3.35)			(112.25)

NPV at 4% = −20.11
NPV at 12% = +6.49

$$K_{D_{AT}} = 4\% + \left[\frac{-20.11}{-20.11 - 6.49} \times (12\% - 4\%) \right] = 10\%.$$

10. The minimum value of a convertible is the greater of its value as straight debt and its conversion value.

Chapter 17

1. $$K_E = \frac{5(1.07)}{83} + 0.07 = 13.4\% \qquad V_E = 24m \times 83p = £19.92m$$

$$K_{D_Q} = \frac{15(1 - 0.35)}{110} = 8.9\% \qquad V_{B_Q} = £25m \times 1.10 = £27.5m$$

$$K_{D_{UQ}} = K_{D_Q} = 8.9\% \text{(assuming similar risk)}.$$

$$P_{B_{UQ}} = \frac{12(1 - 0.35)}{0.089} = £87.64 \qquad \therefore V_{B_{UQ}} = £10m \times 0.8764 = £8.76$$

$$K_L = 14\%(1 - 0.35) = 9.1\% \quad V_L = £3m$$

$$V_0 = £19.92m + £27.5m + £3m = £59.18m$$

$$K_0 = \left(13.4\% \times \frac{19.92}{59.18} \right) + \left(8.9\% \times \frac{27.5}{59.18} \right) + \left(8.9\% \times \frac{8.76}{59.18} \right)$$

$$+ \left(9.1\% \times \frac{3}{59.18} \right) = 10.4\%.$$

2. In the medium to long term the company will maintain a fixed capital structure and it is the overall return on this mix of capital that projects must be able to generate to allow the company to continue in existence.

3. (a) Project is small relative to the size of the company.
   (b) Project will be financed in such a way as not to change the capital structure.
   (c) Project has the same degree of systematic risk as that of the company's existing cash flows.
   (d) All level perpetuity cash flows.

4. Its WACC will reflect its *average* level of systematic risk, and not the particular level of systematic risk of any one of its individual business activities. Thus the WACC is an unsuitable NPV discount rate with which to evaluate projects in any one of the company's areas of activity.

5. The CAPM produces an NPV discount rate which is tailor-made to the level of systematic risk of the individual project. The WACC only reflects the company's existing, *average* systematic risk level.

6. Because companies, but not individual investors, can get tax relief on debt interest.

7. Companies should finance themselves almost entirely with debt capital.

8. The gearing or leverage ratio is usually measured as $V_B \times V_E$, although it is sometimes measured, as a percentage, as: $V_B \div V_0$.

Chapter 18

1. Given

$$K_{E_g} = K_{E_{ug}} + (K_{E_{ug}} - K_D)\frac{V_B}{V_E} \text{ then}$$

$$20\% = K_{E_{ug}} = (K_{E_{ug}} - 10\%)\frac{1}{4}$$

$$20\% = K_{E_{ug}} + 0.25K_{E_{ug}} - 2.5\%$$

$$20\% + 2.5\% = 1.25K_{E_{ug}}$$

$$\frac{22.5\%}{1.25} = K_{E_{ug}} = 18\%.$$

2. Again using the M and M equation:

$$K_{E_g} = 18\% + (18\% - 10\%)\frac{3}{5} = 22.8\%.$$

In a no-tax world, the gearing ratio does *not* affect the WACC. So the change in capital structure will leave K_0 unchanged:

$$K_O = 20\% \times \frac{4}{5} + 10\% \times \frac{1}{5} = 18\%.$$

$$K_O = 22.8\% \times \frac{5}{8} + 10\% \times \frac{3}{8} = 18\%.$$

3. Sell your shares in company A for £100 cash and buy £25 of debt in company B and £75 of company B's equity.

4. In arbitrage it is necessary to show the *pure* gain that can be made with no change in either business or financial risk. Business risk does not cause problems as the two companies involved in the arbitrage would be in the same business risk class (same asset betas). However, if a shareholder in a geared company wished to arbitrage into another company, care must be taken in order to preserve the existing degree of financial risk held. This is maintained by substituting home-made for corporate gearing.

5. Financial risk is borne by the shareholders in a geared company. It arises out of the fact that, because debt interest has to be paid in full before equity dividends can be paid, then shareholders are at risk that the company may have insufficient cash flow to pay dividends because it has all gone out in interest payments. This is financial risk.

6. As $K_D = r_F = 10\%$, then we can assume $\beta_{debt} = 0$
   Using CAPM, $20\% = 10\% + (15\% - 10\%)\,\beta_{equity}$

   $$\text{therefore } \frac{20\% - 10\%}{(15\% - 10\%)} = \beta_{equity} = 2.0$$

   $$\beta_{assets} = 2.0 \times \frac{2}{3} + 0 \times \frac{1}{3} = 1.33$$

7. $$\beta_{equity} = \beta_{assets} \times \frac{V_O}{V_E} = 1.33 \times \frac{7}{5} = 1.87.$$

8. For two companies to be in the same business risk class, they should have the same asset betas and – in a no-tax world – the same WACC. As the WACCs of the two companies are *not* the same, we can conclude that they are not in the same business risk class:

   $$K_O = 20\% \times \frac{2}{3} + 10\% \times \frac{1}{3} = 16.67\%.$$

   $$K_O = 20\% \times \frac{5}{7} + 10\% \times \frac{2}{7} = 17.14\%.$$

   Alternatively, the asset beta of the question 6 company is 1.33. The asset beta of the question 8 company is:

   $$\left(2.0 \times \frac{5}{7}\right) + \left(0 \times \frac{2}{7}\right) = \beta_{assets} = 1.43.$$

Chapter 19

1.

$$\text{Using}: K_{E_g} = K_{E_{ug}} + (K_{E_{ug}} + K_D)\frac{V_B(1-T_C)}{V_E}$$

then : $25\% = K_{E_{ug}} + (K_{E_{ug}} - 10\%)\dfrac{1(1-0.35)}{3}$

$25\% = K_{E_{ug}} + 0.217\,K_{E_{ug}} - 2.17\%$

$25\% + 2.17\% = 1.217\,K_{E_{ug}}$

$27.17\% \div 1.217 = K_{E_{ug}} = 22.32\%.$

2.

$$K_{0_g} = K_{E_{ug}}\left(1 - \frac{V_B T_C}{V_0}\right), \text{therefore} :$$

$$K_{0_g} = 22.32\%\left(1 - \frac{1 \times 0.35}{1+2}\right)$$

$K_{0_-} = 22.32\% \times 0.8833 = 19.7\%.$

3. $V_{0_g} = V_{E_{ug}} + V_B T_C$, therefore

$V_{0_g} = £40m + (£10 \times 0.35) = £43.5m.$

Shareholder wealth would have increased by the value of the tax shield:

$$V_B T_C = £10m \times 0.35 = £3.5m.$$

4.

$$K_{0_g} = K_{E_{ug}}\left(1 - \frac{V_B T_C}{V_0}\right).$$

5. The tax shield represents the present value of the tax relief on debt interest. It is the source of the increase in shareholders' wealth that arises from increasing the level of gearing.

6. Debt capacity describes an asset's ability to act as security for a loan. Specifically, an asset's percentage debt capacity indicates the size of loan it would act as security for, expressed as a percentage of the asset's worth.

7. Using: $V_{0_g} = V_{E_{ug}} + V_B T_C - E(b/c)$

then: $£40m = V_{E_{ug}} + (£10m \times 0.35) - (0.05 \times £1m)$

$£40m - £3.5m + £0.05m = V_{E_{ug}} = £36.55m.$

8.

$$V_{0_g} = V_{E_{ug}} + V_B\left[1 - \frac{(1-T_C)(1-T_E)}{1-T_D}\right].$$

Chapter 20

1. $$\frac{\text{Long-term debt and short-term debt} - \text{Cash balances}}{\text{Shareholders' funds}}.$$

    However, the definitions of debt, etc. are not entirely unproblematical and thought needs to be given to items such as the capitalized value of leases.

2. $$\frac{\text{Earnings available for shareholders (after tax and interest)}}{\text{Number of shares in issue}}.$$

3. Gearing ratios cannot be viewed as being high or low in absolute terms (within reason), but only in relative terms. Thus whether, at 50%, a company could be considered to have a high or low level of gearing would depend on the gearing ratio of other companies in its industry group.

    This is likely to be related to the business risk of the particular industry, cost structures, etc.

4. Financial risk is all systematic. It is not unsystematic.

5. There are two main factors:

    (a) the revenue sensitivity of the company;
    (b) the proportion of fixed to variable operating costs.

6. $$\frac{\text{Revenues} - \text{Variable operating costs}}{\text{Earnings before interest and tax}}.$$

7. DOG gives the percentage change in EBIT for every 1% change in revenues.

8. The greater the DOG value, the greater the systematic business risk of a company in comparison with similar companies. Thus the company with a DOG of 2.50 has a greater degree of systematic business risk than a similar company whose DOG value is only 1.50.

Chapter 21

1. Because the project's NPV will add to the market value of the equity.

2. The return required from the project which purely reflects its systematic *business* risk (i.e. it assumes the project is all-equity financed).

3. What the NPV of the project would be, if it was all-equity financed.

4. An operating lease is essentially a marketing device to encourage sales and can be viewed as an operating cash flow. A financial lease is a particular method of project financing.

5. $$\beta_{\text{assets}} = 1.45 \times \frac{5}{5 + 2(1 - 0.35)} + 0.25 \times \frac{2(1 - 0.35)}{5 + 2(1 - 0.35)} = 1.20.$$

6. The equity beta reflects both the business and financial systematic risk. The asset beta purely reflects the business systematic risk. Therefore the financial systematic risk is reflected in a beta value of: $1.45 - 1.20 = 0.25$.

7. Debt capacity concerns an asset's ability to act as security for a loan.

8. The PV of the tax shield is based on debt capacity. Therefore the PV of the tax shield can be calculated as:

$$£2500 \times 0.10 = £250 \times 0.35 = £87.50 = \text{Annual tax relief}$$
$$\text{PV of tax relief: } £87.50 \, A_{5\neg 0.10} \, (1.10)^{-1} = £301.54.$$

Chapter 22

1. The dividend decision could be said to be irrelevant because it does not affect the overall return on the shares, but simply determines how that return is split up between dividend and capital gain.

2. Given the irrelevancy argument of the dividend decision, a company should invest as much of its retained earnings as possible in positive NPV projects. If all earnings cannot be utilized in this way, then the residual should be paid out as a dividend. In this way, shareholder wealth will be maximized.

3. If dividends are to be truly irrelevant, then companies must be indifferent between financing projects with retained earnings and financing via cash raised externally. For this to be the case, the company's capital structure must also be an irrelevant consideration.

4. The bird-in-the-hand argument is that dividends, because they represent a certain current cash flow, are worth more than retained earnings which represent an uncertain future cash flow. Hence dividends are preferred to capital gains.

5. Investors with high marginal rates of personal tax are likely to prefer capital gains to dividends. There are two reasons. The first is that the marginal rate of capital gains tax is likely to be less than the marginal rate of tax on dividends. Secondly, the investor can control the time at which he takes his capital gains to give the greatest degree of tax efficiency. In contrast dividends must be taken when the company decides to pay them.

6. The clientele effect implies that companies should follow a consistent dividend policy to attract a specific clientele of investors.

7. There are two main classes of evidence. One is that companies seem reluctant to face a situation where they have to reduce dividends from one year to the next. Thus dividend growth lags behind earnings growth. The other evidence suggests that share prices react significantly to unexpected changes in dividends.

8. Given the evidence on signalling, to retain an expected dividend for capital investment purposes might be thought of as unwise. The market might interpret the decision as a signal about an unfavourable financial position.

There is, however, evidence that so long as shareholders are properly prepared by the company, the withholding of a dividend for investment purposes can be seen as a good thing.

Chapter 23

1.

Spot	85.10	−	85.90
Less premium	1.20		1.10
Forward	83.90		84.80

2. As the forward rate is at a premium, the first currency (¥) is appreciating against the second currency (DM). Therefore, it follows that the DM must be depreciating against the ¥.

3. DM350 000 × 85.10 = ¥29.785m cost.

4. ¥3.5m ÷ 84.80 = DM41 273 receipt.

5.

£/DM	=	0.3946	−	0.3956
¥/DM	=	85.10	−	85.90
¥/£	=	85.10	−	85.90
		$\overline{0.3946}$		$\overline{0.3956}$
¥/£	=	215.66	−	217.14

6. ¥85.10. $(1 + 0.03)^4 \times (1 - 0.10)^2 = ¥77.58$ Year 6 forward.

7. Using the IRPT:

$$\text{US bills yield} = \left(1.05 \times \frac{1.5815}{1.5210}\right) - 1 = 9.18\%.$$

8. Using the PPPT:

$$\text{Future \$/£ spot} : \frac{1.05}{1.03} \times 1.4550 = 1.4832.$$

9.

$$\frac{0.05 - 0.06}{1.06} = -0.0094$$

$$1.5835(1 - 0.0094) = 1.5686 \quad \text{Year 1}$$

$$\frac{0.07 - 0.07}{1.07} = 0$$

$$1.5686(1 + 0) = 1.5686 \quad \text{Year 2}$$

$$\frac{0.09 - 0.05}{1.05} = +0.038$$

$1.5686(1 + 0.038) = 1.6282$ Year 3

Current \$/£ spot	: 1.5835
Year 1 forecast	: 1.5686
Year 2 forecast	: 1.5686
Year 3 forecast	: 1.6282

Chapter 24

1. For forward rates: Add discount, Subtract premium; therefore:

2.3440	–	2.3460
180		165
2.3260	–	2.3295

Buy \$ = sell DM ∴ FX rate = 2.3295
Cost of buying \$1000 = 1000 × 2.3295 = 2329.5 DM.

2. (a) Forces of supply and demand for currencies from

(i)   'hot money';
(ii) international trade and investment.

(b) Differences in interest rates between countries (IRPT). Movements in FX rates will take up differences in interest rates. Thus the currency of the country with high interest rates can be expected to depreciate.

(c) Differences in inflation rates between countries (PPPT). Movements in FX rates will take up differences in inflation rates. Thus currency of the country with higher inflation can be expected to depreciate.

3. (a) Sell DM10 000 one month forward to yield:

10 000 ÷ 2.3295 = \$4292.77 in one month.

(b) Create a matching one-month DM10 000 liability. Approach: Borrow DMx for 1 month at 0.83% (10% + 12) so that capital plus interest accumulates to DM10 000.

DMx (1 + 0.0083) = DM10 000
DMx = 10 000 ÷ 1.0083 = DM9917.36 one-month DM loan
Convert DM loan immediately into dollars at 2.3460 to yield DM9917.36 ÷ 2.3460 = \$4227.35 now.

(c) First, which of the two hedges is best? Put them on a common point of time for comparison purposes. Assume \$4227.35 from money market hedge is placed on dollar deposit for one month at 11/12% to yield:

\$4227.35 (1 + 0.00917) = \$4266.11.

As this is less than the forward market hedge, that hedging device must be best.
The max discount must be where the company is indifferent between discount and the best alternative hedge (forward hedge).

Again to place the two alternatives at a common point in time, the minimum amount in dollars that the US company would be willing to receive now is x, where

$$\$x \, (1 + 0.00917) = \$4292.77$$
$$\$x = \$4292.77 + 1.00917 = \$4253.76.$$

At a spot rate of exchange, this represents:

$$\$4253.76 \times 2.3460 = DM9979.33$$

which represents a discount on the original invoiced amount of:
$(10\,000 - 9979.33) \div 10\,000 = 0.0021$, or just under 0.25%.

4. $\$/\pounds = \dfrac{9.8040}{5.1020} = 1.9216.$

5.   Exercise of put option will generate $\$100\,000 \div 1.80 = \pounds55\,555.56.$
     (a)   (i)   A spot sale of $\$100\,000$ at 1.95 will produce only £51 282.05. Therefore, exercise option.
          (ii)   A spot sale of $\$100\,000$ at 1.70 will yield: £58 823.53 therefore allow option to lapse and sell currency in spot market.
     (b)   (i)   A spot purchase of $\$100\,000$ at 1.95 will only cost £51 282.05. Therefore spot purchase $\$100\,000$ and then sell them through exercising the option to yield a profit of: £55 555.56 − £51 282.05 = £4273.51.
          (ii)   A spot purchase of $\$100\,000$ at 1.70 would cost £58 823.53, therefore it is not worth exercising the option – allow it to lapse.

6.   The deal will be done at the worst rate to forward sell the dollar: 1.7650.

7.   (a)   OTC options available in large numbers of currencies, traded currency options available only in major currencies.
     (b)   OTC options available in cross-currencies, traded currency options are only available against dollars.
     (c)   OTC options are available for any reasonable exercise date; traded currency options only 3/6/9 months forward.
     (d)   OTC option prices determined by bank. Thus a big company can use its financial strength to strike a better deal.
     (e)   A *very* large transaction may be difficult to arrange on a traded currency option exchange (LIFFE).
     (f)   OTC currency options are not dependent on the option exchange being open to deal or exercise.
     (g)   OTC currency options are available for any amount of currency; traded currency options come in standardized amounts (i.e. £25 000 is the unit in sterling options).

8.   (a)   Target: $\$526\,000 \div 0.4090 = DM1\,286\,064$
         Hedge: $\$526\,000 \div 0.41 = DM1\,282\,927$

$$\frac{1\,282\,927}{80\,000} = 16 \text{ DM futures contracts.}$$

In August, we will want to sell \$526 000 in order to buy DM. Therefore, we hedge by buying 16 September DM futures contracts at \$0.41 each.

(b) In August, we receive \$526 000 from our customer and sell at spot to receive:

$$\$526\,000 \div 0.4170 = \text{DM1}\,261\,391, \text{ which is DM24 673 less}$$
than target (i.e. a loss).

We close out our futures position by reversing the earlier deal: sell 16 September futures at \$0.41$\frac{1}{2}$.

Profit on futures deal:

Buy: 16 × DM80 000 = 1.28m DM at an exchange rate of \$0.41, therefore the cost is: 1.28m × 0.41 = \$0.5248m.

Sell: 13 × DM80 000 DM = 1.28m DM at an exchange rate of \$0.41$\frac{1}{2}$, therefore we receive: 1.28 m × 0.4150 = \$0.5312m.

Profit: \$531 200 − £524 800 = \$6400. If sold at spot this would yield: \$6400 ÷ 0.4170 = DM15 348.

Hedge efficiency: $\dfrac{\text{Profit}}{\text{Loss}} = \dfrac{15\,348}{24\,673} = 62.2\%.$

9. (a) Buy \$297 500 forward to October at a rate of \$1.7000.
Cost: \$297 500 ÷ 1.7000 = £175 000.

(b) Number of futures: $\dfrac{£175\,000}{£12\,500} = 14 \text{ contracts.}$

Hedge position: Sell 14 sterling December futures at \$1.70 each. In October, close out the futures position by buying 14 December sterling futures contracts at the going price. At same time buy \$297 500 on spot market to pay supplier.

(c) Cost of paying invoice:

$$\$297\,500 \div 1.7800 = £167\,135.$$

Outcome of futures market deals:

Bought   14 × £12 500 × 1.78   =   \$311 500   Cost
Sold   14 × £12 500 × 1.70   =   \$297 500   Received
                                    \$14 000   Loss

These dollars would then have to be bought at spot to pay off the loss: \$14 000 ÷ 1.3800 = £7865 cost.
Therefore the net cost of invoice: £167 135 + £7865 = £175 000, which is the same as the outcome of the forward market hedge.

Chapter 25

1. $$\frac{1+\text{inflation}_\$}{1+\text{inflation}_\pounds} = \frac{\text{Forward rate}}{\text{Spot rate}} \quad \text{or} \quad \frac{\$\,\text{inflation} - \pounds\,\text{inflation}}{1+\pounds\,\text{inflation}}$$

2.
$$\frac{1.8420 \times 1.25}{1.9050} - 1 = 0.209 \text{ or } 20.9\% \text{ approx.}$$

3. $1.9280(1 - 0.07)^3 = 1.5508.$

4. $1.7940
   less 150
   $\overline{\$1.7790}$ = two-month forward rate

5. (a) Project's dollar cash flows are discounted by dollar discount rate to give a dollar NPV which is then converted at spot to a sterling NPV; or

   (b) Project's dollar cash flows are converted into sterling cash flows and then discounted at the sterling discount rate to give a sterling NPV.

6. Because they may well affect the cash flow available to be remitted back to the parent.

7. Property fixed assets and working capital, finance in the overseas currency. Non-property fixed assets, finance via the export of sterling.

8. (a) Dividends;
   (b) interest;
   (c) management charges;
   (d) royalty payments;
   (e) transfer prices.

9. The risk that the host government might adversely change the 'rules of the game' after the company have undertaken the investment.

10. Economic risk describes the risk that a company is exposed to from unexpected FX rate movements and their resulting impact on the sterling worth of a foreign project's cash flows.

Index